CONTENTS AT A GLANCE

www.whitebook.co.uk

Welcome to...

THE ESSENTIAL DIRECTORY FOR THE EVENTS INDUSTRY

The White Book contains every event resource in one place, which is why it has has been the go-to guide to the live events industry for more than 30 years.

In both print and online, The White Book features full postal addresses, phone numbers and websites for event production services and equipment as well as listing venues in a logical, easy-to-navigate format.

So whether you are looking for wifi services, trailers or recording studios, The White Book 2017 should be your first port of call.

The website www.whitebook.co.uk is regularly updated, and ruthlessly checked to ensure you find what you want, when you want it – in an instant.

The White Book is the essential tool to make 2017 a successful year for your business.

Senior Account Manager Richard Dove
020 8481 11 22
Group Production Manager Simon Hadley
Production Controller Elizabeth Nixon
Production Assistant Ryan Begley

The White Book, 2nd Floor Applemarket House,
17 Union Street, Kingston-Upon-Thames KT1 1RR
Tel: 020 8481 11 22 **Fax:** 020 8481 11 44
ISBN 2017: 97809576478-4-8

Mash Media

ENTERTAINMENT / ATTRACTIONS

Action / Adventure Days

Altitude Events
Old Brookhouse Barn, Brookhouse Lane, Framfield
Sussex TN22 5QJ 07832 227 571
e: mail@altitudeevents.org
w: www.altitudeevents.org

Big Bang Promotions International Ltd
MAGNA Science Adventure Centre, Sheffield Road,
Templeborough, Rotherham
Yorkshire S60 1DX 0845 319 2767
e: info@bigbang-promotions.com
w: www.bigbang-promotions.com

Highline Adventure
Mill Farmhouse , Mill Road , Shouldham Thorpe , Kings Lynn
PE33 0EA... 08454 091 303
e: highlinemd@highlineadventure.co.uk
w: www.highlineadventure.co.uk

Izorb
Victoria House, Great Ancoats Street, Manchester
M4 7EA... 07779 150 145
e: martin@izorb.org
w: www.izorb.org

Just Add Water Sports
Unit 27, Graphite way, Hadfield
Derbyshire SK13 1QH 01457 238285
e: info@jawsltd.co.uk
w: www.jawsltd.co.uk

Sky High Bungee
145 Carr Lane, Dronfield Wood House, Dronfield
Derbyshire S18 8XF 0114 289 0173
e: info@skyhighbungee.com
w: www.skyhighbungee.com

Skyfall Mobile Zip Wire Hire
Mayfield House, 133 Walmsersley Rd, Bury
Lancashire Bl9 5AY 01625 532098
w: www.mobileziplinehire.co.uk

The Gnat Display Team
HERITAGE AIRCRAFT LIMITED, Hangar 4a, North Weald Airfield,
Epping
CM16 6HR 07942 800 921
e: info@gnatdisplayteam.com
w: www.gnatdisplayteam.com

Uk Bungee Club
Magna Science Adventure Centre, Sheffield Road,
Templeborough, Rotherham
S60 1DX 01709 366 660
e: info@ukbungee.co.uk
w: www.visitmagna.co.uk

All Terrain / Off Road / 4WD

Driveme.net - Driving Experiences
Seighford Airfield, Seighford, Stafford
Staffordshire ST18 9QE.. 01244 833 895
e: nicci@driveme.net
w: www.driveme.net

Animals

Animal Dramatics
Porkers Cottage and Stables, Baughurst Road, Aldermaston
RG7 4PJ 07831 409457
e: jackie@animaldramatics.co.uk
w: www.animaldramatics.co.uk

Celebrity Reptiles
11 Tramway Close, Penge
London SE20 7DF 020 8659 0877
e: info@celebrityreptiles.co.uk
w: www.celebrityreptiles.co.uk

Creature Feature
Gibhill Farm, Dumfries
Dumfries & Galloway DG1 1RL.............................. 01387 860648
e: david@creaturefeature.co.uk
w: www.creaturefeature.co.uk

The Exotic Animal ENCOUNTER
.... 7714745033
e: exoticanimalencounters@live.com
w: www.theexoticanimalencounter.co.u

Tricky Tykes Terrier Racing Display Team
Cilyblaidd Manor, Pencarreg, Llanybydder
Carmarthenshire SA40 9QL................................. 01570 480090
e: info@trickytykes.co.uk
w: www.trickytykes.co.uk

Aquatic / Marine Displays

Amazing Animals
Heythrop Zoological Gardens Ltd, Heythrop, Chipping Norton
Oxfordshire OX7 5TU... 01608 683389
e: jclubb@amazinganimals.co.uk
w: www.amazinganimals.co.uk

Aquabatix
24 Sidney Road, Beckenham
Kent BR3 4QA... 020 8144 2782
e: info@aquabatix.com
w: www.aquabatix.com

Archery

Archery4All
First Floor, 41 Roseheath, Hemel Hempstead
HP1 2NG....................................01442 245700 // 07850 843005
e: grandaffairsgroup@gmail.com
w: www.archery4all.co.uk

Corporate Archery Events
11 Allington Road, Southville
Bristol BS3 1PS....................................07770 982 290
e: info@corporatearcheryevents.co.uk
w: www.corporatearcheryevents.co.uk

On Target Archery
1 Otterbourne, 7 Surrey Road, Bournemouth
BH2 6BP..................01202 779072 // 0780 1643 404 // 0780 16
e: info@archery.me.uk
w: www.archery.me.uk

The Ackers
Golden Hillock Road, Small Heath, Birmingham
B11 2PY 0121 772 5111
e: info@ackers-adventure.co.uk
w: www.ackers-adventure.co.uk

Balloon Sculptures

Balloons for Events
....08456 524848
e: info@balloonsforevents.co.uk
w: www.weddingballoons.biz

Bloon
....08454 860 200
e: bloononline@gmail.com
w: www.bloon.co.uk

Rainbow Faces Ltd
101 High Street, Newport
Shropshire TF10 7AY.........................01952 811 544
e: sales@rainbowfaces.co.uk
w: www.rainbowfaces.co.uk

Bar Mitzvahs

Gamewagon Ltd
113 - 115 Oyster Lane, Byfleet
KT14 7JZ..0845 319 4263
e: admin@gamewagon.co.uk
w: www.gamewagon.info

Big Fun Outdoor Games

Aquazorbs
....07889 845393
e: info@aquazorbs.com
w: www.aquazorbs.com

Department Of Enjoyment
21 Bar Terrace, Whitworth, Rochdale
Lancashire OL12 8TB 0800 292 2049
e: events@enjoy.co.uk
w: www.enjoy.co.uk

S&D Leisure Rides
1 Chadwick's Depot, Collingham Street, Manchester
M8 8RQ ....07791 941731 // 0797 007 1560
e: events@sdlrides.com
w: www.sdlrides.com

Sunshine Events
Event House, 52 - 54 Tulketh Road, Ashton On Ribble, Preston
PR2 1AQ 01772 970 389
w: www.sunshineevents.co.uk

Birthday Events

Gamewagon Ltd
113 - 115 Oyster Lane, Byfleet
KT14 7JZ..0845 319 4263
e: admin@gamewagon.co.uk
w: www.gamewagon.info

Casinos

1st Call Cabaret Casino
Ten Acre Farm, Stonehill Road, Ottershaw
Surrey KT16 0AQ 08450 008 007
e: enquiry@cabaretcasino.co.uk
w: www.cabaretcasino.co.uk

A Mobile Fun Casino
9230 Fishingline Road, , Enfield, Redditch
Worcestershire B98 0FX 01527 518082
e: info@centralenglandcasinos.com
w: www.centralenglandcasinos.com

Abc Events
Unit 12 Castle Court, Bankside Industrial Est, Grangemouth, Falkirk
FK2 7UU 0845 602 4139
e: louise@abc-events.co.uk
w: www.abc-events.co.uk

Big Indoor Games Company Ltd
Birches Wood, Crackley Lane, Kenilworth
Warwickshire CV8 2JT...01926 863090
e: sales@bigindoorgames.co.uk
w: www.bigindoorgames.co.uk

Classic Casino Entertainments
Unit G, Emms Court, Meeting Lane, Brierley Hill
DY5 3LB 01384 265793
e: info@classiccasino.co.uk
w: www.classiccasino.co.uk

CASINOS / CHILDREN'S ENTERTAINMENT / CHOCOLATE FOUNTAIN / CLAY/TARGET SHOOTING
COMMUNITY EVENTS / COMPANY FUN DAYS / CONFETTI / CORPORATE ENTERTAINMENT/EVENTS   9

ENTERTAINMENT/
ATTRACTIONS

Diamond Fun Casino
31 Kennel Lane, Fetcham
Surrey KT22 9PQ 0845 6123707
e: info@diamondfc.com
w: www.diamondfc.com

Grosvenor Fun Casino
Statesman House, Stafferton Way, Maidenhead
SL6 1AY 01628 504000
e: zoe.westerman@rank.com

Perfect Fun Casino
Caddington
LU1 .... 07864 149102
e: info@perfectfuncasino.co.uk

Viva Vegas
144a Old South Lambeth Road, London
SW8 1XX 020 7820 0999
e: enquiries@vivavegas.co.uk
w: www.vivavegas.co.uk

Children's Entertainment

The Wheelie Good Party Company
.... 0845 0451076
e: partyhq@wheeliegoodparty.co.uk
w: www.wheeliegoodparty.co.uk

Chocolate Fountain

Chocolate Fondue Company
Livermores, Boars Tye Road, Silver End, Witham
Essex CM8 3PN 01376 584669
e: info@chocolatefonduecompany.co.uk
w: www.chocolatefonduecompany.co.uk

Vital Attractions Ltd
.... 0151 733 7788 // 07986 174193
e: naomi@tatu.co.uk
w: www.vitalattractions.co.uk

Clay / Target Shooting

CMSC Corporate Entertainment
.... 01782 397961
e: chris@executivedays.co.uk
w: www.executivedays.co.uk

Laser Like A Shot
Grovebeck Grange, North Drove, Quadring Fen, Spalding
Lincolnshire PE11 4QS... 01775 750456
e: info@laserlikeashot.co.uk
w: www.laserlikeashot.co.uk

Sporting Targets Ltd
Knotting Lane, Sharnbrook Road, Riseley
MK44 1BX 01234 708893
e: eventbookings@sportingtargets.co.uk
w: www.sportingtargets.co.uk

Community Events

Gamewagon Ltd
113 - 115 Oyster Lane, Byfleet
KT14 7JZ... 0845 319 4263
e: admin@gamewagon.co.uk
w: www.gamewagon.info

Company Fun Days

Ace Tones Group
11 Thorpe Road, Peterborough, PE3 6AB, Peterborough
PE3 6AB 0845 189 5858
e: enquiry@acetonesgroup.com
w: www.acetonesgroup.com

Confetti

Confetti Master
8 Badgers Folly, Castle Cary
Somerset BA7 7BF... 01963 350960
e: hello@confettimaster.com
w: www.confettimaster.com

Flutter Fetti
....01992 893340 // 07738 177699
e: flutterfetti@btconnect.com
w: www.flutterfetti.co.uk

Corporate Entertainment

Team Building Solutions
Unit 7, Ampress Lane, Lymington Enterprise Centre, Lymington
Hampshire SO41 8LZ.. 0845 121 1194
e: info@teambuildingsolutions.co.uk
w: www.teambuildingsolutions.co.uk

The Jammy Showgirls
Century House South, North Station Road, Colchester
Essex CO1 1RE 07796 138884
e: anthony@jammyshowsandproductions.co.uk
w: www.jammyshowsandproductions.co.u

Corporate Events

Chuckle Pod Limited
.... 07770 692499
e: info@chucklepod.co.uk
w: www.chucklepod.co.uk

JS Ent
Unit 5-7a, 109 Maybank Rd, South Woodford, London
E18 1EJ... 020 8505 8222
e: sales@jsent.co.uk
w: www.jsent.co.uk

Team Building Solutions
Unit 7, Ampress Lane, Lymington Enterprise Centre, Lymington
Hampshire SO41 8LZ... 0845 121 1194
e: info@teambuildingsolutions.co.uk
w: www.teambuildingsolutions.co.uk

Disco Equipment

SilentArena
.... 0800 122 3314
e: bookings@silentarena.com
w: www.silentarena.com

Sound Of Music Mobile Disco DJ Hire Agency Croydon
.... 07402 700695
e: soundofmusicdjagency@hotmail.com
w: www.soundofmusicmobiledisco.com

DJ

Sound Of Music Mobile Disco DJ Hire Agency Croydon
.... 07402 700695
e: soundofmusicdjagency@hotmail.com
w: www.soundofmusicmobiledisco.com

Driving / Motor Racing Days

Chris Birkbeck Corporate Entertainment
Low Farm, Manx Lodge, Brotton, Saltburn
North Yorkshire TS12 2QX.................................... 01287 677512
e: sales@gorallyschool.co.uk
w: www.gorallyschool.co.uk

Speedkarting Warrington Uk
Unit 2, Bank Quay Trading Estate, Warrington
Cheshire WA1 1PJ 01925 415114
e: sales@speedkarting.co.uk
w: www.speedkarting.co.uk

The Racing Bug Ltd
29 Latimer Close, Little Chalfont
Buckinghamshire HP6 6QS 07767 870191
e: info@theracingbug.co.uk
w: www.theracingbug.co.uk

Entertainment

Electric Cabaret
107 High St, Brackley
NN13 7BN 07714 089 763
e: info@electriccabaret.co.uk
w: www.electriccabaret.co.uk

Gamewagon Ltd
113 - 115 Oyster Lane, Byfleet
KT14 7JZ.. 0845 319 4263
e: admin@gamewagon.co.uk
w: www.gamewagon.info

IAMBE Productions Limited
376 London Road, Hadleigh, Essex, SS7 2DA ...... 01702 300865 / 07970 685982
e: admin@iambeproductions.com
w: www.iambeproductions.com

Team Building Solutions
Unit 7, Ampress Lane, Lymington Enterprise Centre, Lymington
Hampshire SO41 8LZ... 0845 121 1194
e: info@teambuildingsolutions.co.uk
w: www.teambuildingsolutions.co.uk

The Jammy Showgirls
Century House South, North Station Road, Colchester
Essex CO1 1RE 07796 138884
e: anthony@jammyshowsandproductions.co.uk
w: www.jammyshowsandproductions.co.u

The Wheelie Good Party Company
.... 0845 0451076
e: partyhq@wheeliegoodparty.co.uk
w: www.wheeliegoodparty.co.uk

Face Painting

Brushstroke Ltd
Brushstroke Media Make-Up School, Shepperton Studios, Studios Road, Shepperton
Surrey TW17 0QD 01932 592463
e: info@brushstroke.co.uk
w: www.brushstroke.co.uk

Face In A Crowd
Mumble Farm, Pasturefields, Great Haywood, Stafford
Staffordshire ST18 0RB 07976 289 234
e: siany711@hotmail.co.uk
w: www.faceinacrowd.net

Facepaint Uk
188 Brixton Road, London
SW9 6AR 020 7735 5719
e: info@facepaint-uk.com
w: www.facepaint-uk.com

Faces for Fun
.... 07859 054 237
e: fran@facesforfun.com
w: www.facesforfun.com

Funky Faces
40 Blumfield Crescent, , Burnham, Slough
Berkshire SL1 6NH 07976 671309
e: jenquille@hotmail.com
w: www.funkyfaces.co.uk

Rainbow Faces Ltd
101 High Street, Newport
Shropshire TF10 7AY... 01952 811 544
e: sales@rainbowfaces.co.uk
w: www.rainbowfaces.co.uk

Fairground / Funfair Attractions

Coopers Leisure
.... 7446123141
e: info@coopersleisure.co.uk
w: www.ridesforhirenortheast.co.uk

Dodgems Direct
20 Westend Parade, Gloucester
Gloucestershire GL1 2RY.. 01452 300356
e: dodgemsandfunfairs@hotmail.co.uk
w: www.dodgemsdirect.co.ue

Events With A Difference
Unit 12, Riverside Trading Estate, Station Road, Penketh,
Warrington, Cheshire WA5 2UL.............................. 01925 725252
e: enquiries@eventswithadifference.co.uk
w: www.eventswithadifference.co.uk

Irvin Amusements
Unit 3, Rosies Way, off Buckles Lane , South Ockendon
Essex RM15 6RW 07966 548140
e: info@irvinamusements.co.uk
w: www.irwinamusements.co.uk

John Parnham Funfairs
Bernard House, New Road Feltham, Feltham, Hounslow
London TW14 9BQ 07956 245531
e: johnparnham@aol.com
w: www.parnhamfunfairs.co.uk

Premier Rides Limited
Woodstock House, Woodstock Close, Horsham
West Sussex RH12 5YT.. 01403 270 076
e: info@premierrides.com
w: www.premierrides.com

Race Time Ltd
Unit 3 3 Wigan Road, Skelmersdale
Lancashire WN8 8NB 01695 722 700
e: enquiries@race-time.co.uk
w: www.race-time.co.uk

S&d Leisure Ltd
1 Chadwicks Depot, Collingham Street, Cheetham Hill,
Manchester
M8 8RQ 0161 835 2758
e: enquiries@sdleisure.com
w: www.sdleisure.com

Sideshow Illusions
18 Church Street, Sutton-on-Hull
East Yorkshire HU7 4TS.. 01482 709939
e: jon@sideshowillusions.com
w: www.sideshowillusions.com

Traditional Fun Fair
93 Hertford Drive , Tyldesley , Manchester
M29 8LU... 01942 799831
e: s.laidlaw3@ntlworld.com
w: www.traditionalfunfair.com

Wantafunfair.com Ltd
Unit 13-14, Enterprise House, Thomlinson Road, Hartlepool
TS25 1NS 01429 263256
e: office@wantafunfair.com
w: www.wantafunfair.com

Fairground Amusements

Blenheim Amusements
.... 07970 588417
e: samantha.brixton@btinternet.com
w: www.blenheimamusements.co.uk

Coopers Leisure
.... 7446123141
e: info@coopersleisure.co.uk
w: www.ridesforhirenortheast.co.uk

Fireworks / Pyrotechnics

Alchemy Fireworks Ltd
Barn 7, The Old Dairy, Beadlow, Shefford
Bedfordshire SG17 5PL...................................... 08000 66 58 37
e: rob@alchemyfireworks.co.uk
w: www.alchemyfireworks.co.uk

Aquabatics
Symondshyde Farm, Hatfield
AL10 9BB 01707 269574
e: office@aquabatics.co.uk
w: www.aquabatics.co.uk

Dragonfire Ltd
Tuthill Rise, Stoke Lacy, Bromyard
Herefordshire HR7 4QZ 01885 490538
e: info@dragonfire.co.uk
w: www.dragonfire.co.uk

Essex Pyrotechnics Ltd
.... 01223 264563
e: office@essex-pyrotechnics.com
w: www.essex-pyrotechnics.co.uk

Fantastic Fireworks
Rocket Park, Pepperstock, Luton
LU1 4LL... 01582 485 555
e: info@fantasticfireworks.co.uk
w: www.fantasticfireworks.co.uk

Firework Crazy
Unit 21 Eckersley Road, Chelmsford
Essex CM1 1SL..01245 354422
e: mark@fireworkcrazy.com
w: www.fireworkcrazy.com

Fireworks Direct
Unit 3, Doal Trading Estate , Rolfe Street, Smethwick, Birmingham
West Midlands B66 ....0844 556 1300
e: manni@fireworks-direct.co.uk
w: www.fireworks-direct.co.uk

Fireworks International Ltd
West Pyro Site, Fauld Industrial Estate, Tutbury, Burton on Trent
Staffordshire DE13 9HS 01283 521 174
w: www.fireworksinternational.co.uk

Frontier Fireworks Ltd
23 Southfield, Polegate
BN26 5LX 01323 488 866
e: info@frontierfireworks.co.uk
w: www.frontierfireworks.co.uk

Fully Fused Fireworks
....01462 817640
w: www.fullyfusedfireworks.com

Kimbolton Fireworks Ltd
7 High Street, Kimbolton, Huntingdon
Cambridgeshire PE28 0HB 01480 860988
e: info@kimboltonfireworks.co.uk
w: www.kimboltonfireworks.co.uk

Magic and Miracle Fireworks
Arthur Mee Road, Stapleford, Nottingham
Nottinghamshire NG9 7EW.........0845 094 9170 // 07921189706
e: info@magicandmiracle.co.uk
w: www.magicandmiracle.co.uk

MLE Pyrotechnics Ltd
Units 14 - 16, Bentley Way, Royal Oak Industrial Estate, Daventry
Northamptonshire NN11 8QH................................01327 876037
e: mail@mlepyrotechnics.co.uk
w: www.mlepyrotechnics.co.uk

Pains Fireworks Ltd
Romsey Road, Whiteparish, Salisbury
Wiltshire SP5 2SD...01794 884 040
e: sales@painsfireworks.com
w: www.painsfireworks.com

Paul Jubb Fireworks
2 Shacklegate Lane, Teddington
London TW11 8SH 020 8977 4742
e: pauljubb@gmail.com
w: www.pauljubbfireworks.co.uk

Pyro 1- Firework Displays
Symondshyde Farm, Hatfield
AL10 9BB 01707 269566
e: contactus@pyro1.com
w: www.pyro1.com

Quicksilver Uk Limited
17 Hyde Road, Denton, Manchester
Greater Manchester M34 3AF 0161 320 7232
e: sales@quicksilversfx.co.uk
w: www.quicksilversfx.co.uk

Sandling Fireworks
First Floor Offices, SE45 Gloucestershire Airport, Staverton
GL51 6SP 01452 855915
e: sales@sandlingfireworks.co.uk
w: www.sandlingfireworks.co.uk

Shell Shock Fireworks Ltd
....01664 454994 // 07768 684910
w: www.shellshockfireworks.co.uk

Shellscape Pyrotechnics Ltd
Butchers Lane, White Waltham, Maidenhead
Berkshire SL6 3SD..01628 829 401
e: blast@shellscape.com
w: www.shellscape.com

Skyburst - The Firework Co
 Unit 1A, Peartree Indurstrial Estate, Bath Road, Upper Langford,
Bristol BS40 4DJ...08000 744 636
w: www.skyburst.co.uk

Starlight Fireworks Ltd
....01494 766901
e: displays@starlightfireworks.co.uk
w: www.starlightfireworks.co.uk

Viking Fireworks
....01843 823545 // 01843 596717
e: enquiries@vikingfireworks.co.uk
w: www.tplpyro.co.uk

Fun Fairs

Blenheim Amusements
....07970 588417
e: samantha.brixton@btinternet.com
w: www.blenheimamusements.co.uk

Hire A Funfair
Mowbray Farm, Low Catton, York
YO41 1EA 01759 371786
e: sara@awkwardentertainments.com
w: www.hireafunfair.com

I need a funfair
....7970430309
e: ineedafunfair@hotmail.co.uk
w: www.ineedafunfair.co.uk

Gaming

Gamewagon Ltd
113 - 115 Oyster Lane, Byfleet KT14 7JZ............0845 319 4263
e: admin@gamewagon.com
w: www.gamewagon.info

GLADIATOR GAMES/IT'S A KNOCKOUT / GO-KARTING / GOLF
HEN NIGHTS / HISTORICAL RE-ENACTMENTS / HOT AIR BALLOONS / ICE RINKS   13
ICE SCULPTURES / INFALTABLES/BOUNCY CASTLES

ENTERTAINMENT/
ATTRACTIONS

Gladiator Games / It's a Knockout

1st Leisure Supplies
Leisure House, 137 Hankinson Road, Charminster
Dorset BH9 1HR...01202 525223
e: info@1stleisuresupplies.com
w: www.1stleisuresupplies.com

Knockout Challenge Limited
PO Box 5167, South Woodham Ferrers
CM3 5EH 01245 328221
e: info@knockout-challenge.co.uk
w: www.knockout-challenge.co.uk

Peach
Peach, Unit D, Daux Road Ind Est, Billingshurst
West Sussex RH14 9SJ..01403 780 900
e: info@peach-ent.co.uk
w: www.peach-ent.co.uk

Go-Karting

Kiddi Karts Ltd
Hellerman House, Harris Way, Sunbury on Thames
Surrey TW16 7EW...01932 770770
e: enquiries@kiddikarts.co.uk
w: www.kiddikarts.co.uk

Golf

Golfsim (mobile Golf Simulator Hire)
30 Elvington, Kings Lynn
Norfolk PE30 4TA...01553 767685
e: info@golfsimulation.co.uk
w: www.golfsimulation.co.uk

Manor Of Groves
High Wych, Sawbridgeworth
Hertfordshire CM21 0JU 01279 600777
e: info@manorofgroves.com
w: www.manorofgroves.com

Hen Nights

Gamewagon Ltd
113 - 115 Oyster Lane, Byfleet
KT14 7JZ..0845 319 4263
e: admin@gamewagon.co.uk
w: www.gamewagon.info

Historical Re-enactments

Knights Of Arkley
Glyn Sylen Farm, Five Roads, Llanelli
Carmarthenshire SA15 5BJ....................................01269 861001
e: penny@knightsofarkley.fsnet.co.uk
w: www.knightsofarkley.com

Hot Air Balloons

Peter Drury Bird Ltd
Crossways, West Stoughton, Wedmore
Somerset BS28 4PW...07973 931675
e: p.bird@thedrurypartnership.com

Ice Rinks

Ice Magic
....0845 5196544
e: simon@ice-magic.com
w: www.synthetic-ice-rinks.com

Ice Sculptures

Eskimo Ice
Unit A 45-48, New Covent Garden Market, Nine Elms Lane
SW8 5EE..................................020 7720 4883 // 07831 260 813
w: www.eskimo-ice.co.uk

Ice Immediate
....0800 169 3991
e: enquiries@iceimmediate.com
w: www.iceimmediate.com

Inflatables / Bouncy Castles

ABC Inflatables
4 Wildmere Close, Wildmere Industrial Estate, Banbury
OX16 3TL..0845 0508 600
e: sales@abcinflatables.co.uk
w: www.abcinflatables.co.uk

ABC Leisure
139A Queslett Road East Streetly, Sutton Coldfield, Birmingham
West Midlands B74 2AJ...07980 225375
e: info@abcleisure.net
w: www.abcleisure.net

About2Bounce Mansfield
....01623 553891
e: m.kirkwood.86@hotmail.co.uk
w: www.about2bouncemansfield.co.uk

Ace Inflatables
8 Totease Cottages, High Street, Buxted, Uckfield
TN22 4LD 07760 752840
e: peter@aceinflatables.com
w: www.aceinflatables.com

Activity Day
Littleheath Road, Bexleyheath
Kent DA7 5HF ....0203 589 6303 // 07795 174782
e: mail@activityday.co.uk
w: www.activityday.co.uk

Airdancer Wales
Unit D1 Capel Hendre Industrial Estate, Capel Hendre, Ammanford
SA18 3SJ....................................01269 512010 // 07957 928962
e: info@racearchesuk.co.uk
w: www.airdancerwales.co.uk

Airtechs Ltd
Unit 18, Halesworth Business Centre, Norwich Road, Halesworth
IP19 8QJ...01986 835 724
w: www.airtechs.co.uk

Bounce Krazee
14 Green Leys, High Wycombe
Buckinghamshire HP13 5UH 01494 464902
e: info@bouncekrazee.co.uk
w: www.bouncekrazee.co.uk

Bounce-Mania
18 Tennyson Avenue, Rustington
West Sussex BN16 2PB 01903 771863
e: info@bounce-mania.co.uk
w: www.bouncemaniaevents.co.uk

Circuit Entertainments
Springbank, 160 Withersfield Road, Haverhill
CB9 9HQ..01440 707307
e: circuitents@btopenworld.com
w: www.circuitentertainments.co.uk

Factory of Fun
47 Lutterworth Road, Leicester
LE2 8PH...07860 422134
e: factoryoffun@aol.com
w: www.factory-of-fun.co.uk

Funtime Hire
Finchingfield Nurseries, Bardfield Road, Finchinfield
CM7 4LL..01371 811381
w: www.funtimehire.co.uk

GazInflatables
47 LUTTERWORTH ROAD, Leicester
LE2 8PH...07860 422134
e: gazinflate@aol.com
w: www.gazinflatables.co.uk

Huff N Puff Events
Unit 3A, Welwyn Garden City, Swallowfields
AL7 1JD..01707 696797
w: www.hpcastles.co.uk

Location Inflation
....07966 165658
e: info@locationinflation.com
w: www.locationinflation.com

Rascals Bouncy Castles and Inflatables
Wellstead Way, Hedge End, Eastleigh, Southampton
SO30 2BH...07745 696 848
w: www.rascalscastles.co.uk

Jukeboxes

Mightymast Leisure Ltd
58 Bentwaters Park, , Rendlesham, Woodbridge
Suffolk IP12 2TW 01394 460896
e: info@mightymast.com
w: www.mightymast.com

The Jukebox Company
633 Eastern Avenue, Illford
Essex IG2 6PW...0208 554 5757
e: info@jukeboxco.com
w: www.jukeboxco.com

Lasers

Lightfantastics Laser
5 Haugh Road, Burntisland
Fife KY3 0BZ..+44 (0) 131 5100218
e: show@lightfantastics.com
w: www.lightfantastics.co.uk

Lights

Lightfantastics Laser
5 Haugh Road, Burntisland
Fife KY3 0BZ..+44 (0) 131 5100218
e: show@lightfantastics.com
w: www.lightfantastics.co.uk

Mobile Disco

Sound Of Music Mobile Disco DJ Hire Agency Croydon
....07402 700695
e: soundofmusicdjagency@hotmail.com
w: www.soundofmusicmobiledisco.com

Photo Booth Hire

Booth Nation
7 Ezra Street, London
E2 7RH 020 7613 5576
e: info@boothnation.com
w: www.boothnation.com

Chuckle Pod Limited
....07770 692499
e: info@chucklepod.co.uk
w: www.chucklepod.co.uk

cityphotobooths
18 Tennyson Avenue, Rustington
West Sussex BN16 2PB 01903 771863
e: info@cityphotobooths.co.uk
w: www.cityphotobooths.co.uk

Foxy Photo Booth
82 Lammermuir Way, Chapelhall
Lanarkshire ML6 8BE.................0141 413 4096 - 07751 613 265
e: info@foxyphotobooth.com
w: www.foxyphotobooth.com

Funsnaps Photobooth
.... 7871613924
e: mail@funsnapsphotobooth.co.uk
w: www.funsnapsphotobooth.co.uk

HR Entertainment Ltd
.... 1706220338
e: jason@hrentertainment.co.uk
w: www.photoboothhire.org

JS Ent
Unit 5-7a, 109 Maybank Rd, South Woodford, London
E18 1EJ.. 020 8505 8222
e: sales@jsent.co.uk
w: www.jsent.co.uk

Megabooth
Unit 4, Rear of 41/43 Roebuck Road, Hainault Industrial Estate
Essex IG6 3TU... 020 3053 4333
e: info@megabooth.com
w: www.megabooth.com

Say Fromage
J109-110, The Biscuit Factory, 100 Clements Road, London
SE16 4DG 020 7237 1648
w: www.sayfromage.co.uk

Seasons Photobooth
Birmingham
West Midlands B68 8SS....................................... 079 9001 9006
w: www.seasonsphotobooth.co.uk

Snappabox Party & Event Photo Booth
The Powerhouse, 87 West Street, Harrow on the Hill
Middlesex HA1 3EL.. 0845 680 8995
w: www.snappabox.com

Style Booth
.... 0208 0900 105
e: hello@stylebooth.co.uk
w: www.stylebooth.co.uk

The Party Photo Booth
26 Granville Road, Bournemouth
Dorset BH5 2AQ.. 07894 477106
e: info@thepartyphotobooth.co.uk
w: www.thepartyphotobooth.co.uk

Zeven Media Ltd
Suite 3 Nexus, 4 Brindley Road, Manchester
M16 9HQ 020 7717 5408
e: info@zeven.co.uk
w: www.zevenmedia.com

Puppet Workshops

Puppet Works
....01603 470005 / 07833 972192
e: puppetworks@live.co.uk
w: www.puppetworks.net

Roller Rinks

Roller Magic
.... 07887 505693
e: simon@ice-magic.com
w: www.roller-skate-rink-hire.com

Sailing / Marine

All Marine Watersports
Unit 8 , 2 Ulwell Road, Swanage
BH19 1LH.. 0755 126 3434
e: info@allmarinewatersports.com
w: www.allmarinewatersports.com

Showgirls

The Jammy Showgirls
Century House South, North Station Road, Colchester
Essex CO1 1RE 07796 138884
e: anthony@jammyshowsandproductions.co.uk
w: www.jammyshowsandproductions.co.uk

Simulators

Golf At Home Ltd
Stable Cottage, Cherry Garden Lane, Maidenhead
Berkshire SL6 3QD 07905 163391
e: karen@golf-at-home.net
w: www.golf-at-home.net

Jemlar Ltd
P.O. Box 7416, Towcester
Northamptonshire NN12 6WB 0870 765 0536
e: sales@jemlar.com
w: www.jemlar.com

Premier Simulation
Woodstock House, Woodstock Close, Horsham
West Sussex RH12 5YT.. 01403 270076
e: mandi.lucas@virgin.net
w: www.mobilesimulators.co.uk

Simworx Limited
Second Avenue, The Pensett Estate, Kingswinford
West Midlands DY6 7UL....................................... 01384 295733
e: sales@simworx.co.uk
w: www.simworx.co.uk

ENTERTAINMENT/ ATTRACTIONS

16   SKY DIVING/PARACHUTISTS / SLOT CAR RACING / STAG NIGHTS / STEAM ENGINES/VEHICLES
STREET ENTERTAINMENT / TEAM BUILDING / VIDEO GAMING

Sky Diving / Parachutists

David Morris Action Sports
2 Daleside, Cotgrave
Nottinghamshire NG12 3QA 0115 989 3538
e: info@flatfly.co.uk
w: www.flatfly.co.uk

Slot Car Racing

Corporace
13 Carey Close, Moulton, Northampton
NN3 7SN...07713 121515
e: info@corporace.com
w: www.facebook.com/corporace

Stag Nights

Gamewagon Ltd
113 - 115 Oyster Lane, Byfleet
KT14 7JZ..0845 319 4263
e: admin@gamewagon.co.uk
w: www.gamewagon.info

Steam Engines / Vehicles

Bluebell Railway
Sheffield Park Station, Uckfield
East Sussex TN22 3QL...01825 720800
e: info@bluebell-railway.co.uk
w: www.bluebell-railway.co.uk

Great Central Railway Plc
Great Central Road, Loughborough
Leicestershire LE11 1RW.....................................01509 230726
e: booking_office@gcrailway.co.uk
w: www.gcrailway.co.uk

Paignton & Dartmouth Steam Railway
Queens Park Station, Torbay Road, Paignton
Devon TQ4 6AF..01803 555872
e: pdsr@talk21.com

Steamreplicas Ltd
82 Birmingham Road , , Great Barr , Birmingham
West Midlands B43 6NT 0121 580 8893
e: enquiries@steamreplicas.co.uk
w: www.steamreplicas.co.uk

Vintage Trains & Shakespeare Express
670 Warwick Road , , Tyseley, Birmingham
West Midlands B11 2HL...0121 708 4960
e: office@vintagetrains.co.uk
w: www.vintagetrains.co.uk

Street Entertainment

Electric Cabaret
107 High St, Brackley
NN13 7BN..07714 089 763
e: info@electriccabaret.co.uk
w: www.electriccabaret.co.uk

Team Building

Accolade Corporate Events
17 Chalford Avenue, The Reddings, Cheltenham
Gloucestershire GL51 6UF....................................01452 857 172
e: enquiries@accolade-corporate-events.com
w: www.accolade-corporate-events.com

Adventure Scotland Ltd
Croft House, 12 Croftside, Kingussie
Highlands PH22 1QJ...01479 811 411
e: info@adventure-scotland.com
w: www.adventure-scotland.com

All-terrain Services
Greetham Valley, Wood Lane , Greetham, Rutland
Leicestershire LE15 7NP......................................01792 862 669
e: info@4x4events.co.uk
w: www.4x4events.co.uk

Altitude Events Mobile Rock Climbing Walls
Old Brookhouse Barn, Brookhouse Lane, Framfield
East Sussex TN22 5QJ...07832 227571
e: mail@altitudeevents.org
w: www.altitudeevents.org

Anglia Sporting Activities
Hungarian Hall, , Pettistree, Woodbridge
Suffolk IP13 0JF 01394 460 475
e: enquiries@angliasport.co.uk
w: www.angliasport.co.uk

Arena Pursuits Ltd
Rosemary House, Rosemary Lane, Flimwell, Wadhurst
East Sussex TN5 7PT...01580 879 614
e: info@arenapursuits.com
w: www.arenapursuits.com

Ashcombe Adventure Centre Ltd
Colley Lane, , Ashcombe, Near Dawlish
Devon EX7 0QD 01626 866 766
e: info@ashcombeadventure.co.uk
w: www.ashcombeadventure.co.uk

Avalanche Adventure
The Wrongs, Welford Raod, Sibbertoft, Market Harborough
Leicestershire LE16 9UJ 01858 880 613
e: info@avalancheadventure.co.uk
w: www.avalancheadventure.co.uk

Awesome Events
Argo House, Argo Business Centre, Kilburn Park Road
London N56 5LF 0845 644 6510
e: sales@awesome-events.co.uk
w: www.awesome-events.co.uk

Banzai Action Sports Ltd
Stratton Court Barn, Pool Farm, Stratton Audley, Bicester
Oxfordshire OX27 9AJ... 01869 278199
e: info@banzaievents.com
w: www.banzaievents.com

Circomedia
St Paul's Church, Portland Square, Bristol
Avon BS2 8SJ.. 0117 947 7288
e: info@circomedia.com
w: www.circomedia.com

Creative Action
69 Highgate Road, Woodley, Reading
RG5 3ND... 0118 948 7058
e: andy@creative-action.co.uk
w: www.creative-action.co.uk

D&s Events
The Circuit Office, Donington Park, Derby
Derbyshire DE74 2RP 01332 810007
e: enquiries@dandsevents.co.uk
w: www.dandsevents.co.uk

Hatt Adventures
PO Box 5157, Brighton
BN50 9TW 01273 358359
e: adventures@thehatt.co.uk
w: www.thehatt.co.uk/adventures

Manby Motorplex
Manby Showground,, Manby, Louth
Lincolnshire LN11 8UZ... 01507 328855
e: info@manbymotorplex.com
w: www.manbymotorplex.com

Off Limits Corporate Events
East View Terrace, Langley Mill
NG16 4DF.. 01773 766047
e: links@actiondays.co.uk
w: www.actiondays.co.uk

Priory Events
Sandy Lane, Nutfield
Surrey RH1 4EJ 01737 822 484
e: info@prioryevents.co.uk
w: www.prioryevents.co.uk

Progressive Resources
Unit 6 Dell Buildings, Efford Park, Milford Road, Lymington
Hampshire SO41 0JD 01590 676599
e: info@teambuilding.co.uk
w: www.teambuilding.co.uk

Sno!zone Ltd
602 Marlborough Gate, Milton Keynes
Buckinghamshire MK9 3XS................................... 01908 680824
e: eventsmk@snozoneuk.com
w: www.snozoneuk.com

Spy Games
Coates Grounds, Singlebrough, Milton Keynes
Buckinghamshire MK17 0RF................................. 0845 1303 007
e: info@spy-games.com
w: www.spy-games.com

Sushi Team Building
.... 020 3287 2299
e: info@sushi-teambuilding.co.uk
w: www.sushi-teambuilding.co.uk

Team Building Solutions
Unit 7, Ampress Lane, Lymington Enterprise Centre, Lymington
Hampshire SO41 8LZ... 0845 121 1194
e: info@teambuildingsolutions.co.uk
w: www.teambuildingsolutions.co.uk

Teamday.co.uk
The Potters Barn, Roughwood Lane, Hassall Green,
Sandbach, Cheshire
CW11 4XX 01270 884080
e: breakthemould@teamday.co.uk
w: www.teamday.co.uk

Wild Events Ltd
The Valley, , Lamarsh, Bures
Suffolk CO8 5EZ.. 01787 269 819
e: info@wildevents.co.uk
w: www.wildevents.co.uk

Wingbeat Sporting Events
10 Strawberry Green, Whitby, Ellesmere Port
Cheshire CH66 2TX.. 0151 356 1208
e: wingbeat@lineone.net
w: www.wingbeatsportingevents.co.uk

Xtreme Vortex
85 Chessington Avenue , Bexleyheath
Kent DA7 5HF 07739 560990
e: mail@xtremevortex.co.uk
w: www.xtremevortex.co.uk

Video Gaming

Gamewagon Ltd
113 - 115 Oyster Lane, Byfleet
KT14 7JZ... 0845 319 4263
e: admin@gamewagon.co.uk
w: www.gamewagon.info

Vintage Vehicles / Car Displays

Coys Of Kensington
2-4 Queens Gate Mews, London
SW7 5QT 020 7584 7444
e: sales@coys.co.uk
w: www.coys.co.uk

Virtual Reality / Futuristic Games

Psw Events Ltd
The Old Chapel, 36 North Street, Burwell, Cambridge
Cambridgeshire CB25 0BA.................................. 0845 3703 660
e: sales@pswevents.co.uk
w: www.corporate-entertainment-hire.

Weddings

Chuckle Pod Limited
.... 07770 692499
e: info@chucklepod.co.uk
w: www.chucklepod.co.uk

Gamewagon Ltd
113 - 115 Oyster Lane, Byfleet
KT14 7JZ.. 0845 319 4263
e: admin@gamewagon.co.uk
w: www.gamewagon.info

Wine / Wine Tasting / Champagne

Charles Salt Fine Wines
Corner Cottage, 2 Park Row Cottages, Dawlish
Devon EX7 9NP... 0162 686 4381
e: salt@charliethewineman.co.uk
w: www.charliethewineman.co.uk

Grape Escapes Ltd
The Manor House, High Street, Buntingford
Hertfordshire SG9 9AB... 08456 430 860
e: mark@grapeescapes.net
w: www.grapeescapes.net

Lovely Bubbly
PO Box 330, Newcastle upon Tyne
Tyne & Wear NE3 1ZS.. 0845 2572754
e: info@lovelybubbly.co.uk
w: www.lovelybubbly.co.uk

Taste Of The Vine
Jeroboam House, Sandy Lane, Grayswood, Haselmere
Surrey GU27 2DG... 01428 656319
e: events@tasteofthevine.co.uk
w: www.tasteofthevine.co.uk

The Tasting Quarter
West Lodge Farm, Low Road, Easton, Norwich
NR9 5EN... 01603 340 084
e: info@thetastingquarter.com
w: www.thetastingquarter.com

Thirty Fifty Wine Tastings
24 Chestnut Road, Twickenham
London TW2 5QZ 0208 288 0314
e: chris.scott@thirtyfifty.co.uk
w: www.thirtyfifty.co.uk

Vinisus Wines
Loveletts, Gossops Green, Crawley
West Sussex RH11 8EG 01293 734664
e: info@vinisus.com
w: www.vinisus.com

Vintellect
Heronsmere, Ashtead Woods Rd, Ashtead
Surrey KT21 2ET.. 01372 272295
e: info@vintellect.co.uk
w: www.vintellect.co.uk

West London Wine School
2b Silver Crescent, , Chiswick, London
Greater London W4 5SE...................................... 020 8144 2444
e: info@westlondonwineschool.com
w: www.westlondonwineschool.com

Winfield Wine Events
38 The Avenue
London W13 8LP... 0208 997 4718
e: gilbert@winfieldwines.co.uk
w: www.winfieldwines.co.uk

Access Towers / Tools

A

24 Hour Lightning Locksmiths
RUSSET WAY, KINGS HILL, WEST MALLING
ME19 4FJ 7526103597
e: info@24hrlightninglocksmiths.com
w: www.24hrlightninglocksmiths.com/

Access Platform Sales Ltd
LEEWOOD BUSINESS PARK, UPTON, HUNTINGDON
Cambridgeshire PE28 5YQ 0845 108 4000
e: sales@iapsgroup.com
w: www.accessplatforms.co.uk

Accesscaff International Ltd
37 CROYDON ROAD, BECKENHAM
Kent BR3 4AB 0844 848 7784
e: mraccess@mraccessuk.com
w: www.accesscaffinternational.com

Acorn Event Structures
MOXON WAY, MOOR LANE TRADING ESTATE, SHERBURN IN
ELMET, LEEDS
West Yorkshire LS25 6ES 0800 078 7916
e: info@acorn-events.com
w: www.acorn-events.com

Advanced Access Platforms
ACCESS HOUSE, UNIT 1, 299 GANDER GREEN LANE, , SUTTON
Surrey SM3 9QE 020 8641 7050
e: info@advancedaccessplatforms.co.uk
w: www.advancedaccessplatforms.co.uk

Alloy Access Ltd
THE SCAFFMAN, 120 BEDDINGTON LANE, CROYDON
Surrey CR0 4TD 020 8684 6999
e: info@precipitous.co.uk
w: www.alloyaccess.net

Caunton Access Ltd
UNIT 88, ROAD B, BOUGHTON INDUSTRIAL ESTATE, NEWARK
Nottinghamshire NG22 9LD 0800 246 5815
e: info@cauntonaccess.co.uk
w: www.cauntonaccess.co.uk

Certex (UK) Ltd
UNIT C1 HARWORTH INDUSTRIAL ESTATE, BRYANS CLOSE,
HARWORTH
Nottinghamshire DN11 8RY...................................01302 756 777
e: sales@certex.co.uk
w: www.certex.co.uk

Claydon Yield o Meter Limited
BUNTERS ROAD , WICKHAMBROOK, NEWMARKET
Suffolk CB8 8XY..1440820327
e: stephen.ball@claydondrill.com
w: www.claydondrills.com

CLM Access Ltd
PLAZA BUILDING, 102 LEE HIGH ROAD, LEWISHAM, LONDON
Greater London SE13 5PQ.....................................07599 999 219
e: info@clmaccess.co.uk
w: www.clmaccess.co.uk

DGM Services UK Ltd
25 WOOD LANE, COTTON END, BEDFORD
MK45 3AJ...01234 743573
e: darren@dgmservices.co.uk
w: www.dgmservices.co.uk

Elev8 Access Platforms Ltd
UNIT 2B, CLAY STREET, SHEFFIELD
South Yorkshire S9 2PF..0845 274 3627
e: hiredesk@elev8hire.com
w: www.elev8hire.com

Essex Hire & Sales
245 ONGAR ROAD , BRENTWOOD
Essex CM15 9DZ 01277 222 382
e: essexhireandsale@aol.com
w: www.essexhire.co.uk

Fairport Plate Compactors
BLAGDEN STREET, SHEFFIELD
South Yorkshire S2 5QS 01142 767 921
e: sales@fairport.uk.com
w: www.fairport.uk.com

Gem Tool Hire & Sales Ltd
28 WEDGWOOD ROAD, BICESTER
Oxfordshire OX26 4UL.. 01869 245945
e: info@gem-tools.co.uk
w: www.gem-tools.co.uk

Herts Tool Co.
LYON WAY, HATFIELD ROAD, ST. ALBANS
Hertfordshire AL4 0LR...01727 832 131
e: info@hertstools.co.uk
w: www.hertstools.co.uk

Hewden
SALTIRE COURT, 20 CASTLE TERRACE, EDINBURGH
Edinburgh EH1 2EN...0845 60 70 111
e: hirenow@hewden.co.uk
w: www.hewden.co.uk

Hiremech
UNIT 1, TARIFF ROAD, TOTTENHAM, LONDON
Greater London N17 0EB 020 8880 3322
e: sales@hiremech.co.uk
w: www.hiremech.co.uk

HiTech Engineering
HEATHFIELD WAY, , UNIT 108-111 K2 HOUSE, NORTHAMPTON
Northamptonshire NN5 7QP ....
.... 01604586175 / 01604 757 414 / 078 94 62
e: office@hitecheng.co.uk
w: www.hitecheng.co.uk

HSS Hire
25 WILLOW LANE, MITCHAM
Surrey CR4 4TS .... 08457 28 28 28 / 08456 02 19 61
w: www.hsseventhire.com

JMS Plant Hire Ltd
32 COLDHARBOUR LANE, HARPENDEN
Hertfordshire AL5 4UN 0845 4670000
e: hire@jms-access.co.uk
w: www.jms-planthire.co.uk

Kimberly Access (London)
COURT LANE ESTATE, IVER
Buckinghamshire SL0 9HL....................................0870 066 6684
e: makecontact@kimberlyaccess.co.uk
w: www.kimberlyaccess.co.uk

Lakeside-Hire
BRETTS FARM, ROMFORD RD, AVELEY
Essex RM15 4XD 0333 920 2076
e: hire@lakeside-hire.co.uk
w: www.lakeside-hire.co.uk

Nationwide Platforms
UNIT 15 MIDLAND COURT, CENTRAL PARK, LUTTERWORTH
Leicestershire LE17 4PN..01455 558874
e: webadmin@lavendongroup.com
w: www.nationwideplatforms.co.uk

Nationwide Services Group Ltd
NATIONWIDE HOUSE, 2 FRANKTON WAY, GOSPORT
Hampshire PO12 1FR................. 02392 604479 // 02392 604300
e: sales@nationwideservices.co.uk
w: www.nationwideservices.co.uk

Newburn Power Rental
NIT 36, LIDGATE CRESCENT, , LANGTHWAITE BUSINESS
PARK,SOUTH KIRKBY, PONTEFRACT
West Yorkshire WF9 3NR 0845 077 6693
e: info@npr-uk.com
w: www.newburnpowerrental.com

Outreach Ltd
ABBOTS ROAD, MIDDLEFIELD INDUSTRIAL ESTATE, FALKIRK
Stirlingshire FK2 9AR 01324 889000
e: mailbox@outreachltd.co.uk
w: www.outreachltd.co.uk

Power Platform Services
LYN HOUSE, IVY MILL LANE, GODSTONE
Surrey RH9 8NR...01883 744 766
w: www.pps.co.uk

Premier Plant Hire
48A BURBAGE ROAD , GIANT ARCHES 12-23 , LONDON
 SE24 9HE 020 3582 7691
e: premierplant@hotmail.com
w: www.premierplanthire.co.uk/

RS Power Solutions Ltd
868 PLYMOUTH ROAD, SLOUGH TRADING ESTATE, SLOUGH
Berkshire SL1 4PL 01753 568 050
e: hire@rspowersolutions.co.uk
w: rspowersolutions.co.uk

Smart Platform Rental Ltd........................0333 800 6000
e: sales@smartplatforms.co.uk
w: www.smartplatforms.co.uk

Southern Plant & Tool Hire Ltd
UNIT 10, CENTENARY BUSINESS PARK, STATION RD,
HENLEY ON THAMES
Oxfordshire RG9 1DS .... 01491 576 063 /
01491 573515

e: info@southernplant.co.uk
w: www.southernplant.co.uk

Speedy Events
CHASE HOUSE, 16 THE PARKS, NEWTON-LE-WILLOWS
Merseyside WA12 0JQ .... 01942 720000 /
0845 609 9998

e: customerservices@speedyhire.com
w: www.speedyservices.com

Turner Access Ltd
65 CRAIGTON ROAD, GLASGOW
Glasgow G51 3EQ 0141 309 5555
e: enquiries@turner-access.co.uk
w: www.turner-access.co.uk

Winner Events
1 NORTH MOORS, SLYFIELD INDUSTRIAL ESTATE, GUILDFORD
Surrey GU1 1SE 0845 601 5427
e: sales@winnerevents.com
w: www.winnerevents.com

Working At Height Limited
AMBERLEY COURT, OLD ELSTEAD ROAD, MILFORD
Surrey GU8 5EB 01483 415410
e: workingatheightlocal2@outlook.com
w: www.workingatheightltd.com

Youngman Group Limited
THE CAUSEWAY, MALDON
Essex CM9 4LJ 01621 745 900
e: uk.customercare@wernerco.com
w: www.youngmangroup.com

Accommodation

Applehouse Travel
UNIVERSAL HOUSE, 20-22 HIGH ST, IVER
Buckinghamshire SL0 9NG 0844 855 8140
w: www.applehousetravel.co.uk

Baden Powell House
65-67 QUEEN'S GATE, LONDON
Greater London SW7 5JS.....................................020 7590 6909
e: bph.conferences@scout.org.uk
w: www.towntocountry.co.uk/bpHouse/

A

Brickhouse Farm Cottages
BRICKHOUSE LANE , POULTON-LE-FYLDE, HAMBLETON
Lancashire FY6 9BG...1253702122
e: info@brickhousecottages.co.uk
w: www.brickhousecottages.co.uk

Brook House Farm
WALL UNDER HEYWOOD, CHURCH STRETTON, HEYWOOD
Shropshire SY6 7DS..01694 771599
e: info@brookcottageandcamping.co.uk
w: www.brookcottageandcamping.co.uk

Duddings Country Cottages
TIMBERSCOMBE, DUNSTER, MINEHEAD
 TA24 7TB..01643 841123
e: richard@duddings.co.uk
w: www.duddings.co.uk

Highland Club Direct
.............................0800 731 6651 / 02032390894 / 0758403396
e: info@highlandclubdirect.com
w: www.highlandclubdirect.com

Middleham House
KIRKGATE, MIDDLEHAM
North Yorkshire DL8 4PG.......................................020 77335716
e: info@themiddlehamhouse.com
w: www.themiddlehamhouse.com

Oakdale Apartments
WEST MEAD HOUSE , WESTMEAD FARNBOROUGH
Hampshire GU14 7LP..0800 246 1126
e: info@oakdaleapartments.co.uk
w: www.oakdaleapartments.co.uk

PKL Group (UK) Ltd
STELLA WAY, BISHOPS CLEEVE, CHELTENHAM
Gloucestershire GL52 7DQ....................................01242 663 000
e: postbox@pkl.co.uk
w: www.pkl.co.uk

Plas Hafod Ltd
GWERNYMYNYDD, MOLD
 CH7 5JS 01352 700177
e: reception@plashafodhotel.com
w: www.plashafod.co.uk

The Apartment Service
5-6 FRANCIS GROVE, WIMBLEDON, LONDON
Greater London SW19 4DT....................................020 8944 1444
w: www.apartmentservice.com

The Cranley Hotel
10 BINA GARDENS, SOUTH KENSINGTON, LONDON
Greater London SW5 0LA......................................020 7373 0123
e: reception@cranleyhotel.com
w: www.cranleyhotel.com

THE HOLLINS HEY HOTEL
191, VICTORIA ROAD, NEW BRIGHTON, WIRRAL
Merseyside CH45 0JY..0151 6911171
e: hhhenquiry@aol.com
w: www.hollinsheyhotel.co.uk

The Landmark London
222 MARYLEBONE ROAD
Greater London NW1 6JQ .... +44 20 7631 8000
e: thelandmarklon@viziamail.com
w: www.landmarklondon.co.uk

Travel Counsellors Ltd
TRAVEL HOUSE, 43 CHURCHGATE, BOLTON
Lancashire BL1 1TH................... 01773 318910 / 07973 306280
e: louise.cutting@travelcounsellors.com
w: www.tctravelmanagement.co.uk/loui

Acoustic / Noise Control

Advanced Acoustics
UNIT B MAUNSIDE, GREENLINES IND EST, MANSFIELD
Nottinghamshire NG18 5GU 01623 643609
e: info@advancedacoustics-uk.com
w: www.advancedacoustics-uk.com

Attend2IT
UNIT 8, PARK FARM INDUSTRIAL ESTATE, BUNTINGFORD
Hertfordshire SG9 9AZ 01763 877 477
w: www.attend2it.co.uk

DACS Ltd
UNIT A19, STONEHILLS, SHIELDS ROAD, PELAW, GATESHEAD
 NE10 0HW 0191 438 2500
e: sales@dacs-audio.com
w: www.dacs-audio.com

EarpieceOnline
19 MEON ROAD, BASINGSTOKE
Hampshire RG23 7AL..0845 838 7109
e: sales@earpieceonline.co.uk
w: www.earpieceonline.co.uk

F1 Acoustics Company Ltd
38 BRITON HILL ROAD, SANDERSTEAD,, SOUTH CROYDON
Surrey CR2 0JL..01227 770 890
e: info@f1acoustics.com
w: www.f1acoustics.com

Industrial Acoustics Company
IAC HOUSE, MOORSIDE ROAD, WINCHESTER
Hampshire SO23 7US 01962 873 000
e: info@iacl-uk.com
w: www.iac-acoustics.com

Rock-Tech Projects
UNIT 2, FRYORS COURT, MURTON
Yorkshire YO19 5UY 01904 481 700
e: info@rock-tech.co.uk
w: www.rock-tech.co.uk

A

Shaun Murkett Acoustic Consultants Ltd
1 CLISSOLD ROAD, STOKE NEWINGTON, LONDON
Greater London N16 9EX.......................................020 7923 7275
e: murkett@aol.com
w: www.shaunmurkett-acoustics.co.uk

Sound Advice Acoustics
2 WEST LINKS, TOLLGATE, CHANDLERS FORD
Hampshire SO53 3TG 02380 253 010
e: info@soundadviceacoustics.co.uk
w: www.soundadviceacoustics.co.uk

Sound Advice Acoustics Ltd
2 WEST LINKS, TOLLGATE , CHANDLERS FORD
Hampshire SO53 3TG .... 07976630808 / 02380253010
e: info@soundadviceacoustics.co.uk
w: www.soundadviceacoustics.co.uk/

StageCore
UNIT 6 EAST GATE BUSINESS PARK, ARGALL WAY, LONDON
Greater London E10 7PG.....................................020 3697 3888
e: info@stagecore.co.uk
w: www.stagecore.co.uk

Studio Wizard
MELTON PARK , MELTON CONSTABLE
Norfolk NR24 2NJ 01263 862 999
e: info@studiowizard.com
w: www.studiowizard.com

Symphotech Ltd
....0871 711 5264
e: info@symphotech.co.uk
w: www.symphotech.co.uk

Three Spires Acoustics Ltd
2 SYKE INGS, RICHINGS PARK, IVER HEATH
Buckinghamshire SL0 9ET .... 01753 651185 // 07939 324 063
e: chris@threespiresacoustics.co.uk
w: www.threespiresacoustics.co.uk

Veale Associates Ltd
16 NORTH ROAD, STEVENAGE
Hertfordshire SG1 4AL 01438 747666
w: www.va-studiodesign.com/

VNV Sounds
UNITS 10 AND 10A ASHLEY HOUSE, ASHLEY ROAD, LONDON
Greater London N17 9LZ.......................................0203 021 1370
e: info@vnvlive.co.uk
w: www.vnvsounds.co.uk

Action / Adventure Days

Altitude Events
OLD BROOKHOUSE BARN, BROOKHOUSE LANE, FRAMFIELD
Sussex TN22 5QJ 07832 227 571
e: mail@altitudeevents.org
w: www.altitudeevents.org

Big Bang Promotions International Ltd
MAGNA SCIENCE ADVENTURE CENTRE, SHEFFIELD ROAD,
TEMPLEBOROUGH, ROTHERHAM
Yorkshire S60 1DX 0845 319 2767
e: info@bigbang-promotions.com
w: www.bigbang-promotions.com

Highline Adventure
MILL FARMHOUSE , MILL ROAD , SHOULDHAM THORPE ,
KINGS LYNN
PE33 0EA..08454 091 303
e: highlinemd@highlineadventure.co.uk
w: www.highlineadventure.co.uk

Izorb
VICTORIA HOUSE, GREAT ANCOATS STREET, MANCHESTER
M4 7EA..07779 150 145
e: martin@izorb.org
w: www.izorb.org

Just Add Water Sports
UNIT 27, GRAPHITE WAY, HADFIELD
Derbyshire SK13 1QH 01457 238285
e: info@jawsltd.co.uk
w: www.jawsltd.co.uk

Sky High Bungee
145 CARR LANE, DRONFIELD WOOD HOUSE, DRONFIELD
Derbyshire S18 8XF 0114 289 0173
e: info@skyhighbungee.com
w: www.skyhighbungee.com

Skyfall Mobile Zip Wire Hire
MAYFIELD HOUSE, 133 WALMSERSLEY RD, BURY
Lancashire BI9 5AY 01625 532098
w: www.mobileziplinehire.co.uk

The Gnat Display Team
HERITAGE AIRCRAFT LIMITED, HANGAR 4A, NORTH WEALD
AIRFIELD, EPPING
CM16 6HR 07942 800 921
e: info@gnatdisplayteam.com
w: www.gnatdisplayteam.com

Uk Bungee Club
MAGNA SCIENCE ADVENTURE CENTRE, SHEFFIELD ROAD,
TEMPLEBOROUGH, ROTHERHAM
S60 1DX 01709 366 660
e: info@ukbungee.co.uk
w: www.visitmagna.co.uk

Advertising Agencies

A2ZLeapfrog
.... +9715 52323941
e: robsz@a2zleapfrog.com
w: www.a2zleapfrogonline.com

A

Aboveline Ltd
UNIT 4G, WISTASTON ROAD BUSINESS CENTRE   , WISTASTON ROAD, CREWE
Cheshire CW2 7RP..01270 848650
e: info@aboveline.co.uk
w: www.aboveline.co.uk

Adam & Eve DDB
12 BISHOPS BRIDGE ROAD, LONDON
Greater London W2 6AA..020 7258 3979
e: hello@adamandeveddb.com
w: www.adamandeveddb.com

Allsee Technologies Ltd
UNIT 5, WOODGATE BUSINESS PARK, KETTLES WOOD DRIVE, , BIRMINGHAM, BARTLEY GREEN
West Midlands B32 3DB 0121 421 4458
e: info@allsee-tech.com
w: www.allsee-tech.com

Aroma Company (europe) Ltd
HILLIARD HOUSE, LESTER WAY, WALLINGFORD
Oxfordshire OX10 9TA..01491 835510
e: info@aromaco.co.uk
w: www.aromaco.co.uk

Bartle Bogle & Hegarty
60 KINGLY STREET, LONDON
Greater London W1B 5DS 020 7734 1677
e: tim.harvey@bartleboglehegarty.com
w: www.bartleboglehegarty.com

Command D Ltd
10 MARGARET STREET, LONDON
Greater London W1W 8RL....................................020 3008 4994
w: www.commandhq.co.uk

Creative Advertising Ltd
11A GILDREDGE ROAD, EASTBOURNE
East Sussex BN21 4RB 01323 725472
w: www.creative-ad.co.uk

Ecobikeads
2 BEECHES LODGE, FOREST ROAD , CUDDINGTON, NORTHWICH
CHESTER CW8 2EH.......... 1244960193
e: info@ecobikeads.co.uk
w: www.ecobikeads.co.uk/

Flemington House
FLEMINGTON STREET, SPRINGBURN, GLASGOW
G21 4BF .... 0141 889 8000 / 0141 558 3541
e: flemingtonhouseuk@gmail.com
w: flemingtonhouse.com/

Fluid
12 TENBY STREET, BIRMINGHAM
West Midlands B1 3AJ..0121 212 0121
e: info@fluiddesign.co.uk
w: www.fluiddesign.co.uk

Hannon Homes
K204 THE BISCUIT FACTORY, TOWER BRIDGE BUSINESS COMPLEX,100 CLEMENTS ROAD, LONDON
SE16 4DG..2072375326
e: info@hannon-homes.co.uk
w: www.hannon-homes.co.uk

Hatch Creations Ltd
MERIDIAN HOUSE, 365 WESTHORNE AVENUE, GREENWICH PARK, LONDON
Greater London SE12 9AB....................................0208 297 1200
e: info@hatchcreations.co.uk
w: www.hatchcreations.co.uk

Hhc Lewis
THREEFIELD HOUSE, THREEFIELD LANE, SOUTHAMPTON
Hampshire SO14 3LP... 02382 021319
e: enquiries@hhc-lewis.co.uk
w: www.hhc-lewis.co.uk

Home Counties Estate Agents
108 HIGH STREET, POTTERS BAR, HERTS
EN6 5AT..1707245555
e: rlowry@home-counties.com
w: www.home-counties.com

Hps Group
ATLAS HOUSE, THIRD AVENUE, GLOBE PARK, MARLOW
Buckinghamshire SL7 1EY....................................01628 894700
e: hello@hpsgroup.co.uk
w: www.hpsgroup.co.uk

Iconic Brand Agency
FLAXMAN COURT , 112-114 WARDOUR STREET , LONDON
W1F 0TS..2072872037
e: julia@iconicbrand.co.uk
w: www.iconicbrand.co.uk/

Jack Morton Worldwide
16-18 ACTON PARK ESTATE, STANLEY GARDENS, LONDON
Greater London W3 7QE.......................................020 8735 2000
e: victoria_yates@jackmorton.co.uk
w: www.jackmorton.com

JK Advertising Ltd
730 PERSHORE ROAD, SELLY PARK, BIRMINGHAM
West Midlands B29 7NJ..0121 472 1000
e: info@jkadvertising.co.uk
w: www.jkadvertising.co.uk

Koala Limited
18 SOHO SQUARE, SOHO, WESTMINSTER
Greater London W1D 3QL.....................................2030210260
e: hello@koalatv.com
w: koalatv.com

Leapfrog
....1222144557
e: robsz@a2zleapfrog.com
w: www.a2zleapfrog.com

Mydisplays.co.uk
16 UPPER WOBURN PLACE, LONDON
WC1H 0BS...0 203 794 7626
e: info@mydisplays.co.uk
w: www.mydisplays.co.uk

Ontrac Agency
BERWYN HOUSE, 46 MOCHDRE ENTERPRISE PARK, NEWTOWN,
BS48 4NP.. 01686 620400
e: info@ontracagency.com
w: www.ontracagency.com

Resource Advertising Ltd
....01202 746900
e: zoe@resourceadvertising.co.uk
w: www.resourceadvertising.co.uk

Response Uk
48 CHARLOTTE STREET, LONDON
Greater London W1T 2NS.................................. 020 3008 5533 /
07831 875888
e: info@responseuk.com
w: www.responseuk.com

Rock Kitchen Harris
32 POCKLINGTONS WALK, LEICESTER
Leicestershire LE1 6BU...0116 233 7500
e: hello@rkh.co.uk
w: www.rkh.co.uk

Root
UNIT 9, 37 - 42 CHARLOTTE ROAD, SHOREDITCH, LONDON
Greater London EC2A 3PG 0207 7392277
e: info@thisisroot.co.uk
w: www.thisisroot.co.uk

Sans Frontiere Marketing Communications
73 HIGH STREET, LEWES
East Sussex BN7 1XG 01273 487 800
e: info@sansfrontiere.co.uk
w: www.sansfrontiere.co.uk

Sigma Marketing & Advertising Ltd
64 CREMYLL STREET, STONEHOUSE, PLYMOUTH
Devon PL1 3RE..01752 668813
e: admin@sigma-marketing.co.uk
w: www.sigma-marketing.co.uk

Small Back Room
5 WOOTTON STREET, LONDON
Greater London SE1 8TG.......................................020 7902 7600
e: b.slade@smallbackroom.co.uk
w: www.smallbackroom.com

Smart Moving Media UK Ltd
96 SEYMOUR PLACE, LONDON
Greater London W1H 1NB .... 08000 324340 / 020 3544 8173
e: uk@smartmovingmedia.co.uk
w: www.smartmovingmedia.co.uk

The Advertising Bike Company
1 UNDERCROFT, YORK
Yorkshire YO19 5RP 07712 887551
e: sales@advertisingbikeco.net
w: www.advertisingbikeco.net

The Big Cat Group Ltd
GRIFFIN HOUSE, 18-19 LUDGATE HILL, BIRMINGHAM
West Midlands B3 1DW..0121 200 0910
e: info@bcguk.com
w: www.bigcatgroup.co.uk/

The Main Stage
....0800 321 3406
e: hello@themainstage.com
w: https://themainstage.com/

Agricultural Shows

Bath & West of England Society
BATH & WEST SHOWGROUND, SHEPTON MALLET
Somerset BA4 6QN 01749 822200
e: info@bathandwest.co.uk
w: www.bathandwest.com

Fusion Events
KILLINGTON HALL, KILLINGTON, KIRKBY LONSDALE, CARNFORTH
Lancashire LA6 2HA 0845 4900 142
e: admin@farm-smart.co.uk
w: www.farm-smart.co.uk

North Of England Horticultural Society
REGIONAL AGRICULTURAL CENTRE, GREAT YORKSHIRE
SHOWGROUND, HARROGATE
North Yorkshire HG2 8NZ 01423 546158
e: info@flowershow.org.uk
w: www.flowershow.org.uk

Royal Agricultural Society of England
THE ARTHUR RANK CENTRE, STONELEIGH PARK,, KENILWORTH,
Warwickshire CV8 2LZ...02476 692 470
e: emilys@rase.org.uk
w: www.rase.org.uk

South Of England Agricultural Society
SOUTH OF ENGLAND CENTRE , ARDINGLY, HAYWARDS HEATH
West Sussex RH17 6TL...01444 892700
e: seas@btclick.com
w: www.seas.org.uk

Air Con / H&V

Air Systems Mechanical Services
280 MAIN ROAD, WALTERS ASH, HIGH WYCOMBE
Buckinghamshire HP14 4TJ....................................01494 566001
e: info@as-ms.co.uk
w: www.as-ms.co.uk

A

Andrews Sykes
ST DAVID'S COURT, UNION STREET, WOLVERHAMPTON
West Midlands WV1 3JE...0800 211 611
w: www.andrews-sykes.com

Carrier Rental Systems
UNIT 3, THORPE INDUSTRIAL ESTATE, CRABTREE ROAD, THORPE
Surrey TW20 8RJ..0870 182 9824
e: info@carrierrentalsystems.co.uk
w: www.carrierrentalsystems.co.uk

Speedy Events
CHASE HOUSE, 16 THE PARKS, NEWTON-LE-WILLOWS
Merseyside WA12 0JQ
.... 01942 720000 / 0845 609 9998
e: customerservices@speedyhire.com
w: www.speedyservices.com

Surrey Air Conditioning
244 GRAND DRIVE, RAYNES PARK, LONDON
SW20 9NE 020 8542 6100
e: phil@surreyairconditioning.com
w: www.surreyairconditioning.com

Tower Productions
23 ALBERT ROAD , EDINBURGH
Edinburgh EH6 7DP ....
.... +44 131 552 0100
e: enquiries@tower-productions.com
w: www.tower-productions.com

Watkins Hire Ltd
UNITS 24-28, BURNBANK INDUSTRIAL ESTATE, BURNBANK
ROAD, FALKIRK
Stirlingshire FK2 7PE 01324 664 222
e: cameron.loftus@wakinshire.co.uk
w: www.watkinshire.co.uk

Watkins Hire Ltd (Skelmersdale)
GARDINERS PLACE, WEST GILLIBRANDS, SKELMERSDALE
Lancashire WN8 9SP 01695 724888
e: alan.ferguson@watkinshire.co.uk
w: www.watkinshire.co.uk

Watkins Hire Ltd (Walsall)
BRINETON STREET, QUAYSIDE DRIVE, WALSALL
West Midlands WS2 9LA 01922 634797
e: chris.easterlow@wakins.co.uk
w: www.watkinshire.co.uk

All Terrain / Off Road / 4WD

Driveme.net - Driving Experiences
SEIGHFORD AIRFIELD, SEIGHFORD, STAFFORD
Staffordshire ST18 9QE..01244 833 895
e: nicci@driveme.net
w: www.driveme.net

Animals

Animal Dramatics
PORKERS COTTAGE AND STABLES, BAUGHURST ROAD,
ALDERMASTON
RG7 4PJ 07831 409457
e: jackie@animaldramatics.co.uk
w: www.animaldramatics.co.uk

Celebrity Reptiles
11 TRAMWAY CLOSE, PENGE
London SE20 7DF 020 8659 0877
e: info@celebrityreptiles.co.uk
w: www.celebrityreptiles.co.uk

Creature Feature
GIBHILL FARM, DUMFRIES
Dumfries & Galloway DG1 1RL..............................01387 860648
e: david@creaturefeature.co.uk
w: www.creaturefeature.co.uk

The Exotic Animal ENCOUNTER
....7714745033
e: exoticanimalencounters@live.com
w: www.theexoticanimalencounter.co.u

Tricky Tykes Terrier Racing Display Team
CILYBLAIDD MANOR, PENCARREG, LLANYBYDDER
Carmarthenshire SA40 9QL..................................01570 480090
e: info@trickytykes.co.uk
w: www.trickytykes.co.uk

Aquatic / Marine Displays

Amazing Animals
HEYTHROP ZOOLOGICAL GARDENS LTD, HEYTHROP,
CHIPPING NORTON
Oxfordshire OX7 5TU..01608 683389
e: jclubb@amazinganimals.co.uk
w: www.amazinganimals.co.uk

Aquabatix
24 SIDNEY ROAD, BECKENHAM
Kent BR3 4QA...020 8144 2782
e: info@aquabatix.com
w: www.aquabatix.com

Archery

Archery4All
FIRST FLOOR, 41 ROSEHEATH, HEMEL HEMPSTEAD
HP1 2NG.................................. 01442 245700 // 07850 843005
e: grandaffairsgroup@gmail.com
w: www.archery4all.co.uk

A

Corporate Archery Events
11 ALLINGTON ROAD, SOUTHVILLE
Bristol BS3 1PS......................................07770 982 290
e: info@corporatearcheryevents.co.uk
w: www.corporatearcheryevents.co.uk

On Target Archery
1 OTTERBOURNE, 7 SURREY ROAD, BOURNEMOUTH
BH2 6BP..................01202 779072 // 0780 1643 404 // 0780 16
e: info@archery.me.uk
w: www.archery.me.uk

The Ackers
GOLDEN HILLOCK ROAD, SMALL HEATH, BIRMINGHAM
B11 2PY 0121 772 5111
e: info@ackers-adventure.co.uk
w: www.ackers-adventure.co.uk

Artist Liaison

Artist Needs Ltd
41 ST PAUL'S STREET , LEEDS
West Yorkshire LS1 2JG 0113 244 0410
e: info@artistneeds.com
w: www.artistneeds.com

Black and White Live
....0208 422 0042
e: info@blackandwhitelive.com
w: www.blackandwhitelive.com

Multiversal Events
261 DITCHLING ROAD, BRIGHTON
East Sussex BN1 6JH.......................... 01273 900221 /
07880 704378
e: info@multiversalevents.co.uk
w: www.multiversalevents.co.uk

Sevens7
3RD FLOOR , 46A ROSEBERY AVENUE, LONDON
Greater London EC1R 4RP 020 3096 1348
e: info@sevens7.co.uk
w: www.sevens7.co.uk

Associations / Organisations

Advertising Association
7TH FLOOR NORTH ARTILLERY HOUSE, 11-19 ARTILLERY ROW, LONDON
Greater London SW1P 1RT...................................020 7340 1100
e: aa@adassoc.org.uk
w: www.adassoc.org.uk

Association For Conferences & Events
MARSH WAY , RAINHAM
Essex RM13 8EU....................................0208 596 5458
e: ace@ace-international.org
w: www.ace-international.co.uk

Association Of British Professional Conference Organisers
BARN DOWN , 2 POOL ROW, WILLERSEY
Gloucestershire WR12 7PJ....................................0138 685 8886
e: hello@abpco.org
w: www.abpco.org

Association Of Event Organisers (AEO)
119 HIGH STREET, BERKHAMSTED
Hertfordshire HP4 2DJ 01442 285810
e: info@aeo.org.uk
w: www.aeo.org.uk

Association Of Event Venues (aev)
119 HIGH STREET , BERKHAMSTED
Hertfordshire HP4 2DJ 01442 285811
e: info@aev.og.uk
w: www.aev.org.uk

Association Of Festival Organisers
FOLKARTS ENGLAND , PO BOX 296, MATLOCK
Derbyshire DE4 3XU...01629 827014
e: info@festivalorganisers.org
w: www.festivalorganisers.org

Association Of Lighting Designers (ald)
PO BOX 955, SOUTHSEA
Hampshire PO1 9NF 07817 060189
e: office@ald.org.uk
w: www.ald.org.uk

Association Of Professional Recording Services (APRS)
PO BOX 22, TOTNES
Devon TQ9 7YZ...01803 868600
e: admin@aprs.co.uk
w: www.aprs.co.uk

Auto-cycle Union
ACU HOUSE, WOOD STREET, RUGBY
Warwickshire CV21 2YX...01788 566400
e: admin@acu.org.uk
w: www.acu.org.uk

BAFTA
195 PICCADILLY, LONDON
Greater London W1J 9LN 0207 7340022
e: info@bafta.org
w: www.bafta.org

Bath Conference Plus
....01225 322435
e: tourism@bathtourism.co.uk
w: www.bathconference.co.uk

British & International Federation Of Festivals
FESTIVALS HOUSE, 198 PARK LANE, MACCLESFIELD
Cheshire SK11 6UD 01625 428297
e: info@federationoffestivals.org.uk
w: www.federationoffestivals.org.uk

A

British Amateur Rugby League Association
WEST YORKSHIRE HOUSE, 4 NEW NORTH PARADE,
HUDDERSFIELD
West Yorkshire HD1 5JP..01484 599113
e: secretary@barla.org.uk
w: www.barla.org.uk

British Horse Society
ABBEY PARK, STARETON, KENILWORTH
Warwickshire CV8 2XZ..02476 840500
e: enquiry@bhs.org.uk
w: www.bhs.org.uk

British Hospitality Association (bha)
AUGUSTINE HOUSE, 6A AUSTIN FRIARS, LONDON
Greater London EC2N 2HA 020 7404 7744
e: bha@bha.org.uk
w: www.bha.org.uk

British Universities Film & Video Council
77 WELLS STREET, LONDON
Greater London W1T 3QJ......................................020 7393 1500
e: ask@bufvc.ac.uk
w: www.bufvc.ac.uk

British Video Association
3 SOHO SQUARE, LONDON
Greater London W1D 3HD 020 7439 8817
e: general@bva.org.uk
w: www.bva.org.uk

Community Media Association
15 PATERNOSTER ROW, SHEFFIELD
South Yorkshire S1 2BX 0114 279 5219
e: info@commedia.org.uk
w: www.commedia.org.uk

Concert Promoters Association (CPA)
6 ST MARK'S ROAD, HENLEY ON THAMES
Oxfordshire RG9 1LJ...01491 575060
e: carolesmith.cpa@virgin.net
w: www.concertpromotersassociation.c

Confederation Of Aerial Industries Ltd
COMMUNICATIONS HOUSE, 41A MARKET STREET, WATFORD
Hertfordshire WD18 0PN 01923 803030
e: office@cai.org.uk
w: www.cai.org.uk

Contemporary Dance Trust
THE PLACE THEATRE, 17 DUKES ROAD, LONDON
Greater London WC1H 9PY....................................0207 121 1100
e: info@theplace.org.uk
w: www.theplace.org.uk

Drama UK
WOBURN HOUSE, 20 TAVISTOCK SQUARE, LONDON
Greater London WC1H 9HQ 020 3393 6141
e: info@dramauk.co.uk
w: www.dramauk.co.uk

EHA (Event Hire Association)
2450 REGENTS COURT, THE CRESCENT, BIRMINGHAM BUSINESS
PARK, SOLIHULL
West Midlands B37 7YE 0121 380 4602
e: mail@eha.org.uk
w: www.eha.org.uk

Entertainment Retailers Association (ERA)
3 SOHO SQUARE (3RD FLOOR), LONDON
Greater London W1D 3HD 020 7440 1595
e: admin@eraltd.org
w: www.eraltd.org

Event Supplier And Services Association (essa)
119 HIGH STREET, BERKHAMSTED
Hertfordshire HP4 2DJ 01442 285812
e: info@essa.uk.com
w: www.essa.uk.com

Eventia (the Events Industry Assoc)
5TH FLOOR GALBRAITH HOUSE, 141 GREAT CHARLES STREET,
BIRMINGHAM B3 3LG..0121 212 1400
e: info@eventia.org.uk
w: www.eventia.org.uk

Federation Against Copyright Theft (FACT)
REGAL HOUSE, 70 LONDON ROAD, TWICKENHAM
Middlesex TW1 3QS...020 8891 1217
e: contact@fact-uk.org.uk
w: www.fact-uk.org.uk

Freeman
PROLOGIS PARK , IMPERIAL ROAD , RYTON
CV8 3LF... 07973 869155 /
02477 601601
e: sarah.mayo@freemanxp.com
w: www.freeman-emea.com/

Gaelic Arts Agency
56 SEAFORTH ROAD, STORNOWAY
HS1 2SD 01851 704493
e: pne@gaelic-arts.com
w: www.gaelic-arts.com

Generator
CLUNY ANNEX, 36 LIME STREET, NEWCASTLE UPON TYNE
Tyne and Wear NE1 2PQ 0191 231 4016
e: mail@generator.org.uk
w: www.generator.org.uk

Guild Of Int'l Songwriters & Composers
32 HILLGARTH, CASTLESIDE, CONSETT
Durham DH8 9QD 01207 500825
e: gisc@btconnet.com
w: www.songwriters-guild.co.uk

Incorporated Society Of Musicians
4-5 INVERNESS MEWS, LONDON
Greater London W2 3JQ..020 7221 3499
e: membership@ism.org
w: www.ism.org

Institution Of Lighting Engineers (ILE)
REGENT HOUSE, RUGBY
Warwickshire CV21 2PN 01788 576492
e: info@theilp.org.uk
w: www.theilp.org.uk

ISBA - The Voice Of British Advertisers
12 HENRIETTA STREET, LONDON
Greater London WC2E 8LH....................................0207 291 9020
e: answers@isba.org.uk
w: www.isba.org.uk

JCB Power Products
.... 01889 272200 / 0800 083 8015
e: generator.sales@jcb.com
w: www.jcbpowerproducts.co.uk

Lighting Association
STAFFORD PARK 7, TELFORD
Shropshire TF3 3BQ...01952 290905
e: info@thelia.org.uk
w: www.thelia.org.uk

National Operatic & Dramatic Assoc'n
15 THE METRO CENTRE, PETERBOROUGH
Cambridgeshire PE2 7UH......................................01733 374 790
e: info@noda.org.uk
w: www.noda.org.uk

National Outdoor Events Association (NOEA)
PO BOX 4495, WELLS
Somerset BA5 9AS 01749 674 531
e: secretary@noea.org.uk
w: www.noea.org.uk

National Youth Theatre
111 BUCKINGHAM PALACE ROAD, LONDON
Greater London SW1W 0DT...................................020 3696 7066
e: info@nyt.org.uk
w: www.nyt.org.uk

Pasma
PO BOX 26969, GLASGOW
Glasgow G3 9DR..0845 230 4041
e: info@pasma.co.uk
w: www.pasma.co.uk

Plasa
1 EDWARD ROAD , EASTBOURNE
East Sussex BN23 8AS 01323 524120
e: info.eu@plasa.org
w: www.plasa.org

PPL (Phonographic Performance Ltd)
1 UPPER JAMES STREET, LONDON
Greater London W1F 9DE......................................020 7534 1000
e: info@ppluk.com
w: www.ppluk.com

Production Services Association (psa)
PO BOX 2709, BATH
Somerset BA1 3YS..01225 332 668
e: gm@psa.org.uk
w: www.psa.org.uk

Productions Managers Association
EALING STUDIOS, EALING GREEN, EALING, LONDON
Greater London W5 5EP 0208 758 8699
e: pma@pma.org.uk
w: www.pma.org.uk

RadioCentre
6TH FLOOR, 55 NEW OXFORD STREET, LONDON
Greater London WC1A 1BS....................................020 7010 0600
e: info@radiocentre.org
w: www.radiocentre.org

Royal Academy Of Dance
36 BATTERSEA SQUARE, LONDON
Greater London SW11 3RA....................................020 7326 8000
e: info@rad.org.uk
w: www.rad.org.uk

Royal Agricultural Society of England
THE ARTHUR RANK CENTRE, STONELEIGH PARK,, KENILWORTH,
Warwickshire CV8 2LZ...02476 692 470
e: emilys@rase.org.uk
w: www.rase.org.uk

Royal Television Society
KILDARE HOUSE, 3 DORSET RISE, LONDON
Greater London EC4Y 8EN....................................0207 822 2810
e: info@rts.org.uk
w: www.rts.org.uk

Scottish Screen
249 WEST GEORGE STREET, GLASGOW
Glasgow G2 4QE...0845 300 7300
e: info@scottishscreen.com
w: www.scottishscreen.com

Sesac International
1 PRIMROSE ST, LONDON
Greater London EC2A 2EX....................................020 7616 9284
w: www.sesac.com

Showmen's Guild Of Gb
151A KING STREET, DRIGHLINGTON, LEEDS
West Yorkshire BD11 1EJ.......................................01132 853341
e: denise@showmensguild.com
w: www.showmensguild.com

Society Of Event Organisers (SEO)
29A MARKET SQUARE, BIGGLESWADE
Bedfordshire SG18 8AQ 01767 312986
e: info@seoevent.co.uk
w: www.seoevent.co.uk

South West Scotland Screen Commission
28 EDINBURGH ROAD, DUMFRIES
Dumfriesshire DG1 1JQ 01387 263666
e: screencom@dumgal.gov.uk
w: www.sw-scotland-screen.com

Sport England
SPORTPARK, 3 OAKWOOD DRIVE, LOUGHBOROUGH
Leicestershire LE11 3QF 08458 508 508
e: funding@sportengland.org
w: www.sportengland.org

Stage Management Association
89 BOROUGH HIGH STREET, FIRST FLOOR, LONDON
Greater London SE1 1NL..0207 403 7999
e: admin@stagemanagementassociation.co.uk
w: www.stagemanagementassociation.co

Sustainable Events
2ND FLOOR, FOURWAYS HOUSE, 57 HILTON STREET,
MANCHESTER
Greater Manchester M1 2EJ 0161 2735107
e: admin@sustainableeventsltd.com
w: www.sustainableeventsltd.com

The Event Services Association (TESA)
ASSOCIATION HOUSE, 18C MOOR STREET, CHEPSTOW
Monmouthshire NP16 5DB....................................01291 636341
e: admin@tesa.org.uk
w: www.tesa.org.uk

United Kingdom Copyright Bureau
110 TRAFALGAR ROAD, BRIGHTON
BN41 1GS..01273 277333
e: info@copyrightbureau.co.uk
w: www.copyrightbureau.co.uk

Voice Of The Listener & Viewer (VLV)
THE OLD RECTORY BUSINESS CENTRE, SPRINGHEAD ROAD,
NORTHFLEET
Kent DA11 8HN..01474 338716
e: info@vlv.org.uk
w: www.vlv.org.uk

AV Equipment

Absolute Audio Visual Solutions
NEW CAMBRIDGE HOUSE, LITLINGTON
Cambridgeshire SG8 0SS.......................................01763 852222
e: info@absoluteavs.co.uk
w: www.absoluteavs.co.uk

Access Audio Ltd
WINTONFIELD HOUSE, NEW WINTON
East Lothian EH33 2NN..0131663 0777
e: info@accessaudio.co.uk
w: www.accessaudio.co.uk

Active Presentation Services Ltd
NUTCOMBE LODGE, HINDHEAD ROAD, HINDHEAD
Surrey GU26 6AZ .... +44 (0)1428 607453 // +44 (0)7979 788711
e: info@activepresentations.co.uk
w: www.activepresentations.co.uk

Active Visual Supplies Ltd
5 HIGH STREET, WELLINGTON, TELFORD
Shropshire TF1 1JW...0800 5421726
e: sales@activeuk.com
w: www.activevisuals.co.uk

adi.tv
PITTMAN COURT, PITTMAN WAY, FULWOOD, PRESTON
Lancashire PR2 9ZG 01772 708 200
e: info@adi.tv
w: www.adi.tv

Adlib Audio Limited
ADLIB HOUSE, FLEMING ROAD, SPEKE, LIVERPOOL
Merseyside L24 9LS 0151 486 2214
e: info@adlibsolutions.co.uk
w: www.adlib.co.uk/

Advanta Conference Productions
....0845 225 5908
e: enquiries@advantaproductions.com
w: www.advantaproductions.com

AJR Services
CORNER HOUSE, 114 WINDMILL STREET, MACCLESFIELD
Cheshire SK11 7LB...01625 615090
e: mail@ajrservices.com
w: www.ajrservices.com

Andycam Audiovisual
9 INDUSTRIAL COTTAGES, LONG LEYS ROAD, LINCOLN
Lincolnshire LN1 1DZ...01522 533039
e: andy@andycam.tv
w: www.andycam.tv

Arc Sound Ltd
16 CLIPPER PARK, THURROCK PARK WAY , TILBURY
Essex RM18 7HG..+44(0)1375 857 227
e: info@arcsound.co.uk
w: www.arcsound.com

Arcstream Av
GARTH HOUSE, 141 GARTH ROAD, MORDEN
Greater London SM4 4LG.......................................01372 742 682
e: info@arcstreamav.com
w: www.arcstreamav.com

Asets (uk) Ltd
37 R/O WESTMINSTER ROAD, BLACKPOOL
Lancashire FY1 2QE...01253 294920
e: info@asets.com
w: www.asets.com

At Communications (atc) Ltd
UNIT 5, LANDSBERG, LICHFIELD ROAD INDUSTRIAL ESTATE ,
TAMWORTH, Staffordshire B79 7XB.........................01827 301010
e: atcmidlands@atcomms.co.uk
w: www.atcomms.co.uk

Attend2IT
UNIT 8, PARK FARM INDUSTRIAL ESTATE, BUNTINGFORD
Hertfordshire SG9 9AZ 01763 877 477
w: www.attend2it.co.uk

Audio Gold
308 - 310 PARK ROAD, LONDON
Greater London N8 8LA..020 8341 9007
e: info@audiogold.co.uk
w: www.audiogold.co.uk

Audio Source Ltd
31 MONGLEATH AVENUE, FALMOUTH
Cornwall TR11 4PP .... 07971 607172 /
07867 525016 / 01326 3115
e: hire@audio-source.co.uk
w: www.audio-source.co.uk

Audio Visual Unit Ltd
243 FELIXSTOWE ROAD, IPSWICH
Suffolk IP3 9BN...01473 705205
e: info@avunit.com
w: www.avunit.com

Audiotech Services Ltd
UNIT 18 MIDDLEWOODS WAY , WHARNCLIFFE BUSINESS PARK,
CARLTON, BARNSLEY
South Yorkshire S71 3HR 01226 208327
e: rachael@audiotechuk.com
w: www.audiotechuk.com

Audiowall Systems Limited
2/3 BASSETT COURT, BROAD STREET, NEWPORT PAGNELL
Buckinghamshire MK16 0JN..... 01908 951 470 / 01908 615 365
e: info@audiowall.co.uk
w: www.audiowall.co.uk

AV Department Limited
UNIT 83, EAST WAY,, HILLEND INDUSTRIAL PARK, DALGETY BAY
Fife KY11 9JF 01383 825 709
e: info@avdept.co.uk
w: www.avdept.co.uk

AV Direct CC
70 NARUNA CRESCENT, SOUTHFIELD,
CAPE TOWN, SOUTH AFRICA 7800...................+27 021 706 6730
e: cpt@avdirect.co.za
w: www.avdirect.co.za

AV Joint Resource
CORNER HOUSE, 114 WINDMILL STREET, MACCLESFIELD
Cheshire SK11 7LB................ 01625 61 50 90 - 01253 85 12 02
e: hello@avjr.eu
w: www.avjointresource.com

AV Matrix
UNIT 120, STREET 7, THORP ARCH TRADING ESTATE,
WEMBLEY, LONDON
Greater London LS23 7FL 0800 1950 600
e: jen@av-matrix.com
w: www.av-matrix.com

AV Projections
AV PROJECTIONS LTD THE ARCHES, 65 WEBBER STREET,
LONDON
Greater London SE1 0QP.......................................020 7620 2001
e: info@avprojections.co.uk
w: www.avprojections.co.uk

AV Unit
243 FELIXSTOWE ROAD, IPSWICH
Suffolk IP3 9BN...01473 705205
e: adam@avunit.com
w: www.avunit.com

AVC Live Ltd
UNIT 103, BUSINESS DESIGN CENTRE , 52 UPPER STREET,
ISLINGTON, LONDON
Greater London N1 0QH 020 7288 6561
e: info@avcliveltd.com
w: www.avcliveltd.com

AVC Media Enterprises Ltd
GRANDHOLM MILL, GRANDHOLM VILLAGE, ABERDEEN
AB22 8BB 01224 392828
e: accounts@avcmedia.com
w: www.avcmedia.com

Avcom Hire
STANLAKE MEWS, SHEPHERDS BUSH, LONDON
Greater London W12 7HS.....................................0208 735 3424
e: sales@avcom.co.uk
w: www.avcom.co.uk

AVLS
....01226 764435
e: info@avls.co.uk
w: www.avls.co.uk

AVM Creative Solutions
11618 PERRY RD, HOUSTON, TEXAS 77064
e: info@avmcreativesolutions.com
w: www.avmcreativesolutions.com

AVM Impact
EUROPE HOUSE, 170 WINDMILL ROAD WEST,
SUNBURY ON THAMES
Middlesex TW16 7HB...0845 2626 200
e: info@avmi.com
w: www.avmi.com/

AVT Connect
AVT HOUSE, 7 STONE STREET , BRIGHTON
East Sussex BN1 2HB 441273299001
e: connect@avtconnect.com
w: www.avtconnect.com

A

AXICO
Lancashire 01524 847265
e: production@axico.co.uk
w: www.axico.com

Aztec Event Services Ltd
UNITS 1-2, FALCON BUSINESS CENTRE, 14 WANDLE WAY,
MITCHAM
Surrey CR4 4FG 020 7803 4000
e: sales@aztecuk.com
w: www.aztecuk.com

Blackjack Event Co
ALPHA 6, , MASTERLORD OFFICE VILLAGE WEST ROAD, IPSWICH
Suffolk IP3 9SX.................................08448 400 123
e: info@blackjackevents.co.uk
w: www.blackjackuk.co.uk

Blueparrot Production & Events
UNIT 8, FORTH INDUSTRIAL ESTATE, SEALCARR STREET,
EDINBURGH
Edinburgh EH5 1RF.............................0131 510 3333
e: info@blueparrotevents.com
w: www.blueparrotevents.com

Board Repairs
....0844 683 9901
e: info@boardrepairs.co.uk
w: www.boardrepairs.co.uk

Brahler ICS UK Ltd
UNIT 2, THE BUSINESS CENTRE, CHURCH END, CAMBRIDGE
Cambridgeshire CB1 3LB.......................01223 411601
e: rentals@brahler.co.uk
w: www.brahler.co.uk

Britannia Row Productions Ltd
104 THE GREEN, TWICKENHAM, LONDON
Greater London TW2 5AG.....................020 8893 4997
e: info@britanniarow.com
w: www.britanniarow.com

Brown Cow Audio Visual Ltd
37 MOUNT ROAD, ROCHESTER
Kent ME1 3NH 0163 4311 657
e: info@browncowav.co.uk
w: www.browncowav.co.uk

Businessav
UNIT E, SCHAPPE BUILDING, LLAY INDUSTRIAL UNITS, LLAY,
WREXHAM
LL12 0PG...0800 587 9908
e: info@businessav.co.uk
w: www.businessav.co.uk

Cameron Presentations & All Event Hire
BURNFIELD ROAD, GIFFNOCK, GLASGOW
Glasgow G46 7TH................................0141 637 0368
e: hire@cameronpres.co.uk
w: www.cameronpres.co.uk

Capitol House Productions
CAPITOL HOUSE, 662 LONDON ROAD, CHEAM
Surrey SM3 9BY 020 8644 6194
e: mail@capitol.co.uk
w: www.capitol.co.uk

Central Event Productions Ltd
ASTON ROAD, NUNEATON
Warwickshire CV11 5EL 0 7812 8420 60
e: office@centralevent.co.uk
w: www.centralevent.co.uk

CFM Audio Visual Sound and Lighting Hire
....0843 289 2798
e: info@cfmeventhire.co.uk
w: www.cfmentertainments.co.uk

CH Vintage Audio
PO Box 116
Northwich, Cheshire
CW9 5UG

t: 01565 734066 or 07970 219701
e: enquiries@chvintageaudio.com

CH Vintage Audio have the largest stock of Vintage Musical Sound
Equipment for hire or sale in the UK!
WEM 1960's and 1970's HH, Vox, Marshall, Shure, Selmer, Carlsbro,
Martin Audio Vox, Fender, Marshall, Music Man, Selmer, Peavey
available!

www.chvintageaudio.com

City Audio Visual
UNIT 19 KINGS MEADOW, FERRY HINKSEY ROAD, OXFORD
Oxfordshire OX2 0DP 01865 722800
e: info@cityav.co.uk
w: www.cityav.co.uk/

Clever Connections
UNIT 3 WARWICK COURT, SAXON BUSINESS PARK,HANBURY
ROAD, BROMSGROVE
West Midlands B60 4AD 01527 833 338
e: info@cleverconnections.co.uk
w: www.cleverconnections.co.uk

Complete Production Services Group
UNIT 14, AIRFIELD ROAD, CHRISTCHURCH
Dorset BH23 3TG...01202 572000
e: enquiries@cpsgroup.co.uk
w: www.cpsgroup.co.uk

Conference Engineering
.... +44 (0)1625 426916
e: hello@conferenceengineering.co.uk
w: www.conferenceengineering.co.uk

CoNi Ltd
WEST END ESTATE, BRUNTCLIFFE ROAD, MORLEY
West Yorkshire LS27 0LQ......................................0113 289 7700
e: hire@co-ni.co.uk
w: www.co-ni.co.uk

CreateAV (UK) Ltd
UNIT 14 STUDIO HOUSE, DELAMARE ROAD, CHESHUNT, LONDON
Greater London EN8 9SH......................................01992 789 759
e: connect@createav.com
w: www.createav.com

Creative Lighting & Sound (CLS)
UNIT 6, SPIRES BUSINESS CENTRE, MUGIMOSS RD , ABERDEEN
Aberdeen AB21 9NY...01224 683 111
e: info@clsaberdeen.co.uk
w: www.clsaberdeen.co.uk

Creative Staging Limited
INNOVATION HOUSE, 17-27 STIRLING ROAD, ACTON, LONDON
Greater London W3 8DJ......................................020 8752 3939
e: info@creativestaging.co.uk
w: www.creativestaging.co.uk

Cricklewood Electronics
40-42 CRICKLEWOOD BROADWAY, LONDON
Greater London NW2 3ET.......... 020 8450 0995 // 020 84520161
e: accounts@cricklewoodelectronics.com
w: www.cricklewoodelectronics.com

Dance2 Sound & Light Hire
107 WOODBRIDGE ROAD, GUILDFORD
Surrey GU1 4PY..01483 451 002
e: in2dance2@hotmail.com
w: www.dance2.co.uk

Dancefloor DJs & Events
THISTLEY CLOSE, THORPE ASTLEY, LEICESTER
Leicestershire LE3 3RZ.......................................0116 348 0146
e: dancefloordjs85@gmail.com
w: dancefloor-djs-events.com/

Db Systems Ltd
ASHCHURCH BUSINESS CENTRE, ALEXANDRA WAY, TEWKESBURY
Gloucestershire GL20 8TD...................................0845 226 3083
e: hiredesk@dbsystems.co.uk
w: www.dbsystems.co.uk

Definition Audio Visual
3D HARROGATE ROAD, RAWDON, LEEDS
West Yorkshire LS19 6HW.......... 07548 347594 // 08435 235470
e: mark@definitionaudiovisual.co.uk
w: www.definitionaudiovisual.co.uk

Devs AV Company
BARCELONA...................... ....+34 938010612
e: Barcelona@devsavcompany.com
w: www.avrentalspain.com

Devs Av Rental Group Europe
....34938010612
e: devs@devsavrentalgroup.com
w: www.devsavrentalgroup.com

Digital Design & Media
17 ST CLEMENTS RD, POOLE
Dorset BH15 3PB 01202 802 975
e: mail@digitaldesignandmedia.com
w: www.digitaldesignandmedia.com

Dimension Audio
UNITS 2-4, MANOR GATE MANOR ROYAL, CRAWLEY
West Sussex RH10 9SX..01293 582005
e: info@dimension.co.uk
w: www.dimension.co.uk

DJ and Studio
19 ERLESMERE GARDENS, EALING, LONDON
Greater London W13 9TZ 020 8840 8480
e: enquiries@djandstudio.co.uk
w: www.djandstudio.co.uk

DLC Events
STREET 22, AL QUOZ IND 3, DUBAI
PO Box 282841,................................ +971 4 347 0484
e: office@dlcevents.com
w: www.dlcevents.com

DM Audio Ltd
UNIT 7/1 NEWHAILES INDUSTRIAL ESTATE, NEWHAILES ROAD,
EDINBURGH
Edinburgh EH21 6SY 0131 665 5615
e: hire@dmaudio.co.uk
w: www.dmaudio.co.uk

DMI Productions
UNIT 8, LITTLETON HOUSE, LITTLETON ROAD,
ASHFORD, AMIDDLESEX,
TW15 1UU 01784 421212
e: contactus@dmiproductions.co.uk
w: www.dmiproductions.co.uk

Drinkle & Mann Ltd
UNIT 2 PEEL GREEN TRADING ESTATE, PEEL GREEN, ECCLES,
MANCHESTER
Greater Manchester M30 7HF 0161 707 7588
e: bryan@drinklemann.co.uk
w: drinklemann.co.uk/

Easirent Limited
UNIT B3- BAESPOINT BUSINESS & INNOVATION CENTRE, 110
BUTTERFIELD, GREAT MARLINGS, LUTON
Bedfordshire LU2 8DL.......................... +44 (0)845 845
8585 // +44 (0)1582 43377
e: sales@firstrental.co.uk
w: www.firstrental.co.uk/

East Anglia Leisure
UNIT 4, CIVIC INDUSTRIAL ESTATE, HOMEFIELD ROAD, HAVERHILL
Suffolk CB9 8QP 01440 714204

e: info@ealeisure.co.uk
w: www.ealeisure.co.uk

Eclipse Presentations Ltd
PRESENTATIONS HOUSE, 5 CHAFFINCH BUSINESS PARK,
CROYDON ROAD, BECKENHAM
Kent BR3 4AA 0208 662 6444
e: info@eclipse-service.co.uk
w: www.eclipse-presentations.co.uk

Elation DJs Ltd
7 RINGHAY ROAD, BRADFORD
West Yorkshire BD4 0TZ........... 01274 800 460 // 07811 200 293
e: info@elationdjs.co.uk
w: www.elationdjs.co.uk

EMF Technology Ltd
....020 8003 3344
e: info@emftechnology.co.uk
w: www.emftechnology.co.uk

Enlightened Lighting Ltd
26-28 EMERY ROAD, BRISLINGTON
Bristol BS4 5PF......................................01179 727 123
e: info@enlx.co.uk
w: www.enlightenedlighting.co.uk

Entertainment Toolbox Ltd
WOLVERHAMPTON BUSINESS AIRPORT, UNIT 23B, BOBBINGTON,
STOURBRIDGE
West Midlands DY7 5DY..01384 221083
e: info@etx-ltd.com
w: www.etx-ltd.com

ETASound
BURNT MEADOW HOUSE, NORTH MOONS MOAT, REDDITCH
Worcestershire B98 9PA 01527 528822
e: enquiries@sseaudio.com
w: www.sseaudiogroup.com

European Communications Technology Ltd
PO BOX 4020, PANGBOURNE
Berkshire RG8 8TX...0118 984 1141
e: support@ect-av.com
w: www.ect-av.com

Euroscreens Ltd
UNIT 11 LONGRIDGE TRADING ESTATE, KNUTSFORD
Cheshire WA16 8PR 01565 654 004
w: www.euroscreens.co.uk

Event Hire Wales
....07494 169599
e: info@eventhire.wales
w: www.eventhire.wales

Firefly Audio Visual Solutions Ltd
UNIT 31 BARKSTON HOUSE, CROYDON STREET, LEEDS
West Yorkshire LS11 9RT 01133 320042
e: hire.leeds@fireflyav.co.uk
w: www.fireflyav.co.uk

A

First Network Ltd
ROWDELL ROAD, NORTHOLT
Middlesex UB5 5QR 020 8842 1222
e: info@first-network.com
w: www.first-network.com

Flare Audio
UNIT 8 CHARTWELL BUSINESS CENTRE, 42 CHARTWELL RD,
LANCING
West Sussex BN15 8FB...01903 761000
e: info@flareaudio.com
w: www.flareaudio.com

Focus 21 Hire & Events
123-127 DEEPCUT BRIDGE ROAD, DEEPCUT, CAMBERLEY
Surrey GU16 6SD...08452 707453
e: F21Sales@focus21.co.uk
w: www.focus21.co.uk

Fonix LED
SANDBOURNE HOUSE, DOMINION ROAD, BOURNEMOUTH
Dorset BH11 8LH 0203 012 5566
e: info@fonix.co.uk
w: www.fonix.co.uk

FT Audio Visual
UNITS 4 & 5 GROVE PARK VIEW, HARROGATE
North Yorkshire HG1 4BT......................................0800 5316715
e: info@ftav.co.uk
w: www.ftav.co.uk

Future Media Systems Limited
UNIT 2, GRANGE RD INDUSTRIAL ESTATE, CHIRSTCHURCH
Dorset BH23 4JD 01425 270511
e: webenquiries@futuremediasystems.co.uk
w: www.futuremediasystems.co.uk

Gab Audio Engineers
BARBRETHAN, KIRKMICHAEL, MAYBOLE
Ayrshire KA19 7PS...01655 740330
e: jimbryan@gab-audio.co.uk
w: www.gab-audio.co.uk

Gearhouse In2Structures
PO BOX 751391, GARDENVIEW, JOHANNESBURG
 2047.. +27 (0) 112 163 000
e: jhb@gearhouse.co.za
w: www.gearhouse.co.za

Gordon Audio Visual
THE OLD TORPEDO FACTORY, ST LEONARD'S ROAD, LONDON
Greater London NW10 6ST...................................020 8537 1000
w: www.gav.co.uk

Group Dynamics Ltd
21 WADSWORTH ROAD, GREENFORD
Middlesex UB6 7LQ 020 8991 9559
e: webinfo@groupdynamics.co.uk
w: www.groupdynamics.co.uk

Halo Lighting
98-124 BREWERY ROAD, LONDON
Greater London N7 9PG 0207 607 4444
e: info@halo.co.uk
w: www.halo.co.uk

Hamilton Rentals
UNIT 2, MAPLE CENTRE, DOWNMILL ROAD , BRACKNELL
Berkshire RG12 1QS 01344 456600
e: info@hamilton.co.uk
w: www.hamilton.co.uk

Harkness Screens Ltd
UNIT A NORTON ROAD, STEVENAGE
Hertfordshire SG1 2BB...01438 725200
e: sales@harkness-screens.com
w: www.harkness-screens.com

Heathrow Sound Hire
UNITS 9 & 10- POD BUSINESS CENTRE, HARRIS WAY,
SUNBURY ON THAMES
Surrey TW16 7EW....................... 0208 4322310 // 07834520290
e: enquiries@heathrowsoundhire.co.uk
w: www.heathrowsoundhire.co.uk

Hi-Lights
18E WHITEROSE WAY, FOLLINGSBY PARK, GATESHEAD
Tyne and Wear NE10 8YX.....................................0191 495 0608
e: martin@hi-lights.tv
w: www.hi-lights.tv

hi-Vision Systems Ltd
WAREHAM HOUSE, 263 BROAD LANE, TILE HILL , COVENTRY
West Midlands CV5 7AQ 0870 428 1159
e: web@hi-vision.co.uk
w: www.hi-vision.co.uk

High Lite Touring
MITROVICKA 359/45, OSTRAVA - NOVA BELA
 72400...00420 596 731 034
e: info@highlite.cz
w: www.highlite.cz

Hire Intelligence Uk
UNIT 5, ACTON PARK ESTATE, THE VALE, LONDON
Greater London W3 7QE..0208 749 9900
e: enquiries@hire-intelligence.co.uk
w: www.hire-intelligence.co.uk

Hire Manager
2 SWANSTONS ROAD, GREAT YARMOUTH
 NR30 3NQ 01493 845577
e: info@paddyhall.com
w: www.paddyhall.com

HTT Limited
3 THE NEW ROAD, COOKHAM, MAIDENHEAD
Berkshire SL6 9HB..01628 525130
e: info@httltd.co.uk
w: www.httltd.co.uk

Hyde AV
UNIT 22, 33 NOBEL SQUARE, BURNT MILLS, BASILDON
Essex SS13 1LT .... 01268 729636 // 07713 917137
e: info@hyde-av.co.uk
w: www.hyde-av.co.uk

ICTHUS Group
OFFICE 2, HOMESTEAD FARM, NORTH HOUGHTON, STOCKBRIDGE
Hampshire SO20 6LG 01264 810356
e: info@icthusgroup.co.uk
w: www.icthusgroup.co.uk

Indivisual Limited
UNIT 3, 140, MOWBRAY DRIVE, BLACKPOOL
Lancashire FY3 7UN 01253 300 002
e: info@indivisual.co.uk
w: www.indivisual.co.uk

Inovaplus Limited
....020 3326 8505
e: info@inovaplus.com
w: www.inovaplus.com

Install uk Ltd (Events)
UNITS 1 & 2, LINGEN ROAD, LUDLOW
Shropshire SY8 1XD...1584711119
e: events@install-uk.com
w: www.install-uk.com

Istead Business Presentations Ltd
14 HERALD BUSINESS PARK, GOLDEN ACRES LANE, COVENTRY
West Midlands CV3 2SY 024 7663 5530
e: enquiry@istead.co.uk
w: www.istead.co.uk

Joy's Production Services
5 ST JOHN'S LANE, LONDON
  EC1M 4BH 020 7549 1697
e: info@joys.com
w: www.joys.com

Julianas Leisure Services Ltd
MARIA MILSTEAD, PIPPIN GROVE, 628 LONDON ROAD,
COLNBROOK
Berkshire SL3 8QH 020 70996875
e: maria@julianas.com
w: www.julianas.com

Just Lite Productions
UNIT 31 FINGLAS BUSINESS CENTRE, JAMESTOWN ROAD,
FINGLAS, DUBLIN 11
.... + 353 1 806 8333
e: info@justlite.com
w: justlite.com

Key Audio Visual Services
BLACK TOWER STUDIOS, 15 BRACONDALE, NORWICH
Norfolk NR1 2AL 01603 616661
e: info@keyav.com
w: www.keyav.com

Just Lite Productions
Unit 31, Finglas Business Centre, Jamestown road,
Finglas, Dublin 11

t: +353 1 8068333
Paul Smith: +353 872525183 / pauls@justlite.com
Alan Smith: +353 872361162 / alans@justlite.com

As Ireland's leading production company, Just Lites' reputation
has been won through a keen understanding of client expectation
and its ability to amplify that vision. Just Lite Productions provides
Lighting, Audio, Staging, Visual Systems, Dance Floors, Lasers and
Draping and can facilitate events on all scales.

www.justlite.com

Kick Audio Visual
UNIT 4, THE BOX WORKS, HEYSHAM ROAD, AINTREE, LIVERPOOL
L30 6UR 0151 430 7000
e: info@kickpa.co.uk
w: www.kickpa.co.uk

Lapp Limited
UNIT 3 PERIVALE PARK, HORSENDEN LANE SOUTH, GREENFORD
Middlesex UB6 7RL..020 8758 7800
e: sales@lapplimited.com
w: www.lapplimited.com

LCI Productions Ltd
55 MERTHYR TERRACE, BARNES, LONDON
Greater London SW13 8DL....................................020 8741 5747
e: contact@lci-uk.com
w: www.lci-uk.com

LED Screen Hire Europe Ltd
UNIT D7A FAIROAKS AIRPORT, CHERTSEY ROAD, CHOBHAM
Surrey GU24 8HU 01276 859 480
e: info@screenhire.com
w: www.screenhire.com

Lightmedia Displays Ltd
HUDDLESTON GRANGE, NEWTHORPE, SOUTH MILFORD, LEEDS
West Yorkshire LS25 6JU 0333 600 6000
e: sales@lightmedia.co.uk
w: www.lightmedia.co.uk

Lindos Electronics
SANDY LANE, LITTLE BEALINGS, WOODBRIDGE
Suffolk IP13 6LP 01473 611133
e: info@lindos.co.uk
w: www.lindos.co.uk

Live Audio Production
GROSVENOR WAY, CLAPTON
Greater London E5 9ND .... 020 3713 0502 / 07909 993125
e: liveaudioproduction@gmail.com
w: www.liveaudioproduction.co.uk

Loft Sound LLP
16 KILBEGS ROAD, ANTRIM
 BT41 4NN...08452 99 33 77
e: info@loftsound.co.uk
w: www.loftsound.co.uk

London Audio Ltd
ROBERT DASHWOOD WAY, CAMBERWELL, LONDON
Greater London SE17 3PZ......................................0207 701 9444
e: info@londonaudiovisual.co.uk
w: www.london-audio.co.uk

LRS Associates Ltd
UNIT 12, BROOK ROAD, , BICTON INDUSTRIAL PARK, KIMBOLTON,
Cambridgeshire PE28 0LR .... 01480 861186 / 01480 860267
e: info@lrs-associates.com
w: www.lrs-associates.com

Mastermix Dj.com
HAWTHORNE HOUSE, 5-7 FITZWILLIAM STREET, PARKGATE,
ROTHERHAM
S62 6EP...01709 710022
e: support@mastermixdj.com
w: www.mastermixdj.com

Matt Bunday Events
 .... 023 8055 3736 // 07730 604 869
e: info@mattbundayevents.com
w: www.mattbundayevents.com

MCL (Glasgow)
UNIT C, MOORPARK CENTRAL, 40 DAVA STREET, GLASGOW
Glasgow G51 2BQ...0141 425 2016
e: glasgow@mclcreate.com
w: mclcreate.com/

MCL (Manchester)
18 LORD BYRON SQUARE, STOWELL TECHNICAL PARK, SALFORD
QUAYS, MANCHESTER

Greater Manchester M50 2XH...............................0161 745 9933
e: manchester@mclcreate.com
w: mclcreate.com/

MCL Create
UNIT 500, CATESBY PARK, ECKERSALL ROAD, KINGS NORTON,
BIRMINGHAM, West Midlands B38 8SE 0121 433 8899
e: birmingham@mclcreate.com
w: mclcreate.com

MCM Creative Group
SOUTH AVENUE STUDIOS, SOUTH AVENUE, KEW
Greater London TW9 3LY.......................................020 8741 7576
e: info@mcmcreativegroup.com
w: www.mcmcreativegroup.com

Mediatheme Ltd
UNIT 18A OAKHAM ENTERPRISE PARK, ASHWELL ROAD, OAKHAM
Rutland LE15 7TU..01572 771363
e: info@mediatheme.com
w: www.mediatheme.com

MJ Visual
UNIT 1, ATLANTIC HOUSE, 119 THIRD AVENUE, ALMODINGTON,
CHICHESTER, West Sussex PO20 7LB 01243 780816
e: sales@mjvisual.co.uk
w: www.mjvisual.co.uk

MTS
UNIT 37, MOUNTHEATH TRADING , ESTATE PRESTWICH ,
MANCHESTER
Greater Manchester M25 9WE 1617739933
e: Keith@massivetech.co.uk
w: www.massivetech.co.uk

Multimedia Plus
PRODUCTION STUDIO, HENLEY-ON-THAMES
Oxfordshire RG9 5DT 01491 628110
e: info@multimediaplus.co.uk
w: www.multimediaplus.co.uk

Neon Arena Services
UNIT 305, THE ARGENT CENTRE, 60 FREDERICK STREET,
HOCKLEY, BIRMINGHAM
West Midlands B1 3HS...0121 236 5555
e: info@neonarenaservices.co.uk
w: www.neonsportsfloors.co.uk

Neuron Pro Audio Ltd
DOWNTEX WAREHOUSE, 17 MARY STREET, MANCHESTER
Greater Manchester M3 1NH..................................0161 408 1545
e: enquiries@neuronproaudio.co.uk
w: www.neuronproaudio.co.uk

New Day
44 BOVERTON DRIVE, BROCKWORTH
Gloucestershire GL3 4DA 01452 618619
e: sales@newday.tv
w: www.newdayhire.co.uk

New Day Hire
 44 BOVERTON DRIVE, BROCKWORTH, GLOUCESTER
Gloucestershire GL3 4DA 08450 618619
e: sales@newday.tv
w: www.newdayhire.co.uk

Nightair Productions
UNIT ONE, EASTFIELD SIDE, SUTTON IN ASHFIELD
Nottinghamshire NG17 4JW...................................01623 557 040
e: sales@nightair.co.uk
w: www.nightair.co.uk

Novum AV
56 KEPLER, LICHFIELD ROAD INDUSTRIAL ESTATE, TAMWORTH
Staffordshire B79 7XE...0121 673 8385
e: hire@novumav.com
w: www.novumav.com

NSR Communications Ltd
16 CAXTON WAY, WATFORD BUSINESS PARK, WATFORD
Hertfordshire WD18 8UA......................................01923 209640
e: sales@nsrcommunications.co.uk
w: www.nsrcommunications.co.uk

A

NSR Communications Ltd
16 Caxton Way, Watford Business Park
Watford, Herts
WD16 8UA

t: 01923 209640
f: 01923 218196
e: sales@nsrcommunications.co.uk

NSR supplies technical services to events nationwide for hire
or sale including public address (PA) systems, audio and visual
equipment, judges/commentary/hospitality units, two-way radio
communications & sports/equestrian timing equipment. NSR also
supplies and installs permanent sound & vision.

www.nsrcommunications.co.uk

P&G Photographics Ltd
....07860 234 582
e: website@poulson.info
w: www.poulson.info

Paragon Projection Ltd
WALKERS RISE, RUGELEY ROAD, HEDNESFORD
Staffordshire WS12 0QU 01543 451111
w: www.paragonprojection.co.uk

Perception Events Ltd
ARCH 26, BONDWAY, VAUXHALL, LONDON
Greater London SW8 1SQ 0845 527 5667
e: events@perceptionlive.com
w: www.perceptionlive.com

Perception Live
ARCH 26, HANDEL BUSINESS CENTRE, 73 BONDWAY, VAUXHALL
, LONDON
Greater London SW8 1SQ 0845 527 5667
e: events@perceptionlive.com
w: www.perceptionlive.com

Pete Cornish
....01435 813393
e: info@petecornish.co.uk
w: www.petecornish.co.uk

Piccadilly Live
13 CONSUL ROAD, RUGBY
CV21 1PB 01788 576296
e: rugby@piccadilly-live.com
w: www.picc.co.uk

Picture Works Ltd, The
UNIT 23, GREENFORD PARK, GREENFORD, LONDON
Greater London UB6 0AZ.......................................0845 310 8321
e: enquiry@pictureworks.com
w: www.pictureworks.com

Plastic Monkey Ltd
LONDON
Greater London SW6 4DX 07931 585100
e: info@plasticmonkey.co.uk
w: www.plasticmonkey.co.uk

Point Source Productions Ltd
UNIT 5 KIMPTON TRADE & BUSINESS CENTER, MINDEN ROAD,
SUTTON
Surrey SM3 9PF..020 8254 2620
e: info@pslx.co.uk
w: www.pslx.co.uk

Positive Image Ltd
PROVIDIAN HOUSE, 16-18 MONUMENT STREET, LONDON
Greater London EC3R 8AJ 020 7868 5233
e: theoffice@positiveimage.co.uk
w: www.positiveimage.co.uk

Precise Events
UNIT K14 CLYDE WORKSHOPS, FULLARTON ROAD, GLASGOW
Glasgow G32 8YL 0141 255 0740
e: info@PreciseEvents.co.uk
w: www.preciseaudio.co.uk

Premier UK Events Ltd
UNIT 2, ROOKERY LANE, THURMASTON, LEICESTER
Leicestershire LE4 8AU...1162029953
e: ben@premier-ltd.com
w: premier-event-solutions.com/

Present Communications Ltd
ZEAL HOUSE, 8 DEER PARK ROAD, WIMBLEDON, LONDON
Greater London SW19 3UU 0208 770 0655
e: office@presentcommunications.com
w: www.presentcommunications.com

Presentation Rentals Ltd
UNIT 6, WINDSOR CENTRE, , ADVANCE ROAD, LONDON
Greater London SE27 9NT.....................................0208 670 5000
e: hello@prlive.co
w: www.prlive.co/

Prestige Sound and Light
UNIT 1, MARLIN PARK, CENTRAL WAY, FELTHAM, LONDON
Greater London TW14 0AN....................................07584 292070
e: info@prestigesoundandlight.co.uk
w: www.prestigesoundandlight.co.uk

Prism
....0203 287 7338
e: sales@prism-av.com
w: www.prism-av.com

Pro Display Ltd
UNIT 5, SHORTWOOD BUSINESS PARK, HOYLAND
South Yorkshire S74 9LH.......................................01226 740 007
e: info@prodisplay.com
w: www.prodisplay.com

Pro-Audio Systems

BLYNK HOUSE, YOUNG STREET, BRADFORD
West Yorkshire BD8 9RE 01274 497 261
e: hello@blynkgroup.com
w: pasystems.co.uk/

Production AV Ltd
UNIT 3 BAMEL WAY, GLOUCESTER BUSINESS PARK, ,
GLOUCESTER
Gloucestershire GL3 4BH 0845 370 0024
e: info@productionav.co.uk
w: www.productionav.co.uk

Production Light & Sound Ltd
PO BOX 96, LEEDS
West Yorkshire LS12 4XS 0113 2360951
e: info@productionlightandsound.com
w: www.productionlightandsound.com

Production Support Services Ltd
UNIT 18 ASTON ROAD, ASTON FIELDS INDUSTRIAL ESTATE,
BROMSGROVE
Worcestershire B60 3EX 0845 838 1123
e: chris@production-support.net
w: www.production-support.net

Projector Point
2 HIGH STREET, TEDDINGTON
Middlesex TW11 8EW .... 0808 278 8882 /
0208 977 5882
w: www.projectorpoint.co.uk

Proscreens
....0845 309 6369 // 07876755357
e: info@proscreens.net
w: www.proscreens.net

Protec (Production Technology LLC)
PLOT NO. 548 - 597, DUBAI INVESTMENT PARK 2,
DUBAI, UNITED ARAB EMIRATES.......................+971 4 880 0092
e: eventrental@productiontec.com
w: www.productiontec.com

PSAV Presentation Services
UNIT 3, HERON TRADING ESTATE, ALLIANCE ROAD, LONDON
W3 0RA 0208 896 6120
e: infoeurope@psav.com
w: www.psav.com

PSCo Ltd
UNIT B, 1-3 ACRE ROAD, READING
Berkshire RG2 0SU 0118 372 3300
e: enquiries@psco.co.uk
w: www.psco.co.uk

Puxley Limited
11 HARRIER COURT , WESTCOTT LANE , EXETER
EX5 2DR 01392 364900
e: info@puxley.com
w: www.puxley.com

Pyramid
22 REYNOLDS PARK, BELL CLOSE, PLYMOUTH
Devon PL7 4FE .... 0800 0185933 /
01752 335000
e: hires@pyramidav.co.uk
w: www.pyramidav.co.uk

Q7db Limited
32 ROWDEN ROAD, WEST EWELL, EPSOM
Surrey KT19 9PN .... 020 8397 0197 //
07957 972595
e: enquiry@q7db.co.uk
w: www.q7db.co.uk

QED Productions
UNIT 11, SUMMIT ROAD, CRANBORNE INDUSTRIAL ESTATE,
POTTERS BAR, Hertfordshire EN6 3QW.................01707 648 800
e: info@qed-productions.com
w: www.qed-productions.com

Quadrant Events - Birmingham
49 PHOENIX PARK, AVENUE CLOSE, ASTON, BIRMINGHAM
West Midlands B7 4NU 0121 359 6377
e: info@quadrantevents.com
w: www.quadrantevents.com

Quadrant Events - Nottingham
12 LONGWALL AVENUE, QUEENS DRIVE INDUSTRIAL ESTATE,
NOTTINGHAM
Nottinghamshire NG2 1NA 0115 8402 288
e: info@quadrantevents.com
w: www.quadrantevents.com

Quality Rental Ltd
UNIT 5 KING'S COURT, GLEN TYE ROAD, STIRLING
Stirlingshire FK7 7LH 01786 479077
w: www.qualityrental.co.uk

Quiz Systems
195 THORNHILL ROAD, SURBITON
Surrey KT6 7TG 020 8288 0246
e: web@quizsystems.co.uk
w: www.quizsystems.co.uk

Raw State
THE OLD MALTHOUSE, UNIT 4, LEVEL 2, CLARENCE STREET, BATH
Somerset BA1 5NS 01225 466464
e: info@rawstate.com
w: home.btconnect.com/rawstate/welco

RealSound and Vision Ltd
120C OLYMPIC AVENUE, MILTON PARK, ABINGDON
Oxfordshire OX14 4SA...................................... +44 1235 833944
e: sales@realsound.co.uk
w: www.realsound.co.uk

Rent It
DENMORE INDUSTRIAL ESTATE, BRIDGE OF DON
Aberdeen AB23 8JW .... 01224 853104 // 0800 298 5186
e: sales@rentit.biz
w: www.rentit.biz

A

Rhythm Group
RHYTHM HOUSE, KING STREET, CARLISLE
Cumbria CA1 1SJ 01228 515 141
e: info@rhythm.co.uk
w: www.rhythm.co.uk

River Pro Audio
UNIT 6, BELVEDERE BUSINESS PARK, CRABTREE MANORWAY
SOUTH, BELVEDERE
Kent DA17 6AH..020 8311 7077
e: sales@riverproaudio.co.uk
w: www.riverproaudio.co.uk

Roland Systems Group UK
ATLANTIC CLOSE, SWANSEA ENTERPRISE PARK, SWANSEA
SA7 9FJ...01792 702701
e: simon.kenning@rolandsg.co.uk
w: www.rolandsystemsgroup.co.uk

RT Event Ltd
.... 01704 541069 // 07990 546007
e: info@rtevent.co.uk
w: www.rtevent.co.uk

S1b.com
NEW HOUSE, MEWITH LANE, BENTHAN, LANCASTER
North Yorkshire LA2 7AW 015242 61010
e: info@s1b.com
w: www.s1b.com

Sabre International Ltd
UNITS 5, 6 & 7 HEADLEY PARK 8, HEADLEY ROAD EAST,
WOODLEY, READING
RG5 4SA 0118 938 0683
e: sales@sabre-international.com
w: www.sabre-international.com

Saville Audio Visual
UNIT 5, MILLFIELD LANE, NETHER POPPLETON, YORK
Yorkshire YO26 6PQ 0870 606 1100
e: head.office@saville-av.com
w: www.saville-av.com

Seen & Heard Limited
3 WOOD POTTERY, STEPNEY BANK, NEWCASTLE UPON TYNE
Tyne and Wear NE1 2NP 0191 232 5736
e: sales@seenandheard.co.uk
w: www.seenandheard.co.uk

SES Technical Ltd
UNIT 6 MARLOW ROAD INDUSTRIAL ESTATE, LEICESTER
Leicestershire LE3 2BQ............ 0845 226 0330 // 0116 289 4745
e: sales@sestechnical.co.uk
w: www.sestechnical.co.uk

SFL Group
UNIT 5- HEADLEY PARK 10, HEADLEY ROAD EAST,
WOODLEY, READING
Berkshire RG5 4SW 0118 969 0900
e: info@sflgroup.co.uk
w: www.sflgroup.co.uk

SHMS
LAURELS FARM, BARMBY MOOR, YORK
Yorkshire YO42 4EJ...01759 307863
e: enquiry@shms.co.uk
w: www.shms.co.uk

Show Partners
481 QUARTIER INDUSTRIEL, LOTISSEMENT AL MASSAR, ROUTE
DE SAFI, MARRAKECH, MOROCCO 40 100
....+212 524 35 58 91
e: showpartners@gmail.com
w: www.show-partners.ma

Show Solutions Limited
....01562 863 500
e: mail@showsolutions.co.uk
w: www.showsolutions.co.uk

Showscape Ltd
HOLLY FARM BUSINESS PARK, HONILEY
Warwickshire CV8 1NP 01926 484591
e: enquiries@showscape.co.uk
w: www.showscape.co.uk

Smart AV
5 CENTRAL ROAD, HARLOW
Essex CM20 2ST .... 0845 078 0326 // 01279 624 840
e: info@smart-av.com
w: www.smart-av.com

Smash Productions Ltd
50 ALBERT RD
Bristol BS2 0XW..0117 329 0109
w: www.smashproductions.com

Smile Events
392 GALLEY HILL,, HEMEL HEMPSTEAD,
Hertfordshire HP1 3LA 01923 750 525
e: info@smileevents.co.uk
w: www.smileevents.co.uk

Sony Broadcast & Professional Uk
THE HEIGHTS, BROOKLANDS, WEYBRIDGE
Surrey KT13 0XW... +44 1932 816000
e: enquiries.ses@eu.sony.com
w: www.sonybiz.net/uk

Sound & Vision Av Ltd (edinburgh)
16 DRYDEN ROAD, BILSTON GLEN INDUSTRIAL ESTATE,
LOANHEAD, LOANHEAD
Edinburgh EH20 9LZ 0131 334 3324
e: edinburgh@visionevents.co.uk
w: www.visionevents.co.uk

Sound Barrier Systems
UNIT 20, PALMERSTON BUSINESS PARK, NEWGATE LANE,
FAREHAM
Hampshire PO14 1DJ...07855 165 781
e: enquiries@soundbarriersystems.com
w: www.soundbarriersystems.com

EVENT EQUIPMENT RENTAL **I** TECHNICAL EXPERTISE **I** DESIGN SUPPORT

CONSISTENLY RELIABLE CREATIVELY RESOURCEFUL

AV & Staging

productiontec.com   eventrental@productiontec.com   Dubai & Abu Dhabi

Sound Division
430 HIGH ROAD, LONDON
Greater London NW10 2DA 0208 3495 200
e: info@sounddivision.com
w: www.sounddivision.com

Sound Of Music Ltd
.... 08456 448 550 // 07946 739 384
e: info@pahire.com
w: www.pahire.com

Sound-Link ProAudio Ltd
BICESTER, Oxfordshire............. 01869 600 817 // 07973 633 634
w: www.sound-link.co.uk

Sounds Commercial (Swindon)
5 THE MEADS BUSINESS CENTER, ASHWORTH ROAD,
BRIDGEMEAD, SWINDON
Wiltshire SN5 7YJ 01793 513777
e: info@soundscommercial.co.uk
w: www.sounds-commercial.co.uk

Spectrum Event Technologies
SANAYI CAD. TURIN IS MERKEZI 95. , BLOK NO:5 KAGITHANE,
34403 ISTANBUL - TURKEY
34403... +90 212 294 9162
e: info@spectrum.web.tr
w: www.spectrum.web.tr

Spectrum Hire
UNIT 1 HESTON INDUSTRIAL MALL, HESTON, MIDDLESEX
TW5 OLD...07944 001174
e: info@spectrumhire.co.uk
w: www.spectrumhire.co.uk

Spherevision
UNIT 1A SHEPPERTON STUDIOS, STUDIOS ROAD, SHEPPERTON
Middlesex TW17 0QD..0208 783 1972
e: info@arithmetica.com
w: www.spherevision.com

SPL Audio Services
STUDIO THIRTEEN , 2 SIDMOUTH ROAD, SALE
Cheshire M33 5FX .... 0161 962 5151 // 07788 725 726
e: info@splaudioservices.co.uk
w: www.splaudioservices.co.uk

Spyder UK Ltd
UNIT 3, ATTRILLS YARD, THE DUVER, ST HELENS
Isle of Wight PO33 1YB 01983 779337
e: hire@spyderuk.com
w: www.spyderuk.com

Stage Connections
UNIT 1B, ACTON STREET , LONG EATON, NOTTINGHAM
Nottinghamshire NG10 1FT........0115 938 6354 / 07976 00 5769
e: info@stageconnections.co.uk
w: www.stageconnections.co.uk/

StageCore
UNIT 6 EAST GATE BUSINESS PARK, ARGALL WAY, LONDON
Greater London E10 7PG.....................................020 3697 3888
e: info@stagecore.co.uk
w: www.stagecore.co.uk

Stagelogic Ltd
UNIT 21 EVANS BUSINESS CENTRE, DUNNS CLOSE, NUNEATON
Warwickshire CV11 4NF.................................... 0845 600 3961 //
024 7632 2232 // 07595
e: hire@stagelogic.co.uk
w: www.stagelogic.co.uk

Storm Events London Ltd
....0207 993 6077 / 07733 352631
e: messages@storm-events.co.uk
w: www.storm-events.co.uk

Studio Wizard
MELTON PARK , MELTON CONSTABLE
Norfolk NR24 2NJ...01263 862 999
e: info@studiowizard.com
w: www.studiowizard.com

SWG Events
VINE HOUSE, NORTHWICK ROAD, PILING
Bristol BS35 4HA .... +44(0)1454 633635
e: ask@swgevents.co.uk
w: www.swgevents.co.uk

SXS Events
....0870 080 2342
e: hello@sxsevents.co.uk
w: www.sxsevents.co.uk

Team Visual Solutions Ltd
1ST FLOOR ENAVANT HOUSE, REFORM ROAD, MAIDENHEAD
Berkshire SL6 8BT... +44 1753 569967
// +44 1753 569453
e: create@team-solutions.co.uk
w: www.team-solutions.co.uk

Technical Hire Ltd
12-13 BONVILLE ROAD, BRISLINGTON
Bristol BS4 5QG..0844 854 3900
e: info@technicalhire.com
w: www.technicalhire.com

Technology4events
SPIRELLA BUILDING BRIDGE ROAD, LETCHWORTH GARDEN CITY
Hertfordshire SSG6 4ET 01462 476118
e: info@technology4events.co.uk
w: www.technology4events.co.uk

Techpro Events Ltd
UNITS 10 - 12, CAVENDISH, LICHFIELD ROAD IND. EST.,
TAMWORTH
Staffordshire B79 7XH 01827 310750
e: hello@techpro.co.uk
w: www.techproevents.co.uk

A

Tega AV
148 SCULCOATES LANE, HULL
East Yorkshire HU5 1EE..01482 444666
e: av@tega.co.uk
w: www.tega.co.uk

The Hire Company (UK) Ltd
UNITS 5 & 6, CHRISTCHURCH BUSINESS PARK, RADAR WAY,
CHRISTCHURCH
Dorset BH23 4FL 01425 272002
e: scott@thehireco.co.uk
w: www.thehireco.co.uk

The Home Cinema Specialist
10 ORCHARD CLOSE , BRIXHAM , DEVON
TQ5 9QA 0800 880 3127
e: enquiries@thehomecinemacompany.co.uk
w: www.thehomecinemacompany.co.uk

The LED Studio
HANGER WAY, PETERSFIELD
Hampshire GU31 4QE 020 3617 1979
e: sales@theledstudio.co.uk
w: www.theledstudio.co.uk

The Presentation Business
9 BUCKSTONE RISE, EDINBURGH
Edinburgh EH10 6UW................ 0131 466 8254 // 07977566727
e: info@tide-motion.co.uk
w: www.tide-motion.co.uk

The Production Works
UNIT 5- EXMOUTH COURT, EXMOUTH ROAD, CHELTENHAM
Gloucestershire GL53 7NR 01242 807841
e: contact@the-production-works.co.uk
w: www.the-production-works.co.uk

The Small PA Company
NEWHAM
Greater London .... 020 8536 0649 // 077 8558 4279
e: ian@thesmallpacompany.com
w: www.soundengineer.co.uk

The Wicked Company
UNIT 2, BLACKETT ROAD, DARLINGTON
Durham DL1 2BJ ....01325 789382 /
07725 164507
e: info@thewickedcompany.co.uk
w: www.thewickedcompany.co.uk

Tower Showrental
UNIT 8- FORTH INDUSTRIAL CENTRE, SEALCARR STREET
Edinburgh EH5 1RF...0131 552 0100
e: enquiries@tower-productions.com
w: www.tower-productions.com

Transmission Tx Ltd
UNIT 1A, SHEPPERTON STUDIOS, STUDIOS ROAD, SHEPPERTON
Middlesex TW17 0QD................................. + 44 (0)20 8783 1972
w: www.ttx.co.uk

True Sound Hire
UNIT 2, MANOR PARK INDUSTRIAL EST, WYNDHAM STREET,
ALDERSHOT
Hampshire GU12 4NZ ....01252 313154 / 01252 313154
e: info@truesoundhire.co.uk
w: www.truesoundhire.co.uk

UK Event Services
UNIT 56- ENFIELD INDUSTRIAL ESTATE, REDDITCH
Worcestershire B97 6DE .... 08456 43 48 49 // 08456 44 65 70
e: websitecontact@ukeventservices.co.uk
w: www.ukeventservices.co.uk

Unicol Engineering
GREEN ROAD, OXFORD
Oxfordshire OX3 8EU..01865 767676
e: sales@unicol.com
w: www.unicol.com

Universal Live
GUY STREET, BRADFORD
West Yorkshire BD4 7BB 01274 200292
e: bradford@universal-live.com
w: www.universal-live.com

VDC Trading Ltd
VDC HOUSE, 4 BRANDON ROAD, KINGS CROSS, LONDON
Greater London N7 9AA ....020 7700 2777 / 20 7697 9974
e: sales@vdctrading.com
w: www.vdctrading.com

Velvet Twenty
....020 8675 4870
e: enquiries@velvettwenty.co.uk
w: www.velvettwenty.co.uk

VER - Video Equipment Rentals
DOWNLAND CLOSE, UNITS 3-4, LONDON
Greater London N20 9LB.................................... +44 (0) 20 8445
0267
e: info@verrents.com
w: www.verrents.com

Video Conferencing London
ARLINGHAM HOUSE ST. ALBANS ROAD, POTTERS BAR
Hertfordshire EN6 3PH 08458 380 562
e: cs@videoconferencinglondon.co.uk
w: www.videoconferencinglondon.co.uk

Video Village
BLUE TOWER, MEDIACITYUK, SALFORD
M50 2ST..8000096880
e: hire@videovillage.tv
w: videovillage.tv

VisionSound AV
751 SOUTH WEIR CANYON ROAD, SUITE 157-223, ANAHEIM, CA
92808..001 714 280
8201
e: sales@visionsoundav.com
w: www.visionsoundav.com

Visual Response Ltd
WILD RENTS STUDIO, 20-30 WILDS RENTS, LONDON
Greater London SE1 4QG 020 7378 7731
w: www.visualresponse.com

VME Ltd
UNIT 11, LONDRIDGE TRADING ESTATE, KNUTSFORD
Cheshire WA16 8PR...01565 652 202
e: rental@vme-uk.com
w: www.vme-uk.com

VNV Sounds
UNITS 10 AND 10A ASHLEY HOUSE, ASHLEY ROAD, LONDON
Greater London N17 9LZ......................................0203 021 1370
e: info@vnvlive.co.uk
w: www.vnvsounds.co.uk

West End Studios Ltd
THE OLD BISCUIT FACTORY, FINMERE CLOSE, EASTBOURNE
East Sussex BN22 8QN...01323 732130
e: info@teamwestend.com
w: www.west-end-studios.co.uk

West Ent
UNIT 2, CAMBRIAN BUSINESS PARK, CARMARTHEN
Carmathenshire SA31 3RB....................................01267 243957
e: carmarthen@westent.co.uk
w: www.westent.co.uk

Western Cine-video Services
RUTHERFORD HOUSE, 30 ALPHINGTON ROAD, EXETER
 EX2 8HN 01392 256651

WM Event Design
19 ST JAMES'S DRIVE, WANDSWORTH COMMON, LONDON
Greater London SW17 7RN 020 3837 4926
e: info@williammoyse.com
w: www.wmeventdesign.com

AV Supply

Bertram Library Services
CENTURION HOUSE, CENTURION WAY, CLECKHEATON
West Yorkshire BD19 3QE 01603 648164
e: blscustomer.services@bertrams.com
w: libraryservices.bertrams.com

CM Vintage Audio
 ....07970 219 701
e: chrishewitt@cmvintageaudio.com
w: cmvintageaudio.com

Aviation / Marine Charter

Activ Power and Sail
19 CROSSWAYS AVE, EAST GRINSTEAD
 RH19 1JF..01342 300236
e: ernie@activpowerandsail.co.uk
w: www.activpowerandsail.co.uk

Air Charter Global
83 DUCIE STREET , MANCHESTER
Greater Manchester M1 2JQ 020 8242 1845
e: contact@aircharterglobal.co.uk
w: www.aircharterglobal.co.uk

Air Charter Service Plc
MILLBANK HOUSE , 171 - 185 EWELL ROAD , SURBITON
Surrey KT6 6AP...0 20 8339 8588
e: lonprivate@aircharterservice.com
w: www.aircharter.co.uk

Air Partner
2 CITY PLACE, BEEHIVE RING ROAD, GATWICK
 RH6 0PA .... +44 1293 844 888
e: info@airpartner.com
w: www.airpartner.com

Aircraft Chartering Services Ltd
NIGHTINGALE HOUSE, 46/48 EAST STREET, EPSOM
Surrey KT17 1HQ..01372 749 692
e: sales@aircraft-chartering.co.uk
w: www.aircraft-chartering.com

Allport Ltd
HOUSE 1, COWLEY , BUSINESS PARK HIGH STREET, UXBRIDGE
 ....01895 206000
e: info@uk.allportcargoservices.com
w: www.allportcargoservices.com

Aquatech Camera Boats
2 COBBIES ROCK, EPNEY, GLOUCESTER
Gloucestershire GL2 7LN 01452 740559
e: office@aquatech-uk.com
w: www.aquatech-uk.com

Atlas Helicopters
LASHAM AIRFIELD, ALTON
Hampshire GU34 5SP 0125 663 5000
e: info@atlashelicopters.co.uk
w: www.atlashelicopters.co.uk

Bateaux London
EMBANKMENT PIER, VICTORIA EMBANKMENT, LONDON
Greater London WC2N 6NU ....(0)20 7695 1800
e: sales@bateauxlondon.com
w: www.bateauxlondon.com

Blackbushe Aviation
BLACKBUSHE AIRPORT, CAMBERLEY
Surrey GU17 9LB 01252 877727
e: info@blackbusheaviation.com
w: www.blackbusheaviation.com

Bristol Packet Boat Trips
WAPPING WHARF, GAS FERRY ROAD, BRISTOL
Bristol BS1 6UN 0117 926 8157
w: www.bristolpacket.co.uk

A

Bruntingthorpe Aerodrome & Proving Ground
C WALTON LTD, LUTTERWORTH, LEICESTER
Leicestershire LE17 5QS......................................0116 247 8000
w: www.bruntingthorpe.com

Castle Air
TREBROWN, LISKEARD
Cornwall PL14 3PX 01503 240543
e: info@castleair.co.uk
w: www.castleair.co.uk

Centreline Air Charter
THE BRISTOL FLYING CENTRE, SILVER ZONE, BRISTOL AIRPORT, BRISTOL
Bristol BS48 3DP 01275 474357
e: operations@centrelineair.co.uk
w: www.centrelineair.co.uk

Chapman Freeborn Air Charter
3 CITY PLACE, BEEHIVE RING ROAD, GATWICK
West Sussex RH6 0PA...01293 832 318
e: ukcargo@chapman-freeborn.com
w: www.chapman-freeborn.com

Diamond Jets
43 - 45 HIGH ROAD, BUSHEY HEATH
Hertfordshire WD23 1EE 020 8421 7000
e: enquiries@diamondjets.co.uk
w: www.diamondjets.co.uk

Event Group
BRAYE ROAD, VALE
 GY3 5PB 01481 243 334
e: admin@eventgroup.gg
w: www.eventgroup.gg

Flight Logistics
....020 8202 5667
e: operations@flight-logistics.co.uk
w: www.flightlogistics.tv

Flying Flicks
EAGLE & EAGLE LTD, 15 MARLBOROUGH ROAD, LONDON
Greater London W4 4EU..0208 995 1884
e: producer@eagletv.co.uk
w: www.eagletv.co.uk

GB Helicopters
CASTLE HILL COURT, MILL LANE, ASHLEY
Cheshire WA15 0RE 0800 030 4105
e: ops@gbhelicopters.com
w: www.gbhelicopters.com

Heli Adventures
THE OLD FIRE STATION, COTSWOLD AIRPORT, KEMBLE, CIRENCESTER
Gloucestershire GL7 6BA 01285 719222
e: ops@heliadventures.co.uk
w: www.heliadventures.co.uk

Hunt & Palmer Plc
THE TOWER, GOFF'S PARK ROAD, CRAWLEY
 RH11 8XX 01293 558000
e: enquiry@huntandpalmer.com
w: www.huntandpalmer.com

JetAir (Brokers) Ltd
3 CITY PLACE, BEEHIVE RING ROAD, LONDON GATWICK AIRPORT, GATWICK
West Sussex RH6 0PA...01293 566 040
e: aircraft@jetair.co.uk
w: www.jetair.co.uk

KB Event Ltd
PLYMOUTH AVENUE, BROOKHILL INDUSTRIAL ESTATE, PINXTON
Nottinghamshire NG16 6NS 01773 811136
e: info@kbevent.com
w: www.kbevent.com

Las Vegas Charter Private Jet Flights
922 E BRIDGER AVE, LAS VEGAS, NEVADA
 89101.. +1 702 872 3229
e: info@lasvegasjetcharter.net
w: www.lasvegasjetcharter.net

Logwin Air + Ocean Ltd
1 BETAM RD, HAYES
 UB3 1SR 0870 729 5700
w: www.logwin-logistics.com

Lomas Helicopters
LAKE HELIPORT, ABBOTSHAM, BIDEFORD
Devon EX39 5BQ...01237 421054
e: mail@lomashelicopters.com
w: www.lomashelicopters.com

Marine Film Services Ltd
15 CHURCH ROAD, EAST MOLESEY
Surrey KT8 9DR 020 8224 9246
w: www.marinefilm.co.uk

Ocean Leisure
11-14 NORTHUMBERLAND AVENUE, LONDON
Greater London WC2N 5AQ 020 7930 5050
e: internetsales@oceanleisure.co.uk
w: www.oceanleisure.co.uk

Patriot Aviation Ltd
ANSON HOUSE, COVENTRY AIRPORT WEST, BAGINTON, COVENTRY
West Midlands CV8 3AZ..0845 356 3008
e: sales@patriot.uk.com
w: www.patriot.uk.com

Premier Aviation (uk) Ltd
THE TOWER, 48 GOFFS PARK ROAD, SOUTHGATE, CRAWLEY
West Sussex RH11 8XX...01293 558080
e: operations@premieraviation.com
w: www.premieraviation.com

Private Jet Charter

GABLE HOUSE, 239 REGENTS PARK ROAD, LONDON
Greater London N3 3LF...020 8897 8979
e: sales@privatejetcharter.co.uk
w: www.privatejetcharter.com

RIMA Travel Ltd
7 ANGEL GATE CITY ROAD, LONDON
Greater London EC1V 2PT....................................020 7833 5071
e: ernie.garcia@rima-travel.co.uk
w: www.rima-travel.co.uk

Rowland Nichols Air Charter Ltd
SUITE 121, 69 STEWARD STREET, BIRMINGHAM
West Midlands B18 7AF 0121 285 0052
e: info@rowland-nichols.com
w: www.rowland-nichols.com

Rum Jungle
38 SOUTHAMPTON ROAD, LYMINGTON
Hampshire SO41 9GG 01590 676796
e: info@rumjungle.co.uk
w: www.rumjungle.co.uk

Statesman Travel Group
SENATOR HOUSE, 85 QUEEN VICTORIA STREET, LONDON
Greater London EC4V 4AB.....................................020 3667 1000
e: enquiries@statesmantravel.com
w: www.statesmantravel.com

Steve Hill Marine
5 TAMARIND COURT, WETTON PLACE, HIGH STREET, EGHAM
Surrey TW20 9EZ 0784 0937015
e: stevehillmarine@btinternet.com
w: www.stevehillmarine.co.uk

Thames Luxury Charters Ltd
KNOT HOUSE, 2-7 BREWERY SQUARE, LONDON
Greater London SE1 2LF 020 7357 7751
e: enquiries@thamesluxurycharters.co.uk
w: www.thamesluxurycharters.co.uk

Titan Airways Ltd
ENTERPRISE HOUSE, BASSINGBOURN ROAD, LONDON STANSTED
AIRPORT, STANSTED
Essex CM24 1RN 01279 680 616
e: charter@titan-airways.co.uk
w: www.titan-airways.com

Topsail Charters
COOKS YARD, THE HYTHE, MALDON
Essex CM9 5HN 01621 857567
e: info@top-sail.co.uk
w: www.top-sail.co.uk

TravelandMore Ltd
ACORN BUSINESS CENTRE, 18 SKATERS WAY, WERRINGTON,
PETEBOROUGH
 PE4 6NB 0800 6800252
e: info@travelandmore.co.uk
w: www.travelandmore.co.uk

Award Manufacturers

A

Aspect Signs & Engraving
UNIT C1D, BOUNDS GREEN INDUSTRIAL ESTATE, NORTH WAY,
LONDON
Greater London N11 2UL..020 8368 9017
e: info@aspectsigns.com
w: www.aspectsigns.com

Award EFX
ETTINGTON PARK , STRATFORD UPON AVON
 CV37 8BT 1789450005
e: awardefx@email.com
w: www.awardefx.co.uk/

Awards EFX
ETTINGTON PARK , STRATFORD UPON AVON
 CV37 8BT 1789450005
e: awardefx@email.com
w: www.awardefx.co.uk/

Gaudio Awards
UNIT H THE COURTYARD, , TEWKESBURY BUSINESS PARK,
TEWKESBURY
Gloucestershire GL20 8GD 01242 232383
e: sales@gaudio.co.uk
w: www.gaudio-awards.com

Jamy Ltd
33 ROMAN WAY, GODMANCHESTER, HUNTINGDON, CAMBRIDGE
Cambridgeshire PE29 2LN 01480 456391
e: sales@jamy.co.uk
w: www.jamy.co.uk

Laser Crystal Ltd
UNIT 4 SOVEREIGN BUSINESS PARK, WILLIS WAY, POOLE
Dorset BH15 3TB 01202 675 000
e: sales@lasercrystal.co.uk
w: www.lasercrystal.co.uk

Podium Designs
33 MAIN STREET, GOADBY MARWOOD
Leicestershire LE14 4LN 020 3764 0805
e: enquiries@podium-designs.co.uk
w: www.podium-designs.co.uk

Rosettes Direct
THE OLD CHAPEL, YORK STREET, OSWALDTWISTLE, ACCRINGTON
Lancashire BB5 3NU..01254 393711
e: sales@rosettesdirect.com
w: www.rosettesdirect.com

Special Efx Ltd
ETTINGTON PARK BUSINESS CENTRE, STRATFORD-ON-AVON
Warwickshire CV37 8BT...01789 450 005
e: award@efx.co.uk
w: www.awardefx.co.uk

B

B

Backdrops

3D Creations
BERTH 33, MALTHOUSE LANE, GORLESTON, GREAT YARMOUTH
Norfolk NR31 0GW...01493 652055
e: info@3dcreations.co.uk
w: www.3dcreations.co.uk

Acre Jean Ltd
UNIT 7 THE KIMBER CENTRE, 54 KIMBER ROAD, LONDON
Greater London SW18 4PP......................................020 8877 3211
e: enquiries@acrejean.com
w: www.acrejean.com

Architen Landrell Associates Limited
STATION ROAD INDUSTRIAL YARD, STATION ROAD, CHEPSTOW
Gloucestershire NP16 5PF 01291 638200
e: mail@architen.com
w: www.architen.com

Back2front
14 MILL LANE, WINGRAVE
HP22 4PL 01296 681222
e: info@back2front.com
w: www.back2front.com

Brilliant Backdrops
.... 01296 749070 // 07842 249481
e: michellebambrick4@gmail.com
w: www.brilliantbackdrops.co.uk

Bristol (UK) Ltd
UNIT 1, SUTHERLAND COURT, TOLPITS LANE, WATFORD
Hertfordshire WD18 9SP 01923 779 333
e: tech.sales@bristolpaint.com
w: www.bristolpaint.com

Cameo Curtains
LILYHOLT LODGE, 25A LILYHOLT ROAD, BENWICK, MARCH
Cambridgeshire PE15 0XQ 01354 677796
e: info@cameocurtains.co.uk
w: www.cameocurtains.co.uk

Complete Avenue Ltd
OLD BARN, BLACKBIRD FARM,BLACKBIRD LANE, ALDENHAM
West Midlands WD25 8BS......................................07854 007483
w: www.completeavenue.co.uk

Cover It Up Ltd
UNIT 12 LILFORD BUSINESS CENTRE, 61 LILFORD ROAD,
LONDON
Greater London SE5 9HY......................................0207 326 7900
e: info@cover-it-up.com
w: www.cover-it-up.com

DAP Studio
39A HIGH STREET,, CARSHALTON
Surrey SM53BB .... 0208 6698223 / 07973 406830
e: james@dapstudio.co.uk
w: www.dapstudio.co.uk

Dave Parkinson Murals
LANGSTONE, 6 AVENUE ROAD, ABERGAVENNY
Monmouthshire NP7 7DA......................................07946 830446
e: dave@daveparkinsonmurals.co.uk
w: www.daveparkinsonmurals.co.uk

Four Star Events
UNIT 35 GRASMERE WAY, BLYTH
Northumberland NE24 4RR 7971754904
e: alanfourstarevents@gmail.com
w: www.fourstarevents.co.uk

Georgia Stage Inc.
3765 PEACHTREE CREST DRIVE, DULUTH
 30097...001 770 931 1600
e: info@gastage.com
w: www.gastage.com

Gerriets Great Britain Ltd
18 VERNEY ROAD, LONDON
Greater London SE16 3DH 020 7639 7704
e: general@gerriets.co.uk
w: www.gerriets.co.uk

House Couturier Ltd
STUDIO 116, 30 RED LION STREET, RICHMOND UPON THAMES
Surrey TW9 1RB 0207 371 9255
e: info@housecouturier.eu
w: www.housecouturier.eu

Ideal Event Services
310 UNTHANK ROAD, NORWICH
Norfolk NR4 7QD 01603 280176
e: hello@idealeventservices.co.uk
w: www.idealeventservices.co.uk

Invision Display Services Ltd
10 HIGH STREET, THAMES DITTON
Surrey KT7 0RY 0208 9729285
e: sales@invisiondisplayservices.co.uk
w: www.invisiondisplayservices.co.uk

J&C Joel Limited (Head Office)
CORPORATION MILL, CORPORATION STREET, SOWERBY BRIDGE,
HALIFAX
Yorkshire HX6 2QQ...01422 833835
e: uksales@jcjoel.com
w: www.jcjoel.com

JD McDougall Ltd
4 MCGRATH ROAD, STRATFORD, LONDON
Greater London E15 4JP.......................................0208 534 2921
e: mail@mcdougall.co.uk
w: www.mcdougall.co.uk

Leisure Interiors 2000 Ltd
47F BROAD STREET, BANBURY
Oxfordshire OX16 5BT..01295 252551
e: info@leisure-interiors.com
w: www.leisure-interiors.com

Lightmedia Displays Ltd
HUDDLESTON GRANGE, NEWTHORPE, SOUTH MILFORD, LEEDS
West Yorkshire LS25 6JU 0333 600 6000
e: sales@lightmedia.co.uk
w: www.lightmedia.co.uk

Magnet Schultz Ltd
3-4 CAPITAL PARK, OLD WOKING, SURREY
Sussex GU22 9LD 01483 794700
e: sales@magnetschultz.co.uk
w: www.magnetschultz.co.uk

Mediaco Graphic Solutions
CHURCHILL POINT, CHURCHILL WAY, TRAFFORD PARK,
MANCHESTER
Greater Manchester M17 1BS..............................0161 875 2020
e: customerservice@mediaco.co.uk
w: www.mediaco.co.uk

Non Facture Design
STUDIO 520, GREENHOUSE, CUSTARD FACTORY, BIRMINGHAM
West Midlands B9 4AA...0121 794 0245
e: non@nonfacture.co.uk
w: www.nonfacture.co.uk

Perry Scenic Creative
UNIT 53 LANGTHWAITE BUSINESS PARK, SOUTH KIRKBY,
WAKEFIELD,West Yorkshire WF9 3NR 01977 659800
e: jonathan.perry@perryscenic.com
w: www.perryscenic.com

Planet Gold Decor
UNIT 4 ROMARSH, FOWLSWICK BUSINESS PARK , ALLINGTON
Wiltshire SN14 6QE...07747 015 170
e: info@planetgolddecor.co.uk
w: www.planetgolddecor.co.uk or www.

Rockdrops Ltd
....08455 197 791
e: info@rockdrops.com
w: www.rockdrops.com

Rutters
UNIT 6, SOUTH CAMBRIDGESHIRE BUSINESS PARK, BARBRAHAM
ROAD, SAWSTON
Cambridgeshire CB22 3JH....................................01223 833522
e: info@ruttersuk.com
w: www.ruttersuk.com

S + H Technical Support Ltd
MULLACOTT INDUSTRIAL ESTATE, STARCLOTH WAY, ILFRACOMBE
Devon EX34 8PL 01271 866832
e: shtsg@aol.com
w: www.starcloth.co.uk

Scene Set Ltd
UNIT 11, KELVIN WAY INDUSTRIAL , KELVIN WAY ESTATE,
WEST BROMWICH
West Midlands B70 7TN...0121 246 8283
e: info@sceneset.co.uk
w: www.sceneset.co.uk

Sculpture Studios
UNIT 3F HARVEY ROAD, NEVENDON INDUSTRIAL ESTATE,
BASILDON
Essex SS13 1DA 01268 726470
e: aden.hynes@hotmail.com
w: www.sculpturestudios.co.uk

Secrets Of
....0161 4080582
e: info@secretsof.co.uk
w: www.secretsof.co.uk

SIGA CreativeFX
UNIT F1-F3 HEATH PLACE, BOGNOR REGIS
West Sussex PO22 9SL...01243 837 835
e: hello@sigacreativefx.com
w: www.sigacreativefx.com

Spectrum Event Technologies
SANAYI CAD. TURIN IS MERKEZI 95. , BLOK NO:5 KAGITHANE,
34403 ISTANBUL - TURKEY
34403.. +90 212 294
9162
e: info@spectrum.web.tr
w: www.spectrum.web.tr

Splinter Scenery
THE GASWORKS , HIGGINSHAW LANE, OLDHAM
OL1 3LB 0161 633 6787
e: alec@splinterscenery.co.uk
w: www.splinterscenery.co.uk

Tildenet Ltd
JOURNAL HOUSE, HARTCLIFFE WAY
Bristol BS3 5RJ...0117 966 968
e: info@tildenet.co.uk
w: www.tildenet.co.uk

Vision Events (Edinburgh)
16 DRYDEN ROAD, BILSTON GLEN INDUSTRIAL ESTATE,
LOANHEAD
Edinburgh EH20 9LZ 0131 334 3324
e: edinburgh@visionevents.co.uk
w: www.visionevents.co.uk

Wallunica
15 DOXEY ROAD, STAFFORD ST16 2EW
.... +49 (0) 40 414 310 0922
e: service@wallunica.com
w: www.wallunica.com

Whaleys Bradford Ltd
HARRIS COURT, GREAT HORTON, BRADFORD
West Yorkshire BD7 4EQ 01274 576718
w: www.whaleys.co.uk

Backline Equipment

B

Backline for Bands
42 WOODSTOCK ROAD EAST, BEGBROKE, OXFORD
Oxfordshire OX5 1RG 01865 842 840
e: info@backlineforbands.com
w: www.backlineforbands.com

Bell Percussion Ltd
6 GREENOCK ROAD, ACTON, LONDON
Greater London W3 8DU.......................................020 8896 1200
e: info@bellperc.com
w: www.bellperc.com

Black Box Pro Audio
THE COURTYARD, 22 HAYBURN STREET, GLASGOW
Glasgow G11 6DG...0141 404 5719
e: info@blackboxproaudio.com
w: www.blackboxproaudio.com

Celestion Ltd
CLAYDON BUSINESS PARK, GREAT BLAKENHAM, IPSWICH
SUFF IP6 0NL...01473 835 300
e: info@celestion.com
w: www.celestion.com

Clear and Loud
....0191 64 54 645
e: bookings@clearandloudpahire.co.uk
w: www.clearandloudpahire.co.uk

Creative Lighting & Sound (CLS)
UNIT 6, SPIRES BUSINESS CENTRE, MUGIMOSS RD , ABERDEEN
Aberdeen AB21 9NY...01224 683 111
e: info@clsaberdeen.co.uk
w: www.clsaberdeen.co.uk

ESP Music Rentals
UNIT 4, 67 TRADESTON ST, GLASGOW
 G5 8BL .... 0141 649 8952 //
07973 478 850
e: info@esp-musicrentals.co.uk
w: www.esp-musicrentals.co.uk

ESS (Entertainment Sound Specialists)
UNIT 2 MAUN CLOSE, HERMITAGE LANE, MANSFIELD
Nottinghamshire NG18 5GY 01623 647291
e: richardmjohn@me.com
w: www.esspahire.co.uk

Inta Sound PA
UNIT 15 , HIGH GROVE FARM IND EST, PINVIN, PERSHORE
Worcestershire WR10 2LF.......................................01905 841591
e: sales@intasoundpa.co.uk
w: www.intasoundpa.co.uk

John Henry's Ltd
16-24 BREWERY ROAD, LONDON
Greater London N7 9NH.......................................020 7609 9181
e: info@johnhenrys.com
w: www.johnhenrys.com

Langley Rehearsal Studios
126 MEADFIELD ROAD, LANGLEY, SLOUGH
Berkshire SL3 8JF 01753 542720
e: langleyguitarcentre@hotmail.com
w: www.langleyguitarcentre.co.uk

Live Systems Ltd
UNITS 1-2, NORTH LEITH SANDS,, LEITH, EDINBURGH
Edinburgh EH6 4ER..0131 555 5200
e: info@livesystems.co.uk
w: www.livesystems.co.uk

LRS Associates Ltd
UNIT 12, BROOK ROAD, , BICTON INDUSTRIAL PARK, KIMBOLTON,
Cambridgeshire PE28 0LR .... 01480 861186 / 01480 860267
e: info@lrs-associates.com
w: www.lrs-associates.com

Matt Snowball Music
UNIT 2, 3-9 BREWERY ROAD, LONDON
Greater London N7 9QJ 020 7700 6555
e: enquiries@mattsnowball.com
w: www.mattsnowball.com

Music Bank Hire
BUILDING D, TOWER BRIDGE BUSINESS COMPLEX, 100
CLEMENTS ROAD, LONDON
Greater London SE16 4DG 0207 252 0001
e: info@musicbank.org
w: www.musicbank.org

Ooosh! Tours Ltd
COMPASS HOUSE, 7 EAST STREET, PORTSLADE, BRIGHTON
 BN41 1DL .... 01273 911382 / 07719 568409
e: jon@oooshtours.co.uk
w: www.oooshtours.co.uk

Pete Cornish
....01435 813393
e: info@petecornish.co.uk
w: www.petecornish.co.uk

Peter Webber Hire Co Ltd
110-112 DISRAELI ROAD, PUTNEY, LONDON
Greater London SW15 2DX 07973 731359
e: ben@peterwebberhire.com
w: www.peterwebberhire.com

Pick N Styx
2 NAPIER STREET, COVENTRY
West Midlands CV1 5PR.......................................024 76 550070
e: info@picknstyx.co.uk
w: www.picknstyx.co.uk

Plastic Monkey Ltd
, LONDON
Greater London SW6 4DX 07931 585100
e: info@plasticmonkey.co.uk
w: www.plasticmonkey.co.uk

B

Premier Exhibition Systems Ltd
3 SMITHY CLOSE, OFF LINGWOOD LANE , WOODBOROUGH,
NOTTINGHAM
Nottinghamshire NG14 6RX 0800 5427739
e: sales@premex.co.uk
w: www.premex.co.uk

Protec (Production Technology LLC)
PLOT NO. 548 - 597, DUBAI INVESTMENT PARK 2,
DUBAI, UNITED ARAB EMIRATES
....+971 4 880 0092
e: eventrental@productiontec.com
w: www.productiontec.com

STS Touring Productions
GROUND FLOOR UNIT 1, APOLLO BUSINESS CENTRE, ARDWICK,
MANCHESTER
Greater Manchester M12 6AW 0161 273 5984
e: office@ststouring.co.uk
w: www.ststouring.co.uk

Badges

PDC Big Badges
6 HAMPTON HILL BUSINESS PARK, HIGH STREET, HAMPTON HILL
Greater London TW12 1NP.....................................21 8614 8980
e: sales@pdc-big.co.uk
w: www.big.co.uk

Badging / Passes

1KPL Badge
PO BOX 662, BOURNEMOUTH
Dorset BH8 0YB .... 01202 397 070 / 0759 454 7845
e: admin@1kpl.com
w: www.1kpl.com

A.J Gilbert (Birmingham) Ltd
66 - 77 BUCKINGHAM STREET, HUCKLEY, BIRMINGHAM
West Midlands B19 3HU .... 0121 236 7774 / 0121 233 1394
w: www.ajgilbert.co.uk

AAA Badges Of Quality
37 DUCKERY WOOD WALK, GREAT BARR, BIRMINGHAM
West Midlands B43 7DW 0121 403 30 30
e: enquiries@aaabadgesofquality.co.uk
w: www.aaabadgesofquality.co.uk

Aspinline
EXHIBITION HOUSE, HAYWARD INDUSTRIAL ESTATE, 1-2 NORTH
VIEW, SOUNDWELL, BRISTOL
Gloucestershire BS16 4NT 0117 9566657
e: sales@aspinline.co.uk
w: www.aspinline.co.uk

Badgemaster
HAZELFORD WAY INDUSTRIAL PARK, NEWSTEAD, NOTTINGHAM
Nottinghamshire NG15 0DQ...................................01623 723112
e: customerservices@badgemaster.co.uk
w: www.badgemaster.co.uk

Badges Plus
BADGES PLUS LIMITED, 1-2 LEGGE LANE, BIRMINGHAM
West Midlands B1 3LD..0121 236 1612
e: sales@badgesplus.co.uk
w: www.badgesplus.co.uk

Band Pass Ltd
1ST FLOOR 20 SUNNYDOWN, WITLEY, GODALMING
Surrey GU8 5RP..01428 684926
e: maxine@band-pass.co.uk
w: www.band-pass.co.uk

Conference Badges
2 HIGH STREET, TEDDINGTON
Middlesex TW11 8EW .... 0800 082 1448 // 0208 614 4134
w: www.conferencebadges.co.uk

D2i Systems Ltd
41-43 HAMILTON SQUARE, WIRRAL, BIRKENHEAD
Merseyside CH41 5BP 0151 6495150
e: info@d2isystems.com
w: www.d2isystems.com

Databac Group Ltd
1 THE ASHWAY CENTRE, ELM CRESCENT,
KINGSTON UPON THAMES
Surrey KT2 6HH 0208 546 9826
e: enquiries@databac.com
w: www.databac.com

Durable
10 NIMROD WAY, WIMBORNE
Dorset BH21 7SH..01202 897071
e: customeroperations@durable-uk.com
w: www.durable-uk.com

Enterprise Products
UNIT 7, TINWELL LODGE FARM , 18 STEADFOLD LANE,
STAMFORD
Lincolnshire PE9 3UN...01780 740075
e: sales@ebadges.co.uk
w: www.buttons.co.uk

Event Merchandising Ltd
UNIT 11, THE EDGE, HUMBER ROAD, LONDON
Greater London NW2 6EW.....................................020 8208 1166
e: event@eventmerch.com
w: www.eventmerchandising.com

G4S Events
SOUTHSIDE, 105 VICTORIA STREET, LONDON
Greater London SW1E 6QT....................................0207 963 3100
w: www.g4s.uk.com

GI Security Pvt. Ltd
3RD AND 4TH FLOOR, 20/1, ASHUTOSH CHOWDHURY AVENUE,
KOLKATA, WEST BENGAL
700 019...+91 98307 22234
e: info@gisecurity.com
w: www.gisecurity.com

B

Harrison Products
STERLING HOUSE, MORETON ROAD, LONGBOROUGH
Gloucestershire GL56 0QJ 01451 830083
e: sales@harrisonprodcuts.net
w: www.harrisonproducts.net

ID&C Ltd
1 -2 DECIMUS PARK , KINGSTANDING WAY , TUNBRIDGE WELLS
Kent TN2 3GP 0845 450 7085
e: sales@idcband.co.uk
w: www.idcband.co.uk

Identilam Plc
UNIT 1 FAYGATE BUSINESS CENTRE, FAYGATE LANE, HORSHAM
West Sussex RH12 4DN..01293 851711
e: sales@identilam.co.uk
w: www.identilam.co.uk

Lanyards Etc Ltd
2 DUCHY ROAD, CREWE
Cheshire CW1 6ND 01270 216 369
e: info@lanyardsetc.com
w: www.lanyardsetc.com

Melville Data Services
SILVERSTONE DRIVE, GALLAGHER BUSINESS PARK, COVENTRY
West Midlands CV6 6PA..02476 380 000
e: enquiry@ges.com
w: www.ges.com

Name Badge Company
UNIT 26 ISEMILL ROAD, BURTON LATIMER
Nottinghamshire NN15 5XU 03330 124 648
e: sales@namebadges.co.uk
w: www.namebadges.co.uk/

Nicholas Hunter Ltd
UNIT 3 OXBRIDGE COURT, OSNEY MEAD INDUSTRIAL ESTATE,
OXFORD, Oxfordshire OX2 0ES.............................01865 251136
e: office@nicholashunter.com
w: www.nicholashunter.com

Orakel Ltd
PANTHEON CENTRE, FFORDD CELYN, LON PARCWR BUSINESS
PARK, RUTHIN
Denbighshire LL15 1NJ 01824 702214
e: enquiries@orakel.co.uk
w: www.orakel.co.uk

Original Thing
TOP FLOOR, 30 TORCROSS ROAD, RUSLIP
Middlesex HA4 0TB..020 8841 1252
e: source@orginalthing.com
w: www.originalthing.com

P3 Medical
1 NEWBRIDGE CLOSE , BRISTOL
Bristol BS4 4AX...0117 972 8888
e: sales@p3-medical.com
w: www.p3-medical.com

Pac 3000 Ltd
UNIT 1, SOUTH PARK BUSINESS CENTRE, HOBSON STREET,
MACCLESFIELD
Cheshire SK11 8BS...01625 442020
e: sales@wristbands.co.uk
w: www.wristbands.co.uk

Pinpoint Badges & Promotions
MALTINGS MEWS, SIDCUP
Kent DA15 7DG..020 8302 8008
e: sales@pinpointbadges.com
w: www.pinpointbadges.com

Ribbon Works
WILSON BUSINESS PARK, HILLINGTON, GLASGOW
G52 4NQ...01355 813301
e: info@ribbonworks.co.uk
w: https://www.ribbonworks.co.uk

Rocket Badge Company
6 VALE ROYAL , LONDON
Greater London N7 9AP 0333 7000 132
e: sales@rocketbadge.co.uk
w: www.rocketbadge.co.uk

Security Solutions UK Ltd
THE COURT HOUSE, POLICE STATION LANE, , DROXFORD,
Hampshire SO32 3RF...................................... +44 1489 877700
e: info@securitysolutionsuk.com
w: www.securitysolutionsuk.com

Stablecroft Conference Products Ltd
KINNINGHALL FARMHOUSE, CAVERS, HAWICK
Berwickshire TD9 8LH 01450 373373
e: louise@stablecroft.com
w: www.stablecroft.com

The Conference People
UPPERTON FARM HOUSE, 2 ENYS RD, EASTBOURNE
East Sussex BN21 2DE 01323 644644
e: info@confpeople.co.uk
w: www.confpeople.co.uk

Ticket Alternative
UNIT 333, ASHLEY ROAD, TOTTENHAM
Greater London N17 9LN 0208 880 4167
e: uk@ticketalternative.com
w: www.ticketalternative.co.uk

Trademark Clothing
TRADEMARK HOUSE, RAMSHILL, PETERSFIELD
Hampshire GU31 4AT...01730 711140
e: sales@tm-clothing.com
w: www.tm-clothing.com

WCM&A Ltd
UNITS 1 - 4, WOODEND BUSINESS PARK, STOKE LACY,
BROMYARD HR7 4HQ...01885 490 500
e: info@wcma.co.uk
w: www.wcma.co.uk

B

Words Bureau Systems
13 JOHN STREET, STRATFORD-UPON-AVON
Warwickshire CV37 6UB .... +44 01926 330209
e: sales@wordsoft.co.uk
w: www.wordsbureau.co.uk

Wristbands UK
OAKTREE HOUSE, ASPEN WAY, PAIGNTON
Devon TQ4 7QR .... +44 01803 668099
e: wristbands@longcombe.co.uk
w: www.wristbandsuk.co.uk

Xtreme
5A CHURCH SQUARE, MARKET HARBOROUGH
Leicestershire LE16 7NB..01858 434700
e: info@xtremeid.co.uk
w: www.xtremeid.co.uk

Balloon Sculptures

Balloons for Events
....08456 524848
e: info@balloonsforevents.co.uk
w: www.weddingballoons.biz

Bloon
....08454 860 200
e: bloononline@gmail.com
w: www.bloon.co.uk

Rainbow Faces Ltd
101 HIGH STREET, NEWPORT
Shropshire TF10 7AY..01952 811 544
e: sales@rainbowfaces.co.uk
w: www.rainbowfaces.co.uk

Bar Mitzvahs

Gamewagon Ltd
113 - 115 OYSTER LANE, BYFLEET
 KT14 7JZ..0845 319 4263
e: admin@gamewagon.co.uk
w: www.gamewagon.info

Bars Mobile Licenced

ABC Marquees
1 HAWTHORN WAY, PORTSLADE, BRIGHTON & HOVE
East Sussex BN41 2HR 01273 891511
e: info@abcmarquees.co.uk
w: www.abcmarquees.co.uk

Abraxas Bar Solutions Ltd
.... 01271817861 / 07468 566822
e: info@abraxasbars.co.uk
w: www.abraxasbars.co.uk

Airstream Facilities
....01885 400223
e: talk@airstreamfacilities.com
w: www.airstreamfacilities.com

Bar Hire UK
28 BACK LANE, LEEDS
West Yorkshire LS20 8EB .... 078 35893295 / 08450 661 662
e: info@barhireuk.co.uk
w: www.barhireuk.co.uk

Bar4Hire
UNIT 3 , HILLS COURT, BLAYDON, NEWCASTLE UPON TYNE
Tyne and Wear NE21 5NH 0191 908 6827
e: info@bar4hire.com
w: www.bar4hire.com

Bars2You
25 LARKSPUR GROVE, SAXON PARK, WARRINGTON
 WA5 1BP.................................... 01925 633 131 / 07709888809
e: enquiries@bars2you.co.uk
w: www.bars2you.co.uk

Beetle Juice
....07872 122 882
e: info@beetle-juice.co.uk
w: www.beetle-juice.co.uk

Blast Event Hire
UNIT 1 & 2 BONVILLE BUSINESS ESTATE, DIXON ROAD,
BRISLINGTON, Bristol BS4 5QQ 0117 370 2660
e: info@blasteventhire.co.uk
w: www.blasteventhire.co.uk

Blue Water Bars
....7481093758
e: info@bluewaterbars.co.uk
w: www.bluewaterbars.co.uk

Event Hire Wales
....07494 169599
e: info@eventhire.wales
w: www.eventhire.wales

Ideal Event Services
310 UNTHANK ROAD, NORWICH
Norfolk NR4 7QD 01603 280176
e: hello@idealeventservices.co.uk
w: www.idealeventservices.co.uk

Mambo Mobile Bar
29A VICTOR CRESCENT, SANDIACRE
Derbyshire NG10 5JY..08450 563 953
e: hello@mambomobilebars.co.uk
w: www.mambomobilebars.co.uk

Obelisk Bar Services
PRESTON DEANERY, NORTHAMPTON
Northamptonshire NN7 2DX 01604 844444
e: enquiries@obeliskbarservices.co.uk
w: www.obeliskbarservices.co.uk

B

Stoneham Springs
LOWER STONEHAM FARM, UCKFIELD ROAD, LEWES
East Sussex BN8 5RJ...07881 943059
e: mail@stonehamsprings.com
w: www.stonehamsprings.com

Tactical Management & Events
NEWPORT ROAD , ALBRIGHTON WV7 3AJ...............07950 534672
e: tacticalmanagement@email.com
w: www.thetacticalgroup.yolasite.com

The Mobile Bar People
....07736 323 575
e: richard.todd@mobilebarpeople.com
w: www.mobilebarpeople.com

WM Event Design
19 ST JAMES'S DRIVE, WANDSWORTH COMMON, LONDON
Greater London SW17 7RN 020 3837 4926
e: info@williammoyse.com
w: www.wmeventdesign.com

Big Fun Outdoor Games

Aquazorbs
....07889 845393
e: info@aquazorbs.com
w: www.aquazorbs.com

Department Of Enjoyment
21 BAR TERRACE, WHITWORTH, ROCHDALE
Lancashire OL12 8TB 0800 292 2049
e: events@enjoy.co.uk
w: www.enjoy.co.uk

S&D Leisure Rides
1 CHADWICK'S DEPOT, COLLINGHAM STREET, MANCHESTER
M8 8RQ .... 07791 941731 // 0797 007 1560
e: events@sdlrides.com
w: www.sdlrides.com

Sunshine Events
EVENT HOUSE, 52 - 54 TULKETH ROAD, ASHTON ON RIBBLE,
PRESTON PR2 1AQ 01772 970 389
w: www.sunshineevents.co.uk

Birthday Events

Gamewagon Ltd
113 - 115 OYSTER LANE, BYFLEET
KT14 7JZ..0845 319 4263
e: admin@gamewagon.co.uk
w: www.gamewagon.info

Books & AV Supply

Dawson Books Limited
1 BROADLAND BUSINESS PARK, NORWICH
Norfolk NR7 0WF 01603 648137
e: enquiries@dawsonbooks.co.uk
w: www.dawsonbooks.co.uk

Broadcast Hire

adi.tv
PITTMAN COURT, PITTMAN WAY, FULWOOD, PRESTON
Lancashire PR2 9ZG 01772 708 200
e: info@adi.tv
w: www.adi.tv

Audiovisual Joint Resource
AJR, CORNER HOUSE, 114 WINDMILL STREET, MACCLESFIELD
Cheshire SK11 7LB..1625615090
e: events@avjr.eu
w: www.avjr.eu

BORIS TV Ltd
BRIDGE HOUSE, BRANKSOME PARK ROAD, CAMBERLEY
Surrey GU15 2AQ...01276 612 22
e: info@boris.tv
w: www.boris.tv

British Broadcast Audio
....7538152390
e: ivor.richards@britishbroadcastaudio.co.uk
w: www.britishbroadcastaudio.co.uk

Debrouillard Ltd
....0114 220 0667
e: jonathan@debrouillard.tv
w: www.debrouillard.tv

Finepoint Broadcast Ltd
HILL HOUSE , FURZE HILL, KINGSWOOD
Surrey KT20 6EZ..01737 370033
e: sales@finepoint.co.uk
w: www.finepoint.co.uk

Hyperactive Broadcast Limited
UNIT 5, THE ROYSTON CENTRE, LYNCHFORD LANE, ASH VALE
GU12 5PQ...01252 519191
e: hire@hyperactivebroadcast.com
w: www.hyperactivebroadcast.com

Ide Systems
UNIT 3 SWAFFIELD PARK, HYSSOP CLOSE, CANNOCK
Staffordshire WS11 7FU..01543 574 111
e: enquiries@idesystems.co.uk
w: www.idesystems.co.uk

Lightmedia Displays Ltd
HUDDLESTON GRANGE, NEWTHORPE, SOUTH MILFORD, LEEDS
West Yorkshire LS25 6JU 0333 600 6000
e: sales@lightmedia.co.uk
w: www.lightmedia.co.uk

Max WiFi (UK) Ltd
8 BELBINS BUSINESS PARK, CUPERNHAM LANE, ROMSEY
Hampshire SO51 7JF 0203 727 9520
e: events@maxwifi.co.uk
w: maxwifi.co.uk

Megahertz Broadcast Systems Ltd
UNIT 39 LANCASTER WAY BUSINESS PARK, WITCHFORD, ELY
Cambridgeshire CB6 3NW......................................01353 645000
e: sales@megahertz.co.uk
w: www.megahertz.co.uk

Mike Weaver Communications Ltd
UNIT 10 REDLAND CLOSE, ALDERMANS GREEN INDUSTRIAL
ESTATE, COVENTRY
West Midlands CV2 2NP..024 7660 2605
e: sales@mwc.co.uk
w: www.mwc.co.uk

MTR Ltd
FORD HOUSE, 58 CROSS ROAD, BUSHEY
Hertfordshire WD19 4DQ..01923 234050
e: MTRLtd@aol.com
w: www.mtraudio.com

OptaNet
95 QUEENS RD, BRIGHTON
East Sussex BN1 3XE...2034753610
e: nicholas@optanet.com
w: www.optanet.com

OptaNet
95 QUEENS RD, BRIGHTON
East Sussex BN1 3XE...2034753610
e: nicholas@optanet.com

S L Vision Ltd
70-74 STEWARTS ROAD, LONDON
Greater London SW8 4DE......................................020 7720 6464
e: shoot@slvision.co.uk
w: www.slvision.co.uk

Satstream
8, BRAMLEY COURT, HEREFORD
Herefordshire HR4 0SB 0844 8008785
e: info@satstream.co.ukw: www.satstream.co.uk

Sis Live
2 WHITEHALL AVENUE, KINGSTON, MILTON KEYNES
Buckinghamshire MK10 0AX..................................01908 865656
e: sales@sislive.tv
w: www.sislive.tv

stream7
THE STUDIO, 36 SEAGRAVE ROAD, SHEFFIELD
South Yorkshire S12 2JS..01143 605 060
e: hello@stream7.co.uk
w: www.stream7.co.uk

Synergy Audio
THE OLD BAKERY, FRAMLINGHAM
Suffolk IP13 9DT...07941 552418
e: info@synergyaudio.co.uk
w: www.synergyaudio.co.uk

The LED Studio
HANGER WAY, PETERSFIELD
Hampshire GU31 4QE 020 3617 1979
e: sales@theledstudio.co.uk
w: www.theledstudio.co.uk

Urban Entertainment
UNIT 516, THE WORKSTATION, 15 PATERNOSTER ROW,
SHEFFIELD
South Yorkshire S1 2BX .... 01142 210295 /
07916 161053
e: info@urbanentertainment.org.uk
w: www.urbanentertainment.org.uk

C

C

Cable / Satellite Equipment

Attend2IT
UNIT 8, PARK FARM INDUSTRIAL ESTATE, BUNTINGFORD
Hertfordshire SG9 9AZ 01763 877 477
w: www.attend2it.co.uk

Conference Engineering
.... +44 (0)1625 426916
e: hello@conferenceengineering.co.uk
w: www.conferenceengineering.co.uk

Frontline Network Service
98 GLOUCESTER ROAD, HAMPTON
TW12 2UJ...0800 458 2010
e: enquiries@frontline-ns.com
w: www.frontline-ns.com

JNB Aerials
55 ST GEORGES CRESCENT, SALFORD
Greater Manchester M6 8JN.................................0161 825 9099
e: j.higgins@jnbaerials.co.uk
w: www.jnbaerials.co.uk

Lapp Limited
UNIT 3 PERIVALE PARK, HORSENDEN LANE SOUTH, GREENFORD
Middlesex UB6 7RL...020 8758 7800
e: sales@lapplimited.com
w: www.lapplimited.com

Max WiFi (UK) Ltd
8 BELBINS BUSINESS PARK, CUPERNHAM LANE, ROMSEY
Hampshire SO51 7JF...0203 727 9520
e: events@maxwifi.co.uk
w: maxwifi.co.uk

UK Cables Ltd
LONDON 01708 864464
e: london.016@ukcables.co.uk
w: www.ukcables.co.uk

VDC Trading Ltd
VDC HOUSE, 4 BRANDON ROAD, KINGS CROSS, LONDON
Greater London N7 9AA .... 020 7700 2777 / 20 7697 9974
e: sales@vdctrading.com
w: www.vdctrading.com

Video Village
BLUE TOWER, MEDIACITYUK, SALFORD
M50 2ST...8000096880
e: hire@videovillage.tv
w: videovillage.tv

Carpets

Reeds Carpeting Contractors Ltd
183 TORRINGTON AVE, COVENTRY
West Midlands CV4 9UQ 02476 694 114
e: martincairns@reedscarpets.co.uk
w: www.reeds-carpets.co.uk

Cash / Payment Machines

123 Hire Ltd
120 LEMAN STREET, LONDON
Greater London E1 8EU......................................0800 54 23 123
e: sales@123hire.net
w: www.123hire.net

123Send
.... 0800 54 24 123 / 02073929740
e: opowell@decibeldigital.com
w: www.123send.net/

Acceptcards
THE WHEATSHEAF, BRIGGATE, ELLAND
West Yorkshire HX5 9HG 0345 2696650
e: info@acceptcards.co.uk
w: www.acceptcards.co.uk

Cash On The Move
PO BOX COTM, LONDON
Greater London WC1N 3XX................................020 7794 3664
e: sales@cashonthemove.com
w: www.cashonthemove.com

Wireless Terminal Solutions
GROUND FLOOR, 14 DANBURY MEWS, MANOR ROAD,
WALLINGTON
Greater London SM6 0BY.....................................0845 459 9984
e: sales@wirelessterminalsolutions.co.uk
w: www.wirelessterminalsolutions.co.

Casinos

1st Call Cabaret Casino
TEN ACRE FARM, STONEHILL ROAD, OTTERSHAW
Surrey KT16 0AQ..08450 008 007
e: enquiry@cabaretcasino.co.uk
w: www.cabaretcasino.co.uk

A Mobile Fun Casino
9230 FISHINGLINE ROAD, , ENFIELD, REDDITCH
Worcestershire B98 0FX 01527 518082
e: info@centralenglandcasinos.com
w: www.centralenglandcasinos.com

Abc Events
UNIT 12 CASTLE COURT, BANKSIDE INDUSTRIAL EST,
GRANGEMOUTH, FALKIRK
FK2 7UU 0845 602 4139
e: louise@abc-events.co.uk
w: www.abc-events.co.uk

Big Indoor Games Company Ltd
BIRCHES WOOD, CRACKLEY LANE, KENILWORTH
Warwickshire CV8 2JT 01926 863090
e: sales@bigindoorgames.co.uk
w: www.bigindoorgames.co.uk

Classic Casino Entertainments
UNIT G, EMMS COURT, MEETING LANE, BRIERLEY HILL
 DY5 3LB 01384 265793
e: info@classiccasino.co.uk
w: www.classiccasino.co.uk

Diamond Fun Casino
31 KENNEL LANE, , FETCHAM
Surrey KT22 9PQ 0845 6123707
e: info@diamondfc.com
w: www.diamondfc.com

Grosvenor Fun Casino
STATESMAN HOUSE, STAFFERTON WAY, MAIDENHEAD
 SL6 1AY...01628 504000
e: zoe.westerman@rank.com

Perfect Fun Casino
, CADDINGTON
 LU1...07864 149102
e: info@perfectfuncasino.co.uk

Viva Vegas
144A OLD SOUTH LAMBETH ROAD, LONDON
 SW8 1XX 020 7820 0999
e: enquiries@vivavegas.co.uk
w: www.vivavegas.co.uk

Caterers

Aaron's catering service
42 ASHINGDON ROAD ROCHFORD
 SS4 1RD .... 07432635597 /
01702 531 600
e: singh.1972@yahoo.co.uk
w: aaroncatering.co.uk/

ABC Marquees
1 HAWTHORN WAY, PORTSLADE, BRIGHTON & HOVE
East Sussex BN41 2HR 01273 891511
e: info@abcmarquees.co.uk
w: www.abcmarquees.co.uk

Acclaim Food Ltd
82 BARWELL BUSINESS PARK, LEATHERHEAD ROAD,
CHESSINGTON
Surrey KT9 2NY 020 8397 8999
e: info@acclaimfood.co.uk
w: www.acclaimfood.co.uk

Al-Bader Restaurant
178-182 LADYPOOL ROAD SPARKBROOK, BIRMINGHAM
 B12 8JS...1217739818
e: info@al-bader.co.uk
w: www.al-bader.co.uk

Alisan
THE JUNCTION, ENGINEERS WAY , WEMBLEY
 HA9 0EG 0208 903 3888
e: mail@alisan.co.uk
w: www.alisan.co.uk

Alistair-Hugo Catering & Events
UNIT 20 ACTON PARK ESTATE, ACTON
 W3 7QE 020 8735 4050
e: yasemin@getmanic.co.uk

Allson Wholesale
 ....01592 715545
e: allsonsd@aol.com
w: www.allsonwholesale.co.uk

Anglian Events - First For Festival Food
BUILDING 726, BENTTWATERS PARKS, RENDLESHAM,
WOODBRIDGE
Suffolk IP12 2TW 01394 461546
e: food@anglianevents.co.uk
w: www.anglianevents.co.uk

Aniseed Catering Ltd
UNIT 7, ST GABRIEL'S BUSINESS PARK, EASTON
Bristol BS5 0RT......................................0117 954 2251
e: info@aniseedcatering.co.uk
w: www.aniseedcatering.co.uk

At Home
40 HIGH STREET, COBHAM
Surrey KT11 3EB 01932 862026
e: parties@athomecatering.co.uk
w: www.athomecatering.co.uk

Bad Ass Cakes
FULHAM, LONDON
Greater London SW6.............................07854 400459
e: contact@badasscakes.co.uk
w: www.badasscakes.co.uk

Bexleys
561 PRESCOT ROAD, OLD SWAN, LIVERPOOL
Merseyside L13 5UX..............................0151 259 4380
e: info@bexleys.co.uk
w: www.bexleys.co.uk

Blast Event Hire
UNIT 1 & 2 BONVILLE BUSINESS ESTATE, DIXON ROAD,
BRISLINGTON
Bristol BS4 5QQ 0117 370 2660
e: info@blasteventhire.co.uk
w: www.blasteventhire.co.uk

Blue Strawberry
OPB HOUSE, 26-28 SIDNEY ROAD
 SW9 0TS 020 7733 3151
e: enquiries@bluestrawberry.co.uk
w: www.bluestrawberry.co.uk

Bovingdons
16 EDGEL STREET, LONDON
Greater London SW18 1SR....................020 8874 8032
e: charlotte@bovingdons.co.uk
w: www.bovingdons.co.uk

C

C

Buzz Events & Catering Ltd
CHESTERFIELD RD, WORTHING
West Sussex BN12 6BY .... 07914 971 306 //
01903 501 613
e: info@becatering.co.uk
w: becatering.co.uk

Cafe2U
10 FUSION COURT, ABERFORD ROAD, GARFORTH, LEEDS
West Yorkshire LS25 2GH.......................................08456 444708
e: events@uk.cafe2u.com
w: www.cafe2u.co.uk

Caketoppers Ltd
UNIT 4 HURLANDS BUSINESS CENTRE, FARNHAM
Surrey GU9 9JE .... 01252 726 790 // 0845 200 9820
e: sales@caketoppers.co.uk
w: www.caketoppers.co.uk

Canapes Gastronomiques
....020 7794 2017
e: enquiries@canapes-gastronomiques.co.uk
w: www.canapes-gastronomiques.co.uk

Cater Hire Ipswich
UNIT 1 DALES COURT BUSINESS CENTRE, DALES ROAD, IPSWICH
Suffolk IP1 4JR 01473 462 989
e: info@caterhireipswich.co.uk
w: www.hatfieldscatering.co.uk

Catered-Events
CROWN WORKS KITCHEN, COMMERCIAL ROAD,
WOLVERHAMPTON
West Midlands WV1 3QS 01902 456661
e: chef@callthecaterers.co.uk
w: www.catered-events.co.uk

Celico Event Catering
....07849 002620
e: stephen.celico@gmail.com

ChefNOW! Personal Chef Services
ENGLANDS COTTAGE, CLYST HYDON, EXETER
Devon EX15 2NF... 01884 277336 //
07540 492987
e: information@chefnow.com
w: www.chefnow.com

Coca-Cola Enterprises Ltd - Event Services
ENTERPRISE HOUSE, BAKERS ROAD, UXBRIDGE
Middlesex UB8 1EZ...01895 231 313
e: gbeventservices@cokecce.com
w: www.cokecce.com

Con Gusto Catering
WOOLWICH ROYAL ARSENAL, LONDON
SE18 6PL...020 7112 8544
e: congustocatering@outlook.com
w: www.congustocatering.co.uk/

Cook And Waiter
UNIT B8 - ALPHA BETA CENTRE, 8 STANDARD ROAD, LONDON
Greater London NW10 6EU 0208 537 1200
e: reception@cookandwaiter.com
w: www.cookandwaiter.com

Cranford Catering Solutions Ltd
PO BOX 150, CHEPSTOW, MONMOUTHSHIRE
NP16 5AP .... 01633 265787 /
07795 207909
e: info@cranfordcateringsolutions.co.uk
w: www.cranfordcateringsolutions.co.

Create Food & Party Design
24 ENDEAVOUR WAY, LONDON
Greater London SW19 8UH 020 8944 4900
e: info@createfood.co.uk
w: www.createfood.co.uk

Cult Events
UNIT 3, AUTUMN YARD, AUTUMN STREET, LONDON
Greater London E3 2TT .... 020 8983 5459 -
07540782176
e: info@culte.co.uk
w: www.culte.co.uk

Del Fuego
1A LINKWAY PARADE, LINKWAY, FLEET
Hampshire GU52 7UL...07873 777 740
e: info@del-fuego.co.uk
w: www.del-fuego.co.uk

Delicious North East
UNIT 8, PENNYWELL BUSINESS CENTRE, PORTSMOUTH ROAD,
SUNDERLAND
Tyne and Wear SR4 9AR 0191 5341681
e: info@deliciousnortheast.com
w: www.deliciousnortheast.com

Delightful Catering
82 DRAYTON WOOD RD, NORWICH
 NR6 5BZ..01603 442061
e: delightful.catering@ntlworld.com
w: www.delightfulcatering.co.uk

doesfood
....2033227576
e: jane@doesfood.com
w: www.doesfood.com

Eat To The Beat
GLOBAL INFUSION COURT, NASHLEIGH HILL, CHESHAM
Buckinghamshire HP5 3HE 01494 790 700
e: hello@eattothebeat.com
w: www.eattothebeat.com

Eatopia Event Catering
HORLEY GREEN HOUSE, HALIFAX
West Yorkshire HX3 6AS..07872 451693
e: info@eatopia.eu
w: www.eatopia.eu

Eight Day Events
....01925 262820
e: info@eightdayevents.co.uk
w: www.eightdayevents.co.uk

Elegant Cuisine
....01865 391888
e: enquiries@elegantcuisine.com
w: www.elegantcuisine.com

Empty Plates Catering Services Limited
NAUGHTON FIELDS, 241 LIVERPOOL ROAD, WIDNES
Cheshire WA8 7HL 07562 001967
e: info@emptyplates.co.uk
w: www.emptyplates.co.uk

Exclusive Occasions
LESTER HOUSE, TAMWORTH ROAD, LICHFIELD
West Midlands WS14 9PU.....................................01543 433 554
e: info@exclusive-occasions.co.uk
w: www.exclusive-occasions.co.uk

Fayre Do's Location Caterers
NORSTED MANOR FARM, NORSTED LANE, PRATTS BOTTOM,
ORPINGTON,Kent RR6 7PB 0207 237 6691
e: info@fayredos.co.uk
w: www.fayredos.co.uk

Feedback Event Cuisine Ltd
....+ 44 (0) 7912964100
w: www.feedbackeventcuisine.com

Flying Saucers Ltd
PO BOX 4, HALESWORTH
Suffolk IP19 9AL...01986 784298
e: val@flyingsaucerscatering.com
w: www.flyingsaucerscatering.com

Four Gables Fine Dining
FOUR GABLES FARM, ASHLEY COURT, ASHTEAD WOODS ROAD,
ASHTEAD
Surrey KT21 2ET...01372 275276
e: Info@fourgablesgroup.com
w: www.fourgablesfinedining.com

Fresh Catering
WIZZO & CO. , 47 BEAK STREET, LONDON
 W1F 9SE..07721 472 157
e: maxfresh@sky.com
w: www.freshcatering.org

Fresh Food Event Catering
.... 01633 251864 // 07896 654596
e: lesley@freshfoodevents.co.uk
w: www.freshfoodevents.co.uk

GIG...fyi
GLOBAL INFUSION COURT, NASHLEIGH HILL, CHESHAM
Buckinghamshire HP5 3HE 01494 790700
e: hellogigfyi@gigfyi.com
w: www.gigfyi.com

Global Infusion Group
GLOBAL INFUSION COURT, NASHLEIGH HILL, CHESHAM
Buckinghamshire HP5 3HE 01494 790700
e: hello@globalinfusiongroup.com
w: www.globalinfusiongroup.com

Happy Days Cakes
....7975533724
e: info@happy-days-cakes.co.uk
w: www.happy-days-cakes.co.uk

Hotco Hires
....2036034066
e: info@hotcohires.co.uk
w: www.hotcohires.co.uk

Hughes Caterers
THE OLD CREAMERY, FOUR CROSSES, , LLANYMYNECH
Shropshire SY22 6LP...01691 830 055
e: info@hughescaterers.co.uk
w: hughescaterers.co.uk

Indigo Food
WINCHESTER
Hampshire SO23 7LX................. 0845 527 0208 / 07968 991781
e: info@indigofood.co.uk

Inn Credible Bars
.... 020 8894 3765 // 07970 531981
e: inncred@msn.com
w: www.inncrediblebars.com

John Ginster Catering Ltd
ABACUS HOUSE, 129 NORTH HILL,, PLYMOUTH
Devon PL4 8JY .... 0117 902 5275 // 07775 852484
e: info@jgcatering.co.uk
w: www.jgcatering.co.uk

K&N Catering
.... 01213 530566 // 07860 523 312
e: info@kandncatering.com
w: www.kandncatering.com

KK Catering
....0844 740 5001
w: www.kkcatering.co.uk

Lettice Party Design & Catering
18 STANNARY STREET, LONDON
Greater London SE11 4AA.....................................020 7820 1161
e: stevie@letticeparty.com
w: www.letticeparty.com

Life's Kitchen
....0800 915 0978
e: info@lifeskitchen.com
w: www.lifeskitchen.com

C

C

Luxury Shropshire Events
INNAGE LANE, BRIDGNORTH, SHROPSHIRE
WV16 4HJ..7958516941
e: info@luxuryshropshireevents.co.uk
w: www.luxuryshropshireevents.co.uk/

Mange On The Move Ltd
61 CENTRAL STREET, LONDON
Greater London EC1V 3AF....................................020 7263 5000
e: info@mange.co.uk
w: www.mange.co.uk

Marmalade Hospitality
HAM MANOR GOLF CLUB, WEST DRIVE, ANGMERING
West Sussex Bn16 4JE 0844 414 5516
e: marmaladehospitality@gmail.com
w: www.marmaladehospitality.com

Mat-Crewing
UNIT 3 GILLMOSS INDUSTRIAL ESTATE, HERMES ROAD, LIVERPOOL
Merseyside L11 0ED .... 0845 680 7129 // 07738 439 551
e: info@ineedcrew.co.uk
w: www.ineedcrew.co.uk

Mecco
UNIT 3 , I.O.CENTRE , JUGGLERS CLOSE , BANBURY
Oxfordshire OX16 3TA...01295 254556
e: info@mecco.co.uk
w: www.mecco.co.uk

MJ Events
24 MARKET PLACE, BRACKLEY
Northamptonshire NN13 5DP
.... 01280 701702 // 07850 511 877
e: mark@e8t.co.uk
w: www.mjevents.co.uk

Moodies Ltd
BLAIR HOUSE, THREE GATES LANE, HASLEMERE, HASLEMERE
Surrey GU27 2LD .... 01428 644310 // 01428 652244
e: info@moodies.co.uk
w: www.moodies.co.uk

Mossimann's Party Services
11B WEST HALKIN STREET, LONDON
Greater London SW1X 8JL 020 7235 9625
e: events@mosimann.com
w: www.mosimann.com

MSL Global
BUILDING 91, SEME, BUDDS LANE, BORDON
Hampshire GU35 0JE 01420 471000
w: www.mslglobal.com

Ninety Nine Catering Limited
UNIT 16 FERRYBRIDGE WORKSPACE, PONTEFRACT ROAD, FERRYBRIDGE
West Yorkshire WF11 8PL 01977 277260
e: info@99events.co.uk
w: www.99events.co.uk

Paella Fella Ltd
FEN PLACE FARM BUSINESS PARK, EAST STREET, TURNERS HILL
West Sussex RH10 4QA 01342 777846
e: enquire@paellafella.co.uk
w: www.paellafella.co.uk

Party Ingredients Private Caterers
CATERING SERVICES LIMITED, 34 MASTMAKER COURT, LONDON
Greater London E14 9UB.......................................020 7517 3500
e: sales@partyingredients.co.uk
w: www.partyingredients.co.uk

PenniBlack Caterers
65 QUEENSTOWN ROAD, BATTERSEA, LONDON
Greater London SW8 3RG 0800 3896107
e: info@penniblack.co.uk
w: www.penniblack.co.uk

Peppers Cafe
UNIT G1 BALLYMOUNT DRIVE, DUBLIN 12
.... 01 4292040
e: colm@peppers.ie
w: www.peppers.ie

Place Settings (London) Ltd
UNIT C2, SIX BRIDGES TRADING ESTATE, MARLBOROUGH GROVE, LONDON
Greater London SE1 5JT 020 7740 1234
e: london@placesettingseventhire.com
w: www.placesettingseventhire.com

Plato Catering Hire
BIDFORD ROAD, BROOM
Warwickshire B50 4HF...01789 491133
e: sales@platohire.com
w: www.platohire.com

Purple Grape Catering
14 CUMBERLAND AVENUE, LONDON
Greater London NW10 7QL 020 8453 3310
e: events@purplegrapecatering.co.uk
w: www.purplegrapecatering.co.uk

Randall & Aubin Catering
14-16 BREWER STREET, SOHO, LONDON
Greater London W1F 0SG.....................................020 7287 4447
e: info@randallandaubin.com
w: www.randallandaubin.com

Red Herring Catering Company
SETLEY BARN, SETLEY, BROCKENHURST
Hampshire SO42 7UF...01590 622222
e: info@redherringevents.com
w: www.redherringevents.com

Sapphire London Ltd
.... 020 8127 5400 / 07895 007 951
e: info@sapphirelondon.com
w: www.sapphirelondon.com

Seaholme Marquees
COLEMAN'S PARK, SHAVESWOOD LANE, ALBOURNE
West Sussex BN6 9DY 01273 857577
e: info@seaholmemarquees.co.uk
w: www.seaholmemarquees.co.uk

Seasoned Events
13 BISHOPSGATE, Greater London EC2N 3BA........020 7236 2149
e: hello@seasonedevents.co.uk
w: www.seasonedevents.co.uk

Shirleys Catering
9 WESTBOURNE DRIVE, CHELTENHAM
Gloucestershire GL52 2QG 1242238924
e: shirleys_catering@yahoo.co.uk
w: www.shirleyscatering.co.uk

Simply Taste Ltd
....01279 444714
e: info@simplytaste.co.uk
w: www.simplytaste.co.uk

Smart Hospitality
30 MAIDEN LANE, COVENT GARDEN, LONDON
Greater London WC2E 7JS....................................0207 836 1033
e: enquiries@smartgroupltd.co.uk
w: www.smarthospitality.co.uk

Snakatak
THE HOLLIES, 51 WESTBOURNE ROAD, BROOMHILL, SHEFFIELD
South Yorkshire S10 2QT 0114 268 0860
e: lisa@snakatak.freeserve.co.uk
w: www.snakatakcatering.com

Snap Crew UK
....07837 592361
e: info@snapcrew.co.uk
w: www.snapcrew.co.uk

Stem London Ltd
....07958 707119
e: martin@stem-london.com
w: www.stem-london.com

Sushi Events
....020 3287 2299
e: info@sushi-events.com
w: www.sushi-events.com

Sweet Basil Experience
5 LINGFIELD CLOSE, OLD BASING, BASINGSTOKE
Hampshire RG24 7ED 01256 811 560
e: jo@sweetbasil.co.uk
w: www.sweetbasil.co.uk

Ta-maki Sushi Ltd
UNIT 206, UPPER LEVEL, CENTRE COURT SHOPPING CENTRE, 4
QUEEN'S ROAD , WIMBLEDON
Greater London SW19 8YE.......................................2088796271
e: wimbledon@ta-makisushi.net
w: www.ta-makisushi.com

Tastes Catering Ltd
....020 7232 2325
e: orders@tastescatering.com
w: www.tastescatering.co.uk

The Barista
15G SPRINGFIELD COMMERCIAL CENTRE, BAGLEY LANE,
FARSLEY
West Yorkshire LS28 5LY......................................0845 257 5900
e: info@thebarista.co.uk
w: www.thebarista.co.uk

The Caterers Ltd
33 MOAT HOUSE ROAD,, KIRTON LINDSEY, GAINSBOROUGH
Lincolnshire DN21 4DD..1652649343
e: chefs@thecaterers.co.uk
w: www.thecaterers.co.uk

The Clay Oven
197 EALING ROAD, WEMBLEY
Middlesex HA0 4LW...020 8903 8800
e: theclayoven4@gmail.com
w: www.theclayoven.co.uk/

The Fantastic Sandwich Co
63 NORTH ROAD, ST. ANDREWS, BRISTOL
 BS6 5AD..01179 420470
e: admin@fantasticsandwich.co.uk
w: www.fantasticsandwichco.co.uk

The Flying Pig Hog Roast Company
UNIT 6, HOPEWELL BUSINESS CENTRE, 105 HOPEWELL DRIVE,
CHATHAM
Kent ME5 7DX 07597 1304 88
e: sally@flyingpighogroast.co.uk
w: www.flyingpighogroast.co.uk

The Garden Bars
....0800 028 2817
e: info@thegardencatering.com
w: www.thegardenbars.com

The Happy Buffet Co.
19 VICARAGE LANE, UPPER HALE, FARNHAM
Surrey GU9 0PF 01252 723875
e: jon@thehappybuffet.co.uk
w: www.thehappybuffet.co.uk

The Little Kitchen Company
ELM ROAD, WINCHESTER
Hampshire SO22 5AG 7522927567
e: info@thelittlekitchencompany.com
w: www.thelittlekitchencompany.com

The Vintage Catering Co.
97B CAMBERWELL STATION ROAD, LONDON
Greater London SE5 9JJ......................................020 7738 7842
e: info@thevintagecateringcompany.com
w: www.thevintagecateringcompany.com

C

Tom's Kitchen
FARE ACRES FARM, DRY DRAYTON ROAD, OAKINGTON
Cambridgeshire CB24 3BD 01223 237 666
e: tom@toms-kitchen.com
w: www.toms-kitchen.com

Urban Caprice
63-65 GOLDNEY ROAD, MAIDA VALE
 W9 2AR 020 7286 1700
e: events@urbancaprice.co.uk
w: www.urbancaprice.co.uk

Vip Location Catering
PO BOX 16290, GLASGOW
Glasgow G13 9BT .... 0141 950 2716 // 07976 458 662
e: info@vip-locationcatering.co.uk
w: www.vip-locationcatering.co.uk

Whole Hog
....01305 813232
e: mark@thewholehog.ltd.uk
w: www.thewholehog.ltd.uk

WM Event Design
19 ST JAMES'S DRIVE, WANDSWORTH COMMON, LONDON
Greater London SW17 7RN 020 3837 4926
e: info@williammoyse.com
w: www.wmeventdesign.com

Catering Concessions

Blast Event Hire
UNIT 1 & 2 BONVILLE BUSINESS ESTATE, DIXON ROAD,
BRISLINGTON, Bristol BS4 5QQ 0117 370 2660
e: info@blasteventhire.co.uk
w: www.blasteventhire.co.uk

Con Gusto Catering
WOOLWICH ROYAL ARSENAL, LONDON
SE18 6PL...020 7112 8544
e: congustocatering@outlook.com
w: www.congustocatering.co.uk/

Cult Events
UNIT 3, AUTUMN YARD, AUTUMN STREET, LONDON
Greater London E3 2TT .... 020 8983 5459 - 07540782176
e: info@culte.co.uk
w: www.culte.co.uk

Sweet&Chilli Ltd.
ARCH 4, 1 CRUCIFIX LANE, LONDON
Greater London SE1 3JW 020 7407 4430
e: helloUK@sweetandchilli.com
w: www.sweetandchilli.com

The Barista
15G SPRINGFIELD COMMERCIAL CENTRE, BAGLEY LANE,
FARSLEY,West Yorkshire LS28 5LY........................0845 257 5900
e: info@thebarista.co.uk
w: www.thebarista.co.uk

The Clay Oven
197 EALING ROAD, WEMBLEY
Middlesex HA0 4LW 020 8903 8800
e: theclayoven4@gmail.com
w: www.theclayoven.co.uk/

WM Event Design
19 ST JAMES'S DRIVE, WANDSWORTH COMMON, LONDON
Greater London SW17 7RN 020 3837 4926
e: info@williammoyse.com
w: www.wmeventdesign.com

Catering Equipment

Band International
SUNNYSIDE, FRESHWATER, ISLE OF WIGHT
Isle of Wight PO40 9RW 01983 755 858
e: enquiries@band.co.uk
w: www.band.co.uk

Bash Bars Ltd
UNIT 1, REDHILL 23, 29 HOLMETHORPE AVENUE, REDHILL
Surrey RH1 2GD...01737 210979
e: info@bashbars.co.uk
w: www.bashbars.co.uk

Bath Vintage Hire
CLUTTON, BRISTOL
....7854368541
e: info@bathvintagehire.co.uk
w: www.bathvintagehire.co.uk

Bentley Brown Catering Hire Ltd
10 WOODBRIDGE MEADOWS, GUILDFORD
Surrey GU1 1BA...01483 506720
e: info@bentleybrownco.uk
w: www.bentleybrown.co.uk

Birmingham Catering and Event Hire Ltd
THE HENRY MILLS BUILDING, 30 CHESTER STREET, ASTON,
BIRMINGHAM
West Midlands B6 4BE...0800 910 1317
e: sales@birminghamcateringhire.com
w: www.birminghamcateringhire.com

Blackwood's Ice Delivery
THE GREEN BARN, HAYDEN LANE, HENLEY ON THAMES
Oxfordshire RG9 5TX...01491 642299
e: sales@blackwoods.co.uk
w: www.blackwoodsfoods.co.uk

Cameo Event Hire
UNIT 16, GARDNER INDUSTRIAL ESTATE, KENT HOUSE LANE, ,
BECKENHAM
Kent BR3 1QZ...020 8659 8000
w: www.cameoeventhire.co.uk

Classic Crockery
CLASSIC CROCKERY HIRE, UNIT 10 - 11 MAPLE, FELTHAM,
WEST LONDON, Greater London TW13 7AW
.... 020 3582 9818 / 07584 993 498
e: hire@classiccrockery.co.uk
w: www.classiccrockery.co.uk

CMR International (UK)
CHANNEL HOUSE, 27 QUEEN STREET, ASHFORD
Kent TN23 1RF...07773 885556
e: info@cmr-catering-equipment.co.uk
w: www.cmr-catering-equipment.co.uk

Co-Ordination Catering Hire
15 GATWICK INTERNATIONAL DISTRIBUTION CENTRE, COBHAM
WAY, CRAWLEY
West Sussex RH10 9RX 01293 553 040
e: info@co-ordination.net
w: www.co-ordination.net/

Coronet Hire Services
PARLES FARMS, BANK LANE, WARTON
Lancashire PR4 1TB 01772 634771
e: nikki.nye@tiscali.co.uk
w: www.coronetuk.co.uk

Dragon Marquee & Events Limited
 710 GOWER ROAD, UPPER KILLAY, SWANSEA
 SA2 7HQ...01792 709477
e: enquiries@dragonevents.co.uk
w: www.dragonevents.co.uk

Eight Day Events
....01925 262820
e: info@eightdayevents.co.uk
w: www.eightdayevents.co.uk

Florida Marquees Ltd
THE OLD FORGE, BURY STREET, VALLEY ROAD, SHEFFIELD
South Yorkshire S8 9QQ..0800 731 1676
e: admin@floridamarquees.com
w: www.marqueehiresales.com

Four Candles Ltd
TALLY HO FARM, CROUCH LANE,WINKFIELD, ASCOT
Berkshire SL4 4RZ...8006444944
e: lthomas471@btinternet.com
w: www.four-candles.net

Four-Candles
TALLY HO FARM, CROUCH LANE, WINKFIELD, ASCOT
Berkshire SL4 4RZ...01344 883934
e: lthomas471@btinternet.com
w: www.four-candles.net

Hallmark Catering & Equipment Hire Co.
27-49 WILLOW WAY, LONDON
Greater London SE26 4QP.....................................0208 2919339
e: hireenquiries@hallmarkcatering.com
w: www.hallmarkcatering.com

Hughes Caterers
THE OLD CREAMERY, FOUR CROSSES, , LLANYMYNECH
Shropshire SY22 6LP 01691 830 055
e: info@hughescaterers.co.uk
w: hughescaterers.co.uk

Johnsons Stalbridge Linen Services
JOHNSONS APPARELMASTER LTD , PITTMAN WAY, FULWOOD,
PRESTON
Lancashire PR2 9ZD 0800 093 9933
e: info@stalbridge-linen.com
w: www.stalbridge-linen.com

Jongor Ltd
KINGSLAND TRADING ESTATE, ST PHILIPS, BRISTOL
Bristol BS2 0JZ...0117 955 6739
e: bristol@jongor.co.uk
w: www.jongor.co.uk

Just Hire Catering Equipment Ltd
....020 8595 8877
e: info@justhire.co.uk
w: www.justhire.co.uk

Millie Miles Event Hire Ltd
WESTON GROUNDS FARM, WESTON ON THE GREEN, BICESTER
Oxfordshire OX25 3QX 01869 351 603
e: info@milliemiles.co.uk
w: www.milliemiles.co.uk

Mobile Kitchens Ltd
....0845 812 0800
e: info@mk-hire.co.uk
w: www.mk-hire.co.uk

On Site Refrigeration
....01923 777 736
e: info@osrltd.com
w: www.osrltd.com

On-Site Kitchens
HILLHOUSE INTERNATIONAL BUSINESS PARK, NORTH ROAD, ,
THORNTON CLEVELEYS
Lancashire FY5 4QD 01253 863305
e: info@onsitekitchens.co.uk
w: www.onsitekitchens.co.uk

Party Line Hire Service
42 MORLEY ROAD, BASINGSTOKE
Hampshire RG21 3LW 01256 469255
e: orders@partyline.co
w: www.partyline.co

PKL Group (UK) Ltd
STELLA WAY, BISHOPS CLEEVE, CHELTENHAM
Gloucestershire GL52 7DQ 01242 663 000
e: postbox@pkl.co.uk
w: www.pkl.co.uk

C

Purple & Fine Linen
97 PAVENHILL, PURTON, Wiltshire SN5 4DB 01491 638184
w: www.purpleandfine.com

Rayners Catering Hire Ltd
BANQUET HOUSE, 118-120 GARRATT LANE, LONDON
Greater London SW18 4DJ.................................020 8870 6000
e: info@rayners.co.uk
w: www.rayners.co.uk

Teppanyaki Hire
LESTER HOUSE, TAMWORTH ROAD, LICHFILED
 WS14 9PU 01543 433 554
e: gb@teppanyakihire.co.uk
w: www.teppanyakihire.co.uk

The Event Hire Company
HIRE HQ, 855 LONDON ROAD, WEST THURROCK
Essex RM20 3LG..01708 335184
e: hello@tehcltd.co.uk
w: www.eventhireonline.co.uk

The Mobile Sink Company
THE MOBILE SINK COMPANY LTD , UNIT B6 187 PARK LANE ,
CASTLE VALE , BIRMINGHAM
West Midlands B35 6AN 0121 747 1179
e: info@mobilesink.com
w: www.mobilesink.com

Thorns Furniture & Catering Hire (Birmingham)
19-21 PORTLAND STREET, ASTON, BIRMINGHAM
West Midlands B6 5RX...0121 328 4666
e: hello@thorns.co.uk
w: www.thorns.co.uk

Thorns Furniture & Catering Hire (London)
WELHAM DISTRIBUTION CENTRE, TRAVELLERS LANE, WELHAM
GREEN, NORTH MYMMS, HATFIELD, HERTS
Hertfordshire AL9 7HN 020 8801 4444
e: hello@thorns.co.uk
w: www.thorns.co.uk

Thorns Furniture & Catering Hire (Manchester)
UNIT D, LYNTOWN TRADING ESTATE, LYNWELL ROAD, ECCLES,
MANCHESTER
Greater Manchester M30 9QG.............................0161 788 9064
e: hello@thorns.co.uk
w: www.thorns.co.uk

Well Dressed Tables
4 DEER PARK ROAD, SOUTH WIMBLEDON, LONDON
Greater London SW19 3GY....................................020 8545 6000
e: enquiries@welldressedtables.co.uk
w: www.welldressedtables.co.uk

Whitehouse Crockery
71 SHENTONFIELD ROAD, SHARSTON INDUSTRIAL ESTATE,
MANCHESTER
Greater Manchester M22 4RW 0161 491 5209
e: info@whitehousecrockery.co.uk
w: www.eventcrockeryhire.co.uk

WM Event Design
19 ST JAMES'S DRIVE, WANDSWORTH COMMON, LONDON
Greater London SW17 7RN 020 3837 4926
e: info@williammoyse.com
w: www.wmeventdesign.com

Youcan Hire Ltd
YOUCAN HEAD OFFICE, LOSCOE CLOSE OFF FOXBRIDGE WAY,
NORMANTON, West Yorkshire WF6 1TW 0870 6004007
w: www.youcanhire.co.uk

CCTV

2CL Communications Ltd
UNIT C, WOODSIDE TRADE CENTRE, PARHAM DRIVE, EASTLEIGH
Hampshire SO50 4NU .... +44 (0) 23 8064 8500
e: contact@2cl.co.uk
w: www.2cl.co.uk

Attend2IT
UNIT 8, PARK FARM INDUSTRIAL ESTATE, BUNTINGFORD
Hertfordshire SG9 9AZ 01763 877 477
w: www.attend2it.co.uk

Cricklewood Electronics
40-42 CRICKLEWOOD BROADWAY, LONDON
Greater London NW2 3ET.......... 020 8450 0995 // 020 84520161
e: accounts@cricklewoodelectronics.com
w: www.cricklewoodelectronics.com

Etherlive
INTERFACE BUSINESS PARK UNIT 13, ROYAL WOOTTON BASSETT
Wiltshire SN4 8SY...01666 800129
e: info@etherlive.co.uk
w: www.etherlive.co.uk

JS Electrical Services
6 BEACON SQUARE , PENRITH
CA11 8AJ 07540 418933
e: jselectricalservices.penrith@gmail.com
w: www.jselectricalservices.co.uk

Mobile CCTV
UNIT 8 CAMBERLEY BUSINESS CENTRE, BRACEBRIDGE,
CAMBERLEY, Surrey GU15 3DP 01276 469 084
e: info@mobilecctv.co.uk
w: www.mobilecctv.co.uk

Phase 1 Security Services - Security Guard Company
7 NAPIER HAUSE, ELVA WAY, BEXHILL
Sussex TN39 5BF...0800 009 6898
e: info@phaseonesecurity.co.uk
w: www.phaseonesecurity.co.uk

RockIT Networks
26 BROOM CLOSE, TEDDINGTON
Middlesex TW11 9RJ 07956 920581
e: marty@RockIT-Networks.com
w: www.rockit-networks.com

Security In Action Guards Limited
THIRD FLOOR, 207 REGENT STREET, LONDON
Greater London W1B 3HH 0800 009 6898
e: sales@phaseonesecurity.co.uk
w: www.sia-guards.com

Total Care Security Ltd
UNIT 3 , BRUNEL DRIVE, NEWARK
Nottinghamshire NG24 2DE 0800 917 47 67
e: info@totalcaresecurity.co.uk
w: www.totalcaresecurity.com

Chauffeur / Limousine Services

5 Star Cars
1 KEY HOUSE, COW LANE, READING, RG1 8NA.....01189 50 50 50
e: info@5starcar.co.uk
w: www.5starcar.co.uk

AA Executive Wedding Cars Kent
4 ARLINGTON CLOSE, SIDCUP
Kent DA15 8JW 0208 3081500
e: tom@aaexecutive.co.uk
w: www.aaexecutiveweddingcars.co.uk

ADM Taxis Fleet
2 GALLOWAY CLOSE, ANCELLS FARM, FLEET
Hampshire .... 01252884098 // 07449520283
e: info@admtaxisfleet.co.uk
w: www.admtaxisfleet.co.uk

Atlantic Cars
FIRST FLOOR OFFICE 10 LONGBARN LANE, READING
Berkshire RG2 7SZ 0118 910 1010
e: info@atlanticcars.co.uk
w: www.atlanticcars.co.uk

Beat The Street
WYNYARD MIL, BASKERVILLE, MALMESBURY
Wiltshire SN16 9BS .... +44.(0)1666.825171
e: garry@beatthestreet.net
w: www.beatthestreet.net

Brigade Security Consultants Ltd
SUITE 65, 2 LANSDOWNE ROW, BERKELEY SQUARE, LONDON
Greater London W1J 6HL 0800 389 0893
e: daniel@brigadesecurity.com
w: www.brigadesecurity.com

C & C Cars
THE AUDLEYS, FORDHAM ROAD, FRECKENHAM, NEWMARKET
Suffolk IP28 8JB 1638724155
e: info@candckars.co.uk
w: www.candckars.co.uk

C M Executive Cars Ltd
31 STARTS HILL ROAD, ORPINGTON
Kent BR6 7AR .... 0168 9859 555 // 07768 961339
e: info@cmexecutivecars.co.uk
w: www.cmexecutivecars.co.uk

C M Executive Cars Ltd
31 STARTS HILL ROAD, ORPINGTON
Kent BR6 7AR 01689 859555
e: info@cmexecutivecars.co.uk
w: www.cmexecutivecars.co.uk

Celebration Cars Ltd
BOTLEY ROAD, WEST END, SOUTHAMPTON
Hampshire SO30 3XH...............................07881 248856
e: celebrationcarsltd@me.com
w: www.celebration-cars.co.uk

Celestial Cars
Warwickshire 7531257853
e: stuartdobbie@btinternet.com
w: www.celestial-cars.co.uk

Central Chauffeur Services
23 CITY ROAD, LONDON, Greater London EC1Y 1AE
.... (0)370 042 2752 // 0800 069 9060
e: info@centralchauffeur.com
w: www.centralchauffeur.com

Chauffeur Link
38 COMBE PARK, WESTON, BATH
Somerset BA1 3NR 01225 840880
e: select@chauffeurlink.co.uk
w: www.chauffeurlink.co.uk

Civilised Car Hire Company Ltd
CAMBERWELL TRADING ESTATE, 117-119 DENMARK ROAD, LONDON
Greater London SE5 9LB.......................................020 77387 788
e: darren@londoncarhire.com
w: www.londoncarhire.com

Crosswinds Chauffeur Services
42 YORK ROAD, RAYLEIGH
Essex SS6 8SB 07939 052 921
e: info@crosswindschauffeurs.co.uk
w: www.crosswindschauffeurs.com

Destinations PTC Ltd
6 TEMPLE COURT, TEMPLE WAY, COLESHILL, BIRMINGHAM
West Midlands B46 1HH 01675 461800
e: operations@destinationsptc.com
w: www.destinationsptc.com

Devine's Chauffeur Services
....0035 316 269092
e: res@devinescs.com
w: www.devinescs.com

Driven Executive Hire
MODA BUSINESS CENTRE, STIRLING WAY, BOREHAMWOOD
Hertfordshire WD6 2BW .... 020 8243 8873 / 07956 466 125
e: info@drivenexecutivehire.co.uk
w: www.drivenexecutivehire.co.uk

C

C

Easychauffeur Ltd
222 LONG LANE, HILLINGDON, UXBRIDGE
Middlesex UB10 9PB .... 01895 546241 // 07971 125516
e: info@easychauffeur.com
w: www.easychauffeur.com

Elegance Wedding Cars
109 ELMCROFT AVENUE, WANSTEAD, LONDON
Greater London E11 2BS.......... 020 8530 6401 // 020 8491 0103
e: info@eleganceweddingcars.co.uk
w: www.eleganceweddingcars.co.uk

European Travelplan Ltd
STOCKBURY HOUSE, CHURCH STREET, STORRINGTON
RH20 4LD 01903 745451
e: travel@travplan.co.uk
w: www.travplan.co.uk

First Class Cars Ltd
KENSAL HOUSE , PRESIDENT WAY, LUTON AIRPORT, LUTON
Bedfordshire LU2 9NR 0203 4757070
e: sales@firstclasscars.co.uk
w: www.firstclasscars.co.uk

Flights Hallmark
COACH TRAVEL CENTRE,, BEDFONT ROAD, STANWELL,
Middlesex TW19 7LZ 01784 425600
e: sales@hallmark-connections.com
w: www.vipcoach.co.uk/

Four Seasons Travel
....01361 884 714
e: info@fourseasonstravel.co.uk
w: www.fourseasonstravel.co.uk

Galaxy Cruiser
11 CURLEW WAY, MORETON, WIRRAL
CH46 7SP 0151 538 9320
e: paul@galaxycruiser.co.uk
w: www.galaxycruiser.co.uk

Gleneagles Chauffeur Drive
AUCHTERARDER, PERTHSHIRE
PH3 1NF 0800 731 9219
e: glenlimos@btconnect.com
w: www.gleneagles.com

Gold Choice Wedding Cars
4 MCKAY PLACE, EAST KILBRIDE
G74 4SP 01355 220 228
e: mail@goldchoiceweddingcars.co.uk
w: www.goldchoiceweddingcars.co.uk

Green Metro Cars Reading
UNIT 1 ROBERT CORT IND EST., BRITTEN ROAD, READING
RG2 0AU 0118 666 656
e: info@greenmetrocars.co.uk
w: www.greenmetrocars.co.uk

Grosvenor Classic Cars
LITTLETON HALL , LITTLETON LANE , LITTLETON, CHESTER
Cheshire CH3 7DJ.................... 0800 999 5151 // 07776 248 592
e: classiccars@littletonhall.com
w: www.grosvenorclassiccars.co.uk

J S Cars
.... 01765 603171 / 07824 467636
w: www.ripontaxi.co.uk

LHC Chauffeurs
45 WRIGHTS LANE, PRESTWOOD, GREAT MISSENDEN
Buckinghamshire HP16 0LQ 07702 409424
e: lhcchauffeurs@gmail.com
w: www.lhcchauffeurs.com

London VIP Transfers
.... 07482361190 / 078434172 78
e: bookings@londonviptransfers.co.uk
w: www.londonviptransfers.co.uk

Marvel Cars
4 LISLE STREET, PICCADILLY, LONDON
Greater London WC2H 7BG 020 7439 8444
e: info@marvel-cars.co.uk
w: www.marvel-cars.co.uk

MyMan & Co
6 CLEVELAND DRIVE, ELLESMERE PORT
Cheshire CH66 4XY.................... 0151 2001302 / 07774 184459
e: info@mymanandco.co.uk
w: www.mymanandco.co.uk

Northern Ferrari Hire
YONDERLEA, PORTENCROSS, WEST KILBRIDE
Ayrshire KA23 9PY... 01244 43 44 55
e: info@northernferrarihire.com
w: www.northernferrarihire.com

Panache Chauffeur Hire
90 LONG ACRE, COVENT GARDEN, LONDON
Greater London WC2E 9RZ....... 020 7870 3766 // 0800 054 6974
e: website@panache-chauffeur.com
w: www.panache-chauffeur.com

Paragon Travel PHC Ltd
UNIT 3A, TELFORD RD, FERNDOWN,
Dorset BH21 7QN....................... 01202 929862 // 08001303054
e: info@paragontravelphc.co.uk
w: www.paragontravelphc.co.uk

Park Executive
4 ADMIRAL WAY , SUNDERLAND
SR3 3WX 0191 5250495
e: info@parkexecutive.co.uk

Parkers Executive Chauffeurs
GROUND FLOOR, FORTH BANKS HOUSE, SKINNERBURN ROAD,
NEWCASTLE UPON TYNE, Tyne and Wear NE1 3RH....... 0333 666 1777
e: enquiries@parkerschauffeurs.com
w: www.parkerschauffeurs.com

Pinnacle Chauffeur Transport
31 NOTTINGHAM ROAD, NOTTINGHAM
Nottinghamshire NG9 8AB 0800 783 4107
e: info@wedriveyou.co.uk
w: www.wedriveyou.co.uk

Pinnacle Chauffeur Transport - Essex
31 NOTTINGHAM ROAD, NOTTINGHAM
Nottinghamshire NG9 8AB 0330 330 4107
e: info@wedriveyou.co.uk
w: www.wedriveyou.co.uk

Pinnacle Chauffeur Transport - London
14 LUCERNE CLOSE, LONDON
Greater London N13 4QJ .... 07866 523851 // 0800 783 4107
e: alandpinner@wedriveyou.co.uk
w: www.yourchauffeur.co.uk

Pinnacle Chauffeur Transport - Peterborough
PO BOX 1202, KINGS LYNN
 PE30 9DU 07854 491 219
e: markpaflin@wedriveyou.co.uk
w: www.wedriveyou.co.uk

Platinum Executive Travel
1272 COVENTRY ROAD, YARDLEY, BIRMINGHAM
West Midlands B25 8BS.......................................0121 706 2900
e: sales@platinumet.co.uk
w: www.platinumet.co.uk

Platinum Limousines
1391 LONDON ROAD, , LEIGH ON SEA
 SS9 2SA 0845 612 5565
e: admin@1stplatinum.com
w: www.1stplatinum.com

Prestige Wedding Cars
36 PORTLAND RD, BOURNMOUTH
Dorset BH9 1NQ..01202 535083
e: weds@talktalk.net
w: www.prestige-weddingcars.co.uk

Primus Protective Consultants Ltd
EARLSWOOD RD, LLANISHEN, CARDIFF
 CF14 5GH 02920 757 578
e: info@primusprotection.com
w: www.primusprotection.com

Silverline LandFlight Ltd
ARGENT HOUSE, VULCAN ROAD, SOLIHULL
West Midlands B91 2JY 0121 705 5555
e: silverline@landflight.co.uk
w: www.landflight.co.uk

Simon James Executive Ltd
UNIT 75, 2 SAWLEY ROAD, MANCHESTER
Greater Manchester M40 8BB...............................0161 914 8003
e: enquiries@sjexecutive.co.uk
w: www.sjexecutive.co.uk

Sutherland Specialist Cars
THE CATTLE MARKET, CHEW ROAD, WINFORD
Somerset BS40 8HB .... 01275 472 252 // 07813 961 494
e: info@sutherlandcars.com
w: www.sutherlandcars.com

The Limousine Bureau
HIGH STREET , WICKFORD
Essex SS12 9AQ 1268350228
e: thelimousinebureau@gmail.com
w: www.thelimousinebureau.co.uk

TMR Executive Cars
....01489 580483
e: alex@tmr-executive-cars.co.uk
w: www.tmr-executive-cars.co.uk

Total Chauffeur Service
SUITE G02 150 MINORIES, LONDON
Greater London EC3N 1LS 020 7264 2263
e: bookings@totalchauffeurs.co.uk
w: www.totalchauffeurs.co.uk

Tranzcare Travel Ltd
1B BEALEY IND EST, DUMERS LANE, RADCLIFFE, MANCHESTER
Greater Manchester M26 2BD.. 0845 680 2408 // 0161 725 8300
e: enquiries@tranzcaretravel.co.uk
w: www.tranzcaretravel.co.uk

Travel Counsellors Ltd
TRAVEL HOUSE, 43 CHURCHGATE, BOLTON
Lancashire BL1 1TH................... 01773 318910 / 07973 306280
e: louise.cutting@travelcounsellors.com
w: www.tctravelmanagement.co.uk/loui

Tristar Worldwide Chauffeur Services
HORTON ROAD, WEST DRAYTON
Middlesex UB7 8BQ .... +44(0) 1895 432001
e: events@tristarworldwide.com
w: www.tristarworldwide.com

Voyager Executive Cars Ltd
....01223 245450
e: info@vecl.co.uk
w: www.vecl.co.uk

Children's Entertainment

The Wheelie Good Party Company
....0845 0451076
e: partyhq@wheeliegoodparty.co.uk
w: www.wheeliegoodparty.co.uk

Chocolate Fountain

Chocolate Fondue Company
LIVERMORES, BOARS TYE ROAD, SILVER END, WITHAM
Essex CM8 3PN 01376 584669
e: info@chocolatefonduecompany.co.uk
w: www.chocolatefonduecompany.co.uk

Vital Attractions Ltd
.... 0151 733 7788 // 07986 174193
e: naomi@tatu.co.uk
w: www.vitalattractions.co.uk

Classic Bus Hire

Ensignbus Hire
JULIETTE CLOSE, PURFLEET INDUSTRIAL PARK, PURFLEET
Essex RM15 4YF..01708 865656
e: nick.pirie@ensignbus.com
w: www.ensignbushire.com

Starsleeper Limited
10 LOCHSIDE PLACE, EDINBURGH PARK, EDINBURGH
Edinburgh EH12 9RG 07708 273200
e: derek@starsleeper.co.uk
w: starsleeper.co.uk

The London Bus Company Ltd
UNITS 1-4, NORTHFLEET INDUSTRIAL ESTATE, LOWER ROAD, NORTHFLEET
Kent DA11 9SN..01474 361199
e: info@thelondonbuscompany.co.uk
w: www.thelondonbuscompany.co.uk

Clay / Target Shooting

CMSC Corporate Entertainment
....01782 397961
e: chris@executivedays.co.uk
w: www.executivedays.co.uk

Laser Like A Shot
GROVEBECK GRANGE, NORTH DROVE, QUADRING FEN, SPALDING
Lincolnshire PE11 4QS..01775 750456
e: info@laserlikeashot.co.uk
w: www.laserlikeashot.co.uk

Sporting Targets Ltd
KNOTTING LANE, SHARNBROOK ROAD, RISELEY
MK44 1BX 01234 708893
e: eventbookings@sportingtargets.co.uk
w: www.sportingtargets.co.uk

Cleaning Services / Litter Clearance

A1 Event & Exhibition Cleaners
THE COURT YARD, 63A WORCESTER ROAD, LONDON
Greater London E17 5QT........... 0845 241 2719 / 0208 523 1516
e: cleaners@a1eventandexhibitioncleaners.co.uk
w: www.a1eventandexhibitioncleaners.

AA Cleaning Services
12 WILLOW HERB CLOSE, RUSHDEN, NORTHSMPTON
Northamptonshire NN10 0GB................................01933 311 354
e: sales@aacleaningservices.co.uk
w: www.aacleaningservices.co.uk

ABA Cleaners
UNIT 4, MARSHALL BUSINESS CENTRE , FARADAY ROAD ,
HEREFORD HR4 9NS................. 01432 298 686 / 01432 343 733
e: sales@abacleaners.com
w: www.abacleaners.com

All Gleaming Clean
77 KINGSWAY, WEST WICKHAM
Greater London BR4 9JE.....................................020 8462 6050
e: info@allgleamingclean.com
w: www.allgleamingclean.com

Apple Maid Cleaning Events
CHANDOS BUSINESS CENTRE, 87 WARWICK STREET, ,
ROYAL LEAMINGTON SPA
Warwickshire CV32 4RJ.......................................0843 886 1401
e: alfreton@applemaidcleaning.co.uk
w: www.applemaidcleaning.co.uk

Assertio Cleaning Company London
UNIT F30, HASTINGWOOD TRADING ESTATE,, HARBET ROAD,
EDMONTON, LONDON
Greater London N18 3HT 0844 8006806
e: info@assertioservices.com
w: www.assertioservices.com

Barringtons Cleaning Ltd
24 CADDICK ROAD, KNOWSLEY BUSINESS PARK, LIVERPOOL
Merseyside L34 9HP..0151 549 4000
e: cleaning@barringtonscleaning.co.uk
w: www.barringtonscleaning.co.uk

Bluebell Cleaning Company Ltd
....020 8813 6489
e: info@bluebellcleaningcompany.co.uk
w: www.bluebellcleaningcompany.co.uk

Brother Home Improvement Ltd
162 ACACIA RD, MITCHAM, LONDON
CR4 1SU...7845566639
e: brothers.home.improvement.ltd@gmail.com
w: www.bhimprovement.co.uk

Carlisle Support Services
800 CAPABILITY GREEN, LUTON
LU1 3BA 073420 58614
e: alex.leake@carlislesupportservices.com
w: www.carlislesupportservices.com/

DC Site Services Ltd
FENLAND DISTRICT INDUSTRIAL ESTATE, STATION ROAD,
WHITTLESEY, PETERBOROUGH
Cambridgeshire PE7 2EY 01733 200713
e: admin@dcsiteservices.com
w: www.dcsiteservices.com

Dream Clean Services
5 UPLANDS, COVENTRY
West Midlands CV2 3FY 07568 374 864
e: dreamcleanservicescoventry@hotmail.co.uk
w: www.dreamcleanservicescoventry.co

Ecoven
324 WEST WAY, BROADSTONE
Dorset BH18 9LF 07530 925484
e: paul.spencer70@yahoo.co.uk
w: www.ecoven.co.uk

Emprise Services Plc
186 CITY ROAD, LONDON
Greater London EC1V 2NT.....................................020 7549 0800
e: info@emprise.co.uk
w: www.emprise.co.uk

Environmental Production Services
77 ARDLEIGH ROAD, HORNCHUCH
 RM15 5SJ...07976 440992
e: info@environmentalproductionservices.com
w: www.environmentalproductionservic

Fresh Solution Uk
 98B TIPTON STREET, SHEFFIELD
South Yorkshire S9 1DF .... 0114 2448837 // 07504866362
e: freshsolutionenquiry@gmail.com
w: www.freshsolutionuk.co.uk

Green Machine Events
 ....07850 631153
w: www.greenmachineevents.co.uk

Gutter Art Aluminum Seamless Guttering
130 STOCKPORT ROAD HYDE
Cheshire SK14 5RA..8000868312
e: info@gutterartcheshire.co.uk
w: www.gutterartcheshire.co.uk

Herts Cleaning and Maintenance Services Ltd
6 ELM GROVE, WATFORD
Hertfordshire WD24 5NA.......................................0845 108 5656
e: info@hertscleaning.co.uk
w: www.hertscleaning.co.uk

IDEAL Facilities Management Ltd
DIGITAL WORLD CENTRE, 1 LOWRY PLAZA, SALFORD
Greater Manchester M50 3UB..............................0845 0779 776
e: sales@idealfm.co.uk
w: www.idealfm.co.uk

Insite Managed Services Ltd
7 STATION PARADE, SUNNINGDALE, ASCOT
SL5 0EP...01344 620381
e: j.spence@cleanmyevent.com

Karpet Kleen Services.................................013 028 88877
e: patgittins2@hotmail.com
w: www.karpetkleenservices.co.uk

KCC Cleaning Services Ltd
.... 0800 9754 992 // 07767 893648
e: enquiry@kcccleaning.com
w: www.kcccleaning.com

Love Your Cleaning
LOVE YOUR CLEANING, KEMP HOUSE, 152 - 160 CITY ROAD,
London EC1V 2NX...................... 020 3581 4113 /0800 061 4392
e: info@loveyourcleaning.co.uk
w: www.loveyourcleaning.co.uk

Mags Cleaning Services
35 - 37 WEST ST, OLDLAND COMMON, BRISTOL
Bristol BS30 9QT 0333 202 7733
e: magscleaning@yahoo.com
w: www.magscleaning.co.uk

MJ CLEANING AGENCY
IMPERIAL HOUSE, 64, WILLOUGHBY LN , LONDON
N17 0AS..0757242 1229
e: mjcleaningagency@gmail.com
w: www.mj-cleaning-services.co.uk

Nu Kleen Services
UNIT 2 ABBEY GRANGE WORKS, LONDON
Greater London IG11 8BL......................................020 8594 0800
e: sales@nukleen.com
w: www.nukleen.com

Property Services Ltd
21 ELLERTON ROAD, BIRMINGHAM
West Midlands B44 0QD 0121 647 7203
e: propertyservicesuk@live.co.uk
w: www.birmingham-and-midlands-clean

Rawley Event Toilets
HARVEY ROAD, BURNT MILLS, BASILDON
SS13 1RP..01268 722300
e: info@rawley.co.uk
w: www.rawley.co.uk

Rising Star Cleaning Services Limited
4 BLACKTHORN ROAD, HOUGHTON REGIS, DUNSTABLE
Bedfordshire LU5 5JP .... 07474 134748 // 07733043169
e: info@risingstarcleaners.co.uk
w: www.risingstarcleaners.co.uk

Roze Cleaning Services Ltd
35 ETHELBERT GARDENS, ILFORD
Essex IG2 6UN 07926 492813
e: contact@rozecleaningservices.co.uk
w: www.rozecleaningservices.co.uk

Salima Ltd
2A BACCHUS HOUSE, CALLEVA PARK, ALDERMASTON, READING
Berkshire RG7 8EN .... 0845 458 1699 / 07825 586 083
e: info@salima-ltd.co.uk
w: www.salima-ltd.co.uk

C

C

Sam's Flat Cleaning London
....020 3404 2268
e: nathanwilkinsonmail@gmail.com
w: www.flatcleaninglondon.co.uk/

SCS Cleaning Services Limited
3A BUTLERFIELD IND. ESTATE, BONNYRIGG, EDINBURGH
Edinburgh EH19 3JQ...01875 820080
e: contact@scscleaningservices.com
w: www.scscleaningservices.com

Shine Smart Services Ltd.
52 BERKSHIRE GARDENS , LONDON
Greater London N13 6AB 020 3727 2588
e: enquiries@shinesmartservices.co.uk
w: www.shinesmartservices.co.uk

Silky Starlight Ltd
18 RYLSTON ROAD, FULHAM, LONDON
Greater London SW67HJ...07722 914522
e: silkystarlight1967@gmail.com
w: www.silkystarlight.co.uk

Skweeky Kleen
1 WELLINGTON PARK, CLIFTON, BRISTOL
Bristol BS8 2UR 0117 9706211
e: skweekykleen123@gmail.com
w: www.skweekykleen.co.uk

Slim Maintenance
3.1 STANLEY HOUSE, KELVIN WAY , CRAWLEY WEST
Sussex RH10 9SE..01293 277489 / 07792 004700 / 07754 6189
e: info@slimmaintenance.co.uk
w: www.slimmaintenance.co.uk

SPS Environmental Ltd
97 IMPERIAL WAY   , ASHFORD, KENT
 TN23 5HT 01233 695978
e: spsenvironmental@gmail.com
w: www.spsenvironmental.co.uk

Squeaky Event Cleaning Limited
59 BRADFORD STREET, WALSALL
West Midlands WS1 3QD 0800 865 4832
e: info@squeakyeventcleaning.co.uk
w: www.squeakyeventcleaning.co.uk

Watford Cleaners
....01923 865044
e: office@watfordcleaners.co.uk
w: www.watfordcleaners.co.uk

White Knight Cleaning Service
.... 01204852515 / 07792408615
e: marcusdowns@talktalk.net
w: www.white-knight-cleaning.co.uk

Coach / Minibus Hire

247 Coach Hire
105 MAYES ROAD, OFFICE NO.7, LONDON
N22 6UP 020 31 500 522
e: contact@247coachhire.com
w: www.247coachhire.com

Abbey Travel
UNIT N3 EUROPA TRAD EST , FRASER ROAD, ERITH
Greater London DA8 1QL .... 020 8312 9514 / 08000 857 827
e: enquiries@abbeytravel.com
w: www.abbeytravel.com

Adaptable Travel
ADAPTABLE TRAVEL, THE LODGE CONDICOTE,
CHELTENHAM GLOS.
Gloucestershire GL54 1EY.....................................01451 832133
e: info@adaptabletravel.co.uk
w: www.adaptabletravel.co.uk

Beat The Street
WYNYARD MIL, BASKERVILLE, MALMESBURY
Wiltshire SN16 9BS .... +44.(0)1666.825171
e: garry@beatthestreet.net
w: www.beatthestreet.net

BM Coaches
BM HOUSE, SILVERDALE ROAD, HAYES
Middlesex UB3 3BH 020 8848 7711
e: info@bmcoaches.co.uk
w: www.bmcoaches.co.uk

Central Chauffeur Services
23 CITY ROAD, LONDON
Greater London EC1Y 1AE...... (0)370 042 2752 // 0800 069 9060
e: info@centralchauffeur.com
w: www.centralchauffeur.com

Chauffeur Link
38 COMBE PARK, WESTON, BATH
Somerset BA1 3NR 01225 840880
e: select@chauffeurlink.co.uk
w: www.chauffeurlink.co.uk

CMAC Group
SUITE 12, THE GLOBE CENTRE, ST JAMES SQUARE, ACCRINGTON
Lancashire BB5 0RE .... 03333 207 100 / 01254 355120
e: chloe.cumby@coachhirebooking.co.uk
w: cmacgroup.co.uk/

Coach Logistics
Herefordshire 078 7089 8905
e: events@coachlogistics.com
w: www.coachlogistics.com

Coaches Excetera
20-22 WENLOCK ROAD, LONDON
 N1 7GU...2086655561
e: listings@coachesetc.com
w: www.coachesetc.com

Commbus.com Ltd
BLYTHE ROAD,, COLESHILL, BIRMINGHAM
West Midlands B46 2AF...01675 463555
e: sales@commbus.com
w: www.commbus.com

Destinations PTC Ltd
6 TEMPLE COURT, TEMPLE WAY, COLESHILL, BIRMINGHAM
West Midlands B46 1HH 01675 461800
e: operations@destinationsptc.com
w: www.destinationsptc.com

t: 01675 461800
f: 01675 461808
e: operations@destinationsptc.com

Passenger Transport is our speciality - a single Car or
1000 Coaches. We can supply Executive Cars, Chauffeurs,
Minicoaches, Coaches & also provide a Transport Manager for
your Event all over the UK.

www.destinationsptc.com

Direct Minibuses
SUITE 128, 3 RAVENSBOURNE ROAD , BROMLEY
BR1 1HN...1732252272
e: directminibuses@gmail.com
w: www.directminibushire.co.uk/Shepp

Direct Minibuses
SUITE 128 , 3 RAVENSBOURNE ROAD , BROMLEY
BR1 1HN...1732252272
e: directminibuses@gmail.com
w: www.directminibushire.co.uk/Shepp

European Travelplan Ltd
STOCKBURY HOUSE, CHURCH STREET, STORRINGTON
RH20 4LD 01903 745451
e: travel@travplan.co.uk
w: www.travplan.co.uk

Fastway (Eclipse Touring Ltd)
UNIT 17 CASTLEFIELDS INDUSTRIAL ESTATE, BINGLEY
West Yorkshire BD16 2AF.......................................01274 568888
e: sales@fastway.uk.com
w: www.fastway.uk.com

Flights Hallmark
COACH TRAVEL CENTRE,, BEDFONT ROAD, STANWELL,
Middlesex TW19 7LZ 01784 425600
e: sales@hallmark-connections.com
w: www.vipcoach.co.uk/

Four Seasons Travel
....01361 884 714
e: info@fourseasonstravel.co.uk
w: www.fourseasonstravel.co.uk

Go Explore Motorhome Hire
CONWY RD, LLANDUDNO JUNCTION, CONWY
LL31 9LU..01492 583913
e: info@goexplore.biz
w: www.goexploremotorhomehire.co.uk

John Houghton Luxury Mini Coaches
2 ELGAR AVENUE, EALING, LONDON
Greater London W5 3JU .... 020 8567 0056 // 07831 117131
e: john@luxuryminicoaches.co.uk
w: www.luxuryminicoaches.co.uk

Jumbocruiser
PO BOX 30, SEATON
Devon EX12 3WZ 01297 24717
e: sales@jumbocruiser.com
w: www.jumbocruiser.com

London Bus Export Company
PO BOX 12, CHEPSTOW
Gloucestershire NP16 5UZ 01291 689741
e: enquiries@londonbuspromotions.com
w: www.london-bus.co.uk

Macpherson Coaches Ltd
THE GARAGE, HILL STREET, DONISTHORPE
Derbyshire DE12 7PL 01530 414101
e: travel@macphersoncoaches.co.uk
w: www.macphersoncoaches.co.uk

Marshalls Coaches
FIRBANK WAY, LEIGHTON BUZZARD
Bedfordshire LU7 4YP 01525 376 077
e: info@marshalls-coaches.co.uk
w: www.marshalls-coaches.co.uk

Mint Coaches
3 COVENTRY CLOSE, LONDON
Greater London NW6 5TJ.......................................020 7624 6796
e: info@mintcoaches.com
w: mintcoaches.co.uk

MM Band Services Ltd
ACER GLADE, BLACK TUP LANE, ARNOLD, HULL
East Yorkshire HU11 5JA..01964 563 464
e: enquiries@mmbandservices.co.uk
w: www.mmbandservices.co.uk

Motts Travel
GARSIDE WAY, STOCKLAKE, AYLESBURY
Buckinghamshire HP20 1BH 01296 398300
e: info@mottstravel.com
w: www.mottstravel.com

C

Nova Bussing Ltd
ROCK CHANNEL, RYE
East Sussex TN31 7HJ .... 0800 6444 118 // 020 7118 1140
e: info@novabussing.co.uk
w: www.novabussing.co.uk

On The Run Touring
THE OLD BARFLO BUILDING LHS, COPPARDS LANE IND ESTATE,
COPPARDS LANE, NORTHIAM
East Sussex TN31 6QR 01797 253753
e: info@ontheruntouring.co.uk
w: www.ontheruntouring.co.uk

P & M Coaches
PIPPS HILL ROAD NORTH, BILLERICAY
Essex CM11 2UJ..................... 01268 534 454 // 07891 286 476
e: pmcoaches@hotmail.co.uk
w: www.pmcoaches.co.uk

Parkers Executive Chauffeurs
GROUND FLOOR, FORTH BANKS HOUSE, SKINNERBURN ROAD,
NEWCASTLE UPON TYNE
Tyne and Wear NE1 3RH 0333 666 1777
e: enquiries@parkerschauffeurs.com
w: www.parkerschauffeurs.com

Redwing Coaches
10 DYLAN ROAD, HERNE HILL, LONDON
Greater London SE24 0HL.....................................020 7733 1124
e: redwingsales@redwing-coaches.co.uk
w: www.redwing-coaches.co.uk

RIMA Travel Ltd
7 ANGEL GATE CITY ROAD, LONDON
Greater London EC1V 2PT.....................................020 7833 5071
e: ernie.garcia@rima-travel.co.uk
w: www.rima-travel.co.uk

Selwyns Travel Ltd
CAVENDISH FARM ROAD, WESTON, RUNCORN
Cheshire WA7 4LU 01928 529 036
e: info@selwyns.co.uk
w: www.selwyns.co.uk

SilverGray & Niteflite Bussing
UNIT 8 THE HORTON DEPOT, STANWELL ROAD, HORTON
Berkshire SL3 9PE .... 01797 343900 // 02088180101
e: enquiries@silvergray.co.uk
w: www.silvergray.co.uk

Silverline LandFlight Ltd
ARGENT HOUSE, VULCAN ROAD, SOLIHULL
West Midlands B91 2JY 0121 705 5555
e: silverline@landflight.co.uk
w: www.landflight.co.uk

South Lakes Motorhome Hire
....01229 440113
e: info@southlakesmotorhomehire.com
w: www.southlakesmotorhomehire.com

Spires Of Oxford
P.O.BOX 24, WHEATLEY
Oxfordshire OX33 1RA 01865 875 539
e: info@spiresofoxford.co.uk
w: www.spiresofoxford.co.uk

Starsleeper Limited
10 LOCHSIDE PLACE, EDINBURGH PARK, EDINBURGH
Edinburgh EH12 9RG 07708 273200
e: derek@starsleeper.co.uk
w: starsleeper.co.uk

Studio Moves Ltd
54A CONINGHAM ROAD, BASEMENT FLAT, LONDON
Greater London W12 8BH.......... 020 8746 9329 // 07970 518217
e: info@studiomoves.co.uk
w: www.studiomoves.co.uk

TBR Global Chauffeuring
15 BIRKMYE ROAD, GLASGOW
Glasgow G51 3JH 0870 0589 504
e: corporate.uk@tbrglobal.com
w: www.tbrglobal.com

The Kings Ferry- VIP Services
NATIONAL EXPRESS HOUSE, BIRMINGHAM COACH STATION, MILL
LANE, DIGBETH, BIRMINGHAM
West Midlands B5 6DD 0845 257 9909
e: sales@thekingsferry.co.uk
w: www.vipcoachhire.co.uk

Tiger Tours Ltd
81 - 83 WEMBLEY HILL ROAD, WEMBLEY
Middlesex HA9 8BU 0208 9021 006
e: info@tigertours.co.uk
w: www.tigertours.co.uk

Tranzcare Travel Ltd
1B BEALEY IND EST, DUMERS LANE, RADCLIFFE, MANCHESTER
Greater Manchester M26 2BD ..0845 680 2408 // 0161 725 8300
e: enquiries@tranzcaretravel.co.uk
w: www.tranzcaretravel.co.uk

van rental maidenhead
37 JEROME CLOSE MARLOW
SL7 1TX...01628 302029
e: transportwizard@gmail.com
w: www.vanhiremaidenhead.co.uk/about

Vans For Bands Ltd
42 WOODSTOCK ROAD EAST, BEGBROKE, OXFORD
Oxfordshire OX5 1RG 01865 842 840
e: info@vansforbands.co.uk
w: www.vansforbands.co.uk

VIP Coach Hire
.... 0800 9755589 // 07725071076
e: info@vipcoachhire.com
w: www.vipcoachhire.com

Wagon Wheels On Location
....07974 765792
e: info@wagonwheels.tv
w: www.wagonwheelsonlocation.com

West Ten Travel
.... 0208 962 8796 / 07999795006
e: westtentravel@gmail.com
w: www.westtentravel.co.uk

Wheal's Far-Go
UNIT 5, 13-15 SUNBEAM ROAD, LONDON
Greater London NW10 6JP....................................0208 965 4600
e: wfg@whealsfargo.com
w: www.whealsfargo.com

Wiseguides Ltd
PO BOX 63, PRESTWICH, MANCHESTER
Greater Manchester M25 3DB..............................0161 773 0692
e: operations@wiseguides.co.uk
w: www.wiseguides.co.uk

WKN Coaches Ltd
WKN COACHES 13 KILLICK COTTAGES , BENOVER ROAD YALDING,
KENT ME18 6EW...01622 815573
e: info@wkncoaches.co.uk
w: www.wkncoaches.co.uk

Wright Bros Coaches Ltd
CENTRAL GARAGE, NENTHEAD, ALSTON
Cumbria CA9 3NP .... +44 01434 381200
e: info@wrightscoaches.co.uk
w: www.wrightscoaches.co.uk

Coffee / Smoothie Bars

Coffee Solutions
UNIT 3, RECTORY FARM, BREWERY ROAD, PAMPISFORD,
CAMBRIDGE
Cambridgeshire CB22 3EN....................................01223 833 661
e: info@simplygreatcoffee.co.uk
w: www.simplygreatcoffee.co.uk

Lavazza On The Road
....0845 519 8316
e: events@brooklands-uk.com
w: www.lavazza.uk.com

Lovecoffee
5 HEDGEROW WAY, LANG FARM, DAVENTRY
NN11 0SH..07969 195 022
e: lovecoffee@roccocatering.co.uk
w: www.roccocatering.co.uk

Markey Coffee Communication
28 PARK FARM IND EST, ERMINE STREET, BUNTINGFORD
Hertfordshire SG9 9AZ 0870 241 0812
e: info@markey.co.uk
w: www.markey.co.uk

Volkscafe Mobile Specialist Coffee Van
34 LULWORTH PARK, KENILWORTH
Warwickshire , CV8 2XG........... 01926 864156 / 07500 33 46 78
e: mail@volkscafe.co.uk
w: www.volkscafe.co.uk

Community Events

Gamewagon Ltd
113 - 115 OYSTER LANE, BYFLEET
KT14 7JZ...0845 319 4263
e: admin@gamewagon.co.uk
w: www.gamewagon.info

Company Fun Days

Ace Tones Group
11 THORPE ROAD, PETERBOROUGH, PE3 6AB, PETERBOROUGH
PE3 6AB 0845 189 5858
e: enquiry@acetonesgroup.com
w: www.acetonesgroup.com

Computer Graphics

Annix Ltd
580 EASTSIDE COMPLEX, PINEWOOD STUDIOS, IVER HEATH
SL0 0NH 01753 656728
e: stuart@annix.com
w: www.annix.com

Capricorn Digital
41B MONTAGU ROAD
NW4 3ER 0208 202 9594
e: info@capricorn-digital.com
w: www.capricorn-digital.com

Cine Wessex Ltd
2 MOORSIDE PLACE, MOORSIDE ROAD, WINCHESTER
Hampshire SO23 7FX...01962 844900
e: info@cinewessex.co.uk
w: www.cinewessex.co.uk

Compuhire
....020 3137 0599
e: info@compuhire.com
w: www.compuhire.com

Cubic Space
LUMINOUS HOUSE, 300 SOUTH ROW, MILTON KEYNES
Buckinghamshire MK9 2FR....................................01908 889 294
e: meeting@cubicspace.com
w: www.cubicspace.com

Freehand Ltd
BUILDING 52, DUNSFOLD PARK, CRANLEIGH
Surrey GU6 8TB 01483 200 111
e: info@freehand.co.uk
w: www.freehand.co.uk

C

Greenfield Television Ltd
STUDIO 4 SALT LANE, HYDESTILE, GODALMING
Surrey GU8 4DG...01483 202206
e: website@greenfieldtv.com
w: www.greenfieldtv.com

Hotbox Studios Ltd
UNIT 1, MIDDLE YARD, HOME FARM ROAD, ELVETHAM
Hampshire RG27 8AW...0845 355 0604
e: info@hotboxstudios.co.uk
w: www.hotboxstudios.co.uk

Liquid TV
10 AMWELL STREET, LONDON
Greater London EC1R 1UQ 020 7833 8633
e: hello@liquid.co.uk
w: www.liquid.co.uk

MS Media Solutions
15 SPRINGFIELD RD, ABERDEEN
AB15 7RU 01224 314999
e: mark@ms-media.co.uk
w: www.ms-media.co.uk

Concert Promoters

AEG Live (UK) Ltd
ALMACK HOUSE, 28 KING STREET, LONDON
SW1Y 6QW 0207 536 2626
e: help@aeglive.co.uk
w: www.aeglive.co.uk

Arran Events C.I.C
GATE COTTAGE, MACHRIE, ISLE OF ARRAN
Ayrshire KA27 8DS 07884 482 524
e: info@arranevents.com
w: www.arranevents.com

Festival Republic
35 BOW STREET, COVENT GARDEN , LONDON
Greater London WC2E 7AU....................................020 7009 3001
e: info@festivalrepublic.com
w: www.festivalrepublic.com

Gigsnconcerts
18 MILLBAY GDNS, DUNDEE
DD25JR 7511421579
e: andy@gigsnconcerts.com

Highgain Promotions
HYC, HURST ROAD , HORSHAM
RH12 2DN...01403 888005
e: sam.albrow@horshamlive.co.uk
w: www.highgainlive.co.uk

Jar Music Live
75 SHELTON STREET, COVENT GARDEN , LONDON
Greater London WC2H 9JQ....................................020 8732 8495
e: info@jarmusiclive.com
w: www.jarmusiclive.com

Maestro Music International
14 CROWN LANE, , THEALE
Berkshire RG7 5BQ 0118-930-3239
e: mail@birminghamtattoo.co.uk
w: www.maestromusicinternational.co.

Marshall Arts
PO BOX 66142, LONDON
Greater London NW1W 8PA..................................020 7586 3831
e: info@marshall-arts.co.uk
w: www.marshall-arts.com

Mrs Casey Music
PO BOX 296, MATLOCK
Derbyshire DE4 3XU...01629 827 012
e: info@mrscasey.co.uk
w: www.mrscasey.co.uk

PBF Motion Pictures
PORTSMOUTH ROAD, RIPLEY
Surrey GU23 6ER 01483 225179
e: image@pbf.co.uk
w: www.pbf.co.uk

Sjm Concerts Ltd
ST MATTHEWS, LIVERPOOL ROAD , MANCHESTER
Greater Manchester M3 4NQ 0844 811 0051
e: customercare@seetickets.com
w: www.seetickets.com/CustomerServic

Solid Entertainments
46 WELLOWGATE, GRIMSBY
Lincolnshire DN32 0RA 01472 349222
e: solidentertainment@live.co.uk
w: www.solidentertainment.com

Solo Agency & Promoters
4TH FLOOR CHESTER HOUSE, 81-83 FULHAM HIGH STREET,
LONDON
Greater London SW6 3JW 020 207 384 6644
e: soloreception@solo.uk.com
w: www.soloagencyregs.com

Sound Advice
5 BERGHEM MEWS, BLYTHE ROAD, LONDON
Greater London W14 0HN 020 7229 2219
e: info@soundadvice.uk.com
w: www.soundadvice.uk.com

Conferences

A1 Events & Exhibitions Ltd
SUITE 10, SHENLEY PAVILIONS, CHALKDELL DRIVE, SHENLEY
WOOD, MILTON KEYNES
Buckinghamshire MK5 6LB....................................01908 867555
e: help@a1-events-exhibitions.com
w: www.a1-events-exhibitions.com

Aspect Ltd
SOLAR HOUSE, 915 HIGH ROAD, NORTH FINCHLEY, LONDON
Greater London N12 8QJ 020 8282 7575
e: team@aspect-communications.com
w: www.aspect-communications.com/

Association Of British Professional Conference Organisers
BARN DOWN , 2 POOL ROW, WILLERSEY
Gloucestershire WR12 7PJ.....................................0138 685 8886
e: hello@abpco.org
w: www.abpco.org

Baden Powell House
65-67 QUEEN'S GATE, LONDON
Greater London SW7 5JS.....................................020 7590 6909
e: bph.conferences@scout.org.uk
w: www.towntocountry.co.uk/bpHouse/

Benchmark Conference and Events
14 BLANDFORD SQUARE, NEWCASTLE UPON TYNE
Tyne and Wear NE1 4HZ..0191 241 4523
e: info@echoevents.org
w: www.echoevents.org

Big House Events Ltd
35 ST CLAIR STREET , EDINBURGH
 EH6 8LB 0131 669 6366
e: tash@bighouse-events.co.uk
w: www.bighouse-events.co.uk

Big House Events Ltd
35 ST CLAIR STREET , EDINBURGH
 EH6 8LB 0131 669 6366
e: tash@bighouse-events.co.uk
w: www.bighouse-events.co.uk

Bracken Presentations Ltd
OFFICE SUITE 2, CASTLE COURT, 59 CASTLE BOULEVARD, NOTTINGHAM
Nottinghamshire NG7 1FD 0115 9470555
e: mail@brackenevents.co.uk
w: www.brackenevents.co.uk

Capitol House Productions
CAPITOL HOUSE, 662 LONDON ROAD, CHEAM
Surrey SM3 9BY 020 8644 6194
e: mail@capitol.co.uk
w: www.capitol.co.uk

Conference Bristol
53 QUEEN SQUARE, BRISTOL
Bristol BS1 4LH...0117 946 2200
e: conference@destinationbristol.co.uk
w: www.conference-bristol.co.uk

Conference Engineering
.... +44 (0)1625 426916
e: hello@conferenceengineering.co.uk
w: www.conferenceengineering.co.uk

Conference Shop Ltd
GOWER HOUSE, 18 ASHMERE LANE, FELPHAM
West Sussex PO22 7QT 0845 873 6299
e: sales@conferenceshop.com
w: www.conferenceshop.com

Corporate Events Plus Ltd
LODGE FARM, RECTORY ROAD, BACTON, STOWMARKET
Suffolk IP14 4LE 01449 781355
e: info@corporateeventsplus.co.uk
w: www.corporateeventsplus.co.uk

Createvents Ltd
450 BROOK DRIVE , READING
Berkshire RG2 6UU 01183 340085
e: info@createvents.co.uk
w: www.createvents.co.uk

Crown Business Communications Ltd
12 SOHO SQUARE , LONDON
Greater London W1D 3QF.....................................020 7605 4500
e: contact@crownbc.com
w: www.crownbc.com

CW Events Management
CNC HOUSE, 3 BROOKLANDS, NEW ROAD, BALLYMENA
 BT42 2RT 028 2587 1989
e: info@cweventsni.co.uk
w: www.cweventsni.co.uk

Definitive Events Ltd
UNIT 104 CHORLTON MILL , 3 CAMBRIDGE STREET , MANCHESTER
Greater Manchester M1 5BY .... +971 50 977 2321
e: lisap@definitiveevents.co.uk
w: www.definitiveevents.co.uk

Delfino Logic Limited
DELFINO HOUSE, 261 PRESTON, BRIGHTON
 BN1 6SE 01273 502502
e: ginny_porpora@delfinologic.com
w: www.delfinologic.com

Destinations Unlimited
7 HIGH STREET, RINGWOOD
 BH24 1AB...01425 461311
e: info@dudmc.com
w: www.dudmc.com

Direct Event Services Ltd
69 HIGHGATE ROAD, WOODLEY, READING
Berkshire RG5 3ND...0118 969 9438
e: info@directeventservices.com
w: www.directeventservices.com

East Anglia Leisure
UNIT 4, CIVIC INDUSTRIAL ESTATE, HOMEFIELD ROAD, HAVERHILL
Suffolk CB9 8QP 01440 714204
e: info@ealeisure.co.uk
w: www.ealeisure.co.uk

C

C

Eastwood Park Training and Conference Centre
FALFIELD, WOOTON-UNDER-EDGE
Gloucestershire GL12 8DA 01454 260207
e: reception@eastwoodpark.co.uk
w: www.eastwoodpark.co.uk

Effective Business Events Ltd
IDC HOUSE, VALE, CHALFONT ST PETER
Buckinghamshire SL9 9RZ.....................................01753 279 866
e: sales@effectivebusiness.com
w: www.effectivebusiness.com

Elysium Global Events Ltd
25 CREEK ROAD, HAMPTON COURT, KINGSTON UPON THAMES
Surrey KT8 9BE 020 8481 9900
e: kwaters@elysiumglobalevents.co.uk
w: www.elysiumglobalevents.co.uk

Enigma Creative Solutions
ST STEPHENS HOUSE, ARTHUR ROAD, WINDSOR
Berkshire SL4 1RU.....................................01753 622592
e: info@enigmacs.com
w: www.enigmacs.com

ESA Live
THE CROFT , WESTGATE , NORTH CAVE
East Yorkshire HU15 2NG 01430 470 731
e: scherri@esalive.com
w: www.esalive.com

Event & Conference Organisers Ltd
66 NANDI ROAD, P O BOX 25313, NAIROBI
 603.. +254 722 848465
e: mail@eco.co.ke
w: www.eco.co.ke

Event Concept
UNIT B3 & B4, GALLEY WALL TRADING ESTATE, GALLEY WALL
ROAD, LONDON
Greater London SE16 3PB.....................................020 7740 3988
e: info@eventconcept.co.uk
w: www.eventconcept.co.uk

Eventwise
AXE & BOTTLE COURT, 70 NEWCOMEN, LONDON
Greater London SE1 1YT 020 7378 2975
e: hello@eventwise.co.uk
w: www.eventwise.co.uk

Experience Scotland Conference & Incentives Ltd
2 WEST STREET, PENICUIK
 EH26 9DL 01968 679969
e: enquiries@experiencescotland.co.uk
w: www.experiencescotland.co.uk

Feathers Catering & Event Management
CATER HOUSE, 113 MOUNT PLEASANT, LIVERPOOL
Merseyside L3 5TF 0151 709 2020
e: info@feathers.uk.com
w: www.feathers.uk.com

Firebird Events Ltd
UNIT 3, NIMBUS BUSINESS PARK, HERCULES WAY,
FARNBOROUGH
Hampshire GU14 6UU 01252 545654
e: enquiry@firebirdevents.co.uk
w: www.firebirdevents.co.uk

First Protocol Event Management Ltd
27 WOOTTON STREET, LONDON
Greater London SE1 8TG.....................................020 7787 5995
e: kate.sheridan-hayes@firstprotocol.com
w: www.firstprotocol.com

Focal Exhibitions Ltd
THE OLD BAKERY, ALBION ROAD, NEW MILLS
 SK22 3EX 01663 744066
e: enquiries@focalexhibs.co.uk
w: www.focalexhibitions.co.uk

Fruition Premier Limited
NEW BROAD STREET HOUSE, NEW BROAD STREET, LONDON
Greater London EC2M 1NH 0845 1308826
e: mtasker@fruition.co.uk
w: www.fruition.co.uk

FTF Worldwide Event Management
15 MILL LANE, CAMPTON, SHEFFORD
Bedfordshire SG17 5NX 01462 817640
e: info@ftfworldwide.com
w: www.ftfworldwide.com

Fuelled Ltd
SUITE 48 BARTON ARCADE, DEANSGATE , MANCHESTER
Greater Manchester M3 2BH.....................................0161 359 3216
e: hello@fuel-led.com
w: www.fuel-led.com

Fun Events Group
14A MILL STREET, OTTERY ST. MARY, DEVON
 EX11 1AD 01404 811 849
e: admin@funevents.com
w: www.funevents.com

Go Live Events Ltd
UNIT 4.14, PAINTWORKS, BATH ROAD, BRISTOL
Bristol BS4 3EH 01172 443552
e: info@golive-events.co.uk
w: www.golive-events.co.uk

Hull & East Yorkshire Conferences
WYKELAND HOUSE, 47 QUEEN STREET, HULL
 HU1 1UU.....................................01482 486500
e: conference.bureau@vhey.co.uk
w: www.heyconferences.co.uk

ierek
1069869241
e: ahmed.sami@ierek.com
w: https://www.ierek.com/

Imagine Events Ltd
37A HART STREET, HENLEY ON THAMES
Oxfordshire RG9 2AR 01491 573311
e: hello@imagine-events.com
w: www.imagine-events.com

In Any Event UK Ltd
18B KESTREL COURT, HARBOUR ROAD, PORTISHEAD
Somerset BS20 7AN 01275 266000
e: events@inanyevent-uk.com
w: www.inanyevent-uk.com

Incentivise Limited
.... 07741 254214 / 01925 211 400
e: paul.bradford@incentivise.co.uk
w: www.incentivise.co.uk/

Integrity Intl Event Services
THE COACH HOUSE, 7 ST ALBANS ROAD, EDINBURGH
Edinburgh EH9 2PA...0131 624 6040
e: hello@integrity-events.com Integrity Events
w: www.integrity-events.com

Inventive Events
THE STUDIO, 61 ELM BANK, BARNES, LONDON
Greater London SW13 0NX 020 8392 9222
e: enquiries@inventiveevents.com
w: www.inventiveevents.com

Ivory Worldwide
21 CHELSEA WHARF, 13-14 CHELSEA WHARF, LONDON
Greater London SW10 0QJ...................................020 3327 7020
e: robbie.crittall@ivoryworldwide.com
w: www.ivoryworldwide.com

JF Events
NORTH LODGE, 122 COWFOLD ROAD, WEST GRINSTEAD,
HORSHAM
 RH13 8LU 01403 865000
e: sales@jfevents.biz
w: www.jfevents.biz

JPFoto
 8 LEATHERWORKS WAY, LITTLE BILLING VILLAGE,
NORTHAMPTON Northamptonshire NN3 9BP
.... 01933 628139 // 01604 419112
e: info@jpfoto.co.uk
w: www.jpfoto.co.uk/corporate-event-

Julian Beard Associates Limited
ABBOTS LODGE, THE STREET, DRINKSTONE
Suffolk IP30 9SX...01359 271962
e: enquiries@jba-events.co.uk
w: www.jba-events.co.uk

KCS Group Ltd
CLARKE HOUSE, BRUNEL ROAD, EARLSTREES IND. EST., CORBY
Northamptonshire NN17 4JW.................................01536 206500
e: dealersupport@kcsgroup.co.uk
w: www.kcsgroup.co.uk

KDM Events Ltd
NEWSTEAD TRADING ESTATE , TRENTHAM
Staffordshire ST4 8HX...01782 646300
e: events@kdmevents.com
w: www.kdmevents.co.uk

KWTM Events Consultancy
74 FIVE ASH DOWN, UCKFIELD
 TN22 3AN 01825 731894
w: www.kwtm.co.uk

Large Creative Executive
11 BRIGHTMOOR STREET, NOTTINGHAM
Nottinghamshire NG1 1FD 0115 9881 557
e: info@large-creative.com
w: www.large-creative.com

Leslie Edward Events Ltd
CHARTER HOUSE, 103-105 LEIGH ROAD, LEIGH ON SEA
Essex SS9 1JL..01702 568394
e: info@leevents.co.uk
w: www.leslieedwardevents.com

London Corporate Event Solutions
REGENT SQUARE, BOW
 E3 3HQ 020 8467 7185
e: jacqui@lcesolutions.co.uk
w: www.lcesolutions.co.uk

MaST International
HERMITAGE HOUSE, BATH ROAD, MAIDENHEAD
Berkshire SL6 0AR...01628 784062
e: peoplesolutions@mast.co.uk
w: www.mast.co.uk

MCB Ltd
119 THE HUB, 300 KENSAL ROAD
 W10 5BE..020 8969 6956
e: bpbp@tgis.co.uk
w: www.mcb-ltd.co.uk

Mediacrown Ltd
OWL BARN, NEW BARN LANE, CRAWLEY, WINCHESTER
Hampshire SO21 2PP...01962 776699
e: cwade@mediacrown.co.uk
w: www.mediacrown.co.uk

MediaMaker Ltd
MEDIA HOUSE, PADGE RD, BEESTON, NOTTINGHAM
Nottinghamshire NG9 2RS
.... 01159 255440 // 0203 691 7580
e: hello@mediamaker.co.uk
w: www.mediamaker.co.uk

Mongoose
38 - 50 KINGS REACH , KINGS ROAD, READING
Berkshire RG1 3AA 01672 515 289
e: hello@mongoose.co.uk
w: www.mongoose.co.uk

C

MST Media Productions
OMNIBUS BUSINESS CENTRE, 39-41 NORTH ROAD, LONDON
N7 9DP...020 7724 8917
e: info@mstmedia.tv
w: www.mstcommunications.co.uk

Newbridge Events LLP
28 WILTON ROAD, BEXHILL-ON-SEA
East Sussex TN40 1EZ 0844 549 9450
e: info@newbridgeevents.com
w: www.newbridgeevents.com

Opening Doors & Venues
WASSELL GROVE BUSINESS CENTRE, WASSELL GROVE LANE,
STOURBRIDGE
West Midlands DY9 9JH...............................01562 731788
e: rpadmore@opening-doors.org.uk
w: www.opening-doors.org.uk

Outsourced Events Ltd
BARLEY MOW CENTRE, 10 BARLEY MOW PASSAGE, LONDON
Greater London W4 4PH...............................020 8995 9495
e: info@outsourcedevents.com
w: www.outsourcedevents.com

Pitman's People Event Staff
UNIT G1A STAMFORD WORKS, 3 GILLETT ST., LONDON
Greater London N16 8JH...............................020 3651 3330
e: admin@pitmanspeople.com
w: www.pitmanspeople.com

Presentations International
88 HIGH STREET , ETON, WINDSOR
Berkshire SL4 6AF 01753 833749
e: info@presentationsuk.co.uk
w: www.presentationsinternational.co

Pretty Clever Events
BRIGHTWIRE HOUSE, 114 CHURCH ROAD, BRIGHTON
East Sussex BN3 2EB 0845 413 3030
e: info@prettyclever.co.uk
w: www.prettyclever.co.uk

Promus Productions Ltd
15 STIRLING PARK, LAKER ROAD, ROCHESTER
Kent ME1 3QR 01708 746 111
e: events@promusproductions.com
w: www.promusproductions.com

Protec (Production Technology LLC)
PLOT NO. 548 - 597 DUBAI INVESTMENT PARK 2,
DUBAI, UNITED ARAB EMIRATES...................... +971 4 880 0092
e: eventrental@productiontec.com
w: www.productiontec.com

Quatreus
5 & 6 EASTLANDS INDUSTRIAL ESTATE , KING GEORGES AVENUE,
LEISTON
Suffolk IP16 4LL 07971 350100
e: justine.samouelle@quatreus.com
w: www.quatreus.com/

Rockitfish Ltd
16 MEAD BUSINESS CENTRE , MEAD LANE , HERTFORD
Hertfordshire SG13 7BJ 01992 558820
e: hello@rockitfish.co.uk
w: www.rockitfish.co.uk

Ruby Mear Promotions Ltd
RYDER HOUSE, RYDER COURT, CORBY
Northamptonshire NN18 9NX 0844 848 1405
e: enquiries@rubymear.com
w: www.rubymear.com

SHMS
LAURELS FARM, BARMBY MOOR, YORK
Yorkshire YO42 4EJ...............................01759 307863
e: enquiry@shms.co.uk
w: www.shms.co.uk

Silent Associates Intl Ltd (sail)
9 FIRST AVENUE, WORTHING
West Sussex BN14 9NH.....................................0 870 321 0988
e: mail@silentassociates.com
w: www.silentassociates.com

SJ Events
SJ EVENT CONSULTANCY LTD, NORTH WING, , SWITHLAND HALL
SWITHLAND
Leicestershire LE12 8TJ 1162302040
e: mikewayne@post.com
w: www.sjevents.co.uk/

Stage Right Productions
FAIRFIELD HOUSE, MOULTON LANE, BOUGHTON, NORTHAMPTON
Northamptonshire NN2 8RG...............................01604 844005
e: info@stage-right.co.uk
w: www.stage-right.co.uk

Sterling Events
62 HOPE STREET, LIVERPOOL
Merseyside L1 9BZ...............................0151 709 8979
e: ben@sterlingevents.co.uk
w: www.sterlingevents.co.uk

Steve Lovell Associates
CONFEX HOUSE, 14 ROZELDINE, HINHEAD
Surrey GU26 6TW 01428 605863
e: info@sla.uk.com
w: www.sla.uk.com

Stoneapple Productions Ltd
21 CARYSFORT ROAD, LONDON
Greater London N16 9AA 020 7226 6900
e: mail@stoneapple.co.uk
w: www.stoneapple.co.uk

Straight Productions
TREYARNON HOUSE, WESTBEAMS ROAD, SWAY
Hampshire SO41 6AE...............................07802 753058
e: info@straightproductions.com
w: www.straightproductions.com

TFI Meeting Point
192 VAUXHALL BRIDGE ROAD, LONDON
Greater London SW1V 1DX.....................................020 7233 5644
e: engagement@tfigroup.com
w: www.tfigroup.com

The Conference People
UPPERTON FARM HOUSE, 2 ENYS RD, EASTBOURNE
East Sussex BN21 2DE 01323 644644
e: info@confpeople.co.uk
w: www.confpeople.co.uk

The JWP Group
195 THORNHILL ROAD, SURBITON
Surrey KT6 7TG 020 8288 0246
e: web@jwp.co.uk
w: www.jwp.co.uk

The RMS Group
INTERNATIONAL HOUSE, 33-35 ST DAVIDS ROAD SOUTH,
LYTHAM ST ANNES FY8 1TJ...................................01253 780000
e: enquiries@rms-group.com
w: www.internationalsport.co.uk/

Think Bright
5.5 PAINTWORKS, BATH ROAD
Bristol BS4 3 EH 0117 971 1127
e: alistair@thinkbright.co.uk
w: www.thinkbright.co.uk

TMB Marketing and Communications
MILTON HEATH HOUSE , WESTCOTT ROAD, DORKING
Surrey RH4 3NB..01306 877000
e: info@thinktmb.com
w: www.thinktmb.com

Top Banana Events and Conferences Ltd
THE COMEDY, 6 FFORD FFAGAN, ST MELLONS, CARDIFF
 CF3 2AB 0845 1908728
e: info@topbananaetc.com
w: www.topbananaetc.com

Trade Fair Support Ltd
WEST COURT , ENTERPRISE ROAD, MAIDSTONE
Kent ME15 6JD...01622 754200
e: info@tradefair.co.uk
w: www.tradefair.co.uk

Trigger Concepts Ltd
UNIT A, LAMBS FARM BUSINESS PARK, BASINGSTOKE ROAD,
SWALLOWFIELD, READING
Berkshire RG7 1PQ 0118 988 7800
e: events@trigger.co
w: www.trigger.uk.com

Vivace
WEST END HOUSE, 33 LOWER RICHMOND ROAD, MORTLAKE
Greater London SW14 7EZ....................................020 8392 9922
e: mail@govivace.co.uk
w: www.govivace.co.uk

Wyndham-Leigh Ltd
THE COURTYARD, BODYMOOR GREEN FARM, COVENTRY ROAD,
NR. KINGSBURY Warwickshire B78 2DZ 01827 875700
e: justin.fisher@wlpr.co.uk / sean.lees@wlpr.co.uk
w: www.wyndham-leigh.co.uk

Confetti

Confetti Master
8 BADGERS FOLLY, CASTLE CARY
Somerset BA7 7BF...01963 350960
e: hello@confettimaster.com
w: www.confettimaster.com

Flutter Fetti
.... 01992 893340 // 07738 177699
e: flutterfetti@btconnect.com
w: www.flutterfetti.co.uk

MTFX
VELT HOUSE, VELT HOUSE LANE, ELMORE
Gloucester GL2 3NY..1453 729 903
e: mark@mtfx.com
w: www.mtfx.com

MTFX
Velt House Lane
Elmore, Gloucestershire
GL2 3NY

t: 01452 729 903
e: info@MTFX.com

Specialising in a wide range of confetti effects. We have a huge
range of Confetti Cannons, Blowers and Spinners to create the
perfect confetti effect no matter what you're looking for.

Welcome to MTFX, the ingenious special effects people.

www.MTFX.com

Copywriting Services

20-20 PR
20-20 PUBLIC RELATIONS LTD, LONGCOT, FARINGDON
Oxfordshire SN7 7TG 01793 780780
e: belindaboyd@2020pr.com
w: www.2020pr.com

Ad Hoc
94A HIGH STREET, , INNERLEITHEN
Dumfriesshire EH44 6HF..01896 830830
e: richard@ad-hoc.co.uk
w: www.ad-hoc.co.uk

Angela Jones PR
1 EDWARDS MEADOW, MARLBOROUGH
Wiltshire SN8 1UL...01672 515068
e: info@angelajonespr.co.uk
w: www.angelajonespr.co.uk

Aurora PR
69 CHURCH ROAD, WIMBLEDON, LONDON
Greater London SW19 5AL...................................0208 287 1124
e: jancomer@aurorapr.co.uk
w: www.aurorapr.co.uk

Bridgeland Copyright
BRIDGELAND HOUSE, HIGH STREET, MARDEN
Kent TN12 9DS...01622 832598
e: sales@bridgeland-copyright.co.uk
w: www.bridgeland-copyright.co.uk

Broadbase
1A HAGGERSTON STUDIOS, 284 KINGSLAND ROAD
London E8 4DN...0207 254 6848
e: mail@broad-base.co.uk
w: www.broad-base.co.uk

Charlie Apple
8 CEDAR WALK, KENLEY
Surrey CR8 5JL......................... 020 8668 6921 // 07973 987779
e: info@charlieapple.com
w: www.charlieapple.co.uk

Empica Ltd
1 LYONS COURT, LONG ASHTON BUSINESS PARK, YANLEY LANE,
LONG ASHTON Bristol BS41 9LB 01275 394400
e: info@empica.co.uk
w: www.empica.com

Lawton Communications Group Ltd
4 & 5 GROSVENOR SQUARE, SOUTHAMPTON
Hampshire SO15 2BE 02380 828525
w: www.lawtoncommsgroup.com

Lolly Agency
7 OLD YARN MILLS , SHERBORNE
Dorset DT9 3RQ..01935 816400
e: hello@lolly-agency.co.uk
w: www.lolly-agency.co.uk

Middlemarch Ltd
PO BOX 111, UCKFIELD TN22 5WQ 01825 890773
e: mark@melodyandlyrics.co.uk
w: www.melodyandlyrics.co.uk

Nick Jon
....07772 530791
e: malcolm@freelance-copywriter-uk.com
w: www.freelance-copywriter-uk.com

Oasis Media
....07956 320 486
e: info@oasismedia.co.uk
w: www.oasismedia.co.uk

Red Pencil
5 TYRRELL ROAD, LONDON
Greater London SE22 9NA 020 8425 2406
e: hello@redpencil.co.uk
w: www.redpencil.co.uk

That Girl Communications Ltd
GOOSEGATE HOUSE, HIGH STREET, SWATON, SLEAFORD
NG34 0JP .... 084 4884 5119 / 07816 765 545
e: info@thatgirlcomms.co.uk
w: www.thatgirlcomms.co.uk

Corporate Entertainment

Team Building Solutions
UNIT 7, AMPRESS LANE, LYMINGTON ENTERPRISE CENTRE,
LYMINGTON
Hampshire SO41 8LZ...0845 121 1194
e: info@teambuildingsolutions.co.uk
w: www.teambuildingsolutions.co.uk

The Jammy Showgirls
CENTURY HOUSE SOUTH, NORTH STATION ROAD, COLCHESTER
Essex CO1 1RE 07796 138884
e: anthony@jammyshowsandproductions.co.uk
w: www.jammyshowsandproductions.co.u

Corporate Events

12 Degrees Ltd
1A CHISWICK END , MELDRETH, ROYSTON
Hertfordshire SG8 6LZ 0845 491 8743
w: www.12degreesshop.co.uk

88 Events Company
IBROX BUSINESS PARK, LARCHFIELD COURT, GLASGOW
Glasgow G51 2RQ...0141 445 2288
e: info@88events.com
w: www.88events.com

A1 Events & Exhibitions Ltd
SUITE 10, SHENLEY PAVILIONS, CHALKDELL DRIVE, SHENLEY
WOOD, MILTON KEYNES
Buckinghamshire MK5 6LB....................................01908 867555
e: help@a1-events-exhibitions.com
w: www.a1-events-exhibitions.com

Aardvark Productions Ltd
WITHYWINDS, MILL HILL, EDENBRIDGE
Kent TN8 5DQ..0800 328 5766
e: info@aardvarkproductions.biz
w: www.aardvarkproductions.biz

Ace Tones Group
UNIT 16, SPRINGWATER BUSINESS PARK, STATION RD,
WHITTLESEY
Cambridgeshire PE7 2EU 0845 189 5858
e: enquiry@acetonesgroup.com
w: www.acetonesgroup.com

Activ Power and Sail
19 CROSSWAYS AVE, EAST GRINSTEAD
RH19 1JF...01342 300236
e: ernie@activpowerandsail.co.uk
w: www.activpowerandsail.co.uk

Active Network - Events
11TH FLOOR ONE EUSTON SQUARE, 40 MELTON STREET, LONDON
Greater London NW1 2FD 020 7554 0949
e: emea-support@activenetwork.com
w: www.activenetwork.co.uk

Activefootprint Ltd
15 THE LEYS, ESHER ROAD, HERSHAM
Surrey KT12 4LP..020 8339 9182
e: events@activefootprint.co.uk
w: www.activefootprint.co.uk

AddingValue Agency
THE POWER HOUSE, , 1 LINKFIELD ROAD, ISLEWORTH
Greater London TW7 6QG,.....................................020 8831 7940
e: hello@addingvalue.com
w: www.addingvalue.com

Agenda Bar
MINSTER COURT, 3 MINCING LANE, LONDON
Greater London EC3R 7AA 0207 929 8399
w: www.agendabar.co.uk

AOL Corporate Events Ltd / Stress Free Events
172 BROX ROAD, OTTERSHAW, CHERTSEY
Surrey KT16 0LQ 020 7610 1060
e: info@stressfreeevents.co.uk
w: www.stressfreeevents.co.uk

Aries Leisure
2 - 7 WEBBER ROAD, KNOWSLEY INDUSTRIAL ESTATE, LIVERPOOL
Merseyside L33 7SW 0151 545 0599
e: info@ariesleisure.co.uk
w: www.ariesleisure.co.uk

Artifact Multimedia
76 BERW ROAD, PONTYPRIDD, SOUTH WALES
 CF37 2AB .... 07961 262080 / 01443 400 204
e: info@artifactmultimedia.co.uk
w: www.artifactmultimedia.co.uk

As You Like It Productions
18 OKEOVER MANOR, 20-23 CLAPHAM COMMON NORTHSIDE, LONDON
Greater London SW4 0RH 020 7627 8942
e: info@asyoulikeitproductions.co.uk
w: www.asyoulikeitproductions.co.uk

Aspect Ltd
SOLAR HOUSE, 915 HIGH ROAD, NORTH FINCHLEY, LONDON
Greater London N12 8QJ 020 8282 7575
e: team@aspect-communications.com
w: www.aspect-communications.com/

Baden Powell House
65-67 QUEEN'S GATE, LONDON
Greater London SW7 5JS......................................020 7590 6909
e: bph.conferences@scout.org.uk
w: www.towntocountry.co.uk/bpHouse/

Banana Split Plc
6 CARLISLE ROAD, LONDON
Greater London NW9 0HN....................................020 8200 1234
e: hello@banana-split.com
w: www.banana-split.com

bars2you ltd
.... 01925 633 131 / 07709888809
e: chris@bars2you.co.uk
w: www.bars2you.com

BDD Events Ltd
PARK VIEW HOUSE, 79 BRIDGEWOOD ROAD, WORCESTER PARK
 KT4 8XR 020 8274 8274
e: enquiry@bddevents.co.uk
w: www.bddevents.co.uk

Bella Parties
LEESWOOD COTTAGE, FIR TREE HILL, CHANDLERS CROSS
 WD3 4NA 7789833676
e: info@bellaparties.co.uk
w: www.bellaparties.co.uk

Best Parties Ever
UNITS 2 - 4 TRADE CITY, AVRO WAY, BROOKLANDS INDUSTRIAL ESTATE, WEYBRIDGE
Surrey KT13 0YF...0844 499 4040
e: sales@bestpartiesever.com
w: www.bestpartiesever.com

Big Chief Productions Ltd
81 DUKE ROAD, CHISWICK, LONDON
Greater London W4 2BN.......................................020 8996 0300
e: info@bigchiefproductions.co.uk
w: www.bigchiefproductions.co.uk

Big House Events Ltd
35 ST CLAIR STREET , EDINBURGH
 EH6 8LB 0131 669 6366
e: tash@bighouse-events.co.uk
w: www.bighouse-events.co.uk

Big House Events Ltd
35 ST CLAIR STREET , EDINBURGH
 EH6 8LB 0131 669 6366
e: tash@bighouse-events.co.uk
w: www.bighouse-events.co.uk

Bird Consultancy Ltd
GOLD 73, THE SHARP PROJECT, THORP ROAD , MANCHESTER
Greater Manchester M40 5BJ 0161 839 4846
e: onawire@birdconsultancy.co.uk
w: www.birdconsultancy.co.uk

Blue Chip Hospitality Ltd
HAWTHORNE COTTAGE, THE ROSS, COMRIE
Perthshire PH6 2JU..01764 679 496
e: info@bluechiphospitality.com
w: www.bluechiphospitality.com

C

Boleyn Events Ltd
BOLEYN EVENTS , 592 FOXHALL ROAD , IPSWICH
Suffolk IP3 8NA...01473 712330
e: info@boleyn-events.com
w: www.boleyn-events.com

Bravo Productions
65 PINE AVENUE, SUITE 858, LONG BEACH, CALIFORNIA
90802..001 562 435 0065
e: staff@bravoevents-online.com
w: www.bravoevents-online.com

C

Brian Cook Productions
BRIAN COOK PRODUCTIONS, 51 SOUTH END, BEDALE
North Yorkshire DL8 2DB.......................................07778 444648
e: bcp@production.co.uk
w: www.production.co.uk

Bridgewood Manor
BRIDGEWOOD ROUNDABOUT, WALDERSLADE WOODS, CHATHAM
ME5 9AX...01634 201333
e: bridgewoodmanorevents@qhotels.co.uk
w: www.qhotels.co.uk

Broadstone Security Ltd
50 ST JAMES'S STREET, MAYFAIR, LONDON
SW1A 1JT..08444 745 001
e: enquiries@broadstonesecurity.co.uk
w: www.broadstonesecurity.co.uk

Buzz Events & Catering Ltd
CHESTERFIELD RD, WORTHING
West Sussex BN12 6BY .... 07914 971 306 // 01903 501 613
e: info@becatering.co.uk
w: becatering.co.uk

Cambria House Corporate Hospitality
CAMBRIA HOUSE, 151 ASHBY ROAD, LOUGHBOROUGH
Leicestershire LE11 3AD...01509 237178
e: sandra@cambria-house.com
w: www.cambria-house.com

Catalyst Teambuilding
SUITE 12, BADEN PLACE, CROSBY ROW, LONDON BRIDGE,
LONDON
Greater London SE1 1YW.....................................020 3551 2050
e: info@catalystteambuilding.co.uk
w: www.catalystteambuilding.co.uk

Catered-Events
CROWN WORKS KITCHEN, COMMERCIAL ROAD,
WOLVERHAMPTON
West Midlands WV1 3QS 01902 456661
e: chef@callthecaterers.co.uk
w: www.catered-events.co.uk

Chapman Holmes Events
UNIT 1 PEEL GREEN ESTATES, GREEN STREET, MANCHESTER
Greater Manchester M30 7HF 0161 7893262
e: events@chapmanholmes.co.uk
w: www.chapmanholmes.co.uk

Chuckle Pod Limited
....07770 692499
e: info@chucklepod.co.uk
w: www.chucklepod.co.uk

CJ's Events Warwickshire
THE COW YARD, CHURCH FARM, , CHURCH LANE, BUDBROOKE,
WARWICK
Warwickshire CV35 8QL..01926 800 750
e: info@cjseventswarwickshire.co.uk
w: www.cjseventswarwickshire.co.uk

Clink Clink Events
14 MONTPELIER CENTRAL, MONTPELIER, STATION ROAD,
BRISTOL
Bristol BS6 5EE...0117 924 0033
e: info@clinkclink.co.uk
w: www.clinkclink.co.uk

Conference Bristol
53 QUEEN SQUARE, BRISTOL
Bristol BS1 4LH...0117 946 2200
e: conference@destinationbristol.co.uk
w: www.conference-bristol.co.uk

Corporate Events Plus Ltd
LODGE FARM, RECTORY ROAD, BACTON, STOWMARKET
Suffolk IP14 4LE 01449 781355
e: info@corporateeventsplus.co.uk
w: www.corporateeventsplus.co.uk

Corporate Fun Events
8 BIRTLES ROAD, ORFORD, WARRINGTON
Cheshire WA2 9AG..01925 575683
e: corporatefunevents@googlemail.com
w: www.corporatefunevents.co.uk

Corporate Occasions
LESTER HOUSE, TAMWORTH ROAD, LICHFIELD
Staffordshire WS14 9PU...01543 433554
e: events@corporate-occasions.co.uk
w: www.corporate-occasions.co.uk

Corporate Ski Specialists
....020 9133 9955
e: info@corporateskispecialists.co.uk
w: www.corporateskispecialists.co.uk

Crafts & Giggles
....07824 396645
w: www.craftsandgiggles.com

Create Events Ltd
THE WHEELHOUSE, THE WATERMILL PARK, BROUGHTON HALL,
SKIPTON
Yorkshire BD23 3AE 08000 807 607
e: enquiries@create-event.com
w: www.create-event.com

Createvents Ltd
450 BROOK DRIVE , READING
Berkshire RG2 6UU 01183 340085
e: info@createvents.co.uk
w: www.createvents.co.uk

Crystal Marquee Hire
BRAMBLE FARM, SHERE ROAD, WEST HORSLEY, LEATHERHEAD
Surrey KT24 6ER 01483 283228
e: info@crystalmarqueehire.co.uk
w: www.crystalmarqueehire.co.uk

Dandy Events
259 SCOTSWOOD ROAD, NEWCASTLE UPON TYNE
Tyne and Wear NE4 7AW......................................0191 272 2006
e: events@dandyevents.com
w: www.dandyevents.com

Demon Wheelers
132-154 HARVEST LANE, SHEFFIELD
South Yorkshire S3 8BX 01142 700 330
e: info@demonwheelers.co.uk
w: www.demonwheelers.co.uk

Destinations Unlimited
7 HIGH STREET, RINGWOOD
BH24 1AB..01425 461311
e: info@dudmc.com
w: www.dudmc.com

Diplomat Cruises
3 MORE LONDON RIVERSIDE, LONDON
Greater London SE1 2RE......................................020 3283 4108
e: info@diplomatcruises.co.uk
w: www.diplomatcruises.co.uk

Direct Event Services Ltd
69 HIGHGATE ROAD, WOODLEY, READING
Berkshire RG5 3ND..0118 969 9438
e: info@directeventservices.com
w: www.directeventservices.com

Dubai Experience
ACORN BUSINESS CENTRE, 18 SKATERS WAY, WERRINGTON,
PETERBOROUGH
Cambridgeshire PE4 6NB......................................0843 290 7092
e: sales@dubaiexperience.com
w: www.dubaiexperience.com

Eastwood Park Training and Conference Centre
FALFIELD, WOOTON-UNDER-EDGE
Gloucestershire GL12 8DA 01454 260207
e: reception@eastwoodpark.co.uk
w: www.eastwoodpark.co.uk

Effective Event Solutions
10 WHEATLEY BUSINESS CENTRE, OLD LONDON ROAD,
WHEATLEY
Oxfordshire OX33 1XW...01865 877 877
e: sales@effectiveeventsolutions.com
w: www.effectiveeventsolutions.com

Elite Training European Ltd
3 PARKERS PLACE, MARTLESHAM HEATH, IPSWICH
Suffolk IP5 3UX...020 3290 1473
e: info@elitetraining.co.uk
w: www.elitetraining.co.uk

Entertee Select Ltd
LONGPOND WORKS , WROTHAM ROAD, BOROUGH GREEN
Kent TN15 8DE..01732 781 137
e: select@entertee.com
w: www.entertee.com

Evalpe Events Management
58 RUE DE LA TERRASSIÃ¨RE, GENEVA - SWITZERLAND
1207.. +33 (0) 22 519 08 00
e: contact@evalpe.com
w: www.evalpe.com

Event Concept
UNIT B3 & B4, GALLEY WALL TRADING ESTATE, GALLEY WALL
ROAD, LONDON
Greater London SE16 3PB.....................................020 7740 3988
e: info@eventconcept.co.uk
w: www.eventconcept.co.uk

Event Dynamics Ltd
UNIT 4, MORDEN GRANGE FARM, BALDOCK ROAD, ROYSTON
Hertfordshire SG8 9NR...07970 010 728
e: events@eventdynamics.co.uk
w: www.eventdynamics.co.uk

Event Management Group Ltd
UNIT 6, DELL BUILDING, MILFORD ROAD, LYMINGTON
SO41 0ED...01590 670 999
e: ask@emg.co.uk
w: www.emg.co.uk

Eventelle Limited
69 DUNVEGAN ROAD, BIRMINGHAM
B24 9HH...07961 067 546
e: info@eventelle.co.uk
w: www.eventelle.co.uk

Events A La Carte Ltd
32 ST JOHNS AVENUE, PUTNEY, LONDON
Greater London SW15 6AN 020 8780 9144
e: clientservices@corporatevents.co.uk
w: www.corporatevents.co.uk

Events Unlimited
6 YEATSALL FARM, YEATSALL ROAD, ABBOTS BROMLEY
Staffordshire WS15 3DY.......................................01283 841600
e: info@eventsunlimited.co.uk
w: www.eventsunlimited.co.uk

Evolution Dome
17, HIGHLODE INDUSTRIAL ESTATE, , STOCKING FEN RD,
RAMSEY,, HUNTINGDON
Cambridgeshire PE26 2RB....................................01487 640640
e: info@evolutiondome.co.uk
w: www.evolutiondome.co.uk

C

C

Evolve Events Ltd
6 FILMER ROAD, LONDON
Greater London SW6 7BW.....................................020 7610 2808
e: info@evolve-events.com
w: www.evolve-events.com

Felix - Special Events
VIA PALESTRO 11, ROME, ITALY
....0039 348 5117467
e: felix@felixreid.com
w: www.felixreid.com

Field Station
FIELD STATION, WYTHAM, OXFORD
OX2 8QJ 01423 313931
e: enquiries@fieldstation.co
w: www.fieldstation.co

Find The Treasure
57 THE FAIRWAY, RUISLIP
Greater London HA4 0SP 020 8842 1284
e: info@treasure-hunts.org.uk
w: www.treasure-hunts.org.uk

Firebird Events Ltd
UNIT 3, NIMBUS BUSINESS PARK, HERCULES WAY,
FARNBOROUGH
Hampshire GU14 6UU 01252 545654
e: enquiry@firebirdevents.co.uk
w: www.firebirdevents.co.uk

First City Events
16 LINDEN PARK TERRACE , MILNATHORT , KINROSS
KY13 9XY.. 01577 865498 //
                                                                   07711 432745
e: joyce@firstcityevents.co.uk
w: www.firstcityevents.co.uk

Fishing Breaks
THE MILL, HEATHMAN STREET, NETHER WALLOP, STOCKBRIDGE
Hampshire SO20 8EW...01264 781988
e: info@fishingbreaks.co.uk
w: www.fishingbreaks.co.uk

French DMC
28 RUE DE L'AMIRAL HAMELIN, PARIS
75016... +33 01 49 52 60 07
e: contact@corpo-events.fr
w: www.french-dmc.com

Fun Events Group
14A MILL STREET, OTTERY ST. MARY, DEVON
EX11 1AD 01404 811 849
e: admin@funevents.com
w: www.funevents.com

Gamewagon Ltd
113 - 115 OYSTER LANE, BYFLEET
Surrey KT14 7JZ..0845 319 4263
e: julie.owen@gamewagon.co.uk
w: www.gamewagon.co.uk

Gemma Pears
56 DUNNOCK LANE, COTTAM, PRESTON
PR4 0NX 07870 161135
e: gemmapearsevents@gmail.com
w: www.gemmapears.wordpress.com

Girl Friday Events
25 ROCHESTER TERRACE, LEEDS
LS6 3DF 0113 217 9966
e: info@girlfridayevents.co.uk
w: www.girlfridayevents.co.uk

GolfFish
SUNNINGDALE, 7 BRAGGS LANE, HEMINGFORD GREY,,
HUNTINGDON,
Cambridgeshire PE28 9BW 07899 928077
e: info@golffish.co.uk
w: www.golffish.co.uk

Grand Slam Events Ltd
THORNTON HOUSE, THORNTON ROAD, WIMBLEDON, LONDON
Greater London SW19 4NG 020 8405 6415
e: info@grandslam.uk.com
w: www.grandslam.uk.com

Hainesnet Teambuilding at Abbey Road Studios
TECHNOPOLE, KINGSTON CRESCENT, PORTSMOUTH
Hampshire PO2 8FA..02392 658302
e: philip@hainesnet.com
w: www.hainesnet.com/teambuilding

Hatt Events
PO BOX 5157, BRIGHTON
East Sussex BN50 9TW..01273 358359
e: adventures@thehatt.co.uk
w: www.thehatt.co.uk/events

Henley Group International
MARKET HOUSE, 33 MARKET PLACE, HENLEY-ON-THAMES
Oxfordshire RG9 2AA 01491 570971
e: admin@henley.co.uk
w: www.henley.co.uk

iCatching Events
UNIT D, JOSEPH ADAMSON IND EST, CROFT STREET, HYDE
Cheshire SK14 1EE 0845 833 6372
e: info@icatchingevents.co.uk
w: www.icatchingevents.co.uk

Ice Entertainment Uk
ICE ENTERTAINMENT UK, UNIT C-D DODD LANE IND ESTATE,
CHORLEY OLD ROAD, BOLTON
Greater Manchester BL5 3NA.............................0845 4751020
e: info@iceentertainmentuk.com
w: www.iceentertainmentuk.com

Inca Productions Ltd
THE TOP FLOOR, 7 - 11 ST JOHNS HILL, LONDON
Greater London SW11 1TN....................................02072 235 512
e: info@incaproductions.com
w: www.incaproductions.co.uk

Incentivise Limited
.... 07741 254214 / 01925 211 400
e: paul.bradford@incentivise.co.uk
w: www.incentivise.co.uk/

Initiative Unlimited
57 THE FAIRWAY, RUISLIP
Middlesex HA4 0SP..020 8842 1284
e: info@initiativeunlimited.co.uk
w: www.initiativeunlimited.co.uk

Inside Outside Marquee Hire
UNITS 14 - 15, BOOKHAM INDUSTRIAL PARK, CHURCH ROAD,
BOOKHAM Surrey KT23 3EU 01372 459485
e: sales@inside-outside.co.uk
w: www.inside-outside.co.uk

Jam Events
LOWER GROUND FLOOR, 314 REGENTS PARK ROAD, LONDON
Greater London N3 2JX...020 8371 9080
e: info@jam-events.com
w: www.jam-events.com

JF Events
NORTH LODGE, 122 COWFOLD ROAD, WEST GRINSTEAD,
HORSHAM
RH13 8LU 01403 865000
e: sales@jfevents.biz
w: www.jfevents.biz

Jongleurs Events
20B CHANCELLORS ST, HAMMERSMITH
W9 6RN 08700 111960
e: enquiries@jongleurs.com
w: www.jongleursevents.com

JPFoto
8 LEATHERWORKS WAY, LITTLE BILLING VILLAGE,
NORTHAMPTON
Northamptonshire NN3 9BP .... 01933 628139 //
                                                     01604 419112
e: info@jpfoto.co.uk
w: www.jpfoto.co.uk/corporate-event-

JS Ent
UNIT 5-7A, 109 MAYBANK RD, SOUTH WOODFORD, LONDON
E18 1EJ...020 8505 8222
e: sales@jsent.co.uk
w: www.jsent.co.uk

JSO Productions Ltd
THREEWAYS, RADNAGE COMMON RD, RADNAGE
Buckinghamshire HP14 4DF ..... 0208 8407070 // 01494 387 770
e: parties@jso.co.uk
w: www.jso.co.uk

Julian Beard Associates Limited
ABBOTS LODGE, THE STREET, DRINKSTONE
Suffolk IP30 9SX..01359 271962
e: enquiries@jba-events.co.uk
w: www.jba-events.co.uk

Just Add Water
6 FLITCROFT STREET, ST GILES IN THE FIELDS, LONDON
Greater London WC2H 8DJ.....................................020 7557 4377
e: swim@sojustaddwater.com
w: www.sojustaddwater.com

JVP Events
64 WEIR ROAD, LONDON
Greater London SW19 8UG 020 8947 3410
e: hire@jvp.uk.com
w: www.jvp.uk.com

KCS Group Ltd
CLARKE HOUSE, BRUNEL ROAD, EARLSTREES IND. EST., CORBY
Northamptonshire NN17 4JW..................................01536 206500
e: dealersupport@kcsgroup.co.uk
w: www.kcsgroup.co.uk

KDM Events Ltd
NEWSTEAD TRADING ESTATE , TRENTHAM
Staffordshire ST4 8HX...01782 646300
e: events@kdmevents.com
w: www.kdmevents.co.uk

KP Events Ltd
34 COLNEY HATCH LANE, LONDON
N10 1DU..0208 883 7411
e: info@kpevents.co.uk
w: www.kpevents.co.uk

Kracker
MITCHELL RD, , ROCKINGHAM, CORBY
Northamptonshire NN17 5AF 020 7478 8308
e: james.guess@kracker.co.uk
w: www.kracker.co.uk

Leisure Pursuits
BLACKLAND FARM, GRINSTEAD LANE, EAST GRINSTEAD
West Sussex RH19 4HP 01342 825522
e: mail@leisurepursuits.co.uk
w: www.leisurepursuits.co.uk

Leslie Edward Events Ltd
CHARTER HOUSE, 103-105 LEIGH ROAD, LEIGH ON SEA
Essex SS9 1JL...01702 568394
e: info@leevents.co.uk
w: www.leslieedwardevents.com

Life's Kitchen
....0800 915 0978
e: info@lifeskitchen.com
w: www.lifeskitchen.com

Lillingston
ONE FOLLY MEWS, 223A PORTOBELLO ROAD, LONDON
Greater London W11 1LU......................................020 7221 5820
e: info@lillingston.co.uk
w: www.lillingston.co.uk

C

Lincoln Castle
THOMAS PARKER HOUSE, 13/14 SILVER STREET, LINCOLN
Lincolnshire LN2 1DY..01522 552222
e: customer_services@lincolnshire.gov.uk
w: www.lincolnshire.gov.uk/lincolnca

Line Up
14 BADEN PLACE, CROSBY ROW, BOROUGH, LONDON
Greater London SE1 1YW 020 8747 2200
e: info@lineup.uk.com
w: www.lineup.uk.com

London Audio Ltd
ROBERT DASHWOOD WAY, CAMBERWELL, LONDON
Greater London SE17 3PZ.....................................0207 701 9444
e: info@londonaudiovisual.co.uk
w: www.london-audio.co.uk

Mongoose
38 - 50 KINGS REACH , KINGS ROAD, READING
Berkshire RG1 3AA 01672 515 289
e: hello@mongoose.co.uk
w: www.mongoose.co.uk

Multiversal Events
261 DITCHLING ROAD, BRIGHTON
East Sussex BN1 6JH................. 01273 900221 / 07880 704378
e: info@multiversalevents.co.uk
w: www.multiversalevents.co.uk

Murder, Mystery And Mayhem
57 THE FAIRWAY, RUISLIP
Greater London HA4 0SP 020 8842 1284
e: info@mayhem.org.uk
w: www.mayhem.org.uk

Newbridge Events LLP
28 WILTON ROAD, BEXHILL-ON-SEA
East Sussex TN40 1EZ 0844 549 9450
e: info@newbridgeevents.com
w: www.newbridgeevents.com

Nexlevel Entertainment & Event Management
106A CLARENCE ROAD, HACKNEY
 E5 8HB 0208 985 3165
e: lekan.fakoya@nexlevel.co.uk
w: www.nexlevel.co.uk

Night Train Productions Ltd
 34 MELVILLE STREET, EDINBURGH
Edinburgh EH3 7HA 07802 793 912
e: allaboard@nighttrain.co.uk
w: www.nighttrain.co.uk

Ninth Events Ltd
39 FEATHERSTONE STREET , ISLINGTON , LONDON
 EC1Y 8RE 7879896725
e: info@ninthevents.com
w: www.ninthevents.com

OPM Partnership
STUDIO A1, THE 1927 BUILDING, THE OLD GAS WORKS, 2
MICHAEL ROAD, LONDON
 SW6 2AD 020 7731 1008
e: enquiries@opmpartnership.com
w: www.opmpartnership.com

Orange Tree Events Ltd
26 NORTH END LANE, ASCOT
SL5 0DZ .... 07976 422950 /
01344 297433
e: info@orange-tree-events.co.uk
w: www.orange-tree-events.co.uk

Organise This
2ND FLOOR, FOURWAYS HOUSE, 57 HILTON STREET,
MANCHESTER
Greater Manchester M1 2EJ 0161 273 5107
e: info@organisethis.co.uk
w: www.organisethis.co.uk

Outsourced Events Ltd
BARLEY MOW CENTRE, 10 BARLEY MOW PASSAGE, LONDON
Greater London W4 4PH......................................020 8995 9495
e: info@outsourcedevents.com
w: www.outsourcedevents.com

P&MM Events & Communications
17/18 SHENLEY PAVILIONS, CHALKDELL DRIVE, SHENLEY WOOD,
MILTON KEYNES
Buckinghamshire MK5 6LB..................................01908 764500
e: ideas@zibrantlive.com
w: ourworld.zibrantlive.com/

Pandemonium
PO BOX 1092, HIGH WYCOMBE
Buckinghamshire HP10 8WY................................01494 813170
e: simon@pandemonium.com
w: www.pandemonium.com

Pennine Events
SUITE 1A, RIBBLE HOUSE, MEANYGATE, BAMER BRIDGE,
PRESTON
Lancashire PR5 6UP 01772 447 979
e: support@pennineevents.co.uk
w: www.pennineevents.co.uk

Pink Buddha Events
510 METROPOLITAN WHARF , 70 WAPPING WALL , LONDON
Greater London E1W 3SS....................................020 7702 0202
e: info@pinkbuddha.com
w: www.pinkbuddha.com

Pitman's People Event Staff
UNIT G1A STAMFORD WORKS, 3 GILLETT ST., LONDON
Greater London N16 8JH......................................020 3651 3330
e: admin@pitmanspeople.com
w: www.pitmanspeople.com

C

Premier UK Events Ltd
UNIT 2, ROOKERY LANE, THURMASTON, LEICESTER
Leicestershire LE4 8AU 1162029953
e: ben@premier-ltd.com
w: premier-event-solutions.com/

Private Drama
ISLAND STUDIOS, 22 ST PETER'S SQUARE, LONDON
Greater London W6 9NW..020 8749 0987
e: event@privatedrama.com
w: www.privatedrama.com

Production Plus Ltd
LYRIC HOUSE, BLACKHORSE ROAD , LETCHWORTH GARDEN CITY
Hertfordshire SG6 1HB..01462 684001
e: info@productionplus.co.uk
w: www.productionplus.co.uk

Pumphouse
CHURCH HOUSE, KNEESWORTH ST, ROYSTON
 SG8 5AB 01763 250899
e: info@pumphouse.co.uk
w: www.pumphouse.co.uk

Puxley Limited
11 HARRIER COURT , WESTCOTT LANE , EXETER
 EX5 2DR 01392 364900
e: info@puxley.com
w: www.puxley.com

Qube Events & Productions
16-20 HEATON FOLD, BURY
Greater Manchester BL9 9HF 0845 463 4008
e: info@qubeevents.co.uk
w: www.qubeevents.co.uk

Quiztaztic
THE COACH HOUSE, CRASHMORE LANE, OVERBURY,
TEWKESBURY
Gloucestershire GL20 7NX 01386 725041
e: enquiries@quiztaztic.co.uk
w: www.quiztaztic.co.uk

Rede2 Ltd
THE COURTYARD, TWIGWORTH COURT, , TWIGWORTH
Gloucestershire GL2 9PG 0870 121 7060
e: info@rede2.com
w: www.rede2.com

Rhodes Event Management
 .... 07971 619502
e: enquiries@rhodes-events.co.uk
w: www.rhodes-events.co.uk

Right Angle Events Ltd
UNIT 7 LONGS BUSINESS CENTRE, 232 FAKENHAM ROAD,
TAVERHAM, NORWICH
Norfolk NR8 6QW..0207 1676 717
e: info@rightangleevents.co.uk
w: www.rightangleevents.co.uk

Rock City Stage Crew
LANGSFORD HOUSE, 8 DARKLAKE VIEW, ESTOVER, PLYMOUTH
Devon PL6 7TL 01752 255 933
e: office@rockcitycrew.co.uk
w: www.rockcitycrew.co.uk

Sail Royal Greenwich
10TH FLOOR, 6 MITRE PASSAGE, GREENWICH
Greater London SE10 0ER....................................0203 040 2350
e: info@sailroyalgreenwich.co.uk
w: www.sailroyalgreenwich.co.uk

Saville Audio Visual
UNIT 5, MILLFIELD LANE, NETHER POPPLETON, YORK
Yorkshire YO26 6PQ 0870 606 1100
e: head.office@saville-av.com
w: www.saville-av.com

School Of Booze
50 ROSE BANK, HOLYPORT RD, FULHAM, LONDON
 SW6 6LH 07729 601 590
e: info@school-of-booze.com
w: www.school-of-booze.com

See Events Ltd
4 APPLEWOOD, KENDAL
Cumbria LA9 5EJ..01539 723584
e: info@see-events.co.uk
w: www.see-events.co.uk

Seggy Segway
CARR FARM , CARR LANE, THORNER , LEEDS
West Yorkshire LS14 3HE......................................07515 253893
e: info@seggysegway.co.uk

Segway Events
MAGNA SCIENCE ADVENTURE CENTRE, SHEFFIELD ROAD,
TEMPLEBROUGH, ROTHERHAM
South Yorkshire S60 1DX 0845 319 3747
e: info@segwayevents.co.uk
w: www.segwayevents.co.uk

Shes Gott It! Events
THREE HEDWORTHS, BOWES OFFICES, BOWES ESTATES,
LAMBTON PARK, CHESTER LE STREET
Durham DH3 4AN 0191 385 6619
e: info@shesgottit.com
w: www.shesgottit.com

Show Me The Square Mile
63 ALLISON ROAD, LONDON
Greater London N8 0AN 020 8616 9185
e: info@showmethesquaremile.com
w: www.showmethesquaremile.com

Simply The Best Events
2 LANE END VILLAS, SHINFIELD ROAD, READING
Berkshire RG2 9BS 0800 019 3908
e: sales@simplythebestevents.co.uk
w: www.simplythebestevents.co.uk

C

SiRAstudio LTD
SPRING GROVE, HARROAGTE
North Yorkshire HG1 2HS .... +44 (0)1423 546440
e: hello@sirastudio.com
w: www.sirastudio.com

Solent Events Ltd
UNIT 6 DELL BUILDINGS, MILFORD ROAD, LYMINGTON
Hampshire SO41 0ED 01590 674900
e: admin@solent-events.co.uk
w: www.solent-events.co.uk

South West Lakes Trust
LIDN PARK, QUARRY CRESCENT, PENNYGILLAM, LAUNCESTON
Cornwall PL15 7PF 01566 771930
e: info@swlakestrust.org.uk
w: www.swlakestrust.org.uk

Splash Events Ltd
PO BOX 3384, BARNET
Greater London EN5 9BT.....................................0208 447 5650
e: party@splashevents.co.uk
w: www.splashevents.co.uk

Stablecroft Conference Products Ltd
KINNINGHALL FARMHOUSE, CAVERS, HAWICK
Berwickshire TD9 8LH 01450 373373
e: louise@stablecroft.com
w: www.stablecroft.com

Stratford Manor
WARWICK ROAD , STRATFORD UPON AVON
Warwickshire CV37 0PY............ 01789 731173 // 0845 074 0060
e: stratformanorevents@qhotels.co.uk
w: www.qhotels.co.uk

SunshineEvents.co.uk
FUN TOWERS, NILE CLOSE, NELSON COURT BUSINESS PARK,
PRESTON DOCKLANDS,
Lancashire PR2 2XU 01772 721 511
e: info@sunshineevents.co.uk
w: www.sunshineevents.co.uk

Synergy Event Solutions Ltd
SUITE 114, CASTLE HOUSE, 1 BAKER STREET, STIRLING
Stirlingshire FK8 1AL 08712 249 710
e: ask@synergyeventsolutions.com
w: www.synergyeventsolutions.com

Synergy Sailing Ltd
TWICKENHAM VILLA, ST EDWARDS ROAD, SOUTHSEA
Hampshire PO5 3DH 07985 459 803
e: info@synergysailing.co.uk
w: www.synergysailing.co.uk

Team Building Solutions
UNIT 7, AMPRESS LANE, LYMINGTON ENTERPRISE CENTRE,
LYMINGTON
Hampshire SO41 8LZ..0845 121 1194
e: info@teambuildingsolutions.co.uk
w: www.teambuildingsolutions.co.uk

Team Challenge Company
PO BOX 28036, EDINBURGH
Edinburgh EH17 8YN...0845 6014186
e: info@teamchallenge-company.co.uk
w: www.teamchallenge-company.co.uk

Team Pamper
Greater London 020 369 18233
e: info@teampamper.com
w: www.teampamper.com

Team Spirit Event Management Ltd.
UNIT 16 BOARSHURST BUSINESS PARK, BOARSHURST LANE,
GREENFIELD,, OLDHAM
Lancashire OL3 7ER 01457 875878
e: hello@team-spirit.co.uk
w: www.team-spirit.co.uk

Thames Luxury Charters Ltd
KNOT HOUSE, 2-7 BREWERY SQUARE, LONDON
Greater London SE1 2LF 020 7357 7751
e: enquiries@thamesluxurycharters.co.uk
w: www.thamesluxurycharters.co.uk

The Carter Company
THE RED HOUSE, COLLEGE ROAD NORTH, ASTON CLINTON
Buckinghamshire HP22 5EZ...................................01296 631671
e: hello@the-carter-company.com
w: www.the-carter-company.com

The Chillout Furniture Company
RYE FARM, HOLLANDS LANE, HENFIELD,
East Sussex BN5 9QY 0800 881 5229
e: info@completechillout.com
w: www.completechillout.com

The Copas Partnership
KINGS COPPICE FARM, GRUBWOOD LANE, COOKHAM,
MAIDENHEAD
Berkshire SL6 9UB..01628 474678
e: admin@copas.co.uk
w: www.copas.co.uk

The Embee Diamond Reception
69 NIGHTINGALE LANE, LONDON
Greater London E11 ....0207193 7090
e: info@embee-reception.com
w: www.embee-reception.com

The Event Business
THE HEATH, ALKERTON OAKS BUSINESS PARK, UPTON ESTATE,
BANBURY
Oxfordshire OX15 6EP...01295 678042
e: ellislp@theeventbusiness.co.uk
w: www.theeventbusiness.co.uk

The Events & Tents Company Ltd
HILLTOP FARM, CAYTHORPE HEATH, GRANTHAM
Lincolnshire NG32 3EU 0800 0274492
e: info@eventsandtents.co.uk
w: www.eventsandtents.co.uk

The Finishing Touch
2ND FLOOR, 3 TENTERDEN STREET, LONDON
Greater London W1S 1TD.....................................020 7993 9993
e: events@finishtouchevents.co.uk
w: www.finishingtouchevents.co.uk

The Penthouse London
1 LEICESTER SQUARE, LONDON
Greater London WC2H 7NA 0203 588 1100
e: info@thepenthouselondon.com
w: www.thepenthouselondon.com

The Queen's Club
PALLISER ROAD, WEST KENSINGTON
Greater London W14 9EQ.....................................020 7386 3400
e: marketing@queensclub.co.uk
w: www.queensclub.co.uk

ThinkersLive
15-19 BAKERS ROW, LONDON
Greater London EC1R 3DG....................................020 3967 5716
w: www.thinkerslive.com

TMB Events
2 KINGSTON BUSINESS PARK, KINGSTON BAGPUIZE, ABINGDON
Oxfordshire OX13 5FE...01865 822500
e: hello@tmb-events.com
w: www.tmb-events.com

Transform Venue
UNIT 1 REAR OF 486 PORTSWOOD ROAD, SOUTHAMPTON
Hampshire SO17 3SP 02380 558923
e: info@transform-venue.co.uk
w: www.transform-venue.co.uk

Travel Counsellors Ltd
TRAVEL HOUSE, 43 CHURCHGATE, BOLTON
Lancashire BL1 1TH.................... 01773 318910 / 07973 306280
e: louise.cutting@travelcounsellors.com
w: www.tctravelmanagement.co.uk/loui

Travel Out There
....020 8123 2077.
e: info@traveloutthere.com
w: www.traveloutthere.com

Treasure Hunts Uk
QUICKTHORN HOLLOW, EAST KEAL,
Hertfordshire PE23 4AY..01790 756 940
e: ann@treasurehuntsuk.co.uk
w: www.treasurehuntsuk.co.uk

Twentyfirst Century Communications
MORAY HOUSE, 23-31 GREAT TITCHFIELD STREET, LONDON
Greater London W1W 7PA.....................................020 7291 0444
e: hello@cheerfultwentyfirst.com
w: cheerfultwentyfirst.com/

Twisted Monkey Events Ltd
THE STABLES, HOLME PIERREPONT HALL, NOTTINGHAM
Nottinghamshire NG12 2LD 0115 933 4030
e: info@twistedmonkeyevents.co.uk
w: www.twistedmonkeyevents.co.uk

Twizzle
STUDIO 9, 26 -28 PRIESTS BRIDGE, LONDON
Greater London SW14 8TA....................................020 8392 0860
e: party@twizzle.co.uk
w: www.twizzle.co.uk

UK Bungee Club
MAGNA SCIENCE ADVENTURE CENTRE, SHEFFIELD ROAD,
TEMPLEBOROUGH, ROTHERHAM
South Yorkshire S60 1DX 01709 720002
e: info@ukbungee.co.uk
w: www.visitmagna.co.uk

Uniqueworld
12A ORSMAN ROAD, SHOREDITCH, LONDON
Greater London N1 5QJ .... +44 (0) 207 613 7080
e: christian@uniqueworld.eu
w: www.uniqueworld.eu

Universal Events Services Ltd
UNIT 27, SPACE BUSINESS CENTRE, TEWKESBURY ROAD,
CHELTENHAM
Gloucestershire GL51 9FL......................................01242 530055
e: info@universalevents.co.uk
w: www.universalevents.co.uk

VIP Adrenaline Ltd
9 EDGBARROW RISE, SANDHURST
Berkshire GU47 8QH..07734 391299
e: info@vipadrenaline.com
w: www.vipadrenaline.com

William Bartholomew Party Organising Ltd
20 BRIDGE STREET, HUNGERFORD
Berkshire RG17 0EG 0207 7318328
e: mail@wbpo.com
w: www.wbpo.com

World Star Artists Ltd
4 MONTPELIER STREET, KNIGHTSBRIDGE, LONDON
 SW7 1EE...020 7584 6566
e: london@worldstarartists.com
w: www.worldstarartists.com

X Marks The Spot Ltd
VIVALDI, STOCKING LANE, HUGHENDEN VALLEY
Buckinghamshire HP14 4NE 07801 693001
e: info@xmarksthespot.co.uk
w: www.xmarksthespot.co.uk

Your Right Arm Events Ltd.
....0788 3033 552
e: mary@yourrightarm.co.uk
w: www.yourrightarmevents.co.uk

C

Corporate Hospitality

12 Degrees Ltd
1A CHISWICK END , MELDRETH, ROYSTON
Hertfordshire SG8 6LZ 0845 491 8743
w: www.12degreesshop.co.uk

Aaron's catering service
42 ASHINGDON ROAD ROCHFORD
 SS4 1RD....................................07432635597 / 01702 531 600
e: singh.1972@yahoo.co.uk
w: aaroncatering.co.uk/

Activefootprint Ltd
15 THE LEYS, ESHER ROAD, HERSHAM
Surrey KT12 4LP...020 8339 9182
e: events@activefootprint.co.uk
w: www.activefootprint.co.uk

Agenda Bar
MINSTER COURT, 3 MINCING LANE, LONDON
Greater London EC3R 7AA 0207 929 8399
w: www.agendabar.co.uk

Almanzora Group
THE MANOR, BODDINGTON, CHELTENHAM
Gloucestershire GL51 0TJ....................................0800 180 4359
e: tag@almanzora.co.uk
w: www.almanzora.com

AOL Corporate Events Ltd / Stress Free Events
172 BROX ROAD, OTTERSHAW, CHERTSEY
Surrey KT16 0LQ 020 7610 1060
e: info@stressfreeevents.co.uk
w: www.stressfreeevents.co.uk

Arena Seating
LAMBOURN WOODLANDS, HUNGERFORD
Berkshire RG17 7TQ 01488 674800
e: info@arenaseating.com
w: www.arenagroup.com

Beyond Brilliant Events
54A CHURCH ROAD, BURGESS HILL
West Sussex RH15 9AE...01444 254350
w: www.beyondbrilliant.co.uk

Blue Chip Hospitality Ltd
HAWTHORNE COTTAGE, THE ROSS, COMRIE
Perthshire PH6 2JU...01764 679 496
e: info@bluechiphospitality.com
w: www.bluechiphospitality.com

Business Events Bureau Ltd
SIMMS COTTAGE, BACK LANE, EAST RUSTON
Norfolk NR12 9FH...01692 650229
e: sales@beb.uk.com
w: www.beb.uk.com

Cambria House Corporate Hospitality
CAMBRIA HOUSE, 151 ASHBY ROAD, LOUGHBOROUGH
Leicestershire LE11 3AD.......................................01509 237178
e: sandra@cambria-house.com
w: www.cambria-house.com

Chew Ltd
86-90 PAUL STREET, LONDON
Greater London EC2A 4NE 020 3289 1194
e: info@chewlondon.com
w: www.chewlondon.com

Clockwork Entertainments & Leisure (London) Ltd
4 THE STABLES, BROADFIELD WAY, ALDENHAM
Hertfordshire WD25 8DG......................................01923 635536
e: sales@clockworkentertainment.com
w: www.clockworkentertainment.com

Corporate Fun Events
8 BIRTLES ROAD, ORFORD, WARRINGTON
Cheshire WA2 9AG...01925 575683
e: corporatefunevents@googlemail.com
w: www.corporatefunevents.co.uk

Corporate Ski Specialists
....020 9133 9955
e: info@corporateskispecialists.co.uk
w: www.corporateskispecialists.co.uk

CSL Hospitality
6 LOWER MOUNT STREET, DUBLIN 2, IRELAND
....00 353 1676 6650
e: info@cslhospitality.ie
w: www.cslhospitality.ie

Dash of Sparkle
IDIT GINSBERG, DASH OF SPARKLE , 59 BEECH DRIVE,
BOREHAMWOOD , HERTS
 WD6 4QX................................020 8905 2908 / 07877 927 246
e: office@dashofsparkle.com
w: www.dashofsparkle.com/

Eatopia Event Catering
HORLEY GREEN HOUSE, HALIFAX
West Yorkshire HX3 6AS.......................................07872 451693
e: info@eatopia.eu
w: www.eatopia.eu

Effective Business Events Ltd
IDC HOUSE, VALE, CHALFONT ST PETER
Buckinghamshire SL9 9RZ....................................01753 279 866
e: sales@effectivebusiness.com
w: www.effectivebusiness.com

Effective Event Solutions
10 WHEATLEY BUSINESS CENTRE, OLD LONDON ROAD,
WHEATLEY
Oxfordshire OX33 1XW...01865 877 877
e: sales@effectiveeventsolutions.com
w: www.effectiveeventsolutions.com

C

C

Essex Entertainment Agency
78 HIGH ROAD, LAYER DE LA HAYE, COLCHESTER
Essex CO2 0DT 01206 734164
e: richard@essexents.com
w: www.essexents.com

Event Management Group Ltd
UNIT 6, DELL BUILDING, MILFORD ROAD, LYMINGTON
 SO41 0ED 01590 670 999
e: ask@emg.co.uk
w: www.emg.co.uk

Event Solution And Promotions
BRAESIDE, HIGH STREET, OXSHOTT
Surrey KT22 0JP...01372 841001
e: esp@eventsol.co.uk
w: www.eventsol.co.uk

Eventica
9 QUAYSIDE LODGE, WILLIAM MORRIS WAY, LONDON
Greater London SW6 2UZ......................................0207 183 2560
e: info@eventica.co.uk
w: www.eventica.co.uk

Events International Ltd
OLYMPIC HOUSE, 53 ST OWEN STREET, HEREFORD
Hertfordshire HR1 2JQ 01432 263263
e: sales@eventsinternational.co.uk
w: www.eventsinternational.co.uk

Events Unlimited
6 YEATSALL FARM, YEATSALL ROAD, ABBOTS BROMLEY
Staffordshire WS15 3DY...01283 841600
e: info@eventsunlimited.co.uk
w: www.eventsunlimited.co.uk

Eventuality Uk Ltd
.... 01285 711111 // 07702 265336
e: liam@eventuality.co.uk
w: www.eventuality.co.uk

Fierce Management
26 VILLAGE, WEST KIRBY, WIRRAL
Merseyside CH48 3JW...
e: enquiries@fiercemanagement.co.uk
w: www.fiercemanagement.co.uk

French DMC
28 RUE DE L'AMIRAL HAMELIN, PARIS
75016.. +33 01 49 52 60 07
e: contact@corpo-events.fr
w: www.french-dmc.com

Friday Island Ltd
POOLE KEYNES, CIRENCESTER
Gloucestershire GL7 6ED 01285 770082
e: its-great@friday-island.co.uk
w: www.friday-island.co.uk

GIG...fyi
GLOBAL INFUSION COURT, NASHLEIGH HILL, CHESHAM
Buckinghamshire HP5 3HE 01494 790700
e: hellogigfyi@gigfyi.com
w: www.gigfyi.com

Global Infusion Group
GLOBAL INFUSION COURT, NASHLEIGH HILL, CHESHAM
Buckinghamshire HP5 3HE 01494 790700
e: hello@globalinfusiongroup.com
w: www.globalinfusiongroup.com

Ice Box
UNIT A35/36, NEW COVENT GARDEN MARKET, LONDON
Greater London SW8 5EE......................................020 7498 0800
e: info@theicebox.com
w: www.theicebox.com

In Association
OAKRIDGE CHAMBERS, 1-3 OAKRIDGE ROAD, BROMLEY
Kent BR1 5QW...0208 697 6976
e: steve@inassociation.co.uk
w: www.inassociation.co.uk

International Conferences Ltd
PO BOX 93, ST PETER PORT, GUERNSEY
 GY1 3EQ 01481 713643
e: info@inter-conferences.com
w: www.inter-conferences.com

Irvin Leisure Ltd
35 CURTIS LANE, MAIN STREET, HANWORTH, WEMBLEY
Middlesex HA0 4FW..020 8795 4282
e: info@irvinleisure.com
w: www.irvinleisure.com

KDM Events Ltd
NEWSTEAD TRADING ESTATE , TRENTHAM
Staffordshire ST4 8HX..01782 646300
e: events@kdmevents.com
w: www.kdmevents.co.uk

Keith Prowse
KEITH PROWSE RIVERMEAD, 82 OXFORD ROAD, UXBRIDGE
Middlesex UB9 4BF...01895 451 189
e: enquiries@keithprowse.co.uk
w: www.keithprowse.co.uk

Mansion & Gardens, Port Lympne Wild Animal Park
PORT LYMPNE RESERVE, NR ASHFORD
Kent CT21 4LR...0844 842 4647
e: info@aspinallfoundation.org
w: www.aspinallfoundation.org

Match Point Ltd
16 WALKER STREET, EDINBURGH
Edinburgh EH3 7LP...0131 477 7755
e: edinburgh@matchpoint.co.uk
w: www.matchpoint.co.uk

C

Memorable Events London Ltd
UNIT 10, CRANLEIGH MEWS, BATTERSEA, LONDON
Greater London SW11 2QL.....................................020 3405 1946
e: hello@melonevents.co.uk
w: www.melonevents.co.uk

Milestone Event Management Ltd
WELBECK HOUSE, CLIFTONVILLE, DORKING
Surrey RH4 2JF...01372 204 057
e: lukeparry@milestone-event.com / paulrockett@milestone-event.com
w: www.milestone-event.com

Moodies Ltd
BLAIR HOUSE, THREE GATES LANE, HASLEMERE, HASLEMERE
Surrey GU27 2LD .... 01428 644310 // 01428 652244
e: info@moodies.co.uk
w: www.moodies.co.uk

Mossimann's Party Services
11B WEST HALKIN STREET, LONDON
Greater London SW1X 8JL 020 7235 9625
e: events@mosimann.com
w: www.mosimann.com

MSL Global
BUILDING 91, SEME, BUDDS LANE, BORDON
Hampshire GU35 0JE...01420 471000
w: www.mslglobal.com

Multiversal Events
261 DITCHLING ROAD, BRIGHTON
East Sussex BN1 6JH..................01273 900221 / 07880 704378
e: info@multiversalevents.co.uk
w: www.multiversalevents.co.uk

Mwm Sports Management Group
144 HIGH STREET, HOLYWOOD
BT18 9HS 028 9042 6633
e: info@mwmsports.co.uk
w: www.mwmsports.co.uk

Orange Tree Events Ltd
26 NORTH END LANE, ASCOT
SL5 0DZ ....07976 422950 / 01344 297433
e: info@orange-tree-events.co.uk
w: www.orange-tree-events.co.uk

Origin Hospitality Ltd
55 CRANBURY ROAD, FULHAM
SW6 2NJ 020 7736 5400
e: tsai@originhospitality.co.uk
w: www.originhospitality.co.uk

Pamper Paradise
CROYDON
Surrey.......................................07775 661696 or 07729 49 39 70
e: info@pamperparadise.co.uk
w: www.pamperparadise.co.uk

Pandemonium
PO BOX 1092, HIGH WYCOMBE
Buckinghamshire HP10 8WY.................................01494 813170
e: simon@pandemonium.com
w: www.pandemonium.com

Place Settings (London) Ltd
UNIT C2, SIX BRIDGES TRADING ESTATE, MARLBOROUGH GROVE, LONDON
Greater London SE1 5JT 020 7740 1234
e: london@placesettingseventhire.com
w: www.placesettingseventhire.com

Planet Gold Decor
UNIT 4 ROMARSH, FOWLSWICK BUSINESS PARK, , ALLINGTON
Wiltshire SN14 6QE..07747 015 170
e: info@planetgolddecor.co.uk
w: www.planetgolddecor.co.uk or www.

Production Network Worldwide Services Ltd
UNIT 1, ELSTREE FILM STUDIOS, SHENLEY ROAD, BOREHAMWOOD
Hertfordshire WD6 1JG 020 8324 2669
e: office@pronetworld.com
w: www.pronetworld.com

Rhodes Event Management
.... 07971 619502
e: enquiries@rhodes-events.co.uk
w: www.rhodes-events.co.uk

Richmond Athletic Association Ltd
RICHMOND ATHLETIC GROUND, TWICKENHAM ROAD, RICHMOND
Surrey TW9 2SF...020 8940 0397
e: events@the-raa.co.uk
w: www.the-raa.co.uk

Sail Royal Greenwich
10TH FLOOR, 6 MITRE PASSAGE, GREENWICH
Greater London SE10 0ER.....................................0203 040 2350
e: info@sailroyalgreenwich.co.uk
w: www.sailroyalgreenwich.co.uk

Sanver Sports Private Limited
126 - 127 UDYOG BHAVAN, SONAWALA ROAD, GOREGAON EAST, MUMBAI, INDIA
400063.. +91 22 42200422
e: sales@sanversports.com
w: www.sanversports.com

School Of Booze
50 ROSE BANK, HOLYPORT RD, FULHAM, LONDON
SW6 6LH...07729 601 590
e: info@school-of-booze.com
w: www.school-of-booze.com

Seggy Segway
CARR FARM , CARR LANE, THORNER , LEEDS
West Yorkshire LS14 3HE.......................................07515 253893
e: info@seggysegway.co.uk

SimpliWifi
THE TELEPHONE EXCHANGE, 33 BRIDGE STREET, KINGTON
HR5 3DW...01544 327 310
e: hello@simpliwifi.co.uk
w: https://www.simpliwifi.co.uk/

Simply The Best Events
2 LANE END VILLAS, SHINFIELD ROAD, READING
Berkshire RG2 9BS 0800 019 3908
e: sales@simplythebestevents.co.uk
w: www.simplythebestevents.co.uk

SJ Events
SJ EVENT CONSULTANCY LTD, NORTH WING, , SWITHLAND HALL
, SWITHLAND
Leicestershire LE12 8TJ 1162302040
e: mikewayne@post.com
w: www.sjevents.co.uk/

SP Events
THE LILACS, STREET LANE, BEWERLEY, HARROGATE
North Yorkshire HG3 5HW ....01423 711806 / 07976 402986
e: info@spevents.co.uk
w: www.spevents.co.uk

Sportsworld Group Plc
DST HOUSE,, ST MARKS HILL, SURBITON
Surrey KT6 4BH 020 8971 2966
e: info@sportsworld.co.uk
w: www.sportsworld.co.uk

Sweet Chariot Leisure Ltd
THE CLUB HOUSE, CHURCH ROAD, EPSOM
Surrey KT17 4DZ 01372 725253
e: info@sweetchariot.org
w: www.sweetchariot.org

Team Pamper
Greater London 020 369 18233
e: info@teampamper.com
w: www.teampamper.com

The Moonlighting Group
THE COACH HOUSE, CRASHMORE LANE, OVERBURY,
TEWKESBURY
Gloucestershire GL20 7NX 01386 725600
e: enquiries@moonlightinggroup.co.uk
w: www.moonlightinggroup.co.uk

The RMS Group
INTERNATIONAL HOUSE, 33-35 ST DAVIDS ROAD SOUTH,
LYTHAM ST ANNES
 FY8 1TJ..01253 780000
e: enquiries@rms-group.com
w: www.internationalsport.co.uk/

The Team Building Company
UNIT 6 DELL BUILDING, MILFORD ROAD, LYMINGTON
Hampshire SO41 0ED 01590 676599
e: info@teambuilding.co.uk
w: www.teambuilding.co.uk

Topsail Charters
COOKS YARD, THE HYTHE, MALDON
Essex CM9 5HN 01621 857567
e: info@top-sail.co.uk
w: www.top-sail.co.uk

Travel Counsellors Ltd
TRAVEL HOUSE, 43 CHURCHGATE, BOLTON
Lancashire BL1 1TH....................01773 318910 / 07973 306280
e: louise.cutting@travelcounsellors.com
w: www.tctravelmanagement.co.uk/loui

Ultimate Experience Ltd
AXE AND BOTTLE COURT, 70 NEWCOMEN STREET, LONDON
Greater London SE1 1YT 0207 940 6060
e: hello@weareultimate.co.uk
w: www.weareultimate.co.uk/

Versatile Venues Ltd
WIRELESS HOUSE, WIRELESS HILL, SOUTH LUFFENHAM
Rutland LE15 8NF......................08000 147 338 / 01780 720 217
e: info@versatilevenues.co.uk
w: www.versatilevenues.co.uk

Costumes / Wardrobe

Academy Costumes
50 RUSHWORTH STREET, WATERLOO, LONDON
Greater London SE1 0RB.......................................020 7620 0771
e: info@academycostumes.com
w: www.academycostumes.com

Angels The Costumiers
1 GARRICK ROAD, LONDON
Greater London NW9 6AA 020 8202 2244
e: info@angels.uk.com
w: www.angels.uk.com

Bath Theatrical Costume Hire
UNIT 8 WALLBRIDGE MILLS, FROME , MENDIP
BA11 5JZ...01373 472786
e: baththeatrical@talktalk.net
w: www.baththeatrical.com

Bridal Apparel Leeds Ltd
15 HARROGATE ROAD, RAWDON, LEEDS
LS19 6HW 01132 501616
e: bridalapparel@gmail.com
w: www.bridalapparelleeds.co.uk

Bristol Costume Services Ltd
FILLWOOD HOUSE, FILLWOOD ROAD, BRISTOL
Bristol BS16 3RY..0117 965 9555
e: bcsbristol@aol.com
w: www.bristolcostumeservices.com

Bryan Philip Davies Costumes
25 GLYNLEIGH DRIVE, POLEGATE, EAST SUSSEX
BN26 6LU 01323 304391
e: bryan@bpdcostumes.co.uk
w: www.bpdcostumes.co.uk

C

Charles H Fox Ltd
22 TAVISTOCK STREET, COVENT GARDEN, LONDON
Greater London WC2E 7PY .... +44 20/7240 3111
e: info-uk@kryolan.com
w: www.charlesfox.co.uk

Contemporary Wardrobe Collection
COLONNADE, BLOOMSBURY, LONDON
Greater London WC1N 1JD 020 7713 7370
e: roger@contemporarywardrobe.com
w: www.contemporarywardrobe.com

Costume Hire Direct
 UNIT 2, NEW BUILDINGS FARM, WINCHESTER ROAD, PETESFIELD
Hampshire GU32 3PB 01703 263094
e: hire@costumehiredirect.co.uk
w: www.costumehiredirect.co.uk

Costume Studio Ltd
159-161 BALLS POND ROAD, ISLINGTON
 N1 4BG..020 7275 9614
e: costume.studio@btconnect.com
w: www.costumestudio.co.uk

D.R. Easton Ltd
1 DOROTHY AVENUE, PEACE HAVEN
East Sussex BN10 8LP...01273 588262
e: wigs@derekeastonwigs.co.uk
w: www.derekeastonwigs.co.uk

Fancy Dress Fanatics
212 CHELTENHAM ROAD, BRISTOL
Bristol BS6 5QU 0117 329 0093
e: info@fancydressfanatics.com
w: www.fancydressfanatics.co.uk

FBFX
UNIT 1 DOCKWELLS ESTATE, CENTRAL WAY, FELTHAM,
HOUNSLOW
Middlesex TW14 0RX..020 8751 5321
e: info@fbfx.co.uk
w: www.fbfx.co.uk

Flame Torbay Costume Hire Ltd (Uniform Specialist)
35 MARKET STREET, TORQUAY
Devon TQ1 3AW...01803 211930
e: flametorbay@hotmail.com
w: www.flametorbay.co.uk

Harveys Of Hove
110 TRAFALGAR ROAD, PORTSLADE, BRIGHTON
 BN41 1GS...01273 430323
e: harveys.costume@ntlworld.com
w: www.harveysofhove.co.uk

Hirearchy Classic & Contempory Costume
45 PALMERSTON ROAD, BOSCOMBE, BOURNEMOUTH
Dorset BH1 4HW..001202 391661
e: hirearchy1@gmail.com
w: www.hirearchy.co.uk

Mahogany
28 HIGH STREET, HARLESDEN, LONDON
Greater London NW10 4LX....................................020 8961 4446
e: costumes@mahoganycarnival.com
w: www.mahoganycarnival.com

Modern Age
65 CHALK FARM ROAD, LONDON
Greater London NW1 8AN 07702 958995
e: vintage-clothing@modern-age.co.uk
w: www.modern-age.co.uk

Pam's The Party Specialists
UNIT 30 , CORRINGHAM ROAD INDUSTRIAL ESTATE,
GAINSBOROUGH
Lincolnshire DN21 1QB..0845 230 6763
e: sales@pams.co.uk
w: www.pams.co.uk

Ryszard Andrzejewski Design For Performance
 ....07799 613 277
e: skirich@hotmail.com
w: www.skirich.co.uk

Siam Costumes International Co. Ltd
79/311 SOI PHUMICHIT RAMA 4 ROAD, PRAKHANONG,
KLONG TOEY
10110..020 3290 2711
e: info@siamcostumes.com
w: www.siamcostumes.com

Smiffy's
PECKETT PLAZA, CALDICOTT DRIVE, GAINSBOROUGH
Lincolnshire DN21 1FJ...0800 590 599
e: sales@smiffys.com
w: www.smiffys.com

Vintage Hosiery Co
26 ARUNSIDE, OFF BLACKBRIDGE LANE, HORSHAM
RH12 1SJ 01403 257116
e: vintageHosiery@lycos.com

WILDCHILD WORLD
 .... +1 786 505 9453
e: info@wildchildworld.com
w: wildchildworld.com

Courier Services

A-B 24/7
UNIT 14 MERTON INDUSTRIAL PARK, LEE ROAD, WIMBLEDON,
LONDON
Greater London SW19 3HX...................................0208 0990 247
e: info@ab247.co.uk
w: www.ab247.co.uk

Bascom-BMS
82 FEEDER ROAD, ATLAS STREET, BRISTOL
Bristol BS2 0HH 0117 977 9900
e: sales@bascom.co.uk
w: www.bascom.co.uk

EwePack Shipping
THE MANOR HOUSE HIGH STREET , BUNTINGFORD, HERTS
SG9 9AB .... +44 207 118 7447
e: steve@ewepack.com
w: www.ewepack.com

F1 Logistics Ltd
BUILDING 500, SHEPPERTON STUDIOS, SHEPPERTON
Middlesex TW17 0QD..01932 580900
e: operations@f1logisticslhr.co.uk
w: www.f1logisticslhr.co.uk

Greener Routes Couriers
THE CIDER PRESS, 5 WOODBEER GARDENS, CULLOMPTON,
EXETER Devon EX15 2LN 8000476527
e: info@greenerroutes.co.uk
w: www.greenerroutes.co.uk

MDS Courier Services
35 WINDSOR ROAD, NEWARK
Nottinghamshire NG24 4HX 01636 707445
e: courier@mdsteleservices.co.uk
w: www.mdsteleservices.co.uk

Peters & May Ltd
UNIT 9, GOODWOOD ROAD, EASTLEIGH, SOUTHAMPTON
Hampshire SO50 4NT 02380 480500
e: marine@petersandmay.com
w: www.petersandmay.com

Redcare Logistics (lhr) Ltd
UNIT 5, FORGEWOOD, GATWICK ROAD, CRAWLEY
Kent RH10 9PG ....0844 2722 247 / 07704 880741
e: info@redcare.uk.com
w: www.redcare.uk.com

Spooners Turf
HESTERS YARD, OAK HILL, WOOD STREET VILLAGE, GUILDFORD
Surrey GU3 3ES 1252793748
e: enquiries@Indian-Sandstone.net
w: www.indian-sandstone.net/

Transfer2000 Ltd International Events Couriers
191 VALE ROAD , TONBRIDGE , KENT
TN9 1ST 0345 060 2000
e: info@transfer2000.co.uk
w: www.transfer2000.com

Créche Services

Limehouse Day Nursery
21-23 TRINIDAD STREET , LIMEHOUSE , LONDON
E14 8AA 0207 538 3355
e: limehousechildcare@gmail.com
w: www.limehousedaynursery.co.uk

Woodpecker Nursery
WOODFIELD HOUSE , TANGMERE ROAD, CHICHESTER
PO20 2EU 01243 839905
e: info@woodpeckernursery.co.uk
w: www.woodpeckernursery.co.uk

Crew Services

24c Birmingham - Event Crew
OLD WARWICK ROAD, LAPWORTH
Warwickshire B94 6LU...0845 170 2424
e: crew@24c.co.uk
w: 24c.co.uk

Ace Crew Ltd
UNIT 6, PRINCESS COURT, 1 HORACE ROAD,
KINGSTON UPON THAMES
Greater London KT1 2SL.......................................0207 924 6569
e: admin@acecrew.co.uk
w: www.acecrew.co.uk

Alpha Crew Ltd
28 GRAZEBROOK ROAD, STOKE NEWINGTON, LONDON
Greater London N16 0HS 020 8802 9227
e: info@alphacrew.co.uk
w: www.alphacrew.co.uk

Audio W(av)elength
....07806 859 998
e: joe_killen@audiowavelength.com
w: www.audiowavelength.com

Bath Film Office
LEWIS HOUSE, MANVERS STREET, BATH
Somerset BA1 1JG..01225 477711
e: bath_filmoffice@bathnes.gov.uk
w: www.visitbath.co.uk/site/film-off

Bell Audio Hire
5 GREENOCK ROAD , CHISWICK , LONDON
W3 8DU 2088961200
e: dan@bellperc.com
w: www.bellaudiohire.com/

Celtic Stage Crew
DRAGON HOUSE, LECKWITH QUAY, LECKWITH ROAD, CARDIFF
CF11 8AU 029 20225152
e: office@celticstagecrew.co.uk
w: www.celticstagecrew.co.uk

Connection Crew
23 JACOB STREET, LONDON
Greater London SE1 2BG 0844 822 1515
e: info@connectioncrew.co.uk
w: www.connectioncrew.co.uk

CREW Yorkshire
3 PARK SQUARE EAST, LEEDS
West Yorkshire LS1 2NE.......................................01132 161 252
e: info@yorkshireeventscrew.co.uk
w: www.yorkshireeventscrew.co.uk

Crewsaders Ltd
MILLER 2, 61 ST PAULS SQUARE, BIRMINGHAM
West Midlands B3 1QS 0845 094 4884
e: bookings@crewsaders.com
w: www.crewsaders.com

C

DC3 Productions Ltd
37 BRAMBLE ROAD, HATFIELD
AL10 9RZ....................................020 8123 8765 / 07737 535886
e: dan@dc3productions.co.uk
w: www.dc3productions.co.uk

Event Crewing Group
....0845 644 6898
e: dragon@event-crewing.com
w: www.event-crewing.com

Festival Loo - Poonarnia
FERNHILL FARM, CHEDDAR ROAD, COMPTON MARTIN
Somerset BS40 6LD 07503 769188
e: squeak@festivalloo.co.uk
w: www.festivalloo.co.uk

Fix-d Media
18 HILLSIDE AVENUE, PURLEY, Surrey CR8 2DP.....0203 393 7210
e: sales@fix-d.co.uk
w: www.fix-d.co.uk

G Force Crew
....08455 197 791
e: crew@gforcecrew.com
w: www.gforcecrew.com

Gallowglass Ltd
3RD FLOOR, 199 THE VALE, ACTON , LONDON
W3 7QS 0845 600 8966
e: events@gallowglass.co.uk
w: www.gallowglass.co.uk

Icarusjet
BERKELEY SQUARE, MAYFAIR, LONDON
W1J-6BD...442071838551
e: ashleyjessicaaa@gmail.com
w: www.icarusjet.com/

LondonCrew.Co
....0871 91 8114
e: info@londoncrew.co
w: www.londoncrew.co

MM Band Services Ltd
ACER GLADE, BLACK TUP LANE, ARNOLD, HULL
East Yorkshire HU11 5JA.......................................01964 563 464
e: enquiries@mmbandservices.co.uk
w: www.mmbandservices.co.uk

MP Squares Ltd
FORTIS HOUSE, 160 LONDON ROAD, BARKING
Essex IG11 8BB 020 8214 1125
e: squares@mp-squares.co.uk
w: www.mp-squares.co.uk

Neon Arena Services
UNIT 305, THE ARGENT CENTRE, 60 FREDERICK STREET,
HOCKLEY, BIRMINGHAM, West Midlands B1 3HS ...0121 236 5555
e: info@neonarenaservices.co.uk
w: www.neonsportsfloors.co.uk

Nova Stage & Live Event Crew
UNIT C3 PALMERSVALE BUSINESS CENTRE, PALMERSTON RD,,
BARRY, VALE OF GLAMORGAN
CF63 2XA 01446 734185
e: info@novacrew.co.uk
w: www.novacrew.co.uk

Panther Crew Ltd
....0845 467 1858 / 07789179921
e: info@panthercrew.com
w: www.panthercrew.com

Pibscam
....07711 528 724 / 08454758676
e: paul@pibscam.com
w: www.pibscam.com

Pinnacle Crew
THE WHITE COTTAGE, MERRY HILL GREEN LANE, WINNERSH
Berkshire RG41 5JP...0870 609 1993
e: info@pinnaclecrew.co.uk
w: www.pinnaclecrew.co.uk

Pirate Crew Ltd
BRIARY BARN- HOME FARM BUSINESS PARK, CHURCH WAY,
WHITTLEBURY, TOWCESTER
Northamptonshire NN12 8XS 0333 123 4401
e: enquiries@piratecrew.co.uk
w: www.piratecrew.co.uk

Pitman's People Marquee and Event Structure Crew and Riggers
UNIT G1A STAMFORD WORKS, 3 GILLETT ST., LONDON
Greater London N16 8JH.......................................020 3651 3330
e: admin@pitmanspeople.com
w: www.pitmanspeople.com

Plant and Stage Crew Services
75 DOMINION DRIVE, COLLIER ROW
Essex RM5 2QS .... 020 3651 9263 // 07780 772713
e: info@plantandstagecrewservices.co.uk
w: plantandstagecrewservices.co.uk

Pro Crews Ltd
....020 3457 8423
e: info@procrews.co.uk
w: www.procrews.co.uk

Production Crew Entertainment Private Limited
B - 707, SILICON PARK , JANKALYAN NAGAR, OFF MARVE ROAD
KHARODI, MALAD WEST , MUMBAI, INDIA
400095..93.55353639879800198
e: vikas.menon@productioncrew.in
w: www.productioncrew.in

RES-Crew Ltd
20-22 WENLOCK ROAD, LONDON
Greater London N1 7GU .... 07985565800 // 02038374985
e: hallo@res-crew.co.uk
w: www.res-crew.co.uk

Rock City Stage Crew
LANGSFORD HOUSE, 8 DARKLAKE VIEW, ESTOVER, PLYMOUTH
Devon PL6 7TL 01752 255 933
e: office@rockcitycrew.co.uk
w: www.rockcitycrew.co.uk

Salima Ltd
2A BACCHUS HOUSE, CALLEVA PARK, ALDERMASTON, READING
Berkshire RG7 8EN ....0845 458 1699 / 07825 586 083
e: info@salima-ltd.co.uk
w: www.salima-ltd.co.uk

Sherpa
12 THE TALINA CENTRE, BAGLEY'S LANE FULHAM, LONDON
SW6 2BW 0207 610 8620
e: info@eventsherpa.co.uk
w: www.eventsherpa.co.uk

Showforce
UNIT 001 STRATFORD WORKSHOPS, BURFORD ROAD,
STRATFORD, LONDON
Greater London E15 2SP..0208 519 5252
e: info@showforce.com
w: www.showforce.com

Showstars
BRIDGE HOUSE, 3 MILLS STUDIOS, THREE MILL LANE, LONDON
Greater London E3 3DU 0208 215 3333
e: enquiries@showstars.co.uk
w: www.showstars.co.uk

Silverback Events
THE SPACE PROJECT, 12 VAUGHN STREET, MANCHESTER
Greater Manchester M12 5FQ 08445 617 939
e: info@silverbackuk.com
w: www.silverbackuk.com

Skyfire Event Services
PEN-Y-BANC FARM, LLAWR-Y-GLYN, CAERSWS, POWYS, WALES
SY17 5RN .... 07971 527062 // 01686 430433
e: skyfirestagecrew@gmail.com
w: www.skyfirepyro.com

South East Crew
12 YORK GROVE, BRIGHTON
East Sussex BN1 3TT...01273 882947
e: info@southeastcrew.com
w: www.southeastcrew.com

Stage Crew
404 RUSSELL COURT, LISBURN ROAD, BELFAST
BT9 6JW.. +44 (0)28 9032 9897
e: office@stage-crew.co.uk
w: www.stage-crew.co.uk

Stage Miracles Ltd
WOODLANDS, SCHOOL ROAD, POTTERS BAR
Hertfordshire EN6 1JW 01707 662 500
e: mail@stagemiracles.co.uk
w: www.stagemiracles.com

Stagecraft CSL
UNIT 311, THE CUSTARD FACTORY, GIBB STREET, DIGBETH,
BIRMINGHAM
West Midlands B9 4AA................0121 693 0124/ 0121 693 0125
e: office@stagecraftcrew.co.uk
w: www.stagecraftcrew.co.uk

Stephen J Brand
.... 07976 731725 // 0044 20 8299 1493
e: sjbrand@dop2000.freeserve.co.uk
w: www.sjbrand.com

T J Production Services Llp
AVALON ROAD, EALING W13 0BN.........................07976 322 149
e: Jeff@tjproductionservices.co.uk
w: www.tjproductionservices.co.uk

Temp Fence Supplies Ltd
MERITOR HOUSE , FOLEY STREET, SHEFFIELD
South Yorkshire S4 7YW..0114 2414116
e: sales@tempfence.co.uk
w: www.tempfence.co.uk

The Wicked Company
UNIT 2, BLACKETT ROAD, DARLINGTON
Durham DL1 2BJ ....01325 789382 / 07725 164507
e: info@thewickedcompany.co.uk
w: www.thewickedcompany.co.uk

Touchwood Security Ltd
6 SOUTH BAR, BANBURY
Oxfordshire OX16 9AA...01280 700866
e: info@touchwoodsecuritylimited.co.uk
w: www.touchwoodsecuritylimited.co.u

Tovs
3RD FLOOR (ROOM 340), THE LINEN HALL, 162-168 REGENT
STREET, LONDON
Greater London W1B 5TD.......................................020 7287 6110
e: hello@tovs.co.uk
w: www.tovs.co.uk

Urban Crew Ltd
112 ALEXANDRA ROAD, WIMBLEDON
Greater London SW19 7JY 08452 262 818
e: info@urbancrewltd.com
w: www.urbancrewltd.com

Crowd Barriers / Fencing

Austen Lewis Ltd
UNIT DG, CHELWORTH PARK, CRICKLADE, SWINDON
Wiltshire SN6 6HE...01793 750599
e: info@austen-lewis.co.uk
w: www.austen-lewis.co.uk

Beaver 84
CHURCHILL HOUSE, SOPWITH CRESCENT, HURRICANE WAY,
WICKFORD, Essex SS11 8YU................................01268 727 112
e: sales@beaver84.co.uk
w: www.beaver84.co.uk

C

www.whitebook.co.uk

C

Blok N Mesh Events
UNIT 3, DRIBERG WAY, BRAINTREE
Essex CM7 1NB 0870 950 5744
e: events@bloknmesh.com
w: www.bloknmeshevents.com

Border Barrier Systems Ltd
NATIONAL SALES AND HIRE, HEAD OFFICE, ALSTONBY GRANGE,
CARLISLE
Cumbria CA6 6AF 01228 675 764
e: sales@borderbarriers.com
w: www.borderbarriers.com

Davis Track Hire
103A MAIN STREET, NEWMAINS, WISHAW
Lanarkshire ML2 9BG 01698 352751
e: info@davistrackhire.com
w: www.davistrackhire.com

Daytona Stage Hire
PO BOX 43, HUDDERSFIELD
West Yorkshire HD8 9YU 01484 605555
e: office@daytonastagehire.com
w: www.daytonastagehire.com

Entertee Hire Services
LONGPOND WORKS, WROTHAM ROAD , BOROUGH GREEN
Kent TN15 8DE 01732 781 137
e: hire@entertee.com
w: www.entertee.com

Europalite
MILWARD HOUSE, EASTFIELD SIDE, SUTTON IN ASHFIELD
Nottinghamshire NG17 4JW....................................01623 528760
e: sales@europalite.eu
w: www.europalite.eu

Eve Trakway
BRAMLEY VALE, CHESTERFIELD
Derbyshire S44 5GA...08700 767676
e: mail@evetrakway.co.uk
w: www.evetrakway.co.uk

Events Solution Ltd
SHIREOAKS COMMON , SHIREOAKS, SHEFFIELD
South Yorkshire S81 8NW 0844 870 9802
e: jameswoodevents@aol.com
w: www.eventssolutions.co.uk

Fencehire (southern) Ltd
COMPOUND ONE, FARRINGDON BUSINESS PARK, FARRINGDON
 GU34 3DZ..01420 588481
e: sales@fencehiresouthern.com
w: www.fencehiresouthern.com

Fieldtrack Ltd
MANSE ROAD, FORTH
Lanarkshire ML11 8AN 01555 812812
e: info@fieldtrackltd.co.uk
w: www.fieldtrackltd.co.uk

GT Trax Ltd
HIGH TREE FARM, NEW ROAD, WARBOYS
Cambridgeshire PE28 2SS 01487 823344
e: info@gttrax.co.uk
w: www.gttrax.co.uk

Ideal Event Services
310 UNTHANK ROAD, NORWICH
Norfolk NR4 7QD 01603 280176
e: hello@idealeventservices.co.uk
w: www.idealeventservices.co.uk

KC Lighting
123 PRIORWAY AVENUE, BORROWASH, DERBY
 DE72 3HY .... 01332 674589 // 07860 669323
e: kev@kclighting.co.uk
w: www.kclighting.co.uk

Liniar
FLAMSTEAD HOUSE, DENBY HALL BUSINESS PARK, DENBY
Derbyshire DE5 8JX..01332 883900
e: sales@liniar.co.uk
w: www.liniar.co.uk

Main Event Product Ltd
UNIT 25 COLESHILL INDUSTRIAL ESTATE, STATION ROAD,
COLESHILL, BIRMINGHAM
West Midlands B46 1JP 01675 464 224
e: sales@mainevent.co.uk
w: www.mainevent.co.uk

Mojo Barriers UK Ltd
1 OAKTREES BOROUGH GREEN ROAD, WROTHAM, SEVENOAKS
Kent TN15 7RD 01708 687 440
e: kevin.thorborn@mojobarriers.com
w: www.mojobarriers.com

Orbit Roofs And Staging
UNIT 2, LONG ING LANE, OUZLEDALE FOUNDRY, BURNLEY
 BB18 6BN..01282 816500
e: info@orbitroofsandstaging.co.uk
w: www.orbitroofsandstaging.co.uk

Prolyte Sales UK Ltd.
UNIT 1A, SHORTWOOD BUSINESS PARK, SHORTWOOD WAY,
BARNSLEY S74 9LH...01977 659 800
e: info@prolyte.com
w: www.prolyte.com

R & R Logistics
DOUBLE LODGE, PINEWOOD FILM STUDIOS, IVER HEATH
Buckinghamshire SL0 0NH 01753 654844
e: info@randrlogistics.co.uk
w: www.randrlogistics.co.uk

Road Safety Services Ltd
BRACKENWOOD CENTRE, BRADSHAW LANE, GREENHALGH,
PRESTON
Lancashire PR4 3HQ 01253 596388
e: shaun@road-safety.net
w: www.road-safety.net

Safe Site Facilities
UNIT 1, MARTELLO ENTERPRISE CENTRE,, COURTWICK LANE,
LITTLEHAMPTON
West Sussex BN17 7PA..0330 012 4442
e: info@safesitefacilities.co.uk
w: www.safesitefacilities.co.uk

Securifence UK Ltd
REVELLS FARM, LINTON, ROSS ON WYE
Herefordshire HR9 7SD...01989 720588
e: info@securifence.co.uk
w: securifence.co.uk

Signature (Fencing & Flooring) Systems Europe Ltd
UNIT 1, BLACKETT ROAD, BLACKETT ROAD INDUSTRIAL ESTATE,
DARLINGTON
Durham DL1 2BJ..01642 744990
e: sales@signaturesystemseurope.co.uk
w: www.signaturesystemseurope.co.uk

Solid Entertainments
46 WELLOWGATE, GRIMSBY
Lincolnshire DN32 0RA...01472 349222
e: solidentertainments@live.co.uk
w: www.solidentertainments.com

South Surrey Fencing
1 PARKHURST ROAD, HORLEY
Surrey RH6 8EU....................... 01293 385 787 // 07973 658 116
e: southsurreyfencing@outlook.com
w: www.southsurreyfencing.co.uk

Temp Fence Supplies Ltd
MERITOR HOUSE , FOLEY STREET, SHEFFIELD
South Yorkshire S4 7YW..0114 2414116
e: sales@tempfence.co.uk
w: www.tempfence.co.uk

Temporary Fencing Limited
STAFFORD HOUSE, 10 PRINCE OF WALES ROAD, DORCHESTER
Dorset DT1 1PW..01202 573311
e: temporaryfencing@btconnect.com
w: www.temporaryfencingltd.com

Tensator Ltd
DANBURY COURT, LINFORD WOOD, MILTON KEYNES
Buckinghamshire MK14 6TS.................................01908 684600
e: info@tensator.com
w: www.tensator.com

Vincehire Ltd
BRAMLEY VALE,, CHESTERFIELD,
Derbyshire S44 5GA...08700 767676
e: mail@evetrakway.co.uk
w: www.evetrakway.co.uk

Wade Building Services Ltd
GROVELAND ROAD, TIPTON
West Midlands DY4 7TN..0345 873 2828
e: sales@wade-bs.co.uk
w: www.wade-bs.co.uk

Wernick Event Hire Ltd
JOSEPH HOUSE, NORTHGATE WAY, ALDRIDGE, WALSALL
West Midlands WS9 8ST 0800 970 0231
e: enquiries@wernickevents.co.uk
w: www.wernickeventhire.co.uk

C

D

Dance Floors

A & B Marquees
4 DUDLEY TERRACE, MILL ROD, LISS
Hampshire GU33 7BE 07747 806794
e: info@abmarquees.co.uk
w: www.abmarquees.co.uk

Apollo Party Hire
APOLLO PARTY HIRE, 60 OAKWAY, WOKING
Surrey GU21 8TR .... 01483 821336 // 07986 497388
e: info@apollopartyhire.co.uk
w: www.apollopartyhire.co.uk

British Harlequin Plc
FESTIVAL HOUSE , CHAPMAN WAY, TUNBRIDGE WELLS
Kent TN2 3EF..01892 514888
e: enquiries@harlequinfloors.com
w: www.harlequinfloors.com

Complete Avenue Ltd
OLD BARN, BLACKBIRD FARM,BLACKBIRD LANE, ALDENHAM
West Midlands WD25 8BS.....................................07854 007483
w: www.completeavenue.co.uk

East Anglia Leisure
UNIT 4, CIVIC INDUSTRIAL ESTATE, HOMEFIELD ROAD, HAVERHILL
Suffolk CB9 8QP 01440 714204
e: info@ealeisure.co.uk
w: www.ealeisure.co.uk

First Light Ltd
UNIT 9-10 LAKER ROAD, ROCHESTER AIRPORT, INDUSTRIAL
ESTATE, ROCHESTER
Kent ME1 3QX 01634 685500
e: info@firstlight.events
w: www.djcevents.co.uk/

Four Star Events
UNIT 35 GRASMERE WAY, BLYTH
Northumberland NE24 4RR 7971754904
e: alanfourstarevents@gmail.com
w: www.fourstarevents.co.uk

Fresh Events UK
UNIT D WESLAKE INDUSTRIAL PARK, RYE HARBOUR ROAD, RYE
East Sussex TN31 7TE 07919 512 608
e: info@fresheventsuk.com
w: www.fresheventsuk.com

iCatching Events
UNIT D, JOSEPH ADAMSON IND EST, CROFT STREET, HYDE
Cheshire SK14 1EE 0845 833 6372
e: info@icatchingevents.co.uk
w: www.icatchingevents.co.uk

Ideal Event Services
310 UNTHANK ROAD, NORWICH
Norfolk NR4 7QD 01603 280176
e: hello@idealeventservices.co.uk
w: www.idealeventservices.co.uk

JDB Events
GATEHOUSE TRADING ESTATE, LICHFIELD RD, BROWNHILLS,
WALSALL WS8 6JZ 0121 667 1444
e: info@jdb-events.co.uk
w: www.jdb-events.com

Kudos Music
UNIT 10 TRADE CITY, COWLEY MILL ROAD, UXBRIDGE
 UB8 2DB...01895 207990
e: info@kudosmusic.co.uk
w: www.kudosmusic.co.uk

Le Mark Self Adhesive Ltd
UNIT 1 HOUGHTON HILL INDUSTRIES, SAWTRY WAY, HOUGHTON
Cambridgeshire PE28 2DH....................................01480 494 540
e: info@lemark.co.uk
w: www.lemark.co.uk

Pitstop Marquees
1 HURLEY LANE, HURLEY, ATHERSTONE
Warwickshire CV9 2JJ 01827 872280
e: info@pitstopmarquees.co.uk
w: www.pitstopmarquees.co.uk

Planet Gold Decor
UNIT 4 ROMARSH, FOWLSWICK BUSINESS PARK, , ALLINGTON
Wiltshire SN14 6QE..07747 015 170
e: info@planetgolddecor.co.uk
w: www.planetgolddecor.co.uk or www.

Portable Floormaker
UNIT 4 SYCAMORE ROAD, TRENT LANE INDUSTRIAL ESTATE,
CASTLE DONINGTON
Leicestershire DE74 2NW 01332 814080
e: enquiries@portablefloormaker.co.uk
w: www.portablefloormaker.co.uk

Portable Floors
MORNINGWELL COTTAGE, PIDDLETRENTHIDE, DORCHESTER
Dorset DT2 7QZ 01300 348 726
e: graham@portable-floors.co.uk
w: www.portable-floors.co.uk

Premier UK Events Ltd
UNIT 2, ROOKERY LANE, THURMASTON, LEICESTER
Leicestershire LE4 8AU...1162029953
e: ben@premier-ltd.com
w: premier-event-solutions.com/

Searched It Ltd
UNIT 15 SUITE 8, COOPERAGE GREEN, ROYAL CLARENCE YARD,
WEEVIL LANE, GOSPORT
Hampshire PO12 1AX...0845 604 9952
e: james@enhanse.co.uk
w: www.gosport.com

Sico Europe Ltd
THE LINK PARK, LYMPNE INDUSTRIAL ESTATE, LYMPNE
Kent CT21 4LR..01303 234 000
e: sales@sico-europe.com
w: www.sico-europe.com

D

Signature (Fencing & Flooring) Systems Europe Ltd
UNIT 1, BLACKETT ROAD, BLACKETT ROAD INDUSTRIAL ESTATE, DARLINGTON
Durham DL1 2BJ 01642 744990
e: sales@signaturesystemseurope.co.uk
w: www.signaturesystemseurope.co.uk

Square One
PRODUCTION HOUSE, ENTERPRISE WAY, LEIGHTON BUZZARD
Bedfordshire LU7 4SZ..01525 374078
e: info@squareone.uk.com
w: www.squareone.uk.com

Staging Services Ltd
LEAMORE LANE, BLOXWICH, WALSALL
West Midlands WS2 7BY...01922 405111
e: info@stagingservicesltd.co.uk
w: www.stagingservicesltd.co.uk

The Chillout Furniture Company
RYE FARM, HOLLANDS LANE, HENFIELD,
East Sussex BN5 9QY 0800 881 5229
e: info@completechillout.com
w: www.completechillout.com

True Sound Hire
UNIT 2, MANOR PARK INDUSTRIAL EST, WYNDHAM STREET, ALDERSHOT
Hampshire GU12 4NZ .... 01252 313154 / 01252 313154
e: info@truesoundhire.co.uk
w: www.truesoundhire.co.uk

Digital Agencies

Blue Sky Film & Media
CHELTENHAM FILM STUDIOS, HATHERLEY LANE, ARLE COURT, CHELTENHAM GL51 6PN..01242 506422
e: contact@blueskyuk.com
w: www.blueskyuk.com

BrandFuel Ltd
8TH FLOOR, 22 UPPER GROUND, LONDON
Greater London SE19PD..020 7424 5444
e: hello@brandfuel.co.uk
w: www.brandfuel.co.uk

Decibel Digital
89 WORSHIP ST, LONDON
EC2A 2BF 2073929740
e: opowell@decibeldigital.com
w: https://www.decibeldigital.com/

Digiket
51 SOMESTREET, CAMBRIDGE
Cambridgeshire CB4 3AA...................................0234 567.890.11
e: info@digiket.co.uk
w: www.digiket.co.uk

Digital Satellite Services ltd
17 HIGH STREET, SHEERNESS, KENT
ME12 1NY 1795665977
e: debbie@digitalsatelliteservice.co.uk
w: www.digitalsatelliteservice.co.uk

Distortion Ltd
18 HOLLIDAY ST , BIRMINGHAM
B1 1TS .... 0800 808 5232 / 0121 285 1833
e: jwilliams@distortion.co.uk
w: www.distortion.co.uk/

Ebizpromotion
UNIT 9, FIRST AVENUE , GLOBE PARK , MARLOW
SL7 1YA..01628 823346
e: ebizpromotion@gmail.com
w: www.ebizpromotion.co.uk

Eclipse Communications
71 BARLICH WAY, LODGE PARK, REDDITCH
Worcestershire B98 7JP...01527 522590
e: info@eclipsecomm.com
w: www.eclipsecomm.com

Greenlight Digital
THE VARNISH WORKS, 3 BRAVINGTONS WALK, LONDON
Greater London N1 9AJ...020 7253 7000
e: info@greenlightdigital.com
w: www.greenlightdigital.com

Isa Music
46 ELLIOT STREET, GLASGOW
Glasgow G3 8DZ...0141 248 2266
e: admin@isa-music.com
w: www.isa-music.com

Logicom Sound & Vision
1 PORTLAND DRIVE, WILLEN, MILTON KEYNES
Buckinghamshire MK15 9JW 01908 663848
e: admin@logicom.co.uk
w: www.logicom.co.uk

Lumacoustics Ltd
FOURTH FLOOR, 2-8 SCRUTTON STREET, LONDON
Greater London EC2A 4RT....................................020 7043 2632
e: hello@thisisluma.com
w: www.thisisluma.com

Manamedia
3RD FLOOR, , 152-154 CURTAIN ROAD, LONDON
Greater London EC2A 3AT 0208 962 9652
e: info@manamediauk.com
w: www.manamediagroup.com

Miramedia Ltd
44 NEWTON ROAD, TUNBRIDGE WELLS
Kent TN1 1RU 01892 800136
e: info@miramedia.co.uk
w: www.miramedia.co.uk

D

My Web Presenters
26 BERWICK STREET, SOHO, LONDON
Greater London W1F 8RG.....................................0845 003 8359
w: www.mywebpresenters.com

Netconnexions Ltd
BURGH ROAD INDUSTRIAL ESTATE , MARCONI ROAD, CARLISLE
CUMBRIA
CA2 7NA...01228 210000
e: phillip.harrison@connexionsgroup.co.uk
w: https://www.netconnexions.co.uk

New Media
ELCOT MEWS, ELCOT LANE, MARLBOROUGH
Wiltshire SN8 2AE..1672552352
e: hello@wearenewmedia.co.uk
w: www.wearenewmedia.co.uk/

PAULEY
BLETCHLEY LEYS FARM , WHADDON ROAD, MILTON KEYNES
Buckinghamshire MK17 0EG..................................01908 522532
e: info@pauley.co.uk
w: www.pauley.co.uk

Powerhouse Productions Ltd
395 MONTROSE AVENUE, SLOUGH TRADING ESTATE, SLOUGH
Berkshire SL1 4TJ 01753 696369
e: andy@powerhouseprod.co.uk
w: www.powerhouseprod.co.uk

Rapido3d
UNIT 6, 2 PRINCE EDWARD ROAD, LONDON
Greater London E9 5NN 020 3536 1944
w: www.rapido3d.co.uk

Sightline
DYLAN HOUSE, TOWN END STREET, GODALMING, SURREY
Surrey GU7 1BQ..01483 813 311
e: video@sightline.co.uk
w: www.sightline.co.uk

Sliced Bread Animation
TUDOR HOUSE, 35 GRESSE STREET, LONDON
Greater London W1T 1QY.....................................020 7148 0526
e: info@sbanimation.com
w: www.thebestthingsince.com

The Digital Holdings
UNIT 3A, JUNO WAY, ELIZABETH INDUSTRIAL ESTATE, LONDON
Greater London SE14 5RW....................................0208 691 9191
e: info@thedigitalholdings.com
w: www.thedigitalholdings.com

The UX Agency
12 MELCOMBE PLACE , MARYLEBONE , LONDON
Greater London NW1 6JJ.....................................0207 947 4940
e: enquiries@theuxagency.co.uk
w: www.theuxagency.co.uk

TITIK Security Systems
....7713947977
e: info@titit.uk
w: www.titik.uk

Upstage Communications
STUDIO A, 7 MAIDSTONE BUILDINGS MEWS, 72-76 BOROUGH
HIGH STREET, LONDON
Greater London SE1 1GD 020 7403 6510
e: simon@upstagecommunications.com
w: upstage-engages.com/

Vision Trade Hire Ltd
UNIT E8, EUROGATEWAY, 100 BORRON STREET , PORT DUNDAS
BUSINESS PARK , GLASGOW
G4 9XG .... 01413522240 / 07982418816
e: info@visiontradehire.com
w: www.visiontradehire.com

Vsourz Limited | Web Design London
3RD FLOOR, 100 COLLEGE ROAD, HARROW
Greater London HA1 1BQ 020 3372 5711
e: vsourzlimited@gmail.com
w: www.vsourz.com/

Whynot! Live
60 PARKER STREET, LONDON
Greater London WC2B 5PZ....................................020 3418 8000
e: hello@whynotthinkpeople.com
w: www.whynotthinkpeople.com

Direct Marketing / Mailing Services

Ark-h Handling Ltd
UNIT 1, KENNETH WAY, WILSTEAD INDUSTRIAL PARK, WILSTEAD
MK45 3PD...01234 742777
e: info@arkhgroup.co.uk
w: www.ark-h.co.uk

Bascom-BMS
82 FEEDER ROAD, ATLAS STREET, BRISTOL
Bristol BS2 0HH 0117 977 9900
e: sales@bascom.co.uk
w: www.bascom.co.uk

Bemrose Booth Ltd
STOCKHOLM ROAD, SUTTON FIELDS, HULL
HU7 0XY .... 01482 371398 /
01482 37139
e: sales@advertticket.com
w: www.bemrosebooth.com

Easy Publicity
200 LONDON ROAD, HADLEIGH, BENFLEET
Essex SS7 2PD 01702 427 100
e: enquiries@entertainers.co.uk
w: www.easypublicity.co.uk

D

Impact Distribution
TUSCANY WHARF, 4B ORSMAN ROAD, LONDON
Greater London N1 5QJ 020 7729 5978
e: info@impact.uk.com
w: impactideas.co.uk/

In Association
OAKRIDGE CHAMBERS, 1-3 OAKRIDGE ROAD, BROMLEY
Kent BR1 5QW...0208 697 6976
e: steve@inassociation.co.uk
w: www.inassociation.co.uk

In Your Corner
RIDGEVIEW HOUSE, 99 DERBY ROAD, STANLEY VILLAGE,
HODDESDON, Derbyshire DE7 6EX.......................0115 932 3955
e: info@in-your-corner.co.uk
w: www.in-your-corner.co.uk

Mail Handling International
82 FEEDER ROAD, BRISTOL
Bristol BS2 0TQ 0117 977 6655
e: sales@mhi.co
w: www.mh-international.com

Metromail Ltd
UNIT 6, FOX COVER ENTERPRISE PARK, ADMIRALTY WAY, SEAHAM
Durham SR7 7DN 0191 301 1700
e: enquiries@metromail.co.uk
w: www.metromail.co.uk

PAULEY
BLETCHLEY LEYS FARM , WHADDON ROAD, MILTON KEYNES
Buckinghamshire MK17 0EG..................................01908 522532
e: info@pauley.co.uk
w: www.pauley.co.uk

Photo Snap Marketing
128 CANNON WORKSHOPS, LONDON
Greater London E14 4AS.......................................020 7096 3966
e: info@photosnapmarketing.com
w: www.photosnapmarketing.com

Disabled / Mobility Equipment

ABC Mobility Scooters
8 BIZSPACE BUSINESS PARK, KINGS RD, BIRMINGHAM
West Midlands B11 2AL..0121 605 6927
e: abcmobility@gmail.com
w: www.abcmobility.co.uk

Convenience Company Ltd
INKERSALL GRANGE FARM, NR BILSTHORPE, NEWARK
Nottinghamshire NG22 8TN 07527 547071
e: info@theconco.co.uk
w: www.theconco.co.uk

Hearing and Mobility
182-186 ROBIN HOOD LANE, HALL GREEN, BIRMINGHAM
West Midlands B28 0LG..0121 777 8383
e: chris.morris@hearingandmobility.com
w: www.hearingandmobility.co.uk

Ra'alloy Ramps Ltd
UNIT A3 STAFFORD PARK 15, TELFORD
Shropshire TF3 3BB 01952 291224
e: sales@raalloy.co.uk
w: www.raalloy.co.uk

WM Event Design
19 ST JAMES'S DRIVE, WANDSWORTH COMMON, LONDON
Greater London SW17 7RN 020 3837 4926
e: info@williammoyse.com
w: www.wmeventdesign.com

Disco / Karaoke Equipment

A1 Pro Entertainments
153 LONDON ROAD, EWELL
 KT17 2BT .... 020 8393 3616 / 0800 0187278
e: info@a1proents.com
w: www.a1proents.com

A1 Reliable Discotheques and Karaoke
132 CHASE WAY, LONDON
Greater London N14 5DH....................................0844 334 3954
e: a1disco@gmail.com
w: www.a1reliablediscothequesandkara

All Events Uk
LUTON, CHATHAM
 ME4 5AG 07581 287 705
e: andy@alleventsuk.co.uk
w: www.alleventsuk.co.uk

Avenue Audio
BRIDGE ROAD, PARK GATE, SOUTHAMPTON
Hampshire SO31 7GD 08454 634381
e: mail@avenueaudio.co.uk
w: www.avenueaudio.co.uk

CFM Audio Visual Sound and Lighting Hire
....0843 289 2798
e: info@cfmeventhire.co.uk
w: www.cfmentertainments.co.uk

CMF Event Hire
....0843 289 2798
e: cfmeventhire@aol.com
w: www.cfmeventhire.co.uk

Dizzy Feet Discotheque
32 DELMONT GROVE, STROUD
Gloucestershire GL5 1UN 01453 753366
e: enquiries@dizzyfeet.co.uk
w: www.dizzyfeet.co.uk

East Anglia Leisure
UNIT 4, CIVIC INDUSTRIAL ESTATE, HOMEFIELD ROAD, HAVERHILL
Suffolk CB9 8QP 01440 714204
e: info@ealeisure.co.uk
w: www.ealeisure.co.uk

Elation DJs Ltd
7 RINGHAY ROAD, BRADFORD
West Yorkshire BD4 0TZ.......... 01274 800 460 // 07811 200 293
e: info@elationdjs.co.uk
w: www.elationdjs.co.uk

EPS Hire
34 STANLEY DRIVE, HATFIELD
Hertfordshire AL10 8XX...07973 721329
e: gary@epshire.com
w: www.epshire.com

First Light Ltd
UNIT 9-10 LAKER ROAD, ROCHESTER AIRPORT, INDUSTRIAL
ESTATE, ROCHESTER, Kent ME1 3QX 01634 685500
e: info@firstlight.events
w: www.djcevents.co.uk/

Images Entertainments Store
UNITS 9 & 10 HOUSTON INDUSTRIAL ESTATE, NASMYTH COURT,
LIVINGSTON
West Lothian EH54 5EG 01506 442111
e: sales@images2.co.uk
w: www.images2.co.uk

JDB Events
GATEHOUSE TRADING ESTATE, LICHFIELD RD, BROWNHILLS,
WALSALL
 WS8 6JZ..0121 667 1444
e: info@jdb-events.co.uk
w: www.jdb-events.com

OnStage Professional Discotheques
THE STUDIO, 108 MAYDOWNS ROAD , CHESTFIELD
Kent CT5 3LW...07708 322 421
e: info@onstage-uk.com
w: www.onstage-uk.com

Sheffield PA Hire
THE LION WORKS, BALL ST, SHEFFIELD
South Yorkshire S3 8DB 0114 2789951
e: info@sheffieldpahire.co.uk
w: www.sheffieldpahire.co.uk

Sound 2 Light Hire
.... 07092 316129 // 0845 128 5238
e: info@djequipmenthiredoncaster.co.uk
w: www.djequipmenthiredoncaster.co.u

Sound Stage Systems
77 HIGH ST, NORTHWOLD, THETFORD
Norfolk IP26 5NF...01366 727197
e: soundstagesystems@talk21.com
w: www.soundstagesystems.co.uk/

Spotlight Sound
UNIT 32B, LITTLE BOYTON FARM , BOYTON HALL LANE ,
CHELMSFORD
Essex CM1 4LN 01245 206206
e: info@spotlightsound.co.uk
w: www.spotlightsound.co.uk

Studio 50 Floors
7 PORTAL CLOSE, CHIPPENHAM
Wiltshire SN15 1QJ.................... 01249 661078 / 07713 095975
e: info@studio-50.com
w: www.studio-50.com

VNV Sounds
UNITS 10 AND 10A ASHLEY HOUSE, ASHLEY ROAD, LONDON
Greater London N17 9LZ.......................................0203 021 1370
e: info@vnvlive.co.uk
w: www.vnvsounds.co.uk

Disco Equipment

SilentArena
....0800 122 3314
e: bookings@silentarena.com
w: www.silentarena.com

Sound Of Music Mobile Disco DJ Hire Agency Croydon
....07402 700695
e: soundofmusicdjagency@hotmail.com
w: www.soundofmusicmobiledisco.com

DJ

Sound Of Music Mobile Disco DJ Hire Agency Croydon
....07402 700695
e: soundofmusicdjagency@hotmail.com
w: www.soundofmusicmobiledisco.com

Drapes / Curtains / Blinds

247 Curtains
....0845 4744 247
e: torinewton82@gmail.com
w: www.247curtains.co.uk

Abacus Stagetech
UNIT 9 BROOKLANDS TERRACE , SAYER STREET, HUNTINGDON
CAMBS PE29 3HE .... 01480455780 / 07961 140152
e: abacusstagetech@gmail.com
w: www.abacusstagetech.co.uk

Acre Jean Ltd
UNIT 7 THE KIMBER CENTRE, 54 KIMBER ROAD, LONDON
Greater London SW18 4PP...................................020 8877 3211
e: enquiries@acrejean.com
w: www.acrejean.com

Astra Blinds
18A ALBION STREET, CASTLEFORD
West Yorkshire WF10 1EN 01977 518005
e: astrablinds@btconnect.com
w: www.awnings1.moonfruit.com

D

Back2front
14 MILL LANE, WINGRAVE
HP22 4PL 01296 681222
e: info@back2front.com
w: www.back2front.com

Blackout Ltd
280 WESTERN ROAD, LONDON
Greater London SW19 2QA 020 8687 8400
e: sales@blackout-ltd.com
w: www.blackout-ltd.com

Cameo Curtains
LILYHOLT LODGE, 25A LILYHOLT ROAD, BENWICK, MARCH
Cambridgeshire PE15 0XQ 01354 677796
e: info@cameocurtains.co.uk
w: www.cameocurtains.co.uk

Cover It Up Ltd
UNIT 12 LILFORD BUSINESS CENTRE, 61 LILFORD ROAD,
LONDON
Greater London SE5 9HY.......................0207 326 7900
e: info@cover-it-up.com
w: www.cover-it-up.com

Covers & Linings Ltd
UNIT 10 WOODSIDE ROAD, BOYATT WOOD INDUSTRIAL ESTATE,
EASTLEIGH
Hampshire SO50 4ET.............................02380 623020
e: Sales@eventinteriors.com
w: www.eventinteriors.com

Creative Draping Ltd
100 LONDON ROAD, DUNSTABLE
Bedfordshire LU63EE.............................07966 372 835
e: info@creativedraping.com
w: www.creativedraping.com

Draping Bliss
MAIN BUILDING, OUNDLE MARINA, BARNWELL ROAD, OUNDLE
Cambridgeshire PE8 5PB .... 07792 221 176 / 01832 358160
e: enquiries@drapingbliss.com
w: www.drapingbliss.com

Fabric UK
CARLTON BUSINESS CENTRE, 132 SALTLEY ROAD, SALTLEY,
BIRMINGHAM
West Midlands B7 4TH...........................0121 359 2349
w: www.fabricuk.com

Flat Earth Scenery & Staging Ltd
UNITS A & B, WHITE STREET, BRISTOL
Bristol BS5 0TS....................................0117 954 1102
e: info@flat-earth.co.uk
w: www.flat-earth.co.uk

Four Star Events
UNIT 35 GRASMERE WAY, BLYTH
Northumberland NE24 4RR 7971754904
e: alanfourstarevents@gmail.com
w: www.fourstarevents.co.uk

Georgia Stage Inc.
3765 PEACHTREE CREST DRIVE, DULUTH
 30097..001 770 931 1600
e: info@gastage.com
w: www.gastage.com

Gerriets Great Britain Ltd
18 VERNEY ROAD, LONDON
Greater London SE16 3DH 020 7639 7704
e: general@gerriets.com
w: www.gerriets.co.uk

Gillians Blinds Ltd
2 GATELODGE CLOSE, ROUND SPINNEY, NORTHAMPTON
Northamptonshire NN3 8RJ 0160 4646007
e: info@gilliansblinds.com
w: www.gilliansblinds.com

Hands On Production Services Ltd
79 LOANBANK QUADRANT, GLASGOW
Glasgow G51 3HZ..................................0141 4402005
e: info@hands-on-uk.com
w: www.hands-on-uk.com

Hangman
THE ARTWORKS, SILVERGATE, BLICKLING, NORWICH
Norfolk NR11 6NN 01263 732265
e: info@hangman.co.uk
w: www.hangman.co.uk

House Couturier Ltd
STUDIO 116, 30 RED LION STREET, RICHMOND UPON THAMES
Surrey TW9 1RB 0207 371 9255
e: info@housecouturier.eu
w: www.housecouturier.eu

IBS Group
DUBAI INVESTMENTS PARK - PHASE 2, DUBAI
 P.O. BOX 23566....................................97148847117
e: sales@ibs-group.om
w: www.ibs-group.com

Image Fabrication
UNIT 14 MULBERRY COURT, BOURNE ROAD, CRAYFORD
Kent DA1 4BF 01322 554 455
e: info@imagefabrication.co.uk
w: www.imagefabrication.co.uk

Interior Fx
UNIT 2 MAIZEFIELD, HINCKLEY FIELDS INDUSTRIAL ESTATE ,
HINCKLEY
Leicestershire LE10 1YF 01455 612744
e: info@interiorfx.com
w: www.interiorfx.com

Invision Display Services Ltd
10 HIGH STREET, THAMES DITTON
Surrey KT7 0RY 0208 9729285
e: sales@invisiondisplayservices.co.uk
w: www.invisiondisplayservices.co.uk

J&C Joel Limited (Head Office)
CORPORATION MILL, CORPORATION STREET, SOWERBY BRIDGE,
HALIFAX, Yorkshire HX6 2QQ 01422 833835
e: uksales@jcjoel.com
w: www.jcjoel.com

JD McDougall Ltd
4 MCGRATH ROAD, STRATFORD, LONDON
Greater London E15 4JP 0208 534 2921
e: mail@mcdougall.co.uk
w: www.mcdougall.co.uk

JDB Events
GATEHOUSE TRADING ESTATE, LICHFIELD RD, BROWNHILLS,
WALSALL
WS8 6JZ..0121 667 1444
e: info@jdb-events.co.uk
w: www.jdb-events.com

Leisure Interiors 2000 Ltd
47F BROAD STREET, BANBURY
Oxfordshire OX16 5BT...01295 252551
e: info@leisure-interiors.com
w: www.leisure-interiors.com

Light The Way
UNIT 7 CAVENDISH COURT MILL, WEST STREET, BRADFORD
BD11 1DA..01422 250 819
e: hire@lighttheway.co.uk
w: www.lighttheway.co.uk

Macflex International
MACFLEX HOUSE, HILL FARM, UPPER HEYFORD, NORTHAMPTON
NN7 3NB 01604 833666
e: sales@macflex.com
w: www.macflex.com

Magnet Schultz Ltd
3-4 CAPITAL PARK, OLD WOKING, SURREY
Sussex GU22 9LD 01483 794700
e: sales@magnetschultz.co.uk
w: www.magnetschultz.co.uk

Mille Couleurs London
REGENT STUDIOS, 1 THANE VILLAS, STUDIO 101, ISLINGTON,
LONDON
Greater London N7 7PH 0207 263 3660
e: info@mc-london.com
w: www.mc-london.com

More Production Ltd
103 COVENTRY ROAD, BURBAGE, , HINCKLEY
Leicestershire LE10 2HN..01455 615 746
e: sales@moreproduction.co.uk
w: www.moreproduction.co.uk

Omega Drapes
RIVERSIDE INDUSTRIAL ESTATE, THAMES ROAD, BARKING
Essex IG11 0ND 020 8591 4945
e: contact@omegadrapes.co.uk
w: www.omegadrapes.co.uk

Paramount Blinds Ltd
UNIT 15, SHAFTMOOR IND. ESTATE, SHAFTMOOR LANE, HALL
GREEN. , BIRMINGHAM
 B28 8SP ....08000434240 / 07984 592923
e: sales@paramountblinds.co.uk
w: www.paramountblinds.co.uk

PH Blinds and Curtains Ltd
UNIT 4 COSGROVE BUSINESS PARK, DAISY BANK LANE,
NORTHWICH
Cheshire CW9 6AA...0160 6781953
e: info@phblinds.co.uk
w: www.phblinds.co.uk

Planet Gold Decor
UNIT 4 ROMARSH, FOWLSWICK BUSINESS PARK, , ALLINGTON
Wiltshire SN14 6QE..07747 015 170
e: info@planetgolddecor.co.uk
w: www.planetgolddecor.co.uk or www.

Prompt Side Ltd
14 MULBERRY COURT, BOURNE ROAD, CRAYFORD
Kent DA1 4BF 01322 55 44 55
e: info@promptside.co.uk
w: www.promptside.co.uk

Rex Howard (Drapes) Ltd
UNIT F, TRADING ESTATE ROAD
 NW10 7LU 020 8955 6940
e: rex.howard@hawthorns.uk.com
w: www.rex-howard.co.uk

S + H Technical Support Ltd
MULLACOTT INDUSTRIAL ESTATE, STARCLOTH WAY, ILFRACOMBE
Devon EX34 8PL 01271 866832
e: shtsg@aol.com
w: www.starcloth.co.uk

Showtex
EVERAERTSSTRAAT 69, ANTWERP
 2060...01706 819746
e: suzanne@showtex.com
w: www.showtex.com

Spot-on Theatre Services Ltd
KEIGHLEY BUSINESS CENTRE, UNIT F2B, SOUTH STREET,
KEIGHLEY, West Yorkshire BD21 1SY 01535 691939
e: sales@spot-on.org.uk
w: www.spot-on.org.uk

Stagecraft UK
ST QUENTIN GATE, TELFORD
Shropshire TF3 4JH 01952 281 600
e: sales@stagecraftuk.com
w: www.stagecraftuk.com

Staging Services Ltd
LEAMORE LANE, BLOXWICH, WALSALL
West Midlands WS2 7BY 01922 405111
e: info@stagingservicesltd.co.uk
w: www.stagingservicesltd.co.uk

D

Studio 50 Floors
7 PORTAL CLOSE, CHIPPENHAM
Wiltshire SN15 1QJ......................01249 661078 / 07713 095975
e: info@studio-50.com
w: www.studio-50.com

Tildenet Ltd
JOURNAL HOUSE, HARTCLIFFE WAY
Bristol BS3 5RJ...0117 966 968
e: info@tildenet.co.uk
w: www.tildenet.co.uk

Triple E Ltd
16 AIRPORT INDUSTRIAL ESTATE, MAIN ROAD, BIGGIN HILL
Kent TN16 3BW 01959 570 333
e: info@3-eee.com
w: www.3-eee.com

Universal Stars Incorporated Ltd
BROAD OAK, WHITEWELL, REDBROOK MEALOR, WHITCHURCH
 SY13 3AQ 01948 780 110
e: info@universalstars.co.uk
w: www.universalstars.co.uk

Varia Textiles Ltd
197 KINGS ROAD, KINGSTON-UPON-THAMES
Greater London KT2 5HJ................................. +44 20 8549 8590
e: varia@variatextile.co.uk
w: www.varia-uk.com

Whaleys Bradford Ltd
HARRIS COURT, GREAT HORTON, BRADFORD
West Yorkshire BD7 4EQ 01274 576718
w: www.whaleys.co.uk

Driving / Motor Racing Days

Chris Birkbeck Corporate Entertainment
LOW FARM, MANX LODGE, BROTTON, SALTBURN
North Yorkshire TS12 2QX 01287 677512
e: sales@gorallyschool.co.uk
w: www.gorallyschool.co.uk

Speedkarting Warrington Uk
UNIT 2, BANK QUAY TRADING ESTATE, WARRINGTON
Cheshire WA1 1PJ 01925 415114
e: sales@speedkarting.co.uk
w: www.speedkarting.co.uk

The Racing Bug Ltd
29 LATIMER CLOSE, LITTLE CHALFONT
Buckinghamshire HP6 6QS 07767 870191
e: info@theracingbug.co.uk
w: www.theracingbug.co.uk

E

Editing / Cutting

422.tv Glasgow
DALINTOBER HALL, 40 DALINTOBER STREET, GLASGOW
G5 8NW 0141 420 0900
e: sharon.fullarton@422tv.co.uk
w: www.422.tv

Blank Tape Studios
54 BROMWICH ROAD, SHEFFIELD
South Yorkshire S8 0GG 0752 842 8925
e: blanktape@blueyonder.co.uk
w: www.blanktapestudios.co.uk

Cavalier Studios Ltd
280 WELLINGTON ROAD SOUTH, STOCKPORT
Cheshire SK2 6ND 0161 480 6073
e: hello@cavalierstudios.co.uk
w: www.cavalierstudios.co.uk

Dan Productions
.... 07824 558 858 / 01772 451350
e: dan@danproductions.co.uk
w: www.danproductions.co.uk

Darkside Studios
40 HOLBORN VIADUCT, LONDON
Greater London EC1N 2PB 020 7148 1500
e: sayhello@darksidestudios.uk
w: www.darksidestudios.uk

DBI Communication
21 CONGREVE CLOSE, WARWICK
West Midlands CV34 5RQ 01926 497695
e: information@dbicom.com
w: www.dbicom.com

Finishing Post Creative Ltd
GILTBROOK STUDIOS, 10, GILTWAY, NOTTINGHAM
NG16 2GN 0115 945 8800
w: www.finishing-post.co.uk

Front Element Camera Services
2 BARRICANE, ST JOHNS, WOKING
GU21 7RB.................... 01483 856202 / 07973 194810
e: mail@jeremyirving.tv
w: www.jeremyirving.tv

Ice Productions Ltd
THE MAIL BOX, 52 BLUCHER STREET, BIRMINGHAM
West Midlands B1 1QU 0121 288 4864
e: birmingham@ice-productions.com
w: www.ice-productions.com

JK Advertising Ltd
730 PERSHORE ROAD, SELLY PARK, BIRMINGHAM
West Midlands B29 7NJ......................0121 472 1000
e: info@jkadvertising.co.uk
w: www.jkadvertising.co.uk

Off The Wall
21A ASKEW ROAD, SHEPHERDS BUSH, LONDON
Greater London W12 9DP....................020 8740 5353
e: john@offthewall.co.uk
w: www.offthewall.co.uk

Peak White
1 LATIMER ROAD, TEDDINGTON
TW11 8QA 0845 874 1922
w: www.peakwhite.com

Pink Pigeon Post Production
1A POLAND STREET, SOHO, LONDON
Greater London W1F 8PR 020 7439 3266
e: info@pinkpigeon.net
w: www.pinkpigeon.net

Planet Television London
FELTHAM AVENUE,, HAMPTON COURT
KT8 9BJ................................... 020 8974 6050 / 079122 86658
e: media@planet-television.com
w: www.planet-television.com

Quadrillion TV
17 BALVERNIE GROVE, LONDON
Greater London SW18 5RR 01628 487522
e: enqs@quadrillion.tv
w: www.quadrillion.tv

re:fine
316-318 LATIMER ROAD, LONDON
Greater London W10 6QN 020 8962 2600
e: info@refine-group.com
w: www.refine-group.com

Sarner Ltd
5 PRINCESS MEWS, HORRACE ROAD, KINGSTON UPON THAMES
Greater London KT1 2SZ.....................020 8481 0600
e: info@sarner.com
w: www.sarner.com

Shushstudio
ROCKVILLE, 10 PLAINES CLOSE, CHIPPENHAM , SLOUGH
Berkshire SL1 5TY 01753 537 206
e: studio@shushstudio.com
w: www.shushstudio.com

Spool
ANTENNA MEDIA CENTRE, BECK STREET, NOTTINGHAM
Nottinghamshire NG1 1EQ 0115 859 9806
e: hello@spool.uk.com
w: www.spool.uk.com

SussedFilms
14 MEADWAY, FRIMLEY, CAMBERLEY
Surrey GU16 8TQ...............................01276 504629
e: studio@timsmith.co.uk
w: www.sussedfilms.co.uk

E

Take One Business Communications Ltd
MEDIA HOUSE, 12 MANOR COURTYARD, HUGHENDEN AVENUE,
HIGH WYCOMBE
Buckinghamshire HP13 5RE .... +44 (0) 1494 898 919
e: info@takeonetv.com
w: www.takeonetv.com

The Exchange Mastering Studios
42 BRUGES PLACE, RANDOLPH STREET, CAMDEN
Greater London NW1 0TL.........................0044 (0)208 399 0718
e: studio@exchangemastering.co.uk
w: www.exchangemastering.co.uk

Timbuktu Productions
16 INGESTRE PLACE, LONDON
Greater London W1F 0JJ.......... 07590 399774 // (0)7881 663317
e: info@timbuktuproductions.co.uk
w: www.timbuktuproductions.co.uk

WaveFX - Video, Events & Digital Media
THE STUDIO - 19 EDWARD STREET, CAMBRIDGE
Cambridgeshire CB1 2LS.......................................01223 505600
e: studio@wavefx.co.uk
w: www.wavefx.co.uk

Education

Proquest Information & Learning Ltd
THE QUORUM, BARNWELL DR, CAMBRIDGE
Cambridgeshire CB5 8SW....................................01223 215512
e: julia.garman@proquest.com
w: www.proquest.com

Education / Training

Access To Music Ltd
68 HEATH MILL LANE, DIGBETH, BIRMINGHAM
West Midlands B9 4AR..0330 123 3155
e: atm.birmingham@accesstomusic.ac.uk
w: www.accesstomusic.co.uk

Arts University Bournemouth
WALLISDOWN, POOLE
Dorset BH12 5HH..01202 533011
e: hello@aub.ac.uk
w: www.aub.ac.uk

Association For Conferences & Events
MARSH WAY , RAINHAM
Essex RM13 8EU..0208 596 5458
e: ace@ace-international.org
w: www.ace-international.co.uk

BBC Academy
ROOM A16, BBC WOOD NORTON, EVESHAM
Worcestershire WR11 4YB 0370 010 0264
e: bbcacademy@bbc.co.uk
w: www.bbcacademy.com

Beyond The Blue Training & Consultancy
92 VEGAL CRESCENT, ENGLEFIELD GREEN, ENGLEFIELD GREEN
Surrey TW20 0QF.................... 01784 434 392 / 0800 066 55 24
e: info@btbl.co.uk
w: www.btbl.co.uk

Brit Performing Arts & Technology School
60 THE CRESCENT, CROYDON, LONDON
Greater London CR0 2HN.....................................020 8665 5242
e: info@brit.croydon.sch.uk
w: www.brit.croydon.sch.uk

British Universities Film & Video Council
77 WELLS STREET, LONDON
Greater London W1T 3QJ.....................................020 7393 1500
e: ask@bufvc.ac.uk
w: www.bufvc.ac.uk

Catalyst Therapy & Training Company
DAVENPORT HOUSE, 16 PEPPER STREET, GLENGALL BRIDGE,
CANARY WHARF , LONDON
 E14 9RP .... 01708781927 / 07970 784 609 / 07973 864
e: info@catalysttnt.co.uk
w: www.catalysttnt.co.uk

Chorley Yamaha Bradley Rider Training
EAVES LANE, CHORLEY
Lancashire PR6...1257269066
e: info@bradleyridertraining.co.uk
w: www.bradleyridertraining.co.uk

Chris Elgood Associates Ltd
32 WEST STREET, TADLEY
Hampshire RG26 3SX 0118 982 1115
e: info@chris-elgood.co.uk
w: www.chris-elgood.co.uk

City Acting Ltd
CLAREMONT PROJECT, 24-27 WHITE LION STREET, LONDON
 N1 9PD...0207 193 68 93
e: sophie@cityacting.co.uk
w: www.cityacting.co.uk

Club Training
....7939477189
e: nick.Lawrence@fitnessagents.co.uk
w: www.club-training.com/

Court Theatre Training Company
THE COURTYARD, BOWLING GREEN WALK, 40 PITFIELD STREET,
LONDON
Greater London N1 6EU 020 7729 2202
e: info@thecourtyard.org.uk
w: www.thecourtyard.org.uk

D&AD
BRITANNIA HOUSE, 96 HANBURY ST, , LONDON
Greater London E1 5JL 020 7840 1111
e: contact@dandad.org
w: www.dandad.org

E

E

Dance Base
14-16 GRASSMARKET, EDINBURGH
Edinburgh EH1 2JU...0131 225 5525
e: dance@dancebase.co.uk
w: www.dancebase.co.uk

De-Risk ltd
PO BOX 504, FARNHAM
Surrey GU9 1AF .... 01252734222 / 07866 69981
e: contact@scscleaningservices.com
w: www.de-risk.com

Drama Studio London
GRANGE COURT, 1 GRANGE ROAD, EALING, LONDON
Greater London W5 5QN 020 8579 3897
e: admin@dramastudiolondon.co.uk
w: www.dramastudiolondon.co.uk

Event Management Training Ltd
3RD FLOOR , 207 REGENT STREET LONDON, LONDON
Greater London W1B 3HH 020 8144 9716
e: info@eventtr.co.uk
w: www.eventtr.co.uk

Fast Pass Ltd
UNIT 22 GRANGE WAY, COLCHESTER
Essex CO2 8HF 01206 793399
e: info@fastpassmot.co.uk
w: www.atatraining.co.uk

Guildford School Of Acting
PERIMETER RD, GUILDFORD
Surrey GU2 7JL...1483 682222
e: admissions@surrey.ac.uk
w: www.gsauk.org

Guitar lessons Camberley
30 SILVER HILL   , COLLEGE TOWN, SANDHURST
Berkshire GU47 0QS 7962101386
e: guitarlessonssandhurst@gmail.com
w: www.guitarlessonscamberley.co.uk

Helen O'Grady Drama Academy
NORTH SIDE, VALE, GUERNSEY
 GY3 5TX 01481 200250
e: croydon@helenogrady.co.uk
w: www.helenogrady.co.uk

ierek
....1069869241
e: ahmed.sami@ierek.com
w: https://www.ierek.com/

Jason M Thorne
Ì»¿ JASON M THORNE 32 BARNBROOK RD, KNOWLE SOLIHULL
West Midlands B93 9PW...0771 258 8150
e: info@jasonmthorne.co.uk
w: www.jasonmthorne.co.uk

Leeds Beckett University
CITY CAMPUS, LEEDS
West Yorkshire LS1 3HE...0113 812 0000
e: admissionenquiries@leedsbeckett.ac.uk
w: www.leedsbeckett.ac.uk/

Lets Go Drive
4 KATHERINE CLOSE , CHARFIELD WOTTON UNDER EDGE SOUTH
Gloucestershire GL12 8TU 07971 198 008
e: steve@letsgodrive.com
w: www.letsgodrive.com

Live Audio Engineering Ltd
SCALA, 275 PENTONVILLE ROAD, KINGS CROSS, LONDON
Greater London N1 9NL 0207 833 2022
e: livesoundcourses@gmail.com
w: www.livesoundcourses.com

London Studio Centre
5 NETHER STREET, TALLY HO CORNER, NORTH FINCHLEY, LONDON
Greater London N12 0GA 020 7837 7741
e: info@londonstudiocentre.org
w: londonstudiocentre.org

Lumie's Magicorium Of Expert Spiritual Healing
UNIT 107, 77 BEAK STREET, LONDON
 W1F 9DB 07818 273 914
e: eclat@lumie.me.uk
w: www.lumie.me.uk

Mountview Academy Of Theatre Arts
CLARENDON ROAD, LONDON
Greater London N22 6XF.......................................020 8881 2201
e: enquiries@mountview.org.uk
w: www.mountview.org.uk

National Film and Television School
BEACONSFIELD STUDIOS, STATION ROAD, BEACONSFIELD
Buckinghamshire HP9 1LG 01494 671234
e: info@nfts.co.uk
w: www.nfts.co.uk

Nordoff-Robbins Music Therapy
2 LISSENDEN GARDENS, LONDON
Greater London NW5 1PQ 0207 267 4496
e: reception@nordoff-robbins.org.uk
w: www.nordoff-robbins.org.uk

Oasys Training & Safety Services Ltd
OFFICE 2, GRESWOLDE HOUSE, 197B STATION ROAD, KNOWLE, SOLIHULL
West Midlands B93 0PU...0845 004 1058
e: info@oasystss.co.uk
w: www.oasystss.co.uk

Performers College
CORRINGHAM, STANFORD-LE-HOPE
Essex SS17 8JS...01375 672053
e: lesley@performerscollege.co.uk
w: www.performerscollege.co.uk

Peterborough Regional College
PARK CRESCENT, PETERBOROUGH
Cambridgeshire PE1 4DZ 0845 8728722
e: info@peterborough.ac.uk
w: www.peterborough.ac.uk

Positive Impact
FOURWAYS HOUSE, 57 HILTON STREET, MANCHESTER
Greater Manchester M1 2EJ 0161 2735107
e: info@positive-impact-events.com
w: positiveimpactevents.co.uk

Qualitation
3 FORGE HOUSE, SUMMERLEYS ROAD, PRINCES RISBOROUGH
Buckinghamshire HP27 9DT 7900896975
e: carl.Kruger@qualitation.co.uk
w: www.qualitation.co.uk

Radcliffe Cardiology
UNIT F, FIRST FLOOR, BOURNE PARK, BOURNE END
Buckinghamshire SL8 5AS................................. 0207 193 5381 /
0207 097 1555

e: ecginterpretation2016@gmail.com
w: www.radcliffecardiology.com/conte

Royal Academy Of Dance
36 BATTERSEA SQUARE, LONDON
Greater London SW11 3RA....................................020 7326 8000
e: info@rad.org.uk
w: www.rad.org.uk

Royal Northern College Of Music Library
THE LIBRARY , 124 OXFORD ROAD, MANCHESTER
Greater Manchester M13 9RD..............................0161 907 5200
e: info@rncm.ac.uk
w: www.rncm.ac.uk

Royal School For The Blind (RNIB)
105 JUDD STREET, , LONDON
Greater London WC1h 9NE....................................0845 766 9999
e: helpline@rnib.org.uk
w: www.rnib.org.uk

S.E. Medical Ltd
....0203 286 9993
e: jono@semedical.co.uk
w: www.semedical.co.uk

Salvus Consulting Ltd
SAFETY UNIT 60 BRIMMERS HILL, WIDMER END, HIGH WYCOMBE
Buckinghamshire HP15 6NP 01494 716954
e: info@salvus-consulting.co.uk
w: www.salvus-consulting.co.uk

Showsec Training & Development Centre
REGENT HOUSE, 16 WEST WALK, LEICESTER
Leicestershire LE1 7NA...0116 204 3333
e: joseph.milner@showsec.co.uk
w: www.showsec.co.uk

Somerset Training
.... 01823 431557 // 07843 436895
e: info@somersettraining.co.uk
w: www.somersettraining.co.uk

Stix School Of Rhythm
11 KINGS ARMS YARD, AMPTHILL, BEDFORD
Bedfordshire MK45 2QH 62 878 62135894
e: info@stix.tv
w: www.stixmusic.com

Summit Corporate Training Limited
SUMMIT HOUSE, 10 CHATSWORTH AVENUE, LONDON
Greater London NW4 1HT .... 020 8202 9876 // 7710 146402
e: sales@summit-training.co.uk
w: www.summit-training.co.uk

Sustainable Events
2ND FLOOR, FOURWAYS HOUSE, 57 HILTON STREET,
MANCHESTER
Greater Manchester M1 2EJ 0161 2735107
e: admin@sustainableeventsltd.com
w: www.sustainableeventsltd.com

Symbiotic Security
6 LEWIS HOUSE, 3 SCHOOL ROAD, LONDON
Greater London NW10 6TD 020 8539 4969
e: info@symbiosec.co.uk
w: www.symbiosec.co.uk

The British Gospel Arts
BROOKDALE HOUSE , 75 BROOKDALE RD, WALTHAMSTOW,
LONDON
Greater London E17 6QH 020 8509 7222
e: info@britishgospelarts.com
w: www.britishgospelarts.com

The Pilates Centre
STUDIO 2, SPIRITUAL WARRIOR MARTIAL ARTS CENTRE , 518-
520 FOLESHILL ROAD , COVENTRY
 CV6 5HP 07866 427530
e: sarah@thepilatescentre.org
w: www.thepilatescentre.org

The Recording Workshop
UNIT 10 BUSPACE STUDIOS, CONLAN STREET
Greater London W10 5AP......................................020 8968 8222
w: www.therecordingworkshop.co.uk

The University For The Creative Arts
FARNHAM CAMPUS, FALKNER ROAD, FARNHAM
Surrey GU9 7DS..01252 722441
e: enquiries@ucreative.ac.uk
w: www.uca.ac.uk/

Theatretrain
PO BOX 10343, EPPING
Essex CM16 9DG..01327 300498
e: admin@theatretrain.co.uk
w: www.theatretrain.co.uk

E

ThinkersLive
15-19 BAKERS ROW, LONDON
Greater London EC1R 3DG 020 3967 5716
w: www.thinkerslive.com

Truck School Ltd
4 ONSLOW ROAD, NEW BRIGHTON , WALLASEY, WIRRAL
Merseyside CH45 5AN 0151 637 3060
info@truck-school.co.uk
www.truck-school.co.uk

Unique Solutions
2 MOUNT PLEASANT, SCARTHIN, CROMFORD, MATLOCK
Derbyshire DE4 3QF...01629 691 691
e: info@uniquesolutions.co.uk
w: www.uniquesolutions.co.uk

University Of Huddersfield
SCHOOL OF COMPUTING AND ENGINEERING, QUEENSGATE,
HUDDERSFIELD
West Yorkshire HD1 3DH 01484 422288
e: admissionsandrecords@hud.ac.uk
w: www.hud.ac.uk

Versatile Venues Ltd
WIRELESS HOUSE, WIRELESS HILL, SOUTH LUFFENHAM
Rutland LE15 8NF .... 08000 147 338 / 01780 720 217
e: info@versatilevenues.co.uk
w: www.versatilevenues.co.uk

World Class Teachers Ltd
THE GATEHOUSE , KEW BRIDGE WEST, KEW BRIDGE ROAD,
LONDON
Bedfordshire TW8 0EF .... +44 (0) 208 579 4501
e: Corinne@worldclassteachers.co.uk
w: www.worldclassteachers.co.uk

York University Student Union
SU BUILDING, NEWTON WAY, HESLINGTON, YORK
North Yorkshire YO10 5DD 01904 323724
e: reception@yusu.org
w: www.yusu.org

Electrical Services

Fourth Generation
LUTON
Bedfordshire 02084 502 943
e: laura@fourthgenerationltd.com
w: www.fourthgenerationltd.com

Emergency Services / Equipment

Ambu-kare (uk) Ltd
2 WESTMINSTER PLACE, EMPSON ROAD, PETERBOROUGH
Cambridgeshire PE1 5SY 01733 560972
e: control@ambukare.co.uk
w: www.ambukare.co.uk

Ambulance & Medical Solutions Ltd
....01422 401000
e: info@ambmed.co.uk
w: www.ambmed.co.uk

Arley Medical Services
UNIT 5A ARLEY INDUSTRIAL ESTATE, COLLIERS WAY, ARLEY
Warwickshire CV7 8HN 01676 937 199
e: info@arleymedicalservices.co.uk
w: www.arleymedicalservices.co.uk

Bells & Two-Tones Ltd
THE HOMESTEAD UNIT 14 PARK LANE CHARVIL READING
BERKSHIRE RG10 9TR MAIN ADMIN BUILDING PINEWOOD
STUDIOS, PINEWOOD ROAD, IVER
Buckinghamshire SL0 0NH .... 01753785658 / 07773357660
e: enquiries@bellsandtwotones.co.uk
w: www.bellsandtwotones.co.uk

Criticare UK Ambulance Service
13 THE CRESCENT, MARCHWOOD
Hampshire SO40 4WSi»¿ 0844 351 0684
e: info@criticareuk.net
w: www.criticareuk.net

Dulais Valley Independent Ambulance Services
82 CHURCH ROAD, SEVEN SISTERS, NEATH
SA10 8DT 01639 700050
e: keith@DVIAS.co.uk
w: www.dvias.co.uk

ERS Medical
HETTON COURT, THE OVAL , LEEDS
West Yorkshire LS10 2AT 0333 240 4999
e: info@ersmedical.co.uk
w: www.ersmedical.co.uk

Event Fire & Rescue Services
60 HAYCROFT DRIVE , GLOUCESTER
GL4 6XX 07989 815 619
e: info@eventfire.co.uk
w: www.eventfire.co.uk

ExtinguisHire
5 MORLEY COURT , MORLEY WAY WOODSTON, PETERBOROUGH
Cambridgeshire PE2 7BW 01733 459169
e: gary@extinguishire.co.uk
w: www.extinguishire.co.uk

Gables Flameretarding
THE STRAW BARN, SCHOOL LANE, CROPREDY, BANBURY, OXON
 OX17 1PX 01295 750708
e: sales@gablesflameretarding.co.uk
w: www.gablesflameretarding.co.uk

Griffin Fire
BIRKBECK STREET, BETHNAL GREEN, LONDON
Greater London E2 6JY 020 7251 9379
e: customer.services@griffinfire.co.uk
w: www.griffinfire.co.uk

Hatt Medics
PO BOX 5157, BRIGHTON
East Sussex BN50 9TW...01273 358 359
e: adventures@thehatt.co.uk
w: www.thehatt.co.uk/medics

Immediate Care Medical
SUITE 108, 69 STEWARD STREET, BIRMINGHAM
West Midlands B18 7AF.......................................0121 200 3086
e: office@immediatecaremedical.co.uk
w: www.immediatecaremedical.co.uk

Location Medical Services
THE MEDICAL CENTRE, SHEPPERTON STUDIOS, STUDIOS ROAD,
SHEPPERTON
Surrey TW17 0QD 0870 750 9898
e: mail@locationmedical.com
w: www.locationmedical.com

Mediskills
340 STOCKPORT ROAD, GEE CROSS, HYDE
Cheshire SK14 5RY...0161 368 5508
e: info@mediskills-uk.com
w: www.mediskills-uk.com

Midland Fire Protection Service
UNIT 6 BAYTON WAY, EXHALL, COVENTRY
West Midlands CV7 9ER.......................................02476 367766
e: info@midlandfire.co.uk
w: www.midlandfire.co.uk

Outdoor Medical Solutions Ltd
 TETBURY MOTOR CENTRE,, TETBURY INDUSTRIAL ESTATE,
CIRENCESTER RD, TETBURY
Gloucestershire GL8 8E.......................................01291 440299
e: info@outdoormedicalsolutions.co.uk
w: www.outdoormedicalsolutions.co.uk

ProMedical 2002
38 WOODVILLE ROAD, HARTSHORNE, SWADLINCOTE
Derbyshire DE11 7ET..01283 552232
e: rob@promedical2002.com
w: www.promedical2002.com/

The Mobile Sink Company
THE MOBILE SINK COMPANY LTD , UNIT B6 187 PARK LANE ,
CASTLE VALE , BIRMINGHAM
West Midlands B35 6AN 0121 747 1179
e: info@mobilesink.com
w: www.mobilesink.com

Wallace Cameron Group
26 NETHERHALL ROAD, NETHERTON INDUSTRIAL ESTATE,
WISHAW
Lanarkshire ML2 0JG..01698 354600
e: sales@wallacecameron.com
w: www.wallacecameron.com

Entertainment

Electric Cabaret
107 HIGH ST, BRACKLEY
 NN13 7BN 07714 089 763
e: info@electriccabaret.co.uk
w: www.electriccabaret.co.uk

Gamewagon Ltd
113 - 115 OYSTER LANE, BYFLEET
 KT14 7JZ..0845 319 4263
e: admin@gamewagon.co.uk
w: www.gamewagon.info

Team Building Solutions
UNIT 7, AMPRESS LANE, LYMINGTON ENTERPRISE CENTRE,
LYMINGTON
Hampshire SO41 8LZ...0845 121 1194
e: info@teambuildingsolutions.co.uk
w: www.teambuildingsolutions.co.uk

The Jammy Showgirls
CENTURY HOUSE SOUTH, NORTH STATION ROAD, COLCHESTER
Essex CO1 1RE 07796 138884
e: anthony@jammyshowsandproductions.co.uk
w: www.jammyshowsandproductions.co.u

The Wheelie Good Party Company
....0845 0451076
e: partyhq@wheeliegoodparty.co.uk
w: www.wheeliegoodparty.co.uk

Event Crew Services

Complete Event Crew
WROXTON BUSINESS PARK, BRAGBOROUGH FARM, WELTON ROA,
BRAUNSTON, DAVENTRY
Northamptonshire NN11 7JG .... 0330 221 0299 / 07795 528055
e: jobs@completeeventcrew
w: www.completeeventcrew.co.uk

E

E

BLOK N MESH
EVENTS

✓ Living Hoarding, New Panels and Barriers

✓ Best Prices Guaranteed

✓ Depots Nationwide

Tel: 0870 950 5744   Email: events@bloknmesh.com

Event Fencing

Blok 'n' Mesh
UNIT 1, BEECH HILL INDUSTRIAL PARK, HAMMOND ROAD,
KNOWSLEY INDUSTRIAL PARK, LIVERPOOL
Merseyside L33 7UL 01823 348 123
e: simonmn@bloknmesh.com
w: www.bloknmesh.com

Event Filming

5th Dimension Graphics
TURNER STREET, NORTHAMPTON
Northamptonshire NN1 4JJ........ 0208 123 8884 / 01604 289779
e: info@5dg.org
w: www.5dg.org

A2Z Film Production
13TH FLOOR, 2 FAWEKAH STREET, MOHANDESSIAN,
CAIRO, EGYPT 11234 ....0020 1 2214 4557
e: robsz@leapfrog.com.eg
w: www.a2z.com.eg

adi.tv
PITTMAN COURT, PITTMAN WAY, FULWOOD, PRESTON
Lancashire PR2 9ZG 01772 708 200
e: info@adi.tv
w: www.adi.tv

Amatis Films Ltd
21 MEARE CLOSE, TADWORTH
Surrey KT20 5RZ 02034 189742
e: info@amatis.co.uk
w: www.amatis.co.uk

Ants Productions
....01332 230281
e: ants-productions@hotmail.co.uk
w: www.ants-productions.co.uk

Appliqué Films
.... 01189 019099 // 07876254910
w: www.appliquefilms.co.uk

AV Joint Resource
CORNER HOUSE, 114 WINDMILL STREET, MACCLESFIELD
Cheshire SK11 7LB.................01625 61 50 90 - 01253 85 12 02
e: hello@avjr.eu
w: www.avjointresource.com

Captive8 Media Video Production
26 WINTNEY STREET, FLEET
Hampshire GU51 1AN 0845 834 0250
e: enquiries@captive8media.com
w: www.captive8media.com

Conference Engineering
.... +44 (0)1625 426916
e: hello@conferenceengineering.co.uk
w: www.conferenceengineering.co.uk

EventStreaming TV
STUDIO 24-25, SIGNET COURT, SWANN ROAD , CAMBRIDGE
Cambridgeshire CB5 8LA..01223 855669
e: hello@eventstreaming.tv
w: www.eventstreaming.tv

Fast Lane Entertainment
UNIT 8 -10, GROUND FLOOR, 21 BONNY STREET, LONDON
Greater London NW1 9PE.....................................07974 171 862
e: info@fast-lane.tv
w: fastlaneproductions.tv/

Firehouse Productions Ltd
90 COWCROSS STREET, LONDON
Greater London EC1M 6BH 020 7250 0593
e: hello@firehouse.co.uk
w: www.firehouse.co.uk

Fourth Wall Productions
UNIT 6, ST. JOHN'S BUSINESS PARK, LUTTERWORTH
Leicestershire LE17 4HB.......................................0845 340 0179
w: www.fourthwallproductions.co.uk

ICTHUS Group
OFFICE 2, HOMESTEAD FARM, NORTH HOUGHTON, STOCKBRIDGE
Hampshire SO20 6LG 01264 810356
e: info@icthusgroup.co.uk
w: www.icthusgroup.co.uk

Luckings Screen Services
PINEWOOD STUDIOS, SUITE C-42, IVER HEATH
 SL0 0NL 01753 639872
e: vic.minay@luckings.co.uk
w: www.luckings.co.uk

Maximus Media
INTERNATIONAL HOUSE, SOUTHAMPTON INTERNATIONAL
BUSINESS PARK, SOUTHAMPTON
Hampshire SO18 2RZ 023 8084 8976
e: info@maximusmedia.co.uk
w: www.maximusmedia.co.uk

Offslip
FLAT 4 OAKVIEW APARTMENT STUDIOS, 12 BENHILL ROAD,
LONDON
Greater London SM1 3RL.......................................07912 091979
e: mail@offslip.co.uk
w: www.offslip.co.uk

Photoreverie
27 AVINGTON, GREAT HOLM, MILTON KEYNES
Buckinghamshire MK8 9DG 08445 888333
e: enquiries@photoreverie.com
w: www.photoreverie-event-photograph

Present Communications Ltd
ZEAL HOUSE, 8 DEER PARK ROAD, WIMBLEDON, LONDON
Greater London SW19 3UU 0208 770 0655
e: office@presentcommunications.com
w: www.presentcommunications.com

Rogue Robot Visual Industries
THE TOWN HALL, ST. GEORGE'S ST., HEBDEN BRIDGE
West Yorkshire HX7 7BY..01422 728502
e: contact@roguerobot.co.uk
w: www.roguerobot.co.uk

Satstream
8, BRAMLEY COURT, HEREFORD
Herefordshire HR4 0SB 0844 8008785
e: info@satstream.co.uk
w: www.satstream.co.uk

Saturday Sunday Productions
29 GLOUCESTER PLACE, LONDON
Greater London W1U 8HX......................................01764 679 573
e: amanda@saturdaysunday.co.uk
w: www.saturdaysunday.co.uk

stream7
THE STUDIO, 36 SEAGRAVE ROAD, SHEFFIELD
South Yorkshire S12 2JS.......................................01143 605 060
e: hello@stream7.co.uk
w: www.stream7.co.uk

Studio Megastar
UNIT 1.7 & 1.8, THE ARCHES INDUSTRIAL ESTATE, COVENTRY
West Midlands CV1 3JQ 02476 712 152
e: info@studiomegastar.co.uk
w: www.studiomegastar.co.uk

Surrey Video
51 MALLARD ROAD, CROYDON
Greater London CR2 8PX.......................................0203 252 2055
e: info@surreyvideo.co.uk
w: www.surreyvideo.co.uk

Take-1 Productions
PO BOX 6010, CHELMSFORD
Essex CM1 2FT...01245 614161
e: info@take1.co.uk
w: www.take1.co.uk

Urban Entertainment
UNIT 516, THE WORKSTATION, 15 PATERNOSTER ROW,
SHEFFIELD
South Yorkshire S1 2BX .... 01142 210295 / 07916 161053
e: info@urbanentertainment.org.uk
w: www.urbanentertainment.org.uk

Video Enterprises
12 BARBERS WOOD ROAD, BOOKER, HIGH WYCOMBE
Buckinghamshire HP12 4EP...................................01494 534144
e: videoenterprises@ntlworld.com
w: www.videoenterprises.co.uk

E

E

Vision Events (Edinburgh)
16 DRYDEN ROAD, BILSTON GLEN INDUSTRIAL ESTATE, LOANHEAD
Edinburgh EH20 9LZ 0131 334 3324
e: edinburgh@visionevents.co.uk
w: www.visionevents.co.uk

Visionworks Television Ltd
56 DONEGALL PASS
BT7 1BU 028 9024 1241
e: hello@visionworks.co.uk
w: www.visionworks.co.uk

WaveFX - Video, Events & Digital Media
THE STUDIO - 19 EDWARD STREET, CAMBRIDGE
Cambridgeshire CB1 2LS 01223 505600
e: studio@wavefx.co.uk
w: www.wavefx.co.uk

Webcastmyevent.co.uk
ZEAL HOUSE, 8 DEER PARK ROAD, WIMBLEDON, LONDON
SW19 3UU 020 8770 0655
e: kieron@webcastmyevent.co.uk
w: www.webcastmyevent.co.uk

Zest4.tv Ltd
UNIT 3, BROOKLANDS CLOSE, SUNBURY-ON-THAMES
Middlesex TW16 7DX...01784 441147
e: ask@zest4.tv
w: www.zest4.tv

Event Management / Organisers

A2ZLeapfrog
.... +9715 52323941
e: robsz@a2zleapfrog.com
w: www.a2zleapfrogonline.com

ABC Marquees
1 HAWTHORN WAY, PORTSLADE, BRIGHTON & HOVE
East Sussex BN41 2HR 01273 891511
e: info@abcmarquees.co.uk
w: www.abcmarquees.co.uk

ABZ Events
ABERDEEN
....01224 515375
e: info@abz-events.co.uk
w: www.abz-events.co.uk

Akshyis Events Management Ltd
SOUTHEND ROAD, EASTHAM , LONDON
E6 2AA .... 02084771356 / 079 5141 8145 / 078 5227 5
e: akshyiseventsm@hotmail.com
w: www.akshyisevent.com/

Alana Jones
ME3 9TW...07974 739369
e: dizzy@dizzyodare.com
w: www.dizzyodare.com

Alexander Hire Ltd
WATERSPLASH FARM, FORDBRIDGE RD, SUNBURY-ON-THAMES
TW16 6AU 01932 784445
e: contact@alexanderhire.co.uk
w: www.alexanderhire.co.uk/

Apex
EXHIBITION HOUSE, LONDON ROAD, MACCLESFIELD
Cheshire SK11 7QX..01625 429370
e: mail@apex.co.uk
w: www.apex.co.uk

Artifact Multimedia
76 BERW ROAD, PONTYPRIDD, SOUTH WALES
CF37 2AB .... 07961 262080 / 01443 400 204
e: info@artifactmultimedia.co.uk
w: www.artifactmultimedia.co.uk

ATM Events
17 HOLROYD BUSINESS CENTRE, CARRBOTTOM ROAD, BRADFORD
West Yorkshire BD5 9AG .... +44 127 472 6280
e: enquiries@atmevents.co.uk
w: www.atmevents.co.uk

Black and White Live
....0208 422 0042
e: info@blackandwhitelive.com
w: www.blackandwhitelive.com

Blue Fizz Events
5 CROSS ST, BARNSTAPLE
EX31 1BA 07845 147563
e: enquiries@bluefizzevents.co.uk
w: www.bluefizzevents.co.uk

BPA - Berlin Event Agency
KURFÜRSTENDAMM 234, BERLIN
10719.................................... +49 (0))30 577 026 124
e: events@event-agency-berlin.com
w: www.event-agency-berlin.com

Captiv8 Creative Events Ltd
....0208 299 2405
e: info@captiv8events.com
w: www.captiv8events.co.uk

Captivent Productions
MONMOUTH STUDIOS, MONMOUTH STREET, BATH
Somerset BA1 2AN 01225 320 836
e: events@captivent.com
w: www.captivent.com

Carlisle Support Services
800 CAPABILITY GREEN, LUTON
LU1 3BA 073420 58614
e: alex.leake@carlislesupportservices.com
w: www.carlislesupportservices.com/

Chance Entertainment
321 FULHAM ROAD, LONDON
Greater London SW10 9QL....................................020 7376 5995
e: info@chanceorganisation.co.uk
w: www.chanceorganisation.co.uk

Charlie Apple
8 CEDAR WALK, KENLEY
Surrey CR8 5JL........................ 020 8668 6921 // 07973 987779
e: info@charlieapple.com
w: www.charlieapple.co.uk

Chase Dream Events
.... 07930 069 551 / 07985349861
e: info@chasedreamevents.co.uk
w: www.chasedreamevents.co.uk

CJ's Events Warwickshire
THE COW YARD, CHURCH FARM, CHURCH LANE, BUDBROOKE,
WARWICK
Warwickshire CV35 8QL.......................................01926 800 750
e: info@cjseventswarwickshire.co.uk
w: www.cjseventswarwickshire.co.uk

Clink Clink Events
14 MONTPELIER CENTRAL, MONTPELIER, STATION ROAD,
BRISTOL
Bristol BS6 5EE..0117 924 0033
e: info@clinkclink.co.uk
w: www.clinkclink.co.uk

Collection 26
66 PORCHESTER ROAD, LONDON
Greater London W2 6ET 08450 553290
e: info@collection26.com
w: www.collection26.com

Concise
5 THE QUADRANT CENTRE , 135 SALUSBURY ROAD , LONDON
NW6 6RJ .... +44 (0)20 7644 6444
e: phil.obrien@concisegroup.com
w: www.concisegroup.com/uk/

Conference Contacts Ltd
CHARTAM HOUSE, 16A COLLEGE AVENUE, MAIDENHEAD
Berkshire SL6 6AX...01628 773300
e: enquiries@conferencecontacts.co.uk
w: www.conferencecontacts.co.uk

Conference Shop Ltd
GOWER HOUSE, 18 ASHMERE LANE, FELPHAM
West Sussex PO22 7QT 0845 873 6299
e: sales@conferenceshop.com
w: www.conferenceshop.com

Crowded House Entertainments Ltd
CROWDED HOUSE ENTERTAINMENTS LTD, THE ENTERPRISE
CENTRE, POTTERS BAR
Hertfordshire EN6 3DQ..7719701188
e: office@crowdedh.com
w: www.crowdedh.com

Cult Events
UNIT 3, AUTUMN YARD, AUTUMN STREET, LONDON
Greater London E3 2TT .... 020 8983 5459 - 07540782176
e: info@culte.co.uk
w: www.culte.co.uk

Curve Box
NORTH HOUSE, 198 HIGH STREET, TONBRIDG
Kent N9 0BE 01795 892098
e: hello@curvebox.co.uk
w: www.curvebox.co.uk

CW Events Management
CNC HOUSE, 3 BROOKLANDS, NEW ROAD, BALLYMENA
BT42 2RT 028 2587 1989
e: info@cweventsni.co.uk
w: www.cweventsni.co.uk

DLP Festival Management
1 ELIZA PLACE, GOSPORT
Hampshire PO12 4UN .... 07825 392 364 / 02392 798 818
w: www.dlpfestivalmanagement.co.uk

Double Vision Events
....7580775517
e: doublevisionevents1@gmail.com
w: www.doublevision.events

Eastern Illusion
....07958 734311
e: info@easternillusion.com
w: www.easternillusion.com

Electra Events & Exhibitions
ADNEC HOUSE, PO BOX 95001,
ABU DHABI, UNITED ARAB EMIRATES
.... +971 2 406 4377
e: info@electradubai.ae
w: www.electra-exhibitions.com

EM UK
COPSE FARM, MOORHURST LANE, HOLMWOOD, DORKING
Surrey RH5 4LJ..01306 712451
e: nick@emuk.org
w: www.eventmanagementuk.org

Enigma Visual Solutions
UNIT 9, FIRST AVENUE GLOBE PARK , MARLOW
Buckinghamshire SL7 1YA.......... 01628624754 / 0845 314 3803
e: companyenigma@gmail.com
w: eni.co.uk/

Enteetainment Ltd
GROUND FLOOR, ELMWOOD BUILDING, SOUTHEND ROAD,
BRADFIELD SOUTHEND, READING
Berkshire RG7 6EU 0118 974 1910
e: info@dicktee.com
w: www.dicktee.com

Envisage
MIDLANDS
....01782 213444
e: rick.hewitt@enviz.co.uk
w: www.enviz.co.uk

Evalpe Events Management
58 RUE DE LA TERRASSIÃRE, GENEVA - SWITZERLAND
1207... +33 (0) 22 519 08 00
e: contact@evalpe.com
w: www.evalpe.com

E

Eventelle Limited
69 DUNVEGAN ROAD, BIRMINGHAM
B24 9HH...07961 067 546
e: info@eventelle.co.uk
w: www.eventelle.co.uk

Eventerprise
UNIT 120, MASON'S PRESS , 7 RAVENSCRAIG ROAD
7925...27729469652
e: johan@eventerprise.com
w: www.eventerprise.com

Events Organised Limited
8 RIDGEWAY ROAD, GILLINGHAM
Dorset SP8 4GH........................ 0845 519 46 54 / 01747 835433
e: info@eventsorganised.co.uk
w: www.eventsorganised.co.uk

Events to inspire
....7979745997
e: michelle@enticier.co.uk
w: www.eventstoinspire.co.uk

EW Production Services
UNIT C, WESLAKE INDUSTRIAL PARK , RYE HARBOUR
TN31 7TE 1797225166
e: paul@ewpsl.com
w: www.ewpsl.com/

Exclusive Occasions
LESTER HOUSE, TAMWORTH ROAD, LICHFIELD
West Midlands WS14 9PU.....................................01543 433 554
e: info@exclusive-occasions.co.uk
w: www.exclusive-occasions.co.uk

Fabled Events
21 TIDEWAY YARD, MORTLAKE HIGH STREET, LONDON
 SW14 8SN 07790 003 790
e: hello@fabledevents.com
w: www.fabledevents.com

Firefly Audio Visual Solutions Ltd
UNIT 31 BARKSTON HOUSE, CROYDON STREET, LEEDS
West Yorkshire LS11 9RT 01133 320042
e: hire.leeds@fireflyav.co.uk
w: www.fireflyav.co.uk

Fossett Events Ltd
PETTICOAT LANE , WIGAN
WN2 2LS 7599394256
e: fossettevents@outlook.com
w: www.fossettevents.com

Freshly Squeezed
THE JOHN BANNER CENTRE, 620 ATTERCLIFFE ROAD, SHEFFIELD
South Yorkshire S9 3QS 0114 2210312
e: info@freshly-squeezed.co.uk
w: www.freshly-squeezed.co.uk

Frontman
....0203 664 1156
e: al@frontman.tv
w: www.frontman.tv

Fun Events Group
14A MILL STREET, OTTERY ST. MARY, DEVON
EX11 1AD 01404 811 849
e: admin@funevents.com
w: www.funevents.com

Gain Audio
47 GORSEY LANE , CLOCK FACE , ST HELENS
WA9 4QS .... 08438861162 / 07896045416
e: justgainaudio@gmail.com
w: www.gainaudio.co.uk/

Gamewagon Ltd
113 - 115 OYSTER LANE, BYFLEET
Surrey KT14 7JZ...0845 319 4263
e: julie.owen@gamewagon.co.uk
w: www.gamewagon.co.uk

Glow Event Management
54 MALTINGS PLACE, 169 TOWER BRIDGE ROAD, LONDON
Greater London SE1 3LJ 0845 308 8300
e: hello@gowithglow.com
w: www.gowithglow.com

GMC Professional
HOZA 51, WARSAW
 00-681 .... 0048 507 164 924 / 0048 601 375 295
e: info@gmcpro.pl
w: www.gmcpro.pl

Go2Show
113 LINCOLN ROAD, LONDON
Greater London EN1 1LH.......................................020 8292 6103
e: bookings@gotoshow.co.uk
w: www.gotoshow.co.uk

Group Se7en Events
97 PARK LANE, MAYFAIR , LONDON
Greater London W1K 7TG.......................................0207 659 4430
e: info@group7events.co.uk
w: www.group7events.co.uk

Harlequin Marquees & Event Management
34 SANDHILL WAY, FAIRFORD LEYS, AYLESBURY
Buckinghamshire HP19 8GU ...... 01296 581524 // 07771 860908
e: info@harlequinevents.com
w: www.harlequinevents.com

Harrisons Events
THE MALTING BARN, MALTING LANE, DAGNALL, BERKHAMSTEAD
HP4 1QY 07846 380474
e: info@harrisonsevents.co.uk
w: www.harrisonsevents.co.uk

Heather Robinson Live Communication
MINERVA MILL, STATION ROAD, ALCESTER
Warwickshire B49 5ET..01789 761 353
w: www.heatherrobinson.co.uk

House of Bestival
3 LOUGHBOROUGH STREET, LONDON
SE11 5RB 0207 604 2944
e: hello@houseofbestival.net

HPSS Event Associates Limited
UNIT 5, DAIRYCOATES INDUSTRIAL ESTATE, WILTSHIRE ROAD,
KINGSTON UPON HULL
East Yorkshire HU4 6PA..01482 309321
e: info@hpssevents.co.uk
w: www.hpssevents.co.uk

Ian Nolan Events
HURST STREET STUDIOS, OXFORD
Oxfordshire OX4 1HD 01865 200780
e: info@iannolanevents.com
w: www.iannolanevents.com

Ideal Event Services
310 UNTHANK ROAD, NORWICH
Norfolk NR4 7QD 01603 280176
e: hello@idealeventservices.co.uk
w: www.idealeventservices.co.uk

INAANIAH Limited
THE LANSDOWNE BUILDING , 2 LANSDOWNE ROAD , CROYDON
Surrey CR9 2ER 7533001780
e: earthvillageevents@gmail.com
w: www.earthvillageevents.co.uk

Inspiration Events
14 STANHOPE MEWS WEST , LONDON
Greater London SW7 5RB 020 7370 4646
e: info@inspirationevents.com
w: www.inspirationevents.com

Install uk Ltd (Events)
UNITS 1 & 2, LINGEN ROAD, LUDLOW
Shropshire SY8 1XD...1584711119
e: events@install-uk.com
w: www.install-uk.com

International Creative Talent
18 SOHO SQUARE, LONDON
Greater London W1D 3QL......................................020 3544 6316
e: info@ictalentagency.com
w: www.ictalentagency.com

Jacqui Leigh Production Management Services
11 MAFEKING ROAD, ENFIELD
EN1 3SS 07971 660089
e: jacqui@jacquileigh.co.uk
w: www.jacquileigh.com

Jade Green Events
56 BLOOMSBURY STREET, LONDON
WC1B 3QT..020 7580 2600
e: info@jadegreenevents.com
w: www.jadegreenevents.com

JDB Events
GATEHOUSE TRADING ESTATE, LICHFIELD RD, BROWNHILLS,
WALSALL
WS8 6JZ...0121 667 1444
e: info@jdb-events.co.uk
w: www.jdb-events.com

Kudos Events
OLAYA MAIN STREET, AKARIA PLAZA GATE D, LEVEL 6 ,
KINGDOM OF SAUDI ARABIA P.O BOX 86334
Riyadh .... +966 (0) 11 486 8591 / +44 (0) 207 268 4
e: kudos.events.sa@gmail.com
w: kudos.events

Kudos Music
UNIT 10 TRADE CITY, COWLEY MILL ROAD, UXBRIDGE
UB8 2DB...01895 207990
e: info@kudosmusic.co.uk
w: www.kudosmusic.co.uk

KWTM Events Consultancy
74 FIVE ASH DOWN, UCKFIELD
TN22 3AN 01825 731894
w: www.kwtm.co.uk

Leapfrog
....1222144557
e: robsz@a2zleapfrog.com
w: www.a2zleapfrog.com

Liberty Events
UNIT 6, SOUTHAMPTON ROW, LONDON
WC1B 4DA...0845 644 6510
e: denis@awesome-events.co.uk
w: www.christmasatthelodge.com

Life's Kitchen
....0800 915 0978
e: info@lifeskitchen.com
w: www.lifeskitchen.com

E

E

Light Motif
26 TALINA CENTRE, 23A BAGLEYS LANE, LONDON
Greater London SW6 2BW.....................................020 7183 5381
e: info@lightmotif.co.uk
w: www.lightmotif.co.uk

MacEvents Event Management
HULTON HOUSE, 11 EWALD ROAD, LONDON
Greater London SW6 3NA .... 020 7736 6606 // 07973 667624
e: cm@macevents.co.uk
w: www.macevents.co.uk

Magnum Opus Events
....0207 607 0953
e: info@magnumopusevents.london

Marmalade Events
....0852 9382 0619
e: hello@thisismarmalade.com
w: www.thisismarmalade.com

Matt Bunday Events
.... 023 8055 3736 // 07730 604 869
e: info@mattbundayevents.com
w: www.mattbundayevents.com

McKenzie Arnold Security
MCKENZIE HOUSE, 11 CRITALL DRIVE, BRAINTREE
Essex CM7 2RT..01376 749572
e: lucille@mckenziearnold.com
w: www.mckenziearnold.com

Medusa Events
MCG PLAZA CUMHURIYET MAH., ADNAN MENDERES CAD.
NO:22/D KAT:3 Ã‡EKMEKÃ¶Y, INSTABUL
....0216 444 0 891
e: info@medusaplus.com
w: www.medusaplus.com

Mode for...Events
.... 07846 996597 // 07901672598
e: modeforevents@gmail.com
w: www.modeforevents.co.uk

Multiversal Events
261 DITCHLING ROAD, BRIGHTON
East Sussex BN1 6JH.................. 01273 900221 / 07880 704378
e: info@multiversalevents.co.uk
w: www.multiversalevents.co.uk

National Event Welfare Service
....447799377632
e: corinne@eventwelfare.co.uk
w: www.eventwelfare.co.uk

Nexlevel Entertainment & Event Management
106A CLARENCE ROAD, HACKNEY
 E5 8HB 0208 985 3165
e: lekan.fakoya@nexlevel.co.uk
w: www.nexlevel.co.uk

Nomadic Display U.K
NOMADIC HOUSE 71 , ST. JOHNS ROAD , ISLEWORTH
TW7 6XQ .... 0208 326 0000 / 0208 326 5555
e: info@nomadicdisplay.co.uk
w: www.nomadicdisplay.co.uk/

One Events Management and Production
31B THE COURTYARD, BROOK STREET, GRANTHAM
Lincolnshire NG31 6RX 01476 978184
e: mail@oneevents.org.uk
w: www.oneevents.org.uk

Paragon
HOLBROOKE PLACE , 28-32 HILL RISE, RICHMOND
TW10 6UD .... 020 8332 8640 / 020 8003 2739
e: sayhello@thisisparagon.co.uk
w: https://www.thisisparagon.co.uk/

Porter & Smith Event Planners
1 FOREST DRIVE, WOODFORD GREEN
Essex IG8 9NG 07796 966 805
e: info@porterandsmith.co.uk
w: www.porterandsmith.co.uk

Premier UK Events Ltd
UNIT 2, ROOKERY LANE, THURMASTON, LEICESTER
Leicestershire LE4 8AU..1162029953
e: ben@premier-ltd.com
w: premier-event-solutions.com/

Priava
LEVEL 4 282 OXFORD STREET , BONDI JUNCTION , AUSTRALIA
NSW 2022 .... +61 (0)2 8383 4333
e: sales.au@priava.com
w: www.priava.com

Production Support Services Ltd
UNIT 18 ASTON ROAD, ASTON FIELDS INDUSTRIAL ESTATE,
BROMSGROVE
Worcestershire B60 3EX 0845 838 1123
e: chris@production-support.net
w: www.production-support.net

Productions Management Services
22 FRESHFIELD PLACE, BRIGHTON
East Sussex BN2 0BN...01273 623972
e: simon@simonbyfordpms.com
w: www.simonbyfordpms.com

Purple Lamb Events
E-SPACE NORTH , WISBECH ROAD , LITTLEPORT
Cambridgeshire CB6 1RA.......................................01353 831031
e: hello@purplelambevents.co.uk
w: www.purplelambevents.co.uk

QED Productions
UNIT 11, SUMMIT ROAD, CRANBORNE INDUSTRIAL ESTATE,
POTTERS BAR
Hertfordshire EN6 3QW 01707 648 800
e: info@qed-productions.com
w: www.qed-productions.com

Really Now Event Management
SECOND FLOOR , ELEVATOR STUDIOS , PARLIAMENT STREET
L8 5RN 07795 168834
e: talktome@reallynow.co.uk
w: www.reallynow.co.uk

Rhodes Event Management
....07971 619502
e: enquiries@rhodes-events.co.uk
w: www.rhodes-events.co.uk

RMAV
UNIT 9, ACORN BUSINESS CENTRE, CUBLINGTON ROAD,
WING, LEIGHTON BUZZARD
Buckinghamshire LU7 0LB.....................................01296 682548
e: jeb@rmav.co.uk
w: www.rmav.co.uk

Rockitfish Ltd
16 MEAD BUSINESS CENTRE , MEAD LANE , HERTFORD
Hertfordshire SG13 7BJ 01992 558820
e: hello@rockitfish.co.uk
w: www.rockitfish.co.uk

Scarlet Events
THIRD FLOOR , 207 REGENT STREET, LONDON
W1B 3HH 0203 589 4780
e: marc@scarletevents.co.uk
w: www.scarletevents.co.uk

Seaholme Marquees
COLEMAN'S PARK, SHAVESWOOD LANE, ALBOURNE
West Sussex BN6 9DY 01273 857577
e: info@seaholmemarquees.co.uk
w: www.seaholmemarquees.co.uk

Seventh Heaven
....01753 546555
e: info@seventh-heaven-events.co.uk
w: www.seventh-heaven-events.co.uk

Sian Events Ltd
....07415 742291
e: claire.mcdonald@Siangroup.co
w: www.sianevents.com

SilverLine Events
GUNNERY TERRACE, CORNWALLIS ROAD, LONDON
SE18 6SW .... 020 8301 8459 / 07577 558 255
e: jorge@silverline-events.com
w: silverline-events.com/

SJ Events
SJ EVENT CONSULTANCY LTD, NORTH WING, , SWITHLAND HALL
SWITHLAND
Leicestershire LE12 8TJ 1162302040
e: mikewayne@post.com
w: www.sjevents.co.uk/

Smoking Gun Events
UNIT 3, PUMA TRADE PARK, 145 MORDEN RD, LONDON
CR4 4DG........................... +447972776469 / +4420 8150 6527
e: louis@sgeventworld.com
w: www.sgeventworld.com

Spies und Schwarz Event
....498959043942
e: spies@spiesundschwarz.de
w: www.spiesundschwarz.de

Spiral Links Ltd
HESKETH HOUSE, 43-45 PORTMAN SQUARE, LONDON
W1H 6HN.................................. 020 7969 2944 / 07745 139307
e: contact@spirallinks.com
w: www.spirallinks.com

SPS Productions
UNIT 1, LATHAM PARK, ST BLAZEY ROAD, PAR , CORNWALL
PL24 2JA...01726 817380
e: steve@sps-productions.co.uk
w: www.sps-productions.co.uk

Stagecraft UK
ST QUENTIN GATE, TELFORD
Shropshire TF3 4JH 01952 281 600
e: sales@stagecraftuk.com
w: www.stagecraftuk.com

Steve Duggan Events
6 SCRUBS LANE, LONDON
Greater London NW10 6RB 02089 603120
e: info@stevendugganevents.com
w: www.stevendugganevents.com

Straight Productions
TREYARNON HOUSE, WESTBEAMS ROAD, SWAY
Hampshire SO41 6AE..07802 753058
e: info@straightproductions.com
w: www.straightproductions.com

Studio Grade Events
UNIT 4 BRIDGE STREET , WORDSLEY, STOURBRIDGE
DY8 5YU .... 01212704422 / 07833259712
e: info@studiograde.co.uk
w: www.studiograde.co.uk

Tactical Management & Events
NEWPORT ROAD , ALBRIGHTON
WV7 3AJ 07950 534672
e: tacticalmanagement@email.com
w: www.thetacticalgroup.yolasite.com

Tapestry Media and Events Ltd
BATTERSEA STUDIO, 80-82 SILVERTHORNE ROAD, BATTERSEA,
LONDON
Greater London SW8 3HE.....................................020 8945 5100
e: chris@tapestrymediaandevents.com
w: www.tapestrymediaandevents.com

E

E

Tarren Production Ltd
1 - 4 THE COURTYARD, ORCHARD FARM, CHURCH LANE,
BENTHAM, CHELTENHAM
Gloucestershire GL51 4TZ......................................01242 806778
e: chris@tarrenproduction.co.uk
w: www.christarren.co.uk

TechST
....07767 366031
e: info@tech-st.co.uk
w: www.tajiri-events.co.uk

Tenpast Events
27 TAVISTOCK SQUARE, LONDON
WC1H 9HH................................. 020 3143 3243 / 07490 390219
e: nh@tenpast.com
w: www.tenpast.com

The Girl Friday Company
HOLMES CHAPEL
Cheshire 7887768296
e: marie@thegirlfridaycompany.co.uk
w: https://www.thegirlfridaycompany.co.uk

The Halo Group
THE OLD IMPERIAL LAUNDRY, STUDIO G1 & G2, 71-73 WARRINER
GARDENS, LONDON
SW11 4XW 020 7870 3210
e: info@thehalogroup.co.uk
w: www.thehalogroup.co.uk

The JWP Group
195 THORNHILL ROAD, SURBITON
Surrey KT6 7TG 020 8288 0246
e: web@jwp.co.uk
w: www.jwp.co.uk

The Main Stage
....0800 321 3406
e: hello@themainstage.com
w: https://themainstage.com/

The Mermaid
THE MERMAID CONFERENCE & EVENTS CENTRE, PUDDLE DOCK,
BLACKFRIARS, LONDON
EC4V 3DB 2072130704
e: louise.stone@the-mermaid.co.uk
w: www.the-mermaid.co.uk

Theme Traders Ltd
THE STADIUM, OAKLANDS ROAD, LONDON
Greater London NW2 6DL 0208 452 8518
e: enquiries@themetraders.com
w: www.themetraders.com

Total Care Security Ltd
UNIT 3 , BRUNEL DRIVE, NEWARK
Nottinghamshire NG24 2DE 0800 917 47 67
e: info@totalcaresecurity.com
w: www.totalcaresecurity.com

Tour Management Services (Nottinghamshire)
207 PARK ROAD EAST , NOTTINGHAM
Nottinghamshire NG14 6PS....................................07530 431 908
e: mike@tour-management-services.co.uk
w: www.tour-management-services.co.u

Transform Venue
UNIT 1 REAR OF 486 PORTSWOOD ROAD, SOUTHAMPTON
Hampshire SO17 3SP 02380 558923
e: info@transform-venue.co.uk
w: www.transform-venue.co.uk

Twentyfirst Century Communications
MORAY HOUSE, 23-31 GREAT TITCHFIELD STREET, LONDON
Greater London W1W 7PA....................................020 7291 0444
e: hello@cheerfultwentyfirst.com
w: cheerfultwentyfirst.com/

Unibox
GREENGATE INDUSTRIAL ESTATE, GREENSIDE WAY, MIDDLETON
MANCHESTER
M24 1SW..0161 655 2100
e: info@unibox.co.uk
w: www.unibox.co.uk

Universal World Events
ASHFIELD HOUSE, RESOLUTION ROAD, ASHBY DE LA ZOUCH
Leicestershire LE65 1DW................................. +1 215 347 6400
e: info@ashfieldhealthcare.com
w: www.universalworldevents.com

VIP Adrenaline Ltd
9 EDGBARROW RISE, SANDHURST
Berkshire GU47 8QH..07734 391299
e: info@vipadrenaline.com
w: www.vipadrenaline.com

Vjem Events
....020 8819 9919
e: talktous@vjem.co.uk
w: www.vjemevents.com

WM Event Design
19 ST JAMES'S DRIVE, WANDSWORTH COMMON, LONDON
Greater London SW17 7RN 020 3837 4926
e: info@williammoyse.com
w: www.wmeventdesign.com

Your Right Arm Events Ltd.
....0788 3033 552
e: mary@yourrightarm.co.uk
w: www.yourrightarmevents.co.uk

Event Power

Festivals aren't the only event where you'll appreciate our whisper quiet generators

LONDON
+44(0)20 8450 2943
info@fourthgenerationltd.com

LUTON
+44(0)1582 562162
www.fourthgenerationltd.com

FOURTH GENERATION

Event Production

2 Can Productions
SUITE 3, BIG YELLOW, 65 PENARTH ROAD, CARDIFF
Glamorgan CF10 5DL................... 29 2010 0256 / 07968 340270
e: info@2canproductions.com
w: www.2canproductions.com

4D Design & Display Ltd
THE DESIGN WORKS, 64 DEANWAY, CHALFONT ST GILES
Buckinghamshire HP8 4JT....................................01494 870105
e: success@4d-design.co.uk
w: www.4d-design.co.uk

88 Events Company
IBROX BUSINESS PARK, LARCHFIELD COURT, GLASGOW
Glasgow G51 2RQ...0141 445 2288
e: info@88events.com
w: www.88events.com

A&e Marquees Ltd
46 STRETTEN AVE, CAMBRIDGE
Cambridgeshire CB4 3EP.....................................01223 560293
e: info@aandemarquees.co.uk
w: www.aandemarquees.co.uk

A1 Events & Exhibitions Ltd
SUITE 10, SHENLEY PAVILIONS, CHALKDELL DRIVE, SHENLEY
WOOD, MILTON KEYNES
Buckinghamshire MK5 6LB....................................01908 867555
e: help@a1-events-exhibitions.com
w: www.a1-events-exhibitions.com

A2ZLeapfrog
.... +9715 52323941
e: robsz@a2zleapfrog.com
w: www.a2zleapfrogonline.com

Abby Lacey Events
25 HILLTOP ROAD, TWYFORD, READING
RG10 9BJ...07789 756656
e: info@abbylacey.co.uk
w: www.abbylacey.co.uk

Absolute Events
250 YORK ROAD, LONDON
Greater London SW11 3SJ...................................020 7228 9200
e: solutions@absoluteevents.co.uk
w: www.absoluteevents.co.uk

E

ABZ Events
ABERDEEN
....01224 515375
e: info@abz-events.co.uk
w: www.abz-events.co.uk

ACP Productions
....0845 4741992
e: info@acp-productions.co.uk
w: www.acp-productions.co.uk

Ad Events International Limited
STUDIO 4,, VALMAR TRADING ESTATE, VALMAR ROAD,, LONDON
Greater London SE5 9NW.....................................020 7635 7372
e: info@adevents.co.uk
w: www.adevents.co.uk

AddingValue Agency
THE POWER HOUSE, , 1 LINKFIELD ROAD, ISLEWORTH
Greater London TW7 6QG,.....................................020 8831 7940
e: hello@addingvalue.com
w: www.addingvalue.com

Amograe Internacional S.l.
PAMA P.I. LOS MORREROS, CALLE MINA SOLILLOS 109,
AZNALCOLLAR
41870.. +34 654522394
e: graeme@amograe.com
w: www.amograe.com

Andrew Cheeseman Productions
LA GRANGE BLEUE, SALIGOS
65120...0845 474 1992
e: info@acp-productions.co.uk
w: www.acp-productions.co.uk

Andycam Audiovisual
9 INDUSTRIAL COTTAGES, LONG LEYS ROAD, LINCOLN
Lincolnshire LN1 1DZ...01522 533039
e: andy@andycam.tv
w: www.andycam.tv

Arlekino Production
KOSOVSKA 8, ZEMUN, BELGRADE, SERBIA
11080... +381 63 22 95 11
e: office@arlekino.rs
w: www.arlekinoproduction.com

Audiowall Systems Limited
2/3 BASSETT COURT, BROAD STREET, NEWPORT PAGNELL
Buckinghamshire MK16 0JN..... 01908 951 470 / 01908 615 365
e: info@audiowall.co.uk
w: www.audiowall.co.uk

AV Projections
AV PROJECTIONS LTD THE ARCHES, 65 WEBBER STREET,
LONDON
Greater London SE1 0QP.......................................020 7620 2001
e: info@avprojections.co.uk
w: www.avprojections.co.uk

Bamboo London
UNIT 12, THE TALINA CENTRE, BAGLEYS LANE, LONDON
Greater London SW6 2BW.....................................0207 610 8606
e: contact@bamboolondon.com
w: www.bamboolondon.com

Banana Split Plc
6 CARLISLE ROAD, LONDON
Greater London NW9 0HN....................................020 8200 1234
e: hello@banana-split.com
w: www.banana-split.com

Ben Van Grutten
FROG COTTAGE, FROG LANE, TUNBRIDGE WELLS
Kent TN1 1YT..01892 525979
e: info@bvggroup.com
w: www.bvggroup.com

Benchmark Conference and Events
14 BLANDFORD SQUARE, NEWCASTLE UPON TYNE
Tyne and Wear NE1 4HZ.......................................0191 241 4523
e: info@echoevents.org
w: www.echoevents.org

Bentleys Entertainments Ltd
7 SQUARE RIGGER ROW, PLANTATION WHARF, LONDON
Greater London SW11 3TZ....................................020 7223 7900
e: info@bentleys.net
w: www.bentleys.net

Big Chief Productions Ltd
81 DUKE ROAD, CHISWICK, LONDON
Greater London W4 2BN.......................................020 8996 0300
e: info@bigchiefproductions.co.uk
w: www.bigchiefproductions.co.uk

Blast Event Hire
UNIT 1 & 2 BONVILLE BUSINESS ESTATE, DIXON ROAD,
BRISLINGTON
Bristol BS4 5QQ...0117 370 2660
e: info@blasteventhire.co.uk
w: www.blasteventhire.co.uk

Blue Box Ltd
4 SMITH'S BARN FARM, COMPTONS LANE, HORSHAM
Sussex RH13 5NN..07785 730 442
e: mark@bluebox-london.com
w: www.bluebox-london.com

Blue Dog Productions Ltd
HURST FARM, THE HURST, WINCHFIELD
Hampshire RG27 8SL..01252 786 000
e: info@bluedogproductions.co.uk
w: www.bluedogproductions.co.uk

Bracken Presentations Ltd
OFFICE SUITE 2, CASTLE COURT, 59 CASTLE BOULEVARD,
NOTTINGHAM
Nottinghamshire NG7 1FD 0115 9470555
e: mail@brackenevents.co.uk
w: www.brackenevents.co.uk

Bravo Productions
65 PINE AVENUE, SUITE 858, LONG BEACH, CALIFORNIA
90802..001 562 435 0065
e: staff@bravoevents-online.com
w: www.bravoevents-online.com

Broadway Events Ltd
UNIT 3, 3 CROW ARCH LANE, RINGWOOD
Hampshire BH24 1PB 01425 838393
e: info@broadway-events.co.uk
w: www.broadway-events.co.uk

Cameron Presentations & All Event Hire
BURNFIELD ROAD, GIFFNOCK, GLASGOW
Glasgow G46 7TH 0141 637 0368
e: hire@cameronpres.co.uk
w: www.cameronpres.co.uk

Captiv8 Creative Events Ltd
....0208 299 2405
e: info@captiv8events.com
w: www.captiv8events.co.uk

Captivent Productions
MONMOUTH STUDIOS, MONMOUTH STREET, BATH
Somerset BA1 2AN 01225 320 836
e: events@captivent.com
w: www.captivent.com

Catalyst Teambuilding
SUITE 12, BADEN PLACE, CROSBY ROW, LONDON BRIDGE,
LONDON
Greater London SE1 1YW 020 3551 2050
e: info@catalystteambuilding.co.uk
w: www.catalystteambuilding.co.uk

Central Event Productions Ltd
ASTON ROAD, NUNEATON
Warwickshire CV11 5EL 0 7812 8420 60
e: office@centralevent.co.uk
w: www.centralevent.co.uk

Central Image Factory
....7728627216
e: centralimagefactory@gmail.com
w: www.centralimagefactory.co.uk

Chance Entertainment
321 FULHAM ROAD, LONDON
Greater London SW10 9QL.....................................020 7376 5995
e: info@chanceorganisation.co.uk
w: www.chanceorganisation.co.uk

Chaos Management
SORBY HOUSE, 42 SPITAL HILL, SHEFFIELD
South Yorkshire S4 7LG........... 07939 001318 // (0)114 213 2340
e: info@chaos-management.co.uk
w: www.chaos-management.co.uk

Chew Ltd
86-90 PAUL STREET, LONDON
Greater London EC2A 4NE 020 3289 1194
e: info@chewlondon.com
w: www.chewlondon.com

Clever Connections
UNIT 3 WARWICK COURT, SAXON BUSINESS PARK,HANBURY
ROAD, BROMSGROVE
West Midlands B60 4AD 01527 833 338
e: info@cleverconnections.co.uk
w: www.cleverconnections.co.uk

Clink Clink Events
14 MONTPELIER CENTRAL, MONTPELIER, STATION ROAD,
BRISTOL
Bristol BS6 5EE...0117 924 0033
e: info@clinkclink.co.uk
w: www.clinkclink.co.uk

Colour CoOrdinate BP
41 TALBOT AVENUE, LANGLEY
Berkshire SL3 8DE...07001 878 128
e: geoff@cc-bp.co.uk
w: www.cc-bp.co.uk

Colour Sound Experiment
ST LEONARDS ROAD , PARK ROYAL, LONDON
Greater London NW10 6ST 020 8965 9119
e: sales@coloursound.co.uk
w: www.coloursound.co.uk

Conference Shop Ltd
GOWER HOUSE, 18 ASHMERE LANE, FELPHAM
West Sussex PO22 7QT 0845 873 6299
e: sales@conferenceshop.com
w: www.conferenceshop.com

Corporate Events
CORPORATE EVENT SERVICES LTD, UNIT 1, MARSHALL ROAD,
HILLMEAD, SWINDON SN5 5FZ 1793849300
e: corporateeventservices@yahoo.com
w: corporate-events.co.uk/

Creator International Ltd
UNIT 3, HIGHAMS HILL FARM, SHEEP BARN LANE
Surrey CR6 9PQ..01959 542732
e: giles@creator.uk.com
w: www.creator.uk.com

Crewsaders Ltd
MILLER 2, 61 ST PAULS SQUARE, BIRMINGHAM
West Midlands B3 1QS 0845 094 4884
e: bookings@crewsaders.com
w: www.crewsaders.com

Crone & Co
STRANDGADE 98, DENMARK
CPH-1401 .... +45 3210 6655
e: hello@croneandco.com
w: www.croneandco.com

E

Crown Business Communications Ltd
12 SOHO SQUARE , LONDON
Greater London W1D 3QF.......................................020 7605 4500
e: contact@crownbc.com
w: www.crownbc.com

CSE / SSVC
CHALFONT GROVE, NARCOT LANE, GERRADS CROSS
Buckinghamshire SL9 8TN...................................01494 874 461
e: info@bfbs.com
w: www.ssvc.com

CSL Hospitality
6 LOWER MOUNT STREET, DUBLIN 2, IRELAND
....00 353 1676 6650
e: info@cslhospitality.ie
w: www.cslhospitality.ie

Cult Events
UNIT 3, AUTUMN YARD, AUTUMN STREET, LONDON
Greater London E3 2TT .... 020 8983 5459 - 07540782176
e: info@culte.co.uk
w: www.culte.co.uk

CW Event Productions Ltd
ALLSOP HOUSE, 10 PARSONAGE FARM, WINGRAVE, AYLESBURY
Buckinghamshire HP22 4RP 01296 682890
e: hello@cweventproductions.com
w: www.cweventproductions.com

CW Events Management
CNC HOUSE, 3 BROOKLANDS, NEW ROAD, BALLYMENA
BT42 2RT 028 2587 1989
e: info@cweventsni.co.uk
w: www.cweventsni.co.uk

David Barrow Event Services
GLEBE BARNS, CHURCH HILL, SPRIDLINGTON
Lincolnshire LN8 2DX .... 01673 866320 /
07974 653467
e: davidbarrow@dbeventservices.com
w: www.dbeventservices.com

DC3 Productions Ltd
37 BRAMBLE ROAD, HATFIELD
AL10 9RZ.................................. 020 8123 8765 / 07737 535886
e: dan@dc3productions.co.uk
w: www.dc3productions.co.uk

Definitive Events Ltd
UNIT 104 CHORLTON MILL , 3 CAMBRIDGE STREET ,
MANCHESTER
Greater Manchester M1 5BY .... +971 50 977 2321
e: lisap@definitiveevents.co.uk
w: www.definitiveevents.co.uk

Dellar Davies Ltd
RAPIER HOUSE, 4-6 CRANE MEAD, WARE
Hertfordshire SG12 9PW 01920 444800
e: info@dellardavies.com
w: www.dellardavies.com

Delta Production Services
UNIT 4, SPRINGSIDE, LA RUE DE LA MONNAIE, TRINITY
JE3 5DG 01534 865885
e: info@delta-av.com
w: www.delta-av.com

Derek Halliday Productions
21 PRINCES AVENUE, WOOD GREEN
N22 7SB 020 8292 6930
e: contact@dhproductions.co.uk

Designscene Ltd
46A ROSEBERY AVENUE, LONDON
Greater London EC1R 4RP 020 8752 8290
e: mail@designscene.co.uk
w: www.designscene.co.uk

DFA Productions
YORK HOUSE, COTTINGLEY BUSINESS PARK, BRADFORD
West Yorkshire BD16 1PE.....................................0800 644 0662
e: thespark@dfaproductions.co.uk
w: www.dfaproductions.co.uk

DM Audio Ltd
UNIT 7/1 NEWHAILES INDUSTRIAL ESTATE, NEWHAILES ROAD,
EDINBURGH
Edinburgh EH21 6SY 0131 665 5615
e: hire@dmaudio.co.uk
w: www.dmaudio.co.uk

DMI Productions
UNIT 8, LITTLETON HOUSE, LITTLETON ROAD,
ASHFORD, AMIDDLESEX,
TW15 1UU 01784 421212
e: contactus@dmiproductions.co.uk
w: www.dmiproductions.co.uk

DPC Communications Limited
THE STUDIO, WEST ACRE, WHEDDON CROSS, MINEHEAD
Somerset TA24 7BY 07831 093000
e: dpccommunications@gmail.com
w: www.dpccommunications.co.uk

East Anglia Leisure
UNIT 4, CIVIC INDUSTRIAL ESTATE, HOMEFIELD ROAD, HAVERHILL
Suffolk CB9 8QP 01440 714204
e: info@ealeisure.co.uk
w: www.ealeisure.co.uk

Electra Events & Exhibitions
ADNEC HOUSE, PO BOX 95001,
ABU DHABI, UNITED ARAB EMIRATES
.... +971 2 406 4377
e: info@electradubai.ae
w: www.electra-exhibitions.com

Elysium Global Events Ltd
25 CREEK ROAD, HAMPTON COURT, KINGSTON UPON THAMES
Surrey KT8 9BE 020 8481 9900
e: kwaters@elysiumglobalevents.co.uk
w: www.elysiumglobalevents.co.uk

EM UK
COPSE FARM, MOORHURST LANE, HOLMWOOD, DORKING
Surrey RH5 4LJ...01306 712451
e: nick@emuk.org
w: www.eventmanagementuk.org

English Heritage
FIRE FLY AVENUE , SWINDON
Wiltshire SN2 2EH 0870 333 1181
e: customers@english-heritage.org.uk
w: www.english-heritage.org.uk

Enigma Creative Solutions
ST STEPHENS HOUSE, ARTHUR ROAD, WINDSOR
Berkshire SL4 1RU..01753 622592
e: info@enigmacs.com
w: www.enigmacs.com

Enteetainment Ltd
GROUND FLOOR, ELMWOOD BUILDING, SOUTHEND ROAD,
BRADFIELD SOUTHEND, READING
Berkshire RG7 6EU 0118 974 1910
e: info@dicktee.com
w: www.dicktee.com

Entertee Productions Ltd
LONGPOND WORKS , WROTHAM ROAD, BOROUGH GREEN
Kent TN15 8DE 01732 781 137
e: productions@entertee.com
w: www.entertee.com

Entertee Select Ltd
LONGPOND WORKS , WROTHAM ROAD, BOROUGH GREEN
Kent TN15 8DE 01732 781 137
e: select@entertee.com
w: www.entertee.com

Envisage
MIDLANDS
....01782 213444
e: rick.hewitt@enviz.co.uk
w: www.enviz.co.uk

ESA Live
THE CROFT , WESTGATE , NORTH CAVE
East Yorkshire HU15 2NG 01430 470 731
e: scherri@esalive.com
w: www.esalive.com

Essex Entertainment Agency
78 HIGH ROAD, LAYER DE LA HAYE, COLCHESTER
Essex CO2 0DT 01206 734164
e: richard@essexents.com
w: www.essexents.com

Ethix Management
UNIT 15 KEMPTON GATE, OLDFIELD ROAD, HAMPTON
Greater London TW12 2AF 020 8487 3508
e: contactus@ethixmanagement.com
w: www.ethixmanagement.com

ETL Logistics
THE LEGACY CENTRE , HANWORTH TRADING ESTATE, HAMPTON
ROAD WEST , FELTHAM
TW13 6DH 01932 887 711
e: info@etl-logistics.com
w: www.etl-logistics.com/

Eurohire Sound & Light
UNIT 6, BESSEMER PARK, BESSEMER ROAD, BASINGSTOKE
Hampshire RG21 3NB 01256 461 234
e: jools@eurohiresoundandhire.co.uk
w: www.eurohiresoundandlight.co.uk

Euroscope Television Facilities Limited
UNIT 15-17, QUARRY FARM, BODIAM
East Sussex TN32 5RA..01424 830044
e: info@euroscope.tv
w: www.euroscope.tv

Event & Conference Organisers Ltd
66 NANDI ROAD, P O BOX 25313, NAIROBI
603.. +254 722 848465
e: mail@eco.co.ke
w: www.eco.co.ke

Event & Management Services
UNIT 5, EXMOUTH COURT, CHELTENHAM
Gloucestershire GL53 7NR 01242 245444
e: events@eandms.com
w: www.eandms.com

Event Owl
20 WELLGATE, CLITHEROE
Lancashire BB7 2DP 1200429242
e: info@eventowl.co.uk
w: https://eventowl.co.uk

Event Solution And Promotions
BRAESIDE, HIGH STREET, OXSHOTT
Surrey KT22 0JP...01372 841001
e: esp@eventsol.co.uk
w: www.eventsol.co.uk

Eventsforce Solutions Ltd
THE WENLOCK, 50-52 WHARF ROAD, LONDON
Greater London N1 7EU 0207 785 7040
e: info@eventsforce.com
w: www.eventsforce.com

Eventuality Uk Ltd
.... 01285 711111 // 07702 265336
e: liam@eventuality.co.uk
w: www.eventuality.co.uk

Evolution Events LLC
INDUSTRIAL 18, PO BOX 1857, SHARJAH (DUBAI OUTSKIRTS)
SHJ 1857 ....00971 65360574
e: info@evolutionevents.com
w: www.evolutionevents.com

E

E

EW Production Services
UNIT C, WESLAKE INDUSTRIAL PARK , RYE HARBOUR
TN31 7TE 1797225166
e: paul@ewpsl.com
w: www.ewpsl.com/

Experience Scotland Conference & Incentives Ltd
2 WEST STREET, PENICUIK
EH26 9DL 01968 679969
e: enquiries@experiencescotland.co.uk
w: www.experiencescotland.co.uk

Feathers Catering & Event Management
CATER HOUSE, 113 MOUNT PLEASANT, LIVERPOOL
Merseyside L3 5TF 0151 709 2020
e: info@feathers.uk.com
w: www.feathers.uk.com

Feile An Phobail
473 FALLS ROAD, BELFAST
BT12 6DD 02890 313440
e: ciaran@feilebelfast.com
w: www.feilebelfast.com

Festaff
....07702 211030
e: clients@festaff.co.uk
w: www.festaff.co.uk

Fexx Productions Ltd
37 CHERRY TREE STREET, ELSECAR
S74 8DG..0844 664 6574
e: enqs@fexx.co.uk
w: www.fexx.co.uk

Field Services Ltd
UNIT 3, CUMBERLAND AVENUE, LONDON
Greater London NW10 7RX 020 8961 1225
e: enquiries@field-services.co.uk
w: www.field-services.co.uk

Firecracker Works Ltd
OLD AIRCRAFT HANGAR, WIMBLEDON WEST GOODS YARD,
DUNDONALD ROAD, WIMBLEDON, LONDON
Greater London SW19 3QJ.....................................0207 228 6111
e: info@firecrackerworks.com
w: www.firecrackerworksltd.com

Firefly Audio Visual Solutions Ltd
UNIT 31 BARKSTON HOUSE, CROYDON STREET, LEEDS
West Yorkshire LS11 9RT 01133 320042
e: hire.leeds@fireflyav.co.uk
w: www.fireflyav.co.uk

First City Events
16 LINDEN PARK TERRACE , MILNATHORT , KINROSS
KY13 9XY................................... 01577 865498 // 07711 432745
e: joyce@firstcityevents.co.uk
w: www.firstcityevents.co.uk

First Protocol Event Management Ltd
27 WOOTTON STREET, LONDON
Greater London SE1 8TG.......................................020 7787 5995
e: kate.sheridan-hayes@firstprotocol.com
w: www.firstprotocol.com

Fisher Productions
118 GARRATT LANE, LONDON
Greater London SW18 4DJ....................................020 8871 1978
e: enquiries@fisherproductions.co.uk
w: www.fisherproductions.co.uk

Fresh Events UK
UNIT D WESLAKE INDUSTRIAL PARK, RYE HARBOUR ROAD, RYE
East Sussex TN31 7TE 07919 512 608
e: info@fresheventsuk.com
w: www.fresheventsuk.com

Fruition Premier Limited
NEW BROAD STREET HOUSE, NEW BROAD STREET, LONDON
Greater London EC2M 1NH 0845 1308826
e: mtasker@fruition.co.uk
w: www.fruition.co.uk

FTF Worldwide Event Management
15 MILL LANE, CAMPTON, SHEFFORD
Bedfordshire SG17 5NX 01462 817640
e: info@ftfworldwide.com
w: www.ftfworldwide.com

Fuelled Ltd
SUITE 48 BARTON ARCADE, DEANSGATE , MANCHESTER
Greater Manchester M3 2BH................................0161 359 3216
e: hello@fuel-led.com
w: www.fuel-led.com

Fun Events Group
14A MILL STREET, OTTERY ST. MARY, DEVON
EX11 1AD 01404 811 849
e: admin@funevents.com
w: www.funevents.com

funk:tion events
6 KINGS BUILDING, KING STREET, CHESTER
Cheshire CH1 2AJ...0161 341 0052
e: info@funktionevents.co.uk
w: www.funktionevents.co.uk

Gemma Pears
56 DUNNOCK LANE, COTTAM, PRESTON
PR4 0NX 07870 161135
e: gemmapearsevents@gmail.com
w: www.gemmapears.wordpress.com

GMC Professional
HOZA 51, WARSAW
00-681 .... 0048 507 164 924 / 0048 601 375 295
e: info@gmcpro.pl
w: www.gmcpro.pl

Gorilla Marketing & Events Ltd
PAPER STOCK HOUSE, AMERSHAM ROAD, CHALFONT ST. GILES
Buckinghamshire HP8 4RU 01494 876 876
e: info@gorillauk.com
w: www.gorillauk.com

Grandslam
PASSATGE TOLEDO,11, BARCELONA, SPAIN
8014..0034 9 3296 5084
e: sam@grandslam.es
w: www.grandslam.es

Great Big Events
UNIT 27, 8 HORNSEY STREET, LONDON
Greater London N7 8EG 0207 607 9272
e: enquiries@greatbigevents.com
w: www.greatbigevents.com

H2 Business Communication
SHEPPERTON STUDIOS, SHEPPERTON
Surrey TW17 0QD 01932 593 717
e: mail@h2bc.co.uk
w: www.h2bc.co.uk

Heather Robinson Live Communication
MINERVA MILL, STATION ROAD, ALCESTER
Warwickshire B49 5ET..01789 761 353
w: www.heatherrobinson.co.uk

Henley Group International
MARKET HOUSE, 33 MARKET PLACE, HENLEY-ON-THAMES
Oxfordshire RG9 2AA 01491 570971
e: admin@henley.co.uk
w: www.henley.co.uk

Heritage Film Services
....01837 811243
e: info@heritagefilmservices.com
w: www.heritagefilmservices.com

Highgain Promotions
HYC, HURST ROAD , HORSHAM RH12 2DN 01403 888005
e: sam.albrow@horshamlive.co.uk
w: www.highgainlive.co.uk

HMX Corporate Communication
THE OLD STABLES, STATION ROAD, , QUAINTON, AYLESBURY,
Buckinghamshire HP22 4BW 01296 642070
e: info@hmx.cc
w: www.hmx.cc

House of Bestival
3 LOUGHBOROUGH STREET, LONDON
SE11 5RB 0207 604 2944
e: hello@houseofbestival.net

Ian Nolan Events
HURST STREET STUDIOS, OXFORD
Oxfordshire OX4 1HD 01865 200780
e: info@iannolanevents.com
w: www.iannolanevents.com

Inspiration Events
14 STANHOPE MEWS WEST , LONDON
Greater London SW7 5RB 020 7370 4646
e: info@inspirationevents.com
w: www.inspirationevents.com

Integrity Intl Event Services
THE COACH HOUSE, 7 ST ALBANS ROAD, EDINBURGH
Edinburgh EH9 2PA..0131 624 6040
e: hello@integrity-events.com Integrity Events
w: www.integrity-events.com

International Conferences Ltd
PO BOX 93, ST PETER PORT, GUERNSEY
GY1 3EQ 01481 713643
e: info@inter-conferences.com
w: www.inter-conferences.com

International Creative Talent
18 SOHO SQUARE, LONDON
Greater London W1D 3QL.....................................020 3544 6316
e: info@ictalentagency.com
w: www.ictalentagency.com

Iogig Ltd
39 EQUINOX HOUSE, WAKERING ROAD, BARKING
IG11 8RN...0207 1128 907
e: info@iogig.com
w: www.iogig.com

Istead Business Presentations Ltd
14 HERALD BUSINESS PARK, GOLDEN ACRES LANE, COVENTRY
West Midlands CV3 2SY 024 7663 5530
e: enquiry@istead.co.uk
w: www.istead.co.uk

Ivory Worldwide
21 CHELSEA WHARF, 13-14 CHELSEA WHARF, LONDON
Greater London SW10 0QJ....................................020 3327 7020
e: robbie.crittall@ivoryworldwide.com
w: www.ivoryworldwide.com

Jacqui Leigh Production Management Services
11 MAFEKING ROAD, ENFIELD
EN1 3SS 07971 660089
e: jacqui@jacquileigh.co.uk
w: www.jacquileigh.com

Jade Green Events
56 BLOOMSBURY STREET, LONDON
WC1B 3QT 020 7580 2600
e: info@jadegreenevents.com
w: www.jadegreenevents.com

Jammy Shows & Productions Ltd
CENTURY HOUSE SOUTH, NORTH STATION ROAD, COLCHESTER
Essex CO1 1RE 07930 287507
e: info@jammyshowsandproductions.co.uk
w: www.jammyshowsandproductions.co.u

E

JSL Productions
VILLAGE FARM, ALLENSMORE, HEREFORD
HR2 9AF 01432 355 416
e: info@jslproductions.co.uk
w: www.jsltickets.com

Just Lite Productions
UNIT 31 FINGLAS BUSINESS CENTRE, JAMESTOWN ROAD,
FINGLAS, DUBLIN 11.......................................+ 353 1 806 8333
e: info@justlite.com
w: justlite.com

K13.biz Ltd
....07771 814 764
e: info@k13.biz
w: www.k13.biz

Kent Media and Communications
7A MILL ROAD, STURRY, CANTERBURY
CT2 0AJ...01227 711746
e: be@tunbridgewellsevents.co.uk
w: www.tunbridgewellsevents.co.uk

Kinetika Design Studio
119 HIGH HOUSE ARTISTS' STUDIOS, HIGH HOUSE PRODUCTION
PARK, PURFLEET
Essex RM19 1AS 01708 202846
e: info@kinetika.co.uk
w: www.kinetikadesignstudio.com

KP Events Ltd
34 COLNEY HATCH LANE, LONDON
N10 1DU..0208 883 7411
e: info@kpevents.co.uk
w: www.kpevents.co.uk

Kudos Music
UNIT 10 TRADE CITY, COWLEY MILL ROAD, UXBRIDGE
UB8 2DB...01895 207990
e: info@kudosmusic.co.uk
w: www.kudosmusic.co.uk

Larmac Live Limited
241 - 245 LONG LANE, LONDON
Greater London SE1 4PR.....................................0207 940 9820
e: info@larmaclive.com
w: www.larmaclive.com

LCI Productions Ltd
55 MERTHYR TERRACE, BARNES, LONDON
Greater London SW13 8DL...................................020 8741 5747
e: contact@lci-uk.com
w: www.lci-uk.com

Lee James Associates Ltd
P.O. BOX 61, MAIN STREET, YORK
North Yorkshire YO61 1WD..................................07739 227 687
e: leejamesltd@btconnect.com
w: www.leejamesltd.com

Liberty Events
UNIT 6, SOUTHAMPTON ROW, LONDON
WC1B 4DA...0845 644
6510..
e: denis@awesome-events.co.uk
w: www.christmasatthelodge.com

Light Motif
26 TALINA CENTRE, 23A BAGLEYS LANE, LONDON
Greater London SW6 2BW...................................020 7183 5381
e: info@lightmotif.co.uk
w: www.lightmotif.co.uk

Lipfriend Rodd International
18 SPECTRUM HOUSE, 32-34 GORDON HOUSE ROAD, LONDON
Greater London NW5 1LP....................................020 7267 6066
e: info@lipfriend-rodd.co.uk
w: www.lipfriend-rodd.co.uk

Liquid Media Group Ltd
MEDIA HOUSE, WYNDHAM ROAD, SWINDON
Wiltshire SN2 1EJ 01793 433345
e: sales@liquidmediagroup.co.uk
w: www.liquidmediagroup.co.uk

Live Technologies
3445 MILLENNIUM COURT, COLUMBUS, OHIO
43219.. +1 614 278 7777
e: info@reallivepros.com
w: www.reallivepros.com

LS Live
UNIT 53, LANGTHWAITE BUSINESS PARK, SOUTH KIRKBY,
WAKEFIELD
West Yorkshire WF9 3NR.....................................01977 659 888
e: sales@ls-live.com
w: www.ls-live.com

Lucid Illusions
HIGHSTED FARM , HIGHSTED VALLEY, SITTINGBOURNE
Kent ME9 0AG 020 3488 0265
e: info@lucidillusions.co.uk
w: www.lucidillusions.co.uk

Lucy Attwood Events Ltd
26 BERENS ROAD
NW10 5DT 020 8964 2657
e: parties@lucyattwoodevents.com
w: www.lucyattwoodevents.com

Luxton Cultural Associates
PO BOX 2772, BRIGHTON
East Sussex BN1 6FW..01273 330464
e: peter@luxtoncultural.net
w: www.luxtoncultural.net

MacEvents Event Management
HULTON HOUSE, 11 EWALD ROAD, LONDON
Greater London SW6 3NA .... 020 7736 6606 // 07973 667624
e: cm@macevents.co.uk
w: www.macevents.co.uk

Made Up Ltd
28 RAYMOUTH ROAD, LONDON
Greater London SE16 2DB 020 7231 7678
e: info@madeupltd.com
w: www.madeupltd.com

Maestro Music International
14 CROWN LANE, , THEALE
Berkshire RG7 5BQ 0118-930-3239
e: mail@birminghamtattoo.co.uk
w: www.maestromusicinternational.co.

Magnum Opus Events
....0207 607 0953
e: info@magnumopusevents.london

ManaMedia UK
3RD FLOOR, 152-154 CURTAIN ROAD, LONDON
EC2A 3AT..+44 208 962 9652
e: info@manamediauk.com
w: www.manamediagroup.com

Mantaplan Ltd
DOUGLAS DRIVE, GODALMING
Surrey GU7 1IJ..01483 420088
e: production@mantaplan.com
w: www.mantaplan.com

Marmalade Events
....0852 9382 0619
e: hello@thisismarmalade.com
w: www.thisismarmalade.com

Marshall Arts
PO BOX 66142, LONDON
Greater London NW1W 8PA.................................020 7586 3831
e: info@marshall-arts.co.uk
w: www.marshall-arts.com

Masquerade Events
33 REGENTS DRIVE, REPTON PARK, WOODFORD GREEN
IG8 8RZ..07747 868 050
e: ade@masqueradeuk.com
w: www.masqueradeuk.com

MCCP Ltd
63 WINCHESTER STREET, BOTLEY, SOUTHAMPTON
Hampshire SO30 2EB 01489 782 535
e: GetInTouch@mccp.co.uk
w: www.mccp.ltd.uk

Melville Exhibition & Event Services
UNIT 1, PERIMETER ROAD, NATIONAL EXHIBITION CENTRE,
BIRMINGHAM
West Midlands B40 1PJ 0121 780 3025
e: info@melville.co.uk
w: www.melville.co.uk

Mike Bell
....07970 646705
e: mike@mikebell.eu
w: www.mikebell.eu

Milestone Event Management Ltd
WELBECK HOUSE, CLIFTONVILLE, DORKING
Surrey RH4 2JF..01372 204 057
e: lukeparry@milestone-event.com / paulrockett@milestone-event.com
w: www.milestone-event.com

MJ Lights LTD
....029 2009 2700
e: matt@mjlights.co.uk
w: www.mjlights.co.uk

Mode for...Events
.... 07846 996597 // 07901672598
e: modeforevents@gmail.com
w: www.modeforevents.co.uk

MTFX Confetti Effects
VELT HOUSE, VELT HOUSE LANE, ELMORE
Gloucestershire GL2 3NY 01452 729903
e: info@mtfx.com
w: www.mtfx.com

MTFX High Voltage
VELTHOUSE, VELTHOUSE LANE, ELMORE
Gloucestershire GL2 3NY 01452 729903
e: info@mtfx.com
w: www.mtfx.com

MTFX Special Effects
VELT HOUSE, VELT HOUSE LANE , ELMORE
Gloucestershire GL2 3NY 01452 729 903
e: info@mtfx.com
w: www.mtfx.com

MTFX Winter Effects
VELT HOUSE, VELT HOUSE LANE, ELMORE
Gloucestershire GL2 3NY 01452 729903
e: info@mtfx.com
w: www.mtfx.com

NewCom
11, A2, AL MAWLID, SIDI MAAROUF, 20190 CASABLANCA,
MOROCCO
....212665651520
e: contact@newcom-maroc.com
w: en.newcom-maroc.com/

Night Train Productions Ltd
 34 MELVILLE STREET, EDINBURGH
Edinburgh EH3 7HA 07802 793 912
e: allaboard@nighttrain.co.uk
w: www.nighttrain.co.uk

E

E

Nine Yards Ltd
STUDIO 5 THE HANGAR, PERSEVERANCE WORKS, 38 KINGSLAND ROAD, LONDON
Greater London E2 8DD 0207 195 2300
e: production@nine-yards.co.uk
w: www.nine-yards.co.uk

On Event Production Co.
UNIT 16, WILLOW ROAD,, TRENT LANE INDUSTRIAL ESTATE, CASTLE DONINGTON, DERBY
Derbyshire DE74 2NP 01159 222959
e: hello@on-productions.co.uk
w: www.lovingitlive.co.uk

One Events Management and Production
31B THE COURTYARD, BROOK STREET, GRANTHAM
Lincolnshire NG31 6RX 01476 978184
e: mail@oneevents.org.uk
w: www.oneevents.org.uk

Ontrac Agency
BERWYN HOUSE, 46 MOCHDRE ENTERPRISE PARK, NEWTOWN, BS48 4NP 01686 620400
e: info@ontracagency.com
w: www.ontracagency.com

Opening Doors & Venues
WASSELL GROVE BUSINESS CENTRE, WASSELL GROVE LANE, STOURBRIDGE
West Midlands DY9 9JH...01562 731788
e: rpadmore@opening-doors.org.uk
w: www.opening-doors.org.uk

Optimus Events Ltd
CEM GROUP , SMUGGLERS WAY, HURN LANE , ASHLEY
Dorset BH24 2AG...01425 485040
e: charlotte@cemgroup.com
w: www.cemgroup.com

Organise This
2ND FLOOR, FOURWAYS HOUSE, 57 HILTON STREET, MANCHESTER
Greater Manchester M1 2EJ 0161 273 5107
e: info@organisethis.co.uk
w: www.organisethis.co.uk

OX2P
18 VANTAGE BUSINESS PARK, BLOXHAM ROAD, BANBURY
Oxfordshire OX16 9UX...01295 701464
e: tmatthews@ox2p.co.uk
w: www.ox2p.co.uk

P-AV Event Management
THE OLD MALTHOUSE, RECTORY ROAD, TAPLOW, MAIDENHEAD
 SL6 0ET.................................... 07951 760199 // 01628 628591
e: pav@p-av.co.uk
w: www.p-av.co.uk

P&MM Events & Communications
17/18 SHENLEY PAVILIONS, CHALKDELL DRIVE, SHENLEY WOOD, MILTON KEYNES
Buckinghamshire MK5 6LB....................................01908 764500
e: ideas@zibrantlive.com
w: ourworld.zibrantlive.com/

Perception Events Ltd
ARCH 26, BONDWAY, VAUXHALL, LONDON
Greater London SW8 1SQ 0845 527 5667
e: events@perceptionlive.com
w: www.perceptionlive.com

Perception Live
ARCH 26, HANDEL BUSINESS CENTRE, 73 BONDWAY, VAUXHALL LONDON
Greater London SW8 1SQ 0845 527 5667
e: events@perceptionlive.com
w: www.perceptionlive.com

Peter Kent Productions
78/12 PHATSANA SOI 2, EKAMAI SOI 4, SUKHUMVIT SOI 63, PHRA KHANONG NUA, WATTANA .... +66 802 307 477
e: peter@peterkent.com
w: www.peterkent.com

Pink Buddha Events
510 METROPOLITAN WHARF , 70 WAPPING WALL , LONDON
Greater London E1W 3SS....................................020 7702 0202
e: info@pinkbuddha.com
w: www.pinkbuddha.com

Planet Gold Decor
UNIT 4 ROMARSH, FOWLSWICK BUSINESS PARK, , ALLINGTON
Wiltshire SN14 6QE..07747 015 170
e: info@planetgolddecor.co.uk
w: www.planetgolddecor.co.uk or www.

Planit Ghana
PMB CT 71, CANTONMENTS, ACCRA
 233...................................+233 2 04304555 // 233 2 64546565
e: events@planitghana.com
w: www.planitghana.com

Point Source Productions Ltd
UNIT 5 KIMPTON TRADE & BUSINESS CENTER, MINDEN ROAD, SUTTON Surrey SM3 9PF....................................020 8254 2620
e: info@pslx.co.uk
w: www.pslx.co.uk

Porter & Smith Event Planners
1 FOREST DRIVE, WOODFORD GREEN
Essex IG8 9NG...07796 966 805
e: info@porterandsmith.co.uk
w: www.porterandsmith.co.uk

Premier UK Events Ltd
UNIT 2, ROOKERY LANE, THURMASTON, LEICESTER
Leicestershire LE4 8AU...1162029953
e: ben@premier-ltd.com
w: premier-event-solutions.com/

Presentation Factor
THE OLD PUB YARD, 143 HIGH STREET, BARNET
Hertfordshire EN5 5UZ 020 8364 8999
e: events@presentationfactor.com
w: www.presentationfactor.com

Presentations International
88 HIGH STREET , ETON, WINDSOR
Berkshire SL4 6AF 01753 833749
e: info@presentationsuk.co.uk
w: www.presentationsinternational.co

Prime Events
204 ROSEMOUNT PLACE, ABERDEEN
Aberdeen AB25 2XQ 01224 646488
e: info@primeeventmanagement.com
w: www.primeeventmanagement.com

Production Bureau
HALL FARM, GOWTHORPE LANE, SWARDESTON
Norfolk NR14 8DS..01508 578598
e: general@productionbureau.com
w: www.productionbureau.com

Production Plus Ltd
LYRIC HOUSE, BLACKHORSE ROAD , LETCHWORTH GARDEN CITY
Hertfordshire SG6 1HB..01462 684001
e: info@productionplus.co.uk
w: www.productionplus.co.uk

Production Support Services Ltd
UNIT 18 ASTON ROAD, ASTON FIELDS INDUSTRIAL ESTATE,
BROMSGROVE
Worcestershire B60 3EX 0845 838 1123
e: chris@production-support.net
w: www.production-support.net

Productions Management Services
22 FRESHFIELD PLACE, BRIGHTON
East Sussex BN2 0BN 01273 623972
e: simon@simonbyfordpms.com
w: www.simonbyfordpms.com

Protec (Production Technology LLC)
PLOT NO. 548 - 597, DUBAI INVESTMENT PARK 2,
DUBAI, UNITED ARAB EMIRATES
.... +971 4 880 0092
e: eventrental@productiontec.com
w: www.productiontec.com

Pump House Productions Intl Ltd
THE LOCKHOUSE, MEAD LANE, HERFORD
Hertfordshire SG13 7AX 01992 532483
e: mail@pumphouse.co.uk
w: www.pumphouse.co.uk

Pumphouse
CHURCH HOUSE, KNEESWORTH ST, ROYSTON
 SG8 5AB 01763 250899
e: info@pumphouse.co.uk
w: www.pumphouse.co.uk

Pure Solutions
33 BOND STREET, BRIGHTON
East Sussex BN1 1RD 01273 823333
e: info@pure-solutions.co.uk
w: www.pure-solutions.co.uk

Puxley Limited
11 HARRIER COURT , WESTCOTT LANE , EXETER
 EX5 2DR 01392 364900
e: info@puxley.com
w: www.puxley.com

Quatreus
5 & 6 EASTLANDS INDUSTRIAL ESTATE , KING GEORGES AVENUE,
LEISTON
Suffolk IP16 4LL 07971 350100
e: justine.samouelle@quatreus.com
w: www.quatreus.com/

Red Alligator Group Ltd
SUITE 313, DAISYFIELD BUSINESS CENTRE, APPLEBY STREET,
BLACKBURN
Lancashire BB1 3BL 0844 873 1966
e: info@redalligatorgroup.com
w: www.redalligatorgroup.com

Rhythm Masters Entertainments (RME)
29 FOURTH AVENUE, WATFORD
 WD25 9QB................................ 01923 677358 / 07973 217226
e: info@rme-events.com
w: www.rme-events.com

Robbie Williams Productions
1 ANSELM ROAD
 SW6 1LH 020 7381 1385
e: robbie@rwpltd.co.uk
w: www.rwpltd.co.uk

Rock-Tech Projects
UNIT 2, FRYORS COURT, MURTON
Yorkshire YO19 5UY 01904 481 700
e: info@rock-tech.co.uk
w: www.rock-tech.co.uk

Rockit Promotions
30 OAKTREE DRIVE, ECCLESFECHAN, LOCKERBIE
Dumfriesshire DG11 3EH .... 01576 300761 / 07979 417560
e: rockitpromotions@aol.com
w: www.rockitpromotions.co.uk

RSS Events
BRACKENWOOD CENTRE, BRADSHAW LANE, GREENHALGH,
KIRKHAM
Lancashire PR4 3HQ 01253 596388
e: info@rssevents.co.uk
w: www.rssevents.co.uk

RT Event Ltd
.... 01704 541069 // 07990 546007
e: info@rtevent.co.uk
w: www.rtevent.co.uk

E

E

Safe Security & Events Ltd
63 CRESCENT ROAD, OXFORD
Oxfordshire OX4 2NY 07802 541858
e: info@safesecurityltd.co.uk
w: www.safesecurityltd.co.uk

Safon Events
FFORDD Y BARCER, ST FAGANS, CARDIFF
 CF5 4QP 029 21251196
e: info@safon.co.uk
w: www.safon.co.uk

Scenegineering Ltd
74 HYDEPARK STREET, GLASGOW
Glasgow G3 8BW..................................0141 238 8330
e: info@scenegineering.com
w: www.scenegineering.com

Scenegineering Ltd
74 HYDEPARK STREET, GLASGOW
Glasgow G3 8BW..................................0141 238 8330
e: info@scenegineering.com
w: www.scenegineering.com

Secret Productions
59-65 WORSHIP STREET, LONDON
Greater London EC2A 2DU 020 7688 9000
e: info@secretproductions.net
w: www.secretproductions.net

SES Technical Ltd
UNIT 6 MARLOW ROAD INDUSTRIAL ESTATE, LEICESTER
Leicestershire LE3 2BQ.................................... 0845 226 0330 //
                                                          0116 289 4745
e: sales@sestechnical.co.uk
w: www.sestechnical.co.uk

Sevens7
3RD FLOOR , 46A ROSEBERY AVENUE, LONDON
Greater London EC1R 4RP 020 3096 1348
e: info@sevens7.co.uk
w: www.sevens7.co.uk

Seventh Heaven
....01753 546555
e: info@seventh-heaven-events.co.uk
w: www.seventh-heaven-events.co.uk

SHMS
LAURELS FARM, BARMBY MOOR, YORK
Yorkshire YO42 4EJ................................01759 307863
e: enquiry@shms.co.uk
w: www.shms.co.uk

Show Partners
481 QUARTIER INDUSTRIEL, LOTISSEMENT AL MASSAR, ROUTE
DE SAFI, MARRAKECH, MOROCCO
 40 100...+212 524 35 58 91
e: showpartners@gmail.com
w: www.show-partners.ma

Show Solutions Limited
....01562 863 500
e: mail@showsolutions.co.uk
w: www.showsolutions.co.uk

Showplace Hospitality Suites Ltd
3 STOUR HOUSE, CLIFFORD PARK, CLIFFORD ROAD,
STRATFORD UPON AVON
Warwickshire CV37 8HW 01789 262701
e: info@showplace.co.uk
w: www.showplace.co.uk

Sian Events Ltd
....07415 742291
e: claire.mcdonald@Siangroup.co
w: www.sianevents.com

SMi Group Ltd
2ND FLOOR SOUTH, HARLING HOUSE, 47-51 GREAT SUFFOLK
STREET, LONDON
Greater London SE1 0BS......................................020 7827 6000
e: events@smi-online.co.uk
w: www.smi-online.co.uk

Sound Advice
5 BERGHEM MEWS, BLYTHE ROAD, LONDON
Greater London W14 0HN 020 7229 2219
e: info@soundadvice.uk.com
w: www.soundadvice.uk.com

Sound Artist Management Ltd.
UNIT B54, , 56 WOOD LANE, LONDON
Greater London W12 7SB......................................020 71129073
e: info@soundartistmanagement.com
w: www.soundartistmanagement.com

Sounds Commercial (Swindon)
5 THE MEADS BUSINESS CENTER, ASHWORTH ROAD,
BRIDGEMEAD, SWINDON
Wiltshire SN5 7YJ..................................01793 513777
e: info@soundscommercial.co.uk
w: www.sounds-commercial.co.uk

Sounds Commercial Limited
UNITS 13-16 DRAGON COURT, CROFTS END ROAD, ST GEORGE
Bristol BS5 7XX....................................0117 9355255
e: info@soundscommercial.co.uk
w: www.sounds-commercial.co.uk

Sp Productions
322 HOLLY LODGE MANSIONS, OAKESHOTT AVENUE,
HIGHGATE, LONDON
Greater London N6 6EB 020 8341 9397
e: hello@spproductions.co.uk
w: www.spproductions.co.uk

Speakeasy Productions Ltd
WILDWOOD HOUSE, STANLEY
Perthshire PH1 4NH 01738 828524
e: info@speak.co.uk
w: www.speak.co.uk

Special Projects Europe Ltd
GLENVAR, RATTRAY, BLAIRGOWRIE, SCOTLAND
PH10 7DE 07785 390004
e: johnw@specialprojects-uk.com
w: www.specialprojects-uk.com

Specialized Security
4 ROSEBANK ROAD, ROSEBANK PARK, LIVINGSTON
West Lothian EH54 7EJ...01506 411231
e: info@specializedsecurity.co.uk
w: www.specializedsecurity.co.uk

Spectrum Hire Ltd
UNIT 1 HESTON INDUSTRIAL MALL, CHURCH ROAD, , HESTON
Middlesex TW5 0LD 2079936455
e: info@spectrumhire.co.uk
w: www.spectrumhire.co.uk

Spirit Productions Ltd
130 HIGH STREET, BUSHEY
Hertfordshire WD23 3DE 020 8950 9350
e: angela@spiritartists.com
w: www.spiritshows.com

Spring Harvest
14 HORSTED SQUARE, UCKFIELD
East Sussex TN22 1QG 01825 769111;
01825 769000
e: info@springharvest.org
w: www.springharvest.org

Sprout
23 GANTON STREET, , SOHO, LONDON
Greater London W1F 9BW 0207 292 3600
e: michelle@sprout.tv
w: www.sprout.tv

SPS Productions
UNIT 1, LATHAM PARK, ST BLAZEY ROAD, PAR , CORNWALL
PL24 2JA..01726 817380
e: steve@sps-productions.co.uk
w: www.sps-productions.co.uk

Stage Services Event Production
THE COACH HOUSE, MAYALLS FARM, WATERY LANE, UPPER
WELLAND , MALVERN
Worcestershire WR14 4JX.............01684 560022; 07719 730053
e: info@stage-services.net
w: www.stage-services.net

Stagecraft UK
ST QUENTIN GATE, TELFORD
Shropshire TF3 4JH 01952 281 600
e: sales@stagecraftuk.com
w: www.stagecraftuk.com

StageLightSound Ltd
....1929423223
e: info@stagelightsound.com
w: www.stagelightsound.com

Sterling Events
62 HOPE STREET, LIVERPOOL
Merseyside L1 9BZ 0151 709 8979
e: ben@sterlingevents.co.uk
w: www.sterlingevents.co.uk

Steve Duggan Events
6 SCRUBS LANE, LONDON
Greater London NW10 6RB 02089 603120
e: info@stevenduggganevents.com
w: www.stevenduggganevents.com

Steven Duggan Events London
6 SCRUBS LANE, LONDON
Greater London NW10 6RB 020 8960 3120
e: info@stevenduggganevents.com
w: www.stevenduggganevents.com

Sweet Chariot Leisure Ltd
THE CLUB HOUSE, CHURCH ROAD, EPSOM
Surrey KT17 4DZ 01372 725253
e: info@sweetchariot.org
w: www.sweetchariot.org

Swim Productions
24A HOLYWELL ROW, LONDON
Greater London EC2A 4JB....................................020 7770 6160
e: jim@swimproductions.com
w: www.swimproductions.com

SXS Events
....0870 080 2342
e: hello@sxsevents.co.uk
w: www.sxsevents.co.uk

Symphony Event Management Software
BALGRAVIER HOUSE, 115 ROCKINGHAM STREET, SHEFFIELD
South Yorkshire S1 4EB...0114 2794990
e: info@symphonyem.co.uk
w: www.symphonyem.co.uk

Synario (events & Venues) Ltd
SUITES 5-9, 2ND FLOOR, 2ND FLOOR, BRITANNIA BUSINESS
CENTRE, 70-72 SILVER STREET,, DONCASTER
South Yorkshire DN1 1HT......................................01943 468403
e: johnnie@synario.co.uk
w: www.synario.co.uk

Synergy Event Solutions Ltd
SUITE 114, CASTLE HOUSE, 1 BAKER STREET, STIRLING
Stirlingshire FK8 1AL 08712 249 710
e: ask@synergyeventsolutions.com
w: www.synergyeventsolutions.com

Synergy Event Solutions Ltd
SUITE 114, CASTLE HOUSE, 1 BAKER STREET, STIRLING
FK8 1AL...08712 249 710
e: ask@synergyeventsolutions.com
w: www.synergyeventsolutions.com

E

Tapestry Media and Events Ltd
BATTERSEA STUDIO, 80-82 SILVERTHORNE ROAD, BATTERSEA, LONDON
Greater London SW8 3HE......................................020 8945 5100
e: chris@tapestrymediaandevents.com
w: www.tapestrymediaandevents.com

Tarren Production Ltd
1- 4 THE COURTYARD, ORCHARD FARM,, CHURCH LANE, BENTHAM, CHELTENHAM
Gloucestershire GL51 4TZ.....................................01242 806778
e: chris@tarrenproduction.co.uk
w: www.christarren.co.uk

E

Technology4events
SPIRELLA BUILDING BRIDGE ROAD, LETCHWORTH GARDEN CITY
Hertfordshire SSG6 4ET 01462 476118
e: info@technology4events.co.uk
w: www.technology4events.co.uk

TechST
....07767 366031
e: info@tech-st.co.uk
w: www.tajiri-events.co.uk

Tenpast Events
27 TAVISTOCK SQUARE, LONDON
 WC1H 9HH... 020) 3143 3243 /
07490 390219
e: nh@tenpast.com
w: www.tenpast.com

TFI Meeting Point
192 VAUXHALL BRIDGE ROAD, LONDON
Greater London SW1V 1DX....................................020 7233 5644
e: engagement@tfigroup.com
w: www.tfigroup.com

The Alternative.
2 VALENTINE PLACE , SOUTHWARK , LONDON
 SE1 8QH 0207 803 0905
e: hello@thealternative.co.uk
w: www.thealternative.co.uk

The Conference People
UPPERTON FARM HOUSE, 2 ENYS RD, EASTBOURNE
East Sussex BN21 2DE 01323 644644
e: info@confpeople.co.uk
w: www.confpeople.co.uk

The Copas Partnership
KINGS COPPICE FARM, GRUBWOOD LANE, COOKHAM, MAIDENHEAD
Berkshire SL6 9UB...01628 474678
e: admin@copas.co.uk
w: www.copas.co.uk

The Dark Horses
....07740 363889
e: info@thedarkhorses.com
w: www.thedarkhorses.com

The Event Business
THE HEATH, ALKERTON OAKS BUSINESS PARK, UPTON ESTATE, BANBURY
Oxfordshire OX15 6EP..01295 678042
e: ellislp@theeventbusiness.co.uk
w: www.theeventbusiness.co.uk

The Full Effect
MILLENNIUM STUDIOS, BEDFORD TECHNOLOGY PARK, THURLEIGH
Bedfordshire MK44 2YP 0203 553 5747
e: info@tfe.co.uk
w: www.thefulleffect.co.uk

The Halo Group
THE OLD IMPERIAL LAUNDRY, STUDIO G1 & G2, 71-73 WARRINER GARDENS, LONDON
 SW11 4XW 020 7870 3210
e: info@thehalogroup.co.uk
w: www.thehalogroup.co.uk

The Live Group Plc
UNIT 9, PRINCESS MEWS, HORACE ROAD, KINGSTON UPON THAMES
Surrey KT1 2SZ..020 8481 2000
e: live@livegroup.co.uk
w: www.livegroup.co.uk

The Lovely Party Company
WHITEFRIARS WHARF, TONBRIDGE, KENT
Kent TN9 1QP 01732 669812
e: hq@thelovelypartycompany.com
w: www.thelovelypartycompany.com

The Mermaid
THE MERMAID CONFERENCE & EVENTS CENTRE, PUDDLE DOCK, BLACKFRIARS, LONDON
 EC4V 3DB 2072130704
e: louise.stone@the-mermaid.co.uk
w: www.the-mermaid.co.uk

The Moonlighting Group
THE COACH HOUSE, CRASHMORE LANE, OVERBURY, TEWKESBURY
Gloucestershire GL20 7NX 01386 725600
e: enquiries@moonlightinggroup.co.uk
w: www.moonlightinggroup.co.uk

The Outlook Creative Group
THE COURTYARD, ORCHARD HILL, LITTLE BILLING, NORTHAMPTON
Northamptonshire NN3 9AG...................................0845 8383333
e: sales@outlook.co.uk
w: outlookcreative.uk/

The Presentation Business
9 BUCKSTONE RISE, EDINBURGH
Edinburgh EH10 6UW................ 0131 466 8254 // 07977566727
e: info@tide-motion.co.uk
w: www.tide-motion.co.uk

The Presentation Group
2 HOCKEY CLOSE, LOUGHBOROUGH
Leicestershire LE11 5GX 01509 230005
e: enquiries@thepresentationgroup.co.uk
w: www.thepresentationgroup.co.uk

Think Bright
5.5 PAINTWORKS, BATH ROAD
Bristol BS4 3 EH 0117 971 1127
e: alistair@thinkbright.co.uk
w: www.thinkbright.co.uk

ThinkersLive
15-19 BAKERS ROW, LONDON
Greater London EC1R 3DG...................................020 3967 5716
w: www.thinkerslive.com

Tiga Marketing
PO BOX 183, LEEDS
West Yorkshire LS14 3WA.....................................0113 289 6961
e: info@tigamarketing.co.uk
w: www.tigamarketing.co.uk

Tony Ball Associates Plc
158 - 160 NORTH GOWER STREET, LONDON
Greater London NW1 2ND.....................................020 7554 9900
e: info@tbaplc.co.uk
w: www.tbaplc.co.uk

Top Banana Events and Conferences Ltd
THE COMEDY, 6 FFORD FFAGAN, ST MELLONS, CARDIFF
CF3 2AB 0845 1908728
e: info@topbananaetc.com
w: www.topbananaetc.com

Tower Productions
23 ALBERT ROAD , EDINBURGH
Edinburgh EH6 7DP .... +44 131 552
0100
e: enquiries@tower-productions.com
w: www.tower-productions.com

TSC Events
WOODPOND FARM, BUCKINGHAM ROAD, WHADDON
MK17 0EQ 01908 504766
e: pat@theshooting.co.uk
w: www.theshooting.co.uk

TSE Productions
UNIT 9, TRIDENT BUSINESS PARK,, OAKENGROVE YARD, RED LION
LANE, CHICHESTER ROAD
West Sussex PO20 9DY..01243 603 080
e: contact@tseproductions.co.uk
w: www.tseproductions.co.uk

Twizzle
STUDIO 9, 26 -28 PRIESTS BRIDGE, LONDON
Greater London SW14 8TA.....................................020 8392 0860
e: party@twizzle.co.uk
w: www.twizzle.co.uk

UK Event Services
UNIT 56- ENFIELD INDUSTRIAL ESTATE, REDDITCH
Worcestershire B97 6DE .... 08456 43 48 49 // 08456 44 65 70
e: websitecontact@ukeventservices.co.uk
w: www.ukeventservices.co.uk

Unique Events Ltd
GLADSTONE HOUSE, 6A MILL LANE, EDINBURGH
Edinburgh EH6 6TJ ....
e: admin@unique-events.co.uk
w: www.unique-events.co.uk

Unique Solutions
2 MOUNT PLEASANT, SCARTHIN, CROMFORD, MATLOCK
Derbyshire DE4 3QF...01629 691 691
e: info@uniquesolutions.co.uk
w: www.uniquesolutions.co.uk

Unique Solutions
2 MOUNT PLEASANT, SCARTHIN, CROMFORD, MATLOCK
Derbyshire DE4 3QF...01629 691 691
e: info@uniquesolutions.co.uk
w: www.uniquesolutions.co.uk

Universal Events Services Ltd
UNIT 27, SPACE BUSINESS CENTRE, TEWKESBURY ROAD,
CHELTENHAM
Gloucestershire GL51 9FL.....................................01242 530055
e: info@universalevents.co.uk
w: www.universalevents.co.uk

Universal World Events
ASHFIELD HOUSE, RESOLUTION ROAD, ASHBY DE LA ZOUCH
Leicestershire LE65 1DW................................. +1 215 347 6400
e: info@ashfieldhealthcare.com
w: www.universalworldevents.com

Urban Caprice
63-65 GOLDNEY ROAD, MAIDA VALE
W9 2AR 020 7286 1700
e: events@urbancaprice.co.uk
w: www.urbancaprice.co.uk

Velvet Entertainment
71 MASKELL ROAD, LONDON
Greater London SW17 0NL....................................020 8947 8245
e: info@velvetentertainment.net
w: www.velvetentertainment.net

Velvet Twenty
....020 8675 4870
e: enquiries@velvettwenty.co.uk
w: www.velvettwenty.co.uk

VICTORIA LILY EVENTS
....7545600437
e: victoria@victorialilyevents.co.uk
w: www.victorialilyevents.co.uk

E

VirtualStudio.TV
SUITE 3, 35 FOREHILL, ELY
Cambridgeshire CB7 4AA............................ +44(0)1223 520968
e: hello@virtualstudio.tv
w: www.virtualstudio.tv

Vision Dance Co
2 WHITEFRIARS WHARF, TONBRIDGE, KENT
TN9 1QP 01273 418 913
e: enquiries@visiondanceco.com
w: www.visiondanceco.com

Visual Response Ltd
WILD RENTS STUDIO, 20-30 WILDS RENTS, LONDON
Greater London SE1 4QG 020 7378 7731
w: www.visualresponse.com

W1 Productions Ltd
UNIT 7 WOODLANDS BUSINESS PARK, BURY ST EDMUNDS
Suffolk IP30 9ND 0870 2405217
e: info@w1productions.co.uk
w: www.w1productions.co.uk

Wellpleased Events
11 BLAYDS YARD, LEEDS
West Yorkshire LS1 4AD..0113 244 2720
e: info@wellpleased.co.uk
w: www.wellpleased.co.uk

West End Events
27 OLD GLOUCESTER STREET, LONDON
Greater London WC1N 3AN 020 3740 1539
e: bookings@westendevents.co.uk
w: www.westendevents.co.uk

West Ent
UNIT 2, CAMBRIAN BUSINESS PARK, CARMARTHEN
Carmathenshire SA31 3RB.....................................01267 243957
e: carmarthen@westent.co.uk
w: www.westent.co.uk

Whole Nine Yards Productions Limited
ST. NICHOLAS HOUSE, 31-34 HIGH STREET, BRISTOL
Bristol BS1 2AW.. +44 117 315 5220
e: info@wny.uk.com
w: www.wny.uk.com

Wilde Ones International Events Ltd
UNIT 122, WESTMINSTER BUSINESS SQUARE, DURHAM STREET, LONDON
Greater London SE11 5JH.....................................020 7793 7933
e: info@wildeones.co.uk
w: www.wildeones.co.uk

WM Event Design
19 ST JAMES'S DRIVE, WANDSWORTH COMMON, LONDON
Greater London SW17 7RN 020 3837 4926
e: info@williammoyse.com
w: www.wmeventdesign.com

Wrg
MERCHANTS WAREHOUSE, 21 CASTLE STREET,, MANCHESTER
Greater Manchester M3 4LZ .... +44 0845 313 0000
e: hello@wrglive.com
w: www.wrg.uk.com

WRG Live
MERCHANTS WAREHOUSE, 21 CASTLE STREET, MANCHESTER
Greater Manchester M3 4LZ .....084 5313 0000 / 07887 7674000
e: andrew.savill@wrglive.com
w: www.wrglive.com

Yellow Bus Events Ltd
BURNTSTONES LODGE, 49 MOORBANK ROAD, SHEFFIELD
South Yorkshire S10 5TQ 0114 230 4397
e: info@yellowbusevents.co.uk
w: www.yellowbusevents.co.uk

Zerodb Live
38 NIGEL HOUSE, PORTPOOL LANE, LONDON
Greater London EC1N 7UR 020 3332 0049
e: info@zerodblive.com
w: www.zerodblive.com

Event Staff

24c Birmingham - Event Crew
OLD WARWICK ROAD, LAPWORTH
Warwickshire B94 6LU..0845 170 2424
e: crew@24c.co.uk
w: 24c.co.uk

Ace Crew Ltd
UNIT 6, PRINCESS COURT, 1 HORACE ROAD,
KINGSTON UPON THAMES
Greater London KT1 2SL.......................................0207 924 6569
e: admin@acecrew.co.uk
w: www.acecrew.co.uk

Achilleus
HEAD OFFICE 6 ATLANTIC BUSINESS CENTRE,, CHINGFORD, LONDON
Greater London E4 7ES ....020 8221 4180 /
0800 358 0983
e: info@achilleus.co.uk
w: www.achilleus.co.uk

Aesthetics Event Ltd
GAINSBOROUGH HOUSE, 81 OXFORD STREET, LONDON
Greater London W1D 2EU.....................................02476 631 093
e: info@aesthetics.co.uk
w: www.aesthetics.co.uk

Aesthetics International Event Staff
C12 GENERATOR HALL , ELECTRIC WHARF , COVENTRY
West Midlands CV1 4JL 02476 631 093
e: info@aesthetics.co.uk
w: www.aesthetics.co.uk

Anything Audio
32 BARKSTON HOUSE, CROYDON ST, LEEDS
West Yorkshire LS11 9RT 0113 322 5001
e: info@anythingaudio.co.uk
w: www.anythingaudio.co.uk

At Your Service Event Staffing
12 THE TALINA CENTRE, BAGLEYS LANE, LONDON
Greater London SW6 2BW....................................020 7610 8610
e: london@ays.co.uk
w: www.atyourservice.co.uk

Beacon Security Services
8 TEKNOL HOUSE, VICTORIA ROAD, BURGESS HILL
West Sussex RH15 9LH..0800 999 2479
e: info@beacon-services.co.uk
w: www.beacon-services.co.uk

Blast Event Hire
UNIT 1 & 2 BONVILLE BUSINESS ESTATE, DIXON ROAD,
BRISLINGTON
Bristol BS4 5QQ 0117 370 2660
e: info@blasteventhire.co.uk
w: www.blasteventhire.co.uk

Boys and Girls Promotions
81-83 FULHAM HIGH STREET, FULHAM GREEN, LONDON
Greater London SW6 3JA......................................020 7167 6874
e: contact@boysandgirlspromotions.co.uk
w: www.boysandgirlspromotions.co.uk

Cautela Security
132 SAMLET ROAD, LLANSAMLET, SWANSEA, WALES
 SA7 9AF 0845 4759981
e: info@cautelasecurityukltd.co.uk
w: www.cautelasecurityukltd.co.uk

Citrus Event Staffing Ltd
1 SOUTHLANDS, HIGH HEATON, NEWCASTLE UPON TYNE
Tyne and Wear NE7 7YH.......................................0191 6030751
e: info@citruseventstaffing.co.uk
w: www.citruseventstaffing.co.uk

CJ's Events Warwickshire
THE COW YARD, CHURCH FARM, , CHURCH LANE, BUDBROOKE,
WARWICK
Warwickshire CV35 8QL..01926 800 750
e: info@cjseventswarwickshire.co.uk
w: www.cjseventswarwickshire.co.uk

Conferents Ltd
1 CONISTON, WEXHAM STREET, STOKE POGES
Buckinghamshire SL3 6NP....................................01753 664222
e: info@conferents.com
w: www.conferents.com

CREW Yorkshire
3 PARK SQUARE EAST, LEEDS
West Yorkshire LS1 2NE.......................................01132 161 252
e: info@yorkshireeventscrew.co.uk
w: www.yorkshireeventscrew.co.uk

Crewsaders Event Staff
MILLER 2, 61 ST. PAULS SQUARE, BIRMINGHAM
West Midlands B3 1QS 0845 094 4884
e: bookings@crewsaders.com
w: www.crewsaders.com

Dazzle
24 PARK STREET, LEAMINGTON SPA
Warwickshire CV32 4QN 01926 423290
e: ann@dazzlepeople.com
w: www.dazzlepeople.com

DC Site Services Ltd
FENLAND DISTRICT INDUSTRIAL ESTATE, STATION ROAD,
WHITTLESEY, PETERBOROUGH
Cambridgeshire PE7 2EY 01733 200713
e: admin@dcsiteservices.com
w: www.dcsiteservices.com

Doyen AEP Ltd
OSBORNES, MAYPOLE ROAD, CHELSFIELD, ORPINGTON
 BR6 7RB...020 8166 5528
e: enquiries@doyenaep.com
w: www.doyenaep.com

Echo Staffing
SUITE 34, 67-68 HATTON GARDEN, LONDON
Greater London EC1N 8JY 020 3000 6960
e: info@echostaffing.co.uk
w: www.echostaffing.co.uk

eStage Production Ltd
71Â "75 SHELTON STREET, COVENT GARDEN, LONDON
 WC2H 9JQ 2071128903
e: chat@estage.net
w: https://production.estage.net

Event Hosts
71-75 SHELTON ST, COVENT GARDEN, LONDON
Greater London WC2H 9JQ...................................0208 935 55 87
e: info@event-hosts.com
w: www.event-hosts.com

Event Protocol
86-90 PAUL STREET, LONDON
Greater London EC2A 4NE 020 8099 9690
w: www.event-protocol.co.uk

Event Staff
UNIT 27, SPACE BUSINESS CENTRE, TEWKESBURY ROAD,
CHELTENHAM
Gloucestershire GL51 9FL.....................................01242 530055
e: info@event-staff.co.uk
w: www.event-staff.co.uk

Eventeem
ONE CASPIAN POINT, PIERHEAD STREET, CARDIFF WATERSIDE
 CF10 4DQ 02921 676 500
e: hello@eventeem.co.uk
w: www.eventeem.co.uk

E

EW Production Services
UNIT C, WESLAKE INDUSTRIAL PARK , RYE HARBOUR
TN31 7TE...1797225166
e: paul@ewpsl.com
w: www.ewpsl.com/

Festaff
....07702 211030
e: clients@festaff.co.uk
w: www.festaff.co.uk

E

Fizz Experience Ltd
VINE COURT, CHALKPIT LANE, DORKING
Surrey RH4 1AJ 01306 640980
e: fizz@fizzexperience.co.uk
w: www.fizz.co.uk

Flair Event Staffing Ltd
4A ROCK MILL LANE, NEW MILLS
Derbyshire SK22 3BN ....01400 220022 / 07961 988644
e: work@flairevents.co.uk
w: www.eventstaffing.co.uk

Fresh Events UK
UNIT D WESLAKE INDUSTRIAL PARK, RYE HARBOUR ROAD, RYE
East Sussex TN31 7TE 07919 512 608
e: info@fresheventsuk.com
w: www.fresheventsuk.com

G4S Events
SOUTHSIDE, 105 VICTORIA STREET, LONDON
Greater London SW1E 6QT....................................0207 963 3100
w: www.g4s.uk.com

Get Scheduled Ltd
1 LONDON STREET, READING
Berkshire RG1 4QW 084 5299 3459
e: sales@getscheduled.co.uk
w: www.getscheduled.co.uk

Go2Show
113 LINCOLN ROAD, LONDON
Greater London EN1 1LH.......................................020 8292 6103
e: bookings@gotoshow.co.uk
w: www.gotoshow.co.uk

Green Machine Events
....07850 631153
w: www.greenmachineevents.co.uk

Hel's Angels
FIRST FLOOR, 4 GREAT NEWPORT STREET, LONDON
Greater London WC2H 7JB....................................020 3301 3845
e: team@helsangels.net
w: www.helsangels.net

Highjam
HIGHJAM MARKETING, 219 LONG LANE, LONDON
Greater London SE1 4PR..020 7407 7464
e: hello@highjam.co.uk
w: www.highjam.co.uk

Image Hospitality & Castings Ltd
3000 CATHEDRAL HILL, GUILDFORD
Surrey GU2 7YB 01483 243690
e: jane@imagehospitality.co.uk
w: www.imagehospitality.co.uk/

JE Events LTD
26 DAGOBERT HOUSE, SMITHY STREET, LONDON
 E1 3HW 07592 074548
e: staffing@jeevents.co.uk
w: www.jeevents.co.uk

Jobs 2 Go
GIBSON HALL, 13 BISHOPSGATE, LONDON
Greater London EC2N 3BA 020 7334 3929
e: chris@jobs-2-go.co.uk
w: www.jobs-2-go.co.uk

LOLA Events
UNIT 2 NEW NORTH HOUSE, 202-208 NEW NORTH ROAD,
LONDON
Greater London N1 7BJ...020 7043 0652
e: info@lolaevents.co.uk
w: www.lolaevents.co.uk

LondonCrew.Co
....0871 91 8114
e: info@londoncrew.co
w: www.londoncrew.co

Mash Staffing
2 ARTBRAND STUDIOS, 7 LEATHERMARKET ST, LONDON
Greater London SE1 3HN 020 7939 7670
e: hello@mashstaffing.com
w: www.mashstaffing.com

Matching Models
26, CADOGAN SQUARE, LONDON
Greater London SW1X 0JP....................................020 339 74033
e: info@matchingmodels.com
w: www.matchingmodels.com

Metro Hospitality
UNIT B507, OLD BISCUIT FACTORY, 100 CLEMENTS ROAD,
LONDON
Greater London SE16 4DG 020 7237 5516
e: info@metrohospitality.co.uk
w: www.metrohospitality.co.uk

Minimal Risk Consultancy Ltd
MINIMAL RISK CONSULTANCY LTD, SKYLON COURT COLDNOSE
ROAD, HEREFORD
Herefordshire HR2 6JS 01432 359353
w: www.minimalrisk.co.uk

MP Squares Ltd
FORTIS HOUSE, 160 LONDON ROAD, BARKING
Essex IG11 8BB 020 8214 1125
e: squares@mp-squares.co.uk
w: www.mp-squares.co.uk

Nebula Events
8 ENBORNE WAY, BRIMPTON, READING
Berkshire RG7 4TP.. 07930 420 257
e: info@nebula-events.co.uk
w: www.nebula-events.co.uk

Neon Arena Services
UNIT 305, THE ARGENT CENTRE, 60 FREDERICK STREET,
HOCKLEY, BIRMINGHAM
West Midlands B1 3HS..0121 236 5555
e: info@neonarenaservices.co.uk
w: www.neonsportsfloors.co.uk

Newthorn - Event Staffing Solutions
THE MILLHOUSE, STATION ROAD, CASTLE DONINGTON, DERBY
Derbyshire DE74 2NJ...01332 811463
e: info@newthorn.co.uk
w: www.newthorn.co.uk

Nova Stage & Live Event Crew
UNIT C3 PALMERSVALE BUSINESS CENTRE, PALMERSTON RD,,
BARRY, VALE OF GLAMORGAN
 CF63 2XA 01446 734185
e: info@novacrew.co.uk
w: www.novacrew.co.uk

Omega Resource Group Ltd
OMEGA HOUSE, BOND'S MILL, STONEHOUSE
Gloucestershire GL10 3RF.....................................01453 827333
e: info@omegaresource.co.uk
w: www.omegaresource.co.uk

Paam
UNIT 1, MIDDLE YARD, HOME FARM ROAD, ELVETHAM, HOOK
Hampshire RG27 8AW...0845 355 0604
e: info@paamapplication.co.uk
w: www.paamapplication.co.uk

Panther Crew Ltd
....0845 467 1858 / 07789179921
e: info@panthercrew.com
w: www.panthercrew.com

Paratus Limited
THE OLD Q STORES, BROWNING BARRACKS, ALDERSHOT
Hampshire GU11 2BU 01252 341 260
w: www.paratus.org.uk

Phoenix Services Security
....01243 785148
w: www.securitybyphoenix.co.uk

Pitman's People Event Staff
UNIT G1A STAMFORD WORKS, 3 GILLETT ST., LONDON
Greater London N16 8JH..020 3651 3330
e: admin@pitmanspeople.com
w: www.pitmanspeople.com

Positive Protection Solutions
1ST FLOOR OFFICES, 14 NEW KINGSWAY, WEST COYNEY,
STOKE ON TRENT
Staffordshire ST3 6NA 01782 596611
e: info@ppssecurity.co.uk
w: ppssecurity.co.uk/

Pro Crews Ltd
....020 3457 8423
e: info@procrews.co.uk
w: www.procrews.co.uk

Production Team
15C WARWICK AVENUE, LONDON
Greater London W9 2PS..020 7289 7649
e: barbara@productionteam.co.uk
w: www.productionteam.co.uk

Push Promotions
HENWOOD COURT, COMPTON
West Midlands WV6 8PG.......................................0800 002 9791
e: bookings@pushpromotions.co.uk
w: www.pushpromotions.co.uk

Regal Promotions
THE BROADGATE TOWER, 20 PRIMROSE STREET, LONDON
 EC2A 2EW 020 3289 5960
e: info@regalpromotionslondon.com
w: www.regalpromotionslondon.com

RES-Crew Ltd
20-22 WENLOCK ROAD, LONDON
Greater London N1 7GU .... 07985565800 // 02038374985
e: hallo@res-crew.co.uk
w: www.res-crew.co.uk

Rodeo Hire
....8700113993
e: info@rodeohire.com
w: www.rodeohire.com

Roman Co (Gloucester) Limited
UNIT 36/3 MORELANDS TRADING ESTATE, BRISTOL ROAD,,
GLOUCESTER
Gloucestershire GL1 5RZ 07807 850005
e: stuart@roman-co.org
w: www.roman-co.org

Salima Ltd
2A BACCHUS HOUSE, CALLEVA PARK, ALDERMASTON, READING
Berkshire RG7 8EN ....0845 458 1699 / 07825 586 083
e: info@salima-ltd.co.uk
w: www.salima-ltd.co.uk

Shaker Events Mobile Cocktail Bar Services
HEAD OFFICE (MIDLANDS & LONDON), UNIT 312, JUBILEE TRADE
CENTRE, 130 PERSHORE STREET, BIRMINGHAM
West Midlands B5 6ND 08707 202 877
w: www.shaker-events.co.uk

E

E

Show Management Services Ltd
NEWTON MAGNUS CO, ARROWSMITH COURT, STATION
APPROACH, BROADSTONE
Dorset BH18 8AT ....
e: info@showmanagementservices.co.uk
w: www.showmanagementservices.co.uk

Showforce
UNIT 001 STRATFORD WORKSHOPS, BURFORD ROAD,
STRATFORD, LONDON
Greater London E15 2SP 0208 519 5252
e: info@showforce.com
w: www.showforce.com

Showsec Training & Development Centre
REGENT HOUSE, 16 WEST WALK, LEICESTER
Leicestershire LE1 7NA..0116 204 3333
e: joseph.milner@showsec.co.uk
w: www.showsec.co.uk

SilverLine Events
GUNNERY TERRACE, CORNWALLIS ROAD, LONDON
 SE18 6SW ....020 8301 8459 / 07577 558 255
e: jorge@silverline-events.com
w: silverline-events.com/

Snap Crew UK
....07837 592361
e: info@snapcrew.co.uk
w: www.snapcrew.co.uk

Splendid Events
68 SOUTH LAMBETH ROAD, VAUXHALL, LONDON
Greater London SW8 1RL...........0207 100 8884 / 0207 099 4292
e: hannah@splendid.co.uk
w: www.splendid.co.uk

Stage Miracles Ltd
WOODLANDS, SCHOOL ROAD, POTTERS BAR
Hertfordshire EN6 1JW 01707 662 500
e: mail@stagemiracles.co.uk
w: www.stagemiracles.com

T-A-G Promotional Staff
.................................020 8330 6154 / 07710 937 437
e: enquiries@tagprom.com
w: www.tagprom.com

Take On Ltd
32 CLERKENWELL GREEN, LONDON
 EC1R 0DU..020 3701 2310
e: info@takeonservices.com
w: www.takeonservices.com

The Esprit Group
UNIT 4 HURLINGHAM BUSINESS PARK, SULIVAN ROAD, FULHAM
Greater London SW6 3DU 020 7384 4100
e: account.manager@esprit-group.com
w: www.esprit-group.com

The Promotional People Agency
PO BOX 2188, BUCKINGHAM
Buckinghamshire MK18 9BE..................................07496 674732
e: enquiries@promotionalpeople.co.uk
w: www.promotionalpeople.co.uk

The Really Good Bar Company
....01983 730222
e: hello@reallygoodbars.com
w: www.reallygoodbars.com

Tidy Models
KEMP HOUSE, 152-160 CITY ROAD, LONDON
Greater London EC1V 2NX...................................020 3000 7975
e: info@tidymodels.com
w: www.tidymodels.com

Total Care Security Ltd
UNIT 3 , BRUNEL DRIVE, NEWARK
Nottinghamshire NG24 2DE 0800 917 47 67
e: info@totalcaresecurity.com
w: www.totalcaresecurity.com

Touchwood Security Ltd
6 SOUTH BAR, BANBURY
Oxfordshire OX16 9AA...01280 700866
e: info@touchwoodsecuritylimited.co.uk
w: www.touchwoodsecuritylimited.co.u

Twist London
....0208 150 0052
e: giles@twistlondon.com
w: www.twistlondon.com

Urban Crew Ltd
112 ALEXANDRA ROAD, WIMBLEDON
Greater London SW19 7JY 08452 262 818
e: info@urbancrewltd.com
w: www.urbancrewltd.com

Varii Promotional Staff
OFFICE 8A ROCKHILL ESTATE, BRISTOL
 BS31 1PE 1172140251
e: simon@varii.co.uk
w: www.varii-promotions.co.uk/

Varii Promotions
OFFICE 8A ROCKHILL ESTATE, BRISTOL
 BS31 1PE 1172140251
e: simon@varii.co.uk
w: www.varii-promotions.co.uk

Well Done Promotions
3A, SHERBOURNE ROAD, ACOCKS GREEN, BIRMINGHAM
West Midlands B27 6AA.......................................0121 605 9623
e: events@welldonepromotions.co.uk
w: www.welldonepromotions.co.uk

WM Event Design
19 ST JAMES'S DRIVE, WANDSWORTH COMMON, LONDON
Greater London SW17 7RN 020 3837 4926
e: info@williammoyse.com
w: www.wmeventdesign.com

Yes People - Promo Staff
62 DUKE ROAD, BARKINGSIDE
Greater London IG6 1NL.......................................020 3627 1116
e: Accounts@yespeople.co.uk
w: www.yespeople.co.uk

Exhibitions

ACA Creative Exhibition Solutions
WOODCOCK LANE, HORDLE
Hampshire SO41 0FG 0 7771 633993
e: studio@aca-exhibitions.co.uk
w: www.aca-exhibitions.co.uk

Apex
EXHIBITION HOUSE, LONDON ROAD, MACCLESFIELD
Cheshire SK11 7QX..01625 429370
e: mail@apex.co.uk
w: www.apex.co.uk

Arte Laguna Prize
VIA ROMA 29/A, VENICE
45017..0039 0415937242
e: info@artelagunaprize.com
w: www.artelagunaprize.com

Brintex Ltd
32 VAUXHALL BRIDGE ROAD, LONDON
Greater London SW1V 2SS....................................020 7973 6400
e: info@hgluk.com
w: www.brintex.com

Broadway Events Ltd
UNIT 3, 3 CROW ARCH LANE, RINGWOOD
Hampshire BH24 1PB 01425 838393
e: info@broadway-events.co.uk
w: www.broadway-events.co.uk

Dryspace Structures Ltd
BLACK LAMBS FARM, BUNKERS HILL ROAD
Kent TN15 7EY...... 01634 230034 / 01474 812353 / 07885 8890
e: info@dryspace.co.uk
w: www.dryspace.co.uk

Electra Events & Exhibitions
ADNEC HOUSE, PO BOX 95001,
ABU DHABI, UNITED ARAB EMIRATES
.... +971 2 406 4377
e: info@electradubai.ae
w: www.electra-exhibitions.com

English Heritage
FIRE FLY AVENUE , SWINDON
Wiltshire SN2 2EH 0870 333 1181
e: customers@english-heritage.org.uk
w: www.english-heritage.org.uk

Enigma Visual Solutions
UNIT 9, FIRST AVENUE GLOBE PARK , MARLOW
Buckinghamshire SL7 1YA............01628624754 / 0845 314 3803
e: companyenigma@gmail.com
w: eni.co.uk/

Equestrian Management Consultants Ltd
STOCKELD PARK , WETHERBY
West Yorkshire LS22 4AW 01937 587 062
e: info@beta-int.com
w: www.beta-uk.org

Events Contacts Ltd
44 SOUTHDEAN CLOSE, MIDDLETON-ON-SEA
PO22 7TH..01243 538456
e: janesterck@eventscontacts.com
w: www.eventscontacts.com

EwePack Shipping
THE MANOR HOUSE HIGH STREET , BUNTINGFORD, HERTS
SG9 9AB.. +44 207 118 7447
e: steve@ewepack.com
w: www.ewepack.com

Gamewagon Ltd
113 - 115 OYSTER LANE, BYFLEET
Surrey KT14 7JZ...0845 319 4263
e: julie.owen@gamewagon.co.uk
w: www.gamewagon.co.uk

Grid Girls Promotions
36 LANCING CLOSE, LANCING
West Sussex BN15 9NJ 1903537780
e: clothing@grid-girls.co.uk
w: www.gridgirlspromotions.com

Hodgson Events
KEVIS HOUSE, LOMBARD STREET, PETWORTH
West Sussex GU28 0AG 01798 215 007
e: mail@hodgsonevents.com
w: www.hodgsonevents.com

Inhouse Exhibition
.... +91 97693 81737
e: enquiry@inhouseexhibition.com
w: www.inhouseexhibition.com

JPFoto
8 LEATHERWORKS WAY, LITTLE BILLING VILLAGE,
NORTHAMPTON
Northamptonshire NN3 9BP .... 01933 628139 // 01604 419112
e: info@jpfoto.co.uk
w: www.jpfoto.co.uk/corporate-event-

E

Lance Show & Publications Ltd
COURTYARD OFFICE, THE COURTYARD, PARSONS POOL, SHAFTESBURY
Dorset SP7 8AP 01747 854099
e: info@showmans-directory.co.uk
w: www.showmans-directory.co.uk

Large Creative Executive
11 BRIGHTMOOR STREET, NOTTINGHAM
Nottinghamshire NG1 1FD 0115 9881 557
e: info@large-creative.com
w: www.large-creative.com

Liquid Media Group Ltd
MEDIA HOUSE, WYNDHAM ROAD, SWINDON
Wiltshire SN2 1EJ 01793 433345
e: sales@liquidmediagroup.co.uk
w: www.liquidmediagroup.co.uk

Mobex Ltd
UNIT 6 RIGESTATE INDUSTRIAL ESTATE, STATION ROAD, BERKELEY
Gloucestershire GL13 9RL.....................................01453 511 210
e: exhibit@mobex.co.uk
w: www.mobex.co.uk

Nationwide Events Limited
PINNACLE HOUSE, 166A GLOUCESTER ROAD NORTH, PATCHWAY
Bristol BS34 5BG 0117 907 1000
e: enquiries@nwe.co.uk
w: www.nationwide-events.co.uk

Nationwide Exhibitions
PO BOX 20, FISHPONDS
Bristol BS16 5QU...0117 907 1000
e: scott@nwe.co.uk
w: www.nwe.co.uk

Nationwide Media Group
PO BOX 20 , FISHPONDS
Bristol BS16 5QU...0117 907 1000
e: martinc@nwe.co.uk
w: www.swmee.co.uk

Nebrak Ltd
UNIT 1, IPPLEPEN BUSINESS PARK , IPPLEPEN
Devon TQ12 5UG 01803 813900
e: enquiries@nebrak.com
w: www.nebrak.co.uk

Nomadic Display U.K
NOMADIC HOUSE 71 , ST. JOHNS ROAD , ISLEWORTH
 TW7 6XQ ....0208 326 0000 / 0208 326 5555
e: info@nomadicdisplay.co.uk
w: www.nomadicdisplay.co.uk/

Ocean Media Group Ltd (Coventry)
BANK HOUSE , 23 WARWICK ROAD , COVENTRY
West Midlands CV1 2EW.......................................024 76 571100
e: enquiries@oceanmedia.co.uk
w: www.oceanmedia.co.uk

Ocean Media Group Ltd (london)
ONE CANADA SQUARE, CANARY WHARF, LONDON
Greater London E14 5AP.......................................020 7772 8300
e: enquiries@oceanmedia.co.uk
w: www.oceanmedia.co.uk

Orchard Events Ltd
POND HOUSE, 1 PRIORY ROAD, RICHMOND
Surrey TW9 3DQ 020 8332 9595
e: info@orchardevents.co.uk
w: www.festivegiftfair.co.uk

PAULEY
BLETCHLEY LEYS FARM , WHADDON ROAD, MILTON KEYNES
Buckinghamshire MK17 0EG.................................01908 522532
e: info@pauley.co.uk
w: www.pauley.co.uk

Pitman's People Event Staff
UNIT G1A STAMFORD WORKS, 3 GILLETT ST., LONDON
Greater London N16 8JH.......................................020 3651 3330
e: admin@pitmanspeople.com
w: www.pitmanspeople.com

Planet Gold Decor
UNIT 4 ROMARSH, FOWLSWICK BUSINESS PARK, , ALLINGTON
Wiltshire SN14 6QE..07747 015 170
e: info@planetgolddecor.co.uk
w: www.planetgolddecor.co.uk or www.

Plasa
1 EDWARD ROAD , EASTBOURNE
East Sussex BN23 8AS 01323 524120
e: info.eu@plasa.org
w: www.plasa.org

POD Exhibitions
LOWER FARM, HIGH STREET, IRCHESTER
Northamptonshire NN29 7AB 01933 411159
e: enquiries@podweb.co.uk
w: www.pod-exhibition-systems.co.uk

Premier UK Events Ltd
UNIT 2, ROOKERY LANE, THURMASTON, LEICESTER
Leicestershire LE4 8AU...1162029953
e: ben@premier-ltd.com
w: premier-event-solutions.com/

Presentation Factor
THE OLD PUB YARD, 143 HIGH STREET, BARNET
Hertfordshire EN5 5UZ 020 8364 8999
e: events@presentationfactor.com
w: www.presentationfactor.com

Print 2 Media Ltd
UNIT 7 MOORSWATER INDUSTRIAL ESTATE, LISKEARD, CORNWALL
Cornwall PL14 4LN 01579 340985
e: info@print-2-media.com
w: www.print-2-media.com

Promus Productions Ltd
15 STIRLING PARK, LAKER ROAD, ROCHESTER
Kent ME1 3QR 01708 746 111
e: events@promusproductions.com
w: www.promusproductions.com

Sculpture Studios
UNIT 3F HARVEY ROAD, NEVENDON INDUSTRIAL ESTATE,
BASILDON
Essex SS13 1DA 01268 726470
e: aden.hynes@hotmail.com
w: www.sculpturestudios.co.uk

Single Market Events Ltd
GREYHOUND HOUSE, 23-24 GEORGE STREET,
RICHMOND UPON THAMES
Greater London TW9 1HY.......................020 8948 5522
e: info@single-market.co.uk
w: www.single-market.co.uk

Skyline Whitespace
320 WESTERN ROAD, LONDON
Greater London SW19 2QA 0845 260 5440
e: getintouch@skylinewhitespace.com
w: www.skylinewhitespace.com

Sprout
23 GANTON STREET, , SOHO, LONDON
Greater London W1F 9BW 0207 292 3600
e: michelle@sprout.tv
w: www.sprout.tv

Stoneapple Productions Ltd
21 CARYSFORT ROAD, LONDON
Greater London N16 9AA 020 7226 6900
e: mail@stoneapple.co.uk
w: www.stoneapple.co.uk

Team Visual Solutions Ltd
1ST FLOOR ENAVANT HOUSE, REFORM ROAD, MAIDENHEAD
Berkshire SL6 8BT .... +44 1753 569967 // +44 1753 569453
e: create@team-solutions.co.uk
w: www.team-solutions.co.uk

Teem Services Ltd
41 WARWICK ROAD, , OLTON, SOLIHULL
 B92 7HS 0121 707 4222
e: teemservices@aol.com

The Promotional People Agency
PO BOX 2188, BUCKINGHAM
Buckinghamshire MK18 9BE.................07496 674732
e: enquiries@promotionalpeople.co.uk
w: www.promotionalpeople.co.uk

Tony Ball Associates Plc
158 - 160 NORTH GOWER STREET, LONDON
Greater London NW1 2ND 020 7554 9900
e: info@tbaplc.co.uk
w: www.tbaplc.co.uk

Tow Master
UNIT 5, AMBER COURT, OFF WALTHEW HOUSE LANE, MARTLAND
PARK, WIGAN
Greater Manchester WN5 0JY 01942 226633
e: comments@towmasteruk.com
w: www.towmasteruk.co.uk

Twentyfirst Century Communications
MORAY HOUSE, 23-31 GREAT TITCHFIELD STREET, LONDON
Greater London W1W 7PA 020 7291 0444
e: hello@cheerfultwentyfirst.com
w: cheerfultwentyfirst.com/

UBM Live
240 BLACKFRIARS ROAD, LONDON
Greater London SE1 8BF.......................020 7921 5000
e: nmilne@ubm.com
w: www.ubm.com

Vcm Exhibitions
WELLESLEY HOUSE, MANOR ROAD, HASSOCKS
 BN6 9UH...................................01273 836800, 0845 5464 121
e: events@vcm.co.uk info@vcm.co.uk
w: www.vcm.co.uk

Versatile Venues Ltd
WIRELESS HOUSE, WIRELESS HILL, SOUTH LUFFENHAM
Rutland LE15 8NF...................08000 147 338 / 01780 720 217
e: info@versatilevenues.co.uk
w: www.versatilevenues.co.uk

Visual Response Ltd
WILD RENTS STUDIO, 20-30 WILDS RENTS, LONDON
Greater London SE1 4QG 020 7378 7731
w: www.visualresponse.com

Warners Group Publications Plc
EXHIBITION DEPT, THE MALTINGS, WEST STREET, BOURNE
Lincolnshire PE10 9PH..........................01778 391123
e: maxines@warnersgroup.co.uk
w: www.warnersgroup.co.uk

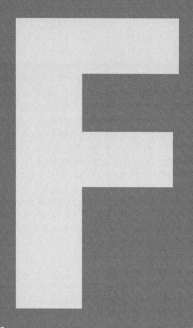

Fabric

Whaley (Bradford) Ltd
HARRIS COURT, GREAT HORTON, BRADFORD
West Yorkshire BD7 4EQ 01274 576718
e: info@whaleysltd.co.uk
w: www.whaleys-bradford.ltd.uk

Face Painting

Brushstroke Ltd
BRUSHSTROKE MEDIA MAKE-UP SCHOOL, SHEPPERTON
STUDIOS, STUDIOS ROAD, SHEPPERTON
Surrey TW17 0QD 01932 592463
e: info@brushstroke.co.uk
w: www.brushstroke.co.uk

Face In A Crowd
MUMBLE FARM, PASTUREFIELDS, GREAT HAYWOOD, STAFFORD
Staffordshire ST18 0RB 07976 289 234
e: siany711@hotmail.co.uk
w: www.faceinacrowd.net

Facepaint Uk
188 BRIXTON ROAD, LONDON
SW9 6AR 020 7735 5719
e: info@facepaint-uk.com
w: www.facepaint-uk.com

Faces for Fun
....07859 054 237
e: fran@facesforfun.com
w: www.facesforfun.com

Funky Faces
40 BLUMFIELD CRESCENT, , BURNHAM, SLOUGH
Berkshire SL1 6NH 07976 671309
e: jenquille@hotmail.com
w: www.funkyfaces.co.uk

Rainbow Faces Ltd
101 HIGH STREET, NEWPORT
Shropshire TF10 7AY..01952 811 544
e: sales@rainbowfaces.co.uk
w: www.rainbowfaces.co.uk

Facilities Companies

Apple Video Facilities
THE STUDIO, 821 CHORLEY OLD ROAD, DOFFCOCKER, BOLTON
Greater Manchester BL1 5SL 01204 847974
e: info@applevideo.co.uk
w: www.applevideo.co.uk

Broadcast Television Facilities
ACUBA HOUSE, LYMM ROAD, LITTLE BOLLINGTON, ALTRINCHAM
WA14 4SY................................. 0161 926 9808 / 07974 151617
e: info@broadcast-tv.co.uk
w: www.broadcast-tv.co.uk

Centreline Video Ltd
CLOSE TO JUNCTION 12 OF M4, READING
Berkshire 0118 9410033
e: mike@centrelinevideo.com
w: www.centrelinevideo.com

Cine Wessex Ltd
2 MOORSIDE PLACE, MOORSIDE ROAD, WINCHESTER
Hampshire SO23 7FX...01962 844900
e: info@cinewessex.co.uk
w: www.cinewessex.co.uk

Conference Technical Facilities Ltd
UNIT 1, LIONGATE ENTERPRISE PARK, 80 MORDEN ROAD,
MITCHAM
Surrey CR4 4NY .... 0845 130 9944 / 020 8687 2720
e: mail@ctf.co.uk
w: www.ctf.co.uk

De-Risk ltd
PO BOX 504, FARNHAM
Surrey GU9 1AF .... 01252734222 / 07866 69981
e: contact@scscleaningservices.com
w: www.de-risk.com

DHP Media
....01753 537105
e: info@dhp-media.co.uk
w: www.star-street-video.com

Euroscope Television Facilities Limited
UNIT 15-17, QUARRY FARM, BODIAM
East Sussex TN32 5RA..01424 830044
e: info@euroscope.tv
w: www.euroscope.tv

Event Locker Solutions
.... 0161 925 0095
e: info@eventlockersolutions.co.uk
w: www.eventlockersolutions.co.uk

ExhibitHire
UNIT J, GREAT WESTERN INDUSTRIAL ESTATE, DEAN WAY ,
LONDON
UB2 4SB 2033840369
e: shane@exhibithire.com
w: www.exhibithire.co.uk

Festival Loo - Poonarnia
FERNHILL FARM, CHEDDAR ROAD, COMPTON MARTIN
Somerset BS40 6LD 07503 769188
e: squeak@festivalloo.co.uk
w: www.festivalloo.co.uk

Finishing Post Creative Ltd
GILTBROOK STUDIOS, 10, GILTWAY, NOTTINGHAM
NG16 2GN 0115 945 8800
w: www.finishing-post.co.uk

F

Freehand Ltd
BUILDING 52, DUNSFOLD PARK, CRANLEIGH
Surrey GU6 8TB 01483 200 111
e: info@freehand.co.uk
w: www.freehand.co.uk

Giltbrook Studios
10, GILTWAY, GILTBROOK, NOTTINGHAM
 NG16 2GN 01157 483035
w: www.giltbrookstudios.co.uk

Gordon Audio Visual
THE OLD TORPEDO FACTORY, ST LEONARD'S ROAD, LONDON
Greater London NW10 6ST...................................020 8537 1000
w: www.gav.co.uk

Heritage Film Services
 ....01837 811243
e: info@heritagefilmservices.com
w: www.heritagefilmservices.com

Matinee Sound & Vision
132-134 OXFORD ROAD, READING
Berkshire RG1 7NL 0118 958 4934
e: Info@matinee.co.uk
w: www.matinee.co.uk

Motivation
124 MANOR ROAD NORTH, , , THAMES DITTON
Surrey KT7 0BH 020 8398 9509
e: info@motivation81.co.uk
w: www.motivation81.co.uk

Planet Television London
FELTHAM AVENUE,, HAMPTON COURT
 KT8 9BJ.................................... 020 8974 6050 / 079122 86658
e: media@planet-television.com
w: www.planet-television.com

The Digital Audio Company
3 CARLETON BUSINESS PARK, CARLETON NEW ROAD, SKIPTON
North Yorkshire BD23 2AA....................................01756 797100
e: info@the-digital-audio.co.uk
w: www.the-digital-audio.co.uk

The Hall (Media Facilities) Ltd
ODDFELLOWS HALL, LONDON ROAD, CHIPPING NORTON
Oxfordshire OX7 5AR 01608 641 592
e: info@the-hall.co.uk
w: www.the-hall.co.uk

The Recording Workshop
UNIT 10 BUSPACE STUDIOS, CONLAN STREET
Greater London W10 5AP.....................................020 8968 8222
w: www.therecordingworkshop.co.uk

Veale Associates Ltd
16 NORTH ROAD, STEVENAGE
Hertfordshire SG1 4AL 01438 747666
w: www.va-studiodesign.com/

Fairground / Funfair Attractions

Coopers Leisure
7446123141
e: info@coopersleisure.co.uk
w: www.ridesforhirenortheast.co.uk

Dodgems Direct
20 WESTEND PARADE, GLOUCESTER
Gloucestershire GL1 2RY.......................................01452 300356
e: dodgemsandfunfairs@hotmail.co.uk
w: www.dodgemsdirect.co.ue

Events With A Difference
UNIT 12, RIVERSIDE TRADING ESTATE, STATION ROAD, PENKETH, WARRINGTON
Cheshire WA5 2UL 01925 725252
e: enquiries@eventswithadifference.co.uk
w: www.eventswithadifference.co.uk

Irvin Amusements
UNIT 3, ROSIES WAY, OFF BUCKLES LANE , SOUTH OCKENDON
Essex RM15 6RW 07966 548140
e: info@irvinamusements.co.uk
w: www.irwinamusements.co.uk

John Parnham Funfairs
BERNARD HOUSE, NEW ROAD FELTHAM, FELTHAM, HOUNSLOW
London TW14 9BQ 07956 245531
e: johnparnham@aol.com
w: www.parnhamfunfairs.co.uk

Premier Rides Limited
WOODSTOCK HOUSE, WOODSTOCK CLOSE, HORSHAM
West Sussex RH12 5YT.......................................01403 270 076
e: info@premierrides.com
w: www.premierrides.com

Race Time Ltd
UNIT 3 3 WIGAN ROAD, SKELMERSDALE
Lancashire WN8 8NB 01695 722 700
e: enquiries@race-time.co.uk
w: www.race-time.co.uk

S&d Leisure Ltd
1 CHADWICKS DEPOT, COLLINGHAM STREET, CHEETHAM HILL, MANCHESTER M8 8RQ 0161 835 2758
e: enquiries@sdleisure.com
w: www.sdleisure.com

Sideshow Illusions
18 CHURCH STREET, SUTTON-ON-HULL
East Yorkshire HU7 4TS...01482 709939
e: jon@sideshowillusions.com
w: www.sideshowillusions.com

Traditional Fun Fair
93 HERTFORD DRIVE , TYLDESLEY , MANCHESTER
 M29 8LU...01942 799831
e: s.laidlaw3@ntlworld.com
w: www.traditionalfunfair.com

F

Wantafunfair.com Ltd
UNIT 13-14, ENTERPRISE HOUSE, THOMLINSON ROAD,
HARTLEPOOL
 TS25 1NS 01429 263256
e: office@wantafunfair.com
w: www.wantafunfair.com

Fairground Amusements

Blenheim Amusements
....07970 588417
e: samantha.brixton@btinternet.com
w: www.blenheimamusements.co.uk

F

Coopers Leisure
....7446123141
e: info@coopersleisure.co.uk
w: www.ridesforhirenortheast.co.uk

Festival Organisers

ACP Productions
....0845 4741992
e: info@acp-productions.co.uk
w: www.acp-productions.co.uk

Association Of Festival Organisers
FOLKARTS ENGLAND , PO BOX 296, MATLOCK
Derbyshire DE4 3XU..01629 827014
e: info@festivalorganisers.org
w: www.festivalorganisers.org

Black and White Live
....0208 422 0042
e: info@blackandwhitelive.com
w: www.blackandwhitelive.com

Chelmsford Borough Council
EVENTS TEAM, CIVIC CENTRE, DUKE STREET, CHELMSFORD
 CM1 1JE..01245 606987
e: arts@essex.gov.uk
w: www.chelmsford.gov.uk/events

David Barrow Event Services
GLEBE BARNS, CHURCH HILL, SPRIDLINGTON
Lincolnshire LN8 2DX .... 01673 866320 / 07974 653467
e: davidbarrow@dbeventservices.com
w: www.dbeventservices.com

DLP Festival Management
1 ELIZA PLACE, GOSPORT
Hampshire   PO12 4UN .... 07825 392 364 / 02392 798 818
w: www.dlpfestivalmanagement.co.uk

End Of The Road Festival
STUDIO 006, NETIL HOUSE, 1 WESTGATE STREET, LONDON
Greater London E8 3RL...
e: info@endoftheroadfestival.com
w: www.endoftheroadfestival.com

Enteetainment Ltd
GROUND FLOOR, ELMWOOD BUILDING, SOUTHEND ROAD,
BRADFIELD SOUTHEND, READING
Berkshire RG7 6EU 0118 974 1910
e: info@dicktee.com
w: www.dicktee.com

Ethix Management
UNIT 15 KEMPTON GATE, OLDFIELD ROAD, HAMPTON
Greater London TW12 2AF 020 8487 3508
e: contactus@ethixmanagement.com
w: www.ethixmanagement.com

Fake Festivals
THE GRANARY OFFICE, OWSTON GRANGE, OWSTON FERRY,
DONCASTER
South Yorkshire DN9 1TZ ....
w: www.fakefestivals.co.uk

Feile An Phobail
473 FALLS ROAD, BELFAST
 BT12 6DD..02890 313440
e: ciaran@feilebelfast.com
w: www.feilebelfast.com

Festival For...
....7725046585
e: festivalforme@gmail.com
w: www.festivalfor.com/

Festival Republic
35 BOW STREET, COVENT GARDEN , LONDON
Greater London WC2E 7AU....................................020 7009 3001
e: info@festivalrepublic.com
w: www.festivalrepublic.com

Festivals Office University Of Edinburgh
13 INFIRMARY STREET, EDINBURGH
Edinburgh EH1 1LT 0131 651 4200
e: festivals@ed.ac.uk
w: www.festivals.ed.ac.uk

Harrogate International Festivals
32 CHELTENHAM PARADE, HARROGATE
North Yorkshire HG1 1DB 01423 562303
e: info@harrogate-festival.org.uk
w: harrogateinternationalfestivals.c

Hay Festivals
THE DRILL HALL, 25 LION STREET, HAY-ON-WYE
 HR3 5AD..01497 822620
e: admin@hayfestival.org
w: www.hayfestival.org

Henley Festival
RIVER & ROWING MUSEUM MILL MEADOWS, MEADOW ROAD,
HENLEY ON THAMES
Oxfordshire RG9 1BE 01491 843400
e: info@henley-festival.co.uk
w: www.henley-festival.co.uk

Jar Music Live
75 SHELTON STREET, COVENT GARDEN , LONDON
Greater London WC2H 9JQ....................................020 8732 8495
e: info@jarmusiclive.com
w: www.jarmusiclive.com

Larmac Live Limited
241 - 245 LONG LANE, LONDON
Greater London SE1 4PR......................................0207 940 9820
e: info@larmaclive.com
w: www.larmaclive.com

Mantaplan Ltd
DOUGLAS DRIVE, GODALMING
Surrey GU7 1HJ...01483 420088
e: production@mantaplan.com
w: www.mantaplan.com

Mrs Casey Music
PO BOX 296, MATLOCK
Derbyshire DE4 3XU..01629 827 012
e: info@mrscasey.co.uk
w: www.mrscasey.co.uk

National Event Welfare Service
....447799377632
e: corinne@eventwelfare.co.uk
w: www.eventwelfare.co.uk

Nine Yards Ltd
STUDIO 5 THE HANGAR, PERSEVERANCE WORKS, 38 KINGSLAND ROAD, LONDON
Greater London E2 8DD 0207 195 2300
e: production@nine-yards.co.uk
w: www.nine-yards.co.uk

Pure Solutions
33 BOND STREET, BRIGHTON
East Sussex BN1 1RD 01273 823333
e: info@pure-solutions.co.uk
w: www.pure-solutions.co.uk

Regather
57-59 CLUB GARDEN ROAD, SHEFFIELD
South Yorkshire S11 8BU 0114 2731258
w: www.regather.net

Remarkable Productions Ltd
54 CHALTON STREET, LONDON
Greater London NW1 1HS 0207 387 1203
e: info@remarkableproductions.org
w: www.remarkableproductions.org

Santa Pod Raceway
AIRFIELD ROAD, PODINGTON, WELLINGBOROUGH, NORTHANTS
Bedfordshire NN29 7XA 01234 782828
w: www.santapod.com

Secret Productions
59-65 WORSHIP STREET, LONDON
Greater London EC2A 2DU 020 7688 9000
e: info@secretproductions.net
w: www.secretproductions.net

Spring Harvest
14 HORSTED SQUARE, UCKFIELD
East Sussex TN22 1QG 01825 769111;
01825 769000
e: info@springharvest.org
w: www.springharvest.org

STR Music Marketing & Management
296 HUGHENDEN ROAD, HIGH WYCOMBE
Buckinghamshire HP13 5PE.................................01494 526 052
e: strmmm@hotmail.co.uk
w: www.strmusicmarketing.co.uk

The Dark Horses
....07740 363889
e: info@thedarkhorses.com
w: www.thedarkhorses.com

The Guardian Hay Festival
THE DRILL HALL, 25 LION STREET, HAY-ON-WYE
Herefordshire HR3 5AD 01497 822 629
e: boxoffice@hayfestival.org
w: www.hayfestival.org

The Original Pop Up Festival Company
VAUXHALL LANE, VAUXHALL LANE, TUNBRIDGE WELLS, KENT TN4 0XD 0800 083 8368
e: enquiries@popup-festival.co.uk
w: www.popup-festival.co.uk

Unique Events Ltd
GLADSTONE HOUSE, 6A MILL LANE, EDINBURGH
Edinburgh EH6 6TJ ....
e: admin@unique-events.co.uk
w: www.unique-events.co.uk

Vjem Events
....020 8819 9919
e: talktous@vjem.co.uk
w: www.vjemevents.com

West End Festival
THE WHITE HOUSE, DOWANHILL PARK, 50 HAVELOCK STREET, GLASGOW
Glasgow G11 5JE 0141 341 0844
e: press@westendfestival.co.uk
w: www.westendfestival.co.uk

Wilde Ones International Events Ltd
UNIT 122, WESTMINSTER BUSINESS SQUARE, DURHAM STREET, LONDON
Greater London SE11 5JH....................................020 7793 7933
e: info@wildeones.co.uk
w: www.wildeones.co.uk

F

Film / TV / Video Production

11th Hour Events Ltd
UNIT G7, SOUTHPOINT INDUSTRIAL PARK, FORESHORE ROAD, CARDIFF
Glamorgan CF10 4SP..02920 794444
e: info@11th-hour-events.com
w: www.11th-hour-events.com

5 Lamps Media Ltd
3 WOBURN HOUSE, VERNON GATE, DERBY
Derbyshire DE1 1UL..01332 383322
e: mail@5lamps.com
w: www.5lamps.com

F

80 Hertz Studios
THE SHARP PROJECT, THORP ROAD, MANCHESTER
Greater Manchester M40 5BJ 0161 850 8088
e: info@80hertz.com
w: www.80hertz.com

A2Z Film Production
13TH FLOOR, 2 FAWEKAH STREET, MOHANDESSIAN, CAIRO, EGYPT
11234...0020 1 2214 4557
e: robsz@leapfrog.com.eg
w: www.a2z.com.eg

Absolute Audio Visual Solutions
NEW CAMBRIDGE HOUSE, LITLINGTON
Cambridgeshire SG8 0SS.....................................01763 852222
e: info@absoluteavs.co.uk
w: www.absoluteavs.co.uk

adi.tv
PITTMAN COURT, PITTMAN WAY, FULWOOD, PRESTON
Lancashire PR2 9ZG 01772 708 200
e: info@adi.tv
w: www.adi.tv

Air-edel Associates Ltd
18 RODMARTON STREET, LONDON
Greater London W1U 8BJ......................................020 7486 6466
e: air-edel@air-edel.co.uk
w: www.air-edel.co.uk

Ali Kubba Videography
....7590321285
e: ali.kubba@hotmail.com
w: https://www.alphacmedia.com

Ants Productions
....01332 230281
e: ants-productions@hotmail.co.uk
w: www.ants-productions.co.uk

Apple Video Facilities
THE STUDIO, 821 CHORLEY OLD ROAD, DOFFCOCKER, BOLTON
Greater Manchester BL1 5SL 01204 847974
e: info@applevideo.co.uk
w: www.applevideo.co.uk

Appliqué Films
.... 01189 019099 // 07876254910
w: www.appliquefilms.co.uk

APS - Athens Production Services
73, KERKYRAS STR, ATHENS, GREECE
11362............................... +30 2106230368 // +30 6937312218
e: info@athensps.com
w: www.athensps.com

ARTtouchesART Films
46 ST. PETERSBURGH PLACE, LONDON
Greater London W2 4LD..07460 303030
e: info@ARTtouchesART.com
w: www.arttouchesart.com

Aspect Film and Video
THE OLD CHAPEL, 16 OAKFIELD ROAD, BRISTOL CITY
BS8 2AP 0117 930 4613
e: tellmemore@aspectfilmandvideo.co.uk
w: www.aspectfilmandvideo.co.uk

Atacama
34B YORK WAY, LONDON
Greater London N1 9AB 020 8099 1731
e: studio@atacama.co.uk
w: www.re3dy.com

Attend2IT
UNIT 8, PARK FARM INDUSTRIAL ESTATE, BUNTINGFORD
Hertfordshire SG9 9AZ 01763 877 477
w: www.attend2it.co.uk

Audiovisual Joint Resource
AJR, CORNER HOUSE, 114 WINDMILL STREET, MACCLESFIELD
Cheshire SK11 7LB...1625615090
e: events@avjr.eu
w: www.avjr.eu

Aura Films
15 QUEEN STREET, COLCHESTER
Essex CO1 2PH..0783 672 62 70
e: info@aurafilms.co.uk
w: www.aurafilms.co.uk

AV Joint Resource
CORNER HOUSE, 114 WINDMILL STREET, MACCLESFIELD
Cheshire SK11 7LB................ 01625 61 50 90 - 01253 85 12 02
e: hello@avjr.eu
w: www.avjointresource.com

AVInteractive - Video Production Studio
MINERVA MILL INNOVATION CENTRE, STATION ROAD, ALCESTER
Warwickshire B49 5ET..01789 761331
e: enquiry@avi.co.uk
w: www.avi.co.uk

AVT Connect
AVT HOUSE, 7 STONE STREET , BRIGHTON
East Sussex BN1 2HB 441273299001
e: connect@avtconnect.com
w: www.avtconnect.com

AXICO
Lancashire 01524 847265
e: production@axico.co.uk
w: www.axico.com

Blow By Blow Productions
PO BOX 565, LINCOLN
Lincolnshire LN2 2YT 01522 754901
e: info@blowbyblow.co.uk
w: www.blowbyblow.co.uk

Blue Sky Film & Media
CHELTENHAM FILM STUDIOS, HATHERLEY LANE, ARLE COURT,
CHELTENHAM
GL51 6PN 01242 506422
e: contact@blueskyuk.com
w: www.blueskyuk.com

Brian Cook Productions
BRIAN COOK PRODUCTIONS, 51 SOUTH END, BEDALE
North Yorkshire DL8 2DB......................................07778 444648
e: bcp@production.co.uk
w: www.production.co.uk

Bright Spark Studios Limited
UNIT 1 'SEVEN-O-SEVEN', CHURCHILL BUSINESS PARK
SLEAFORD ROAD ,BRACEBRIDGE HEATH, LINCOLN
Lincolnshire LN4 2FF 01522 717884
e: enquiries@brightsparkstudios.com
w: www.brightsparkstudios.com

Broad Grin Communications
PERCY LAURIE HOUSE, 217 UPPER RICHMOND ROAD, LONDON
Greater London SW15 6SY....................................020 3239 8722
e: support@broadgrin.com
w: www.broadgrin.com

Broadcast Television Facilities
ACUBA HOUSE, LYMM ROAD, LITTLE BOLLINGTON, ALTRINCHAM
WA14 4SY...0161 926 9808 /
07974 151617
e: info@broadcast-tv.co.uk
w: www.broadcast-tv.co.uk

Bubble Solutions Limited
THE STUDIO , 42 CHAPEL STREET, WATLINGTON
Oxfordshire OX49 5QT 01491 614 505
e: info@bubble-solutions.com
w: www.bubble-solutions.com

Busy Bodies Digital Ltd
....07801 978300
e: phil.goater@busybodies.co.uk
w: www.busybodies.co.uk

Cameron Presentations & All Event Hire
BURNFIELD ROAD, GIFFNOCK, GLASGOW
Glasgow G46 7TH...0141 637 0368
e: hire@cameronpres.co.uk
w: www.cameronpres.co.uk

Captive8 Media Video Production
26 WINTNEY STREET, FLEET
Hampshire GU51 1AN 0845 834 0250
e: enquiries@captive8media.com
w: www.captive8media.com

Cavalier Studios Ltd
280 WELLINGTON ROAD SOUTH, STOCKPORT
Cheshire SK2 6ND 0161 480 6073
e: hello@cavalierstudios.co.uk
w: www.cavalierstudios.co.uk

Centreline Video Ltd
CLOSE TO JUNCTION 12 OF M4, READING
Berkshire 0118 9410033
e: mike@centrelinevideo.com
w: www.centrelinevideo.com

Charlotte Armitage Videography
1A MORLEY ROAD, TWICKENHAM, LONDON
TW1 2HG 07807 284203
w: www.charlottearmitage.com

Cinecosse Video
AB51 3XS, INVERURIE
Aberdeenshire AB51 3XS 01467 670707
e: admin@cinecosse.co.uk
w: www.cinecosse.co.uk

Classlane Media
THE COACHOUSE, NEWPORT GRANGE, MAINE ROAD, NEWPORT
East Yorkshire HU15 2PR 01430 472 055
e: post@classlane.co.uk
w: www.classlane.co.uk

Clockhouse Productions
118 BRAYBROOKE ROAD, HASTINGS
East Sussex TN34 1TG..020 7436 7702
e: mail@clockhouse.co.uk
w: www.clockhouse.co.uk

Cloud 9 Photo
THE MILL, BROME HALL LANE, LAPWORTH, SOLIHULL
Warwickshire B94 5RB 01564 785 799
e: mike@c9dd.com
w: www.cloud9photo.co.uk

Cloud Presenter
....020 89775361
e: matt@cloudpresenter.com
w: www.cloudpresenter.com

F

Comtec Presentations Ltd
COMMUNICATIONS HOUSE, 126-146 FAIRFIELD ROAD,
DROYLSDEN, MANCHESTER
M43 6AT 0161 370 7772
e: info@comtec-presentations.com
w: www.comtec-presentations.com

Conference Engineering
....+44 (0)1625 426916
e: hello@conferenceengineering.co.uk
w: www.conferenceengineering.co.uk

Connections
THE MEADLANDS, 11 OAKLEIGH ROAD, HATCH END
Middlesex HA5 4HB 020 8420 1444
e: mail@connectionsuk.com
w: www.connectionsuk.com

Cornerstone Communications Ltd
49 CHESWICK WAY, SHIRLEY, SOLIHULL
West Midlands B90 4HF..07968 802527
e: bob.shuttleworth@cornerstone-ltd.com
w: www.cornerstone-ltd.com

CTP Photography & Video
TYLER HOUSE, 58-66 MORLEY ROAD, TONBRIDGE
Kent TN9 1RA .... 01959 533268 // 07836 750058
e: chris@takenbychris.co.uk
w: www.ctpimaging.co.uk

CVS International
20 TALLON ROAD, HUTTON INDUSTRIAL ESTATE, BRENTWOOD
Essex CM13 1TJ..01277 262625
e: info@cvsinternational.co.uk
w: www.cvsinternational.co.uk

CW Event Productions Ltd
ALLSOP HOUSE, 10 PARSONAGE FARM, WINGRAVE, AYLESBURY
Buckinghamshire HP22 4RP 01296 682890
e: hello@cweventproductions.com
w: www.cweventproductions.com

CWA
ASHLEIGH ROAD, GLENFIELD, LEICESTER
Leicestershire LE3 8DA...0116 232 7400
e: hello@cwa.co.uk
w: www.cwa.co.uk

Darkside Studios
40 HOLBORN VIADUCT, LONDON
Greater London EC1N 2PB 020 7148 1500
e: sayhello@darksidestudios.uk
w: www.darksidestudios.uk

DBI Communication
21 CONGREVE CLOSE, WARWICK
West Midlands CV34 5RQ 01926 497695
e: information@dbicom.com
w: www.dbicom.com

Deepvisual
PIER HOUSE
SW3 5HG 07801 930 411
e: info@deepvisual.com
w: www.deepvisual.com

DHP Media
....01753 537105
e: info@dhp-media.co.uk
w: www.star-street-video.com

DMI Productions
UNIT 8, LITTLETON HOUSE, LITTLETON ROAD,
ASHFORD, AMIDDLESEX,
TW15 1UU 01784 421212
e: contactus@dmiproductions.co.uk
w: www.dmiproductions.co.uk

DPC Communications Limited
THE STUDIO, WEST ACRE, WHEDDON CROSS, MINEHEAD
Somerset TA24 7BY 07831 093000
e: dpccommunications@gmail.com
w: www.dpccommunications.co.uk

DreamingFish Productions
STUDIO ONE, SILKS YARD , CHURCH HILL , WOKING
GU21 4QE...08444 770355
e: fraser@dreamingfish.co.uk
w: www.dreamingfish.co.uk

Duck Lane Studios
13 BERWICK STREET, LONDON
W1F 0PW..0207 437 1129
e: bookings@ducklanestudios.com
w: www.ducklanestudios.com

Earl Productions
8 COTLEIGH ROAD, LONDON
Greater London NW6 2NP .... 08354 2042 // 7779 625 092
w: www.earl-productions.com

Eclipse Communications
71 BARLICH WAY, LODGE PARK, REDDITCH
Worcestershire B98 7JP...01527 522590
e: info@eclipsecomm.com
w: www.eclipsecomm.com

Eclipse Presentations Ltd
PRESENTATIONS HOUSE, 5 CHAFFINCH BUSINESS PARK,
CROYDON ROAD, BECKENHAM
Kent BR3 4AA 0208 662 6444
e: info@eclipse-service.co.uk
w: www.eclipse-presentations.co.uk

Ecosse Films
BRIGADE HOUSE, 8 PARSONS GREEN, LONDON
Greater London SW6 4TN......................................020 7371 0290
e: info@ecossefilms.com
w: www.ecossefilms.com

Encore London
FILM HOUSE, 142 WARDOUR STREET, LONDON
Greater London W1F 8DD.....................................020 7149 2000
e: london@encorepost.co.uk
w: www.encorepost.co.uk

Enlightenment Interactive
EAST END HOUSE, 24 ENNERDALE, SKELMERSDALE
Lancashire WN8 6AJ...01695 727555
e: mail@trainingmultimedia.co.uk
w: www.trainingmultimedia.co.uk

Event Dynamics Ltd
UNIT 4, MORDEN GRANGE FARM, BALDOCK ROAD, ROYSTON
Hertfordshire SG8 9NR..07970 010 728
e: events@eventdynamics.co.uk
w: www.eventdynamics.co.uk

Extra Veg Broadcast Crews Scotland
GLENLOCKHART HOUSE, 6 THE STEILS, EDINBURGH
 EH10 5XD 0131 446 0444
e: cindy@extraveg.com
w: www.extraveg.com

Fast Lane Entertainment
UNIT 8 - 10, GROUND FLOOR, 21 BONNY STREET, LONDON
Greater London NW1 9PE.....................................07974 171 862
e: info@fast-lane.tv
w: fastlaneproductions.tv/

Film Cut Post Production
30 STAFFORD STREET, EDINBURGH, SCOTLAND
 EH3 7BD 0131 5383989
e: info@filmcut.co.uk
w: www.filmcut.co.uk

FilmNova Sport Production
NEWCASTLE HOUSE, MONARCH ROAD, NEWCASTLE
Tyne and Wear NE4 7YB.......................................020 7550 6000
w: www.filmnova.com

Firehouse Productions Ltd
90 COWCROSS STREET, LONDON
Greater London EC1M 6BH 020 7250 0593
e: hello@firehouse.co.uk
w: www.firehouse.co.uk

Fletcherwilson
UNIT 6, 24A HIGH STREET STRATFORD, LONDON
Greater London E15 2PP......................................0208 534 6999
e: contact@fletcherwilson.com
w: www.fletcherwilson.com

Flying Flicks
EAGLE & EAGLE LTD, 15 MARLBOROUGH ROAD, LONDON
Greater London W4 4EU.......................................0208 995 1884
e: producer@eagletv.co.uk
w: www.eagletv.co.uk

Focal Point Television
1 CAPITAL PARK, COMBE LANE, WORMLEY, GODALMING
Surrey GU8 5TJ 01428 684468
e: hello@focal-point.co.uk
w: www.focal-point.co.uk

fortyfoursixteen LTD
NICHOLSON HOUSE, 41 THAMES STREET, WEYBRIDGE
Surrey KT13 8JG...................... 01932 841 431 / 07810 50 4416
e: brice@44-16.com
w: www.44-16.com

Fourth Wall Productions
UNIT 6, ST. JOHN'S BUSINESS PARK, LUTTERWORTH
Leicestershire LE17 4HB.......................................0845 340 0179
w: www.fourthwallproductions.co.uk

Funhouse Productions Ltd
91 REGENT COURT, NORTH PROMENADE, BLACKPOOL
Lancashire FY1 1RT 01274 619832
e: funhouseproductions1@gmail.com
w: www.funhouse-productions.co.uk

Gemini Productions Ltd
....020 8347 9205
e: events@gemprod.co.uk
w: www.gemprod.co.uk

Gloria Kurnik
KUALA LUMPUR, MALAYSIA
.... + 60 193 436 358 / +44 7443884543
e: gloria.kurnik@gmail.com
w: gloriakurnik.com

Goldcrest Films International
1 LEXINGTON STREET, LONDON
Greater London W1F 9AF 020 7437 7972
e: sales@goldcrestfilms.com
w: www.goldcrestfilms.com

Greenfield Television Ltd
STUDIO 4 SALT LANE, HYDESTILE, GODALMING
Surrey GU8 4DG...01483 202206
e: website@greenfieldtv.com
w: www.greenfieldtv.com

H2 Business Communication
SHEPPERTON STUDIOS, SHEPPERTON
Surrey TW17 0QD 01932 593 717
e: mail@h2bc.co.uk
w: www.h2bc.co.uk

Hallmark Broadcast
30 WOODSIDE ROAD, PARKSTONE, POOLE
Dorset BH14 9JJ...................... 0845 644 5406 / 01202 779000
e: Web@HallmarkBroadcast.tv
w: www.hallmarkbroadcast.tv

F

Hamble Audio & Video Studios
39 MITCHELL POINT, ENSIGN WAY, HMABLE, SOUTHAMPTON
Hampshire SO31 4RF..023 8044 8822
e: biz@focusbiz.co.uk
w: www.focusbiz.co.uk

Hand Made Productions
....01962 777 753
e: action@handmadeproductions.co.uk
w: www.handmadeproductions.co.uk

Handel Productions Ltd
PO BOX 177, HAZEL GROVE, STOCKPORT
Greater Manchester SK7 9AZ... 0161 292 0565 // 07984 407 895
w: www.handelproductions.co.uk

Hartswood Films Ltd
3A PARADISE ROAD, RICHMOND
Surrey TW9 1RX..020 3668 3060
e: films.tv@hartswoodfilms.co.uk
w: www.hartswoodfilms.co.uk

Heather Robinson Live Communication
MINERVA MILL, STATION ROAD, ALCESTER
Warwickshire B49 5ET...01789 761 353
w: www.heatherrobinson.co.uk

Heirloom Media
18 BARDS WAY , TILLICOULTRY FK13 6RR.............01259 752756
e: jsmith@heirloommedia.co.uk
w: www.heirloommedia.co.uk

HMX Corporate Communication
THE OLD STABLES, STATION ROAD, , QUAINTON, AYLESBURY,
Buckinghamshire HP22 4BW 01296 642070
e: info@hmx.cc
w: www.hmx.cc

Ice Productions Ltd
THE MAIL BOX, 52 BLUCHER STREET, BIRMINGHAM
West Midlands B1 1QU 0121 288 4864
e: birmingham@ice-productions.com
w: www.ice-productions.com

Icon Films
3RD FLOOR COLLEGE HOUSE, 32-36 COLLEGE GREEN, BRISTOL
Bristol BS1 5SP..0117 910 2030
e: info@iconfilms.co.uk
w: www.iconfilms.co.uk

Incidium Ltd
54 COBS WAY, NEW HAW, ADDLESTONE
Surrey KT15 3AF.................... 020 8123 5374 // 07515 547 436
e: sales@incidium.net
w: www.incidium.net

Inside-out Branding
UPPER WOODHEAD, BARKISLAND, HALIFAX
West Yorkshire HX4 0EQ.......................................01422 825222
e: info@inside-outbranding.com
w: www.inside-outbranding.com

Jack Taylor Productions
....07919 892239
e: hello@jacktaylorproductions.com
w: www.jacktaylorproductions.com

Jay Film & Video
SANDGATE HOUSE, 102 QUAYSIDE, NEWCASTLE UPON TYNE
Tyne and Wear NE1 3DX 0191 6451702
w: www.jayvideo.com

Jb Communications Ltd
15 BRACKENBURY ROAD, LONDON
Greater London W6 0BE 020 8749 6036
e: inspire@jbcommunications.co.uk
w: www.jbcommunications.co.uk

Jon Collins
....07908 252 703
e: hello@ukjoncollins.com
w: www.ukjoncollins.com

Kartoffel Films
UNIT 25 KARTOFFEL FILMS, 35 CORBRIDGE CRESCENT,
E2 9EZ..020 7112 8331
e: mash@kartoffelfilms.com
w: www.kartoffelfilms.com

King Rollo Films Ltd
DOLPHIN COURT , HIGH STREET, HONITON
Devon EX14 1HT...01404 45218
e: leo@kingrollofilms.co.uk
w: www.kingrollofilms.co.uk

Krystal Displays
22 CHALLENGER DRIVE, SPROTBROUGH, DONCASTER
 DN5 7RY...01302 788095
e: info@krystaldisplays.co.uk
w: www.theshowbusiness.co.uk

Landseer Productions Ltd
27 ARKWRIGHT ROAD, LONDON
Greater London NW3 6BJ....................................020 7794 2523
e: derekbailey2@icloud.com / kchoward1@mac.com
w: www.landseerfilms.com

Leapfrog
....1222144557
e: robsz@a2zleapfrog.com
w: www.a2zleapfrog.com

Light The Way
UNIT 7 CAVENDISH COURT MILL, WEST STREET, BRADFORD
 BD11 1DA...01422 250 819
e: hire@lighttheway.co.uk
w: www.lighttheway.co.uk

Lighthouse Technologies (U.K.) Ltd
2ND FLOOR SARACEN HOUSE, SWAN STREET, ISLEWORTH
Greater London TW76RJ 020 8380 9500
e: infoeurope@lighthouse-tech.com
w: www.lighthouse-tech.com

Line Up
14 BADEN PLACE, CROSBY ROW, BOROUGH, LONDON
Greater London SE1 1YW 020 8747 2200
e: info@lineup.uk.com
w: www.lineup.uk.com

Lion's Den Creatives
86-90 PAUL STREET, LONDON
Greater London EC2A 4NE 07957 973434
e: info@lionsdencreatives.com
w: www.lionsdencreatives.com

Lipfriend Rodd International
18 SPECTRUM HOUSE, 32-34 GORDON HOUSE ROAD, LONDON
Greater London NW5 1LP......................................020 7267 6066
e: info@lipfriend-rodd.co.uk
w: www.lipfriend-rodd.co.uk

Location Rental
....7413669570
e: info@locationrental.co.uk
w: www.locationrental.co.uk

Low Budget Films
23 SHIRLEY GARDENS, EALING, LONDON
Greater London W7 3PT 07973 714901
e: ewan@lowbudgetfilms.co.uk
w: www.lowbudgetfilms.co.uk

Lumiere Studios
3RD FLOOR, 10/11 LOWER JOHN ST, SOHO, LONDON
Greater London W1F 9EB 020 7287 1677
e: info@lumierestudios.co.uk
w: www.lumierestudios.co.uk

Lunar Dragon
....7562939262
e: aybuke.kavas@gmail.com
w: www.lunardragonproductions.com/

Malachite Ltd
EAST KIRKBY, SPILSBY
Lincolnshire PE23 4BX..01790 763538
e: info@malachite.co.uk
w: www.malachite.co.uk

Manamedia
3RD FLOOR, , 152-154 CURTAIN ROAD, LONDON
Greater London EC2A 3AT 0208 962 9652
e: info@manamediauk.com
w: www.manamediagroup.com

Maximus Media
INTERNATIONAL HOUSE, SOUTHAMPTON INTERNATIONAL
BUSINESS PARK, SOUTHAMPTON
Hampshire SO18 2RZ 023 8084 8976
e: info@maximusmedia.co.uk
w: www.maximusmedia.co.uk

MBPtv
SAUCELANDS BARN, COOLHAM, HORSHAM
West Sussex RH13 8QG 01403 741620
e: info@mbptv.com
w: www.mbptv.com

MCCP Ltd
63 WINCHESTER STREET, BOTLEY, SOUTHAMPTON
Hampshire SO30 2EB 01489 782 535
e: GetInTouch@mccp.co.uk
w: www.mccp.ltd.uk

Media Tree
221-222 SHOREDITCH HIGH ST, LONDON
Greater London E1 6PJ 020 7437 3322
e: info@media-tree.com
w: www.media-tree.com

MediaCake
.... 07877 542756 // 07729860465
e: contact@mediacake.co.uk
w: www.mediacake.co.uk

Mediacrown Ltd
OWL BARN, NEW BARN LANE, CRAWLEY, WINCHESTER
Hampshire SO21 2PP...01962 776699
e: cwade@mediacrown.co.uk
w: www.mediacrown.co.uk

MediaMaker Ltd
MEDIA HOUSE, PADGE RD, BEESTON, NOTTINGHAM
Nottinghamshire NG9 2RS .... 01159 255440 //
                                                        0203 691 7580
e: hello@mediamaker.co.uk
w: www.mediamaker.co.uk

Metropolis Group
THE POWERHOUSE, 70 CHISWICK HIGH ROAD, LONDON
Greater London W4 1SY 020 8742 1111
e: hello@thisismetropolis.com
w: www.thisismetropolis.com

MJ Lights LTD
....029 2009 2700
e: matt@mjlights.co.uk
w: www.mjlights.co.uk

Motion Picture Stills & Video
....01264 712135
e: info@mpsv.co.uk
w: www.mpsv.co.uk

Motivation
124 MANOR ROAD NORTH, , , THAMES DITTON
Surrey KT7 0BH 020 8398 9509
e: info@motivation81.co.uk
w: www.motivation81.co.uk

F

F

MS Media Solutions
15 SPRINGFIELD RD, ABERDEEN
 AB15 7RU 01224 314999
e: mark@ms-media.co.uk
w: www.ms-media.co.uk

MWP Digital Media
26 BERWICK STREET, LONDON
Greater London W1F 8RG.....................................0845 003 8359
e: contact@mwpdigitalmedia.com
w: www.mwpdigitalmedia.com

My Web Presenters
26 BERWICK STREET, SOHO, LONDON
Greater London W1F 8RG.....................................0845 003 8359
w: www.mywebpresenters.com

Oasis Media
 ....07956 320 486
e: info@oasismedia.co.uk
w: www.oasismedia.co.uk

Offslip
FLAT 4 OAKVIEW APARTMENT STUDIOS, 12 BENHILL ROAD,
LONDON
Greater London SM1 3RL.......................................07912 091979
e: mail@offslip.co.uk
w: www.offslip.co.uk

On Screen Productions Ltd
ASHBOURNE HOUSE, 33 BRIDGE STREET, CHEPSTOW
Gloucestershire NP16 5GA.....................................01291 636300
e: Action@OnScreenProductions.com
w: www.onscreenproductions.co.uk

P&G Photographics Ltd
 ....07860 234 582
e: website@poulson.info
w: www.poulson.info

Palm Pictures Ltd
1460 BROADWAY, NEW YORK, USA
 10036..001 646 790 1211
e: Kevin.Yatarola@palmpictures.com
w: www.palmpictures.com

Partnership Plus Ltd
43 ALL SAINTS GREEN, NORWICH
Norfolk NR1 3LY..01603 611031
e: pr@partnership-plus.co.uk
w: www.partnership-plus.co.uk

Passion Pictures
33-34 RATHBONE PL, FITZROVIA, LONDON
Greater London W1T1JN 020 7323 9933
e: info@passion-pictures.com
w: www.passion-pictures.com

PBF Motion Pictures
PORTSMOUTH ROAD, RIPLEY
Surrey GU23 6ER 01483 225179
e: image@pbf.co.uk
w: www.pbf.co.uk

Pibscam
.... 07711 528 724 / 08454758676
e: paul@pibscam.com
w: www.pibscam.com

Picture Palace Films
13 EGBERT STREET, LONDON
Greater London NW1 8LJ.....................................020 7586 8763
e: info@picturepalace.com
w: www.picturepalace.com

Pink Pigeon Post Production
1A POLAND STREET, SOHO, LONDON
Greater London W1F 8PR.....................................020 7439 3266
e: info@pinkpigeon.net
w: www.pinkpigeon.net

Positive Image Ltd
PROVIDIAN HOUSE, 16-18 MONUMENT STREET, LONDON
Greater London EC3R 8AJ 020 7868 5233
e: theoffice@positiveimage.co.uk
w: www.positiveimage.co.uk

Powerhouse Productions Ltd
395 MONTROSE AVENUE, SLOUGH TRADING ESTATE, SLOUGH
Berkshire SL1 4TJ 01753 696369
e: andy@powerhouseprod.co.uk
w: www.powerhouseprod.co.uk

Pozzitive Television Ltd
1ST FLOOR, 41 GOODGE STREET, LONDON
Greater London W1T 2PY 020 7255 1112
e: pozzitive@pozzitive.co.uk
w: www.pozzitive.co.uk

Production Network Worldwide Services Ltd
UNIT 1, ELSTREE FILM STUDIOS, SHENLEY ROAD,
BOREHAMWOOD
Hertfordshire WD6 1JG 020 8324 2669
e: office@pronetworld.com
w: www.pronetworld.com

Quadrillion TV
17 BALVERNIE GROVE, LONDON
Greater London SW18 5RR 01628 487522
e: enqs@quadrillion.tv
w: www.quadrillion.tv

Quatreus
5 & 6 EASTLANDS INDUSTRIAL ESTATE , KING GEORGES AVENUE,
LEISTON
Suffolk IP16 4LL 07971 350100
e: justine.samouelle@quatreus.com
w: www.quatreus.com/

Radical Departures
THE PRINTWORKS, 3C BLAKE MEWS, KEW, LONDON
Greater London TW9 3GA.....................................0208 334 7860
e: martin@radical-departures.com
w: www.radical-departures.com

re:fine
316-318 LATIMER ROAD, LONDON
Greater London W10 6QN 020 8962 2600
e: info@refine-group.com
w: www.refine-group.com

Richard Lipman
....07703 061780
w: www.richardlipman.tv

Rock-Tech Projects
UNIT 2, FRYORS COURT, MURTON
Yorkshire YO19 5UY 01904 481 700
e: info@rock-tech.co.uk
w: www.rock-tech.co.uk

Rogue Robot Visual Industries
THE TOWN HALL, ST. GEORGEÂ ™S ST., HEBDEN BRIDGE
West Yorkshire HX7 7BY...01422 720502
e: contact@roguerobot.co.uk
w: www.roguerobot.co.uk

Saturday Sunday Productions
29 GLOUCESTER PLACE, LONDON
Greater London W1U 8HX.......................................01764 679 573
e: amanda@saturdaysunday.co.uk
w: www.saturdaysunday.co.uk

Saxholm Media Communications
203 BASSETT AVENUE, BASSETT, SOUTHAMPTON
 SO16 7HD..023 8076 8274
e: facilities@saxholm.co.uk
w: www.saxholm.co.uk

School Video Productions
12A LYONS FARM ESTATE, LYONS ROAD, SLINFOLD
West Sussex RH13 0QP 01403 791330
e: hello@schoolvideo.co.uk
w: www.schoolvideo.co.uk

Segway Events
MAGNA SCIENCE ADVENTURE CENTRE, SHEFFIELD ROAD,
TEMPLEBROUGH, ROTHERHAM
South Yorkshire S60 1DX 0845 319 3747
e: info@segwayevents.co.uk
w: www.segwayevents.co.uk

Seven Video Productions
COMMER HOUSE, TADCASTER ENTERPRISE PARK, TADCASTER
North Yorkshire LS24 9JF.......................................01937 222102
e: info@sevenvideoproductions.co.uk
w: www.sevenvideoproductions.co.uk

Shorestream Media
EXETER PHOENIX, BRADNINCH PLACE, GANDY STREET, EXETER
Devon EX4 3LS 07765 488101
e: james@shorestreammedia.co.uk
w: www.shorestreammedia.co.uk

Sightline
DYLAN HOUSE, TOWN END STREET, GODALMING, SURREY
Surrey GU7 1BQ..01483 813 311
e: video@sightline.co.uk
w: www.sightline.co.uk

Silverstream TV - The Web Video Experts
NEW MEDIA HOUSE, 2A DE LA HAY AVE, PLYMOUTH
 PL3 4HU 0207 183 6444
e: mail@silverstream.tv
w: www.silverstream.tv

SKYPOD Aerial Media
13 WESTGATE, NORTH BERWICK
East Lothian EH39 4AE .... 01494 523636 // 07710 477880
e: pete@skypod.tv
w: www.skypod.tv

SkyWeb Media
.... 0203 328 9917 / 0753 917 6000
e: will@skyweb.media
w: www.skyweb.media

Sliced Bread Animation
TUDOR HOUSE, 35 GRESSE STREET, LONDON
Greater London W1T 1QY.....................................020 7148 0526
e: info@sbanimation.com
w: www.thebestthingsince.com

Smoking Gun Events
UNIT 3, PUMA TRADE PARK, 145 MORDEN RD, LONDON
 CR4 4DG................ +447972776469 / +4420 8150 6527
e: louis@sgeventworld.com
w: www.sgeventworld.com

Space City Productions
77 BLYTHE ROAD HAMMERSMITH, LONDON
Greater London W14 0HP.....................................020 7371 4000
e: victor@spacecity.co.uk
w: www.spacecity.co.uk

Sparky Film
88 WOOD STREET, 10TH AND 11TH FLOORS, LONDON
Greater London EC2V 7RS....................................020 7412 8924
e: info@sparkyfilm.com
w: www.sparkyfilm.com

Speakeasy Productions Ltd
WILDWOOD HOUSE, STANLEY
Perthshire PH1 4NH 01738 828524
e: info@speak.co.uk
w: www.speak.co.uk

F

F

Spectrecom Films
373 KENNINGTON ROAD, KENNINGTON, LONDON
Greater London SE11 4PT......................................0203 405 2260
e: enquiries@spectrecom.co.uk
w: www.spectrecom.co.uk

Spirit Media
27 OLD GLOUCESTER STREET, LONDON
Greater London WC1N 3AX 020 8960 0108
e: info@spiritmedia.co.uk
w: www.spiritmedia.co.uk

Splinter Scenery
THE GASWORKS , HIGGINSHAW LANE, OLDHAM
OL1 3LB...0161 633 6787
e: alec@splinterscenery.co.uk
w: www.splinterscenery.co.uk

Starlight Productions
3 WYNDHAM ROAD , KINGSTON UPON THAMES
Surrey KT2 5JR..020 8549 3818
e: team@starlightproductions.tv
w: www.starlightproductions.tv

Steadi Facilities Ltd
3000 AVIATOR WAY, MANCHESTER BUSINESS PARK,
MANCHESTER
Greater Manchester M22 5TG..............................0800 689 9866
e: office@steadicam-facilities.co.uk
w: www.steadicam-facilities.co.uk

Stephen J Brand
.... 07976 731725 // 0044 20 8299 1493
e: sjbrand@dop2000.freeserve.co.uk
w: www.sjbrand.com

Steve Lovell Associates
CONFEX HOUSE, 14 ROZELDINE, HINHEAD
Surrey GU26 6TW 01428 605863
e: info@sla.uk.com
w: www.sla.uk.com

Story of Your Day
....07973 459058
e: emma@storyofyourday.co.uk
w: www.storyofyourday.co.uk

Surrey Video
51 MALLARD ROAD, CROYDON
Greater London CR2 8PX......................................0203 252 2055
e: info@surreyvideo.co.uk
w: www.surreyvideo.co.uk

SussedFilms
14 MEADWAY, FRIMLEY, CAMBERLEY
Surrey GU16 8TQ...01276 504629
e: studio@timsmith.co.uk
w: www.sussedfilms.co.uk

Table Top Productions
1 THE ORCHARD, CHISWICK
W4 1JZ..020 8742 0507
e: top@tabletopproductions.com
w: www.tabletopproductions.com

Take 3 Productions
79 ESSEX ROAD, LONDON
Greater London N1 2SF...............................+44(0)20 7354 5577
e: mail@take3.co.uk
w: www.take3.co.uk

Take One Business Communications Ltd
MEDIA HOUSE, 12 MANOR COURTYARD, HUGHENDEN AVENUE,
HIGH WYCOMBE
Buckinghamshire HP13 5RE ....+44 (0) 1494 898 919
e: info@takeonetv.com
w: www.takeonetv.com

Tandem Tv & Film Ltd
17C ALEXANDRA RD, HEMEL HEMPSTEAD
Hertfordshire HP2 5BS..01442 261576
e: info@tandem.tv
w: www.tandem.tv

Tapestry Media and Events Ltd
BATTERSEA STUDIO, 80-82 SILVERTHORNE ROAD, BATTERSEA,
LONDON
Greater London SW8 3HE......................................020 8945 5100
e: chris@tapestrymediaandevents.com
w: www.tapestrymediaandevents.com

Tern Television Productions Ltd
73 CROWN STREET, ABERDEEN
Aberdeen AB11 6EX...01224 211123
e: aberdeen@terntv.com
w: www.terntv.com

The Digital Holdings
UNIT 3A, JUNO WAY, ELIZABETH INDUSTRIAL ESTATE, LONDON
Greater London SE14 5RW....................................0208 691 9191
e: info@thedigitalholdings.com
w: www.thedigitalholdings.com

The Fixer Films and Live Events
.... +971555303393 / +971 4 321 8494
e: Natasha@thefixeragency.com
w: www.thefixeragency.com

The Outlook Creative Group
THE COURTYARD, ORCHARD HILL, LITTLE BILLING,
NORTHAMPTON
Northamptonshire NN3 9AG..................................0845 8383333
e: sales@outlook.co.uk
w: outlookcreative.uk/

The Presentation Group
2 HOCKEY CLOSE, LOUGHBOROUGH
Leicestershire LE11 5GX.......................................01509 230005
e: enquiries@thepresentationgroup.co.uk
w: www.thepresentationgroup.co.uk

Timbuktu Productions
16 INGESTRE PLACE, LONDON
Greater London W1F 0JJ.......... 07590 399774 // (0)7881 663317
e: info@timbuktuproductions.co.uk
w: www.timbuktuproductions.co.uk

Tomfoolery Pictures Ltd
STUDIO I, BALTIC CREATIVE CAMPUS, 49 JAMAICA STREET,
LIVERPOOL
Merseyside L1 0AH..07904 106713
e: info@tomfoolerypictures.co.uk
w: www.tomfoolerypictures.co.uk

Tricaster Operator
....07786 807502
e: simon@tricasteroperator.co.uk
w: www.tricasteroperator.co.uk

Union Street Media Arts
20 EAST UNION ST, MANCHESTER
M16 9AE..1618773124
e: roop@unionstreetmediaarts.com
w: www.unionstreetmediaarts.com/

Video and Film Solutions
52 MADISON SUITES, 41 SEYMOUR GROVE, MANCHESTER
Greater Manchester M16 0NB.............................0161 872 1229
e: enquiries@videoandfilmsolutions.co.uk
w: www.videoandfilmsolutions.co.uk

Video Enterprises
12 BARBERS WOOD ROAD, BOOKER, HIGH WYCOMBE
Buckinghamshire HP12 4EP....................................01494 534144
e: videoenterprises@ntlworld.com
w: www.videoenterprises.co.uk

VidPR
OLD DOWN BUSINESS PARK, EMBOROUGH, RADSTOCK
Somerset BA3 4SA .... +44 (0) 1761 417746
e: info@vidpr.com
w: www.vidpr.com

Vision Events (Edinburgh)
16 DRYDEN ROAD, BILSTON GLEN INDUSTRIAL ESTATE,
LOANHEAD
Edinburgh EH20 9LZ 0131 334 3324
e: edinburgh@visionevents.co.uk
w: www.visionevents.co.uk

Vision Events (Glasgow)
UNIT E6 & 7, EUROGATEWAY, PORT DUNDAS BUSINESS PARK,
GLASGOW
Glasgow G4 9XG...0141 334 3324
e: glasgow@visionevents.co.uk
w: www.visionevents.co.uk

VisionSound AV
751 SOUTH WEIR CANYON ROAD, SUITE 157-223, ANAHEIM, CA
92808..001 714 280 8201
e: sales@visionsoundav.com
w: www.visionsoundav.com

Visionworks Television Ltd
56 DONEGALL PASS
BT7 1BU 028 9024 1241
e: hello@visionworks.co.uk
w: www.visionworks.co.uk

Visual Response Ltd
WILD RENTS STUDIO, 20-30 WILDS RENTS, LONDON
Greater London SE1 4QG 020 7378 7731
w: www.visualresponse.com

Wilkie TV Ltd
6-10 DUNSTON STREET, HAGGERSTON,, LONDON
Greater London E8 4EB...020 35 193 193
e: hello@wilkie.tv
w: www.wilkie.tv

Wizard Video Productions Ltd
PETWORTH ROAD, WITLEY , GODALMING
GU8 5LX 01428 682896
e: info@wizardvideo.co.uk
w: www.wizardvideo.co.uk

WM Event Design
19 ST JAMES'S DRIVE, WANDSWORTH COMMON, LONDON
Greater London SW17 7RN 020 3837 4926
e: info@williammoyse.com
w: www.wmeventdesign.com

Zest4.tv Ltd
UNIT 3, BROOKLANDS CLOSE, SUNBURY-ON-THAMES
Middlesex TW16 7DX...01784 441147
e: ask@zest4.tv
w: www.zest4.tv

Film / Video Equipment

Attend2IT
UNIT 8, PARK FARM INDUSTRIAL ESTATE, BUNTINGFORD
Hertfordshire SG9 9AZ 01763 877 477
w: www.attend2it.co.uk

AV Joint Resource
CORNER HOUSE, 114 WINDMILL STREET, MACCLESFIELD
Cheshire SK11 7LB................. 01625 61 50 90 - 01253 85 12 02
e: hello@avjr.eu
w: www.avjointresource.com

Big-TV (UK) Ltd
HUDSON HOUSE, THE HUDSON, WYKE, BRADFORD
Yorkshire BD12 8HZ..01274 604 309
e: info@big-tv.co.uk
w: www.big-tv.co.uk

Blackstone Film Company
C/ LEVANTE N.16, POL. IND. PARQUE DE LA REINA, 5 MIN TO INT.
AIRPORT TFS, ARONA, S/C DE TENERIFE
38632.. +34 922 739 916
e: service@blackstonefilm.com
w: www.blackstonefilm.com

F

Creative Technology Ltd
UNIT E2, SUSSEX MANOR BUSINESS PARK, , GATWICK ROAD, CRAWLEY
West Sussex RH10 9NH 01293 582 000
e: info@ctlondon.com
w: www.ctlondon.com

Debrouillard Ltd
....0114 220 0667
e: jonathan@debrouillard.tv
w: www.debrouillard.tv

DHP Media
....01753 537105
e: info@dhp-media.co.uk
w: www.star-street-video.com

F

EM UK
COPSE FARM, MOORHURST LANE, HOLMWOOD, DORKING
Surrey RH5 4LJ...01306 712451
e: nick@emuk.org
w: www.eventmanagementuk.org

Finepoint Broadcast Ltd
HILL HOUSE , FURZE HILL, KINGSWOOD
Surrey KT20 6EZ...01737 370033
e: sales@finepoint.co.uk
w: www.finepoint.co.uk

Front Element Camera Services
2 BARRICANE, ST JOHNS, WOKING
 GU21 7RB................................. 01483 856202 / 07973 194810
e: mail@jeremyirving.tv
w: www.jeremyirving.tv

Hamlet Video International Ltd
MAPLE HOUSE, 11 CORINIUM BUSINESS CENTRE, RAANS ROAD, AMERSHAM
Buckinghamshire HP6 6FB............ 0500 625 525 / 1494 723 237
e: enquiry@hamlet.co.uk
w: www.hamlet.co.uk

High Lite Touring
MITROVICKA 359/45, OSTRAVA - NOVA BELA
 72400...00420 596 731 034
e: info@highlite.cz
w: www.highlite.cz

Jon Howes Remote Heads Ltd
....07973 750 719
e: jon@jonhowesremoteheads.co.uk
w: www.jonhowesremoteheads.co.uk

Location One Ltd
UNIT 7, NEW HARBOURS, 75 RIVER ROAD, BARKING
Greater London IG11 0DR .... 07769 910 017 // 0208 099 4291
e: crispin@locationone.co.uk
w: www.locationone.co.uk

Location Rental
....7413669570
e: info@locationrental.co.uk
w: www.locationrental.co.uk

Marine Film Services Ltd
15 CHURCH ROAD, EAST MOLESEY
Surrey KT8 9DR...020 8224 9246
w: www.marinefilm.co.uk

Megahertz Broadcast Systems Ltd
UNIT 39 LANCASTER WAY BUSINESS PARK, WITCHFORD, ELY
Cambridgeshire CB6 3NW.....................................01353 645000
e: sales@megahertz.co.uk
w: www.megahertz.co.uk

Off The Wall
21A ASKEW ROAD, SHEPHERDS BUSH, LONDON
Greater London W12 9DP.....................................020 8740 5353
e: john@offthewall.co.uk
w: www.offthewall.co.uk

Pec Video Ltd
83 CHARLOTTE STREET, LONDON
Greater London W1T 4PR.....................................020 7437 4633
e: sales@pec.co.uk
w: www.pec.co.uk

Picture Works Ltd, The
UNIT 23, GREENFORD PARK, GREENFORD, LONDON
Greater London UB6 0AZ.....................................0845 310 8321
e: enquiry@pictureworks.com
w: www.pictureworks.com

Plasmatising AV Hire London
261 TIMBERLOG LANE, BASILDON
Essex SS14 1PA..01268 550202
e: info@plasmatising.co.uk
w: www.plasmatising.co.uk

Premier UK Events Ltd
UNIT 2, ROOKERY LANE, THURMASTON, LEICESTER
Leicestershire LE4 8AU...1162029953
e: ben@premier-ltd.com
w: premier-event-solutions.com/

QED Productions
UNIT 11, SUMMIT ROAD, CRANBORNE INDUSTRIAL ESTATE, POTTERS BAR
Hertfordshire EN6 3QW..01707 648 800
e: info@qed-productions.com
w: www.qed-productions.com

Rapido3d
UNIT 6, 2 PRINCE EDWARD ROAD, LONDON
Greater London E9 5NN 020 3536 1944
w: www.rapido3d.co.uk

Seen & Heard Limited
3 WOOD POTTERY, STEPNEY BANK, NEWCASTLE UPON TYNE
Tyne and Wear NE1 2NP 0191 232 5736
e: sales@seenandheard.co.uk
w: www.seenandheard.co.uk

Sis Live
2 WHITEHALL AVENUE, KINGSTON, MILTON KEYNES
Buckinghamshire MK10 0AX..................................01908 865656
e: sales@sislive.tv
w: www.sislive.tv

Smoking Gun Events
UNIT 3, PUMA TRADE PARK, 145 MORDEN RD, LONDON
CR4 4DG............................ +447972776469 / +4420 8150 6527
e: louis@sgeventworld.com
w: www.sgeventworld.com

Spectrecom Studios
373 KENNINGTON ROAD, KENNINGTON, LONDON
Greater London SE11 4PT.....................................020 3405 2263
e: studio@spectrecom.co.uk
w: www.spectrecomstudios.co.uk

The Projection Studio
13 TARVES WAY, GREENWICH, LONDON
Greater London SE10 9JP.....................................020 8293 4270
e: info@theprojectionstudio.com
w: www.theprojectionstudio.com

Transmission Tx Ltd
UNIT 1A, SHEPPERTON STUDIOS, STUDIOS ROAD, SHEPPERTON
Middlesex TW17 0QD................................ + 44 (0)20 8783 1972
w: www.ttx.co.uk

Van Diemen Ltd
BRIDGE HOUSE, BRANKSOME PARK ROAD, CAMBERLEY
Surrey GU15 2AQ...+44(0)1276-61222
e: sales@vandiemenbroadcast.co.uk
w: www.vandiemenbroadcast.co.uk

VER - Video Equipment Rentals
DOWNLAND CLOSE, UNITS 3-4, LONDON
Greater London N20 9LB.................................... +44 (0) 20 8445
0267
e: info@verrents.com
w: www.verrents.com

Video Conferencing London
ARLINGHAM HOUSE ST. ALBANS ROAD, POTTERS BAR
Hertfordshire EN6 3PH 08458 380 562
e: cs@videoconferencinglondon.co.uk
w: www.videoconferencinglondon.co.uk

Virtual Reality Hire Ltd
....1630695658
e: info@virtualrealityhire.com
w: virtualrealityhire.com

Vivid Projects
16 MINERVA WORKS, 158 FAZELEY STREET, BIRMINGHAM
West Midlands B5 5RS..
e: info@vividprojects.org.uk
w: www.vividprojects.org.uk

WM Event Design
19 ST JAMES'S DRIVE, WANDSWORTH COMMON, LONDON
Greater London SW17 7RN 020 3837 4926
e: info@williammoyse.com
w: www.wmeventdesign.com

Film / Video Stock Suppliers

F

Attend2IT
UNIT 8, PARK FARM INDUSTRIAL ESTATE, BUNTINGFORD
Hertfordshire SG9 9AZ 01763 877 477
w: www.attend2it.co.uk

AV Joint Resource
CORNER HOUSE, 114 WINDMILL STREET, MACCLESFIELD
Cheshire SK11 7LB................. 01625 61 50 90 - 01253 85 12 02
e: hello@avjr.eu
w: www.avjointresource.com

Location One Ltd
UNIT 7, NEW HARBOURS, 75 RIVER ROAD, BARKING
Greater London IG11 0DR .... 07769 910 017 // 0208 099 4291
e: crispin@locationone.co.uk
w: www.locationone.co.uk

One Stop Media
HAZELWOOD, PERIVALE LANE, PERIVALE
Middlesex UB6 8TL...0208 991 2610
e: phil@onestopmedia.biz
w: www.onestopmedia.biz

Sound & Video Services (UK) Ltd
5 HILLINGDON PARADE, UXBRIDGE ROAD, HILLINGDON,
UXBRIDGE
 UB10 0PE 0844 755 0208
e: sales@svsmedia.com
w: www.svsmedia.com

Film Distributors

Attend2IT
UNIT 8, PARK FARM INDUSTRIAL ESTATE, BUNTINGFORD
Hertfordshire SG9 9AZ 01763 877 477
w: www.attend2it.co.uk

Filmbank Distributors Ltd
WARNER HOUSE, 98 THEOBALD'S ROAD, LONDON
Greater London WC1X 8WB............................... 020 7984 5957/8
e: info@filmbankmedia.com
w: www.filmbankmedia.com

Film Libraries / Archives

Acquire Image Media Picture Library
16 EDGECOMBE WAY, ST ANN'S CHAPEL, GUNNISLAKE
Cornwall PL18 9HJ 01822 833204
e: info@acquireimagemedia.com
w: www.acquireimagemedia.com

BBC Motion Gallery
MEDIA CENTRE, THE GARDEN HOUSE, 1ST FLOOR SOUTH,
WOOD LANE
W12 7TQ 020 8433 2861
e: motiongallery.uk@bbc.com
w: www.bbcmotiongallery.com

Bonded Services
UNITS 4/5, SPACEWAYE, FELTHAM
Greater London TW14 0TH.....................................0 203405 5560
e: CustomerServices@bonded.co.uk
w: www.bonded.com

Environmental Investigation Agency
62-63 UPPER STREET, LONDON
Greater London N1 0NY 020 7354 7960
e: ukinfo@eia-international.org
w: www.eia-international.org

Film Research & Production Services Ltd
PO BOX 28045
SE27 9WZ...020 8670 2959
e: frps@aol.com

Film Rights Ltd
11 PANDORA ROAD, LONDON
Greater London NW6 1TS.....................................0208 001 3040
e: information@filmrights.ltd.uk
w: www.filmrights.ltd.uk

Focal International Ltd
79 COLLEGE ROAD, HARROW
Middlesex HA1 1BD 020 3178 3535
e: info@focalint.org
w: www.focalint.org

Huntley Film Archives Ltd
OLD KING STREET FARM, EWYAS HAROLD, HEREFORD
Herefordshire HR2 0HB 01981 241580
e: films@huntleyarchives.com
w: www.huntleyarchives.com

Last Refuge Ltd
BATCH FARM, PANBOROUGH, NR WELLS
Somerset BA5 1PN 01934 712556
e: info@lastrefuge.co.uk
w: www.lastrefuge.co.uk

Lebrecht Music & Arts Photo Library
3 BOLTON ROAD, LONDON
NW8 0RJ 020 7625 5341
e: pictures@lebrecht.co.uk
w: www.lebrecht.co.uk   www.art-imag

London Transport Museum
COVENT GARDEN PIAZZA, LONDON
Greater London WC2E 7BB....................................020 7379 6344
e: corphire@ltmuseum.co.uk
w: www.ltmuseum.co.uk

New Wave Films
1 LOWER JOHN ST, LONDON
Greater London W1F 9DT 020 3603 7577
e: info@newwavefilms.co.uk
w: www.newwavefilms.co.uk

Showfile
.... +44 (0) 7582 513623
e: enzo@showfile.com
w: www.showfile.com

Skyscan Aerial Photolibrary
OAK HOUSE, TODDINGTON, CHELTENHAM
Gloucestershire GL54 5BY 01242 621357
e: info@skyscan.co.uk
w: www.skyscan.co.uk

Theatresearch
DACRE HALL, DACRE
North Yorkshire HG3 4ET......................................01423 780497
e: office@theatresearch.co.uk
w: www.theatresearch.co.uk

World Television
18 KING WILLIAM STREET, LONDON
Greater London EC4N 7BP 020 7243 7350
e: askus@world-television.com
w: www.world-television.com

Film Processing Labs & Equipment

Attend2IT
UNIT 8, PARK FARM INDUSTRIAL ESTATE, BUNTINGFORD
Hertfordshire SG9 9AZ 01763 877 477
w: www.attend2it.co.uk

Film Storage / Vaults

Bonded Services
UNITS 4/5, SPACEWAYE, FELTHAM
Greater London TW14 0TH.....................................0 203405 5560
e: CustomerServices@bonded.co.uk
w: www.bonded.com

Fireworks

Aardvark FX
UNIT 21 AVON VALLEY FARM, PIXASH LANE, KEYNSHAM
Bristol BS31 1TS..................... 0 1179 863051 / 0 7891 509521
e: enquiries@aardvarkfx.com
w: www.aardvarkfx.com

Alchemy Fireworks Ltd
BARN 7, THE OLD DAIRY, BEADLOW, SHEFFORD
Bedfordshire SG17 5PL.......................................08000 66 58 37
e: rob@alchemyfireworks.co.uk
w: www.alchemyfireworks.co.uk

Aquabatics
SYMONDSHYDE FARM, HATFIELD
 AL10 9BB 01707 269574
e: office@aquabatics.co.uk
w: www.aquabatics.co.uk

Celestial Firework Displays
79 FOREST STREET, SHEPSHED
Leicestershire LE12 9BZ 7751168191
e: sales@celestialdisplays.co.uk
w: www.celestialdisplays.co.uk

Confetti Magic Ltd
ROCKET PARK, PEPPERSTOCK, LUTON
Bedfordshire LU1 4LL 01582 723502
e: ian@confettimagic.com
w: www.confettimagic.com

Dragonfire Ltd
TUTHILL RISE, STOKE LACY, BROMYARD
Herefordshire HR7 4QZ 01885 490538
e: info@dragonfire.co.uk
w: www.dragonfire.co.uk

Essex Pyrotechnics Ltd
 ....01223 264563
e: office@essex-pyrotechnics.com
w: www.essex-pyrotechnics.co.uk

Event FX Ltd
9 GOODWOOD CLOSE, BURGPHFIELD COMMON, READING
Berkshire RG7 3EZ...08000 787707
e: info@eventfx.co.uk
w: www.eventfx.co.uk

Fantastic Fireworks
ROCKET PARK, PEPPERSTOCK, LUTON
 LU1 4LL..01582 485 555
e: info@fantasticfireworks.co.uk
w: www.fantasticfireworks.co.uk

Firework Crazy
UNIT 21 ECKERSLEY ROAD, CHELMSFORD
Essex CM1 1SL..01245 354422
e: mark@fireworkcrazy.com
w: www.fireworkcrazy.com

FIREWORK STORE LTD
49 BUTE GARDENS WEST , WALLINGTON
Surrey SM6 8SP 07748 555 555
e: mark@fireworkstore.co.uk
w: www.fireworkstore.co.uk

Fireworks Direct
UNIT 3, DOAL TRADING ESTATE , ROLFE STREET, SMETHWICK,
BIRMINGHAM
West Midlands B66 ....0844 556 1300
e: manni@fireworks-direct.co.uk
w: www.fireworks-direct.co.uk

Fireworks International Ltd
WEST PYRO SITE, FAULD INDUSTRIAL ESTATE, TUTBURY,
BURTON ON TRENT
Staffordshire DE13 9HS 01283 521 174
w: www.fireworksinternational.co.uk

Frontier Fireworks Ltd
23 SOUTHFIELD, POLEGATE
 BN26 5LX 01323 488 866
e: info@frontierfireworks.co.uk
w: www.frontierfireworks.co.uk

Fully Fused Fireworks
 ....01462 817640
w: www.fullyfusedfireworks.com

Jubilee Fireworks Ltd
UNIT 29 DAWLEY TRADING ESTATE, STALLINGS LANE,
KINGSWINFORD
West Midlands DY6 7AP...1384402255
e: enquiries@jubileefireworks.co.uk
w: www.jubileefireworks.com

Kimbolton Fireworks Ltd
7 HIGH STREET, KIMBOLTON, HUNTINGDON
Cambridgeshire PE28 0HB.....................................01480 860988
e: info@kimboltonfireworks.co.uk
w: www.kimboltonfireworks.co.uk

KJE Technical
 ....01454 631 470
e: info@kjetech.com
w: www.kjetech.com

Komodo Fireworks
61 ALVINGTON WAY, MARKET HARBOROUGH
Leicestershire LE16 7NF 01858 680038
e: enquiries@komodofireworks.com
w: www.komodofireworks.com

Le Maitre Ltd
6 FORVAL CLOSE, WANDLE WAY, MITCHAM
Surrey CR4 4NE...0208 646 2222
e: info@lemaitreltd.com
w: www.lemaitreevents.com

Magic and Miracle Fireworks
ARTHUR MEE ROAD, STAPLEFORD, NOTTINGHAM
Nottinghamshire NG9 7EW......... 0845 094 9170 // 07921189706
e: info@magicandmiracle.co.uk
w: www.magicandmiracle.co.uk

F

MLE Pyrotechnics Ltd
UNITS 14 - 16, BENTLEY WAY, ROYAL OAK INDUSTRIAL ESTATE,
DAVENTRY
Northamptonshire NN11 8QH..................................01327 876037
e: mail@mlepyrotechnics.co.uk
w: www.mlepyrotechnics.co.uk

MTFX Special Effects
VELT HOUSE, VELT HOUSE LANE , ELMORE
Gloucestershire GL2 3NY 01452 729 903
e: info@mtfx.com
w: www.mtfx.com

Pains Fireworks Ltd
ROMSEY ROAD, WHITEPARISH, SALISBURY
Wiltshire SP5 2SD...01794 884 040
e: sales@painsfireworks.com
w: www.painsfireworks.com

Paul Jubb Fireworks
2 SHACKLEGATE LANE, TEDDINGTON
London TW11 8SH...020 8977 4742
e: pauljubb@gmail.com
w: www.pauljubbfireworks.co.uk

Pyro 1- Firework Displays
SYMONDSHYDE FARM, HATFIELD
 AL10 9BB 01707 269566
e: contactus@pyro1.com
w: www.pyro1.com

Pyrotex Fireworx Ltd
THE WILLOWS, COURT FARM LANE, BRANSTON,
BURTON UPON TRENT
Staffordshire DE14 3HA 01283 517600
e: enquiries@pyrotexfireworx.co.uk
w: www.pyrotexfireworx.co.uk

Quicksilver Uk Limited
17 HYDE ROAD, DENTON, MANCHESTER
Greater Manchester M34 3AF 0161 320 7232
e: sales@quicksilversfx.co.uk
w: www.quicksilversfx.co.uk

Sandling Fireworks
FIRST FLOOR OFFICES, SE45 GLOUCESTERSHIRE AIRPORT,
STAVERTON
 GL51 6SP 01452 855915
e: sales@sandlingfireworks.co.uk
w: www.sandlingfireworks.co.uk

Shell Shock Fireworks Ltd
....01664 454994 // 07768 684910
w: www.shellshockfireworks.co.uk

Shellscape Pyrotechnics Ltd
BUTCHERS LANE, WHITE WALTHAM, MAIDENHEAD
Berkshire SL6 3SD...01628 829 401
e: blast@shellscape.com
w: www.shellscape.com

Skyburst - The Firework Co
UNIT 1A, PEARTREE INDURSTRIAL ESTATE, BATH ROAD, UPPER
LANGFORD, BRISTOL
BS40 4DJ 08000 744 636
w: www.skyburst.co.uk

Starlight Fireworks Ltd
....01494 766901
e: displays@starlightfireworks.co.uk
w: www.starlightfireworks.co.uk

The World Famous
BOUNDARY FARM, MAIDSTONE ROAD, HADLOW
Kent ME18 6BY..01732 852002
e: info@theworldfamous.co.uk
w: www.theworldfamous.co.uk

Viking Fireworks
.... 01843 823545 // 01843 596717
e: enquiries@vikingfireworks.co.uk
w: www.tplpyro.co.uk

Walk The Plank
WALK THE PLANK, 72 BROAD STREET, SALFORD
Lancashire M6 5BZ...0161 736 8964
e: info@walktheplank.co.uk
w: www.walktheplank.co.uk

Flags / Banners / Bunting

All About Signs
UNIT 25 CHALLENGE ENTERPRISE CENTRE, SHARPS CLOSE, PORTSMOUTH
Hampshire PO3 5RJ..023 9265 4720
e: enquiries@allaboutsigns.co.uk
w: www.allaboutsigns.co.uk

Balloon & Party Ideas
HICKLEY FARM, RADBOURNE, DERBY
Derbyshire DE6 4LY 01332 824268
w: www.partyplc.com

Blink Giant Media Ltd
COOPER HOUSE 2D, MICHAEL ROAD, LONDON
Greater London SW6 2AD 020 77368822
e: info@blinkgiantmedia.com
w: www.blinkgiantmedia.com

Blueprint Promotional Products
NO. 1 THE EMBASSY, LAWRENCE STREET, LONG EATON, NOTTINGHAM
Nottinghamshire NG10 1JY 0333 1234 400
e: info@blueprintpromo.co.uk
w: www.blueprintpromo.co.uk

Boldscan Ltd
UNIT 4 TONEDALE BUSINESS PARK, WELLINGTON
Somerset TA21 0AW 01823 665849
e: sales@boldscan.co.uk
w: www.boldscan.co.uk

Datum Colour Print (Hatfield) Ltd
UNIT 6, BEACONSFIELD ROAD, HATFIELD
Hertfordshire AL10 8BE..01707 251222
e: sales@datumcp.com
w: www.datumcp.com

Embroiderme
29 UNION STREET, RYDE PO33 2DT 01983 618816
e: embroiderme@btconnect.com
w: www.embroiderme.co.uk

Festival Flags
LAKE VIEW, CAPPNABOUL, KEALKIL, BANTRY, CO. CORK, IRELAND
.... +353 (0)27 66803 / +353 (0)86 355 8030
e: taraflags@gmail.com
w: www.festivalflags.ie

Go Displays
WELBECK WAY, PETERBOROUGH
Cambridgeshire PE2 7WH 01733 232000
e: caroline@go-displays.co.uk
w: www.go-displays.co.uk

GTMS - GT Marketing Services Ltd
1 SILVERTHORNE WAY, WATERLOOVILLE
Hampshire PO7 7XB 0 2392 320 580
e: hello@gtms.co.uk
w: www.gtms.co.uk

Hangman
THE ARTWORKS, SILVERGATE, BLICKLING, NORWICH
Norfolk NR11 6NN 01263 732265
e: info@hangman.co.uk
w: www.hangman.co.uk

Hollywood Monster
THE STUDIOS, REDFERN PARK WAY, TYSELEY, BIRMINGHAM
West Midlands B11 2BF 0121 764 3222
e: sales@hollywoodmonster.co.uk
w: www.hollywoodmonster.co.uk

House Of Flags
BICTON INDUSTRIAL PARK, KIMBOLTON
Cambridgeshire PE28 0LQ 01480 861 678
e: enquiries@flags.co.uk
w: www.flags.co.uk

J&C Joel Limited (Head Office)
CORPORATION MILL, CORPORATION STREET, SOWERBY BRIDGE, HALIFAX
Yorkshire HX6 2QQ...01422 833835
e: uksales@jcjoel.com
w: www.jcjoel.com

Lucid Productions
UNIT 407 GREENHEATH BUSINESS CENTER, THREE COLTS LANE, London E7 0DL...0207 739 0240
e: info@clubdecor.co.uk
w: www.clubdecor.co.uk

Mediaco Graphic Solutions
CHURCHILL POINT, CHURCHILL WAY, TRAFFORD PARK, MANCHESTER
Greater Manchester M17 1BS...............................0161 875 2020
e: customerservice@mediaco.co.uk
w: www.mediaco.co.uk

Newton Newton
THE BISHOP TOZER'S CHAPEL, MIDDLEMARSH ROAD, BURGH-LE-MARSH Lincolnshire PE24 5AD........................01754 768401
e: info@newtonnewtonflags.com
w: www.newtonnewtonflags.com

Non-Stop Party Shop
214-216 KENSINGTON HIGH STREET, LONDON
Greater London W8 7RG...0207 9377201
e: party@nonstopparty.co.uk
w: www.nonstopparty.co.uk

Only Rollers
11 ALBERT PLACE, DARWEN
Lancashire BB3 0QE 0845 3882324
e: info@only-rollers.com
w: www.onlyrollers.com

Oscar Group Ltd
P.O. BOX 7571, MILTON KEYNES
Buckinghamshire MK11 9GL.................................01908 260 333
e: sales@oscar.uk.com
w: www.oscar.uk.com

Piggotts Company Limited
46 STEPFIELD, WITHAM
Essex CM8 3TH 01376 535 750
e: sales@piggotts.co.uk
w: www.piggotts.co.uk

Pink Lizard Design
THE COTTAGE, CASTLE DRIVE, FALMOUTH
TR11 4NG 07761 598254
e: jef@pinklizarddesign.eu
w: www.festival-flags.eu/

Planet Gold Decor
UNIT 4 ROMARSH, FOWLSWICK BUSINESS PARK, , ALLINGTON
Wiltshire SN14 6QE..07747 015 170
e: info@planetgolddecor.co.uk
w: www.planetgolddecor.co.uk or www.

PromotionandEvent.com
UNIT 35 CHARTER GATE, MOULTON INDUSTRIAL PARK,
NORTHAMPTON
NN3 6QB 01604 790762
w: www.promotionandevent.com

Sherwood Signmakers Ltd
A7, ENTERPRISE PARK, BRUNEL DRIVE, NEWARK
Nottinghamshire NG24 2DZ 01636 611950
e: info@sherwoodsigns.co.uk
w: www.sherwoodsigns.co.uk

Sunbaba
SUNBABA HOUSE, VICARAGE CLOSE, DULLINGHAM, NEWMARKET
Suffolk CB8 9XA 01638 507684
e: info@sunbaba.co.uk
w: www.sunbaba.co.uk

Surf & Turf Instant Shelters Ltd
UNIT 7 TATTON COURT, KINGSLAND GRANGE, WARRINGTON
Cheshire WA1 4RR..01925 819608
e: info@surfturf.co.uk
w: www.surfturf.co.uk

The Digitial Print Factory (tdpf)
12-12A ROSEBERY AVENUE, LONDON
Greater London EC1R 4TD 020 7209 5620
e: toby@exhibitionkit.co.uk; info@tdpf.eu
w: www.exhibitionkit.co.uk

Ultimate Banners
151 BORDESLEY MIDDLEWAY, STRATFORD STREET NORTH,
BIRMINGHAM
West Midlands B11 1BN 0800 121 4474
e: askus@ultimatebanners.co
w: www.ultimatebanners.co

Zephyr-the Visual Communicator
MIDLAND ROAD, THRAPSTON
Northamptonshire NN14 4LX 01832 737771
e: info@zephyr-tvc.co.uk
w: www.zephyr-flags.co.uk

Flight Cases

5 Star Cases Ltd
BROADEND INDUSTRIAL ESTATE, BROADEND ROAD, WALSOKEN,
WISBECH
Cambridgeshire PE14 7BQ....................................0845 5000555
e: sales@5star-cases.com
w: www.5star-cases.com

Abs Cases
UNIT 2, EUROPA TRADE PARK, CODY ROAD, LONDON
Greater London E16 4SP......................................020 7474 0333
e: sales@abscases.co.uk
w: www.abscases.co.uk

Adam Hall Ltd
THE SEEDBED BUSINESS CENTRE, VANGUARD WAY,
SHOEBURYNESS
SS3 9QY 01702 613922
e: mail@adamhall.co.uk
w: www.adamhall.com

Adda Super Cases Ltd
PO BOX 366, CAMBRIDGE
Cambridgeshire CB24 3AX....................................01223 233101
e: sales@adda-super-cases.co.uk
w: www.addasupercases.com

CMAC Group
SUITE 12, THE GLOBE CENTRE, ST JAMES SQUARE, ACCRINGTON
Lancashire BB5 0RE .... 03333 207 100 / 01254 355120
e: chloe.cumby@coachhirebooking.co.uk
w: cmacgroup.co.uk/

Condor Cases
14-17 WILLOW FARM BUSINESS PARK, STOWMARKET ROAD,
RICKINGHALL
Suffolk IP22 1LQ..01603 735900
e: sales@condor-cases.co.uk
w: www.condor-cases.co.uk

CP Cases Ltd
UNIT 11, WORTON HALL IND EST, WORTON ROAD, ISLEWORTH
Middlesex TW7 6ER 0208 568 1881
e: info@cpcases.co.uk
w: www.cpcases.com

Dragon Cases
6 THE STUDIO, OLDBURY BUSINESS CENTRE, OLDBURY ROAD,
CWMBRAN
NP44 3JU 01633 791590
e: info@dragoncases.co.uk
w: www.dragoncases.co.uk

EPS Flight Cases
UNIT 3, QUAYSIDE BUSINESS PARK, WEST DOCK STREET, HULL
East Yorkshire HU3 4HH 01482 212887
e: sales@epsflightcases.com
w: www.epsflightcases.com

Ibs Flight Cases Llc
WB2 - ZEDKLYM COMPLEX, DUBAI INVESTMENTS PARK, DUBAI
PO BOX 38365 .... +971.4.339.2982
e: sales@ibsflightcases.com
w: www.ibsflightcases.com

Jetlife Cases
UNIT 8 LEVENS HALL PARK, LUND LANE, KILLINGHALL,
HARROGATE
North Yorkshire HG3 2BG 01423 530716
e: info@jetlifecases.com
w: www.jetlifecases.com

Matt Snowball Music
UNIT 2, 3-9 BREWERY ROAD, LONDON
Greater London N7 9OJ 020 7700 6555
e: enquiries@mattsnowball.com
w: www.mattsnowball.com

Packhorse Ltd
UNIT 7, STEVERN WAY, EDGERLEY DRAIN ROAD, FENGATE,
PETERBOROUGH
Cambridgeshire PE1 5EL.. 01733 897447
e: sales@packhorse.co.uk
w: www.packhorse.co.uk

Quentor Cases Ltd
UNIT 10, FITZMAURICE COURT, RACKHEATH INDUSTRIAL ESTATE,
NORWICH
Norfolk NR13 6PY 01603 721604
e: sales@quentor.com
w: www.quentor.com

Swanflight.com
LOW HARDWICK FARM, SEDGEFIELD, STOCKTON ON TEES
Durham TS21 2EH 01740 623555
e: info@swanflight.com
w: www.swanflight.com

Topper Cases Ltd
16/17 WINDOVER COURT, HUNTINGDON
Cambridgeshire PE29 7EA 01480 457251
e: sales@toppercases.co.uk
w: www.toppercases.co.uk

West Country Cases
7 CAVALIER ROAD, HEATHFIELD INDUSTRIAL ESTATE,
NEWTON ABBOT
TQ12 6TQ 01626 201068
e: sales@westcountrycases.co.uk
w: www.westcountrycases.co.uk

Flooring

A & J Big Top Hire
OXNEY ROAD, PETERBOROUGH
Cambridgeshire PE15YR 01733 222999
e: sales@ajbigtophire.com
w: www.ajbigtophire.com

A T Industries Ltd
UNIT 15 /16 PRIEST COURT, SPRINGFIELD BUSINESS PARK,
SPRINGFIELD ROAD, GRANTHAM
Lincolnshire NG31 7BG 01476 593050
e: sales@atindustries.co.uk
w: www.atindustries.co.uk

Albion Woods Show Tents
CANNARDS FARM, SHEPTON MALLET
Somerset BA4 4LY 01749 346002
e: tents@albionwoods.co.uk
w: www.albionwoods.co.uk

Ascot Structures
ALUTECH HOUSE, GREEN LANE, HEYTHROP
Oxfordshire OX7 5TU... 01608 683999
e: office@ascotstructures.co.uk
w: www.ascotstructures.co.uk

Austen Lewis Ltd
UNIT DG, CHELWORTH PARK, CRICKLADE, SWINDON
Wiltshire SN6 6HE.. 01793 750599
e: info@austen-lewis.co.uk
w: www.austen-lewis.co.uk

AVS Hire
UNIT 4, HIGHAMS FARM, SHEEPBARN LANE, WARLINGHAM
Surrey CR6 9PQ 01959 540 028
e: av_equipment_questions@yahoo.co.uk
w: www.avs-hire.co.uk

British Harlequin Plc
FESTIVAL HOUSE , CHAPMAN WAY, TUNBRIDGE WELLS
Kent TN2 3EF.. 01892 514888
e: enquiries@harlequinfloors.com
w: www.harlequinfloors.com

Bryan & Clark Ltd
UNIT 2 & 3, WESTMORELAND ROAD, KINGBURY, LONDON
Greater London NW9 9RL...................................... 020 8206 2200
e: sales@bryanandclark.co.uk
w: www.bryanandclark.co.uk

Carpet Bright UK
AIRPORT HOUSE, PURLEY WAY, CROYDON
CR0 0XZ 01 689 477100
e: therealnatalietaylor@gmail.com
w: www.carpetbright.uk.com/carpet-cl

Carpets and Vinyls Direct
.... 0190 3743 932 // 07966 212 358
e: leslie.sheeran@unicombox.co.uk
w: www.carpetsandvinylsdirect.co.uk

Churchill Marquees
63 NORWOOD AVENUE, SHIPLEY
West Yorkshire BD18 2AX .... 07758690427 / 07758690427
e: jerry@candsmarquees.co.uk
w: www.candsmarquees.co.uk

F

The largest range of
event and exhibition floor covering
available in Europe.

- ● Installation
- ● Supply
- ● Service
- ● Recycling

Reeds
Carpets

Complete Avenue Ltd
OLD BARN, BLACKBIRD FARM,BLACKBIRD LANE, ALDENHAM
West Midlands WD25 8BS......................................07854 007483
w: www.completeavenue.co.uk

Criterion Flooring
8 FANTAIL LANE, TRING
Hertfordshire HP23 4EN 07850752219/01442 822799
e: info@criterionflooring.co.uk
w: www.criterionflooring.co.uk

CTN Exhibitions Ltd
UNIT G3A, HALESFIELD 19, TELFORD
Shropshire TF7 4QT 01952 680423
e: sales@ctn-uk.com
w: www.ctn-uk.com

Designer Carpets And Remnants Ltd
65 BABINGTON LANE, DERBY
Derbyshire DE1 1TE..01332 346 444
e: info@designer-carpet-remnants.co.uk
w: www.designer-carpet-remnants.co.u

Eco Track & Access Ltd
GEOFF'S DRIVE, WALTON NEW ROAD BUSINESS PARK,
LUTTERWORTH
Leicestershire LE17 5RD.......................................01455 553 700
e: sales@ecotrackway.co.uk
w: www.ecotrackway.co.uk/

Edwards Flooring
57 BECKENHAM LN, BROMLEY
Kent BR2 0DN..2082497646
e: edwardsflooring@live.co.uk
w: www.bromleywoodenflooring.com

Europa International
EUROPA HOUSE, MEAFORD WAY, PENGE, LONDON
Greater London SE20 8RA....................................020 8676 0062
e: contact@europainternational.com
w: www.europainternational.com

Event Decor Group
UNIT 11 PARKROSE INDUSTRIAL ESTATE, MIDDLEMORE ROAD,
BIRMINGHAM West Midlands B66 2DZ..
.... 0121 306 9412 // 07799 353 537
e: admin@eventdecorgroup.co.uk
w: www.eventdecorgroup.co.uk

Event Tents Global
223 ARDGLASS ROAD, DOWNPATRICK
BT30 7ED .... 02844 841 820 / 07872 501861
e: contact@eventtentsglobal.com
w: www.eventtentsglobal.com

Evergreens Uk Ltd
EXTON BLOCK, MARKET OVERTON INDUSTRIAL ESTATE, MARKET
OVERTON, OAKHAM, RUTLAND
Rutland LE15 7TP 01572 768208
e: sales@evergreensuk.com
w: www.evergreensuk.com

ExpressMarqueeFlooring.co.uk
UNIT 18 SEAX COURT, SEAX WAY, BASILDON
Essex SS15 6SL..0126 8412 266
e: sales@expressmarqueeflooring.co.uk
w: https://www.expressmarqueeflooring.co.uk

Flex Furn
THE BARNLANDS, LONDON ROAD, CHELTENHAM
Gloucestershire GL52 6UT 01242 524777
e: info.uk@flexfurn.com
w: www.flexfurn.com

Grass Concrete Ltd
DUNCAN HOUSE, 142 THORNES LANE, THORNES, WAKEFIELD
Warwickshire WF2 7RE 01924 379443
e: info@grasscrete.com
w: www.grasscrete.com

Grassform Plant Hire Ltd
LITTLE WOODBARNS FARM YARD, GREEN STREET, FRYERNING,
INGATESTONE
Essex CM4 0NT 01277 353686
e: info@grassform.co.uk
w: www.grassform.co.uk

Grono Lawns Ltd
ASTRA BUSINESS PARK, 7 TRAFFORD MOSS RD, MANCHESTER
Greater London M17 1SQ.....................................0161 885 5713
e: sales@grono.co.uk
w: www.grono.co.uk

GT Trax Ltd
HIGH TREE FARM, NEW ROAD, WARBOYS
Cambridgeshire PE28 2SS 01487 823344
e: info@gttrax.co.uk
w: www.gttrax.co.uk

Ideal Event Services
310 UNTHANK ROAD, NORWICH
Norfolk NR4 7QD 01603 280176
e: hello@idealeventservices.co.uk
w: www.idealeventservices.co.uk

Impressed Driveways Ltd
4 ASTBURY CLOSE , ALTRINCHAM
WA15 8JA.................................... 01614789929 / 07723378230
e: dmilesroche@hotmail.com
w: www.impresseddriveways.com

JDA Hire
LAURENCE COURT, SHORTLANDS ROAD, LONDON, LEYTON
E10 7AU 07505 221105
e: admin@jdahire.co.uk
w: www.jdahire.co.uk

JMT Indisplay Ltd
UNIT A, VENTURA PARK, OLD PARKBURY LANE, ST. ALBANS
Hertfordshire AL2 2DB 01923 851580
e: sales@jmtindisplay.co.uk
w: www.jmtindisplay.co.uk

F

F

Le Mark Self Adhesive Ltd
UNIT 1 HOUGHTON HILL INDUSTRIES, SAWTRY WAY, HOUGHTON
Cambridgeshire PE28 2DH....................................01480 494 540
e: info@lemark.co.uk
w: www.lemark.co.uk

Made To Measure Windows and Doors Ltd
MAVERICK BUSINESS PARK, 292 MONKMOOR RD,
SHREWSBURY, SHROPSHIRE
SY2 5TF..1743356130
e: madetomeasurewindows@hotmail.co.uk
w: www.madetomeasurewindows.co.uk

Marldon Marquees
111 WINNER STREET, PAIGNTON
Devon TQ3 3BP...01803 524425
e: enquiries@marldonmarquees.co.uk
w: www.marldonmarquees.co.uk

Marquee Carpets Limited
UNIT 8 MAXWELLS WEST, GREAT CAMBRIDGE ROAD, CHESHUNT
Hertfordshire EN8 8XH..01992 629624
e: enquiries@marqueecarpets.com
w: www.marqueecarpets.com

Neon Arena Services
UNIT 305, THE ARGENT CENTRE, 60 FREDERICK STREET,
HOCKLEY, BIRMINGHAM
West Midlands B1 3HS...0121 236 5555
e: info@neonarenaservices.co.uk
w: www.neonsportsfloors.co.uk

Podesta Roofing
15/17 MIDDLE STREET , BRIGHTON
East Sussex BN1 1AL.................. 01273 461367 / 07545 860051
e: alison@podesta-roofing.co.uk
w: podesta-roofing.co.uk/

Polytec Coatings North West Ltd
UNIT 7, MORETON BUSINESS PARK , GLEDRID , CHIRK
LL14 5DG 1691770963
e: polyteccoatings@gmail.com
w: www.polyteccoatings.co.uk

Portable Floors
MORNINGWELL COTTAGE, PIDDLETRENTHIDE, DORCHESTER
Dorset DT2 7QZ..01300 348 726
e: graham@portable-floors.co.uk
w: www.portable-floors.co.uk

Reeds Carpets
183 TORRINGTON AVENUE, COVENTRY
West Midlands CV4 9UQ 02476 694114
e: sales@reeds-carpets.co.uk
w: www.reeds-carpets.co.uk

Rola-Trac
SOUTH BURLINGHAM RD , LINGWOOD , NORWICH
Norfolk NR13 4ET 01493 750 200
e: enquiries@rola-trac.co.uk
w: www.rola-trac.co.uk

SCM EXPO roofing
....1212840902
e: apppical@hotmail.com
w: www.scmroofing.co.uk

Seatchic.co.uk
4 SHENTONFIELD ROAD, SHARSTON INDUSTRIAL ESTATE,
MANCHESTER
Greater Manchester M22 4RW.............................0161 428 8099
e: info@seatchic.co.uk
w: www.seatchic.co.uk

Signature (Fencing & Flooring) Systems Europe Ltd
UNIT 1, BLACKETT ROAD, BLACKETT ROAD INDUSTRIAL ESTATE,
DARLINGTON
Durham DL1 2BJ 01642 744990
e: sales@signaturesystemseurope.co.uk
w: www.signaturesystemseurope.co.uk

Space Photo
37 STRADELLA ROAD , LONDON
SE24 9HN 7717153884
e: general@spacephoto.co.uk
w: www.spacephoto.co.uk

Stretch and Tents
1V5 COOPER HOUSE,, 2 MICHAEL ROAD, LONDON
Greater London SW6 2AD .... 07733326484 // 020 7097 1875
e: info@stretchandtents.co.uk
w: www.stretchandtents.co.uk

Terraplas Plc
HALL FARM HOUSE, HIGH STREET, CASTLE DONINGTON
Derbyshire DE74 2PP..01332 812 813
e: terraplas@checkers-safety.com
w: www.terraplas.com

The Chillout Furniture Company
RYE FARM, HOLLANDS LANE, HENFIELD,
East Sussex BN5 9QY 0800 881 5229
e: info@completechillout.com
w: www.completechillout.com

The Floor Sanding Floor Company Of London Ltd
5 WARWICK ROAD, LONDON
N18 1RR...2070416578
e: thefloorsandingcompanyoflondon@gmail.com
w: www.thefloorsandingcompanylondon.

TSG
HOOKLANDS FARM, LEWERS ROAD, SCAYNES HILL
West Sussex RH17 7NG 01444 831 456
e: info@tsg.uk.com
w: www.tsg.uk.com

Vicarage Marquees
UNIT ONE, CHURCH ROAD, WADHAM PARK STABLES, HOCKLEY
Essex SS5 6AF..01702 232 200
e: info@vicaragemarquees.co.uk
w: www.vicaragemarquees.co.uk

William Armes Ltd
CHURCHFIELD ROAD, SUDBURY
Suffolk CO10 2YA..01787 372988
e: sales@william-armes.co.uk
w: www.william-armes.co.uk

Zigma Ground Solutions Ltd
UNIT 11, M11 BUSINESS LINK, PARSONAGE LANE, STANSTED
Essex CM24 8GF........................ 0845 643 5388 / 01279 647021
e: sales@zigmagroundsolutions.com
w: www.zigmagroundsolutions.com

Floral / Event Decorations

Aerial Promotions
5 HAWKS GREEN LANE, HAWKS GREEN LANE, CANNOCK
Staffordshire WS11 7LG 01543 505755
e: kevin@aerialpromotions.co.uk
w: www.aerialpromotions.co.uk

Appealing Balloons & Events
141 BELVOIR ROAD, COALVILLE
Leicestershire LE67 3PJ 07836 233319
e: enquiries@appealingballoons.com
w: www.appealingballoons.com

Balloon & Party Ideas
HICKLEY FARM, RADBOURNE, DERBY
Derbyshire DE6 4LY 01332 824268
w: www.partyplc.com

Balloon Crazy
UNIT 23B, LOMBARD ROAD, LONDON
Greater London SW19 3TZ....................................020 8543 1133
e: info@ballooncrazy.co.uk
w: www.ballooncrazy.co.uk

Balloon Mad
ASTON ROAD, NUNEATON
Warwickshire CV11 5EL...07473 158698
e: office@balloonmad.co.uk
w: www.balloonmad.co.uk

Balloon.co.uk
10 ABBEY ROAD, BIRMINGHAM
West Midlands B67 5RD 0121 429 9068
e: david@balloon.co.uk
w: www.balloon.co.uk

Changing Chairs and Event Decor
2 BROOKHILL LEYS RD, EASTWOOD, NEW EASTWOOD
Nottinghamshire NG16 3HZ .... 01773 715 982 / 07973 388901
e: covers@changing-chairs.co.uk
w: www.changing-chairs.co.uk

Classic Crockery
CLASSIC CROCKERY HIRE, UNIT 10 -11 MAPLE, FELTHAM,
WEST LONDON
Greater London TW13 7AW .... 020 3582 9818 / 07584 993 498
e: hire@classiccrockery.co.uk
w: www.classiccrockery.co.uk

Dandy Events
259 SCOTSWOOD ROAD, NEWCASTLE UPON TYNE
Tyne and Wear NE4 7AW......................................0191 272 2006
e: events@dandyevents.com
w: www.dandyevents.com

Embroiderme
29 UNION STREET, RYDE
PO33 2DT...01983 618816
e: embroiderme@btconnect.com
w: www.embroiderme.co.uk

Event Decor Group
UNIT 11 PARKROSE INDUSTRIAL ESTATE, MIDDLEMORE ROAD,
BIRMINGHAM
West Midlands B66 2DZ........... 0121 306 9412 // 07799 353 537
e: admin@eventdecorgroup.co.uk
w: www.eventdecorgroup.co.uk

Event Linen Hire
THE HOUGH GRANARY, MALPAS
Cheshire SY14 7JJ...01948 860597
e: info@eventlinen.co.uk
w: www.eventlinen.co.uk

Event Styles Ltd
BARLEY SHEAF SCHOOL HOUSE, HOLLAND FEN, LINCOLN
Lincolnshire LN4 4QH 01205 280469
e: info@event-styles.co.uk
w: www.event-styles.co.uk

GDC Events Ltd
52 KINGSGATE ROAD, KINGSTON UPON THAMES
Surrey KT2 5AA 0208 9479915
e: info@gdc-events.co.uk
w: www.gdc-events.co.uk

Green Interiors Ltd
THE STRAW BARN, SCHOOL LANE, CROPREDY
Oxfordshire OX17 1PX...01295 750205
e: sales@greeninteriors.co.uk
w: www.greeninteriors.co.uk

Hanging Gardens Ltd
WILDMOOR LANE, SHERFIELD-ON-LODDON, HOOK
Hampshire RG27 0JD 01256 880647
e: info@hanginggarden.co.uk
w: www.hanginggarden.co.uk

IVB Direct Ltd
UNITS 3/4, LILFORD BUSINESS CENTRE, 61 LILFORD ROAD,
LONDON
Greater London SE5 9HY.......................................020 7326 7998
e: hire@ivbdirect.com
w: www.ivbdirect.com

Jaffe Et Fils Ltd
THE OLD BRUSHWORKS, CASTLE HILL, AXMINSTER
Devon EX13 5PY 01297 33408
e: info@jaffefeathers.co.uk
w: www.jaffefeathers.co.uk

F

JDA Hire
LAURENCE COURT, SHORTLANDS ROAD, LONDON, LEYTON
E10 7AU 07505 221105
e: admin@jdahire.co.uk
w: www.jdahire.co.uk

JDB Events
GATEHOUSE TRADING ESTATE, LICHFIELD RD, BROWNHILLS, WALSALL
WS8 6JZ...0121 667 1444
e: info@jdb-events.co.uk
w: www.jdb-events.com

F

Kudos Music
UNIT 10 TRADE CITY, COWLEY MILL ROAD, UXBRIDGE
UB8 2DB...01895 207990
e: info@kudosmusic.co.uk
w: www.kudosmusic.co.uk

Lavenders Of London
UNIT 12 THE METRO CENTRE, ST JOHNS ROAD, ISLEWORTH
Greater London TW7 6NJ......................................0208 568 5733
e: info@lavendersoflondon.com
w: www.lavendersoflondon.com

Little Bloomers Florist
70 ST. NICOLAS PARK DRIVE, NUNEATON
Warwickshire CV11 6DJ.......................................02476 351 120
e: susibloomers@yahoo.co.uk
w: www.littlebloomersflorist.co.uk

London Event Rentals
UNIT 7, WILLOW WALK, TOWER BRIDGE, LONDON
Greater London SE1 5SF...................................... 01252 313154
e: info@londoneventrentals.co.uk
w: www.londoneventrentals.co.uk

Non-Stop Party Shop
214-216 KENSINGTON HIGH STREET, LONDON
Greater London W8 7RG.......................................0207 9377201
e: party@nonstopparty.co.uk
w: www.nonstopparty.co.uk

Norah Sleep Events
NO 5, FIRST FLOOR, WESTFIELD HOUSE, MILLFIELD LANE, YORK
North Yorkshire YO26 6GA....................................01904 790123
e: enquiries@norahsleep.co.uk
w: www.norahsleep.co.uk

Om-Creatives
....07599 888869
e: info@om-creatives.com
w: www.om-creatives.com

Palmbrokers
BOTANICA NURSERY, CROWN LANE,, FARNHAM ROYAL
Buckinghamshire SL2 3SG....................................01753 643359
e: ask@palmbrokers.com
w: www.palmbrokers.com

Permabloom
....0843 886 7706
e: sales@permabloom.co.uk
w: www.permabloom.co.uk

Pick A Posy
2A STANHOPE RD, STROOD
Kent ME2 3EJ...01634 716154
e: info@pickaposyflorist.co.uk
w: www.pickaposyflorist.co.uk

Pink Lizard Design
THE COTTAGE, CASTLE DRIVE, FALMOUTH
TR11 4NG 07761 598254
e: jef@pinklizardesign.eu
w: www.festival-flags.eu/

Planet Gold Decor
UNIT 4 ROMARSH, FOWLSWICK BUSINESS PARK, , ALLINGTON
Wiltshire SN14 6QE...07747 015 170
e: info@planetgolddecor.co.uk
w: www.planetgolddecor.co.uk or www.

PromotionandEvent.com
UNIT 35 CHARTER GATE, MOULTON INDUSTRIAL PARK, NORTHAMPTON
NN3 6QB 01604 790762
w: www.promotionandevent.com

PWM - Philip Walters Merchandising
NO.3, THE GARAGES, ST. LUKES AVENUE, MAIDSTONE
Kent ME14 5AL........................... 01622 431871 / 07711 055588
e: philip@pwm.co.uk
w: www.pwm.co.uk

Rachel Morgan Event Flowers
THE FLOWER STUDIO, 104 PLUMSTEAD COMMON ROAD, LONDON
Greater London SE18 3RE.....................................07701 092624
e: rachel@rachelmorganweddingflowers.co.uk
w: www.rachelmorganeventflowers.co.u

Russell & Twining Blooms Ltd
EXHIBITION NURSERIES, MAIN STREET, MURSLEY, MILTON KEYNES
Buckinghamshire MK17 0RT................................01296 720 006
e: rtbflorists@btconnect.com
w: www.rtbflorists.com

Sapphire London Ltd
.... 020 8127 5400 / 07895 007 951
e: info@sapphirelondon.com
w: www.sapphirelondon.com

Seatchic.co.uk
4 SHENTONFIELD ROAD, SHARSTON INDUSTRIAL ESTATE, MANCHESTER
Greater Manchester M22 4RW.............................0161 428 8099
e: info@seatchic.co.uk
w: www.seatchic.co.uk

Seventh Heaven
....01753 546555
e: info@seventh-heaven-events.co.uk
w: www.seventh-heaven-events.co.uk

Silvertree Crystal
THE GLASSWORKS, SPRING LANE, MOORLYNCH, BRIDGWATER
Somerset TA7 9DD...01458 211101
e: nelson@silvertreecrystal.co.uk
w: www.silvertreecrystal.com

Springfields Topiary
1 SPRINGFIELDS , MICKLE TRAFFORD , CHESTER
Cheshire CH2 4EG .... 01244 300696 / 07986679935
e: springfieldstop@aol.com
w: www.springfieldstopiary.co.uk

Studio Soufflé© Ltd
46 BROOKSBY'S WALK, HACKNEY, LONDON
Greater London E9 6DA..................................... 020 7998 4950 /
.... 07882 753215 / 07841 573
e: hello@studiosouffle.com
w: www.studiosouffle.com

Table Art
UNITS 6 & 7, ST. MARY'S ROAD, SYDENHAM INDUSTRIAL ESTATE, LEAMINGTON SPA
Warwickshire CV31 1PR..0845 521 1234
e: info@table-art.co.uk
w: www.table-art.co.uk

The Balloon Works
238 SANDYCOMBE ROAD, KEW, RICHMOND UPON THAMES
Surrey TW9 2EQ..0208 948 8157
e: sales@balloonworks.co.uk
w: www.balloonworks.co.uk

The Chillout Furniture Company
RYE FARM, HOLLANDS LANE, HENFIELD,
East Sussex BN5 9QY 0800 881 5229
e: info@completechillout.com
w: www.completechillout.com

Themes Incorporated
BECKERY ROAD, GLASTONBURY
Somerset BA6 9NX 01458 832602
e: info@themesinc.co.uk
w: www.themesinc.co.uk

Twilight Trees
THE COURTYARD, NORTHFIELDS, FAIR LANE, WINCHESTER
Hampshire SO21 1HF 01962 877644
e: info@twilight-trees.com
w: www.twilight-trees.com

Velvet Twenty
....020 8675 4870
e: enquiries@velvettwenty.co.uk
w: www.velvettwenty.co.uk

Wellpleased Events
11 BLAYDS YARD, LEEDS
West Yorkshire LS1 4AD.......................................0113 244 2720
e: info@wellpleased.co.uk
w: www.wellpleased.co.uk

Zinc Floral Design
38 PELHAM STREET, NOTTINGHAM
NG1 2EG...0115 9585775
e: info@zincfloraldesign.com
w: www.zincfloraldesign.co.uk

Freighting

F

Air Partner
2 CITY PLACE, BEEHIVE RING ROAD, GATWICK
RH6 0PA .... +44 1293 844 888
e: info@airpartner.com
w: www.airpartner.com

Allport Ltd
HOUSE 1, COWLEY , BUSINESS PARK HIGH STREET, UXBRIDGE
....01895 206000
e: info@uk.allportcargoservices.com
w: www.allportcargoservices.com

Anglo Pacific International
5/9 WILLEN FIELD ROAD, PARK ROYAL , LONDON
Greater London NW10 7BQ 020 8965 1234
e: info@anglopacific.co.uk
w: www.anglopacific.co.uk

Cross Transport Ltd
UNIT 3 LYNDONS FARM, POOLHEAD LANE, EARLSWOOD
Surrey B94 5ES 01564 700381
w: www.crosstransport.co.uk

Dragon Cases
6 THE STUDIO, OLDBURY BUSINESS CENTRE, OLDBURY ROAD, CWMBRAN
NP44 3JU 01633 791590
e: info@dragoncases.co.uk
w: www.dragoncases.co.uk

Gem Tool Hire & Sales Ltd
28 WEDGWOOD ROAD, BICESTER
Oxfordshire OX26 4UL.. 01869 245945
e: info@gem-tools.co.uk
w: www.gem-tools.co.uk

Logwin Air + Ocean Ltd
1 BETAM RD, HAYES
UB3 1SR..0870 729 5700
w: www.logwin-logistics.com

Man And Van 2 Go
145-157 ST JOHN STREET, LONDON
Greater London EC1V 4PW........ 0800 612 2731 / 0203 372 5001
e: info@manandvan2go.co.uk
w: www.manandvan2go.co.uk

F

McGuinness Forwarding Ltd
4 ROEBUCK PARK, GOATSTOWN
Dublin 14...003531 296 2281
e: fiona@mcguinness.eu
w: www.mcguinness.eu

Panther Warehousing Plc
LODGE FARM INDUSTRIAL ESTATE,, NORTHAMPTON
Northamptonshire NN5 7US .... 01604 215000 / 01788 823 656
w: www.panthergroup.co.uk

Peters & May Ltd
UNIT 9, GOODWOOD ROAD, EASTLEIGH, SOUTHAMPTON
Hampshire S050 4NT 02380 480500
e: marine@petersandmay.com
w: www.petersandmay.com

Production Freight
UNIT 7, LAKESIDE INDUSTRIAL ESTATE, LAKESIDE ROAD, ,
COLNBROOK
Berkshire SL3 0ED..01784 472 600
e: derek@productionfreight.com
w: www.productionfreight.com

R Jameson Ltd
BENCOMBE COTTAGE, 13 MARLOW BOTTOM ROAD, MARLOW
Buckinghamshire SL7 3LZ .... 01628 483357 / 07823 882394
e: lynne@rjameson-transport.co.uk
w: www.rjameson-transport.co.uk

Redcare Logistics (Ihr) Ltd
UNIT 5, FORGEWOOD, GATWICK ROAD, CRAWLEY
Kent RH10 9PG .... 0844 2722 247 / 07704 880741
e: info@redcare.uk.com
w: www.redcare.uk.com

Rock-it Cargo Ltd
UNIT 6, X2 - HATTON CROSS CENTRE, EASTERN PERIMETER
ROAD, LONDON HEATHROW AIRPORT, HOUNSLOW
Greater London TW6 2GE.....................................020 88 977 977
e: info@rock-it.co.uk
w: www.rock-itcargo.com

Sound Moves (UK) Ltd
ABBEYGATE HOUSE, CHALLENGE ROAD, ASHFORD
Middlesex TW15 1AX .... 01784 424 471 / 07785 735 045
e: martin.corr@soundmoves.co.uk
w: www.soundmoves.com

Southern Van Lines
RIVER WHARF BUSINESS PARK, MULBERRY WAY,
BELVEDERE, KENT
Greater London DA17 6AR 020 8310 8512
e: operations@southernvanlines.com
w: www.southernvanlines.com

Stagefreight Ltd
EVANSTON AVENUE, LEEDS
West Yorkshire LS4 2HR......................................0113 238 0805
e: info@stagefreight.com
w: www.stagefreight.com

Stagetruck Ltd
LARKWHISTLE FARM WORKS, LARKWHISTLE FARM ROAD,
MICHELDEVER
Hampshire SO21 3BG 020 8569 4444
e: enquiries@stagetruck.com
w: www.stagetruck.com

Team Relocations
DRURY WAY, BRENT PARK, WEMBLEY
Greater London NW10 0JN 020 8784 0100
e: uk@teamrelocations.com
w: www.teamrelocations.com

The Freight Company Global Ltd
HELLMANN HOUSE, LAKESIDE INDUSTRIAL ESTATE,
COLNBROOK BY PASS
Berkshire SL3 0EL 0208 844 0600
e: info@tfcglobal.co.uk
w: www.tfcglobal.co.uk

Titan Airways Ltd
ENTERPRISE HOUSE, BASSINGBOURN ROAD, LONDON STANSTED
AIRPORT, STANSTED
Essex CM24 1RN 01279 680 616
e: charter@titan-airways.co.uk
w: www.titan-airways.com

Worldwide Exhibition Specialists Ltd
30 PANTON STREET, CAMBRIDGE
Cambridgeshire CB2 1HP.....................................020 8508 2224
e: info@wes-group.com
w: www.wes-group.com

Fun Fairs

Blenheim Amusements
....07970 588417
e: samantha.brixton@btinternet.com
w: www.blenheimamusements.co.uk

Hire A Funfair
MOWBRAY FARM, LOW CATTON, YORK
YO41 1EA 01759 371786
e: sara@awkwardentertainments.com
w: www.hireafunfair.com

I need a funfair
....7970430309
e: ineedafunfair@hotmail.co.uk
w: www.ineedafunfair.co.uk

Furniture Hire

BE Furniture Ltd
WELBY ROAD, ASFORDBY HILL, MELTON MOWBRAY
Leicestershire LE14 3RD......................................01664 812 627
e: margaret@beeventhire.co.uk
w: www.befurnituresales.co.uk

BE Event Hire

Melton Mowbray, LE14 3RD
t: 01664 812627
e: info@beeventhire.co.uk

Furniture Hire & Sales.
For further information call 01664 812627.

Hire
www.beeventhire.co.uk

Sales
www.befurnituresales.co.uk

Furniture Supply

A-V Custom Image
141 BELVOIR ROAD, COALVILLE
Leicestershire LE67 3PJ 07836 233319
e: enquiries@a-vcustomimage.com
w: www.a-vcustomimage.com

Abinger Marquee Hire
LADYMEAD, GUILDFORD
Surrey GU1 1DL 01483 536270
w: www.abingermarquees.co.uk

All Event Hire
BURNFIELD ROAD, GIFFNOCK, GLASGOW
Glasgow G46 7TH 0141 637 0368/
0131 652 6007
e: info@alleventhire.co.uk
w: www.alleventhire.co.uk

Arena Seating
LAMBOURN WOODLANDS, HUNGERFORD
Berkshire RG17 7TQ 01488 674800
e: info@arenaseating.com
w: www.arenagroup.com

Art Plinths
GROUND FLOOR, 22 CLARENCE MEWS, LONDON
Greater London E5 8HP...07957 754 329
e: info@artplinths.co.uk
w: www.artplinths.co.uk

Band International
SUNNYSIDE, FRESHWATER, ISLE OF WIGHT
Isle of Wight PO40 9RW 01983 755 858
e: enquiries@band.co.uk
w: www.band.co.uk

Be Event Hire
WELBY ROAD, ASFORDBY HILL, MELTON MOWBRAY
Leicestershire LE14 3RD...01664 812627
e: info@beeventhire.co.uk
w: www.beeventhire.co.uk

Beaumont Events Ltd
STAMFORD HOUSE, 57 LIDDON ROAD, BROMLEY
Kent BR1 2SR 0800 591619
e: tracey@beaumontmarquees.co.uk
w: www.beaumontmarquees.co.uk

Big House Events Ltd
35 ST CLAIR STREET , EDINBURGH
 EH6 8LB 0131 669 6366
e: tash@bighouse-events.co.uk
w: www.bighouse-events.co.uk

Big House Events Ltd
35 ST CLAIR STREET , EDINBURGH
 EH6 8LB 0131 669 6366
e: tash@bighouse-events.co.uk
w: www.bighouse-events.co.uk

BlackDog games ltd
....01992 534448
e: peter@blackdoggames.co.uk
w: www.blackdoggames.co.uk

Booths Furniture Ltd
6 16 CHURCH STREET , ECCLES , MANCHESTER
 M30 0DF .... +44 808 178 7195
e: sales@boothsltd.com
w: https://www.boothsfurnitureltd.co.uk

Cameo Event Hire
UNIT 16, GARDNER INDUSTRIAL ESTATE, KENT HOUSE LANE, ,
BECKENHAM
Kent BR3 1QZ 020 8659 8000
w: www.cameoeventhire.co.uk

Cameron Presentations & All Event Hire
BURNFIELD ROAD, GIFFNOCK, GLASGOW
Glasgow G46 7TH 0141 637 0368
e: hire@cameronpres.co.uk
w: www.cameronpres.co.uk

Chichester Canvas
SIDLESHAM COMMON, CHICHESTER
West Sussex PO20 7PY..01243 641164
w: www.chicanvas.co.uk

City Furniture Hire Ltd
WEST ROAD, HARLOW
Essex CM20 2AL 0845 300 5455
e: info@cityfurniturehireltd.com
w: www.cityfurniturehireltd.com/

Classic Crockery
CLASSIC CROCKERY HIRE, UNIT 10 - 11 MAPLE, FELTHAM,
WEST LONDON
Greater London TW13 7AW .... 020 3582 9818 / 07584 993 498
e: hire@classiccrockery.co.uk
w: www.classiccrockery.co.uk

F

F

Complete Avenue Ltd
OLD BARN, BLACKBIRD FARM,BLACKBIRD LANE, ALDENHAM
West Midlands WD25 8BS.......................................07854 007483
w: www.completeavenue.co.uk

Custom Covers (1984) Ltd
QUAYSIDE ROAD, BITTERNE MANOR, SOUTHAMPTON
Hampshire SO18 1AD 023 8033 5744
e: sales@customcovers.co.uk
w: www.customcovers.co.uk

D-Zine Furniture Hire
D-ZINE HOUSE, SEVERN ROAD, STOURPORT-ON-SEVERN
Worcestershire DY13 9EZ 01299 824100
e: info@d-zinefurniture.co.uk
w: www.d-zinefurniture.co.uk

Danco Plc
THE PAVILION CENTRE, FROG LANE, COALPIT HEATH
Bristol BS36 2NW 01454 250 222
e: info@danco.co.uk
w: www.danco.co.uk

Doyles Furniture
GLENOUR, ADAMSTOWN, ENNISCORTHY
 y21 y2a4 ....0539 240 546 / 087 793 5895
e: doylesfurniture@gmail.com
w: www.doylesfurniture.ie

Europa International
EUROPA HOUSE, MEAFORD WAY, PENGE, LONDON
Greater London SE20 8RA....................................020 8676 0062
e: contact@europainternational.com
w: www.europainternational.com

Event Prop Hire
UNIT 197, AVENUE B, THORP ARCH ESTATE, WETHERBY
West Yorkshire LS23 7BJ 0845 0940 816
e: enquiries@eventprophire.com
w: www.eventprophire.com

Event Tents Global
223 ARDGLASS ROAD, DOWNPATRICK
 BT30 7ED ....02844 841 820 / 07872 501861
e: contact@eventtentsglobal.com
w: www.eventtentsglobal.com

ExamTables.co.uk
20 BUGSBY'S WAY, 20 BUGSBY'S WAY, LONDON
Greater London SE7 7SF.......................................0844 567 5753
e: sales@examtables.co.uk
w: www.examtables.co.uk

Field & Lawn Marquees Ltd
EAST MAINS INDUSTRIAL ESTATE, BROXBURN, EDINBURGH
Edinburgh EH52 5NN 01506 857938
e: edinburgh@fieldandlawn.com
w: www.fieldandlawn.com

Fit Hire Ltd
UNIT 2 THE COURTYARD, OLD DITCHAM FARM, DITCHAM, PETERSFIELD
Hampshire GU31 5RQ ....0800 358 7283 / 01730 825050
e: mail@fithire.com
w: www.fithire.com

Flex Furn
THE BARNLANDS, LONDON ROAD, CHELTENHAM
Gloucestershire GL52 6UT 01242 524777
e: info.uk@flexfurn.com
w: www.flexfurn.com

Four-Candles
TALLY HO FARM, CROUCH LANE, WINKFIELD, ASCOT
Berkshire SL4 4RZ...01344 883934
e: lthomas471@btinternet.com
w: www.four-candles.net

Fresh Event Hire
OAK FARM, HETHERSON GREEN, MALPAS
Cheshire SY14 8EJ 01829 720738
e: myorder@fresheventhire.co.uk
w: www.fresheventhire.co.uk

Fresh Events UK
UNIT D WESLAKE INDUSTRIAL PARK, RYE HARBOUR ROAD, RYE
East Sussex TN31 7TE 07919 512 608
e: info@fresheventsuk.com
w: www.fresheventsuk.com

Funky Furniture Hire
LONDON 0203 328 5446
e: info@funkyfurniturehire.co.uk
w: www.funkyfurniturehire.co.uk

Furniture Hire Uk
 FURNITURE HIRE UK OFFICES 201 - 205, UNIT 1, MERIDIAN TRADING ESTATE 20 BUGSBYÂ ™S WAY, LONDON
Greater London SE7 7SF 0844 567 5744
e: sales@furniturehireuk.com
w: www.furniturehireuk.com

Furniture On The Move
THE MODEL MAKING STUDIOS, AARDMAN ANIMATIONS, GAS FERRY ROAD, BRISTOL
Bristol BS1 6UN 0845 459 9875
e: info@furnitureonthemove.co.uk
w: www.furnitureonthemove.co.uk

Geha bedrooms Ltd
UNIT 1 ALBANY HOUSE , 7-17 CHURCH STREET, WILMSLOW
Cheshire Sk9 1AX 01625 529 778
e: daniel@gehauk.com
w: www.gehauk.com

GLD Productions Ltd
UNIT 10A, BENNETTS FIELD TRADING ESTATE, WINCANTON
Somerset BA9 9DT 01963 441155
e: office@gldproductions.com
w: www.gldproductions.com

Gopak Ltd
RANGE ROAD, HYTHE
Kent CT21 6HG 01303 265751
e: gopakinfo@gopak.co.uk
w: www.gopak.co.uk

Greathire
UNIT 4 BAGO HOUSE, 11-15 CHASE ROAD, PARK ROYAL, LONDON
Greater London NW10 6PT....................................020 8965 5005
e: info@greathire.co.uk
w: www.greathire.co.uk

Higgins Furniture Hire Ltd
DONEANY, KILDARE TOWN
R51 H682 .... +353 (45) 526300
e: hire@higgins.ie
w: www.higgins.ie

Hip Props Ltd
UNIT 6 PINNACLE HOUSE, 260 OLD OAK COMMON LANE,
LONDON
Greater London NW10 6DX 020 8961 0070
w: www.hipprops.com

Hire Chiavari Chair
89A GLOUCESTER RD, CROYDON
Surrey CR0 2DN..020 8697 2181
e: hello@hirechiavarichairs.co.uk
w: www.hirechiavarichairs.co.uk

Humberside Marquees
RIVERSIDE HOUSE, 400 WINCOLMLEE, HULL
East Yorkshire HU2 0QL 01482 610102
w: www.humberside-marquees.com

Inner Sanctum
128 NATHAN WAY, THAMESMEAD
Greater London SE28 0AU 020 8317 8851
e: info@innersanctumfurniture.co.uk
w: www.innersanctumfurniture.co.uk

Inspire Hire Ltd
THE BARLEY MOW CENTRE, 10 BARLEY MOW PASSAGE,
CHISWICK, LONDON
W4 4PH 0203 176 6805
e: hireitfurniture@gmail.com
w: www.hireit-eventfurniture.com

IVB Direct Ltd
UNITS 3/4, LILFORD BUSINESS CENTRE, 61 LILFORD ROAD,
LONDON
Greater London SE5 9HY......................................020 7326 7998
e: hire@ivbdirect.com
w: www.ivbdirect.com

JDA Hire
LAURENCE COURT, SHORTLANDS ROAD, LONDON, LEYTON
E10 7AU 07505 221105
e: admin@jdahire.co.uk
w: www.jdahire.co.uk

JMT Indisplay Ltd
UNIT A, VENTURA PARK, OLD PARKBURY LANE, ST. ALBANS
Hertfordshire AL2 2DB 01923 851580
e: sales@jmtindisplay.co.uk
w: www.jmtindisplay.co.uk

Jongor Ltd
KINGSLAND TRADING ESTATE, ST PHILIPS, BRISTOL
Bristol BS2 0JZ...0117 955 6739
e: bristol@jongor.co.uk
w: www.jongor.co.uk

Just Hire Catering Equipment Ltd
....020 8595 8877
e: info@justhire.co.uk
w: www.justhire.co.uk

Loxit Ltd
FIRST AVENUE, POYNTON INDUSTRIAL ESTATE, POYNTON
Cheshire SK12 1YJ 0845 5195191
e: sales@screenlifts.co.uk
w: www.screenlifts.co.uk

Muswell Manufacturing Co Ltd
UNIT 4, MILL RIVER TRADING ESTATE, BRIMSDOWN, ENFIELD
Greater London EN3 7QF 020 84432711
e: sales@muswell.co.uk
w: www.muswell.co.uk

OFCC - Reception Desks Online
UNIT 34 PHOEBE LANE INDUSTRIAL ESTATE , SIDDAL , HALIFAX
West Yorkshire HX3 9EX..01422 382788
e: sales@receptiondesksonline.co.uk
w: www.receptiondesksonline.co.uk

Pink Flamingo Event Furniture Hire
2 NURSERY COTTAGE, HARVEST HILL, WOOBURN COMMON,
HIGH WYCOMBE
HP10 0JH ....01628 531 911 /
07833 990665
e: furniture@pink-flamingo.co.uk
w: www.pink-flamingo.co.uk

Planet Gold Decor
UNIT 4 ROMARSH, FOWLSWICK BUSINESS PARK, , ALLINGTON
Wiltshire SN14 6QE...07747 015 170
e: info@planetgolddecor.co.uk
w: www.planetgolddecor.co.uk or www.

Plato Catering Hire
BIDFORD ROAD, BROOM
Warwickshire B50 4HF...01789 491133
e: sales@platohire.co.uk
w: www.platohire.com

Portable Floormaker
UNIT 4 SYCAMORE ROAD, TRENT LANE INDUSTRIAL ESTATE,
CASTLE DONINGTON
Leicestershire DE74 2NW 01332 814080
e: enquiries@portablefloormaker.co.uk
w: www.portablefloormaker.co.uk

F

F

Principal Furniture Ltd
ARKWRIGHT ROAD, BICESTER
Oxfordshire OX26 4UU 01869 324488
e: sales@principalfurniture.co.uk
w: www.principalfurniture.co.uk

Rap Industries
WELBECK WAY , WOODSTON, PETERBOROUGH
Cambridgeshire PE2 7WH 01733 394941
e: amie@rapind.com
w: www.rapind.com/acatalog/Pop_up_St

Rayners Catering Hire Ltd
BANQUET HOUSE, 118-120 GARRATT LANE, LONDON
Greater London SW18 4DJ....................................020 8870 6000
e: info@rayners.co.uk
w: www.rayners.co.uk

Reception Desks Online
UNIT 34 PHOEBE LANE INDUSTRIAL ESTATE, SIDDAL , HALIFAX
West Yorkshire HX3 9EX...01422 382788
e: sales@receptiondesksonline.co.uk
w: www.receptiondesksonline.co.uk

Rosetone Ltd
UNITS 1 - 3 WREN PARK BUSINESS CENTRE, HITCHIN ROAD,
SHEFFORD
Bedfordshire SG17 5JD..01462 811166
e: sales@rosetone.co.uk
w: www.rosetone.co.uk

Rutland County Garden Furniture Limited
ASHBOURNE HOUSE, 2 DOVECOTE MEADOWS, ASLACKBY
SLEAFORD, LINCS
 NG34 0HZ...1778440803
e: info@rutlandcountygardenfurniture.co.uk
w: www.rutlandcountygardenfurniture.

Sandler Seating
1A FOUNTAYNE ROAD, LONDON
Greater London N15 4QL .... +44 (0) 203 284 8000
e: sales@sandlerseating.com
w: www.sandlerseating.com

Sico Europe Ltd
THE LINK PARK, LYMPNE INDUSTRIAL ESTATE, LYMPNE
Kent CT21 4LR...01303 234 000
e: sales@sico-europe.com
w: www.sico-europe.com

Spaceworks Furniture Hire Ltd
4 DEER PARK ROAD, SOUTH WIMBLEDON, LONDON
Greater London SW19 3GY....................................020 8545 6000
e: sales@spaceworks.co.uk
w: www.spaceworks.co.uk

Strictly Tables and Chairs
57 BURY MEAD ROAD, MEAD INDUSTRIAL ESTATE, HITCHIN
Hertfordshire SG5 1RT 01462 322 520
e: online@stac.co.uk
w: www.strictlytablesandchairs.co.uk

Studio 50 Floors
7 PORTAL CLOSE, CHIPPENHAM
Wiltshire SN15 1QJ......................01249 661078 / 07713 095975
e: info@studio-50.com
w: www.studio-50.com

Tenandahalfthousandthings
STUDIO 4, VALMAR TRADING ESTATE, VALMAR ROAD , LONDON
Greater London SE5 9NW.....................................0207 924 0464
e: enquiries@tenandahalfthousandthings.co.uk
w: www.tenandahalfthousandthings.co.

The Balloon Works
238 SANDYCOMBE ROAD, KEW, RICHMOND UPON THAMES
Surrey TW9 2EQ..0208 948 8157
e: sales@balloonworks.co.uk
w: www.balloonworks.co.uk

The Chillout Furniture Company
RYE FARM, HOLLANDS LANE, HENFIELD,
East Sussex BN5 9QY 0800 881 5229
e: info@completechillout.com
w: www.completechillout.com

The Event Hire Company
HIRE HQ, 855 LONDON ROAD, WEST THURROCK
Essex RM20 3LG...01708 335184
e: hello@tehcltd.co.uk
w: www.eventhireonline.co.uk

The Hire Business
UNIT 5, 46 LEA ROAD, WALTHAM ABBEY
Hertfordshire EN9 1AJ ....0844 800 7508 / 01992 711 600
e: web@thehirebusiness.com
w: www.thehirebusiness.com

The Old Cinema
160 CHISWICK HIGH ROAD, LONDON
Greater London W4 1PR.......................................020 8995 4166
e: sales@theoldcinema.co.uk
w: www.theoldcinema.co.uk

Thorns Furniture & Catering Hire (Birmingham)
19-21 PORTLAND STREET, ASTON, BIRMINGHAM
West Midlands B6 5RX..0121 328 4666
e: hello@thorns.co.uk
w: www.thorns.co.uk

Thorns Furniture & Catering Hire (London)
WELHAM DISTRIBUTION CENTRE, TRAVELLERS LANE, WELHAM
GREEN, NORTH MYMMS, HATFIELD, HERTS
Hertfordshire AL9 7HN 020 8801 4444
e: hello@thorns.co.uk
w: www.thorns.co.uk

Thorns Furniture & Catering Hire (Manchester)
UNIT D, LYNTOWN TRADING ESTATE, LYNWELL ROAD, ECCLES,
MANCHESTER
Greater Manchester M30 9QG.............................0161 788 9064
e: hello@thorns.co.uk
w: www.thorns.co.uk

Velvet Living
71 MASKELL ROAD, LONDON
Greater London SW17 0NL....................................020 8947 8245
e: info@velvetliving.co.uk
w: www.velvetliving.co.uk

Wagstaff Hire
THE WAGSTAFF CENTRE, 15 WHARFSIDE, ROSEMONT ROAD,
WEMBLEY
Greater London HA0 4PE......................................020 8432 1029
e: hire@wagstaffgroup.co.uk
w: www.wagstaffhire.com

Weatherill Brothers Ltd
NEWGREEN BUSINESS PARK, NORWICH ROAD, WATTON
Norfolk IP25 6HW 01953 882394
e: sales@weatherillbrothers.co.uk
w: www.weatherillbrothers.co.uk

Well Dressed Tables
4 DEER PARK ROAD, SOUTH WIMBLEDON, LONDON
Greater London SW19 3GY....................................020 8545 6000
e: enquiries@welldressedtables.co.uk
w: www.welldressedtables.co.uk

Wellpleased Events
11 BLAYDS YARD, LEEDS
West Yorkshire LS1 4AD..0113 244 2720
e: info@wellpleased.co.uk
w: www.wellpleased.co.uk

Yahire Ltd
UNIT 13 CRANFORD WAY, HORNSEY, LONDON
Greater London N8 9DG..020 7112 8511
e: info@yahire.com
w: www.yahire.com

Youcan Hire Ltd
YOUCAN HEAD OFFICE, LOSCOE CLOSE OFF FOXBRIDGE WAY,
NORMANTON
West Yorkshire WF6 1TW 0870 6004007
w: www.youcanhire.co.uk

F

GH

Gaming

Gamewagon Ltd
113 - 115 OYSTER LANE, BYFLEET
KT14 7JZ..0845 319 4263
e: admin@gamewagon.co.uk
w: www.gamewagon.info

Generators / Power / Electrical Services

Apex Generators
CADDER HOUSE, CLOBERFIELD MILNGAVIE
Glasgow G62 7LW..0845 519 2030
e: enquiries@apexgenerators.co.uk
w: www.apexgenerators.co.uk

Complete Elec Ltd
211 PLANK LANE , LEIGH
WN7 4QE ....
.... 07123226645/07725 853578/07833 491107
e: completeelecltd2@gmail.com
w: www.completeelecltd.co.uk

CW Plant Hire
86 HIGH STREET, HARPENDEN
AL5 2SP..01582 716 413
e: harpenden@cwplant.co.uk
w: www.cwplant.co.uk

Dieselec Thistle Generators
CADDER HOUSE, CLOBERFIELD, MILNGAVIE, GLASGOW
Glasgow G62 7LN..0141 956 7764
e: sales@dieselecthistle.co.uk
w: www.dieselecthistle.co.uk

Dynamic Production Solutions
UNIT 13E, BARTON BUSINESS PARK, NEW DOVER ROAD,
CANTERBURY
Kent CT1 3AA 01227 656 599
e: info@dynamicproductionsolutions.co.uk
w: www.dynamicproductionsolutions.co

East Anglia Leisure
UNIT 4, CIVIC INDUSTRIAL ESTATE, HOMEFIELD ROAD, HAVERHILL
Suffolk CB9 8QP 01440 714204
e: info@ealeisure.co.uk
w: www.ealeisure.co.uk

ES Lighting Hire Ltd
UNIT 3 OPTREX BUSINESS PARK, ROTHERWICK
Hampshire RG27 9AY..01256 765 609
e: Sales@eslightinghire.co.uk
w: www.eslightinghire.co.uk

Event Electrix Ltd
THE OLD STABLES, SHOREHAM LANE ST MICHAELS, TENTERDEN
Kent TN30 6NG...0844 800 2833
e: ask@eventelectrix.co.uk
w: www.eventelectrix.co.uk/

Flying Hire Ltd
LANCASTER YARD, WIGSLEY RD , NORTH SCARLE, LINCOLN
Lincolnshire LN6 9HD 01522 778899
e: info@flyinghireevents.co.uk
w: flyinghireevents.co.uk/

Fourth Generation Limited
220 CRICKLEWOOD LANE, LONDON
NW2 2PU 0208 450 2943
e: tweed@fourthgenerationltd.com
w: www.fourthgenerationltd.com

Fresh Events UK
UNIT D WESLAKE INDUSTRIAL PARK, RYE HARBOUR ROAD, RYE
East Sussex TN31 7TE 07919 512 608
e: info@fresheventsuk.com
w: www.fresheventsuk.com

Generator Power
FOXBRIDGE WAY, NORMANTON INDUSTRIAL ESTATE,
NORMANTON
West Yorkshire WF6 1TN 01924 220055
e: info@generator-power.co.uk
w: www.generator-power.co.uk

Ide Systems
UNIT 3 SWAFFIELD PARK, HYSSOP CLOSE, CANNOCK
Staffordshire WS11 7FU 01543 574 111
e: enquiries@idesystems.co.uk
w: www.idesystems.co.uk

London Event Rentals
UNIT 7, WILLOW WALK, TOWER BRIDGE, LONDON
Greater London SE1 5SF 01252 313154
e: info@londoneventrentals.co.uk
w: www.londoneventrentals.co.uk

Matt Bunday Events
.... 023 8055 3736 // 07730 604 869
e: info@mattbundayevents.com
w: www.mattbundayevents.com

Newburn Power Rental
NIT 36, LIDGATE CRESCENT, , LANGTHWAITE BUSINESS
PARK,SOUTH KIRKBY, PONTEFRACT
West Yorkshire WF9 3NR 0845 077 6693
e: info@npr-uk.com
w: www.newburnpowerrental.com

Noble Electrical Contractors Ltd
UNIT 3A, , DAYBROOK BUSINESS CENTER DAYBROOK,
NOTTINGHAM
Nottinghamshire NG5 6AT 0115 783 0359
e: chris@necltd.co.uk
w: www.nobleelectricalcontractors.co

Ocktcom Temporary Power
UNIT 2, BIRD BUSINESS PARK, STATION ROAD, LONG MARSTON
Warwickshire CV37 8RP..01789 722 330
w: www.ocktcomtemporarypower.com

Redline Electronics
....1355512021
e: redlineelectronics@outlook.com
w: www.redlineelectronics.co.uk

Slim Maintenance
3.1 STANLEY HOUSE, KELVIN WAY , CRAWLEY WEST
Sussex RH10 9SE .... 01293 277489 /
07792 004700 / 07754 6189
e: info@slimmaintenance.co.uk
w: www.slimmaintenance.co.uk

Spectrum Hire Ltd
UNIT 1 HESTON INDUSTRIAL MALL, CHURCH ROAD, , HESTON
Middlesex TW5 0LD 2079936455
e: info@spectrumhire.co.uk
w: www.spectrumhire.co.uk

Speedy Events
CHASE HOUSE, 16 THE PARKS, NEWTON-LE-WILLOWS
Merseyside WA12 0JQ .... 01942 720000 / 0845 609 9998
e: customerservices@speedyhire.com
w: www.speedyservices.com

SWG Power
VINE HOUSE, NORTHWICK ROAD, PILNING, BRISTOL
Somerset BS35 4HA 0844 123 6101
e: ask@swgpower.co.uk
w: www.swgpower.co.uk

SXS Events
....0870 080 2342
e: hello@sxsevents.co.uk
w: www.sxsevents.co.uk

Ten 47 Limited
UNIT 2B FRANCES INDUSTRIAL PARK, WEMYSS ROAD, DYSART,
KIRKCALDY
KY1 2XZ...01592 655725
e: admin@ten47.com
w: www.ten47.com

The Powerline (Entertainments) Ltd
Knowle Hill Farm, Beeks Lane
Marshfield, Wiltshire
SN14 8BB

t: 01225 892 336
e: info@thepowerline.co.uk

Powerline offer a complete on site electrical package for Live
Events, Concerts, Festivals and Outside Broadcasts as well as
a comprehensive range of dry hire equipment. We also offer
temperature control services. A 'can do' attitude and broad
experience in our field gives our clients peace of mind.

www.thepowerline.co.uk

The Powerline Entertainment Ltd
KNOWLE HILL FARM, BEEKS LANE, MARSHFIELD
Wiltshire SN14 8BB 01225 892 336
e: rental@thepowerline.co.uk
w: www.thepowerline.co.uk

Tower Productions
23 ALBERT ROAD , EDINBURGH
Edinburgh EH6 7DP .... +44 131 552 0100
e: enquiries@tower-productions.com
w: www.tower-productions.com

Watkins Hire Ltd
UNITS 24-28, BURNBANK INDUSTRIAL ESTATE, BURNBANK
ROAD, FALKIRK
Stirlingshire FK2 7PE 01324 664 222
e: cameron.loftus@wakinshire.co.uk
w: www.watkinshire.co.uk

Gladiator Games / It's a Knockout

1st Leisure Supplies
LEISURE HOUSE, 137 HANKINSON ROAD, CHARMINSTER
Dorset BH9 1HR..01202 525223
e: info@1stleisuresupplies.com
w: www.1stleisuresupplies.com

Knockout Challenge Limited
PO BOX 5167, SOUTH WOODHAM FERRERS
CM3 5EH 01245 328221
e: info@knockout-challenge.co.uk
w: www.knockout-challenge.co.uk

Peach
PEACH, UNIT D, DAUX ROAD IND EST, BILLINGSHURST
West Sussex RH14 9SJ...01403 780 900
e: info@peach-ent.co.uk
w: www.peach-ent.co.uk

Go-Karting

Kiddi Karts Ltd
HELLERMAN HOUSE, HARRIS WAY, SUNBURY ON THAMES
Surrey TW16 7EW..01932 770770
e: enquiries@kiddikarts.co.uk
w: www.kiddikarts.co.uk

Golf

Golfsim (mobile Golf Simulator Hire)
30 ELVINGTON, KINGS LYNN
Norfolk PE30 4TA...01553 767685
e: info@golfsimulation.co.uk
w: www.golfsimulation.co.uk

Manor Of Groves
HIGH WYCH, SAWBRIDGEWORTH
Hertfordshire CM21 0JU 01279 600777
e: info@manorofgroves.com
w: www.manorofgroves.com

Grandstand Seating

A & J Big Top Hire
OXNEY ROAD, PETERBOROUGH
Cambridgeshire PE15YR 01733 222999
e: sales@ajbigtophire.com
w: www.ajbigtophire.com

Ace Seating Hire
NO. 2 ROBERTS LANE, POLEBROOK, PETERBOROUGH
Cambridgeshire PE8 5LS .... 07976 266524 / 07961 358279
e: info@aceseating.co.uk
w: www.aceseating.co.uk

Arena Seating
LAMBOURN WOODLANDS, HUNGERFORD
Berkshire RG17 7TQ 01488 674800
e: info@arenaseating.com
w: www.arenagroup.com

Arena Structures (Head Office)
NEEDINGWORTH ROAD, ST IVES, HUNTINGDON
Cambridgeshire PE27 3ND...................................01480 468888
e: info@arenastructures.com
w: www.arenastructures.com

Arena UK Ltd
ALLINGTON LANE, ALLINGTON, GRANTHAM
Lincolnshire NG32 2EF..01476 591 569
e: office@arenauk.org
w: www.arenauk.com

Austen Lewis Ltd
UNIT DG, CHELWORTH PARK, CRICKLADE, SWINDON
Wiltshire SN6 6HE...01793 750599
e: info@austen-lewis.co.uk
w: www.austen-lewis.co.uk

Carlinden Events Ltd
12 WORDSWORTH CLOSE, BISHOPS WALTHAM, SOUTHAMPTON
Hampshire SO32 1RT.................. 01489 287187 / 07899 892566
e: info@carlinden.co.uk
w: www.carlinden.co.uk

Evertaut Limited
LIONS DRIVE, SHADSWORTH BUSINESS PARK, BLACKBURN
Lancashire BB1 2QS...01254 297880
e: sales@evertaut.co.uk
w: www.evertaut.co.uk

Grandstand Hire Service
7 BRICK MEADOW, BISHOPS CASTLE
Shropshire SY9 5DH 01588 630454
e: sales@grandstandhire.co.uk
w: www.grandstandhire.co.uk

Grandstands Worldwide Ltd
16 COPSE WOOD WAY, NORTHWOOD
Middlesex HA6 2UE 0207 730 2233
e: info@grandstandsworldwide.com
w: www.grandstandsworldwide.com

KL Spectator Seating
167 COLBY DRIVE, THURMASTON, LEICESTER
LE4 8LE .... 0116 269 2117 / 07801 256199
e: klseating@btconnect.com
w: www.tieredseating.com/

Neon Arena Services
UNIT 305, THE ARGENT CENTRE, 60 FREDERICK STREET,
HOCKLEY, BIRMINGHAM
West Midlands B1 3HS...0121 236 5555
e: info@neonarenaservices.co.uk
w: www.neonsportsfloors.co.uk

Pop Up Arena
50 QUEENS ROAD, LONDON
SW19 8LR 020 8879 3030
e: info@popuparena.com
w: popuparena.com

Securifence UK Ltd
REVELLS FARM, LINTON, ROSS ON WYE
Herefordshire HR9 7SD 01989 720588
e: info@securifence.co.uk
w: securifence.co.uk

Tony Hopkins Entertainments Ltd
MAYPINE HOUSE, 7 MERTON PARK PARADE, KINGSTON ROAD,
LONDON
Greater London SW19 3NT....................................0208 795 0919
e: enquiry@tonyhopkinsentertainments.com
w: www.tonyhopkinsentertainments.com

Wernick Event Hire Ltd
JOSEPH HOUSE, NORTHGATE WAY, ALDRIDGE, WALSALL
West Midlands WS9 8ST 0800 970 0231
e: enquiries@wernickevents.co.uk
w: www.wernickeventhire.co.uk

Graphic Design Services

5 Lamps Media Ltd
3 WOBURN HOUSE, VERNON GATE, DERBY
Derbyshire DE1 1UL..01332 383322
e: mail@5lamps.com
w: www.5lamps.com

Absolute Graphics
....(01590) 675614
e: info@absolutegraphics.co.uk
w: www.absolutegraphics.co.uk

Article 10
23 - 28 PENN STREET, LONDON
Greater London N1 5DL 020 7749 4450
e: hello@article10.com
w: www.article10.com

Artifact Multimedia
76 BERW ROAD, PONTYPRIDD, SOUTH WALES
CF37 2AB .... 07961 262080 / 01443 400 204
e: info@artifactmultimedia.co.uk
w: www.artifactmultimedia.co.uk

AXICO
Lancashire 01524 847265
e: production@axico.co.uk
w: www.axico.com

Blueprint Promotional Products
NO. 1 THE EMBASSY, LAWRENCE STREET, LONG EATON,
NOTTINGHAM
Nottinghamshire NG10 1JY 0333 1234 400
e: info@blueprintpromo.co.uk
w: www.blueprintpromo.co.uk

Broadbase
1A HAGGERSTON STUDIOS, 284 KINGSLAND ROAD
London E8 4DN...0207 254 6848
e: mail@broad-base.co.uk
w: www.broad-base.co.uk

C Force Communications Ltd
GAINSBOROUGH HOUSE, CHURCH ROAD, HEDDINGTON
Wiltshire SN11 0PJ 01672 861060
e: info@cforce.co.uk
w: www.cforce.co.uk

Capricorn Digital
41B MONTAGU ROAD
NW4 3ER 0208 202 9594
e: info@capricorn-digital.com
w: www.capricorn-digital.com

Charlie Apple
8 CEDAR WALK, KENLEY
Surrey CR8 5JL......................... 020 8668 6921 // 07973 987779
e: info@charlieapple.com
w: www.charlieapple.co.uk

Checkland Kindleysides
CHARNWOOD EDGE, COSSINGTON
Leicestershire LE7 4UZ 0116 2644700
e: info@checklandkindleysides.com
w: www.checklandkindleysides.com

Colchester Printers
UNIT 5, COLCHESTER BUSINESS CENTRE, 1 GEORGE WILLIAMS
WAY, COLCHESTER
CO1 2JS 01026 588 604

Command D Ltd
10 MARGARET STREET, LONDON
Greater London W1W 8RL 020 3008 4994
w: www.commandhq.co.uk

G
H

Cornerstone Communications Ltd
49 CHESWICK WAY, SHIRLEY, SOLIHULL
West Midlands B90 4HF..07968 802527
e: bob.shuttleworth@cornerstone-ltd.com
w: www.cornerstone-ltd.com

DE22
CHESTNUT HOUSE, 65B FRIAR GATE, DERBY
Derbyshire DE1 1DJ..01332 208862
e: hello@de22.co.uk
w: www.de22.co.uk

DreamingFish Productions
STUDIO ONE, SILKS YARD , CHURCH HILL , WOKING
 GU21 4QE..08444 770355
e: fraser@dreamingfish.co.uk
w: www.dreamingfish.co.uk

Elastic Productions Ltd
103 KINGS CROSS ROAD, LONDON
Greater London WC1X 9LP...................................020 7639 5556
e: daniel@getelastic.co.uk
w: www.getelastic.co.uk

ExhibitionDesigners.org
5A ANGEL COURTYARD,, HIGH STREET, LYMINGTON
Hampshire SO41 9AP 01590 427022
e: creative@exhibitiondesigners.org
w: www.exhibitiondesigners.org

Facemediagroup.co.uk
VICTORIA HOUSE, VALE ROAD, PORTSLADE, BRIGHTON
East Sussex BN41 1GG..0333 8000 888
e: info@facemediagroup.co.uk
w: www.facemediagroup.co.uk

Fletchers The Creative Service Ltd
CHILTON HOUSE, DEPPERS BRIDGE, SOUTHAM
Warwickshire CV47 2SY..01926 614835
e: happy@fletchers.uk.com
w: www.fletchers.uk.com

Fluid
12 TENBY STREET, BIRMINGHAM
West Midlands B1 3AJ..0121 212 0121
e: info@fluiddesign.co.uk
w: www.fluiddesign.co.uk

Gardiner Designer Associates
34 MALTING MEAD, ENDYMION ROAD, HATFIELD
 AL10 8AR...01707 272 185
e: studio@gardinerdesign.co.uk
w: www.gardinerdesign.co.uk

Go Displays
WELBECK WAY, PETERBOROUGH
Cambridgeshire PE2 7WH.....................................01733 232000
e: caroline@go-displays.co.uk
w: www.go-displays.co.uk

Haley Sharpe Design Ltd
11-15 GUILDHALL LANE, LEICESTER
Leicestershire LE1 5FQ..0116 251 8555
e: info@haleysharpe.com
w: www.haleysharpe.com

HASHTAG Ltd
HIGH PARK RD, RICHMOND
Greater London TW9 4BH.....................................0208 0900 105
e: hello@hashtag.co.uk
w: www.hashtag.co.uk

ID Design
 ....01942 203386
e: info@thisisid.com
w: www.iddesignandmarketing.co.uk/

Ideas
DEVONSHIRE HOUSE, DEVONSHIRE AVENUE, LEEDS
West Yorkshire LS8 1AY 0113 240 9822
e: info@ideasthatwork.solutions
w: www.ideasthatwork.solutions/

JP Displays & Exhibitions
UNIT 16A CHALWYN INDUSTRIAL ESTATE, ST CLEMENTS ROAD,
PARK STONE, POOLE Dorset BH12 4PE 01202 715 722
e: contactus@jpdisplays.com
w: www.jpdisplays.com

Jumping Jack
GROUND FLOOR, 8 WESTBURY PARK, LONDON
 BS6 7JB 0117 973 9873
e: jrugg@jumpingjackmarketing.com
w: www.jumpingjackmarketing.com

Leapfrog
1222144557
e: robsz@a2zleapfrog.com
w: www.a2zleapfrog.com

Mansfields
BENTALLS, PIPPS HILL INDUSTRIAL ESTATE, BASILDON
Essex SS14 3BX 01268 520646
w: www.mansfieldsdesign.co.uk

Matthew Stuart Design
11 YEW TREE CLOSE, MIDDLETON CHENEY, BANBURY
 OX17 2SU 01295 713 813
e: info@matthewstuartdesign.co.uk
w: www.matthewstuartdesign.co.uk

Mere PR @BJL
SUNLIGHT HOUSE, QUAY STREET, MANCHESTER
Greater Manchester M3 3JZ 0161 831 7141
e: Info@BJL.co.uk
w: www.bjl.co.uk

Mike Bell
 ....07970 646705
e: mike@mikebell.eu
w: www.mikebell.eu

MST Media Productions
OMNIBUS BUSINESS CENTRE, 39-41 NORTH ROAD, LONDON
N7 9DP...020 7724 8917
e: info@mstmedia.tv
w: www.mstcommunications.co.uk

Netconnexions Ltd
BURGH ROAD INDUSTRIAL ESTATE , MARCONI ROAD, CARLISLE
, CUMBRIA
CA2 7NA..01228 210000
e: phillip.harrison@connexionsgroup.co.uk
w: https://www.netconnexions.co.uk

Noisebox Digital Media
UNIT B, YAREFIELD PARK, OLD HALL ROAD, NORWICH
Norfolk NR4 6FF 01603 767726
e: info@noisebox.co.uk
w: www.noisebox.co.uk

Nomadic Display U.K
NOMADIC HOUSE 71 , ST. JOHNS ROAD , ISLEWORTH
TW7 6XQ .... 0208 326 0000 / 0208 326 5555
e: info@nomadicdisplay.co.uk
w: www.nomadicdisplay.co.uk/

Non Facture Design
STUDIO 520, GREENHOUSE, CUSTARD FACTORY, BIRMINGHAM
West Midlands B9 4AA..0121 794 0245
e: non@nonfacture.co.uk
w: www.nonfacture.co.uk

One2Create
THE FLINT BARN ST CLAIRS FARM, WICKHAM ROAD, DROXFORD
Hampshire SO32 3PW...0844 8040 796
e: INFO@ONE2CREATE.CO.UK
w: www.one2create.co.uk

Out Of Hand Ltd
HEBRON HOUSE, SION ROAD, BEDMINSTER
BS3 3BD..01179 536363
e: info@outofhand.co.uk
w: www.outofhand.co.uk

Paul Solomons Cartoons
1 LYNDHURST AVENUE, MILL HILL, LONDON
Greater London NW7 2AD .... 020 8537 1676 / 07538 238388
e: info@paulsolomons.co.uk
w: www.daftoons.com

Photo Snap Marketing
128 CANNON WORKSHOPS, LONDON
Greater London E14 4AS..020 7096 3966
e: info@photosnapmarketing.com
w: www.photosnapmarketing.com

Resource Advertising Ltd
....01202 746900
e: zoe@resourceadvertising.co.uk
w: www.resourceadvertising.co.uk

Root
UNIT 9, 37 - 42 CHARLOTTE ROAD, SHOREDITCH, LONDON
Greater London EC2A 3PG 0207 7392277
e: info@thisisroot.co.uk
w: www.thisisroot.co.uk

Royale Graphics
VISTA HOUSE, 9 ARCHER ROAD, STAPLEFORD, NOTTINGHAM
Nottinghamshire NG9 7EP......................................0115 9491880
e: sales@royalegraphics.co.uk
w: www.royalegraphics.co.uk

Salivate
ROCKLEY HOUSE, MEADWAY, CAMBERLEY
Surrey GU16 8TQ..01276 504629
e: info@slv8.com
w: www.slv8.com

Service Graphics Ltd
92 LOWER PARLIAMENT STREET, NOTTINGHAM
Nottinghamshire NG1 1EH 0115 958 7379
e: info.notts@servicegraphics.co.uk
w: www.servicegraphics.co.uk

Shorestream Media
EXETER PHOENIX, BRADNINCH PLACE, GANDY STREET, EXETER
Devon EX4 3LS 07765 488101
e: james@shorestreammedia.co.uk
w: www.shorestreammedia.co.uk

Sliced Bread Animation
TUDOR HOUSE, 35 GRESSE STREET, LONDON
Greater London W1T 1QY......................................020 7148 0526
e: info@sbanimation.com
w: www.thebestthingsince.com

Small Back Room
5 WOOTTON STREET, LONDON
Greater London SE1 8TG.......................................020 7902 7600
e: b.slade@smallbackroom.co.uk
w: www.smallbackroom.com

Stable Creative
MEDINA YARD, COWES
Isle of Wight PO31 7PG .... 01983 842 083 / 07885 774 666
e: ben@stablecreative.co.uk
w: www.stablecreative.co.uk

TGV Design & Marketing
MANSFIELDS HOUSE, BENTALLS, BASILDON
Essex SS14 3BX 01268 669403
e: hello@mgroup.co.uk
w: www.tgvdesign.co.uk

The Imagesetting Bureau
18 COLINDEEP LANE, HENDON, LONDON
Greater London NW4 4SG 020 8202 5424
e: contact@imagesetting.com
w: www.imagesetting.com

G
H

The UX Agency
12 MELCOMBE PLACE, MARYLEBONE, LONDON
Greater London NW1 6JJ......................................020 7947 4940
e: enquiries@theuxagency.co.uk
w: www.theuxagency.co.uk

Union Street Media Arts
20 EAST UNION ST, MANCHESTER
M16 9AE..1618773124
e: roop@unionstreetmediaarts.com
w: www.unionstreetmediaarts.com/

Veucom
NORTH BARN, FEATHERBED COURT, MIXBURY
Oxfordshire NN13 5RN..01280 847287
e: info@veucom.com
w: https://veucom.com/

VisualDialogue
16 PRUNUS CLOSE, WEST END, WOKING
Surrey GU24 9NU...01483 289009
e: info@visualdialogue.co.uk
w: www.visualdialogue.co.uk

XYLO Manchester
THE WAREHAUSE, THE NORTHERN QUARTER, MANCHESTER
M4 5JA...0161 839 1082
e: hello@xylomanchester.com <ello@xylomanchester.com>;
w: www.xylomanchester.com

Health & Safety Consultants

Ambulance & Medical Solutions Ltd
....01422 401000
e: info@ambmed.co.uk
w: www.ambmed.co.uk

Ameys Dog Services
....7950324852
e: ameysdogservices@gmail.com
w: www.ameysdogservices.co.uk

Catalyst Therapy & Training Company
DAVENPORT HOUSE, 16 PEPPER STREET, GLENGALL BRIDGE,
CANARY WHARF , LONDON
E14 9RP .... 01708781927 / 07970 784 609 / 07973 864
e: info@catalysttnt.co.uk
w: www.catalysttnt.co.uk

Cath Lloyd
CORBYNS HALL ROAD , PENSNETT, BRIERLEY HILL
West Midlands DY5 4RA..07941 584939
e: makethechange@cathlloyd.co.uk
w: www.cathlloyd.co.uk

City Of London Hypnotherapy Ltd
45 CENTRAL STREET, LONDON
EC1V 8AB 2075030118
e: info@theclerkenwellgroup.co.uk
w: www.cityoflondonhypnotherapy.co.u

City Psychology
2/8 VICTORIA AVENUE, LONDON
EC2M 4NS 8450177838
e: raoul.barducci@citypsychology.com
w: www.city-psychology.co.uk

First Physio Glasgow
2114A POLLOKSHAWS ROAD , GLASGOW SOUTH SIDE
G43 1AT... +44 141 632 7803
e: firstphysioglasgow@yahoo.com
w: www.firstphysioglasgow.co.uk/

Function Jigsaw Limited
FUNCTION JIGSAW , 24 LONG STREET, WIGSTON
Leicestershire LE18 2AH..1163400255
e: julie@functionjigsaw.co.uk
w: functionjigsaw.co.uk/

Location Medical Services
THE MEDICAL CENTRE, SHEPPERTON STUDIOS, STUDIOS ROAD,
SHEPPERTON
Surrey TW17 0QD 0870 750 9898
e: mail@locationmedical.com
w: www.locationmedical.com

M&S AMBULANCE SERVICE
PINEWOOD STUDIOS , PINEWOOD ROAD IVER HEATH
Buckinghamshire SL0 0NH .... 01488638345 / 01753 630388
e: lizzie@msambulance.co.uk
w: www.msambulance.co.uk

MSS Lts
....7961397943
e: eswain999@gmail.com
w: www.stuntsafety.tv/contact

Park Acre Enterprises Ltd
CAENBY CORNER IND. ESTATE, HEMSWELL CLIFF, LINCOLN
Lincolnshire DN21 5TJ.................... 0142766600 / 01427666123
e: g.pennant@park-acre.co.uk
w: www.park-acre.co.uk

Radcliffe Cardiology
UNIT F, FIRST FLOOR, BOURNE PARK, BOURNE END
Buckinghamshire SL8 5AS........ 0207 193 5381 / 0207 097 1555
e: ecginterpretation2016@gmail.com
w: www.radcliffecardiology.com/conte

Ramdev Chemicals Pvt. Ltd
E-5, 3RD FLOOR, NEMIKRISHNA CHS, JETHWA NAGAR, V.L.ROAD,
KANDIVALI, MUMBAI-67 - INDIA
.... 09320010324 /
.... 09320010323 / 09320010322
e: vaibhavsinha432@gmail.com
w: www.ramdevchem.com/

Skin-Science1066
2 CAMBRIDGE RD. , HASTINGS
TN34 1DJ 7709043804
e: info@skin-science1066.co.uk
w: www.skin-science1066.co.uk

Somerset Training
.... 01823 431557 // 07843 436895
e: info@somersettraining.co.uk
w: www.somersettraining.co.uk

Sylvan Therapies
PLATINUM BUSINESS CENTRE, 23 HINTON ROAD ,
BOURNEMOUTH, Dorset BH1 2EF..........................01202 979107
e: lynn@sylvan-therapies.co.uk
w: www.sylvan-therapies.co.uk

The Pilates Centre
STUDIO 2, SPIRITUAL WARRIOR MARTIAL ARTS CENTRE , 518-
520 FOLESHILL ROAD , COVENTRY
 CV6 5HP 07866 427530
e: sarah@thepilatescentre.org
w: www.thepilatescentre.org

The Worsley Centre for Pyscotherapy and Counselling
50 BRIDGEWATER ROAD, WALKDEN, WORSLEY, SALFORD
 M28 3AE....................................... 08000199767 / 07946439491
e: ann.heathcote@btinternet.com
w: www.theworsleycentre.com

Total Access UK Ltd
UNIT 5 RALEIGH HALL INDUSTRIAL ESTATE, ECCLESHALL
Staffordshire ST21 6JL 01785 850 333
e: sales@totalaccess.co.uk
w: www.totalaccess.co.uk

Total Care Security Ltd
UNIT 3 , BRUNEL DRIVE, NEWARK
Nottinghamshire NG24 2DE 0800 917 47 67
e: info@totalcaresecurity.com
w: www.totalcaresecurity.com

Hen Nights

Gamewagon Ltd
113 - 115 OYSTER LANE, BYFLEET KT14 7JZ........0845 319 4263
e: admin@gamewagon.co.uk
w: www.gamewagon.info

Historical Re-enactments

Knights Of Arkley
GLYN SYLEN FARM, FIVE ROADS, LLANELLI
Carmarthenshire SA15 5BJ....................................01269 861001
e: penny@knightsofarkley.fsnet.co.uk
w: www.knightsofarkley.com

Hospitality Units

Blackburn Trailers Ltd
WHITESTONE FARM, MAIN ROAD, BIRDHAM
West Sussex PO20 7HU 01243 513550
e: trailers07@kompak.co.uk
w: www.kompak.co.uk

David Wilson's Trailers Ltd
JUBILEE PARK, HONEYPOT LANE, COLSTERWORTH, GRANTHAM
Lincolnshire NG33 5LZ..01476 860 833
e: info@dwt-exhibitions.co.uk
w: www.dwt-exhibitions.co.uk

Fenwick Mobile Exhibitions Ltd
FENWICK BY-PASS, FENWICK
Ayrshire KA3 6AW..01560 600271
e: enquiries@fmx-ltd.com
w: www.fmx-ltd.com

Function Jigsaw Limited
FUNCTION JIGSAW , 24 LONG STREET, WIGSTON
Leicestershire LE18 2AH..1163400255
e: julie@functionjigsaw.co.uk
w: functionjigsaw.co.uk/

LiteStructures (GB) Ltd
(PART OF THE PROLYTE GROUP), LANGTHWAITE BUSINESS PARK
- UNIT 55, SOUTH KIRKBY, WAKEFIELD
 WF9 3NR 01977 659 800
e: info@prolyte.co.uk
w: www.prolyte.co.uk

London Bus Export Company
PO BOX 12, CHEPSTOW
Gloucestershire NP16 5UZ 01291 689741
e: enquiries@londonbuspromotions.com
w: www.london-bus.co.uk

Lynton Trailers (UK) Ltd
ROSSINGTON INDUSTRIAL PARK, GRAPHITE WAY, HADFIELD,
GLOSSOP
Derbyshire SK13 1QH 01457 852700
e: sales@lyntontrailers.co.uk
w: www.lyntontrailers.co.uk

M&S AMBULANCE SERVICE
PINEWOOD STUDIOS , PINEWOOD ROAD IVER HEATH
Buckinghamshire SL0 0NH .... 01488638345 / 01753 630388
e: lizzie@msambulance.co.uk
w: www.msambulance.co.uk

Mobex Ltd
UNIT 6 RIGESTATE INDUSTRIAL ESTATE, STATION ROAD,
BERKELEY, Gloucestershire GL13 9RL 01453 511 210
e: exhibit@mobex.co.uk
w: www.mobex.co.uk

Motorvation (shows On The Road) Ltd
CHILHAM 3, STATION APPROACH, CHILHAM
Kent CT4 8EG 01227 738 266
e: info@motorv.com
w: www.motorv.com

Neptunus Ltd
COB DRIVE, SWAN VALLEY, NORTHAMPTON
Northamptonshire NN4 9BB .... 01604 593820 // 1604 593820
e: sales@neptunus.co.uk
w: www.neptunus.co.uk

G
H

Open Exhibitions
UNIT 1, ROTHWELL ROAD, WARWICK
Warwickshire CV34 5PY..01926 402 938
e: david.askill@openexhibitions.com
w: www.openexhibitions.co.uk

Paragon
HOLBROOKE PLACE , 28-32 HILL RISE, RICHMOND
 TW10 6UD ....020 8332 8640 / 020 8003 2739
e: sayhello@thisisparagon.co.uk
w: https://www.thisisparagon.co.uk/

Print Designs
EMERALD WAY, STONE BUSINESS PARK, STONE
Staffordshire ST15 0SR..01785 818 111
e: sales@printdesigns.com
w: www.printdesigns.com

Qdos Event Hire
FERNSIDE PLACE, 179 QUEENS ROAD, WEYBRIDGE
Surrey KT13 0AH 0845 862 0952
e: enquiries@qdoseventhire.co.uk
w: www.qdoseventhire.co.uk

Rollalong Hire Ltd
WOOLSBRIDGE INDUSTRIAL PARK , THREE LEGGED CROSS ,
WIMBOURNE
Dorset BH21 6SF 01202 824541
e: enquiries@rollalong.co.uk
w: www.rollalong.co.uk

Showplace Hospitality Suites Ltd
3 STOUR HOUSE, CLIFFORD PARK, CLIFFORD ROAD,
STRATFORD UPON AVON
Warwickshire CV37 8HW 01789 262701
e: info@showplace.co.uk
w: www.showplace.co.uk

Slumbertruck
....7539625498
e: donovan@free-me.com
w: www.slumbertruck.com

Special Event Services Ltd
GROVE FARM, BUCKINGHAM, BRACKLEY
 NN13 5JH..01280 841215
e: info@sesevent.co.uk
w: www.sesevent.co.uk

The Stage Bus
19 PRESTWOOD ROAD, WEOLEY CASTLE, BIRMINGHAM
West Midlands B29 5EB.............07738 900 762 / 0121 585 9264
e: info@thestagebus.com
w: www.thestagebus.com

Torton Bodies Ltd
PILOT WORKS, HOLYHEAD ROAD, OAKENGATES, TELFORD
West Midlands TF2 6BB 01952 612648
e: sales@torton.com
w: www.torton.com

Tow Master
UNIT 5, AMBER COURT, OFF WALTHEW HOUSE LANE, MARTLAND
PARK, WIGAN
Greater Manchester WN5 0JY 01942 226633
e: comments@towmasteruk.com
w: www.towmasteruk.co.uk

Vipex
NUNN BROOK ROAD , HUTHWAITE, SUTTON IN ASHFIELD
Nottinghamshire NG17 2HU 01623 441114
e: info@vipex.co.uk
w: www.vipex.co.uk

Worldwide Structures Ltd
AYRESHIRE FARM , SHARCOTT, PEWSEY
Wiltshire SN9 5PA...01672 565060
e: enquiries@w-sl.com
w: www.smart-spaces.com

Hot Air Balloons

Peter Drury Bird Ltd
CROSSWAYS, WEST STOUGHTON, WEDMORE
Somerset BS28 4PW..07973 931675
e: p.bird@thedrurypartnership.com

G
H

IJK

Ice Rinks

ABC Marquees
1 HAWTHORN WAY, PORTSLADE, BRIGHTON & HOVE
East Sussex BN41 2HR 01273 891511
e: info@abcmarquees.co.uk
w: www.abcmarquees.co.uk

Aggreko UK Ltd (Bristol)
202K SEVERNSIDE TRADING ESTATE, BURCOTT ROAD,
AVONMOUTH
Bristol BS11 8AP...08458 24 7 365
e: hire@aggreko.co.uk
w: www.aggreko.co.uk

Aggreko UK Ltd (Doncaster)
KIRK SANDALL INDUSTRIAL ESTATE, SANDALL STONES ROAD,
DONCASTER
South Yorkshire DN3 1QR....................................08458 24 7 365
e: hire@aggreko.co.uk
w: www.aggreko.co.uk

Arena Seating
LAMBOURN WOODLANDS, HUNGERFORD
Berkshire RG17 7TQ 01488 674800
e: info@arenaseating.com
w: www.arenagroup.com

Fun Ice Ltd
37 ALL SAINTS WAY, SANDY
Bedfordshire SG19 1DX ....01767 222953 / 07967 149608
e: info@hireanicerink.co.uk
w: www.hireanicerink.co.uk

Ice Magic
....0845 5196544
e: simon@ice-magic.com
w: www.synthetic-ice-rinks.com

Ice Tech UK
THE BANK HOUSE, 9A CHURCH STREET, SOUTHWELL
NG25 0HQ 0845 8382310
e: info@icetechuk.com
w: www.icetechuk.com

Icegripper
9 SEAGRY RD, WANSTEAD, LONDON
Greater London E11 2NG 0844 272 3444
e: enquiries@icegripper.co.uk
w: www.icegripper.co.uk

Leisure Skate Ltd
RAVENSGATE, HOLBEACH ST. JOHNS, SPALDING
Lincolnshire PE12 8RD..01775 766999
e: info@leisureskate.co.uk
w: www.leisureskate.co.uk

Ice Sculptures

Eskimo Ice
UNIT A 45-48, NEW COVENT GARDEN MARKET, NINE ELMS LANE
SW8 5EE................................. 020 7720 4883 // 07831 260 813
w: www.eskimo-ice.co.uk

Ice Immediate
....0800 169 3991
e: enquiries@iceimmediate.com
w: www.iceimmediate.com

Inflatables / Bouncy Castles

ABC Inflatables
4 WILDMERE CLOSE, WILDMERE INDUSTRIAL ESTATE, BANBURY
OX16 3TL...0845 0508 600
e: sales@abcinflatables.co.uk
w: www.abcinflatables.co.uk

ABC Leisure
139A QUESLETT ROAD EAST STREETLY, SUTTON COLDFIELD,
BIRMINGHAM
West Midlands B74 2AJ...07980 225375
e: info@abcleisure.net
w: www.abcleisure.net

About2Bounce Mansfield
....01623 553891
e: m.kirkwood.86@hotmail.co.uk
w: www.about2bouncemansfield.co.uk

Ace Inflatables
8 TOTEASE COTTAGES, HIGH STREET, BUXTED, UCKFIELD
TN22 4LD...07760 752840
e: peter@aceinflatables.com
w: www.aceinflatables.com

Activity Day
LITTLEHEATH ROAD, BEXLEYHEATH
Kent DA7 5HF .... 0203 589 6303 // 07795 174782
e: mail@activityday.co.uk
w: www.activityday.co.uk

Airdancer Wales
UNIT D1 CAPEL HENDRE INDUSTRIAL ESTATE, CAPEL HENDRE,
AMMANFORD
SA18 3SJ................................ 01269 512010 // 07957 928962
e: info@racearchesuk.co.uk
w: www.airdancerwales.co.uk

Airtechs Ltd
UNIT 18, HALESWORTH BUSINESS CENTRE, NORWICH ROAD,
HALESWORTH
IP19 8QJ..01986 835 724
w: www.airtechs.co.uk

I
J
K

Bounce Krazee
14 GREEN LEYS, HIGH WYCOMBE
Buckinghamshire HP13 5UH 01494 464902
e: info@bouncekrazee.co.uk
w: www.bouncekrazee.co.uk

Bounce-Mania
18 TENNYSON AVENUE, RUSTINGTON
West Sussex BN16 2PB 01903 771863
e: info@bounce-mania.co.uk
w: www.bouncemaniaevents.co.uk

Circuit Entertainments
SPRINGBANK, 160 WITHERSFIELD ROAD, HAVERHILL
CB9 9HQ..01440 707307
e: circuitents@btopenworld.com
w: www.circuitentertainments.co.uk

Factory of Fun
47 LUTTERWORTH ROAD, LEICESTER
LE2 8PH..07860 422134
e: factoryoffun@aol.com
w: www.factory-of-fun.co.uk

Funtime Hire
FINCHINGFIELD NURSERIES, BARDFIELD ROAD, FINCHINFIELD
CM7 4LL..01371 811381
w: www.funtimehire.co.uk

GazInflatables
47 LUTTERWORTH ROAD, LEICESTER
LE2 8PH..07860 422134
e: gazinflate@aol.com
w: www.gazinflatables.co.uk

Huff N Puff Events
UNIT 3A, WELWYN GARDEN CITY, SWALLOWFIELDS
AL7 1JD..01707 696797
w: www.hpcastles.co.uk

Location Inflation
....07966 165658
e: info@locationinflation.com
w: www.locationinflation.com

Rascals Bouncy Castles and Inflatables
WELLSTEAD WAY, HEDGE END, EASTLEIGH, SOUTHAMPTON
SO30 2BH..07745 696 848
w: www.rascalscastles.co.uk

Insurance Services

Barry Grainger Ltd
20 CHAPMAN WAY, TUNBRIDGE WELLS
Kent TN2 3EF...01892 501 501
e: enquiries@bginsurance.co.uk
w: www.barrygraingerinsurance.co.uk

Blackfriars Group
CANADA HOUSE, 3 CHEPSTOW STREET, MANCHESTER
Greater Manchester M1 5FW 0161 300 2930
e: info@blackfriarsgroup.com
w: www.blackfriarsgroup.com

Blythin & Brown Insurance Brokers Limited
THE POINT , GRANITE WAY, MOUNTSORREL
LE12 7TZ..01509 622 220
w: www.blythinandbrown.co.uk

Britton Financial Ltd
THE COLCHESTER CENTRE, HAWKINS ROAD , COLCHESTER
Essex CO2 8JX 1206266970
e: info@brittonfinancial.co.uk
w: www.brittonfinancial.co.uk

C R Toogood & Co Ltd
....01483 285363
e: info@toogoods.co.uk
w: www.toogoods.co.uk

CoverMarque Ltd
THE BOUNDARY, COXFORD DOWN, WINCHESTER
Hampshire SO21 3BD 01962 774421
e: nick.drew@covermarque.com
w: www.covermarque.com

Coversure Insurance
COVERSURE HOUSE , VANTAGE PARK , WASHINGLEY ROAD ,
HUNTINGDON
Cambridgeshire PE29 6SR 0800 3081 000
e: headoffice@coversure.co.uk
w: www.coversure.co.uk

Doodson Entertainment
CENTURY HOUSE, PEPPER ROAD, HAZEL GROVE, STOCKPORT
Greater Manchester SK7 5BW..............................0161 419 3000
e: info@doodsonbg.com
w: www.doodsonbg.com

Event Assured
HISCOX HOUSE, SHEEPEN ROAD, COLCHESTER
Essex CO3 3XL .... 0800 840 2469 / 01206 773940
e: eventassured@hiscox.com
w: www.event-assured.com

Event Insurance Direct
339 - 343 UNION ROAD, OSWALDTWISTLE
Lancashire BB5 3HS 0845 073 7214
e: contact@eventinsurancedirect.co.uk
w: www.eventinsurancedirect.co.uk

Event Insurance Services Ltd
20A HEADLANDS BUSINESS PARK, RINGWOOD
Hampshire BH24 3PB .... 01425 470360 // 01425 484862
e: info@events-insurance.co.uk
w: www.events-insurance.co.uk

Fidelius Insurance Services Ltd
STRATUS HOUSE, EMPEROR WAY , EXETER BUSINESS PARK ,
EXETER
Devon EX1 3QS..01392 363 111
e: info@fidelius-insurance.co.uk
w: www.fidelius.co.uk

Hencilla Canworth Ltd
SIMPSON HOUSE, 6 CHERRY ORCHARD ROAD, CROYDON
Greater London CR9 6AZ..020 8686 5050
e: mail@hencilla.co.uk
w: www.hencilla.co.uk

Hiscox Event Insurance
25 LONDON ROAD, SITTINGBOURNE
Kent ME10 1PE 01206 773 940
e: eventinsurance@hiscox.com
w: www.hiscox.co.uk

Integro Insurance Brokers Ltd
100 LEADENHALL ST, 2ND FLOOR, LONDON
City of London EC3A 3BP...................................01614 193 000
e: stephanie.less@integrogroup.com
w: www.integrouk.com

Luker Rowe
CENTURY HOUSE, LONDON ROAD, OLD AMERSHAM
Buckinghamshire HP7 0TU 01494 733 337
e: info@lukerrowe.com
w: www.lukerrowe.com

Precision Broking Ltd
59 PRINCE STREET, BRISTOL
Bristol BS1 4QH 0117 922 0420
e: enquiries@precisionbroking.com
w: www.precisionbroking.com

Robertson Taylor Insurance Brokers Ltd
2 AMERICA SQUARE, LONDON
Greater London EC3N 2LU 020 7510 1234
e: enquiries@rtib.co.uk
w: www.rtworldwide.com

Safeonline LLP
80 LEADENHALL ST, LONDON
 EC3A 3DE 020 7954 4400
e: info@safeonline.com
w: https://www.safeonline.com

Towergate Coverex
2 COUNTY GATE, STACEYS STREET,, MAIDSTONE
Kent ME14 1ST..0844 892 1618
e: coverex@towergate.co.uk
w: www.towergatecoverex.co.uk

Worldwide Special Risks
21 VERULAM ROAD, ST ALBANS
Hertfordshire AL3 4DG 01727 843686
e: info@wwsr.co.uk
w: www.worldwidespecialrisks.co.uk

Jukeboxes

Mightymast Leisure Ltd
58 BENTWATERS PARK, , RENDLESHAM, WOODBRIDGE
Suffolk IP12 2TW 01394 460896
e: info@mightymast.com
w: www.mightymast.com

The Jukebox Company
633 EASTERN AVENUE, ILLFORD
Essex IG2 6PW...0208 554 5757
e: info@jukeboxco.com
w: www.jukeboxco.com

I
J
K

208

Lanyards / Wristbands

Aspinline
EXHIBITION HOUSE, HAYWARD INDUSTRIAL ESTATE, 1-2 NORTH VIEW, SOUNDWELL, BRISTOL
Gloucestershire BS16 4NT 0117 9566657
e: sales@aspinline.co.uk
w: www.aspinline.co.uk

Badges Plus
BADGES PLUS LIMITED, 1-2 LEGGE LANE, BIRMINGHAM
West Midlands B1 3LD...0121 236 1612
e: sales@badgesplus.co.uk
w: www.badgesplus.co.uk

Band Pass Ltd
1ST FLOOR 20 SUNNYDOWN, WITLEY, GODALMING
Surrey GU8 5RP 01428 684926
e: maxine@band-pass.co.uk
w: www.band-pass.co.uk

Blueprint Promotional Products
NO. 1 THE EMBASSY, LAWRENCE STREET, LONG EATON, NOTTINGHAM
Nottinghamshire NG10 1JY....................................0333 1234 400
e: info@blueprintpromo.co.uk
w: www.blueprintpromo.co.uk

Event Merchandising Ltd
UNIT 11, THE EDGE, HUMBER ROAD, LONDON
Greater London NW2 6EW.....................................020 8208 1166
e: event@eventmerch.com
w: www.eventmerchandising.com

Global Promotional Solutions Ltd
44 RYDER ST, CARDIFF
 CF11 9BT 02920 227955
e: enquiry@globalpromotionalsolutions.co.uk
w: www.globalpromotionalsolutions.co

ID Card Centre Ltd
19 SCIROCCO CLOSE   , MOULTON PARK, NORTHAMPTON
Northamptonshire NN3 6AP 1604422422
e: b.obrien@idcardcentre.co.uk
w: https://www.idcardcentre.co.uk

JC Leisure
UNIT 1 HAMBURG TECHNOLOGY PARK, HAMBURG ROAD, SUTTON FIELDS, HULL
 HU7 0WD...01482 804514
e: info@jc-leisure.com
w: www.jc-leisure.com

Lanyards Etc Ltd
2 DUCHY ROAD, CREWE
Cheshire CW1 6ND 01270 216 369
e: info@lanyardsetc.com
w: www.lanyardsetc.com

Lanyards Tomorrow
UNIT 5, BUSINESS CENTRE EAST , FIFTH AVENUE , LETCHWORTH GARDEN CITY
Hertfordshire SG6 2TS 441462682020
e: sales@ckb.uk.com
w: www.lanyardstomorrow.co.uk/

Lanyards Trader LTD
9 RUSSELL GARDENS, LONDON
 W14 8EZ 020 3744 2416
e: sales@lanyardstrader.co.uk
w: personalisedlanyards.co/

Nicholas Hunter Ltd
UNIT 3 OXBRIDGE COURT, OSNEY MEAD INDUSTRIAL ESTATE, OXFORD Oxfordshire OX2 0ES...............................01865 251136
e: office@nicholashunter.com
w: www.nicholashunter.com

Orakel Ltd
PANTHEON CENTRE, FFORDD CELYN, LON PARCWR BUSINESS PARK, RUTHIN
Denbighshire LL15 1NJ 01824 702214
e: enquiries@orakel.co.uk
w: www.orakel.co.uk

Pac Wristbands
UNIT 1 SOUTH PARK COURT BUSINESS CENTRE , HOBSON STREET , MACCLESFIELD
Cheshire SK11 8BS...1379872785
w: https://www.wristbands.co.uk/

PDC Big Badges
5 HAMPTON HILL BUSINESS PARK, HIGH STREET, HAMPTON HILL
Greater London TW12 1NP....................................020 8614 8980
e: sales@pdc-big.co.uk
w: www.big.co.uk

PDC Europe
5 HAMPTON HILL BUSINESS PARK, HIGH STREET, HAMPTON HILL
Greater London TW12 1NP....................................020 8614 8880
e: info@vipband-eshop.co.uk
w: www.vipband-eshop.co.uk

Publicity & Display Ltd
DOUGLAS DRIVE, GODALMING
Surrey GU7 1HJ 01483 428 326
e: print@pubdis.com
w: www.pubdis.com

Ribbon Works
WILSON BUSINESS PARK, HILLINGTON, GLASGOW
 G52 4NQ...01355 813301
e: info@ribbonworks.co.uk
w: https://www.ribbonworks.co.uk

Secureticket Ltd
KARAH HOUSE, 10 WILBERFORCE ST, HULL
East Yorkshire HU3 2JR...01482 211168
e: info@secureticket.co.uk
w: www.secureticket.co.uk

Security Solutions UK Ltd
THE COURT HOUSE, POLICE STATION LANE, , DROXFORD,
Hampshire SO32 3RF.. +44 1489 877700
e: info@securitysolutionsuk.com
w: www.securitysolutionsuk.com

Ticket Alternative
UNIT 333, ASHLEY ROAD, TOTTENHAM
Greater London N17 9LN 0208 880 4167
e: uk@ticketalternative.com
w: www.ticketalternative.co.uk

Large Screen / Projection

5th Dimension Graphics
TURNER STREET,, NORTHAMPTON
Northamptonshire NN1 4JJ........ 0208 123 8884 / 01604 289779
e: info@5dg.org
w: www.5dg.org

adi.tv
PITTMAN COURT, PITTMAN WAY, FULWOOD, PRESTON
Lancashire PR2 9ZG 01772 708 200
e: info@adi.tv
w: www.adi.tv

AVC Live Ltd
UNIT 103, BUSINESS DESIGN CENTRE , 52 UPPER STREET,
ISLINGTON, LONDON
Greater London N1 0QH 020 7288 6561
e: info@avcliveltd.com
w: www.avcliveltd.com

Avcom Hire
STANLAKE MEWS, SHEPHERDS BUSH, LONDON
Greater London W12 7HS....................................0208 735 3424
e: sales@avcom.co.uk
w: www.avcom.co.uk

AVS Hire
UNIT 4, HIGHAMS FARM, SHEEPBARN LANE, WARLINGHAM
Surrey CR6 9PQ..01959 540 028
e: av_equipment_questions@yahoo.co.uk
w: www.avs-hire.co.uk

Bay TV Ltd
UNIT C6, SIR ALFRED OWEN WAY, PONTYGWINDY INDUSTRIAL
ESTATE, CAERPHILLY
 CF83 3HU 02920 849668
e: sales@baytv.co.uk
w: www.baytv.co.uk

Bell Theatre Services Ltd
9B CHESTER ROAD, BOREHAMWOOD
Hertfordshire WD6 1LT 020 8238 6000
e: admin@bell-theatre.com
w: www.bell-theatre.com

Big TV
HUDSON HOUSE, THE HUDSON, WYKE, BRADFORD
West Yorkshire BD12 8HZ 0800 001 6000
e: uk@big-tv.co.uk
w: www.big-tv.co.uk

Big-TV (UK) Ltd
HUDSON HOUSE, THE HUDSON, WYKE, BRADFORD
Yorkshire BD12 8HZ...01274 604 309
e: info@big-tv.co.uk
w: www.big-tv.co.uk

Businessav
UNIT E, SCHAPPE BUILDING, LLAY INDUSTRIAL UNITS, LLAY,
WREXHAM
 LL12 0PG..0800 587 9908
e: info@businessav.co.uk
w: www.businessav.co.uk

Cameron Presentations & All Event Hire
BURNFIELD ROAD, GIFFNOCK, GLASGOW
Glasgow G46 7TH..0141 637 0368
e: hire@cameronpres.co.uk
w: www.cameronpres.co.uk

Chauvet
UNIT 1C BROOKHILL INDUSTRIAL ESTATE, PINXTON,
NOTTINGHAM
Nottinghamshire NG16 6NT 01773 511 115
e: uksales@chauvetlighting.com
w: www.chauvetlighting.co.uk

City Audio Visual
UNIT 19 KINGS MEADOW, FERRY HINKSEY ROAD, OXFORD
Oxfordshire OX2 0DP 01865 722800
e: info@cityav.co.uk
w: www.cityav.co.uk/

Conference Technical Facilities Ltd
UNIT 1, LIONGATE ENTERPRISE PARK, 80 MORDEN ROAD,
MITCHAM Surrey
CR4 4NY .... 0845 130 9944 / 020 8687 2720
e: mail@ctf.co.uk
w: www.ctf.co.uk

CreateAV (UK) Ltd
UNIT 14 STUDIO HOUSE, DELAMARE ROAD, CHESHUNT, LONDON
Greater London EN8 9SH 01992 789 759
e: connect@createav.com
w: www.createav.com

Creative Technology Ltd
UNIT E2, SUSSEX MANOR BUSINESS PARK, , GATWICK ROAD,
CRAWLEY
West Sussex RH10 9NH 01293 582 000
e: info@ctlondon.com
w: www.ctlondon.com

L

Db Systems Ltd
ASHCHURCH BUSINESS CENTRE, ALEXANDRA WAY, TEWKESBURY
Gloucestershire GL20 8TD 0845 226 3083
e: hiredesk@dbsystems.co.uk
w: www.dbsystems.co.uk

Deepvisual
PIER HOUSE
 SW3 5HG...07801 930 411
e: info@deepvisual.com
w: www.deepvisual.com

Emphasis Event Production Ltd
UNIT 14, BELGRAVE INDUSTRIAL ESTATE, SOUTHAMPTON
Hampshire SO17 3EA.......................................023 8055 0557
e: enquiries@emphasiseventproduction.co.uk
w: www.prestech.co.uk

European Communications Technology Ltd
PO BOX 4020, PANGBOURNE
Berkshire RG8 8TX..0118 984 1141
e: support@ect-av.com
w: www.ect-av.com

Euroscreens Ltd
UNIT 11 LONGRIDGE TRADING ESTATE, KNUTSFORD
Cheshire WA16 8PR 01565 654 004
w: www.euroscreens.co.uk

Event Equipment Hire
UNIT 2, SYKES STREET, CLECKHEATON
Yorkshire BD19 5HA..01422 200960
e: sales@eventequipmenthire.co.uk
w: www.eventequipmenthire.co.uk

Event Services (SW) Ltd
UNITS 7 & 9, GALLOWS PARK, ,MILLBROOK, TORPOINT
Cornwall PL11 3AX 01752 829 333
e: office@eventservicesonline.com
w: www.eventservicesonline.com

Fresh Events UK
UNIT D WESLAKE INDUSTRIAL PARK, RYE HARBOUR ROAD, RYE
East Sussex TN31 7TE 07919 512 608
e: info@fresheventsuk.com
w: www.fresheventsuk.com

Hamilton Rentals
UNIT 2, MAPLE CENTRE, DOWNMILL ROAD , BRACKNELL
Berkshire RG12 1QS 01344 456600
e: info@hamilton.co.uk
w: www.hamilton.co.uk

Harkness Screens Ltd
UNIT A NORTON ROAD, STEVENAGE
Hertfordshire SG1 2BB..01438 725200
e: sales@harkness-screens.com
w: www.harkness-screens.com

Igloo Vision
UNIT 2 , CRAVEN COURT, STOKEWOOD RD, CRAVEN ARMS
Shropshire SY7 8PF 01588 673337
e: info@igloovision.com
w: www.igloovision.com

iMAG Displays
30-31 HARWELL ROAD, NUFFIELD INDUSTRIAL ESTATE, POOLE
Dorset BH17 0GE...1202282202
e: karley@imagdisplays.co.uk
w: www.imagdisplays.co.uk/contact/

IMAScreen Ltd
UNIT 5, PLOT 7, CLAYMORE, TAME VALLEY INDUSTRIAL ESTATE,
WILNECOTE, TAMWORTH
Staffordshire B77 5DQ 01827 288746
e: info@imascreen.com
w: www.imascreen.com

Indivisual Limited
UNIT 3, 140, MOWBRAY DRIVE, BLACKPOOL
Lancashire FY3 7UN 01253 300 002
e: info@indivisual.co.uk
w: www.indivisual.co.uk

JCS computerent
34 CHARTER GATE, QUARRY PARK CLOSE , MOULTON PARK,
NORTHAMPTON
Northamptonshire NN3 6QB......................................1604495252
e: rentals@computerent.co.uk
w: computerent.co.uk

Joy's Production Services
5 ST JOHN'S LANE, LONDON
 EC1M 4BH 020 7549 1697
e: info@joys.com
w: www.joys.com

K13.biz Ltd
 ....07771 814 764
e: info@k13.biz
w: www.k13.biz

Kudos Music
UNIT 10 TRADE CITY, COWLEY MILL ROAD, UXBRIDGE
 UB8 2DB...01895 207990
e: info@kudosmusic.co.uk
w: www.kudosmusic.co.uk

LED Screen Hire Europe Ltd
UNIT D7A FAIROAKS AIRPORT, CHERTSEY ROAD, CHOBHAM
Surrey GU24 8HU 01276 859 480
e: info@screenhire.com
w: www.screenhire.com

Lighthouse Technologies (U.K.) Ltd
2ND FLOOR SARACEN HOUSE, SWAN STREET, ISLEWORTH
Greater London TW76RJ 020 8380 9500
e: infoeurope@lighthouse-tech.com
w: www.lighthouse-tech.com

Lightmedia Displays Ltd
HUDDLESTON GRANGE, NEWTHORPE, SOUTH MILFORD, LEEDS
West Yorkshire LS25 6JU 0333 600 6000
e: sales@lightmedia.co.uk
w: www.lightmedia.co.uk

Lucid Illusions
HIGHSTED FARM , HIGHSTED VALLEY, SITTINGBOURNE
Kent ME9 0AG 020 3488 0265
e: info@lucidillusions.co.uk
w: www.lucidillusions.co.uk

Mediatec Group
2 PORTERSBRIDGE MEWS, PORTERSBRIDGE STREET, ROMSEY
Hampshire SO51 8DJ 01794 516 787
e: enquiries@mediatecgroup.com
w: www.mediatecgroup.co.uk

MJ Visual
UNIT 1, ATLANTIC HOUSE, 119 THIRD AVENUE, ALMODINGTON, CHICHESTER
West Sussex PO20 7LB...01243 780816
e: sales@mjvisual.co.uk
w: www.mjvisual.co.uk

Mobile CCTV
UNIT 8 CAMBERLEY BUSINESS CENTRE, BRACEBRIDGE, CAMBERLEY
Surrey GU15 3DP...01276 469 084
e: info@mobilecctv.co.uk
w: www.mobilecctv.co.uk

NSR Communications Ltd
16 CAXTON WAY, WATFORD BUSINESS PARK, WATFORD
Hertfordshire WD18 8UA 01923 209640
e: sales@nsrcommunications.co.uk
w: www.nsrcommunications.co.uk

Paragon Projection Ltd
WALKERS RISE, RUGELEY ROAD, HEDNESFORD
Staffordshire WS12 0QU 01543 451111
w: www.paragonprojection.co.uk

Premier Solutions Ltd
11 ASCOT PARK ESTATE, LENTON STREET,, SANDIACRE, NOTTINGHAM
Nottinghamshire NG10 DL 0115 9394122
e: info@premier-solutions.biz
w: www.premier-solutions.biz

Presentation Rentals Ltd
UNIT 6, WINDSOR CENTRE, , ADVANCE ROAD, LONDON
Greater London SE27 9NT....................................0208 670 5000
e: hello@prlive.co
w: www.prlive.co/

Prism
....0203 287 7338
e: sales@prism-av.com
w: www.prism-av.com

Pro Display Ltd
UNIT 5, SHORTWOOD BUSINESS PARK, HOYLAND
South Yorkshire S74 9LH......................................01226 740 007
e: info@prodisplay.co.uk
w: www.prodisplay.com

Proscreens
.... 0845 309 6369 // 07876755357
e: info@proscreens.net
w: www.proscreens.net

QED Productions
UNIT 11, SUMMIT ROAD, CRANBORNE INDUSTRIAL ESTATE, POTTERS BAR
Hertfordshire EN6 3QW..01707 648 800
e: info@qed-productions.com
w: www.qed-productions.com

Quality Rental Ltd
UNIT 5 KING'S COURT, GLEN TYE ROAD, STIRLING
Stirlingshire FK7 7LH 01786 479077
w: www.qualityrental.co.uk

Rap Industries
WELBECK WAY , WOODSTON, PETERBOROUGH
Cambridgeshire PE2 7WH 01733 394941
e: amie@rapind.com
w: www.rapind.com/acatalog/Pop_up_St

Rock-Tech Projects
UNIT 2, FRYORS COURT, MURTON
Yorkshire YO19 5UY 01904 481 700
e: info@rock-tech.co.uk
w: www.rock-tech.co.uk

Smart AV
5 CENTRAL ROAD, HARLOW
Essex CM20 2ST .... 0845 078 0326 // 01279 624 840
e: info@smart-av.com
w: www.smart-av.com

Stagelogic Ltd
UNIT 21 EVANS BUSINESS CENTRE, DUNNS CLOSE, NUNEATON
Warwickshire CV11 4NF.................................... 0845 600 3961 //
024 7632 2232 // 07595
e: hire@stagelogic.co.uk
w: www.stagelogic.co.uk

Techpro Events Ltd
UNITS 10 - 12, CAVENDISH, LICHFIELD ROAD IND. EST., TAMWORTH
Staffordshire B79 7XH 01827 310750
e: hello@techpro.co.uk
w: www.techproevents.co.uk

Tega AV
148 SCULCOATES LANE, HULL
East Yorkshire HU5 1EE..01482 444666
e: av@tega.co.uk
w: www.tega.co.uk

The LED Studio
HANGER WAY, PETERSFIELD
Hampshire GU31 4QE 020 3617 1979
e: sales@theledstudio.co.uk
w: www.theledstudio.co.uk

The Projection Studio
13 TARVES WAY, GREENWICH, LONDON
Greater London SE10 9JP 020 8293 4270
e: info@theprojectionstudio.com
w: www.theprojectionstudio.com

Vision Events (Edinburgh)
16 DRYDEN ROAD, BILSTON GLEN INDUSTRIAL ESTATE,
LOANHEAD
Edinburgh EH20 9LZ 0131 334 3324
e: edinburgh@visionevents.co.uk
w: www.visionevents.co.uk

Visuals
55 SELWOOD ROAD, HOOK, CHESSINGTON
Greater London KT9 1PT.......................................020 8397 1567
e: info@visuals-group.co.uk
w: www.visuals-group.co.uk

VNV Sounds
UNITS 10 AND 10A ASHLEY HOUSE, ASHLEY ROAD, LONDON
Greater London N17 9LZ.......................................0203 021 1370
e: info@vnvlive.co.uk
w: www.vnvsounds.co.uk

YSLV
REDHOUSE FARM, LOWER DUNTON ROAD, UPMINSTER
Greater London RM14 3TD........ 020 8317 7775 / 0800 074 6902
e: london@yslv.co.uk
w: www.yslv.co.uk

Lasers

Arcstream Av
GARTH HOUSE, 141 GARTH ROAD, MORDEN
Greater London SM4 4LG.....................................01372 742 682
e: info@arcstreamav.com
w: www.arcstreamav.com

Continental Lasers (uk) Ltd
B105 PORTVIEW TRADE CTR, 310 NEWTOWNARDS ROAD,
BELFAST BT4 1HE............ ....028 9045 8658
e: info@continental-lasers.com
w: www.continental-lasers.com

DAC Pro-Media Ltd
Surrey 01372 374 600
e: dcrisp@dacpromedia.co.uk
w: www.dacpromedia.co.uk

DLC Events
STREET 22, AL QUOZ IND 3, DUBAI
PO Box 282841.................................... +971 4 347 0484
e: office@dlcevents.com
w: www.dlcevents.com

ER Productions
UNIT 12 SCHOONER PARK, SCHOONER COURT, CROSSWAYS
BUSINESS PARK, DARTFORD
Kent DA2 6NW...01322 293 135
e: info@er-productions.com
w: www.er-productions.com

Event Services (SW) Ltd
UNITS 7 & 9, GALLOWS PARK, ,MILLBROOK, TORPOINT
Cornwall PL11 3AX 01752 829 333
e: office@eventservicesonline.com
w: www.eventservicesonline.com

Fresh Events UK
UNIT D WESLAKE INDUSTRIAL PARK, RYE HARBOUR ROAD, RYE
East Sussex TN31 7TE 07919 512 608
e: info@fresheventsuk.com
w: www.fresheventsuk.com

Heathrow Sound Hire
UNITS 9 & 10- POD BUSINESS CENTRE, HARRIS WAY,
SUNBURY ON THAMES
Surrey TW16 7EW...................... 0208 4322310 // 07834520290
e: enquiries@heathrowsoundhire.co.uk
w: www.heathrowsoundhire.co.uk

Julianas Leisure Services Ltd
MARIA MILSTEAD, PIPPIN GROVE, 628 LONDON ROAD,
COLNBROOK, Berkshire SL3 8QH..........................020 70996875
e: maria@julianas.com
w: www.julianas.com

Laser Electronics Ltd
GUNBY ROAD, ORBY, SKEGNESS
Lincolnshire PE24 5HT...01754 811137
e: clive@laserelectronicsltd.co.uk
w: www.laserelectronicsltd.com

Laser Hire London
UNIT 4 - PACIFIC WHARF, HERTFORD ROAD, BARKING
IG11 8BL .... 0844 664 4455 / 07999 559 995
e: info@laserhirelondon.com
w: www.laserhirelondon.co.uk

Laser Hire Ltd
FOLE SPRING FARM, FOLE, UTTOXETER
Staffordshire ST14 5EF 01889 507 067
e: info@laserhire.co.uk
w: www.laserhire.co.uk

Laserworld (Switzerland) AG
KREUZLINGERSTR. 5, LENGWIL, SWITZERLAND
8574..07714 624355
e: dp@laserworld.com
w: www.laserworld.co.uk

Lightfantastics Laser
5 HAUGH ROAD, BURNTISLAND
Fife KY3 0BZ.. +44 (0) 131 5100218
e: show@lightfantastics.com
w: www.lightfantastics.co.uk

LM Productions Ltd
UNIT 6H SOUTHBOURNE BUSINESS PARK, COURTLANDS ROAD, EASTBOURNE
East Sussex BN22 8UY 01323 432170
e: info@lm-productions.com
w: www.lm-productions.com

True Sound Hire
UNIT 2, MANOR PARK INDUSTRIAL EST, WYNDHAM STREET, ALDERSHOT
Hampshire GU12 4NZ .... 01252 313154 / 01252 313154
e: info@truesoundhire.co.uk
w: www.truesoundhire.co.uk

Licensing

ENcentre
38 BELGRAVE ROAD, SUNBURY
Middlesex TW16 5NQ..01932 761 328
e: info@encentre.co.uk
w: www.encentre.co.uk

F1 Acoustics Company Ltd
38 BRITON HILL ROAD, SANDERSTEAD,, SOUTH CROYDON
Surrey CR2 0JL...01227 770 890
e: info@f1acoustics.com
w: www.f1acoustics.com

Filmbank Distributors Ltd
WARNER HOUSE, 98 THEOBALD'S ROAD, LONDON
Greater London WC1X 8WB............................... 020 7984 5957/8
e: info@filmbankmedia.com
w: www.filmbankmedia.com

PPL (Phonographic Performance Ltd)
1 UPPER JAMES STREET, LONDON
Greater London W1F 9DE......................................020 7534 1000
e: info@ppluk.com
w: www.ppluk.com

Shaun Murkett Acoustic Consultants Ltd
1 CLISSOLD ROAD, STOKE NEWINGTON, LONDON
Greater London N16 9EX......................................020 7923 7275
e: murkett@aol.com
w: www.shaunmurkett-acoustics.co.uk

Lighting

1159 Productions Ltd
2 FALCON WAY, CHELMSFORD
Essex CM2 8AY...01245 227700
e: sales@1159productions.com
w: www.1159productions.com

A.c. Entertainment Technologies Ltd.
CENTAURI HOUSE, HILLBOTTOM ROAD, HIGH WYCOMBE
Buckinghamshire HP12 4HQ..................................01494 446000
e: sales@ac-et.com
w: www.ac-et.com

Absolute Audio Visual Solutions
NEW CAMBRIDGE HOUSE, LITLINGTON
Cambridgeshire SG8 0SS.......................................01763 852222
e: info@absoluteavs.co.uk
w: www.absoluteavs.co.uk

Adam Hall Ltd
THE SEEDBED BUSINESS CENTRE, VANGUARD WAY, SHOEBURYNESS
 SS3 9QY 01702 613922
e: mail@adamhall.co.uk
w: www.adamhall.com

Airstar Lighting Balloons
UNIT A11, PARK ROYAL IND EST, ELDON WAY, LONDON
Greater London NW10 7QQ..................................02033 016 339
e: london@airstar-light.com
w: www.airstar-light.com

AML Group
20-22 WENLOCK ROAD, LONDON
Greater London N1 7GU 8458675679
e: info@amlgroup.biz
w: https://www.amlgroup.biz

Ancient Lights Ltd
HARDWICK PARK FARM, HARDWICK LANE, CHERTSEY
Surrey KT16 0AA 01932 570652
e: info@ancientlights.tv
w: www.ancientlights.tv

Anytronics
5&6 HILLSIDE INDUSTRIAL ESTATE, LONDON ROAD, HORNDEAN
Hampshire PO8 0BL...023 9259 9410
e: sales@anytronics.com
w: www.anytronics.co.uk

Arabian Tent Company
RYE FARM, HOLLANDS LANE, HENFIELD
West Sussex BN5 9QY 0800 88 15 229
e: info@arabiantents.com
w: www.arabiantents.com

Arc Electronics
352 PORTSWOOD ROAD, PORTSWOOD, SOUTHAMPTON
Hampshire SO17 3SB 023 8058 4642
e: info@arcelectronics.co.uk
w: www.arcelectronics.co.uk

Audio Source Ltd
31 MONGLEATH AVENUE, FALMOUTH
Cornwall TR11 4PP .... 07971 607172 /
07867 525016 / 01326 3115
e: hire@audio-source.co.uk
w: www.audio-source.co.uk

Audiowall Systems Limited
2/3 BASSETT COURT, BROAD STREET, NEWPORT PAGNELL
Buckinghamshire MK16 0JN..... 01908 951 470 / 01908 615 365
e: info@audiowall.co.uk
w: www.audiowall.co.uk

L

AVLS
....01226 764435
e: info@avls.co.uk
w: www.avls.co.uk

AVM Creative Solutions
11618 PERRY RD, HOUSTON, TEXAS
77064..
e: info@avmcreativesolutions.com
w: www.avmcreativesolutions.com

Avolites Ltd
184 PARK AVENUE, LONDON
Greater London NW10 7XL...................................020 8965 8522
e: sales@avolites.com
w: www.avolites.com

Backwell PA Hire
.... 07958 516604 / 07860 101512
e: enquiries@backwellpa.co.uk
w: www.backwellpa.co.uk

Bamford Lighting
MILLGATE HOUSE, MARKET STREET, SHAWFORTH, ROCHDALE
Greater Manchester OL12 8NX..............................0800 043 1153
e: Info@bamfordlighting.com
w: www.bamfordlighting.com

Bandshop Ltd
ORCHARD BUSINESS PARK, BADSELL ROAD, TONBRIDGE
Kent TN12 6QU..01622 817818
e: enquiries@bandshophire.co.uk
w: www.bandshophire.co.uk

Bassline Productions
19 OSIERS RD, LONDON
Greater London SW18..0203 609 1230
e: info@basslineproductions.co.uk
w: www.basslineproductions.co.uk

Batmink Ltd
BECKERY ROAD, GLASTONBURY
Somerset BA6 9NX 01458 833186
e: info@batmink.co.uk
w: www.batmink.co.uk

BAV (Boath Audio Visual)
42 NEW ENGLAND ROAD, BRIGHTON
East Sussex BN1 4GG 01273 600678
e: mail@boathaudiovisual.co.uk
w: www.boathaudiovisual.co.uk

Black Light Ltd
WEST SHORE TRADING ESTATE, WEST SHORE ROAD, EDINBURGH
Edinburgh EH5 1QF...0131 551 2337
e: enquiries@black-light.com
w: www.black-light.com

Blacka Acoustics Ltd
UNIT 5, HADFIELD HOUSE, GORDON STREET, LANCASHIRE HILL,
STOCKPORT
Greater Manchester SK4 1RR...............................0161 477 9700
e: info@blackaacoustics.co.uk
w: www.blackaacoustics.co.uk

Blackjack Event Co
ALPHA 6, , MASTERLORD OFFICE VILLAGE WEST ROAD, IPSWICH
Suffolk IP3 9SX..08448 400 123
e: info@blackjackevents.co.uk
w: www.blackjackuk.co.uk

Blueboxx Creative Ltd
UNIT 5 ELSTREE FILM STUDIOS, SHENLEY ROAD,
BOREHAMWOOD
Hertfordshire WD6 1JG 0845 652 2451
e: hire@blueboxx.co.uk
w: www.blueboxx.co.uk

Brunswick Studios
26 MACROOM ROAD, MAIDA VALE, LONDON
Greater London W9 3HY..2089600066
e: info@brunswickstudios.co.uk
w: www.brunswickstudios.co.uk

Bubbles Lighting Ltd
UNITS 20 - 21 BLACK MOOR BUSINESS PARK, NEW ROAD,
MAULDEN
Bedfordshire MK45 2BG..01525 402400
e: info@bubbleslighting.com
w: www.bubbleslighting.com

C.P. Electrical Ltd
BROCKHURST FARM, LYE GREEN ROAD, CHESHAM
 HP5 3NH..01494 793311
e: admin@cpelectricalltd.co.uk
w: www.cpelectricalltd.co.uk

Cameron Presentations & All Event Hire
BURNFIELD ROAD, GIFFNOCK, GLASGOW
Glasgow G46 7TH 0141 637 0368
e: hire@cameronpres.co.uk
w: www.cameronpres.co.uk

Carta Pojects Ltd
5 GEORGE ST, SNAITH
East Yorkshire DN14 9HY 07809 209950
e: martin@cartaprojects.co.uk
w: www.cartaprojects.co.uk

CB Sound Video Light Ltd
UNIT 30 GREENWAY BUSINESS CENTRE, HARLOW BUSINESS
PARK, HARLOW
Essex CM19 5QE 01279 260 160
e: info@cbsvl.co.uk
w: www.cbsvl.co.uk

Central Theatre Supplies
1186 STRATFORD ROAD, HALL GREEN, BIRMINGHAM
West Midlands B28 8AB...0121 778 6400
e: john@centraltheatresupplies.co.uk
w: www.centraltheatresupplies.co.uk

Centre Stage
23 IRON WORKS, 58 DACE ROAD, LONDON
Greater London E3 2NX...01442 255170
e: hire@centrestage.org.uk
w: www.centrestage.org.uk

Chaps Production Co
UNIT 2, 33 BANSTEAD ROAD , CATERHAM-ON-THE-HILL
Surrey CR3 5TS 01883 346789
e: hires@chapsproductionco.com
w: www.chapsproductionco.com

Charles Wilson Instant Power
86 HIGH STREET, HARPENDEN
Hertfordshire AL5 2SP...01582 763 122
e: cw@cwplant.co.uk
w: www.cwplant.co.uk

Chauvet
UNIT 1C BROOKHILL INDUSTRIAL ESTATE, PINXTON,
NOTTINGHAM
Nottinghamshire NG16 6NT 01773 511 115
e: uksales@chauvetlighting.com
w: www.chauvetlighting.co.uk

Cinimod Studio Ltd
UNIT 108, CANALOT STUDIOS, 222 KENSAL ROAD, LONDON
Greater London W10 5BN.......................................020 8969 3960
e: enquiries@cinimodstudio.com
w: www.cinimodstudio.com

Cirro Lite (Europe) Ltd
3 BARRETTS GREEN ROAD, LONDON
Greater London NW10 7AE.....................................020 8955 6700
e: info@cirrolite.com
w: www.cirrolite.com

CMF Event Hire
....0843 289 2798
e: cfmeventhire@aol.com
w: www.cfmeventhire.co.uk

Colour Sound Experiment
ST LEONARDS ROAD , PARK ROYAL, LONDON
Greater London NW10 6ST 020 8965 9119
e: sales@coloursound.co.uk
w: www.coloursound.co.uk

Colourlite Company
DARVIN COURT, WALLISWOOD GREEN ROAD, WALLISWOOD,
DORKING
Surrey RH5 5RD..01306 627664
e: sales@ColourLite.com
w: www.colourlite.com

Complete Production Services Group
UNIT 14, AIRFIELD ROAD, CHRISTCHURCH
Dorset BH23 3TG...01202 572000
e: enquiries@cpsgroup.co.uk
w: www.cpsgroup.co.uk

CoNi Ltd
WEST END ESTATE, BRUNTCLIFFE ROAD, MORLEY
West Yorkshire LS27 0LQ 0113 289 7700
e: hire@co-ni.co.uk
w: www.co-ni.co.uk

CPE Lighting Ltd
UNIT H, 7 CRAIGEND PLACE, GLASGOW
Glasgow G13 2UN..0141 950 6350
e: tech@cpelighting.co.uk
w: www.cpe-lighting.co.uk

Creative Lighting & Sound (CLS)
UNIT 6, SPIRES BUSINESS CENTRE, MUGIMOSS RD , ABERDEEN
Aberdeen AB21 9NY...01224 683 111
e: info@clsaberdeen.co.uk
w: www.clsaberdeen.co.uk

Cricklewood Electronics
40-42 CRICKLEWOOD BROADWAY, LONDON
Greater London NW2 3ET.......... 020 8450 0995 // 020 84520161
e: accounts@cricklewoodelectronics.com
w: www.cricklewoodelectronics.com

Crucial FX
UNIT 4, WATERS BUSINESS PARK, WATERS ROAD,
ELLESMERE PORT
Cheshire CH65 4FF 020 3199 6355
e: info@crucial-fx.com
w: www.crucial-fx.com

DAC Pro-Media Ltd
Surrey 01372 374 600
e: dcrisp@dacpromedia.co.uk
w: www.dacpromedia.co.uk

David Fitch Services Ltd
 176 BEXLEY ROAD, ERITH
Kent DA8 3HF 01322 350351
e: contactus@davidfitchservices.com
w: www.davidfitchservices.com

dbn Lighting Ltd
8 DOWNING ST IND. EST, CHARLTON PLACE, MANCHESTER
Greater Manchester M12 6HH..............................0161 273 4297
e: mail@dbn.co.uk
w: www.dbn.co.uk

DBS Solutions
73 MANCHESTER RD, WOOLSTON, WARRINGTON
Cheshire WA1 4AE 0845 388 0321
e: info@dbs-solutions.co.uk
w: www.dbs-solutions.co.uk

L

DC3 Productions Ltd
37 BRAMBLE ROAD, HATFIELD
AL10 9RZ.................................. 020 8123 8765 / 07737 535886
e: dan@dc3productions.co.uk
w: www.dc3productions.co.uk

DCLX - Lighting Hire and Event Production
UNIT 24, GARDNER INDUSTRIAL ESTATE, KENT HOUSE LANE,
BECKENHAM, KENT BR3 1QZ 020 881 98527
e: info@dclx.co.uk
w: www.dclx.co.uk

Definition Audio Visual
3D HARROGATE ROAD, RAWDON, LEEDS
West Yorkshire LS19 6HW.......... 07548 347594 // 08435 235470
e: mark@definitionaudiovisual.co.uk
w: www.definitionaudiovisual.co.uk

Definitive Special Projects Ltd
HIGH TREE FARM, WOOD END
Hertfordshire SG2 7BB...01438 869005
e: info@laserlightshows.co.uk
w: www.laserlightshows.co.uk

DLC Events
STREET 22, AL QUOZ IND 3, DUBAI
PO Box 282841,................................ +971 4 347 0484
e: office@dlcevents.com
w: www.dlcevents.com

DPL Production Lighitng Limited
UNIT 1 RAWRETH BARDS, DOUBLEGATE LANE, RAWRETH,
WICKFORD
Essex SS11 8UD 01268 732299
e: info@dplx.co.uk
w: www.dplx.co.uk

Dynamic Production Solutions
UNIT 13E, BARTON BUSINESS PARK, NEW DOVER ROAD,
CANTERBURY Kent CT1 3AA 01227 656 599
e: info@dynamicproductionsolutions.co.uk
w: www.dynamicproductionsolutions.co

Earley Creative
2 LISCOMBE WEST, LISCOMBE PARK, SOULBURY,
LEIGHTON BUZZARD,
Bedfordshire LU7 0JL 0333 0556626
e: info@earleycreative.com
w: www.earleycreative.com

East Anglia Leisure
UNIT 4, CIVIC INDUSTRIAL ESTATE, HOMEFIELD ROAD, HAVERHILL
Suffolk CB9 8QP 01440 714204
e: info@ealeisure.co.uk
w: www.ealeisure.co.uk

EC Creative Services Ltd
UNIT 1 LANSDOWNE ROAD, CHADDERTON, OLDHAM
Lancashire OL9 9EF..0161 628 7723
e: info@eccreativeservices.com
w: www.eccreativeservices.com

EJ Productions
12 THE ALBERMARLE , BRIGHTON
BN2 1TX 7971525552
e: Ellis@EJProductions.co.uk
w: www.ejproductions.co.uk/

Electrotechnik UK Ltd
TREDRAGON SPRING, TREDRAGON ROAD, MAWGAN PORTH
Cornwall TR8 4DB..01637 861192
e: service@etuk.co.uk
w: www.etuk.co.uk

Emphasis Event Production Ltd
UNIT 14, BELGRAVE INDUSTRIAL ESTATE, SOUTHAMPTON
Hampshire SO17 3EA..023 8055 0557
e: enquiries@emphasiseventproduction.co.uk
w: www.prestech.co.uk

Enlightened Lighting Ltd
26-28 EMERY ROAD, BRISLINGTON
Bristol BS4 5PF..01179 727 123
e: info@enlx.co.uk
w: www.enlightenedlighting.co.uk

Enliten
20 MERTON INDUSTRIAL PARK, JUBLIEE WAY, WIMBLEDON
SW19 3WL...020 8254 4860
e: paul@enliten.co.uk
w: www.enliten.co.uk

ENTEC Limited
UNIT 13 TIMS BOATYARD, TIMSWAY, STAINS
Middlesex TW18 3JY 02088 424 004
e: barbara@entec-soundandlight.com
w: www.entecaccess.co.uk

Entec Sound & Light
517 YEADING LANE, NORTHOLT
Middlesex UB5 6LN 020 8842 4004
e: sales@entecLIVE.com
w: www.enteclive.com/

Entertainment Toolbox Ltd
WOLVERHAMPTON BUSINESS AIRPORT, UNIT 23B, BOBBINGTON,
STOURBRIDGE
West Midlands DY7 5DY...01384 221083
e: info@etx-ltd.com
w: www.etx-ltd.com

ES Lighting Hire Ltd
UNIT 3 OPTREX BUSINESS PARK, ROTHERWICK
Hampshire RG27 9AY..01256 765 609
e: Sales@eslightinghire.co.uk
w: www.eslightinghire.co.uk

Eurohire Sound & Light
UNIT 6, BESSEMER PARK, BESSEMER ROAD, BASINGSTOKE
Hampshire RG21 3NB...01256 461 234
e: jools@eurohiresoundandhire.co.uk
w: www.eurohiresoundandlight.co.uk

Event and Production Hire
UNITS 2 & 3 IVY HOUSE FARM , GRANGE ROAD ,
SOLIHULL, BIRMINGHAM
West Midlands B94 6PR..01564 770 783
e: warren@eaph.co.uk
w: www.eventproductionhire.com

Event Electrix Ltd
THE OLD STABLES, SHOREHAM LANE ST MICHAELS, TENTERDEN
Kent TN30 6NG..0844 800 2833
e: ask@eventelectrix.co.uk
w: www.eventelectrix.co.uk/

Event Hire Wales
....07494 169599
e: info@eventhire.wales
w: www.eventhire.wales

Event Solutions
UNIT 10 STATION ROAD, HOLMES CHAPEL
Cheshire CW4 8AA..01477 544222
e: sales@eventsolutions.co.uk
w: www.eventsolutions.co.uk

Event Sound & Light Ltd
UNIT 2 WARREN ESTATE, LORDSHIP ROAD, WRITTLE,
CHELMSFORD
Essex CM1 3WT..01245 863863
e: info@eventsoundandlight.com
w: www.eventsoundandlight.com

Event Tents Global
223 ARDGLASS ROAD, DOWNPATRICK
 BT30 7ED .... 02844 841 820 / 07872 501861
e: contact@eventtentsglobal.com
w: www.eventtentsglobal.com

Fantastic Illuminations
E1 FLIGHTWAY, DUNKESWELL BUSINESS PARK, DUNKESWELL
 EX14 4PP...01404 510015
e: info@fantasticilluminations.co.uk
w: www.fantasticilluminations.co.uk

Fenwick Mobile Exhibitions Ltd
FENWICK BY-PASS, FENWICK
Ayrshire KA3 6AW...01560 600271
e: enquiries@fmx-ltd.com
w: www.fmx-ltd.com

Fiend Productions Ltd
46A CHARGROVE ROAD, TOTTENHAM, LONDON
Greater London N17 0JD 0800 148 8269
e: info@fiend-productions.com
w: www.fiend-productions.com

First Network Ltd
ROWDELL ROAD, NORTHOLT
Middlesex UB5 5QR 020 8842 1222
e: info@first-network.com
w: www.first-network.com

Four Star Events
UNIT 35 GRASMERE WAY, BLYTH
Northumberland NE24 4RR 7971754904
e: alanfourstarevents@gmail.com
w: www.fourstarevents.co.uk

Fresh Events UK
UNIT D WESLAKE INDUSTRIAL PARK, RYE HARBOUR ROAD, RYE
East Sussex TN31 7TE 07919 512 608
e: info@fresheventsuk.com
w: www.fresheventsuk.com

FX Productions
UNIT 11D , TANFIELD LEA NORTH INDUSTRIAL ESTATE, STANLEY
Durham DH9 9UU .... 01207 282424 // 07596 728358
e: info@fx-productions.org
w: www.fx-productions.org

Gain Audio
47 GORSEY LANE , CLOCK FACE , ST HELENS
 WA9 4QS .... 08438861162 / 07896045416
e: justgainaudio@gmail.com
w: www.gainaudio.co.uk/

Garden Party Hire
157 EWE LAMB LANE, BRAMCOTE, NOTTINGHAM
Nottinghamshire NG9 3JW....................................0115 849 5686
e: enquiries@garden-party-hire.co.uk
w: www.gardenpartyhire.co.uk

Gearhouse In2Structures
PO BOX 751391, GARDENVIEW, JOHANNESBURG
 2047... +27 (0) 112 163 000
e: jhb@gearhouse.co.za
w: www.gearhouse.co.za

Genie Lighting Ltd
UNIT 4 FELNEX TRADING ESTATE, PONTEFRACT LANE, LEEDS
 LS9 0SL..0113 399 3238
e: sales@genielighting.co.uk
w: www.genielighting.co.uk

L

GLS Lighting
THE ALPHA BUILDING, WILLMENTS SHIPYARD, HAZEL ROAD, SOUTHAMPTON
Hampshire SO19 7HS 023 8043 6622
e: info@glslighting.com
w: www.glslighting.com

GPS Lighting Ltd
UNIT 6 - FEN PLACE FARM, EAST STREET, TURNERS HILL
West Sussex RH10 4QA 020 8123 0409
e: enquiries@gpslighting.com
w: www.gpslighting.com

Gradav Hire and Sales Ltd
SHENLEY ROAD , BOREHAMWOOD
Hertfordshire WD6 1JG 020 8324 2100
e: office@gradav.co.uk
w: www.gradav.co.uk

Halo Lighting
98-124 BREWERY ROAD, LONDON
Greater London N7 9PG 0207 607 4444
e: info@halo.co.uk
w: www.halo.co.uk

Hawthorns
CROWN BUSINESS PARK, OLD DALBY
Leicestershire LE14 3NQ..01664 821111
e: info@hawthorn.biz
w: www.hawthorn.biz/

Heathrow Sound Hire
UNITS 9 & 10- POD BUSINESS CENTRE, HARRIS WAY, SUNBURY ON THAMES
Surrey TW16 7EW....................... 0208 4322310 // 07834520290
e: enquiries@heathrowsoundhire.co.uk
w: www.heathrowsoundhire.co.uk

HFM Lighting Ltd
UNIT 15, MERIDIAN CENTRE, VULCAN WAY, NEW ADDINGTON
Greater London CR0 9UG 01689 848 493
e: hugh@hfmlighting.com
w: www.hfmlighting.co.uk

Hi-Lights
18E WHITEROSE WAY, FOLLINGSBY PARK, GATESHEAD
Tyne and Wear NE10 8YX......................................0191 495 0608
e: martin@hi-lights.tv
w: www.hi-lights.tv

High Lite Touring
MITROVICKA 359/45, OSTRAVA - NOVA BELA
72400..00420 596 731 034
e: info@highlite.cz
w: www.highlite.cz

Hire for Parties Ltd
UNIT C7, J31 PARK, WEST THURROCK
Essex RM20 3XD 07999 488 334
e: info@hireforparties.co.uk
w: www.hireforparties.co.uk

HPSS Ltd
UNIT 5 DAIRYCOATES INDUSTRIAL ESTATE, WHILTSHIRE RD, HULL
East Yorkshire HU4 6PA.......................................01482 221 810
e: webmail@hpss.co.uk
w: www.hpss.co.uk

HSL Productions Ltd
UNITS E & F GLENFIELD PARK, PHILIPS ROAD, BLACKBURN
Lancashire BB1 5PF...01254 698808
e: info@hslgroup.com
w: www.hslgroup.com

Ide Systems
UNIT 3 SWAFFIELD PARK, HYSSOP CLOSE, CANNOCK
Staffordshire WS11 7FU.......................................01543 574 111
e: enquiries@idesystems.co.uk
w: www.idesystems.co.uk

Ideal Event Services
310 UNTHANK ROAD, NORWICH
Norfolk NR4 7QD 01603 280176
e: hello@idealeventservices.co.uk
w: www.idealeventservices.co.uk

Illumination
7 NORTH MEDBURN FARM, WATLING STREET, ELSTREE
Hertfordshire WD6 3AA 020 8953 1414
e: info@illumelec.co.uk
w: www.illumelec.co.uk

IMAX Lighting
UNIT 12-13 BONVILLE ROAD, BRISLINGTON
Bristol BS4 5QG..01179 719625
e: info@imaxlighting.co.uk
w: www.imaxlighting.co.uk

Impact Production Services
29 MOUNT AVENUE , BLETCHLEY , MILTON KEYNES
Buckinghamshire MK1 1LS...................................01908 657950
e: enquiries@impactproductions.co.uk
w: www.impactproductions.co.uk

Inhouse Venue Technical Management (pty) Ltd
PO BOX 905, BELLVILLE, CAPE TOWN
7535 I....................................... +27 (0)86 123 7890
e: info@inhousevtm.com
w: www.inhousevtm.com

Innovation
34 BLIND LANE, NEW SILKSWORTH, SUNDERLAND
Tyne and Wear SR3 1AT.......................................0191 521 0981
e: info@innovationpower.com
w: www.innovationpower.com

Install uk Ltd (Events)
UNITS 1 & 2, LINGEN ROAD, LUDLOW
Shropshire SY8 1XD...1584711119
e: events@install-uk.com
w: www.install-uk.com

Inter Lec Ltd
HOLLAND HILL , LOW ROAD, NORTH WHEATLEY, RETFORD
Nottinghamshire DN22 9DS 01427 880021
e: enquiries2015@inter-lec.co.uk
w: www.inter-lec.co.uk

Intrak
UNIT 5B, CLIFTON BUSINESS PARK,
PRESTON NEW ROAD, CLIFTON
Lancashire PR4 0XQ 01772 633697
e: info@intrak.co.uk
w: www.intraksoundandlight.co.uk

Jacquesolie Lighting Ltd
140 QUEEN ANNE AVENUE, BROMLEY
Kent BR2 0SF .... 07799 143 957 // 0 20 3086 7327
w: www.jacquesolie.co.uk

JMS Plant Hire Ltd
32 COLDHARBOUR LANE, HARPENDEN
Hertfordshire AL5 4UN 0845 4670000
e: hire@jms-access.co.uk
w: www.jms-planthire.co.uk

JS Electrical Services
6 BEACON SQUARE , PENRITH
 CA11 8AJ 07540 418933
e: jselectricalservices.penrith@gmail.com
w: www.jselectricalservices.co.uk

Just Lite Productions
UNIT 31 FINGLAS BUSINESS CENTRE, JAMESTOWN ROAD,
FINGLAS, DUBLIN 11
.... + 353 1 806 8333
e: info@justlite.com
w: justlite.com

KC Lighting
123 PRIORWAY AVENUE, BORROWASH, DERBY
 DE72 3HY .... 01332 674589 // 07860 669323
e: kev@kclighting.co.uk
w: www.kclighting.co.uk

Kes Power & Light Ltd
STATION ROAD, SOUTHAMPTON
Hampshire SO15 4HU 023 8070 4703
e: sales@kes.co.uk
w: www.kes.co.uk

Key Audio Visual Services
BLACK TOWER STUDIOS, 15 BRACONDALE, NORWICH
Norfolk NR1 2AL 01603 616661
e: info@keyav.com
w: www.keyav.com

Keylight Design & Supply
MORSWEG 140, AMSTERDAM
 2332ER 0031 6 4895 8900
e: info@keylight.nu
w: www.keylight.nu

Kick Audio Visual
UNIT 4, THE BOX WORKS, HEYSHAM ROAD, AINTREE, LIVERPOOL
 L30 6UR 0151 430 7000
e: info@kickpa.co.uk
w: www.kickpa.co.uk

Kudos Music
UNIT 10 TRADE CITY, COWLEY MILL ROAD, UXBRIDGE
 UB8 2DB...01895 207990
e: info@kudosmusic.co.uk
w: www.kudosmusic.co.uk

Lamphouse Production Ltd
FLINTSTONES FARM, BUNKERS HILL, RIDLEY
Kent TN15 7EY 1474247670
e: hire@lamphouse.uk.com
w: www.lamphouse.uk.com

Laser Electronics Ltd
GUNBY ROAD, ORBY, SKEGNESS
Lincolnshire PE24 5HT...01754 811137
e: clive@laserelectronicsltd.co.uk
w: www.laserelectronicsltd.com

Laser Lighting & Sound
THE OLD CHAPEL, MANNINGTREE ROAD, IPSWICH
Suffolk IP9 2TA 01473 328897
e: info@laserlighting.co.uk
w: www.laserlighting.co.uk

Leisure Light and Sound (lls)
11 TELFORD ROAD, FERNDOWN IND EST, WIMBOURNE
 BH21 7QP .... 0786 017 9059 / 01985844439
e: info@lls-online.net
w: www.lls-online.net

Leisuretec Distribution Ltd
UNIT L3, CHERRYCOURT WAY, STANBRIDGE ROAD,
LEIGHTON BUZZARD
 LU7 4UH 01525 850085
e: sales@leisuretec.co.uk

Le Maitre Ltd
6 FORVAL CLOSE, WANDLE WAY, MITCHAM
Surrey CR4 4NE...0208 646 2222
e: info@lemaitreltd.com
w: www.lemaitreevents.com

Light Motif
26 TALINA CENTRE, 23A BAGLEYS LANE, LONDON
Greater London SW6 2BW....................................020 7183 5381
e: info@lightmotif.co.uk
w: www.lightmotif.co.uk

Light Processor
20 GREENHILL CRESCENT, WATFORD BUSINESS PARK,
GREENFORD, WATFORD
Hertfordshire WD18 8JA 01923 698090
e: info@lightprocessor.co.uk
w: www.lightprocessor.co.uk

Light The Way
UNIT 7 CAVENDISH COURT MILL, WEST STREET, BRADFORD
BD11 1DA..01422 250 819
e: hire@lighttheway.co.uk
w: www.lighttheway.co.uk

Lightech Sound & Light Ltd
BRAMHALL HILL FARM, NORTH RODE, CONGLETON
Cheshire CW12 2PJ 01260 223666
e: info@lightech.co.uk
w: www.lightech.co.uk

Lightfactor Sales
20 GREENHILL CRESCENT, WATFORD BUSINESS PARK,
GREENFORD, WATFORD
Hertfordshire WD18 8JA 01923 495495
e: performance@coopercontrols.co.uk
w: www.lightfactor.co.uk

Lighting Technology York
18 BROMLEY STREET, -NONE-, -NONE-, YORK
YO26 4YQ 447790902130
e: help@prolx.co.uk
w: www.prolx.co.uk

LightStorm Trading Ltd
8 WILLOW BUSINESS PARK, 61-71 WILLOW WAY, LONDON
SE26 4QP 020 8699 8700
e: sales@lightstormtrading.co.uk
w: www.lightstormtrading.co.uk

Lite Alternative Ltd
UNIT 4 SHADSWORTH BUSINESS PARK, DUTTONS WAY,
BLACKBURN
Lancashire BB1 2QR..01254 279654
w: www.lite-alternative.com

London Event Rentals
UNIT 7, WILLOW WALK, TOWER BRIDGE, LONDON
Greater London SE1 5SF 01252 313154
e: info@londoneventrentals.co.uk
w: www.londoneventrentals.co.uk

London Sound and Light
86 - 90 PAUL STREET, LONDON
Greater London EC2A 4NE 020 3086 7775
e: info@londonsoundandlight.co.uk
w: www.londonsoundandlight.co.uk

Lucid Illusions
HIGHSTED FARM , HIGHSTED VALLEY, SITTINGBOURNE
Kent ME9 0AG 020 3488 0265
e: info@lucidillusions.co.uk
w: www.lucidillusions.co.uk

Lux Technical Ltd
UNIT R, TUNGSTEN PARK, MAPLE DRIVE, HINCKLEY
LE10 3BE..020 3696 0692
e: info@luxtechnical.co.uk
w: www.luxtechnical.co.uk

LX Communications Ltd
UNIT 36, WEST STATION YARD, MALDON
Essex CM9 6TS......................................01621 854075
e: info@lxcommunications.com
w: lightinghireessex.com/

Magnum PA Ltd
HODGESTON, PEMBROKE
Pembrokeshire SA71 5JU 01646 450 172
e: info@magnumpa.com
w: www.magnumpa.com

Mainline Show Productions Ltd
UNIT 21 ETON BUSINESS PARK, ETON HILL ROAD, RADCLIFFE
Greater Manchester M26 2ZS 08432 896 150
e: info@mainlineshow.co.uk
w: www.mainlineshow.co.uk

Markertek
UNIT 4 FALCON BUSINESS CENTRE, 2-4 WILLOW LANE, WILLOW
LANE INDUSTRIAL ESTATE, MITCHAM
Surrey CR4 4NA....................................020 8687 9700
e: sales@markertek.co.uk
w: www.markertek.co.uk

Marklew Production Lighting Hire
UNIT 6 HOCKLEY PORT, BUSINESS CENTRE, ALL SAINTS STREET,
BIRMINGHAM
West Midlands B18 7RL............. 01215 325553 // 07414 728890
e: mail@marklewproductions.com
w: www.marklewproductions.com

Martin Bradley Sound & Light
69A BROAD LANE, HAMPTON
Middlesex TW12 3AX .... 020 8979 0672 //
07973 331451
e: mail@martinbradley.co.uk
w: www.martinbradley.co.uk

Martin Professional Plc
BELVOIR WAY, FAIRFIELD INDUSTRIAL ESTATE, LOUTH
Lincolnshire LN11 0LQ 1507 604 399
e: mpukaccounts@martinpro.co.uk
w: www.martinpro.co.uk

Matt Bunday Events
.... 023 8055 3736 // 07730 604 869
e: info@mattbundayevents.com
w: www.mattbundayevents.com

Microrave
203 STOCKWELL ROAD, LONDON
Greater London SW9 9SL......... 0845 519 1171 // 07590 535 125
e: tom@microrave.biz
w: www.microrave.biz

Middlesex Sound & Lighting Ltd
4-6 VILLAGE WAY EAST, RAYNERS LANE, HARROW
Middlesex HA2 7LU....................................020 8866 5500
e: info@middlesexsound.co.uk
w: www.middlesexsound.co.uk

L

MJ Lights LTD

....029 2009 2700
e: matt@mjlights.co.uk
w: www.mjlights.co.uk

MM Sound and Lighting

UNIT 7 BRYSON STREET IND EST, BRYSON STREET, FALKIRK
FK2 7BT..01324 624598
e: enquiries@mmsoundandlighting.com
w: www.mmsoundandlighting.com

Mode Lighting (UK) Ltd

THE MALTINGS, 63 HIGH ST , WARE
Hertfordshire SG12 9AD...01920 462121
e: sales@modelighting.com
w: www.modelighting.com

Mosaic FX Lighting

THE TYTHE BARN, DOG KENNEL FARM, THE CHARLTON ROAD,
HITCHIN
Hertfordshire SG5 2AB..01462 434445
e: sales@mosaicfx.co.uk
w: www.mosaicfx.co.uk

MTS

UNIT 37, MOUNTHEATH TRADING , ESTATE PRESTWICH ,
MANCHESTER
Greater Manchester M25 9WE 1617739933
e: Keith@massivetech.co.uk
w: www.massivetech.co.uk

Multi-Lite (UK) Ltd

15 AIRLINKS, SPITFIRE WAY, HESTON
Middlesex TW5 9NR..020 8561 4501
e: sales@multi-lite.co.uk
w: www.multi-lite.co.uk

Multiform Technology

SEEDBED BUSINESS CENTRE, VANGUARD WAY, SHOEBURYNESS
Essex SS3 9QY 01702 680021
e: sales@adelto.com
w: www.multiform-lighting.com

Mushroom Event Services Ltd

15 LOW FARM PLACE, MOULTON PARK, NORTHAMPTON
Northamptonshire NN3 6HY 01604 790900
e: info@mushroomevents.co.uk
w: www.mushroomevents.co.uk

Neg Earth Lights

LIGHT HOUSE, WESTERN ROAD, PARK ROYAL, LONDON
Greater London NW10 7LT 020 8963 0327
e: info@negearth.co.uk
w: www.negearth.co.uk

Neolec Lighting

CHURCH LANE, KINWARTON, ALCESTER
Warwickshire B49 6HB 01789 765 667
e: info@neoleclighting.com
w: www.neoleclighting.com

New Day Hire

44 BOVERTON DRIVE, BROCKWORTH, GLOUCESTER
Gloucestershire GL3 4DA 08450 618619
e: sales@newday.tv
w: www.newdayhire.co.uk

Nightair Productions

UNIT ONE, EASTFIELD SIDE, SUTTON IN ASHFIELD
Nottinghamshire NG17 4JW 01623 557 040
e: sales@nightair.co.uk
w: www.nightair.co.uk

NiteLites

UNIT S4, SECOND AVENUE,, TYNE TUNNEL TRADING ESTATE,
NORTH SHIELDS
Tyne and Wear NE29 7SY.......................................0191 296 0100
e: info@nitelites.co.uk
w: www.nitelites.co.uk

Northern Light

NAUTICAL HOUSE, 104 COMMERCIAL STREET, EDINBURGH
Edinburgh EH6 6NF..0131 622 9100
e: contact@northernlight.co.uk
w: www.northernlight.co.uk

Novum AV

56 KEPLER, LICHFIELD ROAD INDUSTRIAL ESTATE, TAMWORTH
Staffordshire B79 7XE...0121 673 8385
e: hire@novumav.com
w: www.novumav.com

Oasis Sound & Lighting

UNIT 19, WINDMILL FARM BUSINESS CENTRE, BARLTEY STREET,
BEDMINSTER
Bristol BS3 4DB .... 0117 966 3663 // 0117 963 7355
e: mail@oasis-online.co.uk
w: www.oasis-online.co.uk

On Event Production Co.

UNIT 16, WILLOW ROAD,, TRENT LANE INDUSTRIAL ESTATE,
CASTLE DONINGTON, DERBY
Derbyshire DE74 2NP 01159 222959
e: hello@on-productions.co.uk
w: www.lovingitlive.co.uk

OneoneTwo.com

112 NORTHWOOD AVENUE, PURLEY CR8 2EQ 020 8660 7143
e: mail@oneonetwo.com
w: www.oneonetwo.com

OX2P

18 VANTAGE BUSINESS PARK, BLOXHAM ROAD, BANBURY
Oxfordshire OX16 9UX..01295 701464
e: tmatthews@ox2p.co.uk
w: www.ox2p.co.uk

Panalux Broadcast & Events

WAXLOW ROAD , LONDON
Greater London NW10 7NU 020 8233 7000
e: info@panalux.biz
w: www.panalux.biz

L

PDS - Sound & Lighting Company
21 IVATT WAY, WESTWOOD, PETERBOROUGH
Cambridgeshire PE3 7PG 01733 261199
e: info@pdssoundandlighting.com
w: www.pdssoundandlighting.com

Perception Live
ARCH 26, HANDEL BUSINESS CENTRE, 73 BONDWAY, VAUXHALL
LONDON
Greater London SW8 1SQ 0845 527 5667
e: events@perceptionlive.com
w: www.perceptionlive.com

PF Events
UNIT 6, EASTGATE BUSINESS PARK, ARGALL WAY, LONDON
Greater London E10 7PG..0208 801 9005
e: sales@pfevents.com
w: www.pfevents.com

Phantom Power Ltd
UNIT 5A, BLACKWELL FARM INDUSTRIAL ESTATE,
TILBROOK, HUNTINGDON
Cambridgeshire PE28 0JQ 07730 865642
e: info@phantompower.co.uk
w: www.phantompower.co.uk

Philip L Edwards (Theatre Lighting)
5 HIGHWOOD CLOSE, GLOSSOP
 SK13 6PH 01457 862811
e: enquiries@pltheatrelighting.co.uk
w: www.pltheatrelighting.co.uk

Photon Beard Ltd
UNIT K3,CHERRYCOURT WAY, LEIGHTON BUZZARD
Bedfordshire LU7 4UH..01525 850911
e: info@photonbeard.com
w: www.photonbeard.com

PKE Lighting
UNIT E7, CROFT COURT, MOSS INDUSTRIAL ESTATE, ST HELENS
ROAD, LEIGH WN7 3PT..01942 678424
e: sales@pkelighting.com
w: www.pkelighting.com

Planet Gold Decor
UNIT 4 ROMARSH, FOWLSWICK BUSINESS PARK, , ALLINGTON
Wiltshire SN14 6QE..07747 015 170
e: info@planetgolddecor.co.uk
w: www.planetgolddecor.co.uk or www.

Precise Events
UNIT K14 CLYDE WORKSHOPS, FULLARTON ROAD, GLASGOW
Glasgow G32 8YL 0141 255 0740
e: info@PreciseEvents.co.uk
w: www.preciseaudio.co.uk

Premier UK Events Ltd
UNIT 2, ROOKERY LANE, THURMASTON, LEICESTER
Leicestershire LE4 8AU..1162029953
e: ben@premier-ltd.com
w: premier-event-solutions.com/

Prestige Sound and Light
UNIT 1, MARLIN PARK, CENTRAL WAY, FELTHAM, LONDON
Greater London TW14 0AN.....................................07584 292070
e: info@prestigesoundandlight.co.uk
w: www.prestigesoundandlight.co.uk

Prime Events
204 ROSEMOUNT PLACE, ABERDEEN
Aberdeen AB25 2XQ 01224 646488
e: info@primeeventmanagement.com
w: www.primeeventmanagement.com

Prism Lighting
UNIT 5A, HAMPTON INDUSTRIAL ESTATE, MALPAS
Cheshire SY14 8LU..01948 820201
e: mail@prismlighting.co.uk
w: www.prismlighting.co.uk

Pro Event Solutions
THEAKLEN DRIVE, , PONSWOOD INDUSTRIAL ESTATE,,
ST LEONARDS
East Sussex TN37 9AZ...8006127427
e: hello@proeventsolutions.co.uk
w: www.proeventsolutions.co.uk

Production Light & Sound Ltd
PO BOX 96, LEEDS
West Yorkshire LS12 4XS 0113 2360951
e: info@productionlightandsound.com
w: www.productionlightandsound.com

Projected Image Uk Ltd
UNIT 17 HOULTS ESTATE, WALKER ROAD,
NEWCASTLE UPON TYNE
Tyne and Wear NE6 2HL...0191 265 9832
e: gobo@projectedimage.com
w: www.projectedimage.com

Protec (Production Technology LLC)
PLOT NO. 548 - 597, DUBAI INVESTMENT PARK 2,
DUBAI, UNITED ARAB EMIRATES.......................+971 4 880 0092
e: eventrental@productiontec.com
w: www.productiontec.com

PSAV Presentation Services
UNIT 3, HERON TRADING ESTATE, ALLIANCE ROAD, LONDON
 W3 0RA 0208 896 6120
e: infoeurope@psav.com
w: www.psav.com

Pulsar Light Of Cambridge Ltd
3 COLDHAMS BUSINESS PARK, NORMAN WAY, CAMBRIDGE
Cambridgeshire CB1 3LH..01223 403500
e: sales@pulsarlight.com
w: www.pulsarlight.com

Puxley Limited
11 HARRIER COURT , WESTCOTT LANE , EXETER
 EX5 2DR 01392 364900
e: info@puxley.com
w: www.puxley.com

QED Productions
UNIT 11, SUMMIT ROAD, CRANBORNE INDUSTRIAL ESTATE,
POTTERS BAR
Hertfordshire EN6 3QW...01707 648 800
e: info@qed-productions.com
w: www.qed-productions.com

Quadrant Events - Nottingham
12 LONGWALL AVENUE, QUEENS DRIVE INDUSTRIAL ESTATE,
NOTTINGHAM Nottinghamshire NG2 1NA 0115 8402 288
e: info@quadrantevents.com
w: www.quadrantevents.com

RealSound and Vision Ltd
120C OLYMPIC AVENUE, MILTON PARK, ABINGDON
Oxfordshire OX14 4SA......................................+44 1235 833944
e: sales@realsound.co.uk
w: www.realsound.co.uk

Rhythm Group
RHYTHM HOUSE, KING STREET, CARLISLE
Cumbria CA1 1SJ 01228 515 141
e: info@rhythm.co.uk
w: www.rhythm.co.uk

Richard Martin Lighting
UNIT 24, SOVEREIGN PARK, CORONATION ROAD, PARK ROYAL,
LONDON NW10 7QP 020 8965 3209
e: info@richardmartinlighting.co.uk
w: www.richardmartinlighting.co.uk

RMAV
UNIT 9, ACORN BUSINESS CENTRE, CUBLINGTON ROAD,
WING, LEIGHTON BUZZARD
Buckinghamshire LU7 0LB.....................................01296 682548
e: jeb@rmav.co.uk
w: www.rmav.co.uk

Roscolab Ltd
KANGLEY BRIDGE ROAD, SYDENHAM, LONDON
Greater London SE26 5AQ 0208 659 2300
e: contact@rosco.com
w: www.rosco.com

S1b.com
NEW HOUSE, MEWITH LANE, BENTHAN, LANCASTER
North Yorkshire LA2 7AW 015242 61010
e: info@s1b.com
w: www.s1b.com

S2 Events
141- 143 NATHAN WAY, LONDON
Greater London SE28 0AB....................................020 7928 5474
e: info@s2events.co.uk
w: www.s2events.co.uk

Scanlite Visual Communications
DATA HOUSE, MOWBRAY DRIVE , BLACKPOOL
Lancashire FY3 7UZ...01253 302723
e: chris.mckendrick@scanlite.co.uk
w: www.scanlite.co.uk

SFL Group
UNIT 5- HEADLEY PARK 10, HEADLEY ROAD EAST,
WOODLEY, READING
Berkshire RG5 4SW 0118 969 0900
e: info@sflgroup.co.uk
w: www.sflgroup.co.uk

Shades Events & Discotheques
4 DEAKIN LEAS, TONBRIDGE
Kent TN9 2JU...01732 363675
e: shadesevents@me.com
w: www.shadesevents.com

SHMS
LAURELS FARM, BARMBY MOOR, YORK
Yorkshire YO42 4EJ...01759 307863
e: enquiry@shms.co.uk
w: www.shms.co.uk

Silver Streak Events
12 STOKE MEADOWS, BRISTOL
 BS329BG... +44 (0) 1179116806
e: info@silverstreakevents.co.uk
w: www.silverstreakevents.co.uk

Siyan Ltd
UNIT L, PROGRESS ROAD, HIGH WYCOMBE
Buckinghamshire HP12 4JD 01494 532820
e: info@siyan.co.uk
w: www.siyan.co.uk

Smash Productions Ltd
50 ALBERT RD
Bristol BS2 0XW...0117 329 0109
w: www.smashproductions.com

Smile Events
392 GALLEY HILL,, HEMEL HEMPSTEAD,
Hertfordshire HP1 3LA 01923 750 525
e: info@smileevents.co.uk
w: www.smileevents.co.uk

Sound & Light Event Management
THE OLD ISOLATION HOSPITAL, VAUXHALL LANE,
TUNBRIDGE WELLS
Kent TN4 0XD 0800 083 8368
e: enquiries@soundandlightgroup.com
w: www.soundandlightgroup.com

Sound 2 Light Hire
.... 07092 316129 // 0845 128 5238
e: info@djequipmenthiredoncaster.co.uk
w: www.djequipmenthiredoncaster.co.u

Sound And Light Guys
36 CUMBERFORD CLOSE, BLOXHAM, BANBURY
Oxfordshire OX15 4HN 01295 720825
e: hire@soundandlightguys.co.uk
w: www.soundandlightguys.com

L

Sound Barrier Systems
UNIT 20, PALMERSTON BUSINESS PARK, NEWGATE LANE, FAREHAM
Hampshire PO14 1DJ... 07855 165 781
e: enquiries@soundbarriersystems.com
w: www.soundbarriersystems.com

Sound Division
430 HIGH ROAD, LONDON
Greater London NW10 2DA 0208 3495 200
e: info@sounddivision.com
w: www.sounddivision.com

Soundstage One Event Services
61 STATION ROAD, THORNEY , PETERBOROUGH
Cambridgeshire PE6 0QE .... 084321 62026 / 07846 349063
e: info@soundstageone.co.uk
w: www.soundstageone.co.uk

Soundwave Audio
UNIT D1 LINCOLN PARK, BOROUGH ROAD, BUCKINGHAM ROAD INDUSTRIAL ESTATE, BRACKLEY
Northamptonshire NN13 7BE 01295 298288
e: info@soundwaveaudio.co.uk
w: https://www.soundwaveaudio.co.uk

Southwest Sound & Light
THE OLD SMITHY, CHURCH ROAD, COCKWOOD, NR EXETER
Devon EX6 8NU... 01626 890806
e: sales@swlighting.co.uk
w: www.swlighting.co.uk

Specialist Lighting Co Limited
49 THE BROADWAY , CHEAM SUTTON
SM3 8BL.. 01202 700569
e: sales@slclightingonline.com
w: slclightingonline.com/

Specialz Limited
UNIT 2, KINGSTON INDUSTRIAL ESTATE, 81-86 GLOVER STREET, BIRMINGHAM
B9 4EN 0121 766 7100
e: info@specialz.co.uk
w: www.specialz.co.uk

Spot-on Theatre Services Ltd
KEIGHLEY BUSINESS CENTRE, UNIT F2B, SOUTH STREET, KEIGHLEY
West Yorkshire BD21 1SY...................................... 01535 691939
e: sales@spot-on.org.uk
w: www.spot-on.org.uk

Spotlight Sound
UNIT 32B, LITTLE BOYTON FARM , BOYTON HALL LANE , CHELMSFORD
Essex CM1 4LN 01245 206206
e: info@spotlightsound.co.uk
w: www.spotlightsound.co.uk

Spyder UK Ltd
UNIT 3, ATTRILLS YARD, THE DUVER, ST HELENS
Isle of Wight PO33 1YB 01983 779337
e: hire@spyderuk.com
w: www.spyderuk.com

Stage Connections
UNIT 1B, ACTON STREET , LONG EATON, NOTTINGHAM
Nottinghamshire NG10 1FT....... 0115 938 6354 / 07976 00 5769
e: info@stageconnections.co.uk
w: www.stageconnections.co.uk/

Stage Control Ltd
20 STATION PARADE, WHITCHURCH LANE, EDGWARE
Greater London HA8 6RW 020 8952 8982
e: admin@stagecontrol.com
w: www.stagecontrol.com

Stage Electrics
UNIT 3 BRITANNIA RD, PATCHWAY TRADING ESTATE, PATCHWAY
Bristol BS34 5TA.. 0117 938 4000
e: bristol@stage-electrics.co.uk
w: www.stage-electrics.co.uk

Stage Light Design Ltd
UNIT 8 CHANCERYGATE BUSINESS CENTRE, 214 RED LION ROAD, SURBITON
Surrey KT6 7RA 020 8397 8691
e: info@stagelightdesign.com
w: www.stagelightdesign.com

Stage Lighting Services Ltd
UNIT A, AVENUE PARK INDUSTRIAL ESTATE, CROESCADARN CLOSE, PENTWYN, CARDIFF
CF23 8HE 02920 613 577
e: info@stagelightingservices.com
w: www.stagelightingservices.com

Stage Right
SHAW LODGE FARM, STONE ROAD, FRADSWELL, STAFFORD
Staffordshire ST18 0HA 01889 502222
e: info@stagerightcreative.co.uk
w: www.stagerightcreative.com

Stage Services Event Production
THE COACH HOUSE, MAYALLS FARM, WATERY LANE, UPPER WELLAND , MALVERN
Worcestershire WR14 4JX............ 01684 560022; 07719 730053
e: info@stage-services.net
w: www.stage-services.net

StageLightSound Ltd
.... 1929423223
e: info@stagelightsound.com
w: www.stagelightsound.com

Storm Lighting Ltd
WARWICK HOUSE, MONUMENT WAY WEST, WOKING
Surrey GU21 5EN.. 01483 757211
e: hire@stormlighting.co.uk
w: www.stormlighting.co.uk

Sussex Lighting
WEST POINT, SPRINGFIELD ROAD, HORSHAM
West Sussex RH12 2PD .... 01403 241933 // 01403 241977
e: info@sussexlighting.co.uk
w: www.sussexlighting.co.uk

SXS Events
....0870 080 2342
e: hello@sxsevents.co.uk
w: www.sxsevents.co.uk

TEC PA & Lighting
PORTLAND BUILDING, UNIVERSITY PARK, NOTTINGHAM
Nottinghamshire NG7 2RD 0115 846 8720
e: info@nottinghamtec.co.uk
w: www.nottinghamtec.co.uk

Tech-ease
AUGUST HOUSE, SAGES END ROAD, HAVERHILL
CB9 7AW 07717 448695
e: enquirys@tech-ease.co.uk
w: www.tech-ease.co.uk

The Hire Company (UK) Ltd
UNITS 5 & 6, CHRISTCHURCH BUSINESS PARK, RADAR WAY,
CHRISTCHURCH
Dorset BH23 4FL 01425 272002
e: scott@thehireco.co.uk
w: www.thehireco.co.uk

The London Candle Company
....2072074458
e: info@londoncandles.uk
w: https://www.londoncandles.uk/

The Manchester Light & Stage Company Ltd
76-78 NORTH WESTERN STREET, ARDWICK, MANCHESTER
Greater Manchester M12 6DY 0161 273 2662
e: info@manchesterlightandstage.com
w: www.manchesterlightandstage.com

The Old Cinema
160 CHISWICK HIGH ROAD, LONDON
Greater London W4 1PR.......................................020 8995 4166
e: sales@theoldcinema.co.uk
w: www.theoldcinema.co.uk

The Powerdrive Drum Co Ltd
UNIT M1 CHERRYCOURT WAY, STANBRIDGE ROAD,
LEIGHTON BUZZARD
Bedfordshire LU7 4UH...01525 370292
e: info@mypowerdrive.com
w: www.mypowerdrive.com

The Powerline
MARSHFIELD, CHIPPENHAM
Wiltshire SN14 8BB 1227 892 352
e: alistair@thepowerline.co.uk
w: www.thepowerline.co.uk

The Production Shop
55 WELLINGTON ROAD, EAST BRISBANE
4169.. +61 1300 099 492
e: sales@productionshop.com.au
w: www.productionshop.com.au

Thunder and Lightning
....01368 459457
e: enquiries@thunderandlightning.org.uk
w: www.thunderandlightning.org.uk

Tiffany Lamps
....8008841041
e: tiffanylampsonline@hotmail.com
w: www.tiffanylampsonline.co.uk

Tower Productions
23 ALBERT ROAD , EDINBURGH
Edinburgh EH6 7DP .... +44 131 552 0100
e: enquiries@tower-productions.com
w: www.tower-productions.com

Trafalgar Lighting Ltd
9 NORTHWAY, CLAVERINGS INDUSTRIAL ESTATE
Greater London N9 0AD 020 8887 0082
e: hire@trafalgarlighting.co.uk
w: www.trafalgarlighting.co.uk

Trilite Ltd
38 CROMWELL ROAD, LUTON
Bedfordshire LU3 1DN 01582 411413
e: UkAdmin@optikinetics.co.uk
w: www.optikinetics.co.uk

True Sound Hire
UNIT 2, MANOR PARK INDUSTRIAL EST, WYNDHAM STREET,
ALDERSHOT
Hampshire GU12 4NZ .... 01252 313154 / 01252 313154
e: info@truesoundhire.co.uk
w: www.truesoundhire.co.uk

TSE Productions
UNIT 9, TRIDENT BUSINESS PARK,, OAKENGROVE YARD, RED LION
LANE, CHICHESTER ROAD
West Sussex PO20 9DY.......................................01243 603 080
e: contact@tseproductions.co.uk
w: www.tseproductions.co.uk

Tusk Showhire
23 COLLUM LANE, SCUNTHORPE
Lincolnshire DN16 2SZ .... 01724 859541 // 07850 307162
e: info@tuskshowhire.co.uk
w: www.tuskshowhire.co.uk

Ultimate Acoustics Ltd
UNIT 2, TOP CAT INDUSTRIAL ESTATE, ESTATE ROAD NO. 8,
GRIMSBY
Lincolnshire DN31 2TG 0845 680 2079
e: info@ultimate-acoustics.co.uk
w: www.ultimate-acoustics.co.uk

L

Universal Stars Incorporated Ltd
BROAD OAK, WHITEWELL, REDBROOK MEALOR, WHITCHURCH
SY13 3AQ 01948 780 110
e: info@universalstars.co.uk
w: www.universalstars.co.uk

Upstage Presentations
UNIT 1 TRIPONTIUM BUSINESS CENTRE, NEWTON LANE, RUGBY
Warwickshire CV23 0TB...01788 860453
e: info@upstagesetdesign.co.uk
w: www.upstagesetdesign.co.uk

UV Light Technology Limited
582-854 HAGLEY ROAD WEST, BIRMINGHAM
West Midlands B68 0BS...0121 423 2000
e: sales@uv-light.co.uk
w: www.uv-light.co.uk

Velvet Entertainment
71 MASKELL ROAD, LONDON
Greater London SW17 0NL.....................................020 8947 8245
e: info@velvetentertainment.net
w: www.velvetentertainment.net

Velvet Twenty
....020 8675 4870
e: enquiries@velvettwenty.co.uk
w: www.velvettwenty.co.uk

Viking Sound & Light Ltd
UNIT 9 WOODSTOCK CLOSE, STANDARD WAY INDUSTRIAL
ESTATE, NORTHALLERTON
North Yorkshire DL6 2NB...............01609 780190, 0798 0023154
e: steve@vikingsound.co.uk
w: www.vikingsound.co.uk

Vision Events (Edinburgh)
16 DRYDEN ROAD, BILSTON GLEN INDUSTRIAL ESTATE,
LOANHEAD
Edinburgh EH20 9LZ...0131 334 3324
e: edinburgh@visionevents.co.uk
w: www.visionevents.co.uk

Visual Poke
THE WORKSHOP, WINTHORPE , BROADWAY, BOURN , CAMBRIDGE
CB23 2TA 8452309001
e: gino@visualpoke.co.uk
w: visualpoke.co.uk/

VME Ltd
UNIT 11, LONDRIDGE TRADING ESTATE, KNUTSFORD
Cheshire WA16 8PR 01565 652 202
e: rental@vme-uk.com
w: www.vme-uk.com

VNV Sounds
UNITS 10 AND 10A ASHLEY HOUSE, ASHLEY ROAD, LONDON
Greater London N17 9LZ...0203 021 1370
e: info@vnvlive.co.uk
w: www.vnvsounds.co.uk

Vortex Lighting
THE OLD CHAPEL, BILLY ROW GREEN, CROOK
Durham DL15 9TA .... 0845 486 7839 / 07971792398
e: sales@vortexlighting.co.uk
w: www.vortexlighting.co.uk

Warwick Corporate Events Ltd
UNIT 5 GLOUCESTER CRESENT, HEATHPARK INDUSTRIAL ESTATE,
HONITON, EXETER
Devon EX14 1DB..0845 3510392
e: enquiries@wce.co.uk
w: www.wce.co.uk

Wellpleased Events
11 BLAYDS YARD, LEEDS
West Yorkshire LS1 4AD...0113 244 2720
e: info@wellpleased.co.uk
w: www.wellpleased.co.uk

West End Studios Ltd
THE OLD BISCUIT FACTORY, FINMERE CLOSE, EASTBOURNE
East Sussex BN22 8QN 01323 732130
e: info@teamwestend.com
w: www.west-end-studios.co.uk

Westminster Electrical
31 - 33 KILBURNLANE, LONDON
Greater London W10 4AE 020 8960 3148
e: sales@westminsterelectrical.com
w: www.westminsterelectrical.com

White Light Ltd
20 MERTON INDUSTRIAL PARK, JUBILEE WAY, WIMBLEDON
Greater London SW19 3WL....................................020 8254 4800
e: live-events@whitelight.ltd.uk
w: www.whitelight.ltd.uk

WM Event Design
19 ST JAMES'S DRIVE, WANDSWORTH COMMON, LONDON
Greater London SW17 7RN 020 3837 4926
e: info@williammoyse.com
w: www.wmeventdesign.com

Wolf Event Services Ltd
UNIT F, WATERSIDE ESTATE, 25-27 WILLIS WAY, POOLE
Dorset BH15 3TD..01202 870794
e: hello@wolf-events.com
w: www.wolf-events.com

YSLV
REDHOUSE FARM, LOWER DUNTON ROAD, UPMINSTER
Greater London RM14 3TD........ 020 8317 7775 / 0800 074 6902
e: london@yslv.co.uk
w: www.yslv.co.uk

Zeal Events
UNIT 6, BESSEMER PARK, BESSEMER ROAD, BASINGSTOKE
Hampshire RG21 3NB 01256 359264
e: info@zeallive.com
w: www.zealevents.com

Zenith Lighting Inc
6557 HAZELTINE NATIONAL DRIVE, SUITE 12, ORLANDO
FL 32822..4078550088
e: zenithlighting.marketin@gmail.com
w: zenithlighting.com/

Zerodb Live
38 NIGEL HOUSE, PORTPOOL LANE, LONDON
Greater London EC1N 7UR....................................020 3332 0049
e: info@zerodblive.com
w: www.zerodblive.com

Zisys Events
PRESTWICK - MAIN OFFICE, GLASGOW PRESTWICK INTNL
AIRPORT, PRESTWICK
Ayrshire KA9 2QA 01292 479 500
e: contact@zisysevents.co.uk
w: www.zisysavmn.co.uk

Lights

Lightfantastics Laser
5 HAUGH ROAD, BURNTISLAND
Fife KY3 0BZ.. +44 (0) 131 5100218
e: show@lightfantastics.com
w: www.lightfantastics.co.uk

Linen Hire

Appealing Balloons & Events
141 BELVOIR ROAD, COALVILLE
Leicestershire LE67 3PJ 07836 233319
e: enquiries@appealingballoons.com
w: www.appealingballoons.com

Atlantic Linen Services Ltd
UNIT 7 TOWER LANE BUSINESS PARK, TOWER LANE, BRISTOL
Bristol BS30 8XY..0117 9604444
e: admin@atlanticlinen.co.uk
w: www.atlanticlinen.co.uk

Band International
SUNNYSIDE, FRESHWATER, ISLE OF WIGHT
Isle of Wight PO40 9RW 01983 755 858
e: enquiries@band.co.uk
w: www.band.co.uk

Birmingham Catering and Event Hire Ltd
THE HENRY MILLS BUILDING, 30 CHESTER STREET, ASTON,
BIRMINGHAM
West Midlands B6 4BE...0800 910 1317
e: sales@birminghamcateringhire.com
w: www.birminghamcateringhire.com

Cameo Event Hire
UNIT 16, GARDNER INDUSTRIAL ESTATE, KENT HOUSE LANE, ,
BECKENHAM
Kent BR3 1QZ...020 8659 8000
w: www.cameoeventhire.co.uk

Changing Chairs and Event Decor
2 BROOKHILL LEYS RD, EASTWOOD, NEW EASTWOOD
Nottinghamshire NG16 3HZ .... 01773 715 982 / 07973 388901
e: covers@changing-chairs.co.uk
w: www.changing-chairs.co.uk

City Furniture Hire Ltd
WEST ROAD, HARLOW
Essex CM20 2AL 0845 300 5455
e: info@cityfurniturehireltd.com
w: www.cityfurniturehireltd.com/

Event Linen Hire
THE HOUGH GRANARY, MALPAS
Cheshire SY14 7JJ..01948 860597
e: info@eventlinen.co.uk
w: www.eventlinen.co.uk

Garden Party Hire
157 EWE LAMB LANE, BRAMCOTE, NOTTINGHAM
Nottinghamshire NG9 3JW....................................0115 849 5686
e: enquiries@garden-party-hire.co.uk
w: www.gardenpartyhire.co.uk

Higgins Furniture Hire Ltd
DONEANY, KILDARE TOWN
R51 H682 .... +353 (45) 526300
e: hire@higgins.ie
w: www.higgins.ie

Johnsons Stalbridge Linen Services
JOHNSONS APPARELMASTER LTD , PITTMAN WAY, FULWOOD,
PRESTON
Lancashire PR2 9ZD 0800 093 9933
e: info@stalbridge-linen.com
w: www.stalbridge-linen.com

Over The Top Rentals Ltd
24 PRINCES PARK AVENUE, LONDON
Greater London NW11 0JP....................................0207 183 2234
e: info@overthetoprentals.co.uk
w: www.overthetoprentals.co.uk

Planet Gold Decor
UNIT 4 ROMARSH, FOWLSWICK BUSINESS PARK, , ALLINGTON
Wiltshire SN14 6QE..07747 015 170
e: info@planetgolddecor.co.uk
w: www.planetgolddecor.co.uk or www.

Spaceworks Furniture Hire Ltd
4 DEER PARK ROAD, SOUTH WIMBLEDON, LONDON
Greater London SW19 3GY...................................020 8545 6000
e: sales@spaceworks.co.uk
w: www.spaceworks.co.uk

Location Caterers

Aaron's catering service
42 ASHINGDON ROAD ROCHFORD
SS4 1RD ....07432635597 / 01702 531 600
e: singh.1972@yahoo.co.uk
w: aaroncatering.co.uk/

Anglian Events - First For Festival Food
BUILDING 726, BENTTWATERS PARKS, RENDLESHAM,
WOODBRIDGE
Suffolk IP12 2TW 01394 461546
e: food@anglianevents.co.uk
w: www.anglianevents.co.uk

Cafe2U
10 FUSION COURT, ABERFORD ROAD, GARFORTH, LEEDS
West Yorkshire LS25 2GH......................08456 444708
e: events@uk.cafe2u.com
w: www.cafe2u.co.uk

Cook And Waiter
UNIT B8 - ALPHA BETA CENTRE, 8 STANDARD ROAD, LONDON
Greater London NW10 6EU 0208 537 1200
e: reception@cookandwaiter.com
w: www.cookandwaiter.com

doesfood
....2033227576
e: jane@doesfood.com
w: www.doesfood.com

Eat To The Beat
GLOBAL INFUSION COURT, NASHLEIGH HILL, CHESHAM
Buckinghamshire HP5 3HE 01494 790 700
e: hello@eattothebeat.com
w: www.eattothebeat.com

Elegant Cuisine
....01865 391888
e: enquiries@elegantcuisine.com
w: www.elegantcuisine.com

Fayre Do's Location Caterers
NORSTED MANOR FARM, NORSTED LANE, PRATTS BOTTOM,
ORPINGTON,
Kent BR6 7PB 0207 237 6691
e: info@fayredos.co.uk
w: www.fayredos.co.uk

Flying Saucers Ltd
PO BOX 4, HALESWORTH
Suffolk IP19 9AL 01986 784298
e: val@flyingsaucerscatering.com
w: www.flyingsaucerscatering.com

Fresh Catering
WIZZO & CO. , 47 BEAK STREET, LONDON
W1F 9SE....................................07721 472 157
e: maxfresh@sky.com
w: www.freshcatering.org

K&N Catering
.... 01213 530566 // 07860 523 312
e: info@kandncatering.com
w: www.kandncatering.com

Luxury Shropshire Events
INNAGE LANE, BRIDGNORTH, SHROPSHIRE
WV16 4HJ....................................7958516941
e: info@luxuryshropshireevents.co.uk
w: www.luxuryshropshireevents.co.uk/

Marmalade Hospitality
HAM MANOR GOLF CLUB, WEST DRIVE, ANGMERING
West Sussex Bn16 4JE 0844 414 5516
e: marmaladehospitality@gmail.com
w: www.marmaladehospitality.com

Mecco
UNIT 3 , I.O.CENTRE , JUGGLERS CLOSE , BANBURY
Oxfordshire OX16 3TA...........................01295 254556
e: info@mecco.co.uk
w: www.mecco.co.uk

MSL Global
BUILDING 91, SEME, BUDDS LANE, BORDON
Hampshire GU35 0JE...........................01420 471000
w: www.mslglobal.com

Red Herring Catering Company
SETLEY BARN, SETLEY, BROCKENHURST
Hampshire SO42 7UF...........................01590 622222
e: info@redherringevents.com
w: www.redherringevents.com

Snakatak
THE HOLLIES, 51 WESTBOURNE ROAD, BROOMHILL, SHEFFIELD
South Yorkshire S10 2QT 0114 268 0860
e: lisa@snakatak.freeserve.co.uk
w: www.snakatakcatering.com

Sweet Basil Experience
5 LINGFIELD CLOSE, OLD BASING, BASINGSTOKE
Hampshire RG24 7ED 01256 811 560
e: jo@sweetbasil.co.uk
w: www.sweetbasil.co.uk

The Happy Buffet Co.
19 VICARAGE LANE, UPPER HALE, FARNHAM
Surrey GU9 0PF 01252 723875
e: jon@thehappybuffet.co.uk
w: www.thehappybuffet.co.uk

Vip Location Catering
PO BOX 16290, GLASGOW
Glasgow G13 9BT .... 0141 950 2716 // 07976 458 662
e: info@vip-locationcatering.co.uk
w: www.vip-locationcatering.co.uk

Whole Hog
....01305 813232
e: mark@thewholehog.ltd.uk
w: www.thewholehog.ltd.uk

WM Event Design
19 ST JAMES'S DRIVE, WANDSWORTH COMMON, LONDON
Greater London SW17 7RN 020 3837 4926
e: info@williammoyse.com
w: www.wmeventdesign.com

Location Research / Management

1st Option
64 UPPER WALKWAY, CAMDEN LOCK, LONDON
Greater London NW1 8AF..0207 28 42345
e: mail@1st-option.com
w: www.1st-option.com

Amazing Space
82 BERWICK STREET, LONDON
Greater London W1F 8TP 020 7251 6661
e: info@amazingspace.co.uk
w: www.amazingspace.co.uk

APS - Athens Production Services
73, KERKYRAS STR, ATHENS, GREECE
11362............................. +30 2106230368 // +30 6937312218
e: info@athensps.com
w: www.athensps.com

Blackstone Film Company
C/ LEVANTE N.16, POL. IND. PARQUE DE LA REINA, 5 MIN TO INT.
AIRPORT TFS, ARONA, S/C DE TENERIFE
38632... +34 922 739 916
e: service@blackstonefilm.com
w: www.blackstonefilm.com

Cindy Thomson - Location Manager
GLENLOCKHART HOUSE, 6 THE STEILS, EDINBURGH
Edinburgh Eh10 5XD..0131 446 0444
e: cindy@extraveg.com
w: www.extraveg.com

Cvent
131-151 GREAT TITCHFIELD STREET, LONDON
Greater London W1W 5BB 0808 234 4540
e: sales@cvent.com
w: www.cvent.com/uk

Elizabeth Marsh Floral Design
P35-42, THE FLOWER MARKET , NEW COVENT GARDEN MARKET,
VAUXHALL, LONDON
SW8 5NA...2077388506
e: admin@elizabethmarsh.co.uk
w: emfd.co.uk/home.aspx?option=1

eStage Production Ltd
71-75 SHELTON STREET, COVENT GARDEN, LONDON
WC2H 9JQ 2071128903
e: chat@estage.net
w: https://production.estage.net

Extra Veg Broadcast Crews Scotland
GLENLOCKHART HOUSE, 6 THE STEILS, EDINBURGH
EH10 5XD 0131 446 0444
e: cindy@extraveg.com
w: www.extraveg.com

Il Bottaccio
4 MANDEVILLE PLACE,, MAYFAIR, LONDON
Greater London SW1U 2BG 020 72359522
e: events@bottaccio.co.uk
w: www.bottaccio.co.uk

Lavish Locations
THE DYE HOUSE, 33 NUTBROOK STREE, LONDON
Greater London SE15 4JU 03337 007 007
e: info@lavishlocations.com
w: www.lavishlocations.com

Location House
VICTORIA HOUSE, BLOOMSBURY SQUARE, LONDON
Greater London WC1B 4DA 020 7269 9750
e: info@locationhouse.co.uk
w: www.locationhouse.co.uk

Location Partnership
82 BERWICK STREET, SOHO, LONDON
Greater London W1F 8TP 020 7734 0456
e: info@locationpartnership.com
w: www.locationpartnership.com

Professional Venue Solutions Ltd
1 CLIFTON COURT, CORNER HALL, HEMEL HEMPSTEAD
Hertfordshire HP3 9XY 01442 835700
e: info@pro-ven.com
w: www.pro-ven.com

TPA Portable Roadways Ltd
DUKERIES MILL, CLAYLANDS AVENUE, WORKSOP
Nottinghamshire S81 7DJ 0870 240 2381
e: enquiries@tpa-ltd.co.uk
w: www.tpa-ltd.co.uk

UK Locations
COMMERCIAL HOUSE, 57 GREAT GEORGE STREET, LEEDS
West Yorkshire LS1 3AJ 0113 269 1596
e: info@uklocations.co.uk
w: www.uklocations.co.uk

WM Event Design
19 ST JAMES'S DRIVE, WANDSWORTH COMMON, LONDON
Greater London SW17 7RN 020 3837 4926
e: info@williammoyse.com
w: www.wmeventdesign.com

L

Logistical Support

Ant Logistics
SUITE 1, ONE HIGH STREET, COLESHILL
West Midlands B46 1AY 01676 7546 4671
e: info@antlogistics.co.uk
w: www.antlogistics.co.uk

Applehouse Travel
UNIVERSAL HOUSE, 20-22 HIGH ST, IVER
Buckinghamshire SL0 9NG 0844 855 8140
w: www.applehousetravel.co.uk

Behind The Scenes Worldwide Logistics (Europe) Limited
BLOXHAM MILL BLOXHAM, BANBURY
Oxfordshire OX15 4FF .... +44 (0) 845 834 0009
e: peter@btsfreight.co.uk
w: www.btsfreight.com

Black and White Live
....0208 422 0042
e: info@blackandwhitelive.com
w: www.blackandwhitelive.com

Brian Yeardley Continental Ltd
STRAND HOUSE, WAKEFIELD ROAD, FEATHERSTONE
West Yorkshire WF7 5BP 01977 708484
e: glenn.savage@brianyeardley.com
w: www.brianyeardley.com

CEI Exhibitions
STONEBRIDGE HOUSE, 28-32 BRIDGE STREET, LEATHERHEAD
Surrey KT22 8BZ .... +44 (0) 1372 869849
e: darryl@ceiexhibitions.co.uk
w: www.ceiexhibitions.co.uk

Channel 16
TOWER BRIDGE BUSINESS COMPLEX, LONDON
Greater London S16 4DG ....07836 693833 / 07595 893020
e: forshow@channel-16.co.uk
w: www.channel-16.co.uk

Clipper Logistics Group
GELDERD ROAD, LEEDS
West Yorkshire LS12 6LT......................................0113 204 2050
w: www.clippergroup.co.uk

Coach Logistics
Herefordshire 078 7089 8905
e: events@coachlogistics.com
w: www.coachlogistics.com

Commbus.com Ltd
BLYTHE ROAD,, COLESHILL, BIRMINGHAM
West Midlands B46 2AF...01675 463555
e: sales@commbus.com
w: www.commbus.com

CS Bull Ltd
PO BOX 872, CANTERBURY
Kent CT4 6WA...01227 831611
e: sales@csbull.ltd.uk
w: www.csbull.ltd.uk

Cvent
131-151 GREAT TITCHFIELD STREET, LONDON
Greater London W1W 5BB 0808 234 4540
e: sales@cvent.com
w: www.cvent.com/uk

ETL Logistics
THE LEGACY CENTRE , HANWORTH TRADING ESTATE, HAMPTON ROAD WEST , FELTHAM
 TW13 6DH 01932 887 711
e: info@etl-logistics.com
w: www.etl-logistics.com/

F1 Logistics Ltd
BUILDING 500, SHEPPERTON STUDIOS, SHEPPERTON
Middlesex TW17 0QD..01932 580900
e: operations@f1logisticslhr.co.uk
w: www.f1logisticslhr.co.uk

Festaxi Ltd
21 DANDBY CLOSE, LITTLE PAXTON
Cambridgeshire PE19 6FA....................................01223 459836
e: info@festaxi.com
w: www.festaxi.com

Fly By Nite Conferences Ltd
THE FBN COMPLEX, SHAWBANK ROAD, LAKESIDE , REDDITCH
Worcestershire B98 8YN 01527 520 720
e: enquiries@flybynite.co.uk
w: www.flybynite.co.uk

Get Scheduled Ltd
1 LONDON STREET, READING
Berkshire RG1 4QW 084 5299 3459
e: sales@getscheduled.co.uk
w: www.getscheduled.co.uk

Global Infusion Group
GLOBAL INFUSION COURT, NASHLEIGH HILL, CHESHAM
Buckinghamshire HP5 3HE 01494 790700
e: hello@globalinfusiongroup.com
w: www.globalinfusiongroup.com

Gorilla Marketing & Events Ltd
PAPER STOCK HOUSE, AMERSHAM ROAD, CHALFONT ST. GILES
Buckinghamshire HP8 4RU 01494 876 876
e: info@gorillauk.com
w: www.gorillauk.com

GPS Logistics
LAKESIDE INDUSTRIAL ESTATE, COLNBROOK BY PASS, COLNBROOK
Berkshire SL3 0EL 020 8150 3300
e: info@gpslogistics.co.uk
w: www.gpslogistics.co.uk

TRUCKINGBY

UK & EUROPEAN LIVE EVENT LOGISTICS

BRIAN YEARDLEY
www.brianyeardley.com

Satellite tracked Euro 6 environmentally friendly trucks of all sizes
Experienced UK and European client friendly tour drivers
On air low ride flat floor high security Mega 100 x m³ box trailers with ramps
FORS Transport for London registered - ISO 9001:2015 - SQAS assessed
Secure backline and set storage in central UK location
Deep sea container and air freight services available

+44 (0)1977 781884
glenn.savage@brianyeardley.com

bpii | A W A
R D S
2 0 1 6
N O M I N E E

BRIAN YEARDLEY
CONTINENTAL LTD
UK I EUROPEAN I GLOBAL LOGISTICS

CONCERTS • FESTIVALS • THEATRE • ROADSHOWS
EXHIBITIONS • CORPORATE EVENTS

KB Event Ltd
PLYMOUTH AVENUE, BROOKHILL INDUSTRIAL ESTATE, PINXTON
Nottinghamshire NG16 6NS 01773 811136
e: info@kbevent.com
w: www.kbevent.com

Lavish Locations
THE DYE HOUSE, 33 NUTBROOK STREE, LONDON
Greater London SE15 4JU......................................03337 007 007
e: info@lavishlocations.com
w: www.lavishlocations.com

Logistics Un Ltd
55 MAIN STREET, LONG COMPTON
Warwickshire CV36 5JS..0845 094 9944
e: contactus@logistics-un.ltd.uk
w: www.logistics-un.ltd.uk

London Close Protection
....08456 521526 / 07879 825 560
e: info@londoncloseprotection.com
w: www.londoncloseprotection.com

M L Environmental Services Ltd
HOLMES WAY, BOSTON ROAD INDUSTRIAL ESTATE,
HORNCASTLE, LINCS
LN9 6JW..1507524040
e: mlenvironmental@aol.com
w: www.mlenvironmentalservices.webs.

Man And Van 2 Go
145-157 ST JOHN STREET, LONDON
Greater London EC1V 4PW.........0800 612 2731 / 0203 372 5001
e: info@manandvan2go.co.uk
w: www.manandvan2go.co.uk

Matco Piano Transport
465 HORNSEY ROAD, LONDON
N19 4DR..020 7281 9555
e: piano@matcomoves.com
w: www.matcomoves.com

North London Piano Transport 2 Ltd
176 MILLICENT GROVE, LONDON
Greater London N13 6HS .... 07711872434 // 020 3441 9463
e: thenorthpiano@googlemail.com
w: www.pianomoveteam.co.uk

Ooosh! Tours Ltd
COMPASS HOUSE, 7 EAST STREET, PORTSLADE, BRIGHTON
BN41 1DL....................................01273 911382 / 07719 568409
e: jon@oooshtours.co.uk
w: www.oooshtours.co.uk

Panther Warehousing Plc
LODGE FARM INDUSTRIAL ESTATE,, NORTHAMPTON
Northamptonshire NN5 7US ....01604 215000 / 01788 823 656
w: www.panthergroup.co.uk

Quatreus
5 & 6 EASTLANDS INDUSTRIAL ESTATE , KING GEORGES AVENUE,
LEISTON
Suffolk IP16 4LL 07971 350100
e: justine.samouelle@quatreus.com
w: www.quatreus.com/

Sherpa
12 THE TALINA CENTRE, BAGLEY'S LANE FULHAM, LONDON
SW6 2BW 0207 610 8620
e: info@eventsherpa.co.uk
w: www.eventsherpa.co.uk

Star Movement Ltd
UNIT 23 LITTLETON HOUSE, LITTLETON ROAD, ASHFORD
Middlesex TW15 1UU................................ +44 (0)1784 558262
e: info@starmovement.co.uk
w: www.starmovement.co.uk

Stardes Ltd
ASHES BUILDINGS, OLD LANE, HALFWAY, SHEFFIELD
South Yorkshire S20 3GZ 0114 251 0051
w: www.stardes.co.uk

Survey Operations
SMITH STREET, WELBOURNE, SKELMERSDALE
Lancashire WN8 8LN 01695 725662
e: mail@survops.co.uk
w: www.survops.co.uk

SXS Events
....0870 080 2342
e: hello@sxsevents.co.uk
w: www.sxsevents.co.uk

Travel Counsellors Ltd
TRAVEL HOUSE, 43 CHURCHGATE, BOLTON
Lancashire BL1 1TH....................01773 318910 / 07973 306280
e: louise.cutting@travelcounsellors.com
w: www.tctravelmanagement.co.uk/loui

TravelandMore Ltd
ACORN BUSINESS CENTRE, 18 SKATERS WAY, WERRINGTON,
PETEBOROUGH
PE4 6NB 0800 6800252
e: info@travelandmore.co.uk
w: www.travelandmore.co.uk

Trucks At Work
18 BIS RUE , EMILE DUCLAUX, SURESNES
92150...09 72 44 37 07
e: exploitation@trucksatwork.fr
w: www.trucksatwork.fr

Velvet Twenty
....020 8675 4870
e: enquiries@velvettwenty.co.uk
w: www.velvettwenty.co.uk

Versatile Venues Ltd
WIRELESS HOUSE, WIRELESS HILL, SOUTH LUFFENHAM
Rutland LE15 8NF......................08000 147 338 / 01780 720 217
e: info@versatilevenues.co.uk
w: www.versatilevenues.co.uk

Visual Response Ltd
WILD RENTS STUDIO, 20-30 WILDS RENTS, LONDON
Greater London SE1 4QG 020 7378 7731
w: www.visualresponse.com

Wellpleased Events
11 BLAYDS YARD, LEEDS
West Yorkshire LS1 4AD.......................................0113 244 2720
e: info@wellpleased.co.uk
w: www.wellpleased.co.uk

WJM Transport
STIRLING WAY INDUSTRIAL ESTATE, STIRLING WAY, CROYDON
Surrey CR0 4XN 07889 515161
e: info@wjmtransport.co.uk
w: www.wjmtransport.co.uk

WM Event Design
19 ST JAMES'S DRIVE, WANDSWORTH COMMON, LONDON
Greater London SW17 7RN 020 3837 4926
e: info@williammoyse.com
w: www.wmeventdesign.com

Worldwide Exhibition Specialists Ltd
30 PANTON STREET, CAMBRIDGE
Cambridgeshire CB2 1HP.....................................020 8508 2224
e: info@wes-group.com
w: www.wes-group.com

Luxury Vehicles

Bradshaw Electric Vehicles
NEW LN, PETERBOROUGH
Cambridgeshire PE8 6LW.......................................1781 782 621
e: sarahg@bradshawelectricvehicles.co.uk
w: www.bradshawelectricvehicles.co.u

MNO

Marketing Consultants / Research

2112 Marketing Ltd
SHAW HOUSE, 17 NEWLANDS, NASEBY
Northamptonshire NN6 6DE 01604 740955
e: info@2112marketing.com
w: www.2112marketing.com

Abucon PR
3-4 BRADFIELD HALL, BRADFIELD COMBUST, BURY ST EDMUNDS
Suffolk IP30 0LU..020 7834 1066
e: info@abucon.co.uk
w: www.abucon.co.uk

Added Insight
BUSWELLS COURT, WATFORD ROAD, CRICK
Northamptonshire NN6 7TT 01788 823 500
e: nanda@addedinsight.co.uk
w: www.addedinsight.co.uk

Arts Media Contacts
PIPE PASSAGE, 151B HIGH STREET, LEWES
BN7 1XU...01273 488996
e: e. subs@artsmediacontacts.co.uk
w: www.artsmediacontacts.co.uk

Barrett Dixon Bell Ltd
CRAIG COURT, 25 HALE ROAD, ALTRINCHAM
Cheshire WA14 2EY 0161 925 4700
e: ideasthatconnect@bdb.co.uk
w: www.bdb.co.uk

Birmingham Security Guards Company
69 WESTGREEN ROAD, LONDON
Greater London N15 5DA .... 020 8432 2236 / 07896 357587
e: info@armstrongsecurity.co.uk
w: www.armstrongsecurity.co.uk

Blackmore Ltd
LONGMEAD, SHAFTESBURY
Dorset SP7 8PX 01747 853034
e: sales@blackmore.co.uk
w: www.blackmore.co.uk

British Performing Arts Yearbook
RHINEGOLD HOUSE, 20 RUGBY ST, LONDON
Greater London WC2N 3QZ 020 7333 1733
e: enquiries@rhingold.co.uk
w: www.rhingold.co.uk

C Force Communications Ltd
GAINSBOROUGH HOUSE, CHURCH ROAD, HEDDINGTON
Wiltshire SN11 0PJ...01672 861060
e: info@cforce.co.uk
w: www.cforce.co.uk

Celebrity Speakers Ltd
CELEBRITY SPEAKERS LTD, BURNHAM
Buckinghamshire SL1 7JT 01628 601 400
e: celebrityspeakersuk@gmail.com
w: www.speakers.co.uk/

Charlie Apple
8 CEDAR WALK, KENLEY
Surrey CR8 5JL........................ 020 8668 6921 // 07973 987779
e: info@charlieapple.com
w: www.charlieapple.co.uk

Comtec Presentations Ltd
COMMUNICATIONS HOUSE, 126-146 FAIRFIELD ROAD,
DROYLSDEN, MANCHESTER
M43 6AT..0161 370 7772
e: info@comtec-presentations.com
w: www.comtec-presentations.com

Cult Events
UNIT 3, AUTUMN YARD, AUTUMN STREET, LONDON
Greater London E3 2TT .... 020 8983 5459 - 07540782176
e: info@culte.co.uk
w: www.culte.co.uk

Cvent
131-151 GREAT TITCHFIELD STREET, LONDON
Greater London W1W 5BB 0808 234 4540
e: sales@cvent.com
w: www.cvent.com/uk

CWA
ASHLEIGH ROAD, GLENFIELD, LEICESTER
Leicestershire LE3 8DA..0116 232 7400
e: hello@cwa.co.uk
w: www.cwa.co.uk

DRSM
27 OLD GLOUCESTER STREET, LONDON
Greater London WC1N 3AX 08701 990100
e: mail@drsmpr.com
w: www.drsmpr.com

Easy Publicity
200 LONDON ROAD, HADLEIGH, BENFLEET
Essex SS7 2PD 01702 427 100
e: enquiries@entertainers.co.uk
w: www.easypublicity.co.uk

Elastic Productions Ltd
103 KINGS CROSS ROAD, LONDON
Greater London WC1X 9LP...................................020 7639 5556
e: daniel@getelastic.co.uk
w: www.getelastic.co.uk

eXecutional Ltd
1200 CENTURY WAY, THORPE PARK BUSINESS PARK,
COLTON, LEEDS
West Yorkshire LS15 8ZA 0330 330 96 29
e: hello@executional.co.uk
w: www.executional.co.uk

Expandys
99 WHITE LION STREET, LONDON
Greater London N1 9PF...0207 723 8327
e: uk@expandys.com
w: www.expandys.com

M
N
O

Fletchers The Creative Service Ltd
CHILTON HOUSE, DEPPERS BRIDGE, SOUTHAM
Warwickshire CV47 2SY...01926 614835
e: happy@fletchers.uk.com
w: www.fletchers.uk.com

Garrett Axford Ltd
BASEPOINT CENTRE, LITTLE HIGH STREET, SHOREHAM BY SEA
West Sussex BN43 5EG 01903 854900
e: mail@garrett-axford.co.uk
w: www.garrett-axford.co.uk

Green 4 Solutions
16-17 MIDLAND COURT, CENTRAL PARK, LUTTERWORTH
Leicestershire LE17 4PN.......................................0845 508 8149
e: beth@green4solutions.com
w: www.green4solutions.com

Greenlight Digital
THE VARNISH WORKS, 3 BRAVINGTONS WALK, LONDON
Greater London N1 9AJ...020 7253 7000
e: info@greenlightdigital.com
w: www.greenlightdigital.com

HavasPeople
6 BRISET STREET, LONDON
Greater London EC1M 5NR 020 7022 4000
w: www.havaspeople.com

Highjam
HIGHJAM MARKETING, 219 LONG LANE, LONDON
Greater London SE1 4PR.......................................020 7407 7464
e: hello@highjam.co.uk
w: www.highjam.co.uk

Hodgson Events
KEVIS HOUSE, LOMBARD STREET, PETWORTH
West Sussex GU28 0AG 01798 215 007
e: mail@hodgsonevents.com
w: www.hodgsonevents.com

Hps Group
ATLAS HOUSE, THIRD AVENUE, GLOBE PARK, MARLOW
Buckinghamshire SL7 1EY 01628 894700
e: hello@hpsgroup.co.uk
w: www.hpsgroup.co.uk

Imagine Events Ltd
37A HART STREET, HENLEY ON THAMES
Oxfordshire RG9 2AR 01491 573311
e: hello@imagine-events.com
w: www.imagine-events.com

Into The Blue
ONE THE PARADE, COWES
Isle of Wight PO31 7QJ 01983 247286
e: hello@intotheblue.biz
w: www.intotheblue.biz

Jack Morton Worldwide
16-18 ACTON PARK ESTATE, STANLEY GARDENS, LONDON
Greater London W3 7QE.......................................020 8735 2000
e: victoria_yates@jackmorton.co.uk
w: www.jackmorton.com

Jumping Jack
GROUND FLOOR, 8 WESTBURY PARK, LONDON
BS6 7JB 0117 973 9873
e: jrugg@jumpingjackmarketing.com
w: www.jumpingjackmarketing.com

Kapow! Consulting
LEXHAM MEWS, LONDON
W8 6JW 020 7193 6885
w: www.kapowconsulting.co.uk

Lam Communications
52 ELMWOOD ROAD, CHISWICK, LONDON
Greater London W4 3DZ.......................................020 8995 9652
e: larry@lamcomms.com
w: www.lamcomms.com

Luxton Cultural Associates
PO BOX 2772, BRIGHTON
East Sussex BN1 6FW...01273 330464
e: peter@luxtoncultural.net
w: www.luxtoncultural.net

Mark Loraine Photography
9 GRANGE VIEW, BALBY, DONCASTER
DN4 0XL ....07789 552900 // 01302 857030 // 07789 55
e: mark@mark-loraine.com
w: www.mark-loraine.com

Mezzo
SYCAMORE HOUSE, MAIN STREET, HUNGARTON
Leicestershire LE7 9JR 0116 259 5367
e: helenwillson@mezzo-consultancy.co.uk
w: www.mezzo-consultancy.co.uk

Mobile Promotions
NEW BROOK, TITCHMARSH, THRAPSTON
Northamptonshire NN14 3DG...............................01832 733460
e: contact@mobilepromotions.com
w: www.mobilepromotions.com

Mobius Media
SUITE 2, SAXON HOUSE,, ANNIE REED ROAD, BEVERLEY
HU17 0LF 014 8224 0260
e: hello@mobiusmedia.co.uk
w: www.mobiusmedia.co.uk

One2Create
THE FLINT BARN ST CLAIRS FARM, WICKHAM ROAD, DROXFORD
Hampshire SO32 3PW...0844 8040 796
e: INFO@ONE2CREATE.CO.UK
w: www.one2create.co.uk

M N O

Online Ventures Group
51 LEVER STREET, THE HIVE, CORE B, 4TH FLOOR, MANCHESTER
Greater Manchester M1 1FN....................................0844 8717291
e: hello@onlineventuresgroup.co.uk
w: www.onlineventuresgroup.co.uk

Optimus Events Ltd
CEM GROUP , SMUGGLERS WAY, HURN LANE , ASHLEY
Dorset BH24 2AG..01425 485040
e: charlotte@cemgroup.com
w: www.cemgroup.com

Photo Snap Marketing
128 CANNON WORKSHOPS, LONDON
Greater London E14 4AS...020 7096 3966
e: info@photosnapmarketing.com
w: www.photosnapmarketing.com

Plaster Creative Communications
LOFT 6, TABACCO FACTORY, RALEIGH ROAD, BRISTOL
Bristol BS3 1TF...0117 953 0320
e: hello@weareplaster.com
w: www.weareplaster.com

Pro-ex Group Ltd
HAMILTON HOUSE, RACKERY LANE, LLAY, WREXHAM
 LL12 0PB...01978 855622
e: enquiries@pro-ex.co.uk
w: www.pro-ex.co.uk

Profound Media & Management Ltd
PO BOX 4222, COVENTRY
West Midlands CV4 0BH...024 76677712
w: www.profoundmedia.co.uk

Right Solution Ltd
DEVONSHIRE BUSINESS CENTRE, 111 MARLOWES,
HEMEL HEMPSTEAD
Hertfordshire HP1 1BB...01442 450422
e: info@rightsolution.co.uk
w: www.rightsolution.co.uk

Salivate
ROCKLEY HOUSE, MEADWAY, CAMBERLEY
Surrey GU16 8TQ..01276 504629
e: info@slv8.com
w: www.slv8.com

Saltwater Communications
22 STRAND STREET, POOLE
Dorset BH15 1SB..01202 669244
e: enquiries@saltwatercoms.com
w: www.saltwatercoms.com

Sanver Sports Private Limited
126 - 127 UDYOG BHAVAN, SONAWALA ROAD, GOREGAON EAST,
MUMBAI, INDIA
 400063... +91 22 42200422
e: sales@sanversports.com
w: www.sanversports.com

Sigma Marketing & Advertising Ltd
64 CREMYLL STREET, STONEHOUSE, PLYMOUTH
Devon PL1 3RE...01752 668813
e: admin@sigma-marketing.co.uk
w: www.sigma-marketing.co.uk

Simpson Mahoney Parrock Ltd
48 CHARLOTTE STREET, LONDON
Greater London W1T 2NS.......................... +44 (0)203 178 3955
e: sayhello@smp.uk.com
w: www.smp.uk.com

STR Music Marketing & Management
296 HUGHENDEN ROAD, HIGH WYCOMBE
Buckinghamshire HP13 5PE................................01494 526 052
e: strmmm@hotmail.co.uk
w: www.strmusicmarketing.co.uk

TA2 Creative Services
236 MERTON ROAD, WIMBLEDON, LONDON
Greater London SW19 1EQ....................................020 8540 4030
e: chris@ta2.co.uk
w: www.ta2.co.uk

That Girl Communications Ltd
GOOSEGATE HOUSE, HIGH STREET, SWATON, SLEAFORD
 NG34 0JP .... 084 4884 5119 / 07816 765 545
e: info@thatgirlcomms.co.uk
w: www.thatgirlcomms.co.uk

The Organisers Ltd
86 REDHILL DRIVE, EDGWARE
Greater London HA8 5JN 020 8933 4821
e: info@theorganisers.co.uk
w: www.theorganisers.co.uk

ThinkersLive
15-19 BAKERS ROW, LONDON
Greater London EC1R 3DG 020 3967 5716
w: www.thinkerslive.com

Tiga Marketing
PO BOX 183, LEEDS
West Yorkshire LS14 3WA 0113 289 6961
e: info@tigamarketing.co.uk
w: www.tigamarketing.co.uk

Tourism Research & Marketing
WOODSIDE TERRACE, CWM-BACH, GLASBURY
Herefordshire HR3 5LS 01497 842 941
e: bill@tram-research.com
w: www.tram-research.com

Tribe Marketing
UNIT 4, THE WOOL HOUSE, 74 BACK CHURCH LANE, LONDON
Greater London E1 1LX 020 7702 3600
e: info@tribemarketing.co.uk
w: www.tribemarketing.co.uk

M
N
O

Versatile Venues Ltd
WIRELESS HOUSE, WIRELESS HILL, SOUTH LUFFENHAM
Rutland LE15 8NF .... 08000 147 338 / 01780 720 217
e: info@versatilevenues.co.uk
w: www.versatilevenues.co.uk

Vital Marketing Ltd
14A CLARENDON AVENUE, LEAMINGTON SPA
Warwickshire CV32 5PZ...01926 338811
e: hello@thevitalagency.co.uk
w: www.thevitalagency.co.uk

WRG Live
MERCHANTS WAREHOUSE, 21 CASTLE STREET, MANCHESTER
Greater Manchester M3 4LZ .... 084 5313 0000 / 07887 7674000
e: andrew.savill@wrglive.com
w: www.wrglive.com

Wyndham-Leigh Ltd
THE COURTYARD, BODYMOOR GREEN FARM, COVENTRY ROAD,
NR. KINGSBURY
Warwickshire B78 2DZ 01827 875700
e: justin.fisher@wlpr.co.uk / sean.lees@wlpr.co.uk
w: www.wyndham-leigh.co.uk

Marquees

A&J Big Top Promotions
AMERICA FARM COTTAGE, OXNEY ROAD, PETERBOROUGH
Cambridgeshire PE1 5YR 1733 222 999
e: sales@ajbigtophire.com
w: www.ajbigtophire.com

Kayam Theatre & Concert Structures
ATTICBEST LTD T/A KAYAM THEATRE & CONCERT STRUCTURES,
THE LAURELS, FRONT STREET, WORSTEAD
Norfolk NR29 9RW 01692 536 025
e: richard@kayam.com
w: kayam.co.uk

Marquees / Temporary Structures

24 Carrot Promotions
Y GAER, CWMCOU, NEWCASTLE EMLYN
Carmathenshire SA38 9PR.......... 01239 711854 / 07989 520637
e: info@24carrotpromotions.co.uk
w: www.24carrotpromotions.co.uk

A & B Marquees
4 DUDLEY TERRACE, MILL ROD, LISS
Hampshire GU33 7BE 07747 806794
e: info@abmarquees.co.uk
w: www.abmarquees.co.uk

A & J Big Top Hire
OXNEY ROAD, PETERBOROUGH
Cambridgeshire PE15YR 01733 222999
e: sales@ajbigtophire.com
w: www.ajbigtophire.com

A-V Custom Image
141 BELVOIR ROAD, COALVILLE
Leicestershire LE67 3PJ 07836 233319
e: enquiries@a-vcustomimage.com
w: www.a-vcustomimage.com

A&A Bell Marquee Hire
HUTSONS YARD, SPITAL ROAD, MALDON, CHELMSFORD
Essex CM9 6EB...07949 907089
e: enquiry@aabellmarqueehire.co.uk
w: www.aabellmarqueehire.co.uk

A&e Marquees Ltd
46 STRETTEN AVE, CAMBRIDGE
Cambridgeshire CB4 3EP 01223 560293
e: info@aandemarquees.co.uk
w: www.aandemarquees.co.uk

Abbas Marquees
WELLHAYES FARM, LOWER WESTHOLME, PILTON
Somerset BA4 4HW 01748 90909
e: enquiry@abbasmarquees.co.uk
w: www.abbasmarquees.co.uk

Abbey Marquees Ltd
TAI MARIAN, MARIAN CWM, DYSERTH
Denbighshire LL18 6HU 01352 720634
e: enquiries@abbeytents.co.uk
w: www.abbeytents.co.uk

ABC Marquees
1 HAWTHORN WAY, PORTSLADE, BRIGHTON & HOVE
East Sussex BN41 2HR 01273 891511
e: info@abcmarquees.co.uk
w: www.abcmarquees.co.uk

Abinger Marquee Hire
LADYMEAD, GUILDFORD
Surrey GU1 1DL 01483 536270
w: www.abingermarquees.co.uk

Acacia Marquees
3 ALBERT TERRACE, HEOL-Y-DWR, HAY-ON-WYE
Herefordshire HR3 5AS .... 01497 820 882 / 07795 958 421
e: mail@acacia-marquees.co.uk
w: www.acacia-marquees.co.uk

Academy Marquees Ltd
FAIROAKS AIRPORT, WOKING
Surrey GU24 8HX...01276 858 111
e: info@academy-marquees.co.uk
w: www.academy-marquees.co.uk

Air-set Ltd
WESTON COLLEY, MICHELDEVER, WINCHESTER, BASINGSTOKE
Hampshire SO21 3AF...01962 774445
e: david@air-set.co.uk
w: www.air-set.co.uk

M N O

Albion Woods Show Tents
CANNARDS FARM, SHEPTON MALLET
Somerset BA4 4LY 01749 346002
e: tents@albionwoods.co.uk
w: www.albionwoods.co.uk

Allsite Structure Rentals
.... +61 408 402 716
e: info@apg-au.com
w: www.allsitestructures.com

Allspan (UK) Ltd
14-16 HEVER ROAD, WEST KINGSDOWN
Kent TN15 6HB 01474 850 550
e: info@allspan.co.uk
w: www.allspan.co.uk

Amazing Tent Company Ltd
2 BLACKNEST COTTAGE, OWLPEN, DURSLEY
Gloucestershire GL11 5BZ 01453 861 131
e: enquiries@amazingtent.co.uk
w: www.amazingtent.co.uk

AMG Marquees
UNIT 9 HEATH FARM, BALSHAM ROAD, FULBOURN
Cambridgeshire CB21 5DA....................................01223 882233
e: enquiries@amgmarquees.co.uk
w: www.amgmarquees.co.uk

Anchor Bloc Ltd
LEA BECK FARM, TRESWELL, RETFORD
Nottinghamshire DN22 0EQ 0800 122 3304
e: sales@anchorbloc.co.uk
w: www.anchor-block.com

Aquila Shelters Ltd
CLAREMONT HOUSE, ST GEORGES ROAD, BOLTON
Greater Manchester BL1 2BY 01204 522424
e: sales@aquila-shelters.co.uk
w: www.aquila-shelters.co.uk

Arabian Tent Company
RYE FARM, HOLLANDS LANE, HENFIELD
West Sussex BN5 9QY 0800 88 15 229
e: info@arabiantents.com
w: www.arabiantents.com

Arena Event Hire
BROADACRES, CHALKS GREEN, HIGH EASTER ROAD, LEADEN
RODING, DUNMOW
Essex CM6 1QG 0800 32 88 638
e: arena01@btconnect.com
w: www.arenaeventhire.com

Arena Seating
LAMBOURN WOODLANDS, HUNGERFORD
Berkshire RG17 7TQ 01488 674800
e: info@arenaseating.com
w: www.arenagroup.com

Arena Structures (Head Office)
NEEDINGWORTH ROAD, ST IVES, HUNTINGDON
Cambridgeshire PE27 3ND....................................01480 468888
e: info@arenastructures.com
w: www.arenastructures.com

Arena UK Ltd
ALLINGTON LANE, ALLINGTON, GRANTHAM
Lincolnshire NG32 2EF..01476 591 569
e: office@arenauk.org
w: www.arenauk.com

Aries Leisure
2 - 7 WEBBER ROAD, KNOWSLEY INDUSTRIAL ESTATE,
LIVERPOOL Merseyside L33 7SW..........................0151 545 0599
e: info@ariesleisure.co.uk
w: www.ariesleisure.co.uk

Ascot Structures
ALUTECH HOUSE, GREEN LANE, HEYTHROP
Oxfordshire OX7 5TU...01608 683999
e: office@ascotstructures.co.uk
w: www.ascotstructures.co.uk

Asia Event Overlay
5TH FLOOR GRAHA ANUGRAH BUILDING, JL. TELUK BETUNG
NO.42, JAKARTA, INDONESIA 10230 .... +6221 314 0287
e: contact@asia-event.com
w: www.asia-event.com

ASJ Luxury Marquees
RIVERDALE FARM, STANTON HILL, STANTON-BY-BRIDGE, DERBY
Derbyshire DE73 7NF.................. 01332 272332 / 07966 261699
e: enquiries@asjluxurymarquees.co.uk
w: www.asjluxurymarquees.co.uk

Audio Source Ltd
31 MONGLEATH AVENUE, FALMOUTH
Cornwall TR11 4PP ....
.... 07971 607172 / 07867 525016 / 01326 3115
e: hire@audio-source.co.uk
w: www.audio-source.co.uk

Austen Lewis Ltd
UNIT DG, CHELWORTH PARK, CRICKLADE, SWINDON
Wiltshire SN6 6HE...01793 750599
e: info@austen-lewis.co.uk
w: www.austen-lewis.co.uk

Baconinflate Ltd
4 OSYTH PARK, BRACKMILLS INDUSTRIAL ESTATE,
NORTHAMPTON
Northamptonshire NN4 7DY 01604 766500
e: sales@baconinflate.co.uk
w: www.baconinflate.co.uk

Baillies Marquees Ltd
1 BARLANARK AVENUE, SPRINGBOIG, GLASGOW
Glasgow G32 0JR 0141 7740830
e: joe@bailliesmarquees.co.uk
w: www.bailliesmarquees.co.uk

**M
N
O**

Hirers of:
**Big tops from 1,000 to 17,000 capacity.
From traditional to the latest in tensile design.
Non slip wooden flooring and tiered seating.**

We cater for private functions • Ballet • Concerts • Conferences
Circus • Theatre • Music festivals • Religious festivals
Corporate entertainment • Fashion shows • Exhibitions etc

**Please visit our website and see the selection
of big tops we have available for hire**

www.ajbigtophire.com

Tel: +44 (0) 1733 222999 **Fax:** +44 (0) 1733 222997
Email: sales@ajbigtophire.com *or* john@ajbigtophire.com

Band International
SUNNYSIDE, FRESHWATER, ISLE OF WIGHT
Isle of Wight PO40 9RW 01983 755 858
e: enquiries@band.co.uk
w: www.band.co.uk

Base Structures Ltd
UNIT A, ST VINCENTS TRADING ESTATE, FEEDER ROAD, BRISTOL
Bristol BS2 0UY..0117 971 2229
e: sales@basestructures.com
w: www.basestructures.com

Beaumont Events Ltd
STAMFORD HOUSE, 57 LIDDON ROAD, BROMLEY
Kent BR1 2SR 0800 591619
e: tracey@beaumontmarquees.co.uk
w: www.beaumontmarquees.co.uk

Beautiful World Tents Ltd
THE GRAIN STORE, POUND FARM, POUND LANE, SHIPLEY
West Sussex RH13 8QB 01403 741299
e: enquiries@beautifulworldtents.co.uk
w: www.beautifulworldtents.co.uk

Bell Tent UK
UNIT 10 COLLEGE FIELDS, PRINCE GEORGES ROAD, COLLIERS
WOOD, LONDON
Greater London SW19 2PT....................................07830 355 993
e: info@belltent.co.uk
w: www.belltent.co.uk

Belle Tents
OWLS GATE, DAVIDSTOW, CAMELFORD
Cornwall PL32 9XY 01840 261 556
e: info@belletents.co.uk
w: www.belletents.com

Berry Marquees
UNITS 11 & 12 CROWTHORNE HOUSE, NINE MILE RIDE,
WOKINGHAM
Berkshire RG40 3GA 01784 471 410
e: sales@berrymarquees.com
w: www.berrymarquees.com

Best Intent Marquees
UNIT 4A, CHARLESFIELD INDUSTRIAL ESTATE, CHARLESFIELD
 TD6 0HH 0800 448 8949
e: info@bestintentmarquees.co.uk
w: www.bestintentmarquees.co.uk

Bigtopmania
SWALLOWS CROFT, CHAPMANS WELL, LAUNCESTON
Cornwall PL15 9SG..01409 211178
e: info@bigtopmania.co.uk
w: www.bigtopmania.co.uk

Boldscan Ltd
UNIT 4 TONEDALE BUSINESS PARK, WELLINGTON
Somerset TA21 0AW 01823 665849
e: sales@boldscan.co.uk
w: www.boldscan.co.uk

Budget Marquees
18 CLIFF HILL, GORLESTON, GREAT YARMOUTH
Norfolk NR31 6DQ .... 01493 300721 / 07909 517141
e: info@budgetmarquees.co.uk
w: www.budgetmarquees.co.uk

C6(n) Technology
UNIT 2 RADAR WAY, CHRISTCHURCH BUSINESS PARK,
CHRISTCHURCH
Dorset BH23 4FL 01425 271 903
e: Sales@c6n.co.uk
w: www.c6n.co.uk

Cameo Event Hire
UNIT 16, GARDNER INDUSTRIAL ESTATE, KENT HOUSE LANE, ,
BECKENHAM
Kent BR3 1QZ...020 8659 8000
w: www.cameoeventhire.co.uk

Carlinden Events Ltd
12 WORDSWORTH CLOSE, BISHOPS WALTHAM, SOUTHAMPTON
Hampshire SO32 1RT................. 01489 287187 / 07899 892566
e: info@carlinden.co.uk
w: www.carlinden.co.uk

Casablanca Hire
UNIT 1, KINGSBURY WORKS, KINGSBURY RD
Greater London NW9 8UP 020 7100 5492
e: heath@casablancahire.com
w: www.casablancahire.com

Cater Hire Ipswich
UNIT 1 DALES COURT BUSINESS CENTRE, DALES ROAD, IPSWICH
Suffolk IP1 4JR..01473 462 989
e: info@caterhireipswich.co.uk
w: www.hatfieldscatering.co.uk

CGSM Events
THE STABLES , HARDWAY HOUSE , BRUTON, SOMERSET
 BA10 0LR 1749813313
e: henry@cgsmevents.com
w: www.cgsmevents.com/

Charles Chipperfield Entertainments
BOGS COTTAGE, PATMORE HALL, ALBURY, WARE,
HERTFORDSHIRE
 SG11 2JU .... 07960 600345 // 07952 651133
e: info@charleschipperfieldentertainments.co.uk
w: www.charleschipperfieldentertainm

Chichester Canvas
SIDLESHAM COMMON, CHICHESTER
West Sussex PO20 7PY..01243 641164
w: www.chicanvas.co.uk

Churchill Marquees
63 NORWOOD AVENUE, SHIPLEY
West Yorkshire BD18 2AX .... 07758690427 / 07758690427
e: jerry@candsmarquees.co.uk
w: www.candsmarquees.co.uk

Classic Chambers
BRANSDALE COTTAGE, STILLINGTON ROAD, BRANDSBY
North Yorkshire YO61 4RS......................................01347 888262
e: info@classicchambers.co.uk
w: www.classicchambers.co.uk

Coopers Marquees
BOLTON LANE, WILBERFOSS, YORK
North Yorkshire YO41 5NX.....................................01759 380190
e: info@coopersmarquees.co.uk
w: www.marqueesuk.co.uk

Countess Marquees Ltd
77 LATCHMERE ROAD, KINGSTON UPON THAMES
Surrey KT2 5TS..020 8546 7373
e: info@countessmarquees.com
w: www.countessmarquees.com

County Marquees
26 HERONDALE CRESCENT, WOLLASTON, STOURBRIDGE
West Midlands DY8 3LH..01384 377749
e: countymarquees@hotmail.co.uk
w: www.marqueehirewestmidlands.com

CoverMarque Ltd
THE BOUNDARY, COXFORD DOWN, WINCHESTER
Hampshire SO21 3BD 01962 774421
e: nick.drew@covermarque.com
w: www.covermarque.com

Covers & Linings Ltd
UNIT 10 WOODSIDE ROAD, BOYATT WOOD INDUSTRIAL ESTATE,
EASTLEIGH
Hampshire SO50 4ET...02380 623020
e: Sales@eventinteriors.com
w: www.eventinteriors.com

Crackerjack Marquee Company
CHURCH FARM, SOUTHWOLD ROAD, BLYFORD, HALESWORTH
Suffolk IP19 9JZ 0845 9000 328
e: hello@crackerjackmarquees.co.uk
w: www.crackerjackmarquees.co.uk

Crystal Marquee Hire
BRAMBLE FARM, SHERE ROAD, WEST HORSLEY, LEATHERHEAD
Surrey KT24 6ER 01483 283228
e: info@crystalmarqueehire.co.uk
w: www.crystalmarqueehire.co.uk

Curlew
34 MILLFIELD GARDENS, NETHER POPPLETON, YORK
North Yorkshire YO26 6NZ.....................................01904 373402
e: admin@secondhand-websites.co.uk
w: www.curlew.co.uk

Custom Covers (1984) Ltd
QUAYSIDE ROAD, BITTERNE MANOR, SOUTHAMPTON
Hampshire SO18 1AD 023 8033 5744
e: sales@customcovers.co.uk
w: www.customcovers.co.uk

Danco Plc
THE PAVILION CENTRE, FROG LANE, COALPIT HEATH
Bristol BS36 2NW 01454 250 222
e: info@danco.co.uk
w: www.danco.co.uk

De Boer Structures (UK) Ltd
CASTLE PARK, BOUNDRY ROAD, BUCKINGHAM ROAD INDUSTRIAL
ESTATE, BRACKLEY
Nottinghamshire NN13 7ES...................................01280 846 500
e: sales.uk@deboer.com
w: www.deboer.com

Dragon Marquee & Events Limited
710 GOWER ROAD, UPPER KILLAY, SWANSEA
SA2 7HQ..01792 709477
e: enquiries@dragonevents.co.uk
w: www.dragonevents.co.uk

Dryspace Structures Ltd
BLACK LAMBS FARM, BUNKERS HILL ROAD
Kent TN15 7EY...... 01634 230034 / 01474 812353 / 07885 8890
e: info@dryspace.co.uk
w: www.dryspace.co.uk

East Anglia Leisure
UNIT 4, CIVIC INDUSTRIAL ESTATE, HOMEFIELD ROAD, HAVERHILL
Suffolk CB9 8QP 01440 714204
e: info@ealeisure.co.uk
w: www.ealeisure.co.uk

ES Global Solutions
UNIT G EAST COATE HOUSE, 1 - 3 COATE STREET, LONDON
Greater London E2 9AG...020 7055 7200
e: info@esglobalsolutions.com
w: www.esglobalsolutions.com

Event Equipment Hire
UNIT 2, SYKES STREET, CLECKHEATON
Yorkshire BD19 5HA..01422 200960
e: sales@eventequipmenthire.co.uk
w: www.eventequipmenthire.co.uk

Event Hire Wales
....07494 169599
e: info@eventhire.wales
w: www.eventhire.wales

Event Tents Global
223 ARDGLASS ROAD, DOWNPATRICK
BT30 7ED .... 02844 841 820 / 07872 501861
e: contact@eventtentsglobal.com
w: www.eventtentsglobal.com

Evolution Dome
17, HIGHLODE INDUSTRIAL ESTATE, , STOCKING FEN RD,
RAMSEY,, HUNTINGDON
Cambridgeshire PE26 2RB....................................01487 640640
e: info@evolutiondome.co.uk
w: www.evolutiondome.co.uk

M N O

Fabric Architecture Limited
UNIT B4, NEXUS, HURRICANE ROAD, GLOUCESTER BUSINESS
PARK, BROCKWROTH
Gloucestershire GL3 4AG 01452 612 800
e: info@fabricarchitecture.com
w: www.fabricarchitecture.com

Fews Marquees Ltd
DITCHFORD BANK ROAD, HANBURY, BROMSGROVE
Worcestershire B60 4HS 01527 821789
e: info@fewsmarquees.co.uk
w: www.fewsmarquees.co.uk

Field & Lawn Marquees Ltd
EAST MAINS INDUSTRIAL ESTATE, BROXBURN, EDINBURGH
Edinburgh EH52 5NN 01506 857938
e: edinburgh@fieldandlawn.com
w: www.fieldandlawn.com

Florida Marquees Ltd
THE OLD FORGE, BURY STREET, VALLEY ROAD, SHEFFIELD
South Yorkshire S8 9QQ 0800 731 1676
e: admin@floridamarquees.com
w: www.marqueehiresales.com

Four Seasons Marquees Ltd
KINGSLEY BARN, GANDERS BUSINESS PARK KINGSLEY, KINGSLEY,
BORDON
Hampshire GU35 9LU..01420 488477
e: sales@fourseasonsmarquees.co.uk
w: www.fourseasonsmarquees.co.uk

Freedomes
1 VISCOUNT WAY, WOODLEY, READING
Berkshire RG5 4DZ 020 3695 4246
e: info@freedomes.co.uk
w: www.freedomes.co.uk

Fresh Events UK
UNIT D WESLAKE INDUSTRIAL PARK, RYE HARBOUR ROAD, RYE
East Sussex TN31 7TE 07919 512 608
e: info@fresheventsuk.com
w: www.fresheventsuk.com

Funtastic Entertainment
57 FRIARS LANE, BARROW IN FURNESS, CUMBRIA
LA13 9NS .... 01229829242 / 07966691178
e: info@funtasticentertainment.co.uk
w: www.funtasticentertainment.co.uk

Gearhouse In2Structures
PO BOX 751391, GARDENVIEW, JOHANNESBURG
2047.. +27 (0) 112 163 000
e: jhb@gearhouse.co.za
w: www.gearhouse.co.za

Gigtent
....01223 870935
e: enquiries@gigtent.co.uk
w: www.gigtent.co.uk

Gill Parker Sculpture
....7885273309
e: bronze@gillparker.co.uk
w: www.gillparker.co.uk

GL Events Owen Brown Ltd
STATION ROAD, CASTLE DONINGTON
Derbyshire DE74 2NL...01332 631 607
e: owenbrown@glevents.co.uk
w: www.glevents.co.uk/

GL Events Snowdens
SECOND DROVE, EASTERN INDUSTRY, FENGATE, PETERBOROUGH
Cambridgeshire PE1 5XA 01733 344110
e: snowdens@glevents.co.uk
w: www.glevents.co.uk

Grandstand Hire Service
7 BRICK MEADOW, BISHOPS CASTLE
Shropshire SY9 5DH 01588 630454
e: sales@grandstandhire.co.uk
w: www.grandstandhire.co.uk

Harlequin Marquees & Event Management
34 SANDHILL WAY, FAIRFORD LEYS, AYLESBURY
Buckinghamshire HP19 8GU .... 01296 581524 //
07771 860908
e: info@harlequinevents.com
w: www.harlequinevents.com

Hoecker Structures (UK) Ltd
1 ROBINSON WAY, TELFORD WAY INDUSTRIAL ESTATE, ROBINSON
CLOSE, KETTERING
Northamptonshire NN16 8PT 01536 316970
e: info@hoeckeruk.com
w: www.hoeckeruk.com

Hotel Bell Tent
UNIT 10 COLLEGE FIELDS, PRINCE GEORGES ROAD, COLLIERS
WOOD, LONDON
Greater London SW19 2PT.....................................07525 050744
e: INFO@HOTELBELLTENT.CO.UK
w: www.hotelbelltent.co.uk

Humberside Marquees
RIVERSIDE HOUSE, 400 WINCOLMLEE, HULL
East Yorkshire HU2 0QL 01482 610102
w: www.humberside-marquees.com

Hummingbird Tipis
.... 07889 288982
e: info@hummingbird-tipis.com
w: www.hummingbird-tipis.com

Ideal Event Services
310 UNTHANK ROAD, NORWICH
Norfolk NR4 7QD 01603 280176
e: hello@idealeventservices.co.uk
w: www.idealeventservices.co.uk

M N O

Indalo Marquees
.... 0121 355 0005 / 07976 928 053
e: info@indalomarquees.co.uk
w: www.indalomarquees.co.uk

Ingenious Inflatables
45 LUDGATE HILL, LONDON
Greater London EC4M 7JU....................................020 7183 7842
e: enquiries@ingeniousinflatables.com
w: www.ingeniousinflatables.co.uk

Inside Out Marquees Ltd
132 BLACKHEATH ROAD, LOWESTOFT
Suffolk NR33 7JH .... 01502 569327 // 07733 381092
e: insideoutmarquees7@gmail.com
w: www.east-anglia-marquee-hire.co.u

Inside Outside Marquee Hire
UNITS 14 - 15, BOOKHAM INDUSTRIAL PARK, CHURCH ROAD, BOOKHAM
Surrey KT23 3EU 01372 459485
e: sales@inside-outside.co.uk
w: www.inside-outside.co.uk

Instant Marquees
UNIT D CENTRAL ESTATE, HIGHFIELD ROAD, CAMELFORD
Cornwall PL32 9RA..01840 213 063
e: shelter@instantmarquees.co.uk
w: www.instantmarquees.co.uk

J & J Carter Ltd
UNIT 2, 34 WALWORTH ROAD, WALWORTH BUSINESS PARK, ANDOVER
Hampshire SP10 5LH...01264 721630
e: sales@jjcarter.com
w: www.jjcarter.com

James Dabbs Marquees
BRETFIELD COURT , BRETTON STREET INDUSTRIAL ESTATE , SAVILE TOWN , DEWSBURY
West Yorkshire WF12 9BB .... 0800 590460 // 01924 459550
e: sales@james-dabbs-marquees.co.uk
w: www.james-dabbs-marquees.co.uk

Jigsaw Events
104 ALMA LANE, UPPER HALE, FARNHAM
GU9 0LP 0116 248 9421
e: info@jigsaw-events.co.uk
w: www.jigsaw-events.co.uk

John Attwooll & Co (tents) Ltd
BRISTOL ROAD, WHITMINSTER
Gloucestershire GL2 7LX.......................................01452 742 222
e: marquees@attwoolls.co.uk
w: www.attwoolls.co.uk

Kayam Theatre Tents
LAURELS FARMHOUSE, WORSTEAD, NORTH WALSHAM
NR28 9RW...01692 536025
e: info@kayam.com
w: www.kayam.com

Kayam
Laurels Farmhouse,
Worstead, North Walsham,
Norfolk, NR28 9RW

t: ++44 1692 536025
f: ++44 1692 535456
e: info@kayam.com

Kayam specialises in modular tensile structures. Our diverse range allows our clients to pick from structures for small intimate venues to mega structures for events, festivals, theatre and more.

www.kayam.com

Key Structures
UNIT 2, GRESHAM WAY, WIMBLEDON, LONDON
SW19 8ED 0208 944 9633
e: info@keystructures.co.uk
w: www.keystructures.co.uk

Killington Marquees
MARQUEES AND TEEPEES, KILLINGTON,, 13 KINGS YARD, SEDBERGH
Cumbria LA10 5BJ..01539 620 602
e: office@killingtonmarquees.co.uk
w: www.killingtonmarquees.co.uk

Kingdom Marquees
NALDERTOWN, WANTAGE
OX12 9EA 07967 390 020
e: mail@kingdommarquees.com
w: www.kingdommarquees.com

Lakeview Events Ltd
OLD BANK END ROAD, FINNINGLEY, DONCASTER
South Yorkshire DN9 3NT.....................................07731 510685
e: lakevieweventsltd@gmail.com
w: www.lakeviewevents.com

Lh Woodhouse & Co Ltd
WOLDS FARM, THE FOSSE, COTGRAVE
Nottinghamshire NG12 3HG 0115 9899899
e: sales@lhwoodhouse.co.uk
w: www.lhwoodhouse.co.uk

LM Productions Ltd
UNIT 6H SOUTHBOURNE BUSINESS PARK, COURTLANDS ROAD, EASTBOURNE
East Sussex BN22 8UY 01323 432170
e: info@lm-productions.com
w: www.lm-productions.com

Losberger UK Ltd
UNIT 14, ROSELAND BUSINESS PARK , LONG BENNINGTON , NEWARK
Nottinghamshire NG23 5FF...................................01949 845070
e: losbergeruk@losberger.com
w: www.losberger.co.uk

M N O

Mahood Marquees
LORDSFOLD, RANFORD, ST HELENS
Merseyside WA11 8HP...01744 884158
e: sales@mahoodmarquees.com
w: www.mahoodmarquees.com

Malton Marquees Ltd
PASTURE FARM, SCRAYINGHAM, YORK
North Yorkshire YO41 1JQ .... 01759 373033 // 07889 956919
e: info@maltonmarquees.co.uk
w: www.maltonmarquees.co.uk

Mar-key Group
SUITE 22A, PEARTREE BUSINESS CENTRE, COBHAM ROAD, WIMBORNE
Dorset BH21 7PT 01202 577111
e: info@mar-key.com
w: www.mar-key.com

Marldon Marquees
111 WINNER STREET, PAIGNTON
Devon TQ3 3BP...01803 524425
e: enquiries@marldonmarquees.co.uk
w: www.marldonmarquees.co.uk

Marquee Carpets Limited
UNIT 8 MAXWELLS WEST, GREAT CAMBRIDGE ROAD, CHESHUNT
Hertfordshire EN8 8XH 01992 629624
e: enquiries@marqueecarpets.com
w: www.marqueecarpets.com

Marquee Express Ltd
11 CANFORD DRIVE, ADDLESTONE
KT15 2HH 08000 029202
e: marquee_express@btinternet.com
w: www.marquee-express.co.uk

Marquee Moments
84 HIGHLANDS GARDENS, ILFORD
IG1 3LD 07961 050 422
e: info@marqueemoments.co.uk
w: www.marqueemoments.co.uk

Mastertent
RIDGEVIEW HOUSE, 99 DERBY ROAD, STANLEY VILLAGE, DERBYSHIRE
DE7 6EX .... 0845 437 4462 / 0115 932 3955
w: www.mastertent.co.uk

Media Structures
87-91, BEDDINGTON LANE, CROYDON
Surrey CR0 4TD 020 8683 3131
e: info@mediastructures.co.uk
w: www.mediastructures.co.uk

Meridian Marquees
READING OFFICE UNIT A, PARSONS FARM , CHURCH LANE, FARLEY HIL
Berkshire RG7 1UY 0800 298 5955
e: meridianmarquees@googlemail.com
w: www.meridianmarquees.co/

Midland Marquees and Leisure
THE OLD VICARAGE, 1 ST MARYS CLOSE, NEWTON SOLNEY, BURTON ON TRENT
Staffordshire DE15 0SE...01283 701936
e: sales@midlandmarquees.co.uk
w: www.midlandmarquees.co.uk

Millie Miles Event Hire Ltd
WESTON GROUNDS FARM, WESTON ON THE GREEN, BICESTER
Oxfordshire OX25 3QX 01869 351 603
e: info@milliemiles.co.uk
w: www.milliemiles.co.uk

Mini Marquees
UNIT 70 - 73, BLOCK 8, OLD MILL PARK, MANSFIELD
Nottinghamshire NG19 9BG 01623 634228
e: sales@mmx3.com
w: www.mmx3.com

Mobex Ltd
UNIT 6 RIGESTATE INDUSTRIAL ESTATE, STATION ROAD, BERKELEY Gloucestershire GL13 9RL....................01453 511 210
e: exhibit@mobex.co.uk
w: www.mobex.co.uk

Mr. Marquee
179 SILKMORE LANE, STAFFORD
Staffordshire ST17 4JB...07710 131450
e: info@mr-marquee.co.uk
w: www.mr-marquee.co.uk

Mudway Workman Marquee Hire
MANOR FARM,, STOKE ORCHARD, CHELTENHAM
Gloucestershire GL52 7RY......................................01242 680204
e: enquiries@mudwayworkman.co.uk
w: www.mudwayworkman.co.uk

National Theatre Tents
THE OLD POST OFFICE, BEATRICE ROAD, LEICESTER
LE3 9FD...0203 287 3253
e: redwagon@letsdotheshowrighthere.com
w: www.letsdotheshowrighthere.com

Neptunus Ltd
COB DRIVE, SWAN VALLEY, NORTHAMPTON
Northamptonshire NN4 9BB .... 01604 593820 // 1604 593820
e: sales@neptunus.co.uk
w: www.neptunus.co.uk

Nicoll Industries Ltd
UNITS 10 & 11, WINDSOR INDUSTRIAL ESTATE, HAWKINS LANE, BURTON ON TRENT
Staffordshire DE14 1QF 01283 510570
e: sales@nicoll-industries.co.uk
w: www.nicoll-industries.co.uk

Northern Event Structures
EVENT HOUSE, 45 COAL PIT LANE, LOWER CUMBERWORTH, HUDDERSFIELD West Yorkshire HD8 8PL................01484 861573
e: info@northernmarquees.co.uk
w: www.northerneventstructures.co.uk

M N O

Oakleaf Marquees
STATION ROAD , STALBRIDGE
Dorset DT10 2RW .... 07714243424 /
.... 01258 520345 / 07770 85134
e: matthew@oakleafmarquees.co.uk
w: www.oakleafmarquees.co.uk/

Olive Marquees
30 GREEN LANE, RADNAGE
Buckinghamshire HP14 4DN................................07717 843 942
e: martin@olivemarquees.co.uk
w: www.olivemarquees.co.uk

Out Is In
BINES FARM BARN, BINES ROAD, PARTRIDGE GREEN, HORSHAM
West Sussex RH13 8EQ 01403 710099
e: info@outisin.co.uk
w: www.outisin.co.uk

Overlay Events Ltd
54 OXFORD ROAD, UXBRIDGE
Middlesex UB9 4DJ...020 3693 4925
e: info@overlayevents.com
w: www.overlayevents.com

Piggotts Company Limited
46 STEPFIELD, WITHAM Essex CM8 3TH...............01376 535 750
e: sales@piggotts.co.uk
w: www.piggotts.co.uk

Pinnacle Marquees (uk) Ltd
UNIT 9, MARKET WEIGHTON BUSINESS CENTRE, YORK ROAD, MARKET WEIGHTON
Yorkshire YO43 3GL 08456 25 55 25
e: tim.betteridge@bettgroup.co.uk
w: www.pinnaclemarquees.co.uk

Pitman's People Marquee and Event Structure Crew and Riggers
UNIT G1A STAMFORD WORKS, 3 GILLETT ST., LONDON
Greater London N16 8JH......................................020 3651 3330
e: admin@pitmanspeople.com
w: www.pitmanspeople.com

Pitstop Marquees
1 HURLEY LANE, HURLEY, ATHERSTONE
Warwickshire CV9 2JJ 01827 872280
e: info@pitstopmarquees.co.uk
w: www.pitstopmarquees.co.uk

PKL Group (UK) Ltd
STELLA WAY, BISHOPS CLEEVE, CHELTENHAM
Gloucestershire GL52 7DQ....................................01242 663 000
e: postbox@pkl.co.uk
w: www.pkl.co.uk

Planet Gold Decor
UNIT 4 ROMARSH, FOWLSWICK BUSINESS PARK, , ALLINGTON
Wiltshire SN14 6QE...07747 015 170
e: info@planetgolddecor.co.uk
w: www.planetgolddecor.co.uk or www.

Pole To Pole Marquees
FOURWAYS FARM, NORTHBROOK, MICHELDEVER, WINCHESTER
Hampshire SO21 3AH .... 01962 774920 // 07787 524951
e: mail@poletopolemarquees.co.uk
w: www.poletopolemarquees.co.uk

Proforme UK Limited
PROFORME UK LIMITED, SWADLINCOTE
Derbyshire DE11 0QB 08443 570210
e: sales@proforme.co.uk
w: www.marquee-sale.co.uk

Protec (Production Technology LLC)
PLOT NO. 548 - 548, DUBAI INVESTMENT PARK 2, DUBAI, UNITED ARAB EMIRATES
.... +971 4 880 0092
e: eventrental@productiontec.com
w: www.productiontec.com

Purvis Marquees
4B EAST MAINS, INGLISTON ROAD, EDINBURGH
Edinburgh EH28 8NB 0131 335 3685
e: sales@purvis-marquees.co.uk
w: www.purvis-marquees.co.uk

Pyramid Marquees
DALTON HOUSE, 60 WINDSOR AVENUE, LONDON
Greater London SW19 2RR 07912 066614
e: info@pyramidmarquees.co.uk
w: www.pyramidmarquees.co.uk

RHI Stretch Tents
UNIT 1, EPIC PARK, BAX STREET,, MAITLAND, CAPE TOWN, SOUTH AFRICA
7405.. +27 021 7090493
e: info@rhitents.com
w: www.rhitents.com

Roder Hts Hocker Gmbh
UNIT 3 LAWRENCE WAY, , STANHOPE ROAD, CAMBERLEY
Surrey GU15 3DL...................... 01276 462600 / 07866 988 863
e: admin@roderhts.com
w: www.roderhts.com

Roder UK
UNIT 16 EARITH BUSINESS PARK, MEADOW DROVE, EARITH
Cambridgeshire PE28 3QF....................................01487 840840
e: sales@roderuk.com
w: www.roderuk.com

Roustabout Ltd
FRONGOCH BOATYARD, SMUGGLER'S COVE, ABERDOVEY
LL35 0RG..01654 767 177
e: info@roustabout.ltd.uk
w: www.roustabout.ltd.uk

Rudi Enos Design
SUITE 2, SEATON BUSINESS PARK, 65 DEEP LANE, SHEFFIELD
South Yorkshire S5 0DU 0114 257 7755
e: info@rudienosdesign.com
w: www.rudienosdesign.com

M N O

Seaholme Marquees
COLEMAN'S PARK, SHAVESWOOD LANE, ALBOURNE
West Sussex BN6 9DY 01273 857577
e: info@seaholmemarquees.co.uk
w: www.seaholmemarquees.co.uk

Seamless Tents
PINGEMEAD HOUSE, PINGEWOOD BUSINESS ESTATE, READING
Berkshire RG30 3UR 01189 754545
e: info@seamlesstents.co.uk
w: www.seamlesstents.co.uk

Sherwood Marquees
RUFFORD COURT, WELLOW ROAD, EAKRING
Nottinghamshire NG22 0DF 01623 872811
e: enquiries@sherwoodmarquees.co.uk
w: www.sherwoodmarquees.co.uk

Silver Stage Event Structures
THE OAKS, MILL DROVE, NORTHWOLD, THETFORD
Norfolk IP26 5LQ...01366 727 310
e: info@silver-stage.com
w: www.silver-stage.com

Southern Inflatables (UK) Ltd
THE YARD, NEW STREET, LUTTERWORTH
Leicestershire LE17 4PJ 01455 559956
e: enquiries@southerninflatables.net
w: www.southerninflatables.net

Spacecadets Air Design Ltd
UNION HOUSE, HALL STREET, , TODMORDEN
West Yorkshire OL14 7AD 01706 814 048
e: hello@spacecadets.com
w: www.spacecadets.com

Special Event Services Ltd
GROVE FARM, BUCKINGHAM, BRACKLEY
 NN13 5JH..01280 841215
e: info@sesevent.co.uk
w: www.sesevent.co.uk

Sshh... Luxury Yurt Hire for Festivals, Events and Weddings
THE DOCK, WILBURY VILLAS, HOVE
East Sussex BN3 6AH .... 01273 359099 // 01273 830855
e: info@sshh.uk.com
w: www.sshh.uk.com

Stretch and Tents
1V5 COOPER HOUSE,, 2 MICHAEL ROAD, LONDON
Greater London SW6 2AD .... 07733326484 //
020 7097 1875
e: info@stretchandtents.co.uk
w: www.stretchandtents.co.uk

Surf & Turf Instant Shelters Ltd
UNIT 7 TATTON COURT, KINGSLAND GRANGE, WARRINGTON
Cheshire WA1 4RR...01925 819608
e: info@surfturf.co.uk
w: www.surfturf.co.uk

Tectonics Uk
1 PROSPECT ROAD, NEW ALRESFORD
Hampshire SO24 9QF...01962 736 316
e: sales@tectonicsuk.co.uk
w: www.tectonicsuk.co.uk

Tectoniks
UNIT 1 KINTON BUSINESS PARK, NESSCLIFFE, SHREWSBURY
Shropshire SY4 1AZ...01743 741199
e: info@tectoniks.com
w: www.tectoniks.com

Tent And Garden
OAK FARM, HETHERSON GREEN, CHOLMONDELEY
Cheshire SY14 8EJ...01829 720032
e: tents@tentandgarden.co.uk
w: www.tentandgarden.co.uk

Tentickle Stretch Tents
.... +27 021 593 6918
e: capetown@tentickletents.co.za
w: www.tentickle-stretchtents.com

Tentnology
.... +800 627 78337 (toll free)
e: tent@tentnology.com
w: www.tentnology.com

The Dome Company
UNIT 4, STATION YARD, STATION ROAD, HALESWORTH
Suffolk IP19 8BZ...07876 673354
e: Info@thedomecompany.co.uk
w: www.thedomecompany.co.uk

The Events & Tents Company Ltd
HILLTOP FARM, CAYTHORPE HEATH, GRANTHAM
Lincolnshire NG32 3EU 0800 0274492
e: info@eventsandtents.co.uk
w: www.eventsandtents.co.uk

The Events Structure
INNOSPACE, THE SHEDS, CHESTER STREET, MANCHESTER
Greater Manchester M1 5GD...............................0161 821 1010
w: www.theeventsstructure.com

The Little Marquee Hire Company
.... 01483 722791 // 0845 500 1151
e: sales@littlemarquee.co.uk
w: www.littlemarquee.co.uk

The Pearl Tent Company
UPPER TILTON BARN, FIRLE, LEWES
East Sussex BN8 6LL...0800 88 15 229
e: info@thepearltentcompany.com
w: www.thepearltentcompany.com

The Stretch Tent Company
1 RIVER ROW, PAVENHAM
Bedfordshire MK43 7NN 01908 668247
e: info@thestretchtent.co.uk
w: www.thestretchtent.co.uk

The Stunning Tents Company
UNIT 4B, ASH PARK BUSINESS CENTRE, , ASH LANE, LITTLE
LONDON, Hampshire RG26 5FL...............................01256 882114
e: enquiries@stunningtents.co.uk
w: www.stunningtents.co.uk

Tony Hopkins Entertainments Ltd
MAYPINE HOUSE, 7 MERTON PARK PARADE, KINGSTON ROAD,
Greater London SW19 3NT...................................0208 795 0919
e: enquiry@tonyhopkinsentertainments.com
w: www.tonyhopkinsentertainments.com

Top Marquees
RATCHER WAY, CROWN FARM INDUSTRIAL PARK, MANSFIELD
Nottinghamshire NG19 0FS....................................01623 415944
e: advice@topmarquees.co.uk
w: www.topmarquees.co.uk

Tops Marquees
UNIT 19A, LOWER MOUNT FARM, LONG LANE, COOKHAM,
MAIDENHEAD
Berkshire SL6 9EE 01628 773566
e: info@topsmarquees.co.uk
w: www.topsmarquees.co.uk

Trade Gazebos & Barriers
19 MEADOW WAY, BRACKNELL
Berkshire RG42 1UE 01344 306082
e: info@heavydutygazebo.co.uk
w: www.heavydutygazebo.co.uk

Trend Marquees Ltd
1 ATTERBURY CLOSE, NORTHAMPTON
 NN6 7AA...3330118833
e: contact@trendmarquees.co.uk
w: www.trendmarquees.co.uk

TSG
HOOKLANDS FARM, LEWERS ROAD, SCAYNES HILL
West Sussex RH17 7NG 01444 831 456
e: info@tsg.uk.com
w: www.tsg.uk.com

TT Tents Ltd
NORTH WALTHAM BUSINESS CENTRE, NORTH WALTHAM,
BASINGSTOKE
Hampshire RG25 2DJ 01256 397551
e: sales@tttents.co.uk
w: www.tttents.co.uk

Utopia Leisure
CUMBERLAND HOUSE, THE COMMON, REDBOURN
Hertfordshire AL3 7QP 01582 793336
e: info@utopialeisure.co.uk
w: www.utopialeisure.co.uk

Vicarage Marquees
UNIT ONE, CHURCH ROAD, WADHAM PARK STABLES, HOCKLEY
Essex SS5 6AF..01702 232 200
e: info@vicaragemarquees.co.uk
w: www.vicaragemarquees.co.uk

Walton's Marquees
51 CHEVIOT VIEW, PONTELAND, NEWCASTLE UPON TYNE
Northumberland NE20 9BH 01661 825528
e: info@waltonsmarquees.com
w: www.waltonsmarquees.co.uk

Wango's Staging Concepts
OLD STATION HOUSE, INGHAM, BURY ST EDMUNDS
Suffolk IP31 1NS...077100 37997
e: info@wangos.com
w: www.wangos.com

Weatherill Brothers Ltd
NEWGREEN BUSINESS PARK, NORWICH ROAD, WATTON
Norfolk IP25 6HW 01953 882394
e: sales@weatherillbrothers.co.uk
w: www.weatherillbrothers.co.uk

Weatherweave Ltd
MARKET PLACE, 12-16 HOCKLEY ROAD, RAYLEIGH
Essex SS6 8ED 01268 774141
e: sales@weatherweave.co.uk
w: www.weatherweave.co.uk

Wellpleased Events
11 BLAYDS YARD, LEEDS
West Yorkshire LS1 4AD..0113 244 2720
e: info@wellpleased.co.uk
w: www.wellpleased.co.uk

Wernick Event Hire Ltd
JOSEPH HOUSE, NORTHGATE WAY, ALDRIDGE, WALSALL
West Midlands WS9 8ST..0800 970 0231
e: enquiries@wernickevents.co.uk
w: www.wernickeventhire.co.uk

Westmorland Marquee Hire
DALTON HALL, BURTON-IN-KENDAL
Cumbria LA6 1NJ...01524 782414
e: info@westmorlandmarqueehire.co.uk
w: www.westmorlandmarqueehire.co.uk

White Horse Marquees Ltd
HILL DEVERILL, WARMINSTER
Wiltshire BA12 7EQ..01985 840705
e: info@whitehorsemarquees.co.uk
w: www.whitehorsemarquees.co.uk

World Inspired Tents
UNIT 17 & 18, COXLEIGH BARTON, SHIRWELL, BARNSTAPLE
Devon EX31 4JL .... +44 (0) 1271 851160
e: info@world-inspired.co.uk
w: www.worldinspiredtents.co.uk

Worldwide Structures Ltd
AYRESHIRE FARM , SHARCOTT, PEWSEY
Wiltshire SN9 5PA..01672 565060
e: enquiries@w-sl.com
w: www.smart-spaces.com

M N O

WSSL - Warner Shelter Systems Ltd
9811 44 STREET SE, CALGARY, ALBERTA, CANADA
T2C 2P7...001 403 279 7662
e: warner@wssl.com
w: www.wssl.com

Massage Therapy

Happy Healthy Holistic
PO BOX 56911, LONDON
Greater London N10 3YJ.......................................0845 223 7110
e: info@happyhealthyholistic.com
w: www.happyhealthyholistic.com

Massage on Tour
....0780 9458 270
e: massageontour@serendipity-spa.co.uk
w: www.serendipity-spa.co.uk

On The Spot
12 VICTOR GARDENS, HOCKLEY
Essex SS5 4DR...07989 280 469
e: sally@sallymorris.co.uk
w: sallymorris.co.uk/

Rolletic Massage London
49 GRANVILLE ROAD, NORTH FINCHLEY, LONDON
N12 0JG 7539864579
e: dorothy@rolleticmassagelondon.co.uk
w: www.rolleticmassagelondon.co.uk

Varii Promotions
49 GRANVILLE ROAD, NORTH FINCHLEY, LONDON
N12 0JG 7539864579
e: dorothy@rolleticmassagelondon.co.uk
w: www.rolleticmassagelondon.co.uk

Medical Support

1st Aid 999
4 SANDRINGHAM ROAD, NOTTINGHAM
Nottinghamshire NG2 4HH 07767 041114
e: mail@1staid999.co.uk
w: www.1staid999.co.uk

A B Medical Services
1 CLIFFORD CRESCENT,, SITTINGBOURNE
Kent ME10 3FL .... 07590 542 513 // 08443 100 150
e: operations@ab-medical.co.uk
w: www.ab-medical.co.uk

Advance Medical Solutions (UK) ltd
C/O 126 CONEYGREE ROAD , STANGROUND , PETERBOROUGH
Cambridgeshire PE2 8LG .... 07510 723849 / 01733 892736
e: info@amsuk.org.uk
w: www.amsuk.org.uk

Ambu-kare (uk) Ltd
2 WESTMINSTER PLACE, EMPSON ROAD, PETERBOROUGH
Cambridgeshire PE1 5SY 01733 560972
e: control@ambukare.co.uk
w: www.ambukare.co.uk

Ambulance & Medical Solutions Ltd
....01422 401000
e: info@ambmed.co.uk
w: www.ambmed.co.uk

Arley Medical Services
UNIT 5A ARLEY INDUSTRIAL ESTATE, COLLIERS WAY, ARLEY
Warwickshire CV7 8HN 01676 937 199
e: info@arleymedicalservices.co.uk
w: www.arleymedicalservices.co.uk

British Red Cross
44 MOORFIELDS, LONDON
Greater London EC2Y 9AL...................................0844 871 11 11
e: information@redcross.org.uk
w: www.redcross.org.uk/eventfirstaid

Criticare UK Ambulance Service
13 THE CRESCENT, MARCHWOOD
Hampshire SO40 4WSi»¿ 0844 351 0684
e: info@criticareuk.net
w: www.criticareuk.net

Desican Inc
5320 FINCH AVE EST , TORONTO, CANADA
ON M1S 5G3................................. 9052942222 / 18773891818
e: desican.inc@gmail.com
w: desican.ca/

Devon Ems
4 ORKNEY CLOSE, TORQUAY
Devon TQ2 7DS 01803 315251
e: services@devonems.org
w: www.devonems.org

Dulais Valley Independent Ambulance Services
82 CHURCH ROAD, SEVEN SISTERS, NEATH
SA10 8DT 01639 700050
e: keith@DVIAS.co.uk
w: www.dvias.co.uk

Event First Aid Services
ALEXANDER HOUSE, 40 WILBURY WAY , HITCHIN
Hertfordshire SG4 0AP 0800 4714852
e: info@event-firstaidservices.com
w: www.event-firstaidservices.net

Event Medicine Company Ltd (the)
UNIT D CENTRAL ESTATE, ALBERT ROAD, ALDERSHOT
Hampshire GU11 1SZ..01252 313 005
e: info@eventmedicinecompany.co.uk
w: www.eventmedicinecompany.co.uk

M N O

Events Medical Services Ltd
PO BOX 4741, COVENTRY
West Midlands CV6 9EW 0844 586 6009
e: office@eventsmedical.co.uk
w: www.eventsmedical.co.uk

Face 2 Face Medical Ltd
Berkshire SL1 8HJ .... 07821 538157 // 08000 475866
e: info@face2facemedical.net
w: www.face2facemedical.net

Film Medical Services
UNIT 5-7, COMMERCIAL WAY, PARK ROYAL, LONDON
Greater London NW10 7XF.....................................020 8961 3222
e: info@filmmedical.co.uk
w: www.filmmedical.co.uk

Glasgow Cognitive Therapy Centre Ltd
2ND FLOOR, ROTHESAY HOUSE, 134 DOUGLAS STREET,
GLASGOW G2 4HF 7846817047
e: admin@thegctc.com
w: www.glasgowcognitivetherapycentre

Hatt Medics
PO BOX 5157, BRIGHTON
East Sussex BN50 9TW...01273 358 359
e: adventures@thehatt.co.uk
w: www.thehatt.co.uk/medics

Immediate Care Medical
SUITE 108, 69 STEWARD STREET, BIRMINGHAM
West Midlands B18 7AF...0121 200 3086
e: office@immediatecaremedical.co.uk
w: www.immediatecaremedical.co.uk

Intrim Medical & Rescue Services Ltd
TRAINING CENTRE, UNIT 3 SWINSTEAD CLOSE, BILBOROUGH,
NOTTINGHAM
Nottinghamshire NG8 3JG......................................0844 3100070
e: feedback@intrim-medical.com
w: www.intrim-medical.com

Location Medical Services
**THE MEDICAL CENTRE, SHEPPERTON STUDIOS, STUDIOS
ROAD, SHEPPERTON
Surrey TW17 0QD 0870 750 9898
e: mail@locationmedical.com
w: www.locationmedical.com**

Medicare Event Medical Services Ltd
UNIT 4, PHILLOWS BARNS BUSINESS CENTRE, HAMMONDS
ROAD, LITTLE BADDOW, CHELMSFORD
Essex CM3 4BG 01245 460 666
e: info@medicare-ems.co.uk
w: www.medicare-ems.co.uk

Medicine Man Pharmacy
18 BRAES MEAD, SOUTH NUTFIELD, REDHILL
Surrey RH1 4JR .... 07966 518 031 // 1737 823269
e: j.powell@med-man.co.uk
w: www.med-man.co.uk

Mediskills
340 STOCKPORT ROAD, GEE CROSS, HYDE
Cheshire SK14 5RY...0161 368 5508
e: info@mediskills-uk.com
w: www.mediskills-uk.com

MedRescue24
UNIT 4, DEWAR COURT, ASTMOOR INDUSTRIAL ESTATE,
RUNCORN
 WA7 1PT...

MRL Limited
ALFRED HOUSE, ROPEWALK, KNOTTINGLEY
West Yorkshire WF11 9AL 01977 622000
e: info@mrl-limited.co.uk
w: www.mrl-limited.co.uk

One Staff Solution Ltd
58 PARK STREET, MAYFAIR, LONDON
Greater London W1K 2JL .... 07523 486905 / 020 7511 7722
e: info@oness.co.uk
w: www.security-company-london.com

Outdoor Medical Solutions Ltd
 TETBURY MOTOR CENTRE,, TETBURY INDUSTRIAL ESTATE,
CIRENCESTER RD, TETBURY
Gloucestershire GL8 8E...01291 440299
e: info@outdoormedicalsolutions.co.uk
w: www.outdoormedicalsolutions.co.uk

M N O

ProMedical 2002
38 WOODVILLE ROAD, HARTSHORNE, SWADLINCOTE
Derbyshire DE11 7ET..01283 552232
e: rob@promedical2002.com
w: www.promedical2002.com/

Protak Event Services
2 CLAREMONT CLOSE, ANGMERING
West Sussex BN16 4PB 0844 807 3654
e: info@protakeventservices.co.uk
w: www.protakeventservices.co.uk

Response First Aid and Medical LTD
....7756086997
e: admin@eventfirstaidcover.com
w: eventfirstaidcover.com

S.E. Medical Ltd
....0203 286 9993
e: jono@semedical.co.uk
w: www.semedical.co.uk

Scott Medical (UK) Ltd
SCOTT HOUSE, BARRY'S LANE INDUSTRIAL ESTATE, SEAMER
ROAD, SCARBOROUGH
YO12 4HA...01723 363225
e: scott.andrew@btconnect.com

Somerset Training
.... 01823 431557 // 07843 436895
e: info@somersettraining.co.uk
w: www.somersettraining.co.uk

St. John Ambulance
27 ST JOHN'S LANE, CLERKENWELL, LONDON
Greater London EC1M 4BU 0207 324 4000
w: www.sja.org.uk

Total Care Security Ltd
UNIT 3 , BRUNEL DRIVE, NEWARK
Nottinghamshire NG24 2DE 0800 917 47 67
e: info@totalcaresecurity.com
w: www.totalcaresecurity.com

Merchandising

Action Jacket Company
PO BOX 1180, STOURBRIDGE
West Midlands DY9 0ZF 01562 887096
e: info@actionjacket.co.uk
w: www.actionjacket.co.uk

Advartex
PICKFORD LANE, TICEHURST
East Sussex TN5 7BL..01580 200 120
e: sales@advartex.co.uk
w: www.advartex.co.uk

Alchemy Carta Ltd
HAZEL DRIVE, LEICESTER
Leicestershire LE3 2JE 0116 282 4824
e: promo@alchemygroup.com
w: www.alchemygroup.co.uk

Aspinline
EXHIBITION HOUSE, HAYWARD INDUSTRIAL ESTATE, 1-2 NORTH
VIEW, SOUNDWELL, BRISTOL
Gloucestershire BS16 4NT 0117 9566657
e: sales@aspinline.co.uk
w: www.aspinline.co.uk

Atelier Screenprint Ltd
UNIT 2, 12 LISLE AVENUE, KIDDERMINSTER
Worcestershire DY11 7DL 01562 743166
e: atelier.screenprint@chessmail.co.uk
w: www.atelier-screenprint.com

Awesome Merchandise
B1-B3 WELLINGTON ROAD INDUSTRIAL ESTATE, WELLINGTON
BRIDGE, LEEDS West Yorkshire LS12 2UA 01132 435667
e: luke@awesomemerchandise.com
w: www.awesomemerchandise.com

Bannerbags.co.uk
UNIT 3B & C RED ROSE COURT, SUNNYHURST ROAD, BLACKBURN
 BB2 1PS 01254 582923
e: info@bannerbags.co.uk
w: www.bannerbags.co.uk

Blueprint Promotional Products
NO. 1 THE EMBASSY, LAWRENCE STREET, LONG EATON,
NOTTINGHAM
Nottinghamshire NG10 1JY 0333 1234 400
e: info@blueprintpromo.co.uk
w: www.blueprintpromo.co.uk

Branded Uk
UNIT 8, RED LION BUSINESS CENTRE, RED LION ROAD,
SURBITON Greater London KT6 7QD 020 8974 2722
e: sales@brandeduk.com
w: www.brandeduk.com

Burst (uk) Ltd
GREY STUD, WHYDOWN ROAD, WHYDOWN, BEXHILL ON SEA
 TN39 4RB 0845 643 0133
e: sales@burstuk.com
w: www.burstuk.com

Buypromoproducts Limited
2 SAINT JAMES COURT , SANDIACRE , NOTTINGHAM
 NG10 5NR............................... 01158542906 / 0333 1234 414
e: sales@buypromoproducts.co.uk
w: www.buypromoproducts.co.uk

Calver Promotional Merchandise
22 THE DRIVE, ORPINGTON
Kent BR6 9AP 01689 898828
e: sales@calver.com
w: www.calver.com

M
N
O

Carole Group Ltd
GOLDOAK HOUSE, OAKLANDS BUSINESS PARK, WOKINGHAM
Berkshire RG41 2FD 01189 771424
e: sales@carolegroup.com
w: www.carolegroup.com

Complete Merchandise
29 WOOLMER WAY, BORDON
Hampshire GU35 9QE 01420 478 866
e: info@completemerchandise.co.uk
w: www.completemerchandise.co.uk

Creative Promotions Ltd
79 WEST REGENT STREET, GLASGOW
 G2 2AW 0141 332 7471
e: enquiries@creativepromotions.co.uk
w: www.creativepromotions.co.uk

Event Merchandising Ltd
UNIT 11, THE EDGE, HUMBER ROAD, LONDON
Greater London NW2 6EW.....................................020 8208 1166
e: event@eventmerch.com
w: www.eventmerchandising.com

Festive Promotions Ltd
THE GROTTO, 70 SANDFIELD ROAD, OXFORD
Oxfordshire OX3 7RL...01865 744711
e: sales@festivepromotions.com
w: www.festivepromotions.com

GP Promowear
THEAKLEN HOUSE, THEAKLEN DRIVE, PONSWOOD INDSTRIAL
ESTATE, ST. LEONARDS-ON-SEA
East Sussex TN38 9AZ...01424 716161
e: info@gppromowear.com
w: www.gppromowear.com

Hambleside Business Gift Solutions Ltd
2-3 LANCER HOUSE, HUSSAR COURT, WESTSIDE VIEW,
WATERLOOVILLE
Hampshire PO7 7SE...023 9235 4960
e: sales@hambleside.co.uk
w: www.hambleside-merchandise.co.uk/

Inprint
58A HEAD STREET , COLCHESTER
Essex CO1 1PB 01206 366 014
e: info@inprintonline.co.uk
w: www.inprintonline.co.uk

Jamy Ltd
33 ROMAN WAY, GODMANCHESTER, HUNTINGDON, CAMBRIDGE
Cambridgeshire PE29 2LN 01480 456391
e: sales@jamy.co.uk
w: www.jamy.co.uk

Logo Promotional Merchandise Ltd
CRESCENT TERRACE, ILKLEY
West Yorkshire LS29 8DL.......................................01943 817238
e: enquiries@logomerchandising.co.uk
w: www.logomerchandising.co.uk

Masons Music Ltd
DRURY LANE, PONSWOOD INDUSTRIAL ESTATE,
ST LEONARDS ON SEA
East Sussex TN38 9BA...01424 427 562
e: web@masonsmusic.co.uk
w: www.masonsmusic.co.uk

Merox Screenprint
ELLIOTT ROAD, WEST HOWE , BOURNEMOUTH
Dorset BH11 8JT 01202 571210
e: sales@merox.co.uk
w: www.merox.co.uk

Metro Merchandise
3 PROSPECT COURT , COURTEENHALL ROAD , BLISWORTH
Northamptonshire NN7 3DG..................................01536 415 005
e: louise@metromerchandise.co.uk
w: www.metromerchandise.uk.clickprom

Microtees
31 BARNFIELD AVENUE, KINGSTON UPON THAMES
Surrey KT2 5RD 020 8546 9606
e: sales@tshirt.co.uk
w: www.tshirt.co.uk

Monogram Group Ltd
GREATWORTH PARK, GREATWORTH, BANBURY
Oxfordshire OX17 2HB 01295 768903
e: sales@monogram.co.uk
w: www.monogram.co.uk

My Tshirt Flashes.com
80 TAMWORTH LANE, MITCHAM
Surrey CR4 1DA...0203-052-375
e: info@mytshirtflashes.com
w: www.mytshirtflashes.com

Native Promotions
110 COAST ROAD, WEST MERSEA, COLCHESTER
Essex CO5 8NA..0845 258 1000
e: info@nativepromotions.com
w: www.nativepromotions.com

Porreda Ltd
COUNTY GATES LANE, WESTBOURNE, BOURNMOUTH
Dorset BH4 9EF .... 01202 769 554 //
01202 765216
e: sales@porreda.com
w: www.porreda.com

Print Designs
EMERALD WAY, STONE BUSINESS PARK, STONE
Staffordshire ST15 0SR..01785 818 111
e: sales@printdesigns.com
w: www.printdesigns.com

Promotional Products Ltd
8 EDEN CLOSE, WILMSLOW
Cheshire SK9 6BG 01625 526050
e: sales@promotionproducts.co.uk
w: www.promotionproducts.co.uk

M
N
O

PWM - Philip Walters Merchandising
NO.3, THE GARAGES, ST. LUKES AVENUE, MAIDSTONE
Kent ME14 5AL........................... 01622 431871 / 07711 055588
e: philip@pwm.co.uk
w: www.pwm.co.uk

Quickfold Business Solutions
CEDAR HOUSE, HILLBOTTOM ROAD, HIGH WYCOMBE
Buckinghamshire HP12 4HJ....................................01494 468888
e: sales@quickfoldsolutions.co.uk
w: www.quickfoldofficesupplies.co.uk

Razamataz
4 DERBY STREET, COLNE
Lancashire BB9 9AA 01282 861099
e: sales@razamataz.co.uk
w: www.razamataz.com

Screen Services
40 MILLMARK GROVE, LONDON
Greater London SE14 6RQ 020 8692 4806
e: info@screenservices.biz
w: www.screenservices.biz

Shirtysomething Ltd
6 PARKYN ROAD, DAYBROOK, NOTTINGHAM
Nottinghamshire NG5 6BG 0115 920 2645
e: chaps@shirtysomething.com
w: www.shirtysomething.com

Sinclair Print
396 ASHLEY ROAD, POOLE
 BH14 0AA...01202 730221
e: sinclairprint@aol.com

Special Efx Ltd
ETTINGTON PARK BUSINESS CENTRE, STRATFORD-ON-AVON
Warwickshire CV37 8BT.......................................01789 450 005
e: award@efx.co.uk
w: www.awardefx.co.uk

Status Promotional Merchandise
FLEET HOUSE, 1 ARMSTRONG ROAD, BENFLEET
Essex SS7 4SS 01268 755055
e: sales@statuspm.co.uk
w: www.statuspm.co.uk

Stop The Press!
FLEMING STREET, GLASGOW
Lanarkshire G31 1PQ...0141 530 8755
e: studio@stop-the-press.co.uk
w: www.stop-the-press.co.uk

Striptees Uk
UNIT 5, GILRAY ROAD, DISS
Suffolk IP22 4EU..01379 652 056
e: info@stripteesuk.com
w: www.stripteesuk.com

Sycal Ltd
UNIT 25, CHANTRY ROAD , WOBURN ROAD INDUSTRIAL ESTATE,
KEMPSTON, BEDFORD
Bedfordshire MK42 7SY.......................................01234 841741
e: sales@sycal.co.uk
w: www.sycal.co.uk

T Shirt & Sons
11 WASHINGTON ROAD, WEST WILTS TRADING ESTATE,
WESTBURY
Wiltshire BA13 4JP 01373 301 645
e: sales@tshirtandsons.co.uk
w: www.tshirtandsons.co.uk

T-print Ltd
APPAREL HOUSE, BRISTOL AVENUE, BISPHAM, BLACKPOOL
 FY2 0JF 01253 359120
e: sales@t-print.co.uk
w: www.t-print.co.uk

Tailor Made Signs & Embroidery
6 PROSPECT WAY, ROYAL OAK INDUSTRIAL ESTATE, DAVENTRY
Northamptonshire NN11 8PL 01327 311125
e: sales@tailormade-online.co.uk
w: www.tailormade-online.co.uk

Team Togs Ltd
THE BASEMENT, 139-141 WATLING STREET, RADLETT, HERTS
Hertfordshire WD7 7NQ.......................................01923 853 104
e: info@team-togs.com
w: www.team-togs.com

Totally Original T-Shirts
13A BANKSIA ROAD, ELEY ESTATE, EDMONTON, LONDON
Greater London N18 3BF......................................020 8887 7900
e: sales@totshirts.co.uk
w: www.totshirts.co.uk

Trademark Clothing
TRADEMARK HOUSE, RAMSHILL, PETERSFIELD
Hampshire GU31 4AT...01730 711140
e: sales@tm-clothing.com
w: www.tm-clothing.com

TTfone
321 CALEDONIAN ROAD, LONDON
 N1 1DR...0330 333 0819
e: info@ttfone.com
w: www.ttfone.com

UK Tentickle Stretch Tents
SUTTON COLDFIELD
West Midlands B75 5LU................................... +447826 843099
e: uk@tentickle-stretchtents.com
w: www.tentickle-stretchtents.com/uk

M N O

Mobile Disco

Sound Of Music Mobile Disco DJ Hire Agency Croydon
....07402 700695
e: soundofmusicdjagency@hotmail.com
w: www.soundofmusicmobiledisco.com

Mobile Exhibition / Hospitality Units

Blackburn Trailers Ltd
WHITESTONE FARM, MAIN ROAD, BIRDHAM
West Sussex PO20 7HU 01243 513550
e: trailers07@kompak.co.uk
w: www.kompak.co.uk

David Wilson's Trailers Ltd
JUBILEE PARK, HONEYPOT LANE, COLSTERWORTH, GRANTHAM
Lincolnshire NG33 5l 7..01476 860 833
e: info@dwt-exhibitions.co.uk
w: www.dwt-exhibitions.co.uk

Fenwick Mobile Exhibitions Ltd
FENWICK BY-PASS, FENWICK
Ayrshire KA3 6AW...01560 600271
e: enquiries@fmx-ltd.com
w: www.fmx-ltd.com

LiteStructures (GB) Ltd
(PART OF THE PROLYTE GROUP), LANGTHWAITE BUSINESS PARK
- UNIT 55, SOUTH KIRKBY, WAKEFIELD
 WF9 3NR 01977 659 800
e: info@prolyte.co.uk
w: www.prolyte.co.uk

London Bus Export Company
PO BOX 12, CHEPSTOW
Gloucestershire NP16 5UZ 01291 689741
e: enquiries@londonbuspromotions.com
w: www.london-bus.co.uk

Lynton Trailers (UK) Ltd
ROSSINGTON INDUSTRIAL PARK, GRAPHITE WAY, HADFIELD, GLOSSOP
Derbyshire SK13 1QH 01457 852700
e: sales@lyntontrailers.co.uk
w: www.lyntontrailers.co.uk

Mobex Ltd
UNIT 6 RIGESTATE INDUSTRIAL ESTATE, STATION ROAD, BERKELEY
Gloucestershire GL13 9RL......................................01453 511 210
e: exhibit@mobex.co.uk
w: www.mobex.co.uk

Motorvation (shows On The Road) Ltd
CHILHAM 3, STATION APPROACH, CHILHAM
Kent CT4 8EG 01227 738 266
e: info@motorv.com
w: www.motorv.com

Neptunus Ltd
COB DRIVE, SWAN VALLEY, NORTHAMPTON
Northamptonshire NN4 9BB .... 01604 593820 // 1604 593820
e: sales@neptunus.co.uk
w: www.neptunus.co.uk

Open Exhibitions
UNIT 1, ROTHWELL ROAD, WARWICK
Warwickshire CV34 5PY..01926 402 938
e: david.askill@openexhibitions.com
w: www.openexhibitions.co.uk

Print Designs
EMERALD WAY, STONE BUSINESS PARK, STONE
Staffordshire ST15 0SR..01785 818 111
e: sales@printdesigns.com
w: www.printdesigns.com

Qdos Event Hire
FERNSIDE PLACE, 179 QUEENS ROAD, WEYBRIDGE
Surrey KT13 0AH 0845 862 0952
e: enquiries@qdoseventhire.co.uk
w: www.qdoseventhire.co.uk

Rollalong Hire Ltd
WOOLSBRIDGE INDUSTRIAL PARK , THREE LEGGED CROSS , WIMBOURNE
Dorset BH21 6SF 01202 824541
e: enquiries@rollalong.co.uk
w: www.rollalong.co.uk

Showplace Hospitality Suites Ltd
3 STOUR HOUSE, CLIFFORD PARK, CLIFFORD ROAD, STRATFORD UPON AVON
Warwickshire CV37 8HW 01789 262701
e: info@showplace.co.uk
w: www.showplace.co.uk

Slumbertruck
....7539625498
e: donovan@free-me.com
w: www.slumbertruck.com

Special Event Services Ltd
GROVE FARM, BUCKINGHAM, BRACKLEY
 NN13 5JH..01280 841215
e: info@sesevent.co.uk
w: www.sesevent.co.uk

The Stage Bus
19 PRESTWOOD ROAD, WEOLEY CASTLE, BIRMINGHAM
West Midlands B29 5EB.................................... 07738 900 762 /
0121 585 9264
e: info@thestagebus.com
w: www.thestagebus.com

Torton Bodies Ltd
PILOT WORKS, HOLYHEAD ROAD, OAKENGATES, TELFORD
West Midlands TF2 6BB 01952 612648
e: sales@torton.com
w: www.torton.com

M N O

Tow Master
UNIT 5, AMBER COURT, OFF WALTHEW HOUSE LANE, MARTLAND PARK, WIGAN
Greater Manchester WN5 0JY 01942 226633
e: comments@towmasteruk.com
w: www.towmasteruk.co.uk

Vipex
NUNN BROOK ROAD , HUTHWAITE, SUTTON IN ASHFIELD
Nottinghamshire NG17 2HU 01623 441114
e: info@vipex.co.uk
w: www.vipex.co.uk

Worldwide Structures Ltd
AYRESHIRE FARM , SHARCOTT, PEWSEY
Wiltshire SN9 5PA...01672 565060
e: enquiries@w-sl.com
w: www.smart-spaces.com

Mobile Stages

Actus Event Technology
UNIT 4, FULLERS YARD, SHEEPHOUSE ROAD, MAIDENHEAD
SL6 8HA 0844 736 5650
e: info@actusevent.com
w: www.actusevent.com

Actus Industries
UNIT K5, FIELD WAY, METROPOLITAN PARK, GREENFORD
Middlesex UB6 8UN 020 8578 7001
w: www.actusindustries.com

Adam Hall Ltd
THE SEEDBED BUSINESS CENTRE, VANGUARD WAY, SHOEBURYNESS
SS3 9QY 01702 613922
e: mail@adamhall.co.uk
w: www.adamhall.com

C&E Structures scaffolding
NORTH MERSEY BUSINESS CENTRE/WOODWARD RD, KNOWSLEY INDUSTRIAL PARK, LIVERPOOL
Merseyside L33 7UY .... 0151 5484 492 -
07775 880 460

e: ian@candestructures.co.uk
w: www.candestructures.co.uk

Elation DJs Ltd
7 RINGHAY ROAD, BRADFORD
West Yorkshire BD4 0TZ........... 01274 800 460 // 07811 200 293
e: info@elationdjs.co.uk
w: www.elationdjs.co.uk

Instant Stage
THE OLD FOUNDRY, WOODHALL STREET , FAILSWORTH, MANCHESTER
Greater Manchester M23 0DD 07515 562 787
e: mobilestagebookings@gmail.com
w: www.instantstage.co.uk

KC Lighting
123 PRIORWAY AVENUE, BORROWASH, DERBY
DE72 3HY .... 01332 674589 // 07860 669323
e: kev@kclighting.co.uk
w: www.kclighting.co.uk

Le Mark Self Adhesive Ltd
UNIT 1 HOUGHTON HILL INDUSTRIES, SAWTRY WAY, HOUGHTON
Cambridgeshire PE28 2DH....................................01480 494 540
e: info@lemark.co.uk
w: www.lemark.co.uk

Stageline Mobile Stage
700 MARSOLAIS, 827 L'ANGE-GARDIEN, L'ASSOMPTION, CANADA
J5W 2G9.. +1 450-589-1063
e: info@stageline.com
w: www.stageline.com

Tow Master
UNIT 5, AMBER COURT, OFF WALTHEW HOUSE LANE, MARTLAND PARK, WIGAN
Greater Manchester WN5 0JY 01942 226633
e: comments@towmasteruk.com
w: www.towmasteruk.co.uk

Modular / Portable Display Systems

A1 Events & Exhibitions Ltd
SUITE 10, SHENLEY PAVILIONS, CHALKDELL DRIVE, SHENLEY WOOD, MILTON KEYNES
Buckinghamshire MK5 6LB....................................01908 867555
e: help@a1-events-exhibitions.com
w: www.a1-events-exhibitions.com

Activteam
BUSINESS DESIGN CENTRE, 52 UPPER STREET, LONDON
Greater London N1 0QH 020 3051 6244
e: project@activteam.co.uk
w: www.activteam.com

Amber & Green
PRECISION HOUSE, 4 PITWOOD PARK, WATERFIELD, TONGHAM
Surrey kt20 5jl...020 8256 5980
e: hi@amberandgreen.com
w: www.amberandgreen.com

Ardan Exhibitions
UNIT 7, NORTH MEDBURN FARM, WATLING STREET, ELSTREE
Hertfordshire WD6 3AA 020 8207 4957
e: inquiries@ardan.co.uk
w: www.ardan.co.uk

Ashfield Displays
FLOOR 2, UNIT 10B STONEY CROSS INDUSTRIAL EST, STONEY GATE ROAD, SPONDON, DERBY
Derbyshire DE21 7RX...01332 477372
e: info@ashfielddisplays.co.uk
w: www.ashfielddisplays.co.uk

M N O

Atg Spectrum Ltd
UNIT 7&8, SHAFTESBURY INDUSTRIAL ESTATE, ICKNIELD WAY,
LETCHWORTH GARDEN CITY
Hertfordshire SG6 1HE..01462 485888
e: exhibitions@atgspectrum.com
w: www.atgspectrum.com

Blueprint Design Partnership
HOLLY COTTAGE, 14 LIBBARDS MEWS, STONEBOW AVENUE,
SOLIHULL West Midlands B91 3UP.......................0121 622 1005
w: www.exhibitionsteelwork.com

Boldlook Exhibition
7 GRANGE LANE, WINSFORD
Cheshire CW7 2BP...01606 558770
e: info@boldlook.co.uk
w: www.exhibition-display.net

C&S Displays Ltd
HIGH BURROW, HIGHER LANE CLOSE, AXMOUTH
Devon EX12 4BU...01297 625 481
e: info@candsdisplays.co.uk
w: www.candsdisplays.co.uk

CEI Exhibitions
STONEBRIDGE HOUSE, 28-32 BRIDGE STREET, LEATHERHEAD
Surrey KT22 8BZ .... +44 (0) 1372 869849
e: darryl@ceiexhibitions.co.uk
w: www.ceiexhibitions.co.uk

Clements & Street Design Build Ltd
UNIT 9, BROAD GROUND ROAD, LAKESIDE, REDDITCH
Worcestershire B98 8YP 01527 510154
e: info@clementsandstreet-db.co.uk
w: www.clementsandstreet-db.co.uk

Clip Display Services
CHURCH ROAD, WICK, BRISTOL
Bristol BS30 5RD 0800 834 298
e: info@clipdisplay.com
w: www.clipdisplay.com

Designworks
UNIT 2 WINDSOR BUSINESS CENTRE, VANSITTART ESTATE,
WINDSOR Berkshire SL4 1SP...............................01753 842 404
e: dw@designworkswindsor.co.uk
w: www.designworksgroup.net

Display Makers UK Ltd
SOVEREIGN HOUSE, 10 LANCASTER PARK, NEEDWOOD,
BURTON ON TRENT
Staffordshire DE13 9PD 01283 575097
e: sales@isoframe.co.uk
w: www.isoframe.co.uk

Display Wizard
UNITS 15 & 16 CREAMERY INDUSTRIAL ESTATE, KENLIS ROAD,
BARNACRE, GARSTANG
Lancashire PR3 1GD 01995 606633
e: matthew@displaywizard.co.uk
w: www.displaywizard.co.uk

Europa International
EUROPA HOUSE, MEAFORD WAY, PENGE, LONDON
Greater London SE20 8RA....................................020 8676 0062
e: contact@europainternational.com
w: www.europainternational.com

Excite Exhibition & Display
UNIT 2, 6 FLUSH PARK, LISBURN
 BT28 2DX 028 9267 3030
e: info@excitedisplay.co.uk
w: www.excitedisplay.co.uk

Exhibit Hire
UNIT J, GREAT WESTERN INDUSTRIAL ESTATE, DEAN WAY,
LONDON
Greater London UB2 4SB 020 3384 0369
e: info@exhibithire.com
w: www.exhibithire.co.uk

Exmedia Ltd
UNIT K2, HERALD WAY, BINLEY IND ESTATE, COVENTRY
West Midlands CV3 2NY..02476 455258
e: info@exmedia.uk.com
w: www.exmedia.uk.com

Flying Monk Graphics
UNIT 9 MALMESBURY BUSINESS PARK, BEUTTELL WAY,
MALMESBURY
Wiltshire SN16 9JU...01666 829228
e: info@flyingmonkgraphics.co.uk
w: www.flyingmonkgraphics.co.uk

Harrisons Signs Ltd
LINK HOUSE, GREEN LANE TRADING ESTATE, CLIFTON, YORK
North Yorkshire YO30 5PY 01904 699600
e: sales@harrisonsigns.co.uk
w: www.harrisonsigns.co.uk

Inhouse Exhibition
 .... +91 97693 81737
e: enquiry@inhouseexhibition.com
w: www.inhouseexhibition.com

JDJ Western
UNIT E LLANTRISANT BUSINESS PARK, LLANTRISANT
 CF72 8LF..01443 23 94 86
e: info@jdjwestern.co.uk
w: www.denbewestern.co.uk

JP Displays & Exhibitions
UNIT 16A CHALWYN INDUSTRIAL ESTATE, ST CLEMENTS ROAD,
PARK STONE, POOLE
Dorset BH12 4PE 01202 715 722
e: contactus@jpdisplays.com
w: www.jpdisplays.com

Love Displays Ltd
CHISWICK HOUSE, CHISWICK GROVE, BLACKPOOL
Lancashire FY3 9TW...01253 769 911
e: info@lovedisplays.co.uk
w: www.lovedisplays.co.uk

M N O

Macflex International
MACFLEX HOUSE, HILL FARM, UPPER HEYFORD, NORTHAMPTON
NN7 3NB 01604 833666
e: sales@macflex.com
w: www.macflex.com

Mardell-Pick Design Ltd
THE STUDIO, 27 THE WOODFIELDS, SANDERSTEAD, CROYDON,
LONDON
Greater London CR2 0HG 020 8651 0248
e: info@mardell-pickdesign.com
w: www.mardell-pickdesign.com

Marler Haley
45 BOOTH DRIVE, PARK FARM INDUSTRIAL ESTATE,
WELLINGBOROUGH
Northamptonshire NN8 6NL 0808 159 2181
e: info@marlerhaley.co.uk
w: www.marlerhaley.co.uk

Melville Exhibition & Event Services
UNIT 1, PERIMETER ROAD, NATIONAL EXHIBITION CENTRE,
BIRMINGHAM
West Midlands B40 1PJ 0121 780 3025
e: info@melville.co.uk
w: www.melville.co.uk

Messagemaker Displays Ltd
UNIT 43 ORMSIDE WAY, HOLMETHORPE INDUSTRIAL ESTATE ,
REDHILL
Surrey RH1 2LG 0800 170 7780
e: sales@messagemaker.co.uk
w: www.messagemaker.co.uk

Networks
THE RIVERSIDE, BAMFORD
Derbyshire S33 0BN 01433 659659
e: networks3d@networks3d.net
w: www.networks3d.net

Nimlok Ltd
NIMLOK HOUSE, BOOTH DRIVE, PARK FARM INDUSTRIAL ESTATE,
WELLINGBOROUGH
Northamptonshire NN8 6NL 0808 256 1220
e: info@nimlok.co.uk
w: www.nimlok.co.uk

Oasis Graphic Co
2ND ENTRANCE, UNIT 7, LOWER MOUNT FARM, LONG LANE,
COOKHAM
Berkshire SL6 9EE 01628 532003
e: info@oasisgraphic.co.uk
w: www.oasisgraphic.co.uk

Open Exhibitions
UNIT 1, ROTHWELL ROAD, WARWICK
Warwickshire CV34 5PY 01926 402 938
e: david.askill@openexhibitions.com
w: www.openexhibitions.co.uk

Oscar Group Ltd
P.O. BOX 7571, MILTON KEYNES
Buckinghamshire MK11 9GL.....................01908 260 333
e: sales@oscar.uk.com
w: www.oscar.uk.com

Paul Turner Displays Ltd
UNIT 29, SHOREBURY POINT, AMY JOHNSON WAY, BLACKPOOL
Lancashire FY4 2RF 01253 891 853
e: paul@paulturnerdisplays.co.uk
w: www.paulturnerdisplays.co.uk

POD Exhibitions
LOWER FARM, HIGH STREET, IRCHESTER
Northamptonshire NN29 7AB 01933 411159
e: enquiries@podweb.co.uk
w: www.pod-exhibition-systems.co.uk

Print Designs
EMERALD WAY, STONE BUSINESS PARK, STONE
Staffordshire ST15 0SR............................01785 818 111
e: sales@printdesigns.com
w: www.printdesigns.com

Proscreens
.... 0845 309 6369 // 07876755357
e: info@proscreens.net
w: www.proscreens.net

Publicity Systems
UNIT 2 PROSPECT HOUSE, LOWER DICKER
East Sussex BN27 4BT 01323 846640
e: sales@publicitysystems.net
w: www.publicitysystems.net

Quadrant2Design
THE FULCRUM, VANTAGE WAY, POOLE
Dorset BH12 4NU....................................01202 723 500
e: designteam@quadrant2design.com
w: www.prestige-system.com

Ral Display & Marketing Ltd
2 CRANMER STREET, LEICESTER
Leicestershire LE3 0QA............................0116 2554640
e: sales@ral-display.co.uk
w: www.ral-display.co.uk

Sovereign Exhibitions
UNITS 1,2 AND 3, ARLEY INDUSTRIAL ESTATE,, COLLIERS WAY,
ARLEY, COVENTRY
West Midlands CV7 8HN 01676 549 000
e: info@sovereignexhibitions.co.uk
w: www.sovereignexhibitions.co.uk

Standit Displays
UNIT 5 ASTON COURT, LEEDS
Yorkshire LS13 2AF.................................0113 8272218
e: neesha@standitdisplays.co.uk
w: www.standitdisplays.co.uk

M N O

The Digitial Print Factory (tdpf)
12-12A ROSEBERY AVENUE, LONDON
Greater London EC1R 4TD 020 7209 5620
e: toby@exhibitionkit.co.uk; info@tdpf.eu
w: www.exhibitionkit.co.uk

The Events Structure
INNOSPACE, THE SHEDS, CHESTER STREET, MANCHESTER
Greater Manchester M1 5GD.................................0161 821 1010
w: www.theeventsstructure.com

The Revolving Stage Company Ltd
CRONDAL ROAD, BAYTON ROAD INDUSTRIAL ESTATE, COVENTRY
Warwickshire CV7 9NH 024 7668 7055
e: enquiries@therevolvingstagecompany.co.uk
w: www.therevolvingstagecompany.co.u

The Searchlight Company
UNIT 9, CROMER HYDE FARM, SYMONDSHYDE LANE, HATFIELD
Hertfordshire AL10 9BB 01707 269681
e: enquiries@searchlight.co.uk
w: www.searchlight.co.uk

Timber Intent
WARREN COTTAGE, HARCOMBE BOTTOM, LYME REGIS
Dorset DT/ 3RN..01297 444 416
e: mail@timberintent.co.uk
w: ww.timberintent.co.uk

Ultima Displays Ltd
49-50 CAUSEWAY ROAD, EARLSTREES INDUSTRIAL ESTATE,
CORBY
Northamptonshire NN17 4DU..................................01536 272250
e: sales@ultimadisplays.co.uk
w: www.ultimadisplays.co.uk

Worth Events
28 LONGFELLOW ROAD, WORTHING
 BN11 4NU...01903 620329
e: info@worthevents.com
w: www.worthevents.com

XL Displays
38-39 MANASTY RD, ORTON SOUTHGATE, PETERBOROUGH
Cambridgeshire PE2 6UP 01733 511030
e: sales@xldisplays.co.uk
w: www.xldisplays.co.uk

Zoom Display
UNIT 9 TABRUMS FARM, TABRUMS LANE, BATTLESBRIDGE
Essex SS11 7QX 01245 325743
e: enquiries@zoomdisplay.co.uk
w: www.zoomdisplay.co.uk

Music / Sound Effects Libraries

Arcadia Production Music (uk)
GREENLANDS, PAYHEMBURY
Devon EX14 3HY...01404 841601
e: info@arcadiamusic.tv
w: www.arcadiamusic.tv

Artisan Audio
46A WOODBRIDGE ROAD , , MOSELEY , BIRMINGHAM
 B13 8EJ...0121 249 0598
e: rebecca@artisanaudio.com
w: www.artisanaudio.com

Br Music Productions Ltd
35 ROYCE GROVE, WATFORD
Hertfordshire WD25 7GB.......................................0 1923 679222
e: info@brmusicproductions.com
w: www.brmusicproductions.com

Bucks Music Group
ROUNDHOUSE, 212 REGENTS PARK ROAD ENTRANCE, LONDON
Greater London NW1 8AW....................................020 7221 4275
e: info@bucksmusicgroup.co.uk
w: www.bucksmusicgroup.com

Candle
44 SOUTHERN ROW
 W10 5AN 020 8960 0111
e: tony@candle.org.uk
w: www.candle.org.uk

Caribbean Music Library
EBREL HOUSE, 2A PENLEE CLOSE, PRAA SANDS, PENZANCE
Cornwall TR20 9SR...01736 762826
e: panamus@aol.com
w: www.panamamusic.co.uk

Caritas Media Music
ACHMORE, MOSS ROAD, ULLAPOOL
Ross-shire IV26 2TF...01854 612236
e: info@caritas-music.co.uk
w: www.caritas-music.co.uk

Christof R Davis
.... 07960170429 / 07791008072
e: chrisdaviscomposer@gmail.com
w: www.christopherdavis.org.uk

Deep East Music
UNIT C, RELIANCE WHARF, 2-10 HERTFORD ROAD, LONDON
Greater London N1 5EW......................................020 7923 1444
e: info@deepeastmusic.com
w: www.deepeastmusic.com

Deepwater Blue
119 THIRD AVENUE, ALMODINGTON
West Sussex PO20 7LB..01243 512000
e: info@deepwaterblue.net
w: www.deepwaterblue.net

Dmc Ltd
PO 89 , SLOUGH
 SL1 8NA 01628 667124
e: info@dmcworld.com
w: www.dmcworld.com

M N O

Earshot Music Production
110 BRUDNELL ROAD, HEADINGLEY, LEEDS
LS6 1LS..0113 2782 174
e: info@earshotmusic.co.uk
w: www.earshot.tv

Fifth Company
SUITE 3, 2 PEPPER STREET, ISLE OF DOGS
E14 9RB 020 7515 1587
e: mikestobbie@btinternet.com

High Action Music Ltd
2 WINDSOR COURT, TILE HILL, COVENTRY
CV4 9GW 07950 614 305
e: info@highactionmusic.com
w: www.highactionmusic.com

Higher Audio Ltd
....1483338008
e: info@higheraudio.uk
w: www.higheraudio.uk

Hull Central Lending Library
GUILDHALL, ALFRED GELDER STREET, HULL
East Yorkshire HU1 2AA 01482 300 300
e: info@hullcc.gov.uk
w: www.hullcc.gov.uk

In Tune XI
34 LATELOW ROAD, KITTS GREEN, BIRMINGHAM
B33 8JZ..07508 346 673
e: drjones404@googlemail.com

Joe & Co (music) Ltd
HAMMER HOUSE, 117 WARDOUR STREET
W1F 0UN 020 7439 1272
e: info@yellowboatmusic.com
w: www.joeandco.com

Joe Williams Music
4 DARNLEY ROAD, LEEDS
LS16 5JF..0113 295 6111
e: joe@joewilliams.co.uk
w: www.joewilliams.co.uk

Kassner Associated Publishers Ltd
UNITS 6-7, 11 WYFOLD ROAD, FULHAM
SW6 6SE 020 7385 7700
e: songs@kassner-music.co.uk
w: www.kassnermusic.com

Lynwood Music
2 CHURCH STREET, WEST HAGLEY
West Midlands DY9 0NA 01562 886625
e: downlyn@globalnet.co.uk
w: www.andrewdownes.com

Michael Freeman
5 SHAFTOE MEWS, HAYDON BRIDGE
NE47 6BA 01434 684535
e: michael.newmusic@virgin.net
w: www.youtube.com/watch?v=7_

Middlemarch Ltd
PO BOX 111, UCKFIELD
TN22 5WQ..01825 890773
e: mark@melodyandlyrics.co.uk
w: www.melodyandlyrics.co.uk

Mohock Records
EBREL HOUSE,2A PENLEE CLOSE,, PRAA SANDS, PENZANCE
Cornwall TR20 9SR..01736 762826
e: panamus@aol.com
w: www.panamamusic.co.uk

Mostyn Music
34 BUCKLEY STREET, , STALYBRIDGE
Cheshire SK15 1TT..0161 304 7590
e: orders@mostynmusic.com
w: www.mostynmusic.com

Mph Music
KEEPERS COTTAGE, GLENSTOCKADALE, LEWWALT, STRANRAER
DG9 0LU..01776 870 473
e: mike@mphmusic.co.uk
w: www.mphmusic.co.uk

Northstar Music Publishing Ltd
PO BOX 868, CAMBRIDGE
Cambridgeshire CB21 4SJ..01787 278256
e: info@northstarmusic.co.uk
w: www.northstarmusic.co.uk

Panama Productions
EBREL HOUSE, 2A PENLEE CLOSE, PRAA SANDS, PENZANCE
Cornwall TR20 9ST..01736 762826
e: panamus@aol.com
w: www.panamamusic.co.uk

Plus Music
36 FOLLINGHAM COURT, DRYSDALE PLACE, HOXTON
N1 6LZ..020 7684 8594
e: info@plusmusic.co.uk
w: www.plusmusic.co.uk

Raw State
THE OLD MALTHOUSE, UNIT 4, LEVEL 2, CLARENCE STREET, BATH
Somerset BA1 5NS..01225 466464
e: info@rawstate.com
w: home.btconnect.com/rawstate/welco

Reliable Source Music Ltd
67 UPPER BERKELEY STREET, LONDON
Greater London W1H 7QX..020 7563 7028
e: MusicTeam@reliable-source.co.uk
w: www.reliable-source.co.uk

Rockcast
34 CONISTON ROAD, NESTON
CH64 0TD..0151 336 6199
e: podcast@rockcast.co.uk
w: www.rockcast.co.uk

**M
N
O**

Silverglade Associates Ltd
205 ENTERPRISE HOUSE, 1-2 HATFIELDS, LONDON
Greater London SE1 9PG..020 7827 9510
e: info@silverglade.com
w: www.silverglade.com

Songlife Music
36 RADNOR PARK ROAD, FOLKESTONE
CT19 5AU 01303 257714
e: songlife@fsmail.net

Songs For Today Ltd
PO BOX 130, HOVE
BN3 6QU...01273 550088
e: publishing@tkogroup.com
w: www.tkogroup.com

StageLightSound Ltd
....1929423223
e: info@stagelightsound.com
w: www.stagelightsound.com

State Music
67 UPPER BERKELEY STREET, MARYLEBONE
W1H 7DH..020 7616 9284
e: recordings@staterecords.co.uk

Stephen Budd Management
59-65 WORSHIP STREET
EC2A 2DU 020 7688 8995
e: info@record-producers.com
w: www.record-producers.com

Tairona Songs Ltd
PO BOX 102, LONDON
Greater London E15 2HH 020 8555 5423
e: tairona@moksha.co.uk
w: www.moksha.co.uk

Musical Instruments / Equipment

Abinger Organs
LITTLE HOE, HOE LANE, ABINGER HAMMER, DORKING
Surrey RH5 6RH..01306 730277
e: hires@abingerorgans.co.uk
w: www.abingerorgans.co.uk

Amadeus Equipment
GREAT BEECH BARN, KANE HYTHE ROAD, BATTLE
East Sussex TN33 9QU 01424 775867
e: info@amadeus-equipment.co.uk
w: www.amadeus-equipment.co.uk

Bell Audio Hire
5 GREENOCK ROAD , CHISWICK , LONDON
W3 8DU 2088961200
e: dan@bellperc.com
w: www.bellaudiohire.com/

Black Cat Music
FESTIVAL HOUSE, CHAPMAN WAY, TUNBRIDGE WELLS
Kent TN2 3EF... 01892 619719 //
0800 0727799
e: sales@blackcatmusic.co.uk
w: www.blackcatmusic.co.uk

Brittens Music Direct Ltd
GROVE HILL ROAD, TUNBRIDGE WELLS
Kent TN1 1RZ 01892 526 659
e: sales@brittensmusic.co.uk
w: www.brittensmusic.co.uk

EJ Productions
12 THE ALBERMARLE , BRIGHTON
BN2 1TX 7971525552
e: Ellis@EJProductions.co.uk
w: www.ejproductions.co.uk/

Elation DJs Ltd
7 RINGHAY ROAD, BRADFORD
West Yorkshire BD4 0TZ.................................... 01274 800 460 //
07811 200 293
e: info@elationdjs.co.uk
w: www.elationdjs.co.uk

Fifth Company
SUITE 3, 2 PEPPER STREET, ISLE OF DOGS
E14 9RB 020 7515 1587
e: mikestobbie@btinternet.com

Gb Musical Enterprises Ltd
1 CASTLE RISE,, PRESTBURY,
Cheshire SK10 4UR...01625 871092
e: info@gabor-pianos.co.uk
w: www.gabor-pianos.co.uk

Graff Of Newark Ltd
WOODHILL ROAD, COLLINGHAM, NEWARK
Nottinghamshire NG23 7NR 01636 893036
e: sales@graffdigitalcopiers.co.uk
w: www.graffdigitalcopiers.co.uk/

Guitar lessons Camberley
30 SILVER HILL   , COLLEGE TOWN, SANDHURST
Berkshire GU47 0QS 7962101386
e: guitarlessonssandhurst@gmail.com
w: www.guitarlessonscamberley.co.uk

Hibernian Violins
10 CAMP HILL, WEST MALVERN
Worcestershire WR14 4BZ 01684 562947
e: contact@hibernianviolins.co.uk
w: www.hibernianviolins.co.uk

Korg Uk Ltd
9 NEWMARKET COURT, KINGSTON, MILTON KEYNES
MK10 0AU 01908 857100
e: info@korg.co.uk
w: www.korg.co.uk

M N O

Marek Koczen Music Services Ltd
7 BARROW POINT AVENUE, PINNER MIDDLESEX
Greater London HA5 3HQ 8007723956
e: info@rentadigitalpiano.co.uk
w: www.rentadigitalpiano.co.uk

Markson Pianos Ltd
7-8 CHESTER COURT, ALBANY STREET, LONDON
Greater London NW1 4BU 0207 935 8682
e: info@marksonpianos.com
w: www.marksonpianos.com

Matco Piano Transport
465 HORNSEY ROAD, LONDON
 N19 4DR 020 7281 9555
e: piano@matcomoves.com
w: www.matcomoves.com

Matt Snowball Music
UNIT 2, 3-9 BREWERY ROAD, LONDON
Greater London N7 9QJ 020 7700 6555
e: enquiries@mattsnowball.com
w: www.mattsnowball.com

Neuron Pro Audio Ltd
DOWNTEX WAREHOUSE, 17 MARY STREET, MANCHESTER
Greater Manchester M3 1NH................................0161 408 1545
e: enquiries@neuronproaudio.co.uk
w: www.neuronproaudio.co.uk

Novel Events
UNIT 3B BARON AVENUE, TELFORD WAY INDUSTRIAL
ESTATE, KETTERING
 NN16 8UW..01536 483 854
e: sales@novel-events.com
w: www.novel-events.com

Orange Audio
9 WARGRAVE ROAD, CLACTON-ON-SEA
Essex CO15 3EQ 07510-726-167
e: info@orangeaudio.co.uk
w: www.orangeaudio.co.uk

Paul Hathway Musical Instruments
47 LANGLEY DRIVE, WANSTEAD
 E11 2LN 020 8530 4317
e: paul@paulhathway.com
w: www.paulhathway.com

River Pro Audio
UNIT 6, BELVEDERE BUSINESS PARK, CRABTREE MANORWAY
SOUTH, BELVEDERE
Kent DA17 6AH...020 8311 7077
e: sales@riverproaudio.co.uk
w: www.riverproaudio.co.uk

Swans Music
THE BELAN, MOSS LANE, KNUTSFORD
Cheshire WA16 7BS...01565 873044
e: bill@swansmusic.co.uk
w: www.swansmusic.co.uk

The PA Company Ltd
UNIT 7, THE ASHWAY CENTRE, ELM CRESCENT,
KINGSTON UPON THAMES
Surrey KT2 6HH 020 8546 6640
e: thepacompany@aol.com
w: www.thepaco.com

Violectra -electric Violins, Violas And Cellos
MOSELEY VIOLINS, 2A TUDOR RD, MOSELEY, BIRMINGHAM
West Midlands B13 8HA..0121 693 1214
e: info@violectra.co.uk
w: www.violectra.co.uk

VNV Sounds
UNITS 10 AND 10A ASHLEY HOUSE, ASHLEY ROAD, LONDON
Greater London N17 9LZ.......................................0203 021 1370
e: info@vnvlive.co.uk
w: www.vnvsounds.co.uk

Wedding Bands Glasgow
73 ALBERT ROAD, GLASGOW
 G42 8DP ....01414234863 / 07590693127
e: info@weddingbandsglasgow.com
w: weddingbandsglasgow.com/

WM Event Design
19 ST JAMES'S DRIVE, WANDSWORTH COMMON, LONDON
Greater London SW17 7RN 020 3837 4926
e: info@williammoyse.com
w: www.wmeventdesign.com

Zenworks
114 CHEDDON ROAD, TAUNTON
Somerset TA2 7DW.......................................+44(0)7814754206
e: zenworksengineer@gmail.com
w: zenworks.wix.com/index

Outside Broadcast Units

adi.tv
PITTMAN COURT, PITTMAN WAY, FULWOOD, PRESTON
Lancashire PR2 9ZG 01772 708 200
e: info@adi.tv
w: www.adi.tv

Attend2IT
UNIT 8, PARK FARM INDUSTRIAL ESTATE, BUNTINGFORD
Hertfordshire SG9 9AZ 01763 877 477
w: www.attend2it.co.uk

Big-TV (UK) Ltd
HUDSON HOUSE, THE HUDSON, WYKE, BRADFORD
Yorkshire BD12 8HZ..01274 604 309
e: info@big-tv.co.uk
w: www.big-tv.co.uk

BORIS TV Ltd
BRIDGE HOUSE, BRANKSOME PARK ROAD, CAMBERLEY
Surrey GU15 2AQ...01276 612 22
e: info@boris.tv
w: www.boris.tv

Bowtie Television Ltd
SOUTHBANK HOUSE, BLACK PRINCE ROAD, LAMBETH, LONDON
Greater London SE1 7SJ......................................08454 900 900
e: info@bowtietv.com
w: www.bowtietv.com

Colin Cradock Ltd
DARWIN HOUSE, CROWBOROUGH HILL, CROWBOROUGH
 TN6 2JA.................................. 0208 133 1716 // 07515 869862
e: info@colincradockltd.com
w: www.colincradockltd.com

Plasmatising AV Hire London
261 TIMBERLOG LANE, BASILDON
Essex SS14 1PA...01268 550202
e: info@plasmatising.co.uk
w: www.plasmatising.co.uk

Proscreens
.... 0845 309 6369 // 07876755357
e: info@proscreens.net
w: www.proscreens.net

Satstream
8, BRAMLEY COURT, HEREFORD
Herefordshire HR4 0SB 0844 8008785
e: info@satstream.co.uk
w: www.satstream.co.uk

Silverstream TV - The Web Video Experts
NEW MEDIA HOUSE, 2A DE LA HAY AVE, PLYMOUTH
 PL3 4HU 0207 183 6444
e: mail@silverstream.tv
w: www.silverstream.tv

Sound Moves
THE OAKS, CROSS LANE, SMALLFIELD, HORLEY
Surrey RH6 9SA..01342 844190
e: soundmoves@gmail.com
w: www.sound-moves.com

Soundguy
72 ARRAN STREET, ROATH, CARDIFF
Glamorgan CF24 3HT..07771 600 552
e: info@soundguy.co.uk
w: www.soundguy.co.uk

Yellow Fish Mobile Studio
CONCORDE HOUSE, 18 MARGARET STREET, BRIGHTON
East Sussex BN1 2TS...01273 900 862
e: info@yellowfishmusicgroup.com
w: www.yellowfishmusicgroup.com

Oyster Shuckers

Oyster Meister
4A FAUCONBERG ROAD, CHISWICK
 W4 3JY 0208 747 8981
e: info@oystermeister.com
w: www.oystermeister.com

M
N
O

PQ

Party Goods / Novelties

All Event Hire
BURNFIELD ROAD, GIFFNOCK, GLASGOW
Glasgow G46 7TH 0141 637 0368/ 0131 652 6007
e: info@alleventhire.co.uk
w: www.alleventhire.co.uk

Balloon Crazy
UNIT 23B, LOMBARD ROAD, LONDON
Greater London SW19 3TZ.....................................020 8543 1133
e: info@ballooncrazy.co.uk
w: www.ballooncrazy.co.uk

Balloon Mad
ASTON ROAD, NUNEATON
Warwickshire CV11 5EL..07473 158698
e: office@balloonmad.co.uk
w: www.balloonmad.co.uk

Blueprint Promotional Products
NO. 1 THE EMBASSY, LAWRENCE STREET, LONG EATON,
NOTTINGHAM
Nottinghamshire NG10 1JY....................................0333 1234 400
e: info@blueprintpromo.co.uk
w: www.blueprintpromo.co.uk

Bounce Entertainment
....1768372967
e: info@bouncycastlehire-cumbria.co.uk
w: www.bouncycastlehire-cumbria.co.u

Charles H Fox Ltd
22 TAVISTOCK STREET, COVENT GARDEN, LONDON
Greater London WC2E 7PY .... +44 20/7240 3111
e: info-uk@kryolan.com
w: www.charlesfox.co.uk

Co Prom Ltd
198 LONDON ROAD, PORTSMOUTH
Hampshire PO2 9JE...01243 575247
e: enquiries@coprom.co.uk
w: www.coprom.co.uk

Eastern Ray - Shisha Catering & Party Solutions
FIRST FLOOR, 2 WOODBERRY GROVE, NORTH FINCHLEY, LONDON
Greater London N12 0DR 07447 104649
e: info@eastern-ray.co.uk
w: www.eastern-ray.co.uk

Global Marketing Group Ltd
GLOBAL HOUSE, SALISBURY ROAD, DOWNTON
Wiltshire SP5 3JJ...01725 514999
e: sales@globalmarketinggroup.co.uk
w: www.globalmarketinggroup.co.uk

Ice Box
UNIT A35/36, NEW COVENT GARDEN MARKET, LONDON
Greater London SW8 5EE.......................................020 7498 0800
e: info@theicebox.com
w: www.theicebox.com

Ilovechocs.com
WYNCHGATE HOUSE, HARROW
HA3 6BS..0844 586 4717
e: Sales@ilovechocs.com
w: www.ilovechocs.com

Jaffe Et Fils Ltd
THE OLD BRUSHWORKS, CASTLE HILL, AXMINSTER
Devon EX13 5PY 01297 33408
e: info@jaffefeathers.co.uk
w: www.jaffefeathers.co.uk

Mirrors for Hire
UNITS 9,10,11 MODULAR BUSINESS PARK, ASPLEY CLOSE, FOUR
ASHES, WOLVERHAMPTON
West Midlands WV10 7DE .... 01902 791207 // 07737 263611
e: info@mirrorsforhire.co.uk
w: www.mirrorsforhire.co.uk

MTFX Confetti Effects
VELT HOUSE, VELT HOUSE LANE, ELMORE
Gloucestershire GL2 3NY 01452 729903
e: info@mtfx.com
w: www.mtfx.com

MTFX Special Effects
VELT HOUSE, VELT HOUSE LANE , ELMORE
Gloucestershire GL2 3NY 01452 729 903
e: info@mtfx.com
w: www.mtfx.com

MTFX Winter Effects
VELT HOUSE, VELT HOUSE LANE, ELMORE
Gloucestershire GL2 3NY 01452 729903
e: info@mtfx.com
w: www.mtfx.com

Pam's The Party Specialists
UNIT 30 , CORRINGHAM ROAD INDUSTRIAL ESTATE,
GAINSBOROUGH Lincolnshire DN21 1QB...............0845 230 6763
e: sales@pams.co.uk
w: www.pams.co.uk

Planet Gold Decor
UNIT 4 ROMARSH, FOWLSWICK BUSINESS PARK, , ALLINGTON
Wiltshire SN14 6QE...07747 015 170
e: info@planetgolddecor.co.uk
w: www.planetgolddecor.co.uk or www.

Studio Soufflé Ltd
46 BROOKSBY'S WALK, HACKNEY, LONDON
Greater London E9 6DA...................................... 020 7998 4950 /
.... 07882 753215 / 07841 573
e: hello@studiosouffle.com
w: www.studiosouffle.com

Tequila-belts.com
73, CHESILTON ROAD, FULHAM, LONDON
Greater London SW6 5AA......................................07807 055 321
e: mail@tequila-belts.com
w: www.tequila-belts.com

P
Q

The Bespoke Goody Bag Company
14 PRIORY ROAD, SALE
M33 2BR 0161 222 8981
e: info@thebespokegoodybagco.co.uk
w: www.thebespokegoodybagco.co.uk

The Diamond Ring Company
SUITE 211, 100 HATTON GARDEN, LONDON
Greater London EC1N 8NX 020 7404 6616
e: thediamondringcompanyuk@gmail.com
w: www.thediamondringcompany.

Photo Booth Hire

Booth Nation
7 EZRA STREET, LONDON
E2 7RH 020 7613 5576
e: info@boothnation.com
w: www.boothnation.com

cityphotobooths
18 TENNYSON AVENUE, RUSTINGTON
West Sussex BN16 2PB 01903 771863
e: info@cityphotobooths.co.uk
w: www.cityphotobooths.co.uk

Chuckle Pod Limited
....07770 692499
e: info@chucklepod.co.uk
w: www.chucklepod.co.uk

Foxy Photo Booth
82 LAMMERMUIR WAY, CHAPELHALL
Lanarkshire ML6 8BE................ 0141 413 4096 - 07751 613 265
e: info@foxyphotobooth.com
w: www.foxyphotobooth.com

Funsnaps Photobooth
....7871613924
e: mail@funsnapsphotobooth.co.uk
w: www.funsnapsphotobooth.co.uk

HR Entertainment Ltd
....1706220338
e: jason@hrentertainment.co.uk
w: www.photoboothhire.org

JS Ent
UNIT 5-7A, 109 MAYBANK RD, SOUTH WOODFORD, LONDON
E18 1EJ...020 8505 8222
e: sales@jsent.co.uk
w: www.jsent.co.uk

Megabooth
UNIT 4, REAR OF 41/43 ROEBUCK ROAD, HAINAULT INDUSTRIAL ESTATE
Essex IG6 3TU......................................020 3053 4333
e: info@megabooth.com
w: www.megabooth.com

Say Fromage
J109-110, THE BISCUIT FACTORY, 100 CLEMENTS ROAD, LONDON
SE16 4DG...020 7237 1648
w: www.sayfromage.co.uk

Seasons Photobooth
BIRMINGHAM
West Midlands B68 8SS.........................079 9001 9006
w: www.seasonsphotobooth.co.uk

Snappabox Party & Event Photo Booth
THE POWERHOUSE, 87 WEST STREET, HARROW ON THE HILL
Middlesex HA1 3EL...............................0845 680 8995
w: www.snappabox.com

Style Booth
....0208 0900 105
e: hello@stylebooth.co.uk
w: www.stylebooth.co.uk

The Party Photo Booth
26 GRANVILLE ROAD, BOURNEMOUTH
Dorset BH5 2AQ...................................07894 477106
e: info@thepartyphotobooth.co.uk
w: www.thepartyphotobooth.co.uk

Zeven Media Ltd
SUITE 3 NEXUS, 4 BRINDLEY ROAD, MANCHESTER
M16 9HQ..020 7717 5408
e: info@zeven.co.uk
w: www.zevenmedia.com

Photocopiers / Faxes / Office Equipment

bars2you ltd
.... 01925 633 131 / 07709888809
e: chris@bars2you.co.uk
w: www.bars2you.com

BlackDog games ltd
....01992 534448
e: peter@blackdoggames.co.uk
w: www.blackdoggames.co.uk

JCS computerent
34 CHARTER GATE, QUARRY PARK CLOSE , MOULTON PARK, NORTHAMPTON
Northamptonshire NN3 6QB......................1604495252
e: rentals@computerent.co.uk
w: computerent.co.uk

WM Event Design
19 ST JAMES'S DRIVE, WANDSWORTH COMMON, LONDON
Greater London SW17 7RN 020 3837 4926
e: info@williammoyse.com
w: www.wmeventdesign.com

P
Q

Photography Services / Studios

Acquire Image Media Picture Library
16 EDGECOMBE WAY, ST ANN'S CHAPEL, GUNNISLAKE
Cornwall PL18 9HJ 01822 833204
e: info@acquireimagemedia.com
w: www.acquireimagemedia.com

Adby Creative Images
VOYAGE, GLENDALE HOUSE, READING ROAD, READING
Berkshire RG7 3BL 020 3239 1084
e: sayhello@adbycreative.co.uk
w: www.adbycreativeimages.co.uk

Allan Staley Photographer
....07831 286343
e: a.staley@btconnect.com
w: www.allanstaley.com

Alvey & Towers
BYTHORN HOUSE, 8 NETHER STREET, HARBY
Leicestershire LE14 4BW 01949 861894
e: office@alveyandtowers.com
w: www.alveyandtowers.com

Andrew Photographic
4 ROBINSON ROAD, BEDWORTH
Warwickshire CV12 0EL 024 7636 4235
e: info@andrewphotographic.co.uk
w: www.andrewphotographic.co.uk

Andy Espin Photography
PO BOX 7776, LEICESTER
Leicestershire LE3 5WT 07767 354052
e: andy@andyespin.com
w: www.andyespin.com

Anthony Mosley Photographer
16 EDGECOMBE WAY, ST ANN'S CHAPEL, GUNNISLAKE
Cornwall PL18 9HJ 01822 833204
e: info@anthonymosley-photographer.co.uk
w: www.anthonymosley-photographer.co

Apollo Photographers Ltd
34 PAYNESFIELD AVENUE, LONDON
Greater London SW14 8DW 07788 443 526
e: info@apollophotographers.co.uk
w: www.apollophotographers.co.uk

Artifact Multimedia
76 BERW ROAD, PONTYPRIDD, SOUTH WALES
 CF37 2AB .... 07961 262080 / 01443 400 204
e: info@artifactmultimedia.co.uk
w: www.artifactmultimedia.co.uk

Artis Studios
56A HIGH STREET, SUNNINGHILL
Berkshire SL5 9NF 01344 870033
e: enquiries@artisstudios.com
w: www.artisstudios.com

Aviation-Images.com
14 HIGH STREET, GORING ON THAMES, READING
Berkshire RG8 9AR 020 8944 5225
e: info@aviation-images.com
w: www.aviation-images.com

Ayesha K Photography
....07525 151535
e: info@ayeshakphotography.co.uk
w: www.ayeshakphotography.co.uk

Bliss Imaging
....07754 829 839
e: info@blissimaging.co.uk
w: www.blissimaging.co.uk

Captured Moment Ltd
212 FLEET ROAD, FLEET
Hampshire GU51 4BY 01252 621926
e: studio@capturedmoment.com
w: www.capturedmoment.com

Carole Latimer
113 LEDBURY ROAD, LONDON
Greater London W11 2AQ.....................................020 7727 9371
e: carole@carolelatimer.com
w: www.carolelatimer.com

Catching the Moments Photography
EDINBURGH EH9 1PB..7517263933
e: info@catchingthemoments.com
w: www.catchingthemoments.com

CheeseBox
....1795668755
e: jenell@cheese-box.co.uk
w: www.cheese-box.co.uk

Cloud 9 Photo
THE MILL, BROME HALL LANE, LAPWORTH, SOLIHULL
Warwickshire B94 5RB 01564 785 799
e: mike@c9dd.com
w: www.cloud9photo.co.uk

Creative Camera
CREATIVE CAMERA STUDIOS, 5 CHURCH BANK, BOLTON
Greater Manchester BL1 1HX...............................07912 117 179
e: simon.kearsley@creative-camera.org
w: www.creative-camera.org

CTP Photography & Video
TYLER HOUSE, 58-66 MORLEY ROAD, TONBRIDGE
Kent TN9 1RA .... 01959 533268 // 07836 750058
e: chris@takenbychris.co.uk
w: www.ctpimaging.co.uk

Damon Murgatroyd Photography
36 BROAD AVENUE, BOURNEMOUTH
 BH8 9HJ .... 07947033697 / 07947 033 698
e: gutsyimages@gmail.com
w: damonmurgatroydphotography.com/

David Lamour & Co
87 WHITEHILL PARK, LIMAVADY
BT49 0QF 07850 192 938
e: info@davidlarmour.co.uk
w: www.davidlarmour.co.uk

Fergus Burnett Photography
....07950 255 877
e: fergus_photography@yahoo.co.uk
w: www.fergusburnett.com

First Option Location Studio
PERSEVERANCE WORKS, KINGSLAND ROAD, SHOREDITCH,
LONDONE2 8DD......................07949 205 560 // 020 7739 0132
e: studio@studiohirefirstoption.com
w: www.studiohirefirstoption.com

Flight Images
UNIT 2B, HENLEY BUSINESS PARK, PIRBRIGHT ROAD, NORMANDY
Surrey GU3 2DX..01483 233395
e: info@flightimages.com
w: www.flightimages.com

For Keeps Photography
8 PERRY ROAD BENFLEET
Essex SS7 5DJ 7816148290
e: swimbledon@gmail.com
w: www.4keepsphotography.co.uk

Gap Studios West
228 -230 UXBRIDGE ROAD, LONDON
Greater London W12 7JD......................................0208 740 1757
e: info@gapstudioswest.co.uk
w: www.gapstudioswest.co.uk

Ginny Marsh Photography
.... 01252 856 937 // 07917 666733
e: info@ginnymarsh.co.uk
w: www.ginnymarsh.co.uk

Grete Photo
.... +44 788 589 9908
e: grete@gretephoto.com
w: www.gretephoto.com

Halo Booth
....0141 374 2401
e: halobooth@gmail.com
w: https://www.halobooth.co.uk/

HASHTAG Ltd
HIGH PARK RD, RICHMOND
Greater London TW9 4BH.....................................0208 0900 105
e: hello@hashtag.co.uk
w: www.hashtag.co.uk

Heliview
BRIDGE ROAD, CAMBERLEY
Surrey GU15 2QR..+44(0)1276 471545
e: sales@heliview.co.uk
w: www.heliview.co.uk

Heni Fourie Photography
24 CAMPION ROAD, WIDMER END
Buckinghamshire HP15 6BU 07809 395062
e: heni@henifouriephotography.co.uk
w: www.henifouriephotography.co.uk

High Level Photography Ltd
STUDIO D1, BUILDING D4, FAIROAKS AIRPORT, COBHAM
Surrey GU24 8HU..020 3355 0274
e: info@highlevel.co.uk
w: www.highlevelphotography.co.uk

ICS Photography
THE STUDIO, 20 FAR MOOR CLOSE, HARLINGTON, DONCASTER
South Yorkshire DN5 7JP 01302 235048
e: roy@icsphotography.co.uk
w: www.icsphotography.com

Ignite Images Photography
456 FOREST ROAD, LONDON
Greater London E17 4PY........... 07867 908608 // 0800 772 0237
e: philip@igniteimages.co.uk
w: www.ignite-images.co.uk

Irene Cooper Photographer
....01977 670031
e: irene@irenecooper.com
w: www.irenecooper.com

James Thorpe Photography
7 BURNS STREET, 7 BURNS STREET
Northamptonshire NN1 3QE .... 01604 289234 // 07531 490150
e: james@jthorpe.net
w: www.jthorpe.net

JK Photography
ARTHUR STREET , DERBY
DE1 3EH 07709 269577
e: john@jkphotography.co.uk
w: jkphotography.co.uk/

JP Images
KEMP HOUSE, 152 CITY ROAD, LONDON
Greater London EC1V 2NX,............................... 020 8133 1906 //
07555 89 06 49
e: hello@jp-images.com
w: www.jp-images.com

JPFoto
8 LEATHERWORKS WAY, LITTLE BILLING VILLAGE,
NORTHAMPTON
Northamptonshire NN3 9BP .... 01933 628139 // 01604 419112
e: info@jpfoto.co.uk
w: www.jpfoto.co.uk/corporate-event-

Just Pose
UNIT 12, BREDHURST BUSINESS PARK, WESTFIELD SOLE ROAD,
BOXLEY
Kent ME14 3EH........................ 0207 112 8962 // 01634 776 511
e: pose@just-pose.com
w: www.just-pose.com

P
Q

Lillian Spibey Photography
....07969 466 572
e: lillian@lillianspibeyphotography.com
w: www.lillianspibeyphotography.com

Link Photographers
....07947 884 517
e: office@linkphotographers.com
w: www.linkphotographers.com

ManaMedia UK
3RD FLOOR, 152-154 CURTAIN ROAD, LONDON
 EC2A 3AT... +44 208 962 9652
e: info@manamediauk.com
w: www.manamediagroup.com

Marc Broussely Photography
391A UPPER RICHMOND ROAD, LONDON
 SW15 5QL 07738 920 225
e: marc@marcbroussely.com
w: www.marcbroussely.com

Marcos Bevilacqua Photography
UNIT 6, 2 LANSDOWNE DRIVE, LONDON
Greater London E8 3EZ .... 07798 764156 / 0207 683 0954
e: info@marcos-book.com
w: www.marcos-book.com

Mark Loraine Photography
9 GRANGE VIEW, BALBY, DONCASTER
 DN4 0XL ....07789 552900 // 01302 857030 // 07789 55
e: mark@mark-loraine.com
w: www.mark-loraine.com

Matt Chung Photography
....07940 278679
e: mattchungphoto@gmail.com
w: www.mattchungphoto.com

Matt Gutteridge
87 ASHLEY ROAD, BRISTOL BS6 5NR.......................7896961479
e: matt@mattgutteridgephotography.co.uk
w: www.mattgutteridgephotography.co.

Meadows Farm Studios
MARLOW ROAD, HENLEY ON THAMES
Orkeny RG9 3AA 01491 577789
e: studio@meadowsfarm.co.uk
w: www.meadowsfarmstudios.co.uk

Mission Photographic Ltd
....0781 685 7450
e: info@missionphotographic.com
w: www.missionphotographic.com

Mission Studio
MISSION STUDIO, 8 GROVE STREET, MANSFIELD WOODHOUSE,
MANSFIELD
Nottinghamshire NG198BU .... 07930 947352 / 01623 438747
e: info@missionstudio.co.uk
w: www.missionstudio.co.uk

Moore & Moore Photography
9 TURGIS ROAD, FLEET
Hampshire GU51 1EL..01252 653193
e: HelenandTony@mooreandmoorephotography.co.uk
w: www.mooreandmoorephotography.co.u

Nak Photography
47 SPENCER ROAD, TWICKENHAM
Greater London TW2 5TG.....................................0208 898 2500
e: studio@nakphotography.co.uk
w: www.nakphotography.co.uk

Nick Burrett Photography
....2380675844
e: info@nickburrett.com
w: www.nickburrett.com

Nick Rutter Photography
....07968 449930
w: www.nickrutterphotography.co.uk

Nickon Events Photos
8 CHARD CLOSE, FOSTERS LANE, WOODLEY, READING
Berkshire RG5 4HU .... 01189 695952 // 0791 782 1777
e: nickonevents@gmail.com
w: www.nickonevents.co.uk

Paparazzi VIP
....7736282698
e: simon@paparazzivip.com
w: https://www.paparazzivip.com/

Pascal Molliere Event Photography
.... 07713 242948 / 020 7736 4770
e: pascal@pascalphoto.co.uk
w: www.pascalphoto.co.uk

Paul Brock Photography
71 WATERMAN WAY
 E1W 2QW 020 7168 7087
e: paul@paulbrockphotography.co.uk
w: www.paulbrockphotography.co.uk

Peter Dazeley Photography
THE STUDIOS, 5 HEATHMANS ROAD, PARSONS GREEN, LONDON
Greater London SW6 4TJ......................................020 7736 3171
e: studio@peterdazeley.com
w: www.peterdazeley.com

Phil Nunez Photography
95 MURRAYFIELDS, WEST ALLOTMENT, NEWCASTLE UPON TYNE
Tyne and Wear NE27 0RF.....................................07825 367431
e: info@philnunez.com
w: www.philnunez.com

Philip Barnett Photography
33 KENDAL ROAD, DOLLIS HILL, LONDON
Greater London NW10 1JG....................................07721 741941
e: phil@fletcherwilson.com
w: www.philipbarnettphotography.co.u

P
Q

Photofusion
17A ELECTRIC LANE, BRIXTON, LONDON
Greater London SW9 8LA.....................................020 7738-5774
e: info@photofusion.org
w: www.photofusion.org

PhotoLesk
4 GOLD STREET, TIVERTON
Devon EX16 6PZ...01884 798 070
e: lesk@photolesk.co.uk
w: www.photolesk.co.uk

Photoreverie
27 AVINGTON, GREAT HOLM, MILTON KEYNES
Buckinghamshire MK8 9DG 08445 888333
e: enquiries@photoreverie.com
w: www.photoreverie-event-photograph

Picture Blast Ltd
UNIT 1.9 , THE ARCHES INDUSTRIAL ESTATE, COVENTRY
West Midlands CV1 3JQ..0800 193 3333
e: info@pictureblast-events.co.uk
w: www.pictureblast.co.uk

Raymond Thatcher Studios
28, RAY MILL ROAD WEST, MAIDENHEAD
Berkshire SL6 8SB...................... 01628 625381 / 07723040696
e: studio@raymondthatcher.co.uk
w: www.raymondthatcher.co.uk

Richmond Pictures
....07877 950137
e: hello@richmondpictures.co.uk
w: www.richmondpictures.co.uk

Rick Foulsham Photographer
LAVENDER HOUSE, MELLS, FROME
BA11 3QN.............................. 01373 812 319 // 07976 605 996
e: foulsham@msn.com
w: www.rickfoulsham.co.uk

River Studio
107A TELSEN, 55 THOMAS STREET, ASTON, BIRMINGHAM
West Midlands B6 4TN...07860 824101
e: info@riverstudio.co.uk
w: www.riverstudio.co.uk

Second Capture Ltd
3 ROCK COTTAGE, ASHFORD
TN25 6AQ .... 07866 426303 // 01233 720242
e: marc@secondcapture.com
w: www.secondcapturephotography.com

Shorestream Media
EXETER PHOENIX, BRADNINCH PLACE, GANDY STREET, EXETER
Devon EX4 3LS 07765 488101
e: james@shorestreammedia.co.uk
w: www.shorestreammedia.co.uk

SiRAstudio LTD
SPRING GROVE, HARROAGTE
North Yorkshire HG1 2HS .... +44 (0)1423
546440
e: hello@sirastudio.com
w: www.sirastudio.com

SmartPicsUK
11 MAYDAY GARDENS, BLACKHEATH,, LONDON
Greater London SE3 8NJ......................................020 8856 4894
e: admin@smartpicsuk.com
w: www.smartpicsuk.com

Sonic Editions
....
e: info@soniceditions.com
w: www.soniceditions.com

Specialist Lighting Co Limited
49 THE BROADWAY , CHEAM SUTTON
SM3 8BL...01202 700569
e: sales@slclightingonline.com
w: slclightingonline.com/

Stephen Wright Photographer
19 QUEEN ANNE'S GATE, CAVERSHAM, READING
RG4 5DU...0118 946 2665
e: stephen@wrightphoto.co.uk
w: www.wrightphoto.co.uk

Stonehouse Photographic
....07714 159 589
e: richard@stonehousephotographic.com
w: www.stonehousephotographic.com

Street Advertising Services
69 MERE GREEN ROAD, BIRMINGHAM
West Midlands B75 5BY.......................................0845 658 9940
e: mail@streetadvertisingservices.com
w: www.streetadvertisingservices.com

Studio 11
UNIT G, ARTHUR BRAY'S YARD, WEST QUAY ROAD, POOLE
BH15 1HT 07791 962441
e: lucy@studio-11.co.uk
w: www.studio-11.co.uk

Studio Megastar
UNIT 1.7 & 1.8, THE ARCHES INDUSTRIAL ESTATE, COVENTRY
West Midlands CV1 3JQ..02476 712 152
e: info@studiomegastar.co.uk
w: www.studiomegastar.co.uk

Studio Q Photography & Framing
LAURIESTON INDUSTRIAL ESTATE, OLD REDDING ROAD,
LAURIESTON, FALKIRK
FK2 9JU...01324 432222
e: info@studioqphotography.co.uk
w: www.studioqphotography.co.uk

Studio Time Ltd (Green Screen)
19 WARBURTON ROAD, HACKNEY, LONDON
Greater London E8 3RT..020 8090 0875
e: info@studiotimephoto.com
w: www.greenscreenuk.co.uk

T Class Ltd
UNIT 1A, SHEPPERTON HOUSE, 83 SHEPPERTON ROAD, LONDON
Greater London N1 3DF 020 7436 8066
e: info@thevowstudio.com
w: www.thevowstudio.com

Tenpast Events
27 TAVISTOCK SQUARE, LONDON
WC1H 9HH............................... 020) 3143 3243 / 07490 390219
e: nh@tenpast.com
w: www.tenpast.com

The Edge Photography
....1245830468
e: info@TheEdgePhotography.co.uk
w: www.theedgephotography.co.uk

The Snapshot Cafe
37 CORTIS ROAD, LONDON
Greater London SW15 3AF............ 07542415261 / 07447460808
e: info@thesnapshotcafe.com
w: www.thesnapshotcafe.com

Tim Hollis Photography
UNIT 12A, WEYBRIDGE BUSINESS CENTRE, 66 YORK ROAD,
WEYBRIDGE
KT13 9DA 07774 664672
e: info@timhollisphotography.co.uk
w: www.timhollisphotography.co.uk

Tim Smith Photography
ROCKLEY HOUSE, 14 MEADWAY, CAMBERLEY
GU16 8TQ..01276 504 629
e: studio@timsmith.co.uk
w: www.timsmith.co.uk

Tudor Photography
21 BEAUMONT COURT, BEAUMONT CLOSE, BANBURY
Oxfordshire OX16 1TG...01295 270681
e: info@tudorphotography.co.uk
w: www.tudorphotography.co.uk

Vanessa J White Photography
....07979 496206
e: vanessawhite@talktalk.net
w: www.vanessawhitephotography.co.uk

VNV Sounds
UNITS 10 AND 10A ASHLEY HOUSE, ASHLEY ROAD, LONDON
Greater London N17 9LZ...0203 021 1370
e: info@vnvlive.co.uk
w: www.vnvsounds.co.uk

Picture Libraries

Dat's Jazz Picture Library
38 KINGS WAY, HARROW
Greater London HA1 1XU 020 8427 7384
e: info@datsjazz.co.uk
w: www.datsjazz.co.uk

Environmental Investigation Agency
62-63 UPPER STREET, LONDON
Greater London N1 0NY 020 7354 7960
e: ukinfo@eia-international.org
w: www.eia-international.org

Heliview
BRIDGE ROAD, CAMBERLEY
Surrey GU15 2QR.. +44(0)1276 471545
e: sales@heliview.co.uk
w: www.heliview.co.uk

Huntley Film Archives Ltd
OLD KING STREET FARM, EWYAS HAROLD, HEREFORD
Herefordshire HR2 0HB 01981 241580
e: films@huntleyarchives.com
w: www.huntleyarchives.com

Last Refuge Ltd
BATCH FARM, PANBOROUGH, NR WELLS
Somerset BA5 1PN 01934 712556
e: info@lastrefuge.co.uk
w: www.lastrefuge.co.uk

London Transport Museum
COVENT GARDEN PIAZZA, LONDON
Greater London WC2E 7BB...................................020 7379 6344
e: corphire@ltmuseum.co.uk
w: www.ltmuseum.co.uk

Skyscan Aerial Photolibrary
OAK HOUSE, TODDINGTON, CHELTENHAM
Gloucestershire GL54 5BY 01242 621357
e: info@skyscan.co.uk
w: www.skyscan.co.uk

Stockfile
15 ARMITAGE COURT, ASCOT
Berkshire SL5 9TA .... +44 7973 719060
e: info@stockfile.co.uk
w: www.stockfile.co.uk

Vinmag Archive
VINMAG HOUSE, 84-90 DIGBY ROAD
E9 6HX 020 8533 7588
e: piclib@vinmagarchive.com
w: www.vinmagarchive.com

P
Q

Plant

365 Plant Hire
75A KING STREET, KNUTSFORD
Cheshire WA16 6DX...0161 926 9000
e: info@365planthire.co.uk
w: www.365planthire.co.uk

A-Plant
102 DALTON AVENUE, BIRCHWOOD PARK, WARRINGTON
Cheshire WA3 6YE 01925 281000
e: enquiries@aplant.com
w: www.aplant.com

Alide Hire Services
UNIT 46, BURNETT BUSINESS PARK,, BURNETT
Bristol BS31 2ED 01225 326 484
e: hire@alidehire.co.uk
w: www.alidehire.co.uk

Bluewater Forklift Hire
ATLANTIC HOUSE, RED LION SQUARE, LONDON
Greater London WC1R 4SG 020 7748 2100
e: mail@bluewater.im
w: www.bluewaterforklift.co.uk

Certex (UK) Ltd
UNIT C1 HARWORTH INDUSTRIAL ESTATE, BRYANS CLOSE,
HARWORTH Nottinghamshire DN11 8RY 01302 756 777
e: sales@certex.co.uk
w: www.certex.co.uk

Channel 16
TOWER BRIDGE BUSINESS COMPLEX, LONDON
Greater London S16 4DG .... 07836 693833 / 07595 893020
e: forshow@channel-16.co.uk
w: www.channel-16.co.uk

CW Plant Hire
86 HIGH STREET, HARPENDEN
 AL5 2SP...01582 716 413
e: harpenden@cwplant.co.uk
w: www.cwplant.co.uk

Grass Concrete Ltd
DUNCAN HOUSE, 142 THORNES LANE, THORNES, WAKEFIELD
Warwickshire WF2 7RE..01924 379443
e: info@grasscrete.com
w: www.grasscrete.com

Herts Tool Co.
LYON WAY, HATFIELD ROAD, ST. ALBANS
Hertfordshire AL4 0LR...01727 832 131
e: info@hertstools.co.uk
w: www.hertstools.co.uk

Hewden
SALTIRE COURT, 20 CASTLE TERRACE, EDINBURGH
Edinburgh EH1 2EN..0845 60 70 111
e: hirenow@hewden.co.uk
w: www.hewden.co.uk

Jackie Middleton Garden Design
.... 07768623652 / 01483 351983
e: jackie@jmgardendesigh.com
w: www.jmgardendesign.com

Jovic Plant
JOVIC PLANT HIRE CHELMSFORD, MAYES LANE, SANDON, ,
CHELMSFORD
Essex CM2 7RP 01268 727 272
e: jovicplant@edmmail.co.uk
w: www.jovicplant.co.uk

Kaizen Bonsai Ltd
PO BOX 241 - GREAT YARMOUTH
 NR30 9AG.................................. 08004580672 / 01493 781834
e: info@kaizenbonsai.com
w: www.kaizenbonsai.com

Morris Leslie Event & Plant Hire
ERROL AIRFIELD, ERROL, PERTH
Perthshire PH2 7TB..01821 642940
e: enquiries@morrisleslie.co.uk
w: www.morrisleslie.com

Nationwide Platforms
UNIT 15 MIDLAND COURT, CENTRAL PARK, LUTTERWORTH
Leicestershire LE17 4PN.......................................01455 558874
e: webadmin@lavendongroup.com
w: www.nationwideplatforms.co.uk

Nationwide Services Group Ltd
NATIONWIDE HOUSE, 2 FRANKTON WAY, GOSPORT
Hampshire PO12 1FR................ 02392 604479 // 02392 604300
e: sales@nationwideservices.co.uk
w: www.nationwideservices.co.uk

Northern Pontoon Ltd
BURTON-IN-KENDAL, CARNFORTH
Lanarkshire LA6 1HR 01524 740790
e: info@northernpontoon.com
w: www.northernpontoon.com

Pickerings Plant Ltd
ASHBY ROAD, MEASHAM, SWADLINGCOTE
Derbyshire DE12 7JW..01530 271618
e: accounts@pickeringsplant.co.uk
w: www.pickeringsplant.co.uk

Plant Solution 4U
2 THE COURTYARD, GREENFIELD FARM INDUSTRIAL ESTATE,
CONGLETON
Cheshire CW12 4TR...01782 740802
e: Daryl@plantsolutions4u.com
w: www.plantsolutions4u.com

Power Platform Services
LYN HOUSE, IVY MILL LANE, GODSTONE
Surrey RH9 8NR..01883 744 766
w: www.pps.co.uk

P
Q

Search (leeds)
MARKET WORKS, WHITEHALL ROAD, LEEDS
West Yorkshire LS12 6EP 0113 263 9081
e: info@wgsearch.co.uk
w: www.wgsearch.co.uk

Southern Plant & Tool Hire Ltd
UNIT 10, CENTENARY BUSINESS PARK, STATION RD,
HENLEY ON THAMES
Oxfordshire RG9 1DS .... 01491 576 063 / 01491 573515
e: info@southernplant.co.uk
w: www.southernplant.co.uk

Turner Access Ltd
65 CRAIGTON ROAD, GLASGOW
Glasgow G51 3EQ 0141 309 5555
e: enquiries@turner-access.co.uk
w: www.turner-access.co.uk

Wilson Access Hire Limited
NORTHERN DEPOT, POPE STREET, NORMANTON, WAKEFIELD
West Yorkshire WF6 2TA.......................................01924 224 384
e: hiredesknorth@wilsonaccess.co.uk
w: www.wilsonaccess.co.uk

Winner Events
1 NORTH MOORS, SLYFIELD INDUSTRIAL ESTATE, GUILDFORD
Surrey GU1 1SE 0845 601 5427
e: sales@winnerevents.com
w: www.winnerevents.com

Plumbing / Drainage Services

Andyloos Limited
UNIT 22 HARTLEBURY TRADING ESTATE, HARTLEBURY
Worcestershire DY10 4JB 0845 671 1111
e: Hartlebury@andyloos.co.uk
w: www.andyloos.co.uk

P
Q

Avanti Environmental Services
YARDLEY ROAD , INDUSTRIAL PARK, KNOWSLEY
Merseyside L33 7SS..0333 240 4027
e: info@avantienvironmentalservices.co.uk
w: www.avantienvironmentalservices.c

Clearmasters Environmental Ltd
UNIT 19, MOORES OPEN STORAGE, REIGATE ROAD,
BETCHWORTH
RH3 7HB...01737 842 509
e: clearmasters@aol.com
w: www.clearmasters.co.uk

Dmj Drainage Ltd
DMJ DRAINAGE LTD, THE OFFICES, MEDLAM LANE, CARRINGTON,
BOSTON
Lincolnshire PE22 7LU..01205 480 958
e: sales@dmjdrainage.co.uk
w: www.dmjdrainage.co.uk

Euro Loo Portable Toilets
EURO HOUSE, WEST HANNINGFIELD ROAD, CHELMSFORD
Essex CM2 7TA...................... 01245 475 700 // 0800 61 22 515
e: sales@euroloo.com
w: www.euroloo.com

FreeFlow
38 CHURCH ROAD, LINSLADE , LEIGHTON BUZZARD
LU7 2LR.................................... 01525634070 / 07928 652 013
e: elty1@hotmail.com
w: www.freeflow-drainage.co.uk

Liberty Event Suites
THE OLD AIRFIELD, BELTON ROAD, SANDTOFT
Lincolnshire DN8 5SX 08450 944487
e: sales@libertyguard.co.uk
w: www.libertyguard.co.uk

Liquiline Event Water Services
ASHTREE HOUSE, TARRANT HINTON, BLANDFORD
Dorset DT11 8JA 01258 830324
e: office@liquiline.co.uk
w: www.liquilineeventwaterservices.c

Outflow
SUITE C, THE BARN PRIORY PARK , BLACKHAM COURT ,
WITHYHAM
East Sussex TN7 4DB 0800 917 0077
e: alex.creasy@outflow-services.co.uk
w: www.outflow-services.co.uk

R and R Plumbing Heating
158 MANOR ROAD, CHESTERFIELD
Derbyshire S43 1NW..01246 411 289
e: info@randrplumbingheating.co.uk
w: www.randrplumbingheating.co.uk

Show Site Services
UNIT 18 WEYBRIDGE BUSINESS CENTRE, 66 YORK
ROAD,, WEYBRIDGE
Surrey KT139DY 01932 228 416
e: info@showsiteservices.co.uk
w: www.showsiteservices.co.uk

Slim Maintenance
3.1 STANLEY HOUSE, KELVIN WAY , CRAWLEY WEST
Sussex RH10 9SE .... 01293 277489 /
.... 07792 004700 / 07754 6189
e: info@slimmaintenance.co.uk
w: www.slimmaintenance.co.uk

Wicked Event Water Services Ltd
4 WILEMAN VILLAS, BECKINGHAM, DONCASTER
Nottinghamshire DN10 4PF...................................07909 771 996
e: info@wews.biz
w: www.wickedeventwaterservices.com

Wincanton Water Services
METHUEN PARK, CHIPPENHAM
Wiltshire SN14 0WT .... +44 (0) 1249 710000
e: getintouch@wincanton.co.uk
w: www.wincanton.co.uk

Poster / Hoarding Advertising

Blackmore Ltd
LONGMEAD, SHAFTESBURY
Dorset SP7 8PX 01747 853034
e: sales@blackmore.co.uk
w: www.blackmore.co.uk

High Level Photography Ltd
STUDIO D1, BUILDING D4, FAIROAKS AIRPORT, COBHAM
Surrey GU24 8HU..020 3355 0274
e: info@highlevel.co.uk
w: www.highlevelphotography.co.uk

Mediaco Graphic Solutions
CHURCHILL POINT, CHURCHILL WAY, TRAFFORD PARK,
MANCHESTER
Greater Manchester M17 1BS..............................0161 875 2020
e: customerservice@mediaco.co.uk
w: www.mediaco.co.uk

Only Rollers
11 ALBERT PLACE, DARWEN
Lancashire BB3 0QE 0845 3882324
e: info@only-rollers.com
w: www.onlyrollers.com

Palmer Publicity Services
ANCHORAGE BUSINESS PARK , CHAIN CAUL WAY , PRESTON
PR2 2YL..01772 733213
e: info@palmerpublicity.co.uk
w: www.palmerpublicity.co.uk

Phillips Digital
20-24 KIRBY STREET
EC1N 8TS 020 7242 2015
e: design@phillips-digital.co.uk
w: www.phillips-digital.com

Powell Outdoor Media
54 MILLMOUNT ROAD, SHEFFIELD
South Yorkshire S8 9EG 0870 005 3123
e: email@futurate.com
w: www.futurate.com

Rutters
UNIT 6, SOUTH CAMBRIDGESHIRE BUSINESS PARK, BARBRAHAM
ROAD, SAWSTON
Cambridgeshire CB22 3JH....................................01223 833522
e: info@ruttersuk.com
w: www.ruttersuk.com

Tenpast Events
27 TAVISTOCK SQUARE, LONDON
WC1H 9HH.............................. 020) 3143 3243 / 07490 390219
e: nh@tenpast.com
w: www.tenpast.com

Power Generators

Fourth Generation
LUTON
Bedfordshire 2085 502 943
e: laura@fourthgenerationltd.com
w: www.fourthgenerationltd.com

PR / Publicity Consultants

20-20 PR
20-20 PUBLIC RELATIONS LTD, LONGCOT, FARINGDON
Oxfordshire SN7 7TG 01793 780780
e: belindaboyd@2020pr.com
w: www.2020pr.com

Abucon PR
3-4 BRADFIELD HALL, BRADFIELD COMBUST, BURY ST EDMUNDS
Suffolk IP30 0LU 020 7834 1066
e: info@abucon.co.uk
w: www.abucon.co.uk

Agitate PR
6 SINCLAIR CLOSE, GILLINGHAM
Kent ME8 9JQ... 07787 935606 /
01634 261288
e: nigel@agitatepr.co.uk
w: www.agitatepr.co.uk

Angela Jones PR
1 EDWARDS MEADOW, MARLBOROUGH
Wiltshire SN8 1UL...01672 515068
e: info@angelajonespr.co.uk
w: www.angelajonespr.co.uk

Aurora PR
69 CHURCH ROAD, WIMBLEDON, LONDON
Greater London SW19 5AL....................................0208 287 1124
e: jancomer@aurorapr.co.uk
w: www.aurorapr.co.uk

Ava Pr
THE OLD SCHOOL HOUSE , 65A LONDON ROAD OADBY ,
LEICESTER
Leicestershire LE2 5DN...0116 216 0441
e: team@avapr.biz
w: www.avapr.biz

Bacall Associates
63 CATHERINE PLACE, LONDON
Greater London SW1E 6DY....................................020 7630 2880
e: pr@bacall.net
w: www.bacallassociates.co.uk

P
Q

Bird Consultancy Ltd
GOLD 73, THE SHARP PROJECT, THORP ROAD , MANCHESTER
Greater Manchester M40 5BJ 0161 839 4846
e: onawire@birdconsultancy.co.uk
w: www.birdconsultancy.co.uk

Blow By Blow Productions
PO BOX 565, LINCOLN
Lincolnshire LN2 2YT...01522 754901
e: info@blowbyblow.co.uk
w: www.blowbyblow.co.uk

Book 'em Danno
2 GLASTONBURY CLOSE, SPENNYMOOR
 DL16 6XP 01629 584 438
e: info@bookemdanno.com
w: www.bookemdanno.com

Creative Advertising Ltd
11A GILDREDGE ROAD, EASTBOURNE
East Sussex BN21 4RB 01323 725472
w: www.creative-ad.co.uk

DRSM
27 OLD GLOUCESTER STREET, LONDON
Greater London WC1N 3AX 08701 990100
e: mail@drsmpr.com
w: www.drsmpr.com

Empica Ltd
1 LYONS COURT, LONG ASHTON BUSINESS PARK, YANLEY LANE,
LONG ASHTON
Bristol BS41 9LB...01275 394400
e: info@empica.co.uk
w: www.empica.com

G Promo Pr
2 STREATLEY MEWS, CORVE STREET, LUDLOW
 SY8 2PN 01584 873211
e: gpromo@btinternet.com
w: www.gpromopr.co.uk

Garrett Axford Ltd
BASEPOINT CENTRE, LITTLE HIGH STREET, SHOREHAM BY SEA
West Sussex BN43 5EG 01903 854900
e: mail@garrett-axford.co.uk
w: www.garrett-axford.co.uk

Gasoline Media Limited
9 DALMORE AVENUE, CLAYGATE
Surrey KT10 0HQ 01372 471472
e: sarahj@gasolinemedia.com
w: www.gasolinemedia.com

Geometry PR
VICTORIA HOUSE, 5 LOWER BOROUGH WALLS, BATH
Somerset BA1 1QR 01225 422051
e: linda@geometrypr.co.uk
w: www.geometrypr.co.uk

Grand Plan Consultancy
 ....01608 654040
e: media@thegpc.co.uk
w: www.thegpc.co.uk

Hall or Nothing
7 DIALS CLUB FIRST FLOOR, 42 EARLHAM STREET COVENT
GARDEN, LONDON
Greater London WC2H 9LA....................................07767 471 681
e: gillian@hallornothing.com
w: www.hallornothing.com

Jb Communications Ltd
15 BRACKENBURY ROAD, LONDON
Greater London W6 0BE.......................................020 8749 6036
e: inspire@jbcommunications.co.uk
w: www.jbcommunications.co.uk

Lawton Communications Group Ltd
4 & 5 GROSVENOR SQUARE, SOUTHAMPTON
Hampshire SO15 2BE 02380 828525
w: www.lawtoncommsgroup.com

Mere PR @BJL
SUNLIGHT HOUSE, QUAY STREET, MANCHESTER
Greater Manchester M3 3JZ 0161 831 7141
e: Info@BJL.co.uk
w: www.bjl.co.uk

Mobile Promotions
NEW BROOK, TITCHMARSH, THRAPSTON
Northamptonshire NN14 3DG.................................01832 733460
e: contact@mobilepromotions.com
w: www.mobilepromotions.com

Noble Pr Ltd
2 PROSPERO ROAD, LONDON
Greater London N19 3RF.......................................020 7272 7772
e: peter@noblepr.co.uk
w: www.noblepr.co.uk

Optimus
OPTIMUS PUBLIC RELATIONS, STOTFOLD
Hertfordshire SG5 4LY...01462 612776
e: info@optimuspr.co.uk
w: www.optimuspr.co.uk

Partnership Plus Ltd
43 ALL SAINTS GREEN, NORWICH
Norfolk NR1 3LY..01603 611031
e: pr@partnership-plus.co.uk
w: www.partnership-plus.co.uk

Paul Smith Associates
MEDIA CONSULTANTS, OVINGTON, LOWER FROYLE , ALTON
Hampshire GU34 4NA 01420 22532
e: newsdesk@paulsmithassociates.co.uk
w: www.paulsmithassociates.co.uk

P
Q

Phipps Public Relations Ltd
17 EXETER STREET, LONDON
Greater London WC2E 7DU 020 7759 7400
e: askus@thisisphipps.com
w: thisisphipps.com/

Planit Ghana
PMB CT 71, CANTONMENTS, ACCRA
 233...................................+233 2 04304555 // 233 2 64546565
e: events@planitghana.com
w: www.planitghana.com

Plaster Creative Communications
LOFT 6, TABACCO FACTORY, RALEIGH ROAD, BRISTOL
Bristol BS3 1TF..0117 953 0320
e: hello@weareplaster.com
w: www.weareplaster.com

Profound Media & Management Ltd
PO BOX 4222, COVENTRY
West Midlands CV4 0BH..024 76677712
w: www.profoundmedia.co.uk

Red Pencil
5 TYRRELL ROAD, LONDON
Greater London SE22 9NA 020 8425 2406
e: hello@redpencil.co.uk
w: www.redpencil.co.uk

Rising PR
16 OLDTOWN ST, COOKSTOWN
 BT80 8EE...028 8676 2946
e: brian@risingpr.com
w: www.risingpr.com

Rock Kitchen Harris
32 POCKLINGTONS WALK, LEICESTER
Leicestershire LE1 6BU...0116 233 7500
e: hello@rkh.co.uk
w: www.rkh.co.uk

Saltwater Communications
22 STRAND STREET, POOLE
Dorset BH15 1SB..01202 669244
e: enquiries@saltwatercoms.com
w: www.saltwatercoms.com

Sans Frontiere Marketing Communications
73 HIGH STREET, LEWES
East Sussex BN7 1XG 01273 487 800
e: info@sansfrontiere.co.uk
w: www.sansfrontiere.co.uk

Sharpe PR Limited
83 HOBSON STREET, MACCLESFIELD
Cheshire SK11 8BD 01625 267152
e: info@sharpepr.co.uk
w: www.sharpepr.co.uk

Splendid Communications
69-85 TABERNACLE STREET, SHOREDITCH, LONDON
Greater London EC2A 4BD 020 7553 7300
e: hi@splendidcomms.com
w: www.splendidcomms.com

Tenpast Events
27 TAVISTOCK SQUARE, LONDON
 WC1H 9HH.............................. 020) 3143 3243 / 07490 390219
e: nh@tenpast.com
w: www.tenpast.com

The Big Cat Group Ltd
GRIFFIN HOUSE, 18-19 LUDGATE HILL, BIRMINGHAM
West Midlands B3 1DW..0121 200 0910
e: info@bcguk.com
w: www.bigcatgroup.co.uk/

The Partners Group
105 THE MOUNT, YORK
Yorkshire YO24 1GY 01904 610077
e: postbox@partners-group.co.uk
w: www.partners-group.co.uk

Three Point PR (3point)
UNIT 3A, J, JUNO WAY, LONDON
Greater London SE14 5RW....................................0208 691 9191
e: info@threepointsolutions.co.uk
w: www.threepointsolutions.co.uk

Vital Marketing Ltd
14A CLARENDON AVENUE, LEAMINGTON SPA
Warwickshire CV32 5PZ..01926 338811
e: hello@thevitalagency.co.uk
w: www.thevitalagency.co.uk

Wendy Bailey PR
 ....07770 665512
e: wendy@wendybaileypr.com
w: www.wendybaileypr.com

Work Hard Pr
35 FARM AVENUE, LONDON
Greater London SW16 2UT....................................020 8677 8466
e: roland@workhardpr.com
w: www.workhardpr.com

P
Q

Presentation Coaching

Celebrity Speakers Ltd
CELEBRITY SPEAKERS LTD, BURNHAM
Buckinghamshire SL1 7JT 01628 601 400
e: celebrityspeakersuk@gmail.com
w: www.speakers.co.uk/

Crewsaders Event Staff
MILLER 2, 61 ST. PAULS SQUARE, BIRMINGHAM
West Midlands B3 1QS 0845 094 4884
e: bookings@crewsaders.com
w: www.crewsaders.com

David Block
....07971 195632
e: davidsamblock@gmail.com
w: www.speechwriting.co.uk

Hand Made Productions
....01962 777 753
e: action@handmadeproductions.co.uk
w: www.handmadeproductions.co.uk

Media Tree
221-222 SHOREDITCH HIGH ST, LONDON
Greater London E1 6PJ 020 7437 3322
e: info@media-tree.com
w: www.media-tree.com

Motivation Magic
82 BOURNSIDE ROAD, CHELTENHAM
Gloucestershire GL51 3AH 01242 242765
e: john@motivationmagic.co.uk
w: www.motivationmagic.co.uk

Paul Jackson Associates
34A CLARENCE ROAD, ST ALBANS
Hertfordshire AL1 4NG 07973 953586
e: info@impro.org.uk
w: www.impro.org.uk

Positive Presence
18A LAMBOLLE PLACE, LONDON
Greater London NW3 4PG 020 7586 7925
e: info@pospres.co.uk
w: www.positivepresence.com

Straight Talking International
15B ABINGDON ROAD
Greater London W8 6AH........................0870 429 2108
e: graham@grahamdavies.co.uk
w: www.straighttalking.co.uk

**P
Q**

Printers

Akcent Media Limited
PO BOX 10, ST NEOTS
 PE19 6WR 01480 880655
e: sales@akcentmedia.com
w: www.akcentmedia.com

Arti Promotions
3 HIGHBRIDGE WHARF, GREENWICH, LONDON
Greater London SE10 9PS....................0208 293 1280
e: info@artipromotions.com
w: www.artipromotions.com

Audioprint Ltd
3-4 WOLSELEY COURT, WOBURN ROAD INDUSTRIAL ESTATE, KEMPSTON
Bedfordshire MK42 7AY 01234 857566
e: info@audioprint.co.uk
w: www.audioprint.co.uk

Bemrose Booth Ltd
STOCKHOLM ROAD, SUTTON FIELDS, HULL
 HU7 0XY .... 01482 371398 / 01482 37139
e: sales@adverticket.com
w: www.bemrosebooth.com

Blink Giant Media Ltd
COOPER HOUSE 2D, MICHAEL ROAD, LONDON
Greater London SW6 2AD 020 77368822
e: info@blinkgiantmedia.com
w: www.blinkgiantmedia.com

Blueprint Promotional Products
NO. 1 THE EMBASSY, LAWRENCE STREET, LONG EATON, NOTTINGHAM
Nottinghamshire NG10 1JY..................................0333 1234 400
e: info@blueprintpromo.co.uk
w: www.blueprintpromo.co.uk

Cbf Group
1-11 ALVIN STREET, GLOUCESTER
Gloucestershire GL1 3EJ 01452 346833
e: info@cbfnet.co.uk
w: www.cbfnet.co.uk

Colchester Printers
UNIT 5, COLCHESTER BUSINESS CENTRE, 1 GEORGE WILLIAMS WAY, COLCHESTER
 CO1 2JS 01026 588 604

Datum Colour Print (Hatfield) Ltd
UNIT 6, BEACONSFIELD ROAD, HATFIELD
Hertfordshire AL10 8BE...01707 251222
e: sales@datumcp.com
w: www.datumcp.com

Facemediagroup.co.uk
VICTORIA HOUSE, VALE ROAD, PORTSLADE, BRIGHTON
East Sussex BN41 1GG 0333 8000 888
e: info@facemediagroup.co.uk
w: www.facemediagroup.co.uk

Final Print UK
94-96 GROSVENOR STREET, MANCHESTER
Greater Manchester M1 7HL................................0161 273 8808
e: info@finalprintuk.com
w: www.finalprintuk.com

Geerings Print Ltd
COBBS WOOD HOUSE,, CHART ROAD, ASHFORD
Kent TN23 1EP...01233 633366
e: Info@geeringsprint.co.uk
w: www.geeringsprint.co.uk

GTMS - GT Marketing Services Ltd
1 SILVERTHORNE WAY, WATERLOOVILLE
Hampshire PO7 7XB 0 2392 320 580
e: hello@gtms.co.uk
w: www.gtms.co.uk

Hatch Creations Ltd
MERIDIAN HOUSE, 365 WESTHORNE AVENUE, GREENWICH PARK,
LONDON
Greater London SE12 9AB.....................................0208 297 1200
e: info@hatchcreations.co.uk
w: www.hatchcreations.co.uk

Ideas
DEVONSHIRE HOUSE, DEVONSHIRE AVENUE, LEEDS
West Yorkshire LS8 1AY 0113 240 9822
e: info@ideasthatwork.solutions
w: www.ideasthatwork.solutions/

Image Fabrication
UNIT 14 MULBERRY COURT, BOURNE ROAD, CRAYFORD
Kent DA1 4BF 01322 554 455
e: info@imagefabrication.co.uk
w: www.imagefabrication.co.uk

Imagink
UNIT 5, MILL HALL BUSINESS ESTATE, MILL HALL, AYLESFORD
Kent ME20 7JZ 01622 791 315
w: www.imagink.co.uk

Impact Distribution
TUSCANY WHARF, 4B ORSMAN ROAD, LONDON
Greater London N1 5QJ 020 7729 5978
e: info@impact.uk.com
w: impactideas.co.uk/

Jarballs Ltd
1-2 THE STREET, CHAPPEL
Essex CO6 2DD..01787 221577
e: info@jarballs.com
w: www.jarballs.com

JCS computerent
34 CHARTER GATE, QUARRY PARK CLOSE , MOULTON PARK,
NORTHAMPTON
Northamptonshire NN3 6QB.......................................1604495252
e: rentals@computerent.co.uk
w: computerent.co.uk

Kristal Digital Imaging Centre
7 CASTLE STREET, KINGSTON UPON THAMES
 KT1 1ST..020 8439 7898
e: support@kristal-photos.com
w: www.kristal-photos.com

Large Format Printing Berlin
KURFÃ¼RSTENDAMM 234, DOWNTOWN, 10719 BERLIN, BERLIN-
CHARLOTTENBURG, GERMANY
 10719 Berlin...30577026118
e: largeformat@hellodisplay.de
w: large-format-printing-berlin.com/

Love Displays Ltd
CHISWICK HOUSE, CHISWICK GROVE, BLACKPOOL
Lancashire FY3 9TW 01253 769 911
e: info@lovedisplays.co.uk
w: www.lovedisplays.co.uk

LS1 Print
MATRIX HOUSE, GOODMAN STREET, LEEDS
West Yorkshire LS10 1NZ.......................................0113 252 1787
e: info@ls1print.co.uk
w: www.ls1print.co.uk

Lynhurst Press Limited
UNITS 4 & 5 YARDLEY BUSINESS PARK, LUCKYN LANE, BASILDON
Essex SS14 3GL 01268 288231
e: info@lynhurstpress.co.uk
w: www.lynhurstpress.co.uk

Mediaco Graphic Solutions
CHURCHILL POINT, CHURCHILL WAY, TRAFFORD PARK,
MANCHESTER
Greater Manchester M17 1BS...............................0161 875 2020
e: customerservice@mediaco.co.uk
w: www.mediaco.co.uk

Moorleys Print & Publishing Ltd
23 PARK ROAD, ILKESTON
Derbyshire DE7 5DA 0115 932 0643
e: webenquiries@moorleys.co.uk
w: www.moorleys.co.uk

Mydisplays.co.uk
16 UPPER WOBURN PLACE, LONDON
 WC1H 0BS..0 203 794 7626
e: info@mydisplays.co.uk
w: www.mydisplays.co.uk

Noisebox Digital Media
UNIT B, YAREFIELD PARK, OLD HALL ROAD, NORWICH
Norfolk NR4 6FF 01603 767726
e: info@noisebox.co.uk
w: www.noisebox.co.uk

Orion Security Print Ltd
4 MERLIN WAY, QUARRY HILL INDUSTRIAL PARK, ILKESTON,
IKESTON
 DE7 4RA .... 0115 930 7517 // 0115 944 2605
e: webenquiries@orionprint.com
w: www.orionprint.com

Out Of Hand Ltd
HEBRON HOUSE, SION ROAD, BEDMINSTER
 BS3 3BD..01179 536363
e: info@outofhand.co.uk
w: www.outofhand.co.uk

Palmer Publicity Services
ANCHORAGE BUSINESS PARK , CHAIN CAUL WAY , PRESTON
 PR2 2YL...01772 733213
e: info@palmerpublicity.co.uk
w: www.palmerpublicity.co.uk

Phillips Digital
20-24 KIRBY STREET
 EC1N 8TS 020 7242 2015
e: design@phillips-digital.co.uk
w: www.phillips-digital.com

P Q

Premier Print & Promotions Ltd
PREMIER HOUSE, THRESHELFORDS BUSINESS PARK, INWORTH ROAD, FEERING
Essex CO5 9SE 01376 574670
e: sales@premierpandp.com
w: www.promotional-gifts.com

Print 2 Media Ltd
UNIT 7 MOORSWATER INDUSTRIAL ESTATE, LISKEARD, CORNWALL
Cornwall PL14 4LN 01579 340985
e: info@print-2-media.com
w: www.print-2-media.com

Print Colchester
9 ST JOHN'S STREET, COLCHESTER
Essex CO2 7NN...01206 368881
e: info@printcolchester.co.uk
w: www.printcolchester.co.uk

Print Designs
EMERALD WAY, STONE BUSINESS PARK, STONE
Staffordshire ST15 0SR...01785 818 111
e: sales@printdesigns.com
w: www.printdesigns.com

Printsome
....0203 5982599
e: luca@printsome.com
w: www.printsome.com

Qmj Publishing Ltd
7 REGENT STREET, NOTTINGHAM
Nottinghamshire NG1 5BS 0115 941 1315
e: mail@qmj.co.uk
w: www.qmj.co.uk

Quadrant Print And Design Ltd
UNIT F, ABBEYGATE BUSINESS CENTRE, HITCHIN ROAD, LUTON
Bedfordshire LU2 0ER..1582410741
e: david@quadrantprint.co.uk
w: www.quadrantprint.co.uk

Royale Graphics
VISTA HOUSE, 9 ARCHER ROAD, STAPLEFORD, NOTTINGHAM
Nottinghamshire NG9 7EP......................................0115 9491880
e: sales@royalegraphics.co.uk
w: www.royalegraphics.co.uk

Service Graphics Ltd
92 LOWER PARLIAMENT STREET, NOTTINGHAM
Nottinghamshire NG1 1EH 0115 958 7379
e: info.notts@servicegraphics.co.uk
w: www.servicegraphics.co.uk

Set Creations Ltd
STUDIO HOUSE DELAMARE ROAD, CHESHUNT
Hertfordshire EN8 9SH 01992 789 759
e: connect@setcreations.com
w: www.setcreations.com

Shirtysomething Ltd
6 PARKYN ROAD, DAYBROOK, NOTTINGHAM
Nottinghamshire NG5 6BG 0115 920 2645
e: chaps@shirtysomething.com
w: www.shirtysomething.com

South Kensington Print
76 OLD BROMPTON ROAD, SOUTH KENSINGTON, LONDON
Greater London SW7 3LQ.....................................020 7581 2604
e: printing@south-kensington-print.co.uk
w: www.south-kensington-print.co.uk

Stop The Press!
FLEMING STREET, GLASGOW
Lanarkshire G31 1PQ..0141 530 8755
e: studio@stop-the-press.co.uk
w: www.stop-the-press.co.uk

Stuart Design
UNIT 5, COLCHESTER BUSINESS CENTRE, 1 GEORGE WILLIAMS WAY, COLCHESTER
Essex CO1 2JS 01206 588 603
e: getmore@stuart-design.co.uk
w: www.stuart-design.co.uk

T Shirt & Sons
11 WASHINGTON ROAD, WEST WILTS TRADING ESTATE, WESTBURY
Wiltshire BA13 4JP 01373 301 645
e: sales@tshirtandsons.co.uk
w: www.tshirtandsons.co.uk

Top Marquees
RATCHER WAY, CROWN FARM INDUSTRIAL PARK, MANSFIELD
Nottinghamshire NG19 0FS...................................01623 415944
e: advice@topmarquees.co.uk
w: www.topmarquees.co.uk

Product Launches

Airstage UK
.... +34 971 641 281 / +34 684 243 321
e: info@airstage.biz
w: www.airstage.biz

Ben Van Grutten
FROG COTTAGE, FROG LANE, TUNBRIDGE WELLS
Kent TN1 1YT...01892 525979
e: info@bvggroup.com
w: www.bvggroup.com

Blue Dog Productions Ltd
HURST FARM, THE HURST, WINCHFIELD
Hampshire RG27 8SL..01252 786 000
e: info@bluedogproductions.co.uk
w: www.bluedogproductions.co.uk

Blue Ribbon Events Ltd
845 FINCHLEY ROAD, LONDON
NW11 8NA..020 8455 2255
e: team@blueribbonevents.com
w: www.blueribbonevents.com

Conference Engineering
.... +44 (0)1625 426916
e: hello@conferenceengineering.co.uk
w: www.conferenceengineering.co.uk

Corporate Occasions
LESTER HOUSE, TAMWORTH ROAD, LICHFIELD
Staffordshire WS14 9PU.......................................01543 433554
e: events@corporate-occasions.co.uk
w: www.corporate-occasions.co.uk

Corporate Ski Specialists
....020 9133 9955
e: info@corporateskispecialists.co.uk
w: www.corporateskispecialists.co.uk

Crafty Arty Parties Ltd
BOOKHAM LANE, BUCKLAND NEWTON, DORCHESTER
DT2 7RP 01300 345 397
e: heather.mitchell@craftyartyparties.com
w: www.craftyartyparties.com

Dellar Davies Ltd
RAPIER HOUSE, 4-6 CRANE MEAD, WARE
Hertfordshire SG12 9PW 01920 444800
e: info@dellardavies.com
w: www.dellardavies.com

Disposable RainPonchos
HORWICH, BOLTON
Greater Manchester BL6 6LJ 0844 251 0807
e: deanramsden@rain-poncho.co.uk
w: www.rain-poncho.co.uk

Emma Boardman Consulting
KENSINGTON, LONDON
W8 6JW..07976 294604
e: ideas@emmaboardman.net
w: www.emmaboardman.net

Enterprise Promotions Ltd
GROVE HOUSE, STANLEY GROVE, NORTHWICH
Cheshire CW9 7NP...01606 41194
e: info@enterpro.co.uk
w: www.enterpro.co.uk

Fizz Experience Ltd
VINE COURT, CHALKPIT LANE, DORKING
Surrey RH4 1AJ 01306 640980
e: fizz@fizzexperience.co.uk
w: www.fizz.co.uk

Gamewagon Ltd
113 - 115 OYSTER LANE, BYFLEET
Surrey KT14 7JZ...0845 319 4263
e: julie.owen@gamewagon.co.uk
w: www.gamewagon.co.uk

Ice Box
UNIT A35/36, NEW COVENT GARDEN MARKET, LONDON
Greater London SW8 5EE.....................................020 7498 0800
e: info@theicebox.com
w: www.theicebox.com

Inca Productions Ltd
THE TOP FLOOR, 7 - 11 ST JOHNS HILL, LONDON
Greater London SW11 1TN...................................02072 235 512
e: info@incaproductions.com
w: www.incaproductions.co.uk

JPFoto
8 LEATHERWORKS WAY, LITTLE BILLING VILLAGE, NORTHAMPTON
Northamptonshire NN3 9BP .... 01933 628139 //
01604 419112
e: info@jpfoto.co.uk
w: www.jpfoto.co.uk/corporate-event-

Kapow! Consulting
LEXHAM MEWS, LONDON
W8 6JW...020 7193 6885
w: www.kapowconsulting.co.uk

Kracker
MITCHELL RD, , ROCKINGHAM, CORBY
Northamptonshire NN17 5AF 020 7478 8308
e: james.guess@kracker.co.uk
w: www.kracker.co.uk

Memorable Events London Ltd
UNIT 10, CRANLEIGH MEWS, BATTERSEA, LONDON
Greater London SW11 2QL...................................020 3405 1946
e: hello@melonevents.co.uk
w: www.melonevents.co.uk

Production Team
15C WARWICK AVENUE, LONDON
Greater London W9 2PS.......................................020 7289 7649
e: barbara@productionteam.co.uk
w: www.productionteam.co.uk

Pump House Productions Intl Ltd
THE LOCKHOUSE, MEAD LANE, HERFORD
Hertfordshire SG13 7AX 01992 532483
e: mail@pumphouse.co.uk
w: www.pumphouse.co.uk

Radical Departures
THE PRINTWORKS, 3C BLAKE MEWS, KEW, LONDON
Greater London TW9 3GA.....................................0208 334 7860
e: martin@radical-departures.com
w: www.radical-departures.com

P
Q

Rede2 Ltd
THE COURTYARD, TWIGWORTH COURT, , TWIGWORTH
Gloucestershire GL2 9PG 0870 121 7060
e: info@rede2.com
w: www.rede2.com

Ruby Mear Promotions Ltd
RYDER HOUSE, RYDER COURT, CORBY
Northamptonshire NN18 9NX 0844 848 1405
e: enquiries@rubymear.com
w: www.rubymear.com

SJ Events
SJ EVENT CONSULTANCY LTD, NORTH WING, , SWITHLAND HALL
, SWITHLAND
Leicestershire LE12 8TJ 1162302040
e: mikewayne@post.com
w: www.sjevents.co.uk/

Skyline Whitespace
320 WESTERN ROAD, LONDON
Greater London SW19 2QA 0845 260 5440
e: getintouch@skylinewhitespace.com
w: www.skylinewhitespace.com

Stage Audio Services
UNIT 2, BRIDGE STREET, WORDSLEY , STOURBRIDGE
West Midlands DY8 5YU...01384 263629
e: kevinmobers@aol.com
w: www.stageaudioservices.com

The Finishing Touch
2ND FLOOR, 3 TENTERDEN STREET, LONDON
Greater London W1S 1TD.......................................020 7993 9993
e: events@finishtouchevents.co.uk
w: www.finishingtouchevents.co.uk

The Full Effect
MILLENNIUM STUDIOS, BEDFORD TECHNOLOGY PARK,
THURLEIGH
Bedfordshire MK44 2YP 0203 553 5747
e: info@tfe.co.uk
w: www.thefulleffect.co.uk

The Media Eye
4B PROWSE PLACE, LONDON
Greater London NW1 9PH 020 7553 6060
e: enquiries@themediaeye.com
w: www.themediaeye.com

Timebased Events Ltd
18 - 20 PENTON STREET, LONDON
Greater London N1 9PS 020 7608 0080
e: info@timebased.co.uk
w: www.timebased.co.uk

Prompting / Cueing Services

Autocue Ltd
BRIDGE HOUSE, HERON SQUARE, RICHMOND
Greater London TW9 1EN.......................................0208 665 2992
e: sales@autocue.com
w: www.autocue.com

Cuebox
UNIT 11 DARES FARM , FARNHAM ROAD, EWSHOT, FARNHAM
 GU10 5BB................................ 0845 880 1290 // 07774 712712
e: info@cuebox.com
w: www.cuebox.com

Cuebox Bristol
IMAGIST STUDIOS, UNIT 8&9, SECOND WAY
 BS11 8DF...0845 8801290
e: info@cuebox.com
w: www.cuebox.com

Cuebox Wales
TELEVISION CENTRE, CULVERHOUSE CROSS
 CF5 6XJ...0845 8801290
e: info@cuebox.com
w: www.cuebox.com

Full Circle Presentations Ltd
17 RAVENWOOD, LANDSWOOD PARK, NORTHWICH
Cheshire CW8 1NW..01606 872968
e: info@fullcirclepresentations.com
w: www.fullcirclepresentations.com

MCB Ltd
119 THE HUB, 300 KENSAL ROAD
 W10 5BE...020 8969 6956
e: bpbp@tgis.co.uk
w: www.mcb-ltd.co.uk

Portaprompt Ltd
LANE END ROAD, SANDS, HIGH WYCOMBE
Buckinghamshire HP12 4JQ 01494 450414
e: helen@portaprompt.co.uk
w: www.portaprompt.co.uk

Prompt Action
UNIT 8, WHITEHALL CROSS, WHITEHALL ROAD, LEEDS
West Yorkshire LS12 5XE 0113 279 9500
e: info@promptaction.com
w: www.promptaction.com

Telescript Ltd
THE STUDIO, FLAT 1 , MERIDEN HOUSE, WESTON ROAD, , BATH
Berkshire BA1 2XZ .... 0 1225 314013 / 07802 276511
e: ukinfo@telescript.com
w: www.telescript.co.uk

P
Q

Prop / Model Makers

2d:3d Ltd
263 ABBEYDALE ROAD, LONDON
Greater London HA0 1TW.....................................020 8998 3199
e: rob@2d3d.co.uk
w: www.2d3d.co.uk

3D Creations
BERTH 33, MALTHOUSE LANE, GORLESTON, GREAT YARMOUTH
Norfolk NR31 0GW...01493 652055
e: info@3dcreations.co.uk
w: www.3dcreations.co.uk

Agog Special Effects Ltd
UNIT 10, GREEN FARM, FRITWELL
Oxfordshire OX27 7QU 020 3475 5745
e: hello@agogspecialeffects.co.uk
w: www.agog.tv

Aspect Signs & Engraving
UNIT C1D, BOUNDS GREEN INDUSTRIAL ESTATE, NORTH WAY,
LONDON N11 2UL..020 8368 9017
e: info@aspectsigns.com
w: www.aspectsigns.com

Coleherne Laser Cutting Ltd
LODGE STREET, , NEWTON, HYDE
Cheshire SK14 4LE 0161 366 6603
e: brian@coleherne.co.uk
w: www.coleherne.co.uk

Colin Holden Associates
111 CUCKMERE WAY, BRIGHTON
East Sussex BN1 8GB .... 01273 556290 / 07817 176929
e: colin@colinholden.co.uk
w: www.colinholden.co.uk

Creating the Impossible
LOW FARM, BROOK ROAD, BASSINGBOURN, ROYSTON
Hertfordshire SG8 5NT 01763 852691
e: info@creatingtheimpossible.co.uk
w: www.creatingtheimpossible.co.uk

Creative Glass Fibre Models
266 RALPH ROAD, SHIRLEY, SOLIHULL
West Midlands B90 3LF .... 0121 744 9226 / 07778 285997
e: steve@creativemodelmaking.co.uk
w: www.creativemodelmaking.co.uk

Designworks
UNIT 2 WINDSOR BUSINESS CENTRE, VANSITTART ESTATE,
WINDSOR Berkshire SL4 1SP..................................01753 842 404
e: dw@designworkswindsor.co.uk
w: www.designworksgroup.net

Dorans Propmakers
53 DERBY ROAD, ASHBOURNE
 DE6 1BH .... 01335 300064 / 07721744774
e: info@doransprops.com
w: www.doransprops.com

Effigy Models & Sets
STUDIO NO 93, SHEPPERTON STUDIOS, STUDIOS ROAD,
SHEPPERTON TW17 0QD .... 01932 241690 / 07860 844165
e: sales@effigyuk.com
w: www.effigyuk.com

FBFX
UNIT 1 DOCKWELLS ESTATE, CENTRAL WAY, FELTHAM,
HOUNSLOW
Middlesex TW14 0RX 020 8751 5321
e: info@fbfx.co.uk
w: www.fbfx.co.uk

Final Creation
THE LOFT STUDIO, 19 HILL LANE IND. EST., MARKFIELD,
LEICESTER
Leicestershire LE67 9PN............ 01530 249 100 / 07884 436885
e: gemma@finalcreation.co.uk
w: www.finalcreation.co.uk

Fineline Limited
THE OLD QUARRY, CLEVEDON ROAD, FAILAND, BRISTOL
Bristol BS8 3TU...01275 395000
e: enquiries@fineline.uk.com
w: www.fineline.uk.com

GLD Productions Ltd
UNIT 10A, BENNETTS FIELD TRADING ESTATE, WINCANTON
Somerset BA9 9DT 01963 441155
e: office@gldproductions.com
w: www.gldproductions.com

Handmade Productions Ltd
UNIT B1, EMPRESS PARK, EMPRESS ROAD, SOUTHAMPTON
Hampshire SO14 0JX..023 8021 1000
e: tonyhand@handmade-productions.co.uk
w: www.handmade-scenery.co.uk

Illusion Design & Construct Ltd
UNIT 1A, ELIZABETH INDUSTRIAL ESTATE, JUNO WAY, LONDON
Greater London SE14 5RW...................................0207 2729 255
e: info@illusiondc.com
w: www.illusiondesignandconstruct.co

Karl Evans Studio
SWN-Y-GAN, CEFN-Y-PANT, LLANBOIDY, WHITLAND
Carmathenshire SA34 0TR...................................01994 419 723
e: info@karlevansstudio.com
w: www.karlevansstudio.com

Keeley Hire (film & Tv) Ltd
UNIT 4A, CHARLTON MEAD LANE SOUTH, HODDESDON
 EN11 0DJ 01992 464040
e: salesdesk@keeleyhire.co.uk
w: www.keeleyhire.co.uk

Machine Shop
180 ACTON LANE, PARK ROYAL, LONDON
Greater London NW10 7NH..................................020 8961 5888
e: info@machineshop.co.uk
w: www.machineshop.co.uk

P
Q

Mahogany
28 HIGH STREET, HARLESDEN, LONDON
Greater London NW10 4LX....................................020 8961 4446
e: costumes@mahoganycarnival.com
w: www.mahoganycarnival.com

Mille Couleurs London
REGENT STUDIOS, 1 THANE VILLAS, STUDIO 101, ISLINGTON,
LONDON
Greater London N7 7PH 0207 263 3660
e: info@mc-london.com
w: www.mc-london.com

Palmbrokers
BOTANICA NURSERY, CROWN LANE,, FARNHAM ROYAL
Buckinghamshire SL2 3SG.....................................01753 643359
e: ask@palmbrokers.com
w: www.palmbrokers.com

Plunge Productions
UNIT 3, BESTWOOD WORKS, DROVE ROAD, PORTSLADE VILLAGE,
BRIGHTON
East Sussex BN41 2PA...01273 423014
e: info@plungeproductions.com
w: www.plungeproductions.com

Prop Studios Ltd
STUDIO 1, 9 THORPE CLOSE NOTTING HILL, LONDON
Greater London W10 5XL 0207 3998664
e: info@propstudios.co.uk
w: www.propstudios.co.uk

Rainbow Productions
UNIT 3, GREENLEA PARK, PRINCE GEORGE'S ROAD, LONDON
Greater London SW19 2JD....................................020 8254 5300
e: info@rainbowproductions.co.uk
w: www.rainbowproductions.co.uk

Russell Beck Studio Ltd
UNIT 11 VALE INDUSTRIAL PARK, 170 ROWAN ROAD, LONDON
Greater London SW16 5BN 020 3241 0000
e: Russell@russellbeckstudio.co.uk
w: www.russellbeckstudio.co.uk

Scruffy Dog
UNIT E3, OYO BUSINESS PARK, PARK LANE, BIRMINGHAM
West Midlands B35 6AN 0800 211 8604
e: info@scruffydogltd.com
w: www.scruffydogltd.com

Sculpture Studios
UNIT 3F HARVEY ROAD, NEVENDON INDUSTRIAL ESTATE,
BASILDON
Essex SS13 1DA 01268 726470
e: aden.hynes@hotmail.com
w: www.sculpturestudios.co.uk

SIGA CreativeFX
UNIT F1-F3 HEATH PLACE, BOGNOR REGIS
West Sussex PO22 9SL..01243 837 835
e: hello@sigacreativefx.com

w: www.sigacreativefx.com

Sponge Creative Ltd
CANNA ENTERPRISE ESTATE, LYSONS AVENUE, ASH VALE,
ALDERSHOT
Hampshire GU12 5QF 01483 740068
e: jeff@spongecreative.co.uk
w: www.spongecreative.co.uk

Spur Creative Ltd
UNIT 2 TABLE TOP FARM, LAMBERHURST QUARTER,
LAMBERHURST, TUNBRIDGE WELLS
Kent TN3 8AL...01892 890608
e: info@spurcreative.co.uk
w: www.spurcreative.co.uk

Stuart Learmonth Film & TV Prop Hire
24 ACTON PARK ESTATE, LONDON
Greater London W3 7QE..0208 749 3100
e: service@stuartlearmonthhire.co.uk
w: www.stuartlearmonthhire.co.uk

Studio Soufflé© Ltd
46 BROOKSBY'S WALK, HACKNEY, LONDON
Greater London E9 6DA.....................................020 7998 4950 /
07882 753215 / 07841 573
e: hello@studiosouffle.com
w: www.studiosouffle.com

Vision Works
9 GARDEN STREET, SHEFFIELD
South Yorkshire S1 4BJ.......................................0114 281 9889 /
07949 760 861
e: trevor@vision-works.co.uk
w: www.vision-works.co.uk

WILDCHILD WORLD
.... +1 786 505 9453
e: info@wildchildworld.com
w: wildchildworld.com

Props / 3D Prop Hire

2d:3d Ltd
263 ABBEYDALE ROAD, LONDON
Greater London HA0 1TW....................................020 8998 3199
e: rob@2d3d.co.uk
w: www.2d3d.co.uk

3D Creations
BERTH 33, MALTHOUSE LANE, GORLESTON, GREAT YARMOUTH
Norfolk NR31 0GW..01493 652055
e: info@3dcreations.co.uk
w: www.3dcreations.co.uk

Ad Events International Limited
STUDIO 4,, VALMAR TRADING ESTATE, VALMAR ROAD,, LONDON
Greater London SE5 9NW.....................................020 7635 7372
e: info@adevents.co.uk
w: www.adevents.co.uk

P
Q

Amazing Parties Ltd
THE FORUM, 277 LONDON ROAD, BURGESS HILL
West Sussex RH15 9QU .... 0 2071 181 088 / 01444 240 165
e: sales@amazingpartythemes.com
w: www.amazingpartythemes.com

American Theme Events Ltd
20 SHIRLEY AVENUE, OLD COULSDON
Surrey CR5 1QU...020 8668 5714
e: info@american-theme.com
w: www.american-theme.com

Applied Arts
22-27 THE OVAL, CAMBRIDGE HEATH, LONDON
Greater London E2 9DT...020 7739 3155
e: info@appliedarts.co.uk
w: www.appliedarts.co.uk

Art Plinths
GROUND FLOOR, 22 CLARENCE MEWS, LONDON
Greater London E5 8HP...07957 754 329
e: info@artplinths.co.uk
w: www.artplinths.co.uk

Circus Equipment Hire
CIRCUS HEADQUARTERS, FNRORNE, NEWBURY
 RG20 OLD 07836 641277
e: martin@circusequipmenthire.co.uk
w: www.circusequipmenthire.co.uk

Colin Holden Associates
111 CUCKMERE WAY, BRIGHTON
East Sussex BN1 8GB ....01273 556290 / 07817 176929
e: colin@colinholden.co.uk
w: www.colinholden.co.uk

Dorans Propmakers
53 DERBY ROAD, ASHBOURNE
 DE6 1BH...01335 300064 /
07721744774

e: info@doransprops.com
w: www.doransprops.com

Event Prop Hire
UNIT 197, AVENUE B, THORP ARCH ESTATE, WETHERBY
West Yorkshire LS23 7BJ 0845 0940 816
e: enquiries@eventprophire.com
w: www.eventprophire.com

Farley
1-17 BRUNEL ROAD, LONDON
Greater London W3 7XR..020 8749 9925
e: props@farley.co.uk
w: www.farley.co.uk

Final Creation
THE LOFT STUDIO, 19 HILL LANE IND. EST., MARKFIELD,
LEICESTER
Leicestershire LE67 9PN.............01530 249 100 / 07884 436885
e: gemma@finalcreation.co.uk
w: www.finalcreation.co.uk

Fineline Limited
THE OLD QUARRY, CLEVEDON ROAD, FAILAND, BRISTOL
Bristol BS8 3TU...01275 395000
e: enquiries@fineline.uk.com
w: www.fineline.uk.com

Furniture Prop Hire London
1 LOWER JOHN STREET, SOHO, LONDON
Greater London W1F 9DT......................................020 7036 8023
e: info@furnitureprophirelondon.co.uk
w: www.furnitureprophirelondon.co.uk

Greathire
UNIT 4 BAGO HOUSE, 11-15 CHASE ROAD, PARK ROYAL, LONDON
Greater London NW10 6PT....................................020 8965 5005
e: info@greathire.co.uk
w: www.greathire.co.uk

Hamilton Ice Sculptors Ltd
54 WIMBLEDON STADIUM BUSINESS CENTRE, LONDON
Greater London SW17 0BA.....................................020 8944 9787
e: info@icesculpture.co.uk
w: www.icesculpture.co.uk

Hands On Production Services Ltd
79 LOANBANK QUADRANT, GLASGOW
Glasgow G51 3HZ..0141 4402005
e: info@hands-on-uk.com
w: www.hands-on-uk.com

Howorth Wrightson Ltd
T/A HWL, CRICKET STREET, DENTON, MANCHESTER
 M34 3DR..0161 335 0220
e: props@hwltd.co.uk
w: www.hwltd.co.uk

It's All Greek
25A MUSEUM ST, LONDON
Greater London WC1A 1JU....................................0207 242 6224
e: hello@itsallgreek.co.uk
w: www.itsallgreek.co.uk

John Slough Of London
OLD FORGE, PETERCHURCH, HEREFORD
Hertfordshire HR2 0SD..............01432 277 237 / 07775 643 762
e: john@johnsloughoflondon.co.uk
w: www.johnsloughoflondon.co.uk

Keeley Hire (film & Tv) Ltd
UNIT 4A, CHARLTON MEAD LANE SOUTH, HODDESDON
 EN11 0DJ 01992 464040
e: salesdesk@keeleyhire.co.uk
w: www.keeleyhire.co.uk

Lassco
THREE PIDGEONS, LONDON ROAD, MILTON COMMON
Oxfordshire OX9 2JN..01844 277 188
e: 3pigeons@lassco.co.uk
w: www.lassco.co.uk

P
Q

Lucid Productions
UNIT 407 GREENHEATH BUSINESS CENTER, THREE COLTS LANE,
LONDON E7 0DL 0207 739 0240
e: info@clubdecor.co.uk
w: www.clubdecor.co.uk

Machine Shop
180 ACTON LANE, PARK ROYAL, LONDON
Greater London NW10 7NH...................................020 8961 5888
e: info@machineshop.co.uk
w: www.machineshop.co.uk

Memory Lane Vintage Omnibus Services
UNITS 1-4 NORTHFLEET INDUSTRIAL ESTATE, LOWER
ROAD, NORTHFLEET
Kent DA11 9SN...01474 361199
e: action@memorylane.co.uk
w: www.memorylane.co.uk

Millington Associates
UNIT 6 Ā " 9 SYDENHAM INDUSTRIAL ESTATE, WESTERLEY
CRESCENT, LONDON
Greater London SE26 5BA....................................020 7231 5770
e: enquiries@millingtonassociates.com
w: www.millingtonassociates.com

More Production Ltd
103 COVENTRY ROAD, BURBAGE, , HINCKLEY
Leicestershire LE10 2HN.......................................01455 615 746
e: sales@moreproduction.co.uk
w: www.moreproduction.co.uk

Prop Studios Ltd
STUDIO 1, 9 THORPE CLOSE NOTTING HILL, LONDON
Greater London W10 5XL 0207 3998664
e: info@propstudios.co.uk
w: www.propstudios.co.uk

Rex Howard (Drapes) Ltd
UNIT F, TRADING ESTATE ROAD
 NW10 7LU 020 8955 6940
e: rex.howard@hawthorns.uk.com
w: www.rex-howard.co.uk

Russell Beck Studio Ltd
UNIT 11 VALE INDUSTRIAL PARK, 170 ROWAN ROAD, LONDON
Greater London SW16 5BN 020 3241 0000
e: Russell@russellbeckstudio.co.uk
w: www.russellbeckstudio.co.uk

Sculpture Studios
UNIT 3F HARVEY ROAD, NEVENDON INDUSTRIAL ESTATE,
BASILDON
Essex SS13 1DA 01268 726470
e: aden.hynes@hotmail.com
w: www.sculpturestudios.co.uk

Secrets Of
 ....0161 4080582
e: info@secretsof.co.uk
w: www.secretsof.co.uk

Spur Creative Ltd
UNIT 2 TABLE TOP FARM, LAMBERHURST QUARTER,
LAMBERHURST, TUNBRIDGE WELLS
Kent TN3 8AL..01892 890608
e: info@spurcreative.co.uk
w: www.spurcreative.co.uk

Stuart Learmonth Film & TV Prop Hire
24 ACTON PARK ESTATE, LONDON
Greater London W3 7QE..0208 749 3100
e: service@stuartlearmonthhire.co.uk
w: www.stuartlearmonthhire.co.uk

Superhire
55 CHASE ROAD, PARK ROYAL, LONDON
Greater London NW10 6LU...................................020 8453 3900
e: info@superhire.com
w: www.superhire.com

Tenandahalfthousandthings
STUDIO 4, VALMAR TRADING ESTATE, VALMAR ROAD , LONDON
Greater London SE5 9NW.....................................0207 924 0464
e: enquiries@tenandahalfthousandthings.co.uk
w: www.tenandahalfthousandthings.co.

Theme Traders Ltd
THE STADIUM, OAKLANDS ROAD, LONDON
Greater London NW2 6DL 0208 452 8518
e: enquiries@themetraders.com
w: www.themetraders.com

Themes Incorporated
BECKERY ROAD, GLASTONBURY
Somerset BA6 9NX 01458 832602
e: info@themesinc.co.uk
w: www.themesinc.co.uk

Visual Impact
ST JOHN'S FOUNDRY, 12 ST JOHN'S ROAD, HAMPTON WICK,
KINGSTON UPON THAMES
Greater London KT1 4AN 020 8977 2577
e: info@visual-impact.co.uk
w: www.visual-impact.co.uk

**P
Q**

Pyrotechnics

MTFX
VELT HOUSE, VELT HOUSE LANE, ELMORE
Gloucester GL2 3NY 1454 729 903
e: mark@mtfx.com
w: www.mtfx.com

MTFX
Velt House Lane
Elmore, Gloucestershire
GL2 3NY

t:　01452 729 903
e:　info@MTFX.com

MTFX create visual drama and stunning scenes with pyrotechnic special effects. We can provide Indoor gas flame effects, walls of coloured stars, waterfall effects, six metre LPG flames, coloured flames and more.

Welcome to MTFX, the ingenious special effects people.

www.MTFX.com

P
Q

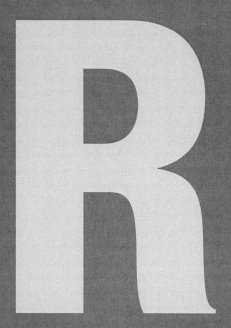

Radio / Telephone Communications

2CL Communications Ltd
UNIT C, WOODSIDE TRADE CENTRE, PARHAM DRIVE, EASTLEIGH
Hampshire SO50 4NU .... +44 (0) 23 8064 8500
e: contact@2cl.co.uk
w: www.2cl.co.uk

Attend2IT
UNIT 8, PARK FARM INDUSTRIAL ESTATE, BUNTINGFORD
Hertfordshire SG9 9AZ 01763 877 477
w: www.attend2it.co.uk

Audiolink Radio Communications
17 IRON BRIDGE CLOSE, NEASDON, WEMBLEY
Greater London NW10 0UF.....................................020 8955 1100
e: info@audiolink.co.uk
w: www.audiolink.co.uk

Barnes-Wilkes Group
....0844 320 0023
e: info@barnes-wilkes.com
w: www.barnes-wilkes.com

Brentwood Communications LTD
BC HOUSE , EAST HANNINGFIELD RD , CHELMSFORD
Essex CM3 8EW..0808 115 2577

Channel 16
TOWER BRIDGE BUSINESS COMPLEX, LONDON
Greater London S16 4DG .... 07836 693833 / 07595 893020
e: forshow@channel-16.co.uk
w: www.channel-16.co.uk

Chatterbox Ltd
1 GUARDS AVENUE, THE VILLAGE, CATERHAM
Surrey CR3 5XL 01883 334792
e: info@chatterboxradio.com
w: www.chatterboxradio.com

CommTrack Ltd
332 STOCKPORT BUSINESS & INNOVATION CENTRE ,
BROADSTONE ROAD, STOCKPORT
Greater Manchester SK5 7DL................................0161 443 4183
w: www.commtrack.co.uk

Communication Specialists Ltd
UNIT 6, MURRELL GREEN BUSINESS PARK, LONDON ROAD, HOOK
Hampshire RG27 9GR 01256 766600
e: enquiries@comm-spec.com
w: www.comm-spec.com

Comsco
PICKWOOD HALL, PICKWOOD AVENUE, LEEK
Staffordshire ST13 5BZ..0800 369 9123
e: sales@comsco.com
w: www.comsco.com

Direct Communications Radio Services Ltd (dcrs)
EDISON ROAD, ST IVES, HUNTINGDON
Cambridgeshire PE27 3LH 01480 466300
e: sales@dcrs.co.uk
w: www.dcrs.co.uk

DLC Events
STREET 22, AL QUOZ IND 3, DUBAI
PO Box 282841,.. +971 4 347 0484
e: office@dlcevents.com
w: www.dlcevents.com

Earcomm
THE OFFICE, CROWN COTTAGE, CROWN LANE, FOUR OAKS,
BIRMINGHAM West Midlands B74 4SU..................0121 371 0880
e: info@earcomm.co.uk
w: www.earcomm.co.uk

Etherlive
INTERFACE BUSINESS PARK UNIT 13, ROYAL WOOTTON BASSETT
Wiltshire SN4 8SY...01666 800129
e: info@etherlive.co.uk
w: www.etherlive.co.uk

Event Communication Services
UNIT G171, CHERWELL BUSINESS VILLAGE, SOUTHAM ROAD,,
BANBURY
Oxfordshire OX16 2SP...02033 284960
e: info@eventgeeks.co.uk
w: www.eventgeeks.co.uk

Event Geeks
UNIT G171, CHERWELL BUSINESS VILLAGE, SOUTHAM ROAD,
BANBURY
Oxfordshire OX16 2SP. 0203 328 4960
e: info@eventgeeks.co.uk
w: www.eventgeeks.co.uk

Frontline Network Service
98 GLOUCESTER ROAD, HAMPTON
TW12 2UJ...0800 458 2010
e: enquiries@frontline-ns.com
w: www.frontline-ns.com

Gradav Hire and Sales Ltd
SHENLEY ROAD , BOREHAMWOOD
Hertfordshire WD6 1JG 020 8324 2100
e: office@gradav.co.uk
w: www.gradav.co.uk

hi-Vision Systems Ltd
WAREHAM HOUSE, 263 BROAD LANE, TILE HILL , COVENTRY
West Midlands CV5 7AQ 0870 428 1159
e: web@hi-vision.co.uk
w: www.hi-vision.co.uk

JNB Aerials
55 ST GEORGES CRESCENT, SALFORD
Greater Manchester M6 8JN 0161 825 9099
e: j.higgins@jnbaerials.co.uk
w: www.jnbaerials.co.uk

R

Limitear Ltd
BOUNDARY HOUSE, BOSTON ROAD, LONDON
Greater London W7 2QE...0845 643 4055
e: information@limitear.com
w: www.limitear.com

Maximon Solutions Ltd
22 SOHO MILLS, WOOBURN GREEN
Buckinghamshire HP10 0PF..................................01628 878066
e: info@maximonsolutions.com
w: www.maximonsolutions.com

Mike Weaver Communications Ltd
UNIT 10 REDLAND CLOSE, ALDERMANS GREEN INDUSTRIAL
ESTATE, COVENTRY
West Midlands CV2 2NP.......................................024 7660 2605
e: sales@mwc.co.uk
w: www.mwc.co.uk

Mobile CCTV
UNIT 8 CAMBERLEY BUSINESS CENTRE, BRACEBRIDGE,
CAMBERLEY Surrey GU15 3DP.............................01276 469 084
e: info@mobilecctv.co.uk
w: www.mobilecctv.co.uk

National Radio Bank
PINFOLD ROAD, BOURNE
Lincolnshire PE10 9HT...01778 393938
e: sales@radiohire.com
w: www.radiohire.com

Orbital Sound & Comunications
57 ACRE LANE, BRIXTON, LONDON
Greater London SW2 5TN.......................................01903 854900
e: information@orbitalsound.com
w: www.orbitalsound.com

Peter Maciuk Installations Ltd
UNIT 2, OLD CHAR WHARF, STATION ROAD, DORKING
Surrey RH4 1EF 01306 883781
e: info@pmihire.co.uk
w: www.pmihire.co.uk

Radio Links Communications Ltd
EATON HOUSE, GREAT NORTH ROAD, EATON SOCON, ST NEOTS
Cambridgeshire PE19 8EG 0500 220221
e: info@radio-links.co.uk
w: www.radio-links.co.uk

Radiocoms Systems Ltd
UNIT 2 & 3, THE CHASE CENTRE, 8 CHASE ROAD, PARK ROYAL,
LONDON NW10 6QD 020 8951 9820
e: websales@radiocoms.co.uk
w: www.radiocoms.co.uk

Radiotek Ltd
UNIT C, SILVER END BUSINESS PARK , BRETTELL LANE ,
BRIERLEY HILL
West Midlands DY5 3LG...0800 5879 774
e: sales@radiotek.co.uk
w: www.radiotek.co.uk

Raycom
LANGTON HOUSE, 19 VILLAGE STREET, HARVINGTON
Worcestershire WR11 8NQ 01789 777040
e: sales@raycom.co.uk
w: www.raycom.co.uk

Red Radio
YORK HOUSE, 140 HIGH TOWN ROAD, LUTON
Bedfordshire LU2 0DJ..01582 481114
e: sales@red-radio.co.uk
w: www.red-radio.co.uk

Show Hire
UNITS 19 & 20 BORDON TRADING ESTATE, OLD STATION WAY ,
BORDON Hampshire GU35 9HH..............................01483 414337
e: info@showhire.co.uk
w: www.showhire.co.uk

Sitelink Communications Ltd
18 BRIDGEWATER ROAD, HERTBURN IND. EST. WASHINGTON,
TYNE & WEAR Tyne and Wear NE37 2SG 020 8508 6688
e: info@sitelink.co.uk
w: www.sitelink.co.uk

Sonifex Ltd
61 STATION ROAD, IRTHLINGBOROUGH
Northamptonshire NN9 5QE 01933 650700
e: sales@sonifex.co.uk
w: www.sonifex.co.uk

Wall To Wall Communications Limited
UNILINK HOUSE, 21 LEWIS ROAD, SUTTON
Surrey SM1 4BR 020 8770 1007
e: info@walltowallcomms.co.uk
w: www.walltowallcomms.co.uk

Wavevend Radio Communications
17B PINDOCK MEWS, LITTLE VENICE, LONDON
Greater London W9 2PY 020 7266 1280
e: info@wavevend.co.uk
w: www.wavevend.co.uk

Radio Microphones

Andrew Sound
4 ROBINSON ROAD, BEDWORTH
Warwickshire CV12 0EL..024 7636 4235
e: info@andrewphotographic.co.uk
w: www.andrewsound.co.uk

Attend2IT
UNIT 8, PARK FARM INDUSTRIAL ESTATE, BUNTINGFORD
Hertfordshire SG9 9AZ 01763 877 477
w: www.attend2it.co.uk

Audio Source Ltd
31 MONGLEATH AVENUE, FALMOUTH
Cornwall TR11 4PP .... 07971 607172 /
.... 07867 525016 / 01326 3115
e: hire@audio-source.co.uk
w: www.audio-source.co.uk

Cardiff M Light & Sound
UNIT 2, THE HIGHWAYMAN, CASTLEVIEW, BRIDGEND
 CF31 1NJ 01656 767388
e: info@cardiffm.co.uk
w: www.cardiffm.co.uk

CommTrack Ltd
332 STOCKPORT BUSINESS & INNOVATION CENTRE ,
BROADSTONE ROAD, STOCKPORT
Greater Manchester SK5 7DL................................0161 443 4183
w: www.commtrack.co.uk

DBS Solutions
73 MANCHESTER RD, WOOLSTON, WARRINGTON
Cheshire WA1 4AE 0845 388 0321
e: info@dbs-solutions.co.uk
w: www.dbs-solutions.co.uk

Earcomm
THE OFFICE, CROWN COTTAGE, CROWN LANE, FOUR OAKS,
BIRMINGHAM
West Midlands B74 4SU..0121 371 0880
e: info@earcomm.co.uk
w: www.earcomm.co.uk

Gb Audio
UNIT D, 51 BRUNSWICK ROAD, EDINBURGH
Edinburgh EH7 5PD 0131 661 0022
e: sales@gbaudio.co.uk
w: www.gbaudio.co.uk

John Hornby Skewes & Co Ltd
SALEM HOUSE, PARKINSON APPROACH, GARFORTH, LEEDS
West Yorkshire LS25 2HR..0113 286 5381
e: webinfo@jhs.co.uk
w: www.jhs.co.uk

London Speaker Hire
ATLAS WHARF, BERKSHIRE ROAD, LONDON
Greater London E9 5NB 020 3333 4444
e: info@londonspeakerhire.com
w: www.londonspeakerhire.com

M.I. Executives Limited
UNIT 2, CRAYFORD COMMERCIAL CENTRE, GREYHOUND WAY,
CRAYFORD, Kent DA1 4HF 01322 552828
e: info@mlexecutives.com
w: www.mlexecutives.com

Mac Sound
1 & 2 ATTENBURYS PARK, PARK ROAD, ALTRINCHAM
Cheshire WA14 5QE..0161 969 8311
e: info@macsound.co.uk
w: www.macsound.co.uk

Midnight Electronics
OFF QUAY BUILDING, FOUNDRY LANE, NEWCASTLE UPON TYNE
Tyne and Wear NE6 1LH..0191 224 0088
e: info@midnightelectronics.co.uk
w: www.midnight.uk.net

Orbital Sound & Comunications
57 ACRE LANE, BRIXTON, LONDON
Greater London SW2 5TN......................................01903 854900
e: information@orbitalsound.com
w: www.orbitalsound.com

Peter Maciuk Installations Ltd
UNIT 2, OLD CHAR WHARF, STATION ROAD, DORKING
Surrey RH4 1EF 01306 883781
e: info@pmihire.co.uk
w: www.pmihire.co.uk

Radiotek Ltd
UNIT C, SILVER END BUSINESS PARK , BRETTELL LANE ,
BRIERLEY HILL West Midlands DY5 3LG 0800 5879 774
e: sales@radiotek.co.uk
w: www.radiotek.co.uk

Skan Pa
THE MERIDIAN BUILDING, 1 BROOKWAY HAMBRIDGE LANE,
NEWBURY Berkshire RG14 5RY 01635 521010
e: enquiries@skanpa.co.uk
w: www.skanpa.co.uk

Sound By Design Ltd
 21 ISLAND FARM AVENUE, WEST MOLESEY
Surrey KT8 2UZ 020 8339 3800
e: enquiries@deltasound.uk
w: www.soundbydesign.net

Wall To Wall Communications Limited
UNILINK HOUSE, 21 LEWIS ROAD, SUTTON
Surrey SM1 4BR 020 8770 1007
e: info@walltowallcomms.co.uk
w: www.walltowallcomms.co.uk

Ramps / Trackway

All Weather Access
COUNTY FARM, RANDS ROAD, HIGH RODING, DUNMOW
Essex CM6 1NQ........................ 01371 700510 / 07801 751 137
e: info@all-weatheraccess.co.uk
w: www.all-weatheraccess.co.uk

All Weather Access Ltd
County Farm, High Roding
Dunmow, Essex
CM6 1NQ

t: 01371 700 510
e: info@all-weatheraccess.co.uk

ALL WEATHER ACCESS
Temporary Access - Ground Protection

Supplying the highest quality ground protection solutions available
and keeping vehicles and pedestrians out of the mud. We have a
wide range of fantastic products ranging from heavy duty 150 tonne
trackway to light weight easy to lay pedestrian flooring.

www.all-weatheraccess.co.uk

C&E Structures scaffolding
NORTH MERSEY BUSINESS CENTRE/WOODWARD RD, KNOWSLEY
INDUSTRIAL PARK, LIVERPOOL
Merseyside L33 7UY .... 0151 5484 492 - 07775 880 460
e: ian@candestructures.co.uk
w: www.candestructures.co.uk

Davis Track Hire
103A MAIN STREET, NEWMAINS, WISHAW
Lanarkshire ML2 9BG 01698 352751
e: info@davistrackhire.com
w: www.davistrackhire.com

Eco Track & Access Ltd
GEOFF'S DRIVE, WALTON NEW ROAD BUSINESS PARK,
LUTTERWORTH
Leicestershire LE17 5RD.......................................01455 553 700
e: sales@ecotrackway.co.uk
w: www.ecotrackway.co.uk/

Eve Trakway
BRAMLEY VALE, CHESTERFIELD
Derbyshire S44 5GA...08700 767676
e: mail@evetrakway.co.uk
w: www.evetrakway.co.uk

Fieldtrack Ltd
MANSE ROAD, FORTH
Lanarkshire ML11 8AN 01555 812812
e: info@fieldtrackltd.co.uk
w: www.fieldtrackltd.co.uk

Grass Concrete Ltd
DUNCAN HOUSE, 142 THORNES LANE, THORNES, WAKEFIELD
Warwickshire WF2 7RE 01924 379443
e: info@grasscrete.com
w: www.grasscrete.com

Grassform Plant Hire Ltd
LITTLE WOODBARNS FARM YARD, GREEN STREET, FRYERNING,
INGATESTONE Essex CM4 0NT..............................01277 353686
e: info@grassform.co.uk
w: www.grassform.co.uk

Groundtrax Systems Ltd
STATION YARD, RIPLEY, HARROGATE
North Yorkshire HG3 3BA 08456 800008
e: info@groundtrax.com
w: www.groundtrax.com

Lh Woodhouse & Co Ltd
WOLDS FARM, THE FOSSE, COTGRAVE
Nottinghamshire NG12 3HG 0115 9899899
e: sales@lhwoodhouse.co.uk
w: www.lhwoodhouse.co.uk

Lion Trackhire Ltd
CLAYLANDS AVENUE , WORKSOP
Nottinghamshire S81 7BQ.....................................01909 212 214
e: enquiries@liontrackhire.com
w: www.liontrackhire.com

Mitchell Bridges Ltd
LONDON ROAD, KINGSWORTHY, WINCHESTER
Hampshire SO23 7QN..01962 885040
e: enquiries@mitchellbridges.com
w: www.temporarybridges.co.uk

Portaramp UK Ltd
UNITS 3 & 4, DOLPHIN BUSINESS PARK, SHADWELL, THETFORD
Norfolk IP24 2RY..01953 681799
e: sales@portaramp.co.uk
w: www.portaramp.co.uk

Profloor Europe B.V.
7 EXPORT DRIVE, BROOKLYN,, VICTORIA
3012 Australia .... +31-416-74 71 13
e: info@profloor.com.au
w: www.pro-floor.eu

Ra'alloy Ramps Ltd
UNIT A3 STAFFORD PARK 15, TELFORD
Shropshire TF3 3BB...01952 291224
e: sales@raalloy.co.uk
w: www.raalloy.co.uk

Rola-Trac
SOUTH BURLINGHAM RD , LINGWOOD , NORWICH
Norfolk NR13 4ET 01493 750 200
e: enquiries@rola-trac.co.uk
w: www.rola-trac.co.uk

Tempower Ltd
UNIT 3B DELTECH EUROPE, PIPERELL WAY, HAVERHILL,
Suffolk CB9 8PH 0845 6066049
e: hire@temppower.co.uk
w: www.temppower.co.uk

The Ramp People
UNIT C3 SANDOWN INDUSTRIAL PARK, ESHER
Surrey KT10 8BL..01372 478960
e: hello@theramppeople.co.uk
w: www.theramppeople.co.uk

TPA Portable Roadways Ltd
DUKERIES MILL, CLAYLANDS AVENUE, WORKSOP
Nottinghamshire S81 7DJ 0870 240 2381
e: enquiries@tpa-ltd.co.uk
w: www.tpa-ltd.co.uk

Trackway Solutions
FOXBRIDGE WAY, NORMANTON INDUSTRIAL ESTATE,
NORMANTON
West Yorkshire WF6 1TN 0845 601 2187
e: info@trackwaysolutions.co.uk
w: www.trackwaysolutions.co.uk

Zigma Ground Solutions Ltd
UNIT 11, M11 BUSINESS LINK, PARSONAGE LANE, STANSTED
Essex CM24 8GF.......................0845 643 5388 / 01279 647021
e: sales@zigmagroundsolutions.com
w: www.zigmagroundsolutions.com

Record Companies / Record Labels

33 Records
65 - 67 BUTE STREET, LUTON
Bedfordshire LU1 2EY 01582 419584
e: info@33jazz.com
w: www.33jazz.com

Abacabe Records
BLUES IN BRITAIN, 11 LANGDON AVENUE, AYLESBURY
Buckinghamshire HP21 9UL..................................0 1296 393877
e: editor@bluesinbritain.org
w: www.bluesinbritain.org

Acoustics Records
PO BOX 350, READING
Berkshire RG6 7DQ 0118 926 8615
e: info@acousticsrecords.co.uk
w: www.acousticsrecords.co.uk

Alchemy Records
P.O. BOX 393, MAIDSTONE
 ME14 5XU...01622 729593
e: alchemist@alchemyrecords.co.uk

Armadillo Music Ltd
PO BOX 3055, STURMINSTER NEWTON
Dorset DT10 2XA 01963 364504
e: mail@bluearmadillo.com
w: www.bluearmadillo.com

Backs Records Ltd
ST MARYS WORKS, ST MARYS PLAIN, NORWICH
 NR3 3AF 01603 626221
e: derek@backsrecords.co.uk

Barn Dance Publications Ltd
20 SHIRLEY AVENUE, OLD COULSDON
 CR5 1QU..020 8668 5714
e: info@barndancepublications.co.uk
w: www.barndancepublications.co.uk

Bearsongs
PO BOX 944, EDGBASTON, BIRMINGHAM
West Midlands B16 8UT...0121 454 7020
e: admin@bigbearmusic.com
w: www.bigbearmusic.com

Big Help Management
THE OVAL ROOM, 4 PARKFIELD ROAD, RUGBY
Warwickshire CV21 1EN 07782 172101
e: studio@bighelp.biz
w: www.bighelp.biz

Bucks Music Group
ROUNDHOUSE, 212 REGENTS PARK ROAD ENTRANCE, LONDON
Greater London NW1 8AW....................................020 7221 4275
e: info@bucksmusicgroup.co.uk
w: www.bucksmusicgroup.com

Caritas Media Music
ACHMORE, MOSS ROAD, ULLAPOOL
Ross-shire IV26 2TF..01854 612236
e: info@caritas-music.co.uk
w: www.caritas-music.co.uk

Circle Sound Services
CIRCLE HOUSE, 14 WAVENEY CLOSE, BICESTER
 OX26 2GP 01869 240051
e: sound@circlesound.net
w: www.circlesound.net

D.o.r
PO BOX 1797, LONDON
 E1 4TX...020 7702 7842
e: contact@dor.co.uk
w: www.dor.co.uk

Discovery Records Ltd
NURSTEED ROAD, DEVIZES
 SN10 3DY 01380 722244
e: info@discovery-records.com

Dmc Ltd
PO 89 , SLOUGH
 SL1 8NA 01628 667124
e: info@dmcworld.com
w: www.dmcworld.com

Emi Records (uk)
EMI HOUSE , 43 BROOK GREEN
 W6 7ET..0207 605 5000
e: matt.edwards@emimusic.com
w: www.emimusic.com

Epic Records
C/O SONY BMG , BEDFORD HOUSE, 69-70 FULHAM HIGH STREET
 SW6 3JW...0207 384 7500
e: info@epicrecords.com
w: www.epicrecords.com

Fellside Recordings Ltd
PO BOX 40, WORKINGTON
Cumbria CA14 3GJ 01900 61556
e: info@fellside.com
w: www.fellside.com

First Night Records
3 WARREN MEWS, LONDON
Greater London W1T 6AN......................................020 7383 7767
e: info@first-night-records.com
w: www.first-night-records.com

Flashlight Records
22 FITZROY COURT, SHEPHERDS HILL, HIGHGATE
 N6 5RD..020 8340 6428
e: info@newjazzsongs.com

R

Floating Earth
UNIT 14, 21 WADSWORTH ROAD, PERIVALE
Middlesex UB6 7LQ 020 8997 4000
e: steve@thesoundcorporation.com
w: www.floatingearth.com

Folksound Records
RICHMOND HOUSE, 127 WESTWOOD HEATH ROAD, COVENTRY
 CV4 8GN...024 7642 2225
e: info@folksound.co.uk

Future Music Management
FUTURE HOUSE, SOUTHAMPTON
 SO15 5EL 02380 529966
e: office@futuremusicmanagement.com
w: www.futuremusicmanagement.com

Greensleeves Records Ltd
UNIT 14, METRO CENTRE, ST JOHNS ROAD, ISLEWORTH
 TW6 6NJ..020 8758 0564
e: info@greensleeves.net
w: www.greensleeves.net

Groovin Records
PO BOX 39, HOYLAKE, WIRRAL
 CH47 2HP...0845 458 0037
e: groovin.records@phonecoop.coop
w: www.groovinrecords.co.uk

Heavenly Recordings Ltd
219 PORTABELLOW ROAD
 W11 1LU...020 7494 2998
e: danny@heavenlyrecordings.com
w: www.heavenlyrecordings.com

Hed Kandi Records
103 GAUNT STREET , LONDON
Greater London SE1 6DP.........................020 7740 8600
e: demo@hedkandi.com
w: www.hedkandi.com

In Tune XI
34 LATELOW ROAD, KITTS GREEN, BIRMINGHAM
 B33 8JZ..07508 346 673
e: drjones404@googlemail.com

Indian Music 4u
LYNTON HOUSE, 304 BENSHAM LANE, THORNTON HEATH
Surrey CR7 7EQ .... 020 86 84 84 77 // 079 18 78 78 78
e: info@audiorec.co.uk
w: www.indianmusic4u.co.uk

Invisible Hands Music
79 WARDOUR STREET , LONDON
Greater London W1D 6UB 2033558878
e: sales@invisiblehands.co.uk
w: www.invisiblehands.co.uk

Irl Record Company
HOPE HOUSE, 40 ST PETERS ROAD, LONDON
 W6 9BD 020 87467461
e: info@spiritmm.com
w: www.irl.org.uk

Isa Music
46 ELLIOT STREET, GLASGOW
Glasgow G3 8DZ....................................0141 248 2266
e: admin@isa-music.com
w: www.isa-music.com

Island Record Group
364-366 KENSINGTON HIGH STREET
 W14 8NS..0207 471 5300
e: info@umusic.com
w: www.islandrecords.co.uk

Joe & Co (music) Ltd
HAMMER HOUSE, 117 WARDOUR STREET
 W1F 0UN 020 7439 1272
e: info@yellowboatmusic.com
w: www.joeandco.com

Jungle Records
RESEARCH HOUSE, FRASER ROAD, PERIVALE
Middlesex UB6 7AQ 020 8537 3444
e: enquiries@jungle-records.com
w: www.jungle-records.net

Kassner Associated Publishers Ltd
UNITS 6-7, 11 WYFOLD ROAD, FULHAM
 SW6 6SE 020 7385 7700
e: songs@kassner-music.co.uk
w: www.kassnermusic.com

Kid Menthal Music
20 MEYRICK CRESCENT, COLCHESTER, ESSEX
 CO2 7QY...01206 549582
e: km@kidmenthal.co.uk
w: www.kidmenthal.co.uk

Krl
PO BOX 5577, NEWTON MEARNS, GLASGOW
 G77 9BH...0141 616 0900
e: krl@krl.co.uk
w: www.krl.co.uk

L S O Live
LONDON SYYMPHONY ORCHESTRA, BARBICAN CENTRE, SILK STREET, LONDON
Greater London EC2Y 8DS 020 7588 1116
e: admin@lso.co.uk
w: www.lso.co.uk

Landstar Management
7A CHAPEL STREET, LANCASTER, LANCASTER
Lancashire LA1 1NZ................................01524 843499
e: turnbuis@hotmail.com
w: www.myspace.com/landstarmanagemen

R

Linn Records
GLASGOW ROAD, WATERFOOT, EAGLESHAM, GLASGOW
Glasgow G76 0EQ.....................................0141 303 5027
e: info@linnrecords.co.uk
w: www.linnrecords.com

Lismor Recordings
46 ELLIOT STREET, GLASGOW
G3 8DZ...0141 248 2266
e: sales@allcelticmusic.com
w: www.allcelticmusic.com

Mastering World
MASTERING WORLD, HAFOD, ST HILARY, CONBRIDGE,
COWBRIDGE
CF71 7DP 01446 775512
e: help@masteringworld.com
w: www.masteringworld.com

Memphis Industries
8 RIPPLEVALE GROVE
N1 1HU..020 7607 2610
e: info@memphis-industries.com
w: www.memphis-industries.com

Meridian Records
PO BOX 317, ELTHAM, LONDON
Greater London SE9 4SF......................020 8857 3213
e: mail@meridian-records.co.uk
w: www.meridian-records.co.uk

Meshhead
PENVALE BARN, , SILVERWELL, TRURO
TR4 8JE..07968 363709
e: info@meshhead.co.uk
w: www.meshhead.co.uk

Metal Mickey Productions Ltd
PO BOX 6936, CLAPTON
E5 8BL..020 8806 4114
e: iwant@metalmickey.com
w: www.metalmickey.com

Microphonic Limited
54 WESLEY ROAD, LEYTON
E10 6JF..0203 039 2979
e: info@microphonic.biz
w: www.microphonic.biz

Moksha Recordings Ltd
PO BOX 102, LONDON
Greater London E15 2HH 020 8555 5423
e: info@moksha.co.uk
w: www.moksha.co.uk

Music Galore Ltd
105 EMLYN ROAD, SHEPHERD'S BUSH
W12 9TG...07985 467970
e: redhotrecs@aol.com

Nervous Records
5 SUSSEX CRESCENT, NORTHOLT
Greater London UB5 4DL 020 8423 7373
e: info@nervous.co.uk
w: www.nervous.co.uk

Nmc Recordings Ltd
3RD FLOOR, SOUTH WING, SOMERSET HOUSE, STRAND, LONDON
Greater London WC2R 1LA....................020 7759 1827
e: nmc@nmcrec.co.uk
w: www.nmcrec.co.uk

Northstar Music Publishing Ltd
PO BOX 868, CAMBRIDGE
Cambridgeshire CB21 4SJ 01787 278256
e: info@northstarmusic.co.uk
w: www.northstarmusic.co.uk

Optimum Records
16 LIMETREES, LLANGATTOCK, CRICKHOWELL
NP8 1LB 01873 810142
e: optimumrecordco@aol.com
w: www.optimumrecords.com

Palm Pictures Ltd
1460 BROADWAY, NEW YORK, USA
10036..001 646 790 1211
e: Kevin.Yatarola@palmpictures.com
w: www.palmpictures.com

Pickwick Group Limited
MERRITT HOUSE, HILL AVENUE, AMERSHAM
Buckinghamshire HP6 5BQ 01494 732 800
e: info@pickwickgroup.com
w: www.pickwickgroup.com

Plus Music
36 FOLLINGHAM COURT, DRYSDALE PLACE, HOXTON
N1 6LZ 020 7684 8594
e: info@plusmusic.co.uk
w: www.plusmusic.co.uk

Polydor
364-366 KENSINGTON HIGH STREET, LONDON
Greater London W14 8NS......................020 8910 4800
e: info@umusic.com
w: www.polydor.co.uk

PPL (Phonographic Performance Ltd)
1 UPPER JAMES STREET, LONDON
Greater London W1F 9DE 020 7534 1000
e: info@ppluk.com
w: www.ppluk.com

Promo Uk
16 LIMETREES, LLANGATTOCK, CRICKHOWELL
NP8 1LB 01873 810 142
e: promogb@aol.com
w: www.promo-uk.co.uk

R

Rdl Records
132 CHASE WAY, SOUTHGATE
N14 5DH...07050 055168
e: alanticartists@yahoo.com
w: www.nkentertainments.8k.com

Real World Records
BOX MILL, MILL LANE, BOX, CORSHAM
Wiltshire SN13 8PL.................................01225 743188
e: records@realworld.co.uk
w: www.realworld.co.uk

Rel Records
86 CAUSEWAYSIDE, EDINBURGH
Edinburgh EH9 1PY..............................0131 668 3366
e: online@relrecords.co.uk
w: www.relrecords.co.uk

Reliable Source Music Ltd
67 UPPER BERKELEY STREET, LONDON
Greater London W1H 7QX 020 7563 7028
e: MusicTeam@reliable-source.co.uk
w: www.reliable-source.co.uk

Scamp Music
EBREL HOUSE , 2A PENLEE CLOSE, PRAA SANDS, PENZANCE
Cornwall TR20 9SR................................01736 762826
e: panamus@aol.com
w: www.panamamusic.co.uk

Seeca Music Ltd
6, DITTON HILL ROAD, LONG DITTON, SURBITON
KT6 5JD .... +44 20 3475 3105
e: info@seeca.co.uk
w: www.seeca.co.uk

Shade Factor Productions Ltd
PO BOX 31945
W2 6YB...020 7402 6477
e: mail@shadefactor.com
w: www.shadefactor.com

Shanelsworldrecords
32 BASSETT ROAD, SITTINGBOURNE
Kent ME10 1JR......................................07800 417915
e: shanel@shanelcuthbert.com
w: www.shanelsworld.com

Sir George Records
231 LOWER CLAPTON ROAD, HACKNEY
E5 8EG 020 8533 7994
e: abrightly@yahoo.com
w: www.brightly.freeserve.co.uk

Solent Records
4 BUCKLERS DRIVE, RYDE,, ISLE OF WIGHT
Isle of Wight PO33 3DB............................. +44 (0)1983 563095
e: johnwatermanhome@hotmail.co.uk
w: www.solentrecords.co.uk

Sonar Records Group
82 LONDON ROAD, COVENTRY
CV1 2JT...01926 842974
e: office@sonar-records.demon.co.uk
w: www.sonar-records.demon.co.uk

State Music
67 UPPER BERKELEY STREET, MARYLEBONE
W1H 7DH...020 7616 9284
e: recordings@staterecords.co.uk

Steve Luck
17 BRAINTREE GARDENS, NEWCASTLE UPON TYNE
Tyne and Wear NE3 3DL........................07970 865243
e: steve@steveluck.com
w: www.steveluck.com

Stiff Records Ltd
SARM MUSIC VILLAGE, 105 LADBROKE GROVE, LONDON
Greater London W11 1PG.....................020 3741 9000
e: info@stiff-records.com
w: www.stiff-records.com

Sv Productions (recording Services)
FLAT 6 STIRLING HALL, 11-13 ELM ROAD, LEIGH-ON-SEA
SS9 1SW 079 4264 7131
e: susana@sv-productions.com
w: www.sv-productions.com

Sylvantone Records
11 SAUNTON AVENUE, REDCAR
North Yorkshire TS10 2RL 01642 479 898
e: tonygoodacre@hotmail.com
w: www.tonygoodacre.com

Tanty Records
PO BOX 557, HARROW
HA2 6ZX 07802 463 154
e: kelvin.r@tantyrecord.com

Temple Records
SHILLINGHILL, TEMPLE, GOREBRIDGE
Midlothian EH23 4SH 01875 830328
e: info@templerecords.co.uk
w: www.templerecords.co.uk

The Music Index
34 CONISTON ROAD, NESTON
Cheshire CH64 0TD 0151 336 6199
e: info@themusicindex.com
w: www.themusicindex.com

Transcend Music Group
MILLENNIUM STUDIOS, BEDFORD TECHNOLOGY PARK, THURLEIGH
MK44 2YP...01234 780170
e: info@transcendrecords.com
w: www.transcendmusicgroup.com

R

Universal Music Group
347-353 CHISWICK HIGH STREET
W4 4HS 0208 910 5454
e: info@umusic.com
w: www.umusic.com

Watermead Music
WATERMEAD APOSTOLATE AT ST JOSEPH'S, 12 GOODWOOD
ROAD, LEICESTER
Leicestershire LE5 6SG 0116 220 7881
e: info@watermead-apostolate.com
w: www.watermead-apostolate.com

Westbury Music Ltd
SUITE B, 2 TUNSTALL ROAD, LONDON
Greater London SW9 8DA 020 7733 5400
e: info@westburymusic.net
w: www.westburymusic.net

Womad Music Ltd
MILL LANE, BOX, CORSHAM
Wiltshire SN13 8PL...0845 1461721
e: publishing@realworld.co.uk
w: www.realworldmusic.com

Recording Studios

80 Hertz Studios
THE SHARP PROJECT, THORP ROAD, MANCHESTER
Greater Manchester M40 5BJ 0161 850 8088
e: info@80hertz.com
w: www.80hertz.com

Air-edel Recording Studios Ltd
18 RODMARTON STREET, LONDON
Greater London W1U 8BJ......................................020 7486 6466
e: bethan.barron@air-edel.co.uk
w: www.air-edel.co.uk

Alan Moore Music
BOX 620, OFFICE 6, SLINGTON HOUSE, RANKINE ROAD,
BASINGSTOKE
RG24 8PH 07837 190461
e: info@alanmooremusic.com
w: www.alanmooremusic.com

Angel Recording Studios Ltd
311-312 UPPER STREET, ISLINGTON, LONDON
Greater London N1 2TU 020 7354 2525
e: bookings@angelstudios.co.uk
w: www.angelstudios.co.uk

Arclite Productions
GROVE MUSIC STUDIOS, 10 LATIMER INDUSTRIAL ESTATE,
LATIMER ROAD
W10 6RQ 02089 649047
e: info@arcliteproductions.com
w: www.arcliteproductions.com

Artisan Audio
46A WOODBRIDGE ROAD , , MOSELEY , BIRMINGHAM
B13 8EJ..0121 249 0598
e: rebecca@artisanaudio.com
w: www.artisanaudio.com

Aspen Media Ltd
11 WINGBURY COURTYARD, WINGRAVE, AYLESBURY
Buckinghamshire HP22 4LW 01296 681313
e: webenquiry@aspen-media.com
w: www.aspen-media.com

Association Of Professional Recording Services (APRS)
PO BOX 22, TOTNES
Devon TQ9 7YZ...01803 868600
e: admin@aprs.co.uk
w: www.aprs.co.uk

Attic Recording Studios
UNIT S25, THE LION WORKS, BALL ST, SHEFFIELD
South Yorkshire S3 8DB 0114 2789951
e: info@atticrecordingstudios.co.uk
w: www.atticrecordingstudios.co.uk

Autograph Sound Recording Ltd
2 SPRING PLACE , LONDON
Greater London NW5 3BA 020 7485 4515
e: studio@autograph.co.uk
w: www.autograph.co.uk

AVC Media Enterprises Ltd
GRANDHOLM MILL, GRANDHOLM VILLAGE, ABERDEEN
AB22 8BB 01224 392828
e: accounts@avcmedia.com
w: www.avcmedia.com

Axis Recording
1 CHEQUER AVENUE, DONCASTER
DN4 5AR...01302 769676
e: info@axisrecording.co.uk
w: www.axisrecording.co.uk

Banana Row
5B - 5C GILES STREET, EDINBURGH
Edinburgh EH6 6DJ...0131 553 5533
e: music@bananarow.com
w: www.bananarow.com

Bark Studio
1A BLENHEIM ROAD, WALTHAMSTOW
E17 6HS 020 8523 0110
e: brian@barkstudio.co.uk
w: www.barkstudio.co.uk

Big Help Management
THE OVAL ROOM, 4 PARKFIELD ROAD, RUGBY
Warwickshire CV21 1EN 07782 172101
e: studio@bighelp.biz
w: www.bighelp.biz

R

Black Island Studios
47 CASTLE STREET, BERKS, READING
Berkshire RG1 7SR 020 8956 5600
e: info@islandstudios.net
w: www.islandstudios.net

Blank Tape Studios
 54 BROMWICH ROAD, SHEFFIELD
South Yorkshire S8 0GG 0752 842 8925
e: blanktape@blueyonder.co.uk
w: www.blanktapestudios.co.uk

Bonafide Studios
13-14 THE VIADUCT , ST JAMES LANE, MUSWELL HILL, LONDON
Greater London N10 3QX .... 0208 883 9641 //
....020 8444 5054
e: info@bonafidestudio.co.uk
w: www.bonafidestudio.co.uk

Candle
44 SOUTHERN ROW
 W10 5AN 020 8960 0111
e: tony@candle.org.uk
w: www.candle.org.uk

Catalyst Studios
UNITS 7-17 CATAPULI TOO, CHARLES STREET, ST HELENS
Merseyside WA10 1LX 01744 733222
e: info@catalyst-studios.co.uk
w: www.catalyst-studios.co.uk

Chamber Recording Studio
120A WEST GRANTON ROAD, EDINBURGH
Edinburgh EH5 1PF..0131 551 6632
e: info@chamberstudio.co.uk
w: www.chamberstudio.co.uk

Circle Sound Services
CIRCLE HOUSE, 14 WAVENEY CLOSE, BICESTER
 OX26 2GP 01869 240051
e: sound@circlesound.net
w: www.circlesound.net

Conversion Studios
MILTON ON STOUR, GILLINGHAM
Dorset SP8 5PX 01747 824729
e: info@conversionstudios.co.uk
w: www.conversionstudios.co.uk

Cool Music Ltd
1A FISHERS LANE, CHISWICK, LONDON
Greater London W4 1RX.......................................020 8995 7766
e: info@coolmusicltd.com
w: www.coolmusicltd.com

De Lane Lea Ltd
75 DEAN STREET, LONDON
Greater London W1D 3PU......................................020 7432 3800
e: helen.alexander@wbdelanelea.com
w: www.delanelea.com

Dean St Studios
59 DEAN ST, LONDON
Greater London W1D 6AN 020 7734 8009
e: info@deanst.com
w: www.deanst.com

Earshot Music Production
110 BRUDNELL ROAD, HEADINGLEY, LEEDS
 LS6 1LS...0113 2782 174
e: info@earshotmusic.co.uk
w: www.earshot.tv

Factory St.studios
UNIT 9, FACTORY STREET, DUDLEY HILL, BRADFORD
West Yorkshire BD4 9NW 01274 682125
e: info@factorystreet.co.uk
w: www.factorystreet.co.uk

First Option Location Studio
PERSEVERANCE WORKS, KINGSLAND ROAD, SHOREDITCH,
LONDON
Greater London E2 8DD .... 07949 205 560 //
....020 7739 0132
e: studio@studiohirefirstoption.com
w: www.studiohirefirstoption.com

Floating Earth
UNIT 14, 21 WADSWORTH ROAD, PERIVALE
Middlesex UB6 7LQ 020 8997 4000
e: steve@thesoundcorporation.com
w: www.floatingearth.com

Foel Studio
LLANFAIR CAEREINON, WELSHPOOL
 SY21 0DS 01938 810758
e: dave@foelstudio.co.uk
w: www.foelstudio.co.uk

Fx Rentals Ltd
38-40 TELFORD WAY, EAST ACTON, LONDON
Greater London W3 7XS..020 8746 2121
e: info@fxgroup.net
w: www.fxgroup.net

G2 Studios Ltd
CLIFTON WORKS, 72 JOHN ST, SHEFFIELD
 S2 4QU..0114 270 6217
e: info@g2studios.co.uk
w: www.g2studios.co.uk

Giltbrook Studios
10, GILTWAY, GILTBROOK, NOTTINGHAM
 NG16 2GN 01157 483035
w: www.giltbrookstudios.co.uk

Hallmark Broadcast
30 WOODSIDE ROAD, PARKSTONE, POOLE
Dorset BH14 9JJ.. 0845 644 5406 /
....01202 779000
e: Web@HallmarkBroadcast.tv
w: www.hallmarkbroadcast.tv

R

Industrial Acoustics Company
IAC HOUSE, MOORSIDE ROAD, WINCHESTER
Hampshire SO23 7US 01962 873 000
e: info@iacl-uk.com
w: www.iac-acoustics.com

Invisible Hands Music
79 WARDOUR STREET , LONDON
Greater London W1D 6UB 2033558878
e: sales@invisiblehands.co.uk
w: www.invisiblehands.co.uk

Jam On Top Music Studios
MELBOURNE HOUSE, CHESHAM STREET, KEIGHLEY
 BD21 4LG 01535 600133
e: info@jamontop.com
w: www.jamontop.com

Livingston Recording Studios Ltd
THE OLD CHURCH HALL, 1 BROOK ROAD, LONDON
Greater London N22 6TR 020 7232 0008
e: bookings@miloco.co.uk
w: www.livingstonstudios.co.uk

Loud Mastering For CD & Vinyl
2-3 WINDSOR PLACE, WHITEHALL, TAUNTON
Somerset TA1 1PG 01823 353123
e: enquiries@loudmastering.com
w: www.loudmastering.com

Low Fold Audio Visual
SHIRESHEAD OLD CHURCH, STONY LANE, FORTON, PRESTON
Lancashire PR3 1DE 01524 792020
e: info@lowfold.com
w: www.lowfold.com

Map Music Ltd
46 GRAFTON ROAD, LONDON
Greater London NW5 3DU 0207 916 0545
e: info@mapmusic.net
w: www.mapmusic.net

Mastering World
MASTERING WORLD, HAFOD, ST HILARY, CONBRIDGE, COWBRIDGE
 CF71 7DP 01446 775512
e: help@masteringworld.com
w: www.masteringworld.com

Matinee Sound & Vision
132-134 OXFORD ROAD, READING
Berkshire RG1 7NL 0118 958 4934
e: info@matinee.co.uk
w: www.matinee.co.uk

Metropolis Group
THE POWERHOUSE, 70 CHISWICK HIGH ROAD, LONDON
Greater London W4 1SY 020 8742 1111
e: hello@thisismetropolis.com
w: www.thisismetropolis.com

Metway Studios
55 CANNING STREET, BRIGHTON
East Sussex BN2 0EF...01273 698171
e: lois@levellers.co.uk
w: www.metwaystudios.co.uk

Millennium Studios Ltd
BEDFORD TECHNOLOGY PARK, THURLEIGH, BEDFORD
Bedfordshire MK44 2YP 01234 780100
e: info@millenniumstudios.co.uk
w: www.millenniumstudios.co.uk

Nam Recording Studios
4-7 FOREWOOD COMMON, HOLT
Wiltshire BA14 6PJ 01225 782281
e: nam@namrecording.com
w: www.namrecording.com

Parr Street Studios
35-45 PARR STREET, LIVERPOOL
Merseyside L1 4JN...0151 707 1050
e: info@parrstreet.co.uk
w: www.parrstreet.co.uk

Peak Recording Studios
18 EAST PARADE, LITTLE GERMANY, BRADFORD
West Yorkshire BD1 5EE..01274 742033
e: info@peak-studios.co.uk
w: www.peak-studios.co.uk

Prism Recording Studios
RINGWAY HOUSE, BRYAN STREET, HANLEY
 ST5 1AJ... 01782 563149 /
....07850 599758
e: prismstudios@aol.com
w: www.prismstudios.co.uk

ProDubbing
UNIT 17, THE QUADRANT, 135 SALISBURY ROAD, QUEENS PARK, LONDON
Greater London NW6 6RJ.....................................020 81449980
e: info@produbbing.com
w: www.produbbing.com

Quadrillion TV
17 BALVERNIE GROVE, LONDON
Greater London SW18 5RR 01628 487522
e: enqs@quadrillion.tv
w: www.quadrillion.tv

Rhythm Rooms
....7961003553
e: info@rhythmrooms.co.uk
w: www.rhythmrooms.co.uk

Sarm Studios
105 LADBROKE GROVE, LONDON
Greater London W11 1PG......................................0203 741 9000
e: jed@sarmstudios.com
w: www.sarmstudios.com

R

Sarner Ltd
5 PRINCESS MEWS, HORRACE ROAD, KINGSTON UPON THAMES
Greater London KT1 2SZ......................................020 8481 0600
e: info@sarner.com
w: www.sarner.com

Shushstudio
ROCKVILLE, 10 PLAINES CLOSE, CHIPPENHAM , SLOUGH
Berkshire SL1 5TY 01753 537 206
e: studio@shushstudio.com
w: www.shushstudio.com

Silk Sound Ltd
THE SILK HOUSE, 13 BERWICK STREET, LONDON
Greater London W1F 0PW 020 7434 3461
e: bookings@silk.co.uk
w: www.silk.co.uk

Silverglade Associates Ltd
205 ENTERPRISE HOUSE, 1-2 HATFIELDS, LONDON
Greater London SE1 9PG......................................020 7827 9510
e: info@silverglade.com
w: www.silverglade.com

Sound Moves
THE OAKS, CROSS LANE, SMALLFIELD, HORLEY
Surrey RH6 9SA...01342 844190
e: soundmoves@gmail.com
w: www.sound-moves.com

Soundguy
72 ARRAN STREET, ROATH, CARDIFF
Glamorgan CF24 3HT...07771 600 552
e: info@soundguy.co.uk
w: www.soundguy.co.uk

Spatial Audio
C/O THE SOUNDHOUSE, UNIT 10 VICTORIA INDUSTRIAL ESTATE,
VICTORIA ROAD, ACTON, LONDON
Greater London W3 6UU...07802 657258
e: gerry@spatial-audio.co.uk
w: www.spatial-audio.co.uk

Spool
ANTENNA MEDIA CENTRE, BECK STREET, NOTTINGHAM
Nottinghamshire NG1 1EQ 0115 859 9806
e: hello@spool.uk.com
w: www.spool.uk.com

Stanbridge Farm Studios
BRIGHTON ROAD (A23), HANDCROSS, HAYWARDS HEATH
Sussex RH17 6BB...01444 400432
e: bob@stanbridgestudio.demon.co.uk
w: www.stanbridgestudio.demon.co.uk

Stevie Vann Lange Productions Ltd
....07507 108 315
e: erika.lee@hotmail.co.uk
w: www.stevielange.com

Studio Alba
54A SEAFORTH ROAD, , STORNOWAY, ISLE OF LEWIS
HS1 2SD..01851 701125
e: info@studioalba.com
w: www.studioalba.com

Studio Studio Recording
UNIT 4, SPODDEN MILL FACIT, WHITWORTH, ROCHDALE
Lancashire OL12 8LJ...01706 853518
e: pete.t@zen.co.uk
w: www.studio-studio.co.uk

The Dairy Studios
43-45 TUNSTALL ROAD, LONDON
Greater London SW9 8BZ......................................020 7738 7777
e: info@thedairy.co.uk
w: www.thedairy.co.uk

The Digital Audio Company
3 CARLETON BUSINESS PARK, CARLETON NEW ROAD, SKIPTON
North Yorkshire BD23 2AA....................................01756 797100
e: info@the-digital-audio.co.uk
w: www.the-digital-audio.co.uk

The Exchange Mastering Studios
42 BRUGES PLACE, RANDOLPH STREET, CAMDEN
Greater London NW1 0TL.......................0044 (0)208 399 0718
e: studio@exchangemastering.co.uk
w: www.exchangemastering.co.uk

The Oxygen Rooms
122 BARR STREET, , HOCKLEY, BIRMINGHAM
West Midlands B19 3DE.......................................0121 551 7001
e: info@theoxygenrooms.com
w: www.theoxygenrooms.com

The Sound House
CUNNINGHAM HOUSE, 429 HOLYWOOD ROAD, BELFAST
BT4 2LN 028 9076 9700
e: info@thesoundhouseni.tv
w: www.thepicturehouse.tv

Touchwood Audio Productions
6 HYDE PARK TERRACE, LEEDS
West Yorkshire LS6 1BJ.......................................0113 278 7180
e: studio@touchwoodaudio.com
w: www.touchwoodaudio.com

Tweeters Rehearsal Studios
UNIT C1, BROOKWAY, KINGSTON ROAD, LEATHERHEAD
Surrey KT22 7NA..01372 386592
e: info@tweeters.ltd.uk
w: www.tweeters.ltd.uk

UnderGround Studios Manchester
76 LIVERPOOL ROAD, ECCLES, MANCHESTER
M30 0WA...07763 586759
e: info@undergroundstudios.co.uk
w: www.undergroundstudios.co.uk

Unsigned Studios
39 TO 40 WESTPOINT BUILDING, WARPLE WAY, LONDON
Greater London W3 0RG...020 8735 2863
e: info@unsignedstudios.com
w: www.unsignedstudios.com

Veucom
NORTH BARN, FEATHERBED COURT, MIXBURY
Oxfordshire NN13 5RN...01280 847287
e: info@veucom.com
w: https://veucom.com/

Warehouse Studios
60 SANDFORD LANE, , KENNINGTON, OXFORD
Oxfordshire OX1 5RW .... 07876 487923 / 01865 736411
e: info@warehousestudios.com
w: www.warehousestudios.com

Westland Studios
5-6 LOMBARD STREET EAST, DUBLIN 2, IRELAND
 NN5-21-YZ7 ....00353 (0)879 668 333
e: westlandstudios@gmail.com
w: www.westlandstudiosdublin.com

Woodbine St Recording Studios Ltd
1 ST MARYS CRESCENT, LEAMINGTON SPA
Warwickshire CV31 1JL...01926 338971
e: studio@woodbinestreet.com
w: www.woodbinestreet.com

Yellow Fish Mobile Studio
CONCORDE HOUSE, 18 MARGARET STREET, BRIGHTON
East Sussex BN1 2TS...01273 900 862
e: info@yellowfishmusicgroup.com
w: www.yellowfishmusicgroup.com

Recruitment

HRGO (Recruitment) Ltd
CITYPOINT, 1 ROPEMAKER ST, LONDON
City of London EC2Y 9HU....................................01604 621 333
e: debby.clayton@hrgo.co.uk
w: www.hrgo.co.uk

R

Refrigeration Units / Services

All Seasons Hire Ltd
HAREWOOD FARM, ANDOVER DOWN, LONDON ROAD, ANDOVER
Hampshire SP11 6LJ 01264 387370
e: info@allseasonshire.eu
w: www.allseasonshire.com

Capital Cooling
EAST MAINS IND. ESTATE , BROXBURN, WEST LOTHIAN
 EH52 5NN................................ 07767 618909 / 0800 644 4004
e: jeff.meacher@capitalcooling.com
w: https://www.capitalcooling.com/

CMR International (UK)
CHANNEL HOUSE, 27 QUEEN STREET, ASHFORD
Kent TN23 1RF...07773 885556
e: info@cmr-catering-equipment.co.uk
w: www.cmr-catering-equipment.co.uk

Container Team Limited
UNIT 9 WESTLAND DISTRIBUTION PARK, WINTERSTOKE ROAD,
WESTON-SUPER-MARE
Somerset BS24 9AB 01934 245027
e: contact@containerteam.co.uk
w: www.containerteam.co.uk

Event Chill
HAGUELANDS FARM , BURMARSH, ROMNEY MARSH
Kent TN29 0JR........................... 01303 875641 // 07816 521559
e: info@event-chill.co.uk
w: www.event-chill.co.uk

Event Support Services
TRITLINGTON OLD HALL, MORPETH
 NE61 3ED 07974 949 756
e: enquiries@eventsupportservices.co.uk
w: www.eventsupportservices.co.uk

Mobile Kitchens Ltd
....0845 812 0800
e: info@mk-hire.co.uk
w: www.mk-hire.co.uk

On Site Refrigeration
....01923 777 736
e: info@osrltd.com
w: www.osrltd.com

PKL Group (UK) Ltd
STELLA WAY, BISHOPS CLEEVE, CHELTENHAM
Gloucestershire GL52 7DQ 01242 663 000
e: postbox@pkl.co.uk
w: www.pkl.co.uk

PW Hire
A5 CITY PARK TRADING ESTATE, DEWSBURY ROAD, FENTON
Staffordshire ST4 2HS 0844 854 8686
e: info@pwhire.co.uk
w: www.pw-hire.co.uk

SHB Hire Ltd
18 PREMIER WAY, ABBEY PARK INDUSTRIAL ESTATE, ROMSEY
Hampshire SO51 9DQ...01794 511458
e: enquiries@shb.co.uk
w: www.shb.co.uk

Simply Chillers
FLEET LANE, WOKINGHAM
Berkshire RG40 4RN .... hello@simplychillers.com
e: hello@simplychillers.com
w: www.simplychillers.com

Team Refrigeration
UNIT 9, WESTON DISTRIBUTION PARK WINTERSTOKE ROAD,
WESTON-SUPER-MARE
Somerset BS24 9AB 01934 245028
e: info@teamrefrigeration.co.uk
w: www.teamrefrigeration.co.uk

Titan Articstore
LONDON ROAD, GRAYS
Essex RM20 4DB 01375 396 456
e: uk@tcmail.eu
w: www.arcticstore.co.uk

Rehearsal Rooms / Studios

Attic Recording Studios
UNIT S25, THE LION WORKS, BALL ST, SHEFFIELD
South Yorkshire S3 8DB 0114 2789951
e: info@atticrecordingstudios.co.uk
w: www.atticrecordingstudios.co.uk

Banana Row
5B - 5C GILES STREET, EDINBURGH
Edinburgh EH6 6DJ..0131 553 5533
e: music@bananarow.com
w: www.bananarow.com

Bonafide Studios
13-14 THE VIADUCT , ST JAMES LANE, MUSWELL HILL, LONDON
Greater London N10 3QX .... 0208 883 9641 // 020 8444 5054
e: info@bonafidestudio.co.uk
w: www.bonafidestudio.co.uk

Catalyst Studios
UNITS 7-17 CATAPULT TOO, CHARLES STREET, ST HELENS
Merseyside WA10 1LX 01744 733222
e: info@catalyst-studios.co.uk
w: www.catalyst-studios.co.uk

Chamber Recording Studio
120A WEST GRANTON ROAD, EDINBURGH
Edinburgh EH5 1PF..0131 551 6632
e: info@chamberstudio.co.uk
w: www.chamberstudio.co.uk

CM Rehearsal Studios
23 LYTHALLS LANE IND EST, COVENTRY
West Midlands CV6 6FL 07852 585 132
e: Bookings@cm-rehearsal-studios.co.uk
w: www.cm-rehearsal-studios.co.uk

Conversion Studios
MILTON ON STOUR, GILLINGHAM
Dorset SP8 5PX 01747 824729
e: info@conversionstudios.co.uk
w: www.conversionstudios.co.uk

Craxton Studios
14 KIDDERPORE AVENUE, HAMPSTEAD, LONDON
Greater London NW3 7SU 0207 435 2965
e: jcraxton@live.co.uk
w: www.craxtonstudios.org.uk

Dean St Studios
59 DEAN ST, LONDON
Greater London W1D 6AN 020 7734 8009
e: info@deanst.com
w: www.deanst.com

Duck Lane Studios
13 BERWICK STREET, LONDON
 W1F 0PW...0207 437 1129
e: bookings@ducklanestudios.com
w: www.ducklanestudios.com

Factory St.studios
UNIT 9, FACTORY STREET, DUDLEY HILL, BRADFORD
West Yorkshire BD4 9NW 01274 682125
e: info@factorystreet.co.uk
w: www.factorystreet.co.uk

Fly By Nite Conferences Ltd
THE FBN COMPLEX, SHAWBANK ROAD, LAKESIDE , REDDITCH
Worcestershire B98 8YN 01527 520 720
e: enquiries@flybynite.co.uk
w: www.flybynite.co.uk

Fx Rentals Ltd
38-40 TELFORD WAY, EAST ACTON, LONDON
Greater London W3 7XS..020 8746 2121
e: info@fxgroup.net
w: www.fxgroup.net

G2 Studios Ltd
CLIFTON WORKS, 72 JOHN ST, SHEFFIELD
 S2 4QU 0114 270 6217
e: info@g2studios.co.uk
w: www.g2studios.co.uk

Gap Studios West
228 -230 UXBRIDGE ROAD, LONDON
Greater London W12 7JD 0208 740 1757
e: info@gapstudioswest.co.uk
w: www.gapstudioswest.co.uk

Jam On Top Music Studios
MELBOURNE HOUSE, CHESHAM STREET, KEIGHLEY
 BD21 4LG..01535 600133
e: info@jamontop.com
w: www.jamontop.com

Langley Rehearsal Studios
126 MEADFIELD ROAD, LANGLEY, SLOUGH
Berkshire SL3 8JF 01753 542720
e: langleyguitarcentre@hotmail.com
w: www.langleyguitarcentre.co.uk

R

LoFi Studios
20 ANCHOR LANE, GLASGOW
Glasgow G1 2HW..01412 485050
e: lofirehearsals@gmail.com
w: www.lofistudios.com

London Studio Centre
5 NETHER STREET, TALLY HO CORNER, NORTH FINCHLEY,
LONDON
Greater London N12 0GA 020 7837 7741
e: info@londonstudiocentre.org
w: londonstudiocentre.org

LS Live
UNIT 53, LANGTHWAITE BUSINESS PARK, SOUTH KIRKBY,
WAKEFIELD West Yorkshire WF9 3NR 01977 659 888
e: sales@ls-live.com
w: www.ls-live.com

Magnet Hire Ltd
UNIT 2 , DAVISELLA HOUSE, NEWARK STREET, SNEINTON,
NOTTINGHAM
Nottinghamshire NG2 4PP.................................... 01159 243324
e: rob@magnetstudios.co.uk
w: www.magnetstudios.co.uk

Map Music Ltd
46 GRAFTON ROAD, LONDON
Greater London NW5 3DU 0207 916 0545
e: info@mapmusic.net
w: www.mapmusic.net

Millennium Studios Ltd
BEDFORD TECHNOLOGY PARK, THURLEIGH, BEDFORD
Bedfordshire MK44 2YP...01234 780100
e: info@millenniumstudios.co.uk
w: www.millenniumstudios.co.uk

Mount Pleasant Studio
51 - 53 MOUNT PLEASANT, LONDON
Greater London WC1X 0AE....................................020 7837 1957
e: info@mountpleasantstudio.com
w: www.mountpleasantstudio.com

National Youth Theatre
111 BUCKINGHAM PALACE ROAD, LONDON
Greater London SW1W 0DT..................................020 3696 7066
e: info@nyt.org.uk
w: www.nyt.org.uk

Panic Music
14 TRADING ESTATE ROAD, LONDON
Greater London NW10 7LU........ 0208 961 9540 / 020 8965 1122
e: panicmusicstudios@gmail.com
w: www.panic-music.co.uk

Peter Webber Hire Co Ltd
110-112 DISRAELI ROAD, PUTNEY, LONDON
Greater London SW15 2DX 07973 731359
e: ben@peterwebberhire.com
w: www.peterwebberhire.com

Pick N Styx
2 NAPIER STREET, COVENTRY
West Midlands CV1 5PR..024 76 550070
e: info@picknstyx.co.uk
w: www.picknstyx.co.uk

Smok Ltd
UNIT 4, CANONBURY YARD, CANONBURY BUSINESS CENTRE ,
190A NEW NORTH ROAD
N1 7BJ..0203 393 3022
e: office@smok.co.uk
w: www.smok.co.uk

Spaceshift
106-108 CROMER STREET, LONDON
Greater London WC1H 8BZ....................................0207 278 4404
e: info@spaceshift.co.uk
w: www.spaceshift.co.uk

Spectrecom Films
373 KENNINGTON ROAD, KENNINGTON, LONDON
Greater London SE11 4PT......................................0203 405 2260
e: enquiries@spectrecom.co.uk
w: www.spectrecom.co.uk

Spectrecom Studios
373 KENNINGTON ROAD, KENNINGTON, LONDON
Greater London SE11 4PT......................................020 3405 2263
e: studio@spectrecom.co.uk
w: www.spectrecomstudios.co.uk

Stanbridge Farm Studios
BRIGHTON ROAD (A23), HANDCROSS, HAYWARDS HEATH
Sussex RH17 6BB...01444 400432
e: bob@stanbridgestudio.demon.co.uk
w: www.stanbridgestudio.demon.co.uk

Stevie Vann Lange Productions Ltd
....07507 108 315
e: erika.lee@hotmail.co.uk
w: www.stevielange.com

Studio Alba
54A SEAFORTH ROAD, , STORNOWAY, ISLE OF LEWIS
HS1 2SD..01851 701125
e: info@studioalba.com
w: www.studioalba.com

SW19
62 WEIR ROAD, WIMBLEDON, LONDON
Greater London SW19 8UG 020 8946 1719
e: info@sw-19.net
w: www.sw-19.net

Terminal Studios
UNIT 17, BERMONDSEY TRADING ESTATE, ROTHERHITHE NEW
ROAD, LONDON
Greater London SE16 3LL 020 7231 4356
e: info@terminal.co.uk
w: www.terminal.co.uk

R

The Joint Ltd
1-6 FIELD STREET, LONDON
Greater London WC1X 9DG 0207 833 3375
e: info@thejoint.org.uk
w: www.thejoint.org.uk

The Oxygen Rooms
122 BARR STREET, , HOCKLEY, BIRMINGHAM
West Midlands B19 3DE...0121 551 7001
e: info@theoxygenrooms.com
w: www.theoxygenrooms.com

Tweeters Rehearsal Studios
UNIT C1, BROOKWAY, KINGSTON ROAD, LEATHERHEAD
Surrey KT22 7NA 01372 386592
e: info@tweeters.ltd.uk
w: www.tweeters.ltd.uk

UnderGround Studios Manchester
76 LIVERPOOL ROAD, ECCLES, MANCHESTER
 M30 0WA..07763 586759
e: info@undergroundstudios.co.uk
w: www.undergroundstudios.co.uk

Warehouse Studios
60 SANDFORD LANE, , KENNINGTON, OXFORD
Oxfordshire OX1 5RW .... 07876 487923 / 01865 736411
e: info@warehousestudios.com
w: www.warehousestudios.com

Rigging Services

Flying by Foy
UNIT 4 BOREHAMWOOD ENTERPRISE CENTRE, THEOBALD
STREET, BOREHAMWOOD
Hertfordshire WD6 4RQ...2083 360 234
e: stephen.wareham@flyingbyfoy.co.uk
w: www.flyingbyfoy.co.uk

Rigging Services Direct
EXCEL, SANDSTONE LANE, LONDON
City of London E16 1BD 02082 151 240
e: ellena.fulcher@riggingservices.co.uk
w: riggingservices.co.uk

Rigging Services / Equipment

Access Platform Sales Ltd
LEEWOOD BUSINESS PARK, UPTON, HUNTINGDON
Cambridgeshire PE28 5YQ 0845 108 4000
e: sales@iapsgroup.com
w: www.accessplatforms.co.uk

Actus Industries
UNIT K5, FIELD WAY, METROPOLITAN PARK, GREENFORD
Middlesex UB6 8UN 020 8578 7001
w: www.actusindustries.com

Alloy Access Ltd
THE SCAFFMAN, 120 BEDDINGTON LANE, CROYDON
Surrey CR0 4TD...020 8684 6999
e: info@precipitous.co.uk
w: www.alloyaccess.net

Avw Controls Ltd
UNIT 12, WILLOW FARM, ALLWOOD GREEN, RICKINGHALL, DISS
Norfolk IP22 1LT 01379 898340
e: sales@avw.co.uk
w: www.avw.co.uk

Base Structures Ltd
UNIT A, ST VINCENTS TRADING ESTATE, FEEDER ROAD, BRISTOL
Bristol BS2 0UY..0117 971 2229
e: sales@basestructures.com
w: www.basestructures.com

Blackout Ltd
280 WESTERN ROAD, LONDON
Greater London SW19 2QA 020 8687 8400
e: sales@blackout-ltd.com
w: www.blackout-ltd.com

Caunton Access Ltd
UNIT 88, ROAD B, BOUGHTON INDUSTRIAL ESTATE, NEWARK
Nottinghamshire NG22 9LD 0800 246 5815
e: info@cauntonaccess.co.uk
w: www.cauntonaccess.co.uk

dbn Lighting Ltd
8 DOWNING ST IND. EST, CHARLTON PLACE, MANCHESTER
Greater Manchester M12 6HH..............................0161 273 4297
e: mail@dbn.co.uk
w: www.dbn.co.uk

DLC Events
 STREET 22, AL QUOZ IND 3, DUBAI
 PO Box 282841,.. +971 4 347 0484
e: office@dlcevents.com
w: www.dlcevents.com

Dynamic Production Solutions
UNIT 13E, BARTON BUSINESS PARK, NEW DOVER ROAD,
CANTERBURY
Kent CT1 3AA 01227 656 599
e: info@dynamicproductionsolutions.co.uk
w: www.dynamicproductionsolutions.co

Enlightened Lighting Ltd
26-28 EMERY ROAD, BRISLINGTON
Bristol BS4 5PF...01179 727 123
e: info@enlx.co.uk
w: www.enlightenedlighting.co.uk

Eventions-rigging Bv
VOLTASTRAAT 5D, EDE
 6716AJ .... +31 (0) 318 69 39 76
e: info@eventions-group.com
w: www.eventions-rigging.nl

Flying By Foy Ltd
UNIT 4, BOREHAMWOOD ENTERPRISE CENTRE, THEOBALD
STREET, BOREHAMWOOD
Hertfordshire WD6 4RQ...0208 236 0234
e: enquiries@flyingbyfoy.co.uk
w: www.flyingbyfoy.co.uk

Focus Rigging & Scaffolding
HEMEL HEMPSTEAD, HEMEL HEMPSTEAD
Hertfordshire HP3 0PA 01442 833 993
e: office@focusmediascaffolding.co.uk
w: www.focusmediascaffolding.co.uk

Gearhouse In2Structures
PO BOX 751391, GARDENVIEW, JOHANNESBURG
2047.. +27 (0) 112 163 000
e: jhb@gearhouse.co.za
w: www.gearhouse.co.za

Halo Lighting
98-124 BREWERY ROAD, LONDON
Greater London N7 9PG 0207 607 4444
e: info@halo.co.uk
w: www.halo.co.uk

Hands On Production Services Ltd
79 LOANBANK QUADRANT, GLASGOW
Glasgow G51 3HZ 0141 4402005
e: info@hands-on-uk.com
w: www.hands-on-uk.com

Hang Fast Rigging
UNIT 18/19 CASTLEFIELD INDUSTRIAL ESTATE, CROSSFLATTS,
BINGLEY
West Yorkshire BD16 2AG 07775 836554
e: info@hangfastrigging.co.uk
w: www.hangfastrigging.co.uk

Hatt Safety
PO BOX 5157, BRIGHTON
East Sussex BN50 9TW..01273 358 359
e: adventures@thehatt.co.uk
w: www.thehatt.co.uk/safety

Hi-fli
18 GREEN COURT DRIVE, MANCHESTER
Greater Manchester M38 0BZ 0161 278 9352
e: mikefrost@hi-fli.co.uk
w: www.hi-fli.co.uk

High Lite Touring
MITROVICKA 359/45, OSTRAVA - NOVA BELA
72400..00420 596 731 034
e: info@highlite.cz
w: www.highlite.cz

J&C Joel Limited (Head Office)
CORPORATION MILL, CORPORATION STREET, SOWERBY BRIDGE,
HALIFAX Yorkshire HX6 2QQ 01422 833835
e: uksales@jcjoel.com
w: www.jcjoel.com

Kirby's Afx Ltd.
8 GREENFORD AVENUE, HANWELL, LONDON
W7 3QP 020 8723 8552
e: mail@afxuk.com
w: www.afxuk.com/

KSG Ltd
117 MERRYLEE ROAD, GLASGOW
G43 2RB 0778 6342 940
e: info@ksg-ltd.co.uk
w: www.ksg-ltd.co.uk

Light The Way
UNIT 7 CAVENDISH COURT MILL, WEST STREET, BRADFORD
BD11 1DA..01422 250 819
e: hire@lighttheway.co.uk
w: www.lighttheway.co.uk

LiteStructures (GB) Ltd
(PART OF THE PROLYTE GROUP), LANGTHWAITE BUSINESS PARK
- UNIT 55, SOUTH KIRKBY, WAKEFIELD
WF9 3NR 01977 659 800
e: info@prolyte.co.uk
w: www.prolyte.co.uk

M&P Survey Equipment Ltd
MERIDIAN HOUSE, STANNEY MILL ROAD, LITTLE STANNEY,
CHESTER CH2 4HX 0151 357 1856
e: marketing@mpsurvey.co.uk
w: www.mpsurvey.co.uk

Marlow Ropes Ltd
ROPEMAKER PARK, DIPLOCKS WAY, HAILSHAM
East Sussex BN27 3GU 01323 444 444
e: info@marlowropes.com
w: www.marlowropes.com

Media Structures
87-91, BEDDINGTON LANE, CROYDON
Surrey CR0 4TD 020 8683 3131
e: info@mediastructures.co.uk
w: www.mediastructures.co.uk

Metalworx Ltd
PONSWOOD INDUSTRIAL ESTATE, DRURY LANE,
ST LEONARDS ON SEA
East Sussex TN38 9BA...01424 446345
e: info@metalworx.com
w: www.metalworx.com

Mushroom Event Services Ltd
15 LOW FARM PLACE, MOULTON PARK, NORTHAMPTON
Northamptonshire NN3 6HY 01604 790900
e: info@mushroomevents.co.uk
w: www.mushroomevents.co.uk

Neg Earth Lights
LIGHT HOUSE, WESTERN ROAD, PARK ROYAL, LONDON
Greater London NW10 7LT 020 8963 0327
e: info@negearth.co.uk
w: www.negearth.co.uk

R

Neon Arena Services
UNIT 305, THE ARGENT CENTRE, 60 FREDERICK STREET,
HOCKLEY, BIRMINGHAM
West Midlands B1 3HS...0121 236 5555
e: info@neonarenaservices.co.uk
w: www.neonsportsfloors.co.uk

Nippy Industries Ltd
BUILDING 15, ALCONBURY AIRFIELD, HUNTINGDON
Cambridgeshire PE28 4WX 01480 443818
e: enquiries@nippyindustries.co.uk
w: www.nippyindustries.co.uk

NLG (Never Let Go)
....0330 016 0030
e: team@neverletgo.uk
w: neverletgo.uk/

Out Board (Sheriff Technology Ltd)
UNIT 4 CHURCH MEADOWS, HASLINGFIELD ROAD, BARRINGTON
Cambridgeshire CB22 7RG......................................01223 871015
e: info@outboard.co.uk
w: www.outboard.co.uk

Outback Rigging Ltd
UNIT 5 KENDAL COURT, KENDAL AVENUE, LONDON
Greater London W3 0RU..020 8993 0066
e: enquiries@outbackrigging.com
w: www.outbackrigging.com

Panalux Broadcast & Events
WAXLOW ROAD , LONDON
Greater London NW10 7NU 020 8233 7000
e: info@panalux.biz
w: www.panalux.biz

Pitman's People Marquee and Event Structure Crew and Riggers
UNIT G1A STAMFORD WORKS, 3 GILLETT ST., LONDON
Greater London N16 8JH..020 3651 3330
e: admin@pitmanspeople.com
w: www.pitmanspeople.com

Premier Plant Hire
48A BURBAGE ROAD , GIANT ARCHES 12-23 , LONDON
 SE24 9HE ....02073260000 / 020 3582 7691
e: premierplant@hotmail.com
w: www.premierplanthire.co.uk/

Production Resource Group
UNIT E, IMBER COURT TRADING ESTATE, ORCHARD LANE EAST
MOLESEY KT8 0BY 020 8335 6000
e: ukinfo@prg.com
w: www.prg.com

Protec (Production Technology LLC)
PLOT NO. 548 - 597, DUBAI INVESTMENT PARK 2,
DUBAI, UNITED ARAB EMIRATES
.... +971 4 880 0092
e: eventrental@productiontec.com
w: www.productiontec.com

Rigging Services (Birmingham)
UNIT B3, MILLER STREET, ASTON, BIRMINGHAM
West Midlands B6 4NF...0121 333 4409
e: birmingham@riggingservices.co.uk
w: www.riggingservices.co.uk

Rigging Services (East London)
3 MILLS STUDIOS, THE ISLAND, THREE MILL LANE, LONDON
 E3 3DU 020 8215 1240
e: london@riggingservices.co.uk
w: www.riggingservices.co.uk

Rigging Services (Manchester)
21 RIVINGTON COURT, HARDWICK GRANGE, WARRINGTON ,
MANCHESTER
Greater Manchester WA1 4RT 01925 251 040
e: manchester@riggingservices.co.uk
w: www.riggingservices.co.uk

Rigging Services (West London)
PINEWOOD STUDIOS, PINEWOOD ROAD, IVER HEATH
Buckinghamshire SL0 0NH 01753 653 529
e: pinewood@riggingservices.co.uk
w: www.riggingservices.co.uk

Rigging Team Ltd
UNIT 16 GUNNELS WOOD PARK, GUNNELS WOOD ROAD,
STEVENAGE SG1 2BH 0203 126 4040
e: office@riggingteam.com
w: https://www.riggingteam.com

Rigorous Technology Limited
....0800 118 2569
e: info@rigorous-technology.co.uk
w: www.rigorous-technology.co.uk

Rock City Stage Crew
LANGSFORD HOUSE, 8 DARKLAKE VIEW, ESTOVER, PLYMOUTH
Devon PL6 7TL 01752 255 933
e: office@rockcitycrew.co.uk
w: www.rockcitycrew.co.uk

Rocky City Rigging & Technical Services
LANGSFORD HOUSE , 8 DARKLAKE VIEW,, PLYMOUTH
Devon PL6 7TL 01752 255 933
e: office@rockcitycrew.co.uk
w: www.rockcitycrew.co.uk

Rope & Marine Services Ltd - Rams
31 YORKSHIRE ROAD, LONDON
Greater London E14 7LR.......... 0207 790 2837 // 0207 790 3795
e: sales@ropemarine.com
w: www.ropemarine.com

Rope and Rigging
UNIT 5, ROSSINGTONS BUSINESS PARK, WEST CARR ROAD,
RETFORD
Nottinghamshire DN22 7SW 01777 948 089
e: jacqui@ropeandrigging.co.uk
w: www.ropeandrigging.co.uk

R

Ropes Direct
HURST'S YARD, LUDHAM ROAD, CATFIELD
Norfolk NR29 5PY ....01692671721 / 07831 291147
e: info@ropesdirect.co.uk
w: www.ropesdirect.co.uk

Salima Ltd
2A BACCHUS HOUSE, CALLEVA PARK, ALDERMASTON, READING
Berkshire RG7 8EN ....0845 458 1699 /
07825 586 083
e: info@salima-ltd.co.uk
w: www.salima-ltd.co.uk

Slingco Ltd
STATION ROAD, FACIT, WHITWORTH
Lancashire OL12 8LJ..01706 855558
e: sales@slingco.com
w: www.slingco.com

Spectrum Hire Ltd
UNIT 1 HESTON INDUSTRIAL MALL, CHURCH ROAD, , HESTON
Middlesex TW5 0LD 2079936455
e: info@spectrumhire.co.uk
w: www.spectrumhire.co.uk

Stage Crew
404 RUSSELL COURT, LISBURN ROAD, BELFAST
BT9 6JW.. +44 (0)28 9032 9897
e: office@stage-crew.co.uk
w: www.stage-crew.co.uk

Stage Electrics
UNIT 3 BRITANNIA RD, PATCHWAY TRADING ESTATE, PATCHWAY
Bristol BS34 5TA...0117 938 4000
e: bristol@stage-electrics.co.uk
w: www.stage-electrics.co.uk

Staging Services Ltd
LEAMORE LANE, BLOXWICH, WALSALL
West Midlands WS2 7BY 01922 405111
e: info@stagingservicesltd.co.uk
w: www.stagingservicesltd.co.uk

Star Events Group Ltd
MILTON ROAD, THURLEIGH, BEDFORD
Bedfordshire MK44 2DF...01234 772233
e: info@StarEventsGroup.com
w: www.stareventsgroup.com

Total Fabrications Ltd
UNITS 3-6, KINGSTON INDUSTRIAL ESTATE, 81-86 GLOVER
STREET, BIRMINGHAM
West Midlands B9 4EN..0121 772 5234
e: info@trussing.com
w: www.trussing.com

Trilite Ltd
38 CROMWELL ROAD, LUTON
Bedfordshire LU3 1DN 01582 411413
e: UkAdmin@optikinetics.co.uk
w: www.optikinetics.co.uk

UK Rigging
110 BRIDGEMAN STREET, BOLTON
Greater Manchester BL3 6BS.................................01204 391343
e: mail@ukrigging.net
w: www.ukrigging.net

Unusual Rigging Ltd
THE WHARF, BUGBROOKE
Northamptonshire NN7 3QB...................................01604 830083
e: info@unusual.co.uk
w: www.unusual.co.uk

Walter Logan & Co Ltd
3 ATHENAEUM ROAD, WHETSTONE, LONDON
Greater London N20 9AA 0208 446 0161
e: info@walterlogan.com
w: www.walterlogan.com

Wolf Event Services Ltd
UNIT F, WATERSIDE ESTATE, 25-27 WILLIS WAY, POOLE
Dorset BH15 3TD...01202 870794
e: hello@wolf-events.com
w: www.wolf-events.com

Youngman Group Limited
THE CAUSEWAY, MALDON
Essex CM9 4LJ...01621 745 900
e: uk.customercare@wernerco.com
w: www.youngmangroup.com

Roller Rinks

Roller Magic
....07887 505693
e: simon@ice-magic.com
w: www.roller-skate-rink-hire.com

R

Sailing / Marine

All Marine Watersports
UNIT 8 , 2 ULWELL ROAD, SWANAGE
BH19 1LH 0755 126 3434
e: info@allmarinewatersports.com
w: www.allmarinewatersports.com

Sales / Promotional Products

A.J Gilbert (Birmingham) Ltd
66 - 77 BUCKINGHAM STREET, HUCKLEY, BIRMINGHAM
West Midlands B19 3HU .... 0121 236 7774 / 0121 233 1394
w: www.ajgilbert.co.uk

Abel Magnets Ltd
BALACLAVA ROAD, SHEFFIELD
South Yorkshire S6 3BG 0114 249 5949
e: info@magnetic-paper.com
w: www.magnetic-paper.com

Action Jacket Company
PO BOX 1180, STOURBRIDGE
West Midlands DY9 0ZF 01562 887096
e: info@actionjacket.co.uk
w: www.actionjacket.co.uk

Advartex
PICKFORD LANE, TICEHURST
East Sussex TN5 7BL 01580 200 120
e: sales@advartex.co.uk
w: www.advartex.co.uk

Aerial Promotions
5 HAWKS GREEN LANE, HAWKS GREEN LANE, CANNOCK
Staffordshire WS11 7LG 01543 505755
e: kevin@aerialpromotions.co.uk
w: www.aerialpromotions.co.uk

Air Artist Ltd
UNIT 19, HALESWORTH BUSINESS CENTRE, NORWICH ROAD,
HALESWORTH
Suffolk IP19 8QJ........................ 01986 874466 / 07785 941 659
e: robin.harries@virgin.net
w: www.airartists.co.uk

Airborne Packaging Ltd
UNIT 6, APPLE BUSINESS PARK, BRIDGWATER
Somerset TA6 4DL 0116 253 6136
e: sales@airbornebags.co.uk
w: www.airbornebags.co.uk

Airstage UK
.... +34 971 641 281 / +34 684 243 321
e: info@airstage.biz
w: www.airstage.biz

Alchemy Carta Ltd
HAZEL DRIVE, LEICESTER
Leicestershire LE3 2JE 0116 282 4824
e: promo@alchemygroup.com
w: www.alchemygroup.co.uk

Arti Promotions
3 HIGHBRIDGE WHARF, GREENWICH, LONDON
Greater London SE10 9PS.....................................0208 293 1280
e: info@artipromotions.com
w: www.artipromotions.com

Article 10
23 - 28 PENN STREET, LONDON
Greater London N1 5DL 020 7749 4450
e: hello@article10.com
w: www.article10.com

Aspinline
EXHIBITION HOUSE, HAYWARD INDUSTRIAL ESTATE, 1-2 NORTH
VIEW, SOUNDWELL, BRISTOL
Gloucestershire BS16 4NT 0117 9566657
e: sales@aspinline.co.uk
w: www.aspinline.co.uk

Atelier Screenprint Ltd
UNIT 2, 12 LISLE AVENUE, KIDDERMINSTER
Worcestershire DY11 7DL 01562 743166
e: atelier.screenprint@chessmail.co.uk
w: www.atelier-screenprint.com

Awesome Merchandise
B1-B3 WELLINGTON ROAD INDUSTRIAL ESTATE, WELLINGTON
BRIDGE, LEEDS West Yorkshire LS12 2UA 01132 435667
e: luke@awesomemerchandise.com
w: www.awesomemerchandise.com

B-loony Ltd
UNIT 3 CHILTERN COURT, ASHERIDGE ROAD, CHESHAM
Buckinghamshire HP5 2PX.....................................01494 774376
e: sales@b-loony.co.uk
w: www.b-loony.com

Bannerbags.co.uk
UNIT 3B & C RED ROSE COURT, SUNNYHURST ROAD, BLACKBURN
BB2 1PS 01254 582923
e: info@bannerbags.co.uk
w: www.bannerbags.co.uk

Barritt Associates Ltd
UNIT 12, BEE MILL,, RIBCHESTER,, PRESTON
Lancashire PR3 3XJ... 01254 820991
e: sales@barrittglassprint.co.uk
w: barrittglassprint.co.uk

Blueprint Promotional Products
NO. 1 THE EMBASSY, LAWRENCE STREET, LONG EATON,
NOTTINGHAM
Nottinghamshire NG10 1JY....................................0333 1234 400
e: info@blueprintpromo.co.uk
w: www.blueprintpromo.co.uk

S

Brand My Clothing Ltd
UNIT 1E THORNTON ROAD INDUSTRIAL ESTATE, HOCKNEY ROAD, BRADFORD
West Yorkshire BD8 9HQ 0800 318 8786
e: sales@brandmyclothing.com
w: www.brandmyclothing.com

British Cushion Supply Co. Ltd
27 CEDAR DRIVE, MARKET BOSWORTH
Leicestershire CV13 0LW 01455 293200
e: sales@britishcushions.com
w: www.britishcushions.com

Burst (uk) Ltd
GREY STUD, WHYDOWN ROAD, WHYDOWN, BEXHILL ON SEA
TN39 4RB 0845 643 0133
e: sales@burstuk.com
w: www.burstuk.com

Calver Promotional Merchandise
22 THE DRIVE, ORPINGTON
Kent BR6 9AP 01689 898828
e: sales@calver.com
w: www.calver.com

Carole Group Ltd
GOLDOAK HOUSE, OAKLANDS BUSINESS PARK, WOKINGHAM
Berkshire RG41 2FD 01189 771424
e: sales@carolegroup.com
w: www.carolegroup.com

Clipkey Products
166 EWELL ROAD, SURBITON
Surrey KT6 6HG 020 8390 5491
e: sales@computercasebadges.com
w: www.computercasebadges.com

Co Prom Ltd
198 LONDON ROAD, PORTSMOUTH
Hampshire PO2 9JE 01243 575247
e: enquiries@coprom.co.uk
w: www.coprom.co.uk

Code Promotional Merchandise
16 CAMELLIA CLOSE, BOLTON
Greater Manchester BL1 4NY...............................0844 879 7323
e: info@codepromotional.co.uk
w: www.codepromotional.co.uk

Creative Promotions Ltd
79 WEST REGENT STREET, GLASGOW
G2 2AW 0141 332 7471
e: enquiries@creativepromotions.co.uk
w: www.creativepromotions.co.uk

Custom T Shirt
NEPTUNE MARINA, IPSWICH
Suffolk IP4 1AX..0800 0787 119
e: sales@custom-t-shirt.biz
w: www.custom-t-shirt.biz

Disposable RainPonchos
HORWICH, BOLTON
Greater Manchester BL6 6LJ 0844 251 0807
e: deanramsden@rain-poncho.co.uk
w: www.rain-poncho.co.uk

Distinctive Confectionery
LANGDALE HOUSE, FOXHILL CLOSE, , HIGH WYCOMBE
Buckinghamshire HP13 5BL................................01494 538 511
e: sales@distinctiveconfectionery.co.uk
w: www.distinctiveconfectionery.com

East Coast Plastics Ltd
ROBERTSON HOUSE, NORTH WALSHAM
Norfolk NR28 0BX...01692 403461
e: sales@east-coast.co.uk
w: www.east-coast-plastics.co.uk

Event Merchandising Ltd
UNIT 11, THE EDGE, HUMBER ROAD, LONDON
Greater London NW2 6EW....................................020 8208 1166
e: event@eventmerch.com
w: www.eventmerchandising.com

Festival Flags
LAKE VIEW, CAPPNABOUL, KEALKIL, BANTRY, CO. CORK, IRELAND
.... +353 (0)27 66803 / +353 (0)86 355 8030
e: taraflags@gmail.com
w: www.festivalflags.ie

Fluid Branding
TREVITHICK, BRUNEL BUSINESS PARK, ST AUSTELL
Cornwall PL25 4TJ...0330 333 3685
e: info@fluidbranding.com
w: www.fluidbranding.com

Gaudio Awards
UNIT H THE COURTYARD, , TEWKESBURY BUSINESS PARK, TEWKESBURY
Gloucestershire GL20 8GD 01242 232383
e: sales@gaudio.co.uk
w: www.gaudio-awards.com

Global Marketing Group Ltd
GLOBAL HOUSE, SALISBURY ROAD, DOWNTON
Wiltshire SP5 3JJ...01725 514999
e: sales@globalmarketinggroup.co.uk
w: www.globalmarketinggroup.co.uk

Global Promotional Solutions Ltd
44 RYDER ST, CARDIFF
CF11 9BT 02920 227955
e: enquiry@globalpromotionalsolutions.co.uk
w: www.globalpromotionalsolutions.co

Gloweasy Promotions
KERENSA STUDIOS, 14 SHARAMAN CLOSE, ST AUSTELL
Cornwall 0843 2896108
e: staff@gloweasy.com
w: www.gloweasy.com

S

GP Promowear
THEAKLEN HOUSE, THEAKLEN DRIVE, PONSWOOD INDSTRIAL
ESTATE, ST. LEONARDS-ON-SEA
East Sussex TN38 9AZ 01424 716161
e: info@gppromowear.com
w: www.gppromowear.com

Green Goblet Ltd
WINCANTON
.... 01963 400 504
e: info@green-goblet.com
w: www.green-goblet.com

Hambleside Business Gift Solutions Ltd
2-3 LANCER HOUSE, HUSSAR COURT, WESTSIDE VIEW,
WATERLOOVILLE
Hampshire PO7 7SE...023 9235 4960
e: sales@hambleside.co.uk
w: www.hambleside-merchandise.co.uk/

Logo Promotional Merchandise Ltd
CRESCENT TERRACE, ILKLEY
West Yorkshire LS29 8DL 01943 817238
e: enquiries@logomerchandising.co.uk
w. www.logomerchandising.co.uk

Luckings Screen Services
PINEWOOD STUDIOS, SUITE C-42, IVER HEATH
SL0 0NL 01753 639872
e: vic.minay@luckings.co.uk
w: www.luckings.co.uk

Lynhurst Press Limited
UNITS 4 & 5 YARDLEY BUSINESS PARK, LUCKYN LANE, BASILDON
Essex SS14 3GL 01268 288231
e: info@lynhurstpress.co.uk
w: www.lynhurstpress.co.uk

M.Brill Limited
55A MORTIMER ROAD , HACKNEY , LONDON
N1 5AR .... 020 7254 0333 / 07956 827 836
e: info@mbrillltd.co.uk
w: www.mbrillltd.co.uk

Metro Merchandise
3 PROSPECT COURT , COURTEENHALL ROAD , BLISWORTH
Northamptonshire NN7 3DG.................................01536 415 005
e: louise@metromerchandise.co.uk
w: www.metromerchandise.uk.clickprom

Minglemore
3 RAMPART ROW, GOSPORT
PO12 1HT 01727 238475
e: info@minglemore.co.uk
w: www.minglemore.co.uk

Monogram Group Ltd
GREATWORTH PARK, GREATWORTH, BANBURY
Oxfordshire OX17 2HB 01295 768903
e: sales@monogram.co.uk
w: www.monogram.co.uk

My Tshirt Flashes.com
80 TAMWORTH LANE, MITCHAM
Surrey CR4 1DA..0203-052-375
e: info@mytshirtflashes.com
w: www.mytshirtflashes.com

Nexus Collections Ltd
BROWNHILLS , LEEBOTWOOD, CHURCH STRETTON
Shropshire SY6 6LU 01694 751777
e: sales@nexuscollections.co.uk
w: www.nexuscollections.com

Original Thing
TOP FLOOR, 30 TORCROSS ROAD, RUSLIP
Middlesex HA4 0TB..020 8841 1252
e: source@orginalthing.com
w: www.originalthing.com

Pinpoint Badges & Promotions
MALTINGS MEWS, SIDCUP
Kent DA15 7DG...020 8302 8008
e: sales@pinpointbadges.com
w: www.pinpointbadges.com

Podium Designs
33 MAIN STREET, GOADBY MARWOOD
Leicestershire LE14 4LN 020 3764 0805
e: enquiries@podium-designs.co.uk
w: www.podium-designs.co.uk

POS Centre
1-2 HORSECROFT ROAD, THE PINNACLES, HARLOW
Essex CM19 5BH 01279 207211
e: sales@poscentre.co.uk
w: www.poscentre.co.uk

Premier Print & Promotions Ltd
PREMIER HOUSE, THRESHELFORDS BUSINESS PARK, INWORTH
ROAD, FEERING
Essex CO5 9SE 01376 574670
e: sales@premierpandp.com
w: www.promotional-gifts.com

Print Designs
EMERALD WAY, STONE BUSINESS PARK, STONE
Staffordshire ST15 0SR...01785 818 111
e: sales@printdesigns.com
w: www.printdesigns.com

Printsome
....0203 5982599
e: luca@printsome.com
w: www.printsome.com

Promotional Products Ltd
8 EDEN CLOSE, WILMSLOW
Cheshire SK9 6BG 01625 526050
e: sales@promotionproducts.co.uk
w: www.promotionproducts.co.uk

PromotionandEvent.com
UNIT 35 CHARTER GATE, MOULTON INDUSTRIAL PARK, NORTHAMPTON
NN3 6QB 01604 790762
w: www.promotionandevent.com

PSK Packaging Supplies of Kidderminster
ACCOUNTS CENTRAL, PO BOX 6847, KIDDERMINSTER
Worcestershire DY12 9AX 01562 743621
e: mail@printedcarrierbags.co.uk
w: www.printedcarrierbags.co.uk

Ribbon Works
WILSON BUSINESS PARK, HILLINGTON, GLASGOW
G52 4NQ..01355 813301
e: info@ribbonworks.co.uk
w: https://www.ribbonworks.co.uk

Ribbonworks
WILSON BUSINESS PARK, HILLINGTON
Glasgow G52 4NQ..1355813301
e: ribbonworksuk@gmail.com
w: https://www.ribbonworks.co.uk

Rocket Badge Company
6 VALE ROYAL , LONDON
Greater London N7 9AP 0333 7000 132
e: sales@rocketbadge.co.uk
w: www.rocketbadge.co.uk

Screen Services
40 MILLMARK GROVE, LONDON
Greater London SE14 6RQ 020 8692 4806
e: info@screenservices.biz
w: www.screenservices.biz

Second Capture Ltd
3 ROCK COTTAGE, ASHFORD
TN25 6AQ.................................... 07866 426303 / 01233 720242
e: marc@secondcapture.com
w: www.secondcapturephotography.com

Status Promotional Merchandise
FLEET HOUSE, 1 ARMSTRONG ROAD, BENFLEET
Essex SS7 4SS 01268 755055
e: sales@statuspm.co.uk
w: www.statuspm.co.uk

Sycal Ltd
UNIT 25, CHANTRY ROAD , WOBURN ROAD INDUSTRIAL ESTATE, KEMPSTON, BEDFORD
Bedfordshire MK42 7SY 01234 841741
e: sales@sycal.co.uk
w: www.sycal.co.uk

T-print Ltd
APPAREL HOUSE, BRISTOL AVENUE, BISPHAM, BLACKPOOL
FY2 0JF 01253 359120
e: sales@t-print.co.uk
w: www.t-print.co.uk

Tailor Made Signs & Embroidery
6 PROSPECT WAY, ROYAL OAK INDUSTRIAL ESTATE, DAVENTRY
Northamptonshire NN11 8PL 01327 311125
e: sales@tailormade-online.co.uk
w: www.tailormade-online.co.uk

Team Togs Ltd
THE BASEMENT, 139-141 WATLING STREET, RADLETT, HERTS
Hertfordshire WD7 7NQ...01923 853 104
e: info@team-togs.com
w: www.team-togs.com

Templecoombe Ltd
THE OLD MALTINGS, 102A HIGH STREET, OLNEY
Buckinghamshire MK46 4BE...................................01234 816748
e: sales@templecoombe.co.uk
w: www.templecoombe.co.uk

TGV Design & Marketing
MANSFIELDS HOUSE, BENTALLS, BASILDON
Essex SS14 3BX 01268 669403
e: hello@mgroup.co.uk
w: www.tgvdesign.co.uk

The Corporate Carrier Company
BRIDGELAND HOUSE, HIGH STREET, MARDEN
Kent TN12 9DS 01622 832318
e: sales@corp-carrier.co.uk
w: www.corp-carrier.co.uk

Totally Original T-Shirts
13A BANKSIA ROAD, ELEY ESTATE, EDMONTON, LONDON
Greater London N18 3BF..020 8887 7900
e: sales@totshirts.co.uk
w: www.totshirts.co.uk

Tribe Marketing
UNIT 4, THE WOOL HOUSE, 74 BACK CHURCH LANE, LONDON
Greater London E1 1LX 020 7702 3600
e: info@tribemarketing.co.uk
w: www.tribemarketing.co.uk

Umbrella Risk Management Ltd
2 THE BARN TOWNHILL FARM, DORTON ROAD CHILTON
HP18 9NA...1844202045
e: info@team-umbrella.co.uk
w: www.team-umbrella.co.uk

Wilson Multiplex
EWOOD HALL, EWOOD LANE, TODMORDEN, TODMODEN
West Yorkshire OL14 7DF.......................................0845 868 8964
e: sales@ukcarrierbags.com
w: www.ukcarrierbags.com

S

Script Services

Bright Spark Studios Limited
UNIT 1 'SEVEN-0-SEVEN', CHURCHILL BUSINESS PARK
SLEAFORD ROAD ,BRACEBRIDGE HEATH, LINCOLN
Lincolnshire LN4 2FF 01522 717884
e: enquiries@brightsparkstudios.com
w: www.brightsparkstudios.com

David Block
....07971 195632
e: davidsamblock@gmail.com
w: www.speechwriting.co.uk

Inside-out Branding
UPPER WOODHEAD, BARKISLAND, HALIFAX
West Yorkshire HX4 0EQ...01422 825222
e: info@inside-outbranding.com
w: www.inside-outbranding.com

Nick Jon
....07772 530791
e: malcolm@freelance-copywriter-uk.com
w: www.freelance-copywriter-uk.com

Samuel French Ltd
52 FITZOY STREET, LONDON
Greater London W1T 5JR 020 7387 9373
e: customerservices@samuelfrench-london.co.uk
w: www.samuelfrench-london.co.uk

Schoolplay Productions Ltd
15 INGLIS ROAD, COLCHESTER
Essex CO3 3HU...01206 540111
e: chrissie@schoolplayproductions.co.uk
w: www.schoolplayproductions.co.uk

Tessa Le Bars Management
54 BIRCHWOOD ROAD, PETTS WOOD, ORPINGTON
Kent BR5 1NZ ....01689 837084 / 07860 287255 (mobile)
e: tessa.lebars@ntlworld.com
w: www.galtonandsimpson.com

The Sharland Organisation
THE MANOR HOUSE, MANOR STREET, RAUNDS
Northamptonshire NN9 6JW..................................01933 626600
e: tso@btconnect.com
w: www.sharlandorganisation.co.uk

Seating

Austen Lewis
CHELWORTH PARKCHELWORTH RD, SWINDON
Wiltshire SN6 6HE..02086 833 131
e: andrew.wilson@mediastructures.co.uk
w: www.austen-lewis.co.uk

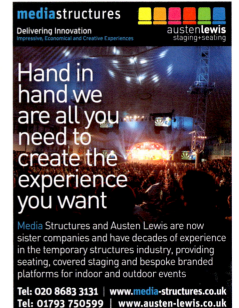
Security

Right Guard Security
3 SIMMONDS RD, CANTERBURY
Kent CT1 3RA 01227 464 588
e: tony.smith@rightguardsecurity.com
w: www.rightguard.co.uk

Security Services

Accent on Security Ltd
UNIT 4, ACCENT PARK, BAKEWELL ROAD, ORTON SOUTHGATE,
PETERBOROUGH. Cambridgeshire PE2 6XS...........0844 499 3939
e: info@accentonsecurity.co.uk
w: www.accentonsecurity.co.uk

Achilleus
HEAD OFFICE 6 ATLANTIC BUSINESS CENTRE, CHINGFORD,
LONDON. Greater London E4 7ES
.... 020 8221 4180 / 0800 358 0983
e: info@achilleus.co.uk
w: www.achilleus.co.uk

Alpha 1 Security Services (U.K) Ltd
3RD FLOOR, 207 REGENT STREET, LONDON
Greater London W1B 3HH 0207 127 4260
e: info@alpha1securityservices.com
w: www.alpha1securityservices.com

AP Security (APS) Ltd
33 METRO CENTRE, DWIGHT ROAD, WATFORD
Hertfordshire WD18 9SB 0844 375 9959
e: info@apsecurity.co.uk
w: www.apsecurity.co.uk

Armour Security Deployment Ltd
11 GRASMEAD AVENUE, LEIGH ON SEA
Essex SS9 3LA...01702 416 201
e: info@armoursecurity.com
w: www.armoursecurity.com

B.W.Y Canine - Specialist Search Dogs
.... 01437 562 103 // 07791 272 650
e: office@bwycanine.co.uk
w: www.bwycanine.co.uk

BCP Security Limited
12-13 HENRIETTA STREET, COVENT GARDEN, LONDON
Greater London WC2E 8LH....................................07771 356332
e: enquiries@bcpsecurity.co.uk
w: www.bcpsecurity.co.uk

Beacon Security Services
8 TEKNOL HOUSE, VICTORIA ROAD, BURGESS HILL
West Sussex RH15 9LH...0800 999 2479
e: info@beacon-services.co.uk
w: www.beacon-services.co.uk

Brigade Security Consultants Ltd
SUITE 65, 2 LANSDOWNE ROW, BERKELEY SQUARE, LONDON
Greater London W1J 6HL 0800 389 0893
e: daniel@brigadesecurity.com
w: www.brigadesecurity.com

Broadstone Security Ltd
50 ST JAMES'S STREET, MAYFAIR, LONDON
SW1A 1JT...08444 745 001
e: enquiries@broadstonesecurity.co.uk
w: www.broadstonesecurity.co.uk

Business & Entertainment Security Ltd
38 ASHTREE ROAD, NORWICH
Norfolk NR5 0LS 01603 441806
e: sales@besecurity.net
w: www.besecurity.co.uk

Carlisle Support Services
800 CAPABILITY GREEN, LUTON
LU1 3BA 073420 58614
e: alex.leake@carlislesupportservices.com
w: www.carlislesupportservices.com/

Cautela Security
132 SAMLET ROAD, LLANSAMLET, SWANSEA, WALES
SA7 9AF 0845 4759981
e: info@cautelasecurityukltd.co.uk
w: www.cautelasecurityukltd.co.uk

Citrus Event Staffing Ltd
1 SOUTHLANDS, HIGH HEATON, NEWCASTLE UPON TYNE
Tyne and Wear NE7 7YH.......................................0191 6030751
e: info@citruseventstaffing.co.uk
w: www.citruseventstaffing.co.uk

CJ's Events Warwickshire
THE COW YARD, CHURCH FARM, , CHURCH LANE, BUDBROOKE,
WARWICK. Warwickshire CV35 8QL 01926 800 750
e: info@cjseventswarwickshire.com
w: www.cjseventswarwickshire.co.uk

Code 9 Security Ltd
80 HIGH STREET, WINCHESTER
Hampshire SO23 9AT..08442 448 448
e: enquiries@code9security.com
w: www.code9security.co.uk

Corvus Security Ltd
HEMSWELL, 4 CHESTNUT COURT , PARC MENAI, BANGOR
LL57 4FH...0845 643 1514
e: info@corvussecurity.co.uk
w: www.corvussecurity.co.uk

Cotswold Security Ltd
DE MONTFORT HOUSE, ENTERPRISE WAY , VALE PARK, EVESHAM
Worcestershire WR11 1GS 1386305051
e: info@cotswold-security.co.uk
w: www.cotswold-security.co.uk

Crewsaders Security
MILLER 2, 61 ST. PAULS SQUARE, BIRMINGHAM
West Midlands B3 1QS 0845 094 4884
e: bookings@crewsaders.com
w: www.crewsaders.com

Cricklewood Electronics
40-42 CRICKLEWOOD BROADWAY, LONDON
Greater London NW2 3ET........... 020 8450 0995 / 020 84520161
e: accounts@cricklewoodelectronics.com
w: www.cricklewoodelectronics.com

CTIH Limited
UNIT 5 TWIGWORTH COURT BUSINESS CENTRE, TEWKESBURY
ROAD, GLOUCESTER
Gloucestershire GL2 9PG 0333 577 9501
e: sales@ctih.co.uk
w: www.ctih.co.uk

Cuff Group
4-6 CLARENCE STREET, GLOUCESTER
Gloucestershire GL1 1DX 01452 856050
e: info@cuffgroup.co.uk
w: www.cuffgroup.co.uk

DC Site Services Ltd
FENLAND DISTRICT INDUSTRIAL ESTATE, STATION ROAD,
WHITTLESEY, PETERBOROUGH
Cambridgeshire PE7 2EY 01733 200713
e: admin@dcsiteservices.com
w: www.dcsiteservices.com

Doyen AEP Ltd
OSBORNES, MAYPOLE ROAD, CHELSFIELD, ORPINGTON
BR6 7RB..020 8166 5528
e: enquiries@doyenaep.com
w: www.doyenaep.com

Enigma Events & Security Ltd
MALBORNE HOUSE   BENYON GROVE, ORTON MALBORN ,
PETERBOROUGH
Cambridgeshire PE2 5ZL 01733 309999
e: office@enigma-security.com
w: www.enigma-security.com

Equinox Security
CHILTERN HOUSE, 24-30 KING STREET, WATFORD
Hertfordshire WD18 0BP 01923 474 020
e: hq@equinoxsecurity.com
w: www.equinoxsecurity.com

Event Staff
UNIT 27, SPACE BUSINESS CENTRE, TEWKESBURY ROAD,
CHELTENHAM
Gloucestershire GL51 9FL..01242 530055
e: info@event-staff.co.uk
w: www.event-staff.co.uk

Exclusec Security Solutions Ltd
THE GUARDIAN BUILDINGS, LONGBRIDGE ROAD, TRAFFORD
PARK, MANCHESTER
Greater Manchester M17 1SN................................0333 344 3991
e: security@exclusec.co.uk
w: www.exclusec.co.uk

Face 2 Face Medical Ltd
Berkshire SL1 8HJ..................... 07821 538157 // 08000 475866
e: info@face2facemedical.net
w: www.face2facemedical.net

Fresh Events UK
UNIT D WESLAKE INDUSTRIAL PARK, RYE HARBOUR ROAD, RYE
East Sussex TN31 7TE 07919 512 608
e: info@fresheventsuk.com
w: www.fresheventsuk.com

FVF Security
UNIT 9 , 9 BRIGHTON TERRACE, LONDON
Greater London SW9 8DJ..0203 763 8580
e: info@fvfsecurity.com
w: www.fvfsecurity.com

G4S Events
SOUTHSIDE, 105 VICTORIA STREET, LONDON
Greater London SW1E 6QT....................................0207 963 3100
w: www.g4s.uk.com

Gallowglass Security
1-5 BEEHIVE PLACE, LONDON
Greater London SW9 7QR .... 0845 2575 648 / 020 7326 7840
e: info@galsec.co.uk
w: gallowglasssecurity.com

GI Security Pvt. Ltd
3RD AND 4TH FLOOR, 20/1, ASHUTOSH CHOWDHURY AVENUE,
KOLKATA, WEST BENGAL 700 019 .... +91 98307 22234
e: info@gisecurity.com
w: www.gisecurity.com

GreyMen Security Solutions
THE TURBINE BUSINESS CENTRE, COACH ROAD, WORKSOP
Nottinghamshire S81 8AP 0333 2070 667
e: info@greymen.co.uk
w: www.greymen.co.uk

JMS Plant Hire Ltd
32 COLDHARBOUR LANE, HARPENDEN
Hertfordshire AL5 4UN 0845 4670000
e: hire@jms-access.co.uk
w: www.jms-planthire.co.uk

K9 Patrol
MONKSWELL HOUSE, UNIT 127, MANSE LANE, KNARESBOROUGH
HG5 8NQ 01423 551526
e: info@k9patrol.co.uk
w: www.k9patrol.co.uk

K9 Protection Ltd
UNIT 4A THE ORION SUITE, ENTERPRISE WAY, NEWPORT, GWENT
NP20 2AQ...01633 504543
e: get@securityguardwales.co.uk
w: www.k9protectionltd.co.uk

Lockerbox
POSTBUS 518, NIEUW VENNEP
 NL-2150 AM 0031 252 623 523
e: info@lockerbox.nl
w: www.lockerbox.nl

London Close Protection
.... 08456 521526 / 07879 825 560
e: info@londoncloseprotection.com
w: www.londoncloseprotection.com

Longmoor Security
WESTMINSTER HOUSE , BLACKLOCKS HILL, BANBURY
Oxfordshire OX17 2BS 1295756380
e: j.fowler@longmoor-security.com
w: www.longmoor-security.com

McKenzie Arnold Security
MCKENZIE HOUSE, 11 CRITALL DRIVE, BRAINTREE
Essex CM7 2RT...01376 749572
e: lucille@mckenziearnold.com
w: www.mckenziearnold.com

Minimal Risk Consultancy Ltd
MINIMAL RISK CONSULTANCY LTD, SKYLON COURT COLDNOSE
ROAD, HEREFORD
Herefordshire HR2 6JS 01432 359353
w: www.minimalrisk.co.uk

S

Mobile CCTV
UNIT 8 CAMBERLEY BUSINESS CENTRE, BRACEBRIDGE, CAMBERLEY
Surrey GU15 3DP..01276 469 084
e: info@mobilecctv.co.uk
w: www.mobilecctv.co.uk

NDSS Ltd
113 - 116 BUTE STREET, MOUNT STUART SQUARE, CARDIFF BAY, CARDIFF
CF10 5EQ 02920 099 993
e: info@ndssltd.co.uk
w: www.ndssltd.co.uk

Oakwood Security Solutions Ltd
UNIT 6-7 PARCHFIELD ENTERPRISE PARK,, COLTON ROAD, RUGELEY
Staffordshire WS15 3HB 01889 570 660
e: info@oakwoodsecurity.co
w: www.oakwoodsecurity.co/

One Staff Solution Ltd
58 PARK STREET, MAYFAIR, LONDON
Greater London W1K 2JL .... 07523 486905 / 020 7511 7722
e: info@oness.co.uk
w: www.security-company-london.com

Paraguard Security
LONDON
.... 0207 1935 762 / 07977 498044
e: info@paraguard.co.uk
w: www.paraguard.co.uk

Paratus Limited
THE OLD Q STORES, BROWNING BARRACKS, ALDERSHOT
Hampshire GU11 2BU 01252 341 260
w: www.paratus.org.uk

Perfect Guards Limited
TALON HOUSE PRESLEY WAY, MILTON KEYNES
MK8 0ES..0844 4145616
e: info@perfect-guards.co.uk
w: www.perfect-guards.co.uk

Phase 1 Security Services - Security Guard Company
7 NAPIER HAUSE, ELVA WAY, BEXHILL
Sussex TN39 5BF...0800 009 6898
e: info@phaseonesecurity.co.uk
w: www.phaseonesecurity.co.uk

Phoenix Services Security
....01243 785148
w: www.securitybyphoenix.co.uk

Pitman's People Event Staff
UNIT G1A STAMFORD WORKS, 3 GILLETT ST. LONDON
Greater London N16 8JH.......................................020 3651 3330
e: admin@pitmanspeople.com
w: www.pitmanspeople.com

Positive Protection Solutions
1ST FLOOR OFFICES, 14 NEW KINGSWAY, WEST COYNEY, STOKE ON TRENT
Staffordshire ST3 6NA 01782 596611
e: info@ppssecurity.co.uk
w: ppssecurity.co.uk

Primus Protective Consultants Ltd
EARLSWOOD RD, LLANISHEN, CARDIFF
CF14 5GH 02920 757 578
e: info@primusprotection.com
w: www.primusprotection.com

Response Security Solutions
TRINITY BUOY WHARF, 33 RIVERSIDE BUILDING, 64 ORCHARD PLACE, , LONDON
Greater London E14 0JY 0845 1661981
e: Info@responsesecuritygroup.co.uk
w: www.responsesecuritygroup.co.uk

Right Guard Security Ltd
4TH FLOOR, HAMILTON HOUSE,, MABLEDON PLACE, LONDON
Greater London WC1H 9BD 0207 241 5525
e: info@rightguard.co.uk
w: www.rightguard.co.uk

Right Guard Security

3 Simmonds Road,
Canterbury, Kent
CT1 3RA

t: 01227 464588
e: info@rightguard.co.uk

Right Guard Security was formed in 1990 in response to an escalation of public order and crowd safety related issues. Our diverse list of services includes Crowd Management for events and venues, Traffic Management, Close Protection and Corporate Security.

www.rightguard.co.uk

Roman Co (Gloucester) Limited
UNIT 36/3 MORELANDS TRADING ESTATE, BRISTOL ROAD,, GLOUCESTER
Gloucestershire GL1 5RZ 07807 850005
e: stuart@roman-co.org
w: www.roman-co.org

Safe Events Security Ltd
....07786 375728
e: info@safe-events-security.co.uk
w: www.safe-events-security.co.uk

Safe Security & Events Ltd
63 CRESCENT ROAD, OXFORD
Oxfordshire OX4 2NY 07802 541858
e: info@safesecurityltd.co.uk
w: www.safesecurityltd.co.uk

S

Safestyle Security Services
EXE SUITE 1, MOTORPOINT ARENA, MARY ANN STREET, CARDIFF
CF10 2EQ 029 20221711
e: office@safestylesecurity.co.uk
w: www.safestylesecurity.co.uk

Securex Security Ltd
FIRST FLOOR, 962 OLD LODE LANE, SOLIHULL
West Midlands B92 8LN.......................................0121 742 4333
e: info@securexsecurity.com
w: www.securexsecurity.com

Security In Action Guards Limited
THIRD FLOOR, 207 REGENT STREET, LONDON
Greater London W1B 3HH 0800 009 6898
e: sales@phaseonesecurity.co.uk
w: www.sia-guards.com

Security Industry Authority
PO BOX 1293, LIVERPOOL
Merseyside L69 1AX 0844 892 1025
e: info@the-sia.org.uk
w: www.the-sia.org.uk

Sentinel Secure Solutions
37 KENSINGTON ROAD, COLCHESTER
Essex CO2 7FF...01206 971362
e: info@sentinelsecuresolutions.com
w: www.sentinelsecuresolutions.com

Showforce
UNIT 001 STRATFORD WORKSHOPS, BURFORD ROAD,
STRATFORD, LONDON
Greater London E15 2SP......................................0208 519 5252
e: info@showforce.com
w: www.showforce.com

Showsec International Ltd (Cardiff)
SUITE 16, CARDIFF INTERNATIONAL ARENA, MARY ANN STREET,
CARDIFF CF10 2EQ 07500 079 441
e: martin.lewis@showsec.co.uk
w: www.crowd-management.com

Showsec International Ltd (Head Office)
REGENT HOUSE, 16 WEST WALK, LEICESTER
Leicestershire LE1 7NA..0116 204 3333
e: joseph.milner@showsec.co.uk
w: www.showsec.co.uk

Showsec International Ltd (London)
THE PHOENIX BREWERY, 13 BRAMLEY ROAD, LONDON
Greater London W10 6SP.......................... +44 (0) 207 190 9110
e: paul.legge@showsec.co.uk;
w: www.crowd-management.com

Showsec International Ltd (Manchester)
13 STANLEY STREET, 52-54 DALE END, MANCHESTER
Greater Manchester M8 8SH................................0116 204 6590
e: mark.wilcock@showsec.co.uk
w: www.showsec.co.uk

Sls Security Ltd
UNIT 5 REDHILL FARM, ELBERTON
Gloucestershire BS35 4AL .... +44(0)1454 419441
e: info@stuartsecurity.co.uk
w: www.stuartsecurity.co.uk

South East Fire & Security Ltd
209 PRINCE AVENUE, SOUTHEND-ON-SEA
Essex SS0 0JU..1702329146
e: mail@southeastfs.co.uk
w: www.southeastltd.com

SpaCES - Complete Event Services
SPA HOUSE, 23 IO CENTRE, , SALBROOK ROAD, SALFORDS ,
REDHILL. Surrey RH1 5GJ 0330 124 1541
e: enquiries@spacesuk.org
w: www.spacesuk.org

Specialized Security
4 ROSEBANK ROAD, ROSEBANK PARK, LIVINGSTON
West Lothian EH54 7EJ...01506 411231
e: info@specializedsecurity.co.uk
w: www.specializedsecurity.co.uk

Stone House Security Guards London
UNIT F30, HASTINGWOOD TRADING ESTATE, HARBOT ROAD,
EDMONTON
Greater London N18 3HT 020 3006 6554
e: david@london-security-guards.com
w: www.london-security-guards.com

Symbiotic Security
6 LEWIS HOUSE, 3 SCHOOL ROAD, LONDON
Greater London NW10 6TD 020 8539 4969
e: info@symbiosec.co.uk
w: www.symbiosec.co.uk

The Safety Officer Ltd
0 BOX 380, 256 BRONTE ROAD,, WAVERLEY
NSW 2024 .... +61 415 885600
e: jc@thesafetyofficer.com
w: www.thesafetyofficer.com

Total Care Security Ltd
UNIT 3, BRUNEL DRIVE, NEWARK
Nottinghamshire NG24 2DE 0800 917 47 67
e: info@totalcaresecurity.com
w: www.totalcaresecurity.com

UK Close Protection Services
....7515 772232
e: info@ukcloseprotectionservices.co.uk
w: ukcloseprotectionservices.co.uk/

Uk Independent Security Ltd
RECULVER ROAD, HERNE BAY
CT6 6LQ 07864 176 767
e: info@ukisecurity.com
w: www.ukisecurity.com

Who gave the organisers confidence?

Showsec did. Because we train only the most motivated, intelligent people to provide the high level of discreet, effective security that venues and event organisers demand.

Showsec are award-winning crowd management and event security specialists who have been delivering high standards of service for over 30 years.

Knowledgeable and approachable, our vigilant professionals discreetly protect your venue, valuable assets and people, while ensuring your customers get the most from their event experience.

SHOWSEC

T: +44(0) 116 204 3333
E: marketing@showsec.co.uk
www.showsec.co.uk

Vespasian Security Ltd
HARBOUR COURT, COMPASS ROAD, NORTH HARBOUR, PORTSMOUTH
Hampshire PO6 4ST..442392295503
e: info@vespasiansecurity.co.uk
w: www.vespasiansecurity.co.uk

Westminster Security
34 BUCKINGHAM PALACE ROAD, LONDON
Greater London SW1W 0RH
.... 0207 123 4544 / 0755 4000 300
e: hello@westminstersecurity.co.uk
w: www.westminstersecurity.co.uk

Whispering Bell
.... + 44 (0) 1202 295 565
e: info@whisperingbell.com
w: www.whisperingbell.com

Session Fixers

Cool Music Ltd
1A FISHERS LANE, CHISWICK, LONDON
Greater London W4 1RX..020 8995 7766
e: info@coolmusicltd.com
w: www.coolmusicltd.com

Generator Power Limited
FOXBRIDGE WAY , NORMANTON INDUSTRIAL ESTATE , NORMANTON
West Yorkshire WF6 1TN 8456012187
e: info@trackwaysolutions.co.uk
w: www.trackwaysolutions.co.uk

Set Design & Construction

Activteam
BUSINESS DESIGN CENTRE, 52 UPPER STREET, LONDON
Greater London N1 0QH 020 3051 6244
e: project@activteam.co.uk
w: www.activteam.com

Air Artist Ltd
UNIT 19, HALESWORTH BUSINESS CENTRE, NORWICH ROAD, HALESWORTH
Suffolk IP19 8QJ........................ 01986 874466 / 07785 941 659
e: robin.harries@virgin.net
w: www.airartists.co.uk

Applied Arts
22-27 THE OVAL, CAMBRIDGE HEATH, LONDON
Greater London E2 9DT..020 7739 3155
e: info@appliedarts.co.uk
w: www.appliedarts.co.uk

S

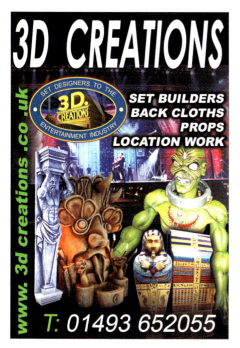

Atlas Event Construction Ltd
UNIT 5, MIDDLEWOODS WAY, CARLTON, BARNSLEY
South Yorkshire S71 3HR 01226 323 656
e: info@atlasec.co.uk
w: www.atlasec.co.uk

Big House Events Ltd
35 ST CLAIR STREET , EDINBURGH
EH6 8LB 0131 669 6366
e: tash@bighouse-events.co.uk
w: www.bighouse-events.co.uk

Big House Events Ltd
35 ST CLAIR STREET , EDINBURGH
 EH6 8LB 0131 669 6366
e: tash@bighouse-events.co.uk
w: www.bighouse-events.co.uk

CEI Exhibitions
STONEBRIDGE HOUSE, 28-32 BRIDGE STREET, LEATHERHEAD
Surrey KT22 8BZ ....+44 (0) 1372 869849
e: darryl@ceiexhibitions.co.uk
w: www.ceiexhibitions.co.uk

Clements & Street Design Build Ltd
UNIT 9, BROAD GROUND ROAD, LAKESIDE, REDDITCH
Worcestershire B98 8YP 01527 510154
e: info@clementsandstreet-db.co.uk
w: www.clementsandstreet-db.co.uk

Colin Holden Associates
111 CUCKMERE WAY, BRIGHTON
East Sussex BN1 8GB .... 01273 556290 / 07817 176929
e: colin@colinholden.co.uk
w: www.colinholden.co.uk

Creator International Ltd
UNIT 3, HIGHAMS HILL FARM, SHEEP BARN LANE
Surrey CR6 9PQ 01959 542732
e: giles@creator.uk.com
w: www.creator.uk.com

Cult Events
UNIT 3, AUTUMN YARD, AUTUMN STREET, LONDON
Greater London E3 2TT .... 020 8983 5459 / 07540782176
e: info@culte.co.uk
w: www.culte.co.uk

EC Creative Services Ltd
UNIT 1 LANSDOWNE ROAD, CHADDERTON, OLDHAM
Lancashire OL9 9EF...0161 628 7723
e: info@eccreativeservices.com
w: www.eccreativeservices.com

Firefly Audio Visual Solutions Ltd
UNIT 31 BARKSTON HOUSE, CROYDON STREET, LEEDS
West Yorkshire LS11 9RT 01133 320042
e: hire.leeds@fireflyav.co.uk
w: www.fireflyav.co.uk

Fitzgaralds Interiors
RIVERSIDE STUDIO,11 STATION ROAD   , LOUDWATER, HIGH WYCOMBE, BUCKS
HP10 9TX .... 01494 443019 / 07775 858106
e: sales@fitzgeraldsinteriors.co.uk
w: www.fitzgeraldsinteriors.co.uk

Global Experience Specialists (GES) Ltd
SILVERSTONE DRIVE, GALLAGHER BUSINESS PARK, COVENTRY
CV6 6PA..02476 380 000
e: enquiry@ges.com
w: www.ges.ae

Gorilla Marketing & Events Ltd
PAPER STOCK HOUSE, AMERSHAM ROAD, CHALFONT ST. GILES
Buckinghamshire HP8 4RU 01494 876 876
e: info@gorillauk.com
w: www.gorillauk.com

Graves & Hobbs Ltd
....7960402612
e: info@gravesandhobbsroofing.co.uk
w: www.gravesandhobbsroofing.co.uk

Illusion Design & Construct Ltd
UNIT 1A, ELIZABETH INDUSTRIAL ESTATE, JUNO WAY, LONDON
Greater London SE14 5RW...................................0207 2729 255
e: info@illusiondc.com
w: www.illusiondesignandconstruct.co

Jason Caley
NEWHOLM HIGH FARM, NEWHOLM, WHITBY
North Yorkshire Y021 3QY 01377 241951
e: thepineman1981@hotmail.com
w: www.jasoncaley.co.uk/

Kinetika Design Studio
119 HIGH HOUSE ARTISTSÂ ™ STUDIOS, HIGH HOUSE
PRODUCTION PARK, PURFLEET
Essex RM19 1AS 01708 202846
e: info@kinetika.co.uk
w: www.kinetikadesignstudio.com

L and B Roofing
4 ROSSKILLING, HELSTON
Cornwall TR13 8JY 07966 367986
e: brad.kirkbride@outlook.com
w: www.landbroofing.co.uk

Leapfrog
....1222144557
e: robsz@a2zleapfrog.com
w: www.a2zleapfrog.com

Light Motif
26 TALINA CENTRE, 23A BAGLEYS LANE, LONDON
Greater London SW6 2BW.....................................020 7183 5381
e: info@lightmotif.co.uk
w: www.lightmotif.co.uk

London Event Rentals
UNIT 7, WILLOW WALK, TOWER BRIDGE, LONDON
Greater London SE1 5SF 01252 313154
e: info@londoneventrentals.co.uk
w: www.londoneventrentals.co.uk

LS Live
UNIT 53, LANGTHWAITE BUSINESS PARK, SOUTH KIRKBY,
WAKEFIELD. West Yorkshire WF9 3NR 01977 659 888
e: sales@ls-live.com
w: www.ls-live.com

Made To Measure Windows and Doors Ltd
MAVERICK BUSINESS PARK, 292 MONKMOOR RD,
SHREWSBURY, SHROPSHIRE
SY2 5TF...1743356130
e: madetomeasurewindows@hotmail.co.uk
w: www.madetomeasurewindows.co.uk

Mardell-Pick Design Ltd
THE STUDIO, 27 THE WOODFIELDS, SANDERSTEAD, CROYDON,
LONDON
Greater London CR2 0HG 020 8651 0248
e: info@mardell-pickdesign.com
w: www.mardell-pickdesign.com

MCM Loft Conversions
31 TORILSDEN WAY HARLOW
Essex cm201au 01279 933023
e: mcmlofts@gmail.com
w: www.mcmloftconversions.co.uk

Patio Awnings 4 Less Ltd
UNIT 9, DERWENT BUSINESS PARK, HAWKINS LANE , BURTON-
UPON-TRENT
Staffordshire DE14 1QA .... 01283567880 / 0800 587 9906
e: davedowning10@hotmail.com
w: patioawnings4less.co.uk/

PAULEY
BLETCHLEY LEYS FARM , WHADDON ROAD, MILTON KEYNES
Buckinghamshire MK17 0EG..................................01908 522532
e: info@pauley.co.uk
w: www.pauley.co.uk

PBM Property Refurbishment
58 ARTHUR VIEW CRESCENT, DANDERHALL, DALKEITH,
EDINBURGH
EH22 1NQ................................... 07955537075 / 0131 2080800
e: andrew.w82@hotmail.com
w: www.pbmrefurbishment.co.uk

Planet Gold Decor
UNIT 4 ROMARSH, FOWLSWICK BUSINESS PARK, , ALLINGTON
Wiltshire SN14 6QE...07747 015 170
e: info@planetgolddecor.co.uk
w: www.planetgolddecor.co.uk or www

Podesta Roofing
15/17 MIDDLE STREET , BRIGHTON
East Sussex BN1 1AL.................. 01273 461367 / 07545 860051
e: alison@podesta-roofing.co.uk
w: podesta-roofing.co.uk/

Rodof LTD
57, SWAN ROAD, WEST DRAYTON, MIDDLESEX
UB7 7JZ...7412623334
e: rodof.limited@gmail.com
w: www.rodof.co.uk

Ryszard Andrzejewski Design For Performance
....07799 613 277
e: skirich@hotmail.com
w: www.skirich.co.uk

Scenex Sets & Staging Ltd
FELDSPAR CLOSE, THE WARRENS INDUSTRIAL PARK, ENDERBY,
LEICESTER
Leicestershire LE19 4SD......................................0116 284 5999
e: hello@scenex.co.uk
w: www.scenex.co.uk

Scenograf
HENDY YNYSFOR, LLANFROTHEN
LL48 6BJ................................... 07717 748 355 / 01766 238451
e: info@scenograf.co.uk
w: www.scenograf.co.uk

SCM EXPO roofing
....1212840902
e: apppical@hotmail.com
w: www.scmroofing.co.uk

Scruffy Dog
UNIT E3, OYO BUSINESS PARK, PARK LANE, BIRMINGHAM
West Midlands B35 6AN 0800 211 8604
e: info@scruffydogltd.com
w: www.scruffydogltd.com

Sculpture Studios
UNIT 3F HARVEY ROAD, NEVENDON INDUSTRIAL ESTATE,
BASILDON
Essex SS13 1DA 01268 726470
e: aden.hynes@hotmail.com
w: www.sculpturestudios.co.uk

Set Creations Ltd
STUDIO HOUSE DELAMARE ROAD, CHESHUNT
Hertfordshire EN8 9SH...01992 789 759
e: connect@setcreations.com
w: www.setcreations.com

Setfree Projects Ltd
UNIT 6, MANOR INDUSTRIAL ESTATE, FLINT
Flintshire CH6 5UY 0800 077 8906
e: info@setfreeprojectsltd.com
w: setfreeprojectsltd.com

Seventh Heaven
....01753 546555
e: info@seventh-heaven-events.co.uk
w: www.seventh-heaven-events.co.uk

Shelly Robinson
....07974 671861
e: Robinsonstonesocialmedia@gmail.com
w: www.robinsonstone.co.uk

SkyWeb Media
.... 0203 328 9917 / 0753 917 6000
e: will@skyweb.media
w: www.skyweb.media

Sovereign Exhibitions
UNITS 1,2 AND 3, ARLEY INDUSTRIAL ESTATE,, COLLIERS WAY,
ARLEY, COVENTRY
West Midlands CV7 8HN 01676 549 000
e: info@sovereignexhibitions.co.uk
w: www.sovereignexhibitions.co.uk

Space Planning UK Ltd
23B VICARAGE CRESCENT, LONDON
Greater London SW11 3LL 2031264880
e: info@spaceplanning-uk.com
w: www.spaceplanning-uk.com

Splinter Scenery
THE GASWORKS , HIGGINSHAW LANE, OLDHAM
OL1 3LB 0161 633 6787
e: alec@splinterscenery.co.uk
w: www.splinterscenery.co.uk

Sprayed Splashbacks
34 RUNFIELD CLOSE, LEIGH
Leicestershire WN7 1EP............ 01942 389 554 / 07551 155 468
e: hello@sprayedsplashbacks.co.uk
w: www.sprayedsplashbacks.co.uk

Stuart Levene
13, NESTOR AVENUE , LONDON
N21 2HE 2082453519
e: info@slsurveying.co.uk
w: www.slsurveying.co.uk

SXS Events
....0870 080 2342
e: hello@sxsevents.co.uk
w: www.sxsevents.co.uk

The Imagesetting Bureau
18 COLINDEEP LANE, HENDON, LONDON
Greater London NW4 4SG 020 8202 5424
e: contact@imagesetting.com
w: www.imagesetting.com

The JWP Group
195 THORNHILL ROAD, SURBITON
Surrey KT6 7TG 020 8288 0246
e: web@jwp.co.uk
w: www.jwp.co.uk

Thomas Ray Limited
....1827713028
e: info@thomasraylimited.co.uk
w: www.thomasraylimited.co.uk

Total Fabrications Ltd
UNITS 3-6, KINGSTON INDUSTRIAL ESTATE, 81-86 GLOVER
STREET, BIRMINGHAM
West Midlands B9 4EN...0121 772 5234
e: info@trussing.com
w: www.trussing.com

Ultima Displays Ltd
49-50 CAUSEWAY ROAD, EARLSTREES INDUSTRIAL ESTATE,
CORBY
Northamptonshire NN17 4DU................................01536 272250
e: sales@ultimadisplays.co.uk
w: www.ultimadisplays.co.uk

Upstage - Set Builders Ltd
UNIT 9 WEST TOWN FARM, LAKE END ROAD, TAPLOW
SL6 0PT...01628 559450
e: office@upstage.org
w: www.upstagesetbuilders.com

Useful Structures Ltd
EUROPARK, A5 WATLING STREET , CLIFTON UPON DUNSMORE,
RUGBY
Warwickshire CV23 0AL...01788 861246
e: usefulstructures@gmail.com
w: www.useful-structures.com

S

Vizone Design
25 SCHOOL CLOSE, , DOWNLEY, HIGH WYCOMBE
Buckinghamshire HP13 5TR 01494 463584
e: info@vizonedesign.co.uk
w: www.vizonedesign.co.uk

Whole Nine Yards Productions Limited
ST. NICHOLAS HOUSE, 31-34 HIGH STREET, BRISTOL
Bristol BS1 2AW.. +44 117 315 5220
e: info@wny.uk.com
w: www.wny.uk.com

WM Event Design
19 ST JAMES'S DRIVE, WANDSWORTH COMMON, LONDON
Greater London SW17 7RN 020 3837 4926
e: info@williammoyse.com
w: www.wmeventdesign.com

Your Home Space
CHISWICK, LONDON
W4.. 07946578933 / 020 81271387
e: hello@yourhomespace.co.uk
w: www.yourhomespace.co.uk

Showgirls

The Jammy Showgirls
CENTURY HOUSE SOUTH, NORTH STATION ROAD, COLCHESTER
Essex CO1 1RE 07796 138884
e: anthony@jammyshowsandproductions.co.uk
w: www.jammyshowsandproductions.co.u

Signs

AA Signs
FANUM HOUSE, BASING VIEW, BASINGSTOKE
Hampshire RG21 4EA..0800 731 7003
e: aasigns@theaa.com
w: www.theaa.com/aasigns

Abel Magnets Ltd
BALACLAVA ROAD, SHEFFIELD
South Yorkshire S6 3BG 0114 249 5949
e: info@magnetic-paper.com
w: www.magnetic-paper.com

All About Signs
UNIT 25 CHALLENGE ENTERPRISE CENTRE, SHARPS CLOSE,
PORTSMOUTH
Hampshire PO3 5RJ...023 9265 4720
e: enquiries@allaboutsigns.co.uk
w: www.allaboutsigns.co.uk

Apollo Signs
5 TANNERY ROAD, GILTBROOK INDUSTRIAL PARK, GILTBROOK
Nottinghamshire NG16 2WP....................................01159 384200
e: info@apollo-signs.co.uk
w: www.apollo-signs.co.uk

Artisan Signs
4 RILEY ROAD, TELFORD WAY INDUSTRIAL ESTATE, ROBINSON
CLOSE, KETTERING
Northamptonshire NN16 8NN................................01536 522777
e: sales@artisansigns.co.uk
w: www.artisansigns.co.uk

Blueprint Promotional Products
NO. 1 THE EMBASSY, LAWRENCE STREET, LONG EATON,
NOTTINGHAM
Nottinghamshire NG10 1JY...................................0333 1234 400
e: info@blueprintpromo.co.uk
w: www.blueprintpromo.co.uk

Display Wizard
UNITS 15 & 16 CREAMERY INDUSTRIAL ESTATE, KENLIS ROAD,
BARNACRE, GARSTANG
Lancashire PR3 1GD 01995 606633
e: matthew@displaywizard.co.uk
w: www.displaywizard.co.uk

Event Exhibition & Design Ltd
THE WAGON YARD, MARLBOROUGH
Wiltshire SN8 1LH...01672 513666
e: david@event-exhibition.co.uk
w: www.event-exhibition.co.uk

FestivalSigns
BATH MARINA, BATH
Somerset BA1 3JT...7854055775
e: info@festivalsigns.co.uk
w: www.festivalsigns.co.uk

Flying Monk Graphics
UNIT 9 MALMESBURY BUSINESS PARK, BEUTTELL WAY,
MALMESBURY
Wiltshire SN16 9JU...01666 829228
e: info@flyingmonkgraphics.co.uk
w: www.flyingmonkgraphics.co.uk

Global Experience Specialists (GES) Ltd
SILVERSTONE DRIVE, GALLAGHER BUSINESS PARK, COVENTRY
CV6 6PA..02476 380 000
e: enquiry@ges.com
w: www.ges.ae

Harrisons Signs Ltd
LINK HOUSE, GREEN LANE TRADING ESTATE, CLIFTON, YORK
North Yorkshire YO30 5PY 01904 699600
e: sales@harrisonsigns.co.uk
w: www.harrisonsigns.co.uk

Ingenious Inflatables
45 LUDGATE HILL, LONDON
Greater London EC4M 7JU....................................020 7183 7842
e: enquiries@ingeniousinflatables.com
w: www.ingeniousinflatables.co.uk

Kennet Sign & Display
UNIT 7 & 8 HOPTON INDUSTRIAL ESTATE, DEVIZES
Wiltshire SN10 2EU...01380 722253
e: sales@kennetsignanddisplay.co.uk
w: www.kennetsignanddisplay.co.uk

Le Mark Self Adhesive Ltd
UNIT 1 HOUGHTON HILL INDUSTRIES, SAWTRY WAY, HOUGHTON
Cambridgeshire PE28 2DH....................................01480 494 540
e: info@lemark.co.uk
w: www.lemark.co.uk

LED Synergy
SYNERGY HOUSE KNIGHTS COURT, MAGELLAN CLOSE
WALWORTH BUSINESS PARK, ANDOVER
Hampshire SP10 5NT..01264 303030
e: sales@ledsynergy.co.uk
w: www.ledsynergy.co.uk

Mediaco Graphic Solutions
CHURCHILL POINT, CHURCHILL WAY, TRAFFORD PARK,
MANCHESTER
Greater Manchester M17 1BS...............................0161 875 2020
e: customerservice@mediaco.co.uk
w: www.mediaco.co.uk

Merox Screenprint
ELLIOTT ROAD, WEST HOWE , BOURNEMOUTH
Dorset BH11 8JT 01202 571210
e: sales@merox.co.uk
w: www.merox.co.uk

Mydisplays.co.uk
16 UPPER WOBURN PLACE, LONDON
WC1H 0BS 0 203 794 7626
e: info@mydisplays.co.uk
w: www.mydisplays.co.uk

Name Badge Company
UNIT 26 ISEMILL ROAD, BURTON LATIMER
Nottinghamshire NN15 5XU 03330 124 648
e: sales@namebadges.co.uk
w: www.namebadges.co.uk/

Neolec Lighting
CHURCH LANE, KINWARTON, ALCESTER
Warwickshire B49 6HB 01789 765 667
e: info@neoleclighting.com
w: www.neoleclighting.com

POS Centre
1-2 HORSECROFT ROAD, THE PINNACLES, HARLOW
Essex CM19 5BH 01279 207211
e: sales@poscentre.co.uk
w: www.poscentre.co.uk

Print 2 Media Ltd
UNIT 7 MOORSWATER INDUSTRIAL ESTATE, LISKEARD,
CORNWALL. Cornwall PL14 4LN............................01579 340985
e: info@print-2-media.com
w: www.print-2-media.com

Publicity & Display Ltd
DOUGLAS DRIVE, GODALMING
Surrey GU7 1HJ 01483 428 326
e: print@pubdis.com
w: www.pubdis.com

Sherwood Signmakers Ltd
A7, ENTERPRISE PARK, BRUNEL DRIVE, NEWARK
Nottinghamshire NG24 2DZ 01636 611950
e: info@sherwoodsigns.co.uk
w: www.sherwoodsigns.co.uk

Sign Industries
GARDYNE, FORFAR, ANGUS, SCOTLAND
DD8 2SQ...01241 828694
e: info@signindustries.com
w: www.signindustries.com

Sign Wizzard
UNIT 6 GRIFFIN INDUSTRIAL MALL, GRIFFIN LANE, AYLESBURY
Buckinghamshire HP19 8BP 01296 398022
e: sales@signwizzard.co.uk
w: www.signwizzard.co.uk

Sinclair Print
396 ASHLEY ROAD, POOLE
BH14 0AA 01202 730221
e: sinclairprint@aol.com

Synergi Exhibition Consultants
CHISWICK HOUSE, CHISWICK GROVE, BLACKPOOL
Lancashire FY3 9TW...01253 769 911
e: mail@synergi.co.uk
w: www.synergi.co.uk

Traffic Management Services
AURILLAC WAY, , HALLCROFT INDUSTRIAL ESTATE, RETFORD
Nottinghamshire DN22 7PX....................................01777 705053
e: info@traffic.org.uk
w: www.traffic.org.uk

Ultima Displays Ltd
49-50 CAUSEWAY ROAD, EARLSTREES INDUSTRIAL ESTATE,
CORBY
Northamptonshire NN17 4DU.................................01536 272250
e: sales@ultimadisplays.co.uk
w: www.ultimadisplays.co.uk

Victory Design Ltd
FOREST BUILDINGS, 41 CRESWELL ROAD, CLOWNE,
CHESTERFEILD
Derbyshire S43 4PN..0844 811 8777
e: sales@victorydesign.co.uk
w: www.victorydesign.co.uk

Walter Logan & Co Ltd
3 ATHENAEUM ROAD, WHETSTONE, LONDON
Greater London N20 9AA 0208 446 0161
e: info@walterlogan.com
w: www.walterlogan.com

S

Zephyr-the Visual Communicator
MIDLAND ROAD, THRAPSTON
Northamptonshire NN14 4LX 01832 737771
e: info@zephyr-tvc.co.uk
w: www.zephyr-flags.co.uk

Simulators

Golf At Home Ltd
STABLE COTTAGE, CHERRY GARDEN LANE, MAIDENHEAD
Berkshire SL6 3QD 07905 163391
e: karen@golf-at-home.net
w: www.golf-at-home.net

Jemlar Ltd
P.O. BOX 7416, TOWCESTER
Northamptonshire NN12 6WB 0870 765 0536
e: sales@jemlar.com
w: www.jemlar.com

Premier Simulation
WOODSTOCK HOUSE, WOODSTOCK CLOSE, HORSHAM
West Sussex RH12 5YT..01403 270076
e: mandi.lucas@virgin.net
w: www.mobilesimulators.co.uk

Simworx Limited
SECOND AVENUE, THE PENSETT ESTATE, KINGSWINFORD
West Midlands DY6 7UL...01384 295733
e: sales@simworx.co.uk
w: www.simworx.co.uk

Site Vehicles

Airstream Facilities
....01885 400223
e: talk@airstreamfacilities.com
w: www.airstreamfacilities.com

Amex Cars
FIRST FLOOR, 10 LONG BARN LANE, READING
Berkshire RG2 7SZ 1189666111
e: mo@amexcars.co.uk
w: www.amexcars.co.uk

Amex Cars
FIRST FLOOR, 10 LONG BARN LANE, READING
Berkshire RG2 7SZ 1189666111
e: mo@amexcars.co.uk
w: www.amexcars.co.uk

Bradshaw Event Vehicles
NEW LANE, STIBBINGTON, PETERBOROUGH
Cambridgeshire PE8 6LW 01780 782621
e: enquiries@eventvehicles.co.uk
w: www.eventvehicles.co.uk

Buggy Hire Uk
LITTLE TY-COCH, ST. BRIDES WENTLOOG, NEWPORT
NP10 8SR...01633 680754
e: hire@hopkinsmachinery.co.uk
w: www.buggyhireuk.com

Caddy Car Company
FARTHINGSTONE GOLF COURSE, FARTHINGSTONE, TOWCESTER
Northamptonshire NN12 8HA 01327 361423
e: info@caddycars.co.uk
w: www.caddycars.co.uk

Contract exhibition services
ALMA PARK , GRANTHAM
Lincolnshire NG31 9SW 2036925232
e: giles@ceseventsupport.com
w: www.ceseventsupport.com

Festaxi Ltd
21 DANDBY CLOSE, LITTLE PAXTON
Cambridgeshire PE19 6FA......................................01223 459836
e: info@festaxi.com
w: www.festaxi.com

Galaxy Cruiser
11 CURLEW WAY, MORETON, WIRRAL
CH46 7SP 0151 538 9320
e: paul@galaxycruiser.co.uk
w: www.galaxycruiser.co.uk

Gator Hire UK
NORSHAW BARN, PUDDING PIE NOOK LANE, PRESTON
Lancashire PR3 2JL 01772 861 049
e: info@gatorhireuk.co.uk
w: www.gatorhireuk.co.uk

Golfbuggyhire Ltd
FLIXTON ROAD, CARRINGTON, URMSTON, MANCHESTER
Greater Manchester M41 6JE 0161 776 5927
e: info@golfbuggyhire.co.uk
w: www.golfbuggyhire.co.uk

Green Metro Cars Limited
UNIT 1 ROBERT CORT IND EST. , BRITTEN ROAD , READING
RG2 0AU...1189666656
e: alanparkinson@greenmetrocars.co.uk
w: www.greenmetrocars.co.uk

Hiremech
UNIT 1, TARIFF ROAD, TOTTENHAM, LONDON
Greater London N17 0EB 020 8880 3322
e: sales@hiremech.co.uk
w: www.hiremech.co.uk

Luckings Live Events Ltd
BOSTON HOUSE, 69-75 BOSTON MANOR ROAD, , BRENTFORD
Middlesex TW8 9JJ..0208 332 2000
e: Info@luckings.co.uk
w: www.luckings.co.uk

S

Nicewheels.net
N1 4EN 07850 818110
e: info@nicewheels.net
w: www.nicewheels.net

Rock City Stage Crew
LANGSFORD HOUSE, 8 DARKLAKE VIEW, ESTOVER, PLYMOUTH
Devon PL6 7TL 01752 255 933
e: office@rockcitycrew.co.uk
w: www.rockcitycrew.co.uk

Tractor Hire Ltd
LITTLE TY-COCH, ST. BRIDES WENTLOOG, NEWPORT
NP10 8SR 01633 680754
e: hire@hopkinsmachinery.co.uk
w: www.buggyhireuk.com

Wagon Wheels On Location
....07974 765792
e: info@wagonwheels.tv
w: www.wagonwheelsonlocation.com

Wheal's Far-Go
UNIT 5, 13-15 SUNBEAM ROAD, LONDON
Greater London NW10 6JP...................................0208 965 4600
e: wfg@whealsfargo.com
w: www.whealsfargo.com

Winner Events
1 NORTH MOORS, SLYFIELD INDUSTRIAL ESTATE, GUILDFORD
Surrey GU1 1SE 0845 601 5427
e: sales@winnerevents.com
w: www.winnerevents.com

Sky Diving / Parachutists

David Morris Action Sports
2 DALESIDE, COTGRAVE
Nottinghamshire NG12 3QA 0115 989 3538
e: info@flatfly.co.uk
w: www.flatfly.co.uk

Slot Car Racing

Corporace
13 CAREY CLOSE, MOULTON, NORTHAMPTON
NN3 7SN...07713 121515
e: info@corporace.com
w: www.facebook.com/corporace

S

Software Providers

AP16
51 THE TANNERY, LAWRENCE STREET, YORK
North Yorkshire YO10 3WH....................................0333 666 1616
e: sophie@ap16.com / contact@ap16.com

Audiovisual Joint Resource Ltd
CORNER HOUSE, 114 WINDMILL STREET, MACCLESFIELD
Cheshire SK11 7LB..1625615090
e: hello@deltrack.co.uk
w: delegatetracking.com/

Beekast
.... +33 983 222 559
w: www.beekast.com

Chris Elgood Associates Ltd
32 WEST STREET, TADLEY
Hampshire RG26 3SX 0118 982 1115
e: info@chris-elgood.co.uk
w: www.chris-elgood.co.uk

Concise
5 THE QUADRANT CENTRE , 135 SALUSBURY ROAD, LONDON
NW6 6RJ .... +44 (0)20 7644 6444
e: phil.obrien@concisegroup.com
w: www.concisegroup.com

D2i Systems Ltd
41-43 HAMILTON SQUARE, WIRRAL, BIRKENHEAD
Merseyside CH41 5BP 0151 6495150
e: info@d2isystems.com
w: www.d2isystems.com

Delegate Select Ltd
SUITE B, 19-23 HIGH STREET, BISHOPS WALK HOUSE, HARROW
Middlesex HA5 5PJ..0208 429 7340
e: info@delegateselect.com
w: www.delegateselect.com

Event Geeks
UNIT G171, CHERWELL BUSINESS VILLAGE, SOUTHAM ROAD, BANBURY
Oxfordshire OX16 2SP. 0203 328 4960
e: info@eventgeeks.co.uk
w: www.eventgeeks.co.uk

Eventbookings.com
BOHUNT MANOR, PORTSMOUTH ROAD, LIPHOOK
GU30 7DL..01428 721 000
e: solutions@eventbookings.com
w: www.eventbookings.com

Eventsforce Solutions Ltd
THE WENLOCK, 50-52 WHARF ROAD, LONDON
Greater London N1 7EU 0207 785 7040
e: info@eventsforce.com
w: www.eventsforce.com

Green 4 Solutions
16-17 MIDLAND COURT, CENTRAL PARK, LUTTERWORTH
Leicestershire LE17 4PN......................................0845 508 8149
e: beth@green4solutions.com
w: www.green4solutions.com

Guestminder
64 ALMA ROAD, CLIFTON
BS8 2DJ 0870 385 1016
e: mick@riotevents.co.uk
w: www.guestminder.co.uk

Guidebook
54 MARSHALL ST. , LONDON
W1F 9BH 020 3575 1095
e: sales.uk@guidebook.com
w: https://guidebook.com/gb/event-apps/

Insphire Ltd
5 CHASE PARK, DALESIDE ROAD, NOTTINGHAM
Nottinghamshire NG2 4GT 0115 979 3377
e: sales@insphire.com
w: www.insphire.com

Iturus Limited
ST HELEN'S HOUSE KING STREET, DERBY
DE1 3EE .... 07884311583 /0203691107
e: richard.brade@iturus.net
w: www.iturus.net

Kent House
ONEUSTONSQ, 40 MELTON STREET, LONDON
NW1 2FD 0203 129 4896
e: london@kenthouse.com
w: www.kenthouse.com

Logicom Sound & Vision
1 PORTLAND DRIVE, WILLEN, MILTON KEYNES
Buckinghamshire MK15 9JW 01908 663848
e: admin@logicom.com
w: www.logicom.com

Mcs Rental Software
ASHWOOD, GROVE BUSINESS PARK, WHITE WALTHAM
Berkshire SL6 3LW 01628 828000
e: moreinfo@mcs.co.uk
w: www.mcs.co.uk

Navigator Systems Ltd
13A CHURCH FARM BUSINESS PARK, CORSTON, BATH
Somerset BA2 9AP..0207 183 0011
e: sales@navigator.co.uk
w: www.navigator.co.uk

Orion Software
5950 CÔTE-DES-NEIGES, SUITE 475, MONTREAL
H3S 1Z8 ....(514) 484-9661 / 1-877 755-212
e: info@orion-soft.com
w: www.orion-soft.com

S

Paam

UNIT 1, MIDDLE YARD, HOME FARM ROAD, ELVETHAM, HOOK
Hampshire RG27 8AW...0845 355 0604
e: info@paamapplication.co.uk
w: www.paamapplication.co.uk

PAULEY

BLETCHLEY LEYS FARM , WHADDON ROAD, MILTON KEYNES
Buckinghamshire MK17 0EG..................................01908 522532
e: info@pauley.co.uk
w: www.pauley.co.uk

Simpli-Fi Ltd

UNIT 11, MOUNT ROAD, FELTHAM,
Middlesex TW13 6AR.................................+44 (0) 8456 123 008
e: info@simpli-fi.co.uk
w: www.simpli-fi.co.uk

Software Partners

OAK TREE HOUSE, STATION ROAD, CLAVERDON
Warwickshire CV35 8PE...01926 842998
e: sales@software-partners.co.uk
w: www.software-partners.co.uk

Somcom Ltd

21 A STUART HOUSE, CROMWELL BUSINESS PARK, BANBURY
ROAD, CHIPPING NORTON
Oxfordshire OX7 5SR 01608 643302
e: sales@somcom.co.uk
w: www.somcom.co.uk

Symphony Event Management Software

BALGRAVIER HOUSE, 115 ROCKINGHAM STREET, SHEFFIELD
South Yorkshire S1 4EB..0114 2794990
e: info@symphonyem.co.uk
w: www.symphonyem.co.uk

Tickets.com Ltd

THE MEZZANINE, CBX2 WEST, 380 MIDSUMMER BOULEVARD,
MILTON KEYNES
Buckinghamshire MK9 2EA......................011-44-1908-232-404
e: sales@tickets.com
w: www.tickets.com

Whygo Video Conferencing

1010 CAMBOURNE BUSINESS PARK, CAMBOURNE, CAMBRIDGE
Cambridgeshire CB23 6DP.....................................020 7183 0460
e: bookings@whygo.eu
w: www.whygo.net

Ya-Ya Regie

13 BODMIN HILL, LOSTWITHIEL, CORNWALL
PL22 0AH 0207 989 2424
e: info@ya-yaregie.com
w: www.ya-yaregie.com

Solicitors / Legal Services

Azule Finance

2-4 HIGH STREET , DATCHET
SL3 9EA..01753 580500
e: info@azule.co.uk
w: www.azule.co.uk

David Wineman Solicitors

101 WIGMORE STREET, LONDON
Greater London W1U 1FA 020 7408 8888
e: info@dwfmbeckman.com
w: www.dwfmbeckman.com

Graham & Rosen Solicitors

8 PARLIAMENT STREET, HULL
HU1 2BB..1482323123
e: flh@graham-rosen.co.uk
w: www.graham-rosen.co.uk/

Howat Avraam LLP

154-160 FLEET STREET, LONDON
EC4A 2DQ...020 78849700
e: info@hasolicitors.co.uk
w: www.howatavraamsolicitors.co.uk

Humphreys & Co

14 KING STREET, BRISTOL
Bristol BS1 4EF..0117 929 2662
e: lawyers@humphreys.co.uk
w: www.humphreys.co.uk

Incorporated Society Of Musicians

4-5 INVERNESS MEWS, LONDON
Greater London W2 3JQ.......................................020 7221 3499
e: membership@ism.org
w: www.ism.org

Irwin Mitchell

RIVERSIDE EAST, 2 MILLSANDS, SHEFFIELD
S3 8DT 0870 1500 100
e: enquiries@irwinmitchell.com
w: www.irwinmitchell.com

Keep It Civil Mediation

37 PARK STREET, LEAMINGTON SPA
CV32 4QN..01926 882255
e: info@keepitcivil.co.uk
w: www.keepitcivil.co.uk

Kidd Rapinet Solicitors

33 QUEEN STREET, MAIDENHEAD
Berkshire SL6 1ND 01628 436015
e: kcoyle@kiddrapinet.co.uk
w: www.kiddrapinet.co.uk

Mathias Gentle Page Hassan LLP

247 TOTTENHAM COURT ROAD, 4TH FLOOR , LONDON
Greater London W1T 7QX 020 7631 1811
e: enquiries@mgph-legal.com
w: www.mgph-legal.com

S

SR Consultancy
102 PEREGRINE DRIVE , SITTINGBOURNE , KENT
ME10 4UP.. 07588727275 /
01795 55759
e: enquiries@srconsultant.co.uk
w: www.srconsultant.co.uk

Taylor Wessing Llp
5 NEW STREET SQUARE, LONDON
Greater London EC4A 3TW.....................................020 7300 7000
e: london@taylorwessing.com
w: www.taylorwessing.com

The Chartered Institute of Legal Executives
KEMPSTON MANOR, KEMPSTON, BEDFORD
Bedfordshire MK42 7AB...01234 841000
e: info@cilex.org.uk
w: www.cilex.org.uk

Turner Parkinson
HOLLINS CHAMBERS, 64A BRIDGE STREET, MANCHESTER
Greater Manchester M3 3BA.................................0161 833 1212
e: tp@tp.co.uk
w: www.tp.co.uk

Sound

ENTEC Limited
UNIT 13 TIMS BOATYARD, TIMSWAY, STAINS
Middlesex TW18 3JY 2089 424 004
e: barbara@entec-soundandlight.com
w: www.entecaccess.co.uk

Entec Sound & Light
517 Yeading Lane
Northolt, Middlesex
UB5 6LN

t: 020 8842 4004
f: 020 8842 3310
e: sales@entecLIVE.com

Entec is the UK's longest established sound & lighting company
covering a huge diversity of events over the years. Convert tours,
live events, corporate shows, exhibitions, television, threatres, open
air festivals, garden parties - you name it - we can do it!

www.entecLIVE.com

Sound / PA

1159 Productions Ltd
2 FALCON WAY, CHELMSFORD
Essex CM2 8AY 01245 227700
e: sales@1159productions.com
w: www.1159productions.com

3d Productions Ltd
UNIT 8, LOTHERTON WAY GARFORTH, LEEDS
West Yorkshire LS25 2JY 0113 236 3700
e: info@3dproductions.co.uk
w: www.3dproductions.co.uk

A.c. Entertainment Technologies Ltd.
CENTAURI HOUSE, HILLBOTTOM ROAD, HIGH WYCOMBE
Buckinghamshire HP12 4HQ 01494 446000
e: sales@ac-et.com
w: www.ac-et.com

A1 Pro Entertainments
153 LONDON ROAD, EWELL
KT17 2BT .... 020 8393 3616 / 0800 0187278
e: info@a1proents.com
w: www.a1proents.com

Absolute Audio Visual Solutions
NEW CAMBRIDGE HOUSE, LITLINGTON
Cambridgeshire SG8 0SS.....................................01763 852222
e: info@absoluteavs.co.uk
w: www.absoluteavs.co.uk

Access Audio Ltd
WINTONFIELD HOUSE, NEW WINTON
East Lothian EH33 2NN...0131663 0777
e: info@accessaudio.co.uk
w: www.accessaudio.co.uk

Ace Vintage Systems
GUYS CLIFFE FARMHOUSE, WARWICK
West Midlands CV34 5YD.......................................07711 887994
e: alex@acevintagesystems.co.uk
w: acevintagesystems.co.uk

Active Visual Supplies Ltd
5 HIGH STREET, WELLINGTON, TELFORD
Shropshire TF1 1JW..0800 5421726
e: sales@activeuk.com
w: www.activevisuals.co.uk

Adam Hall Ltd
THE SEEDBED BUSINESS CENTRE, VANGUARD WAY,
SHOEBURYNESS
SS3 9QY 01702 613922
e: mail@adamhall.co.uk
w: www.adamhall.com

Adlib Audio Limited
ADLIB HOUSE, FLEMING ROAD, SPEKE, LIVERPOOL
Merseyside L24 9LS 0151 486 2214
e: info@adlibsolutions.co.uk
w: www.adlib.co.uk

Allen & Heath Limited
KERNICK IND EST, PENRYN
Cornwall TR10 9LU 01326 372070
e: sales@allen-heath.com
w: www.allen-heath.com

Ampetronic Ltd
UNIT 2, TRENTSIDE BUSINESS VILLAGE, FARNDON ROAD, NEWARK
Nottinghamshire NG24 4XB 01636 610062
e: sales@ampetronic.com
w: www.ampetronic.com

Andrew Sound
4 ROBINSON ROAD, BEDWORTH
Warwickshire CV12 0EL...024 7636 4235
e: info@andrewphotographic.co.uk
w: www.andrewsound.co.uk

Anything Audio
32 BARKSTON HOUSE, CROYDON ST, LEEDS
West Yorkshire LS11 9RT 0113 322 5001
e: info@anythingaudio.co.uk
w: www.anythingaudio.co.uk

Arc Electronics
352 PORTSWOOD ROAD, PORTSWOOD, SOUTHAMPTON
Hampshire SO17 3SB 023 8058 4642
e: info@arcelectronics.co.uk
w: www.arcelectronics.co.uk

Arena Entertainment Systems
....07715 887 457
e: arenainfo1@aol.com
w: www.arenaentertainmentsystems.com

Aspen Media Ltd
11 WINGBURY COURTYARD, WINGRAVE, AYLESBURY
Buckinghamshire HP22 4LW 01296 681313
e: webenquiry@aspen-media.com
w: www.aspen-media.com

Audient Ltd
ASPECT HOUSE, HERRIARD
Hampshire RG25 2PN 01256 381944
e: sales@audient.co.uk
w: www.audient.com

Audio Developments Ltd
23 PORTLAND ROAD, WALSALL
West Midlands WS9 8NS.......................................01922 457007
e: sales@audio.co.uk
w: www.audio.co.uk

Audio Gold
308 - 310 PARK ROAD, LONDON
Greater London N8 8LA...020 8341 9007
e: info@audiogold.co.uk
w: www.audiogold.co.uk

Audio Source Ltd
31 MONGLEATH AVENUE, FALMOUTH
Cornwall TR11 4PP 07971 607172
....07867 525016 / 01326 3115
e: hire@audio-source.co.uk
w: www.audio-source.co.uk

Audio Visual Unit Ltd
243 FELIXSTOWE ROAD, IPSWICH
Suffolk IP3 9BN..01473 705205
e: info@avunit.com
w: www.avunit.com

Audiohire
80 SIDNEY RD, WALTON-ON-THAMES, LONDON
Greater London KT12 2LX 020 8960 4466
e: admin@audiohire.co.uk
w: www.audiohire.co.uk

Audiotech Services Ltd
UNIT 18 MIDDLEWOODS WAY , WHARNCLIFFE BUSINESS PARK, CARLTON, BARNSLEY
South Yorkshire S71 3HR 01226 208327
e: rachael@audiotechuk.com
w: www.audiotechuk.com

Audiowall Systems Limited
2/3 BASSETT COURT, BROAD STREET, NEWPORT PAGNELL
Buckinghamshire MK16 0JN......01908 951 470 / 01908 615 365
e: info@audiowall.co.uk
w: www.audiowall.co.uk

Autograph Sound Recording Ltd
2 SPRING PLACE , LONDON
Greater London NW5 3BA 020 7485 4515
e: studio@autograph.co.uk
w: www.autograph.co.uk

AV Department Limited
UNIT 83, EAST WAY,, HILLEND INDUSTRIAL PARK, DALGETY BAY
Fife KY11 9JF 01383 825 709
e: info@avdept.co.uk
w: www.avdept.co.uk

AV Direct CC
70 NARUNA CRESCENT, SOUTHFIELD,
CAPE TOWN, SOUTH AFRICA. 7800.................+27 021 706 6730
e: cpt@avdirect.co.za
w: www.avdirect.co.za

AV Matrix
UNIT 120, STREET 7, THORP ARCH TRADING ESTATE, WEMBLEY, LONDON. Greater London LS23 7FL.....0800 1950 600
e: jen@av-matrix.com
w: www.av-matrix.com

Avenue Audio
BRIDGE ROAD, PARK GATE, SOUTHAMPTON
Hampshire SO31 7GD 08454 634381
e: mail@avenueaudio.co.uk
w: www.avenueaudio.co.uk

AVM Impact
EUROPE HOUSE, 170 WINDMILL ROAD WEST, SUNBURY ON THAMES
Middlesex TW16 7HB...0845 2626 200
e: info@avmi.com
w: www.avmi.com

S

B&h Sound Services Ltd
UNIT 3, HADDONBROOK, FALLODAN ROAD, ORTON SOUTHGATE, PETERBOROUGH
Cambridgeshire PE2 6YX 01733 371250
e: sound@bhsound.co.uk
w: www.bhsound.co.uk

Backstage Supplies
1 EMPEROR WAY, EXETER BUSINESS PARK, EXETER
Devon EX1 3QS...01392 314042
e: mail@backstagesupplies.co.uk
w: www.backstagesupplies.co.uk

Backwell PA Hire
.... 07958 516604 / 07860 101512
e: enquiries@backwellpa.co.uk
w: www.backwellpa.co.uk

Bassline Productions
19 OSIERS RD, LONDON
Greater London SW18...0203 609 1230
e: info@basslineproductions.co.uk
w: www.basslineproductions.co.uk

Batmink Ltd
BECKERY ROAD, GLASTONBURY
Somerset BA6 9NX 01458 833186
e: info@batmink.co.uk
w: www.batmink.co.uk

BAV (Boath Audio Visual)
42 NEW ENGLAND ROAD, BRIGHTON
East Sussex BN1 4GG 01273 600678
e: mail@boathaudiovisual.co.uk
w: www.boathaudiovisual.co.uk

Bell Theatre Services Ltd
9B CHESTER ROAD, BOREHAMWOOD
Hertfordshire WD6 1LT 020 8238 6000
e: admin@bell-theatre.com
w: www.bell-theatre.com

BES Systems Ltd
155A SOUTH LIBERTY LANE, ASHTON VALE, BRISTOL
Bristol BS3 2TL......................... 0845 224 5967 / 07812 111 646
e: info@b-e-s.co.uk
w: www.bes-systems.co.uk

Big-TV (UK) Ltd
HUDSON HOUSE, THE HUDSON, WYKE, BRADFORD
Yorkshire BD12 8HZ...01274 604 309
e: info@big-tv.co.uk
w: www.big-tv.co.uk

Black Box Pro Audio
THE COURTYARD, 22 HAYBURN STREET, GLASGOW
Glasgow G11 6DG...0141 404 5719
e: info@blackboxproaudio.com
w: www.blackboxproaudio.com

Blacka Acoustics Ltd
UNIT 5, HADFIELD HOUSE, GORDON STREET, LANCASHIRE HILL, STOCKPORT
Greater Manchester SK4 1RR..............................0161 477 9700
e: info@blackaacoustics.co.uk
w: www.blackaacoustics.co.uk

Blackjack Event Co
ALPHA 6, , MASTERLORD OFFICE VILLAGE WEST ROAD, IPSWICH
Suffolk IP3 9SX...08448 400 123
e: info@blackjackevents.co.uk
w: www.blackjackuk.co.uk

Blue Box Ltd
4 SMITH'S BARN FARM, COMPTONS LANE, HORSHAM
Sussex RH13 5NN...07785 730 442
e: mark@bluebox-london.com
w: www.bluebox-london.com

Blueboxx Creative Ltd
UNIT 5 ELSTREE FILM STUDIOS, SHENLEY ROAD, BOREHAMWOOD. Hertfordshire WD6 1JG..............0845 652 2451
e: hire@blueboxx.co.uk
w: www.blueboxx.co.uk

Bonza Sound Sales Ltd
90B HIGH STREET, BRACKLEY
Northamptonshire NN13 7DR...............................01280 843917
e: mark@bonza.co.uk
w: www.bonza.co.uk

Brahler ICS UK Ltd
UNIT 2, THE BUSINESS CENTRE, CHURCH END, CAMBRIDGE
Cambridgeshire CB1 3LB.......................................01223 411601
e: rentals@brahler.co.uk
w: www.brahler.co.uk

Brighton Sound System
BILLY WOOD LTD TA BRIGHTON SOUND SYSTEM, UNIT 2, VICTORIA GROVE, HOVE
East Sussex BN3 2LJ...1273746506
e: info@brightonsoundsystem.co.uk
w: www.brightonsoundsystem.co.uk

Brighton Soundsystem
UNIT 2, VICTORIA GROVE, HOVE
East Sussex BN3 2LJ...01273 746 506
e: info@brightonsoundsystem.co.uk
w: www.brightonsoundsystem.co.uk

Britannia Row Productions Ltd
104 THE GREEN, TWICKENHAM, LONDON
Greater London TW2 5AG.....................................020 8893 4997
e: info@britanniarow.com
w: www.britanniarow.com

Capital Sound Hire Ltd
ABACUS HOUSE, 60 WEIR ROAD, LONDON
Greater London SW19 8UG 020 8944 6777
e: info@capital-sound.co.uk
w: www.capital-sound.co.uk

S

CB Sound Video Light Ltd
UNIT 30 GREENWAY BUSINESS CENTRE, HARLOW BUSINESS PARK, HARLOW
Essex CM19 5QE 01279 260 160
e: info@cbsvl.co.uk
w: www.cbsvl.co.uk

Celestion Ltd
CLAYDON BUSINESS PARK, GREAT BLAKENHAM, IPSWICH
SUFF IP6 0NL...01473 835 300
e: info@celestion.com
w: www.celestion.com

Central Theatre Supplies
1186 STRATFORD ROAD, HALL GREEN, BIRMINGHAM
West Midlands B28 8AB.......................................0121 778 6400
e: john@centraltheatresupplies.co.uk
w: www.centraltheatresupplies.co.uk

Centre Stage
23 IRON WORKS, 58 DACE ROAD, LONDON
Greater London E3 2NX...01442 255170
e: hire@centrestage.org.uk
w: www.centrestage.org.uk

Channel 16
TOWER BRIDGE BUSINESS COMPLEX, LONDON
Greater London S16 4DG .... 07836 693833 / 07595 893020
e: forshow@channel-16.co.uk
w: www.channel-16.co.uk

Chaps Production Co
UNIT 2, 33 BANSTEAD ROAD , CATERHAM-ON-THE-HILL
Surrey CR3 5TS 01883 346789
e: hires@chapsproductionco.com
w: www.chapsproductionco.com

Chaps-PA
78 BUTE ROAD, WALLINGTON
 SM6 8AB 07835 481538
e: Tomwhite183@mac.com
w: www.chaps-pa.co.uk

Chromatec
UNIT 32, BRAMBLES ENTERPRISE CENTRE, WATERBERRY DRIVE, WATERLOOVILLE
Hampshire PO7 7TH 02392 230 085
e: info@chromatec.com
w: www.chromatec.com

Clear and Loud
....0191 64 54 645
e: bookings@clearandloudpahire.co.uk
w: www.clearandloudpahire.co.uk

CMF Event Hire
....0843 289 2798
e: cfmeventhire@aol.com
w: www.cfmeventhire.co.uk

Coast To Coast Concert Productions Ltd.
3, LANE TOP, DENHOLME, BRADFORD
West Yorkshire BD13 4LE......................................01274 835558
e: info@ctc-productions.co.uk
w: www.ctc-productions.co.uk

Complete Production Services Group
UNIT 14, AIRFIELD ROAD, CHRISTCHURCH
Dorset BH23 3TG..01202 572000
e: enquiries@cpsgroup.co.uk
w: www.cpsgroup.co.uk

Concert Sound Clairglobal Ltd
UNIT C, PARK AVENUE INDUSTRIAL ESTATE, SUNDON PARK ROAD, LUTON
 LU3 3BP 01582 565855
e: andywalker@clairglobal.com
w: www.clairglobal.com

Creative Lighting & Sound (CLS)
UNIT 6, SPIRES BUSINESS CENTRE, MUGIMOSS RD , ABERDEEN
Aberdeen AB21 9NY..01224 683 111
e: info@clsaberdeen.co.uk
w: www.clsaberdeen.co.uk

Cricklewood Electronics
40-42 CRICKLEWOOD BROADWAY, LONDON
Greater London NW2 3ET................................ 020 8450 0995 //
020 84520161

e: accounts@cricklewoodelectronics.com
w: www.cricklewoodelectronics.com

Crucial FX
UNIT 4, WATERS BUSINESS PARK, WATERS ROAD, ELLESMERE PORT
Cheshire CH65 4FF...020 3199 6355
e: info@crucial-fx.com
w: www.crucial-fx.com

D&B Audiotechnik Gmbh
NAILSWORTH MILLS ESTATE, AVENING ROAD, NAILSWORTH, STROUD
 GL6 0BS 01453 835884
e: info.gb@dbaudio.com

DACS Ltd
UNIT A19, STONEHILLS, SHIELDS ROAD, PELAW, GATESHEAD
 NE10 0HW..0191 438 2500
e: sales@dacs-audio.com
w: www.dacs-audio.com

Dan Productions
.... 07824 558 858 / 01772 451350
e: dan@danproductions.co.uk
w: www.danproductions.co.uk

Dance2 Sound & Light Hire
107 WOODBRIDGE ROAD, GUILDFORD
Surrey GU1 4PY 01483 451 002
e: in2dance2@hotmail.com
w: www.dance2.co.uk

S

DataRhyme - PA System Hire
CATFORD, LONDON
Greater London SE6 .... 0203 468 3204
e: info@datarhyme.com
w: www.datarhyme.com

DBS Solutions
73 MANCHESTER RD, WOOLSTON, WARRINGTON
Cheshire WA1 4AE 0845 388 0321
e: info@dbs-solutions.co.uk
w: www.dbs-solutions.co.uk

DC3 Productions Ltd
37 BRAMBLE ROAD, HATFIELD
AL10 9RZ.................................. 020 8123 8765 / 07737 535886
e: dan@dc3productions.co.uk
w: www.dc3productions.co.uk

Definition Audio Visual
3D HARROGATE ROAD, RAWDON, LEEDS
West Yorkshire LS19 6HW .... 07548 347594 / 08435 235470
e: mark@definitionaudiovisual.co.uk
w: www.definitionaudiovisual.co.uk

Dimension Audio
UNITS 2-4, MANOR GATE MANOR ROYAL, CRAWLEY
West Sussex RH10 9SX..01293 582005
e: info@dimension.co.uk
w: www.dimension.co.uk

DJ and Studio
19 ERLESMERE GARDENS, EALING, LONDON
Greater London W13 9TZ 020 8840 8480
e: enquiries@djandstudio.co.uk
w: www.djandstudio.co.uk

DM Audio Ltd
UNIT 7/1 NEWHAILES INDUSTRIAL ESTATE, NEWHAILES ROAD,
EDINBURGH
Edinburgh EH21 6SY 0131 665 5615
e: hire@dmaudio.co.uk
w: www.dmaudio.co.uk

Dynamic Production Solutions
UNIT 13E, BARTON BUSINESS PARK, NEW DOVER ROAD,
CANTERBURY
Kent CT1 3AA 01227 656 599
e: info@dynamicproductionsolutions.co.uk
w: www.dynamicproductionsolutions.co

Earley Creative
2 LISCOMBE WEST, LISCOMBE PARK, SOULBURY,
LEIGHTON BUZZARD,
Bedfordshire LU7 0JL 0333 0556626
e: info@earleycreative.com
w: www.earleycreative.com

Easirent Limited
UNIT B3- BAESPOINT BUSINESS & INNOVATION CENTRE, 110
BUTTERFIELD, GREAT MARLINGS, LUTON. Bedfordshire LU2 8DL
.... +44 (0)845 845 8585 / +44 (0)1582 43377
e: sales@firstrental.co.uk
w: www.firstrental.co.uk/

Elation DJs Ltd
7 RINGHAY ROAD, BRADFORD
West Yorkshire BD4 0TZ .... 01274 800 460 / 07811 200 293
e: info@elationdjs.co.uk
w: www.elationdjs.co.uk

Emphasis Event Production Ltd
UNIT 14, BELGRAVE INDUSTRIAL ESTATE, SOUTHAMPTON
Hampshire SO17 3EA...023 8055 0557
e: enquiries@emphasiseventproduction.co.uk
w: www.prestech.co.uk

Encore Group Ltd
UNIT 8, 19 WADSWORTH ROAD, PERIVALE, LONDON
Greater London UB6 7LF............. 020 8991 2612 / 07733051546
e: john@encorepa.co.uk
w: www.encorepa.co.uk

Enlightened Lighting Ltd
26-28 EMERY ROAD, BRISLINGTON
Bristol BS4 5PF..01179 727 123
e: info@enlx.co.uk
w: www.enlightenedlighting.co.uk

Entec Sound & Light
517 YEADING LANE, NORTHOLT
Middlesex UB5 6LN 020 8842 4004
e: sales@entecLIVE.com
w: www.enteclive.com/

Entertainment Toolbox Ltd
WOLVERHAMPTON BUSINESS AIRPORT, UNIT 23B, BOBBINGTON,
STOURBRIDGE
West Midlands DY7 5DY..01384 221083
e: info@etx-ltd.com
w: www.etx-ltd.com

EPS Hire
34 STANLEY DRIVE, HATFIELD
Hertfordshire AL10 8XX..07973 721329
e: gary@epshire.com
w: www.epshire.com

ESS (Entertainment Sound Specialists)
UNIT 2 MAUN CLOSE, HERMITAGE LANE, MANSFIELD
Nottinghamshire NG18 5GY 01623 647291
e: richardmjohn@me.com
w: www.esspahire.co.uk

ETASound
BURNT MEADOW HOUSE, NORTH MOONS MOAT, REDDITCH
Worcestershire B98 9PA 01527 528822
e: enquiries@sseaudio.com
w: www.sseaudiogroup.com

Eurohire Sound & Light
UNIT 6, BESSEMER PARK, BESSEMER ROAD, BASINGSTOKE
Hampshire RG21 3NB 01256 461 234
e: jools@eurohiresoundandhire.co.uk
w: www.eurohiresoundandlight.co.uk

Event and Production Hire
UNITS 2 & 3 IVY HOUSE FARM , GRANGE ROAD ,
SOLIHULL, BIRMINGHAM
West Midlands B94 6PR..01564 770 783
e: warren@eaph.co.uk
w: www.eventproductionhire.com

Event Hire Wales
....07494 169599
e: info@eventhire.wales
w: www.eventhire.wales

Fenwick Mobile Exhibitions Ltd
FENWICK BY-PASS, FENWICK
Ayrshire KA3 6AW...01560 600271
e: enquiries@fmx-ltd.com
w: www.fmx-ltd.com

Fexx Productions Ltd
37 CHERRY TREE STREET, ELSECAR
 S74 8DG..0844 664 6574
e: enqs@fexx.co.uk
w: www.fexx.co.uk

Fiend Productions Ltd
46A CHARGROVE ROAD, TOTTENHAM, LONDON
Greater London N17 0JD 0800 148 8269
e: info@fiend-productions.com
w: www.fiend-productions.com

First Network Ltd
ROWDELL ROAD, NORTHOLT
Middlesex UB5 5QR 020 8842 1222
e: info@first-network.com
w: www.first-network.com

Flare Audio
UNIT 8 CHARTWELL BUSINESS CENTRE, 42 CHARTWELL RD,
LANCING
West Sussex BN15 8FB..01903 761000
e: info@flareaudio.com
w: www.flareaudio.com

Flipside
ALDERNEY WORKS, TIERNEY ROAD, LONDON
Greater London SW2 4QH 02086 710 290
e: hire@flipside-soundsystem.co.uk
w: www.flipside-soundsystem.co.uk

Focus 21 Hire & Events
123-127 DEEPCUT BRIDGE ROAD, DEEPCUT, CAMBERLEY
Surrey GU16 6SD..08452 707453
e: F21Sales@focus21.co.uk
w: www.focus21.co.uk

Fresh Events UK
UNIT D WESLAKE INDUSTRIAL PARK, RYE HARBOUR ROAD, RYE
East Sussex TN31 7TE 07919 512 608
e: info@fresheventsuk.com
w: www.fresheventsuk.com

Future Media Systems Limited
UNIT 2, GRANGE RD INDUSTRIAL ESTATE, CHIRSTCHURCH
Dorset BH23 4JD 01425 270511
e: webenquiries@futuremediasystems.co.uk
w: www.futuremediasystems.co.uk

FX Productions
UNIT 11D , TANFIELD LEA NORTH INDUSTRIAL ESTATE, STANLEY
Durham DH9 9UU .... 01207 282424 / 07596 728358
e: info@fx-productions.org
w: www.fx-productions.org

Gab Audio Engineers
BARBRETHAN, KIRKMICHAEL, MAYBOLE
Ayrshire KA19 7PS..01655 740330
e: jimbryan@gab-audio.co.uk
w: www.gab-audio.co.uk

Gain Audio
47 GORSEY LANE , CLOCK FACE , ST HELENS
WA9 4QS .... 08438861162 / 07896045416
e: justgainaudio@gmail.com
w: www.gainaudio.co.uk/

Gb Audio
UNIT D, 51 BRUNSWICK ROAD, EDINBURGH
Edinburgh EH7 5PD 0131 661 0022
e: sales@gbaudio.co.uk
w: www.gbaudio.co.uk

Globalhire.com
27 NEWTONS WAY, HITCHIN
 SG4 9JR 0845 5194531
e: info@globalhire.com
w: www.globalhire.com

GPS Lighting Ltd
UNIT 6 - FEN PLACE FARM, EAST STREET, TURNERS HILL
West Sussex RH10 4QA 020 8123 0409
e: enquiries@gpslighting.com
w: www.gpslighting.com

Gradav Hire and Sales Ltd
SHENLEY ROAD , BOREHAMWOOD
Hertfordshire WD6 1JG 020 8324 2100
e: office@gradav.co.uk
w: www.gradav.co.uk

H-squared Electronics
CONIFER HOUSE, OLD BRIDGE WAY, SHEFFORD
Bedfordshire SG17 5HQ 01462 851 155
e: sales@h-squared.co.uk
w: www.h-squared.co.uk

S

Halo Lighting
98-124 BREWERY ROAD, LONDON
Greater London N7 9PG 0207 607 4444
e: info@halo.co.uk
w: www.halo.co.uk

Hamble Audio & Video Studios
39 MITCHELL POINT, ENSIGN WAY, HMABLE, SOUTHAMPTON
Hampshire SO31 4RF..023 8044 8822
e: biz@focusbiz.co.uk
w: www.focusbiz.co.uk

Hamlet Video International Ltd
MAPLE HOUSE, 11 CORINIUM BUSINESS CENTRE, RAANS ROAD,
AMERSHAM
Buckinghamshire HP6 6FB............ 0500 625 525 / 1494 723 237
e: enquiry@hamlet.co.uk
w: www.hamlet.co.uk

Hans Kolberg UK
86-90 PAUL STREET, LONDON
EC2A 4NE 020 8123 7095
e: enquiry@hans-kolberg.co.uk
w: www.hans-kolberg.co.uk

Hawthorns
CROWN BUSINESS PARK, OLD DALBY
Leicestershire LE14 3NQ..01664 821111
e: info@hawthorn.biz
w: www.hawthorn.biz

Heathrow Sound Hire
UNITS 9 & 10- POD BUSINESS CENTRE, HARRIS WAY,
SUNBURY ON THAMES
Surrey TW16 7EW........................ 0208 4322310 / 07834520290
e: enquiries@heathrowsoundhire.co.uk
w: www.heathrowsoundhire.co.uk

Hi-Lights
18E WHITEROSE WAY, FOLLINGSBY PARK, GATESHEAD
Tyne and Wear NE10 8YX.......................................0191 495 0608
e: martin@hi-lights.tv
w: www.hi-lights.tv

High Lite Touring
MITROVICKA 359/45, OSTRAVA - NOVA BELA
72400...00420 596 731 034
e: info@highlite.cz
w: www.highlite.cz

Hire for Parties Ltd
UNIT C7, J31 PARK, WEST THURROCK
Essex RM20 3XD 07999 488 334
e: info@hireforparties.co.uk
w: www.hireforparties.co.uk

Hire Manager
2 SWANSTONS ROAD, GREAT YARMOUTH
NR30 3NQ 01493 845577
e: info@paddyhall.com
w: www.paddyhall.com

HPSS Ltd
UNIT 5 DAIRYCOATES INDUSTRIAL ESTATE, WHILTSHIRE RD, HULL
East Yorkshire HU4 6PA...01482 221 810
e: webmail@hpss.co.uk
w: www.hpss.co.uk

Ideal Event Services
310 UNTHANK ROAD, NORWICH
Norfolk NR4 7QD 01603 280176
e: hello@idealeventservices.co.uk
w: www.idealeventservices.co.uk

Inhouse Venue Technical Management (pty) Ltd
PO BOX 905, BELLVILLE, CAPE TOWN
7535 I...+27 (0)86 123 7890
e: info@inhousevtm.com
w: www.inhousevtm.com

Inovaplus Limited
....020 3326 8505
e: info@inovaplus.com
w: www.inovaplus.com

Inta Sound PA
UNIT 15 , HIGH GROVE FARM IND EST, PINVIN, PERSHORE
Worcestershire WR10 2LF......................................01905 841591
e: sales@intasoundpa.co.uk
w: www.intasoundpa.co.uk

Intrak
UNIT 5B, CLIFTON BUSINESS PARK,
PRESTON NEW ROAD, CLIFTON
Lancashire PR4 0XQ 01772 633697
e: info@intrak.co.uk
w: www.intraksoundandlight.co.uk

John Henry's Ltd
16-24 BREWERY ROAD, LONDON
Greater London N7 9NH.......................................020 7609 9181
e: info@johnhenrys.com
w: www.johnhenrys.com

John Hornby Skewes & Co Ltd
SALEM HOUSE, PARKINSON APPROACH, GARFORTH, LEEDS
West Yorkshire LS25 2HR......................................0113 286 5381
e: webinfo@jhs.co.uk
w: www.jhs.co.uk

JSS Audio
UNIT 30B, THE RAYLOR CENTRE, JAMES STREET, YORK
North Yorkshire YO10 3DW......... 01904 431 050 / 07768 064703
e: jem@jssaudio.co.uk
w: www.jssaudio.co.uk

Just Lite Productions
UNIT 31 FINGLAS BUSINESS CENTRE, JAMESTOWN ROAD,
FINGLAS, DUBLIN 11
.... + 353 1 806 8333
e: info@justlite.com
w: justlite.com

S

Kave Theatre Services
UNITS 1 & 2, 55, VICTORIA ROAD, BURGESS HILL
RH15 9LH...01444 245500
e: sales@kave.co.uk
w: www.kave.co.uk

KC Lighting
123 PRIORWAY AVENUE, BORROWASH, DERBY
DE72 3HY .... 01332 674589 / 07860 669323
e: kev@kclighting.co.uk
w: www.kclighting.co.uk

KSG Ltd
117 MERRYLEE ROAD, GLASGOW
G43 2RB 0778 6342 940
e: info@ksg-ltd.co.uk
w: www.ksg-ltd.co.uk

LA Audio
ASPECT HOUSE, HERRIARD
Hampshire RG25 2PN 01256 381944
e: info@laaudio.co.uk
w: www.laaudio.com

Lamphouse Production Ltd
FLINTSTONES FARM, BUNKERS HILL, RIDLEY
Kent TN15 7EY 1474247670
e: hire@lamphouse.uk.com
w: www.lamphouse.uk.com

Laser Lighting & Sound
THE OLD CHAPEL, MANNINGTREE ROAD, IPSWICH
Suffolk IP9 2TA 01473 328897
e: info@laserlighting.co.uk
w: www.laserlighting.co.uk

Leisure Light and Sound (lls)
11 TELFORD ROAD, FERNDOWN IND EST, WIMBOURNE
BH21 7QP.................................. 0786 017 9059 / 01985844439
e: info@lls-online.net
w: www.lls-online.net

Leisuretec Distribution Ltd
UNIT L3, CHERRYCOURT WAY, STANBRIDGE ROAD,
LEIGHTON BUZZARD
LU7 4UH 01525 850085
e: sales@leisuretec.co.uk
Light The Way
UNIT 7 CAVENDISH COURT MILL, WEST STREET, BRADFORD
BD11 1DA...01422 250 819
e: hire@lighttheway.co.uk
w: www.lighttheway.co.uk

Lightfactor Sales
20 GREENHILL CRESCENT, WATFORD BUSINESS PARK,
GREENFORD, WATFORD
Hertfordshire WD18 8JA 01923 495495
e: performance@coopercontrols.co.uk
w: www.lightfactor.co.uk

Lightmedia Displays Ltd
HUDDLESTON GRANGE, NEWTHORPE, SOUTH MILFORD, LEEDS
West Yorkshire LS25 6JU 0333 600 6000
e: sales@lightmedia.co.uk
w: www.lightmedia.co.uk

Live Audio Production
GROSVENOR WAY, CLAPTON
Greater London E5 9ND .... 020 3713 0502 / 07909 993125
e: liveaudioproduction@gmail.com
w: www.liveaudioproduction.co.uk

Live Systems Ltd
UNITS 1-2, NORTH LEITH SANDS,, LEITH, EDINBURGH
Edinburgh EH6 4ER..0131 555 5200
e: info@livesystems.co.uk
w: www.livesystems.co.uk

LMC Audio Systems Ltd (Birmingham)
UNIT 47, PHOENIX PARK, AVENUE CLOSE, ASTON, BIRMINGHAM
West Midlands B7 4NU 0121 359 4535
e: websales@lmcaudio.co.uk
w: www.lmcaudio.co.uk

LMC Audio Systems Ltd (London)
UNIT 10, COWLEY ROAD, LONDON
Greater London W3 7XA..020 8743 4680
e: sales@lmcaudio.co.uk
w: www.lmcaudio.co.uk

Location Audio
....07815 918398
e: locationaudiostage@gmail.com
w: www.locationaudiostagehire.co.uk/

Loft Sound LLP
16 KILBEGS ROAD, ANTRIM
 BT41 4NN...08452 99 33 77
e: info@loftsound.co.uk
w: www.loftsound.co.uk

Logic System Pro Audio Ltd
UNITS 5 & 6 SANDARS ROAD, HEAPHAM ROAD INDUSTRIAL
ESTATE, GAINSBOROUGH
Lincolnshire DN21 1RZ 01427 611791
e: sales@logicsystems.co.uk
w: www.logicsystems.co.uk

London Event Rentals
UNIT 7, WILLOW WALK, TOWER BRIDGE, LONDON
Greater London SE1 5SF 01252 313154
e: info@londoneventrentals.co.uk
w: www.londoneventrentals.co.uk

London Sound and Light
86 - 90 PAUL STREET, LONDON
Greater London EC2A 4NE 020 3086 7775
e: info@londonsoundandlight.co.uk
w: www.londonsoundandlight.co.uk

S

London Speaker Hire
ATLAS WHARF, BERKSHIRE ROAD, LONDON
Greater London E9 5NB 020 3333 4444
e: info@londonspeakerhire.com
w: www.londonspeakerhire.com

Low Fold Audio Visual
SHIRESHEAD OLD CHURCH, STONY LANE, FORTON, PRESTON
Lancashire PR3 1DE 01524 792020
e: info@lowfold.com
w: www.lowfold.com

Lux Technical Ltd
UNIT R, TUNGSTEN PARK, MAPLE DRIVE, HINCKLEY
LE10 3BE..020 3696 0692
e: info@luxtechnical.co.uk
w: www.luxtechnical.co.uk

M.I. Executives Limited
UNIT 2, CRAYFORD COMMERCIAL CENTRE, GREYHOUND WAY,
CRAYFORD
Kent DA1 4HF 01322 552828
e: info@mlexecutives.com
w: www.mlexecutives.com

M&R Communications Ltd
7 BELL INDUSTRIAL ESTATE, 50 CUNNINGTON STREET, LONDON
Greater London W4 5HB..020 8995 4714
e: office@m-rcom.com
w: www.m-rcom.com

Mac Sound
1 & 2 ATTENBURYS PARK, PARK ROAD, ALTRINCHAM
Cheshire WA14 5QE...0161 969 8311
e: info@macsound.co.uk
w: www.macsound.co.uk

Magnum PA Ltd
HODGESTON, PEMBROKE
Pembrokeshire SA71 5JU 01646 450 172
e: info@magnumpa.com
w: www.magnumpa.com

Maltings Audio
....07963 416034
e: info@maltingsaudio.co.uk
w: www.maltingsaudio.co.uk

Markertek
UNIT 4 FALCON BUSINESS CENTRE, 2-4 WILLOW LANE, WILLOW
LANE INDUSTRIAL ESTATE, MITCHAM
Surrey CR4 4NA..020 8687 9700
e: sales@markertek.co.uk
w: www.markertek.co.uk

Martin Bradley Sound & Light
69A BROAD LANE, HAMPTON
Middlesex TW12 3AX .... 020 8979 0672 / 07973 331451
e: mail@martinbradley.co.uk
w: www.martinbradley.co.uk

Martin Professional Plc
BELVOIR WAY, FAIRFIELD INDUSTRIAL ESTATE, LOUTH
Lincolnshire LN11 OLQ 1507 604 399
e: mpukaccounts@martinpro.co.uk
w: www.martinpro.co.uk

Matt Bunday Events
.... 023 8055 3736 / 07730 604 869
e: info@mattbundayevents.com
w: www.mattbundayevents.com

Matt Snowball Music
UNIT 2, 3-9 BREWERY ROAD, LONDON
Greater London N7 9QJ 020 7700 6555
e: enquiries@mattsnowball.com
w: www.mattsnowball.com

Mcl (birmingham)
UNIT 500 CATESBY PARK, ECKERSALL ROAD, KINGS NORTON,
BIRMINGHAM
West Midlands B38 8SE..0121 433 8899
e: birmingham@mclcreate.com
w: mclcreate.com/

Mcl (edinburgh)
UNITS 9Å "13 WEST EDINBURGH BUSINESS PARK, MARNIN WAY
SOUTH GYLE CRESCENT, EDINBURGH
Edinburgh EH12 9GD 0131 314 0650
e: edinburgh@mclcreate.com
w: mclcreate.com

MCM Creative Group
SOUTH AVENUE STUDIOS, SOUTH AVENUE, KEW
Greater London TW9 3LY.......................................020 8741 7576
e: info@mcmcreativegroup.com
w: www.mcmcreativegroup.com

Media Location Services (mls Audio)
2 FORT VIEW HOUSE, CLOCKTOWER DRIVE, MARINE GATE,
SOUTHSEA, PORTSMOUTH
Hampshire PO4 9XR 07860 895498
e: guy.morris@mlsaudio.com
w: www.mlsaudio.com

Microphonic Limited
54 WESLEY ROAD, LEYTON
 E10 6JF..0203 039 2979
e: info@microphonic.biz
w: www.microphonic.biz

Midas Prosound
35 GLENMORE BUSINESS PARK, TELFORD ROAD, SALISBURY
SP2 7GL..07748 115007
e: office@midasprosound.com
w: www.midasprosound.com

Middlesex Sound & Lighting Ltd
4-6 VILLAGE WAY EAST, RAYNERS LANE, HARROW
Middlesex HA2 7LU...020 8866 5500
e: info@middlesexsound.co.uk
w: www.middlesexsound.co.uk

Midnight Electronics
OFF QUAY BUILDING, FOUNDRY LANE, NEWCASTLE UPON TYNE
Tyne and Wear NE6 1LH..0191 224 0088
e: info@midnightelectronics.co.uk
w: www.midnight.uk.net

MM Sound and Lighting
UNIT 7 BRYSON STREET IND EST, BRYSON STREET, FALKIRK
 FK2 7BT...01324 624598
e: enquiries@mmsoundandlighting.com
w: www.mmsoundandlighting.com

MTR Ltd
FORD HOUSE, 58 CROSS ROAD, BUSHEY
Hertfordshire WD19 4DQ..01923 234050
e: MTRLtd@aol.com
w: www.mtraudio.com

MTS
UNIT 37, MOUNTHEATH TRADING , ESTATE PRESTWICH ,
MANCHESTER
Greater Manchester M25 9WE 1617739933
e: Keith@massivetech.co.uk
w: www.massivetech.co.uk

Nam Recording Studios
4-7 FOREWOOD COMMON, HOLT
Wiltshire BA14 6PJ 01225 782281
e: nam@namrecording.com
w: www.namrecording.com

Navigator Systems Ltd
13A CHURCH FARM BUSINESS PARK, CORSTON, BATH
Somerset BA2 9AP...0207 183 0011
e: sales@navigator.co.uk
w: www.navigator.co.uk

Neuron Pro Audio Ltd
DOWNTEX WAREHOUSE, 17 MARY STREET, MANCHESTER
Greater Manchester M3 1NH................................0161 408 1545
e: enquiries@neuronproaudio.co.uk
w: www.neuronproaudio.co.uk

New Day
44 BOVERTON DRIVE, BROCKWORTH
Gloucestershire GL3 4DA 01452 618619
e: sales@newday.tv
w: www.newdayhire.co.uk

NiteLites
UNIT S4, SECOND AVENUE,, TYNE TUNNEL TRADING ESTATE,
NORTH SHIELDS
Tyne and Wear NE29 7SY.....................................0191 296 0100
e: info@nitelites.co.uk
w: www.nitelites.co.uk

NMN Soundproofing Ltd
114 CANBURY PARK ROAD, KINGSTON
Surrey KT2 6JZ...0800 0433319
e: info@londonsoundproofing.co.uk
w: www.londonsoundproofing.co.uk

Northern Light
NAUTICAL HOUSE, 104 COMMERCIAL STREET, EDINBURGH
Edinburgh EH6 6NF...0131 622 9100
e: contact@northernlight.co.uk
w: www.northernlight.co.uk

NSR Communications Ltd
16 CAXTON WAY, WATFORD BUSINESS PARK, WATFORD
Hertfordshire WD18 8UA 01923 209640
e: sales@nsrcommunications.co.uk
w: www.nsrcommunications.co.uk

Nub Sound Ltd
UNIT 1, 23 CLARE PLACE,, COXSIDE, PLYMOUTH
Devon PL4 0JW 01752 255456
e: info@nubsound.com
w: www.nubsound.co.uk

Oasis Sound & Lighting
UNIT 19, WINDMILL FARM BUSINESS CENTRE, BARLTEY STREET,
BEDMINSTER
Bristol BS3 4DB .... 0117 966 3663 / 0117 963 7355
e: mail@oasis-online.co.uk
w: www.oasis-online.co.uk

Offslip
FLAT 4 OAKVIEW APARTMENT STUDIOS, 12 BENHILL ROAD,
LONDON
Greater London SM1 3RL..07912 091979
e: mail@offslip.co.uk
w: www.offslip.co.uk

On Event Production Co.
UNIT 16, WILLOW ROAD,, TRENT LANE INDUSTRIAL ESTATE,
CASTLE DONINGTON, DERBY
Derbyshire DE74 2NP 01159 222959
e: hello@on-productions.co.uk
w: www.lovingitlive.co.uk

OneoneTwo.com
112 NORTHWOOD AVENUE, PURLEY
CR8 2EQ 020 8660 7143
e: mail@oneonetwo.com
w: www.oneonetwo.com

Ooosh! Tours Ltd
COMPASS HOUSE, 7 EAST STREET, PORTSLADE, BRIGHTON
BN41 1DL .... 01273 911382 / 07719 568409
e: jon@oooshtours.co.uk
w: www.oooshtours.co.uk

Orange Audio
9 WARGRAVE ROAD, CLACTON-ON-SEA
Essex CO15 3EQ..07510-726-167
e: info@orangeaudio.co.uk
w: www.orangeaudio.co.uk

S

Panache Audio Systems
A5 SPECTRUM BUSINESS CENTRE, MEDWAY CITY ESTATE,
ROCHESTER
Kent ME2 4NP 01634 720700
e: sales@panacheaudio.co.uk
w: www.panacheaudio.co.uk

PDS - Sound & Lighting Company
21 IVATT WAY, WESTWOOD, PETERBOROUGH
Cambridgeshire PE3 7PG 01733 261199
e: info@pdssoundandlighting.com
w: www.pdssoundandlighting.com

Pg Stage Electrical Ltd
TAMESIDE WORK CENTRE, RYECROFT STREET, ASHTON-UNDER-LYNE
Greater Manchester OL7 0BY.................................0161 830 0303
e: info@pgstage.co.uk
w: www.pgstage.co.uk

Phantom Power Ltd
UNIT 5A, BLACKWELL FARM INDUSTRIAL ESTATE,
TILBROOK, HUNTINGDON
Cambridgeshire PE28 0JQ 07730 865642
e: info@phantompower.co.uk
w: www.phantompower.co.uk

Piccadilly Live
13 CONSUL ROAD, RUGBY CV21 1PB 01788 576296
e: rugby@piccadilly-live.com
w: www.picc.co.uk

Plastic Monkey Ltd
LONDON
Greater London SW6 4DX 07931 585100
e: info@plasticmonkey.co.uk
w: www.plasticmonkey.co.uk

Premier UK Events Ltd
UNIT 2, ROOKERY LANE, THURMASTON, LEICESTER
Leicestershire LE4 8AU...1162029953
e: ben@premier-ltd.com
w: premier-event-solutions.com

Presence Audio
OVERDALE, HAGLANDS LANE, WEST CHILTINGTON, PULBOROUGH
West Sussex RH20 2QR 01798 813133
e: presence@bdlrs.freeserve.co.uk
w: www.presenceaudio.com

Prestige Sound and Light
UNIT 1, MARLIN PARK, CENTRAL WAY, FELTHAM, LONDON
Greater London TW14 0AN....................................07584 292070
e: info@prestigesoundandlight.co.uk
w: www.prestigesoundandlight.co.uk

Pro Event Solutions
THEAKLIN DRIVE, , PONSWOOD INDUSTRIAL ESTATE,
ST LEONARDS
East Sussex TN37 9AZ..8006127427
e: hello@proeventsolutions.co.uk
w: www.proeventsolutions.co.uk

Pro Productions Limited
CASTLEFIELDS FARM, HARVINGTON LANE, NORTON,, EVESHAM
Worcestershire WR114UJ.......................................01386 871901
e: hire@proproductions.co.uk
w: www.proproductions.co.uk

Pro-Audio Systems
BLYNK HOUSE, YOUNG STREET, BRADFORD
West Yorkshire BD8 9RE 01274 497 261
e: hello@blynkgroup.com
w: pasystems.co.uk

Production Light & Sound Ltd
PO BOX 96, LEEDS
West Yorkshire LS12 4XS 0113 2360951
e: info@productionlightandsound.com
w: www.productionlightandsound.com

Proscreens
.... 0845 309 6369 / 07876755357
e: info@proscreens.net
w: www.proscreens.net

Protec (Production Technology LLC)
PLOT NO. 548 - 597, DUBAI INVESTMENT PARK 2,
DUBAI, UNITED ARAB EMIRATES........................ +971 4 880 0092
e: eventrental@productiontec.com
w: www.productiontec.com

Pure Power
STONE FARM, NORWICH ROAD, STOCKTON
Norfolk .... 0845 257 2811 / 07876 241290
e: info@purepower.org.uk
w: www.purepower.org.uk

Puxley Limited
11 HARRIER COURT , WESTCOTT LANE , EXETER
EX5 2DR 01392 364900
e: info@puxley.com
w: www.puxley.com

Q7db Limited
32 ROWDEN ROAD, WEST EWELL, EPSOM
Surrey KT19 9PN .... 020 8397 0197 / 07957 972595
e: enquiry@q7db.co.uk
w: www.q7db.co.uk

QED Productions
UNIT 11, SUMMIT ROAD, CRANBORNE INDUSTRIAL ESTATE,
POTTERS BAR
Hertfordshire EN6 3QW...01707 648 800
e: info@qed-productions.com
w: www.qed-productions.com

Quadrant Events - Birmingham
49 PHOENIX PARK, AVENUE CLOSE, ASTON, BIRMINGHAM
West Midlands B7 4NU 0121 359 6377
e: info@quadrantevents.com
w: www.quadrantevents.com

Raycom
LANGTON HOUSE, 19 VILLAGE STREET, HARVINGTON
Worcestershire WR11 8NQ.....................................01789 777040
e: sales@raycom.co.uk
w: www.raycom.co.uk

RealSound and Vision Ltd
120C OLYMPIC AVENUE, MILTON PARK, ABINGDON
Oxfordshire OX14 4SA...................................... +44 1235 833944
e: sales@realsound.co.uk
w: www.realsound.co.uk

Red Radio
YORK HOUSE, 140 HIGH TOWN ROAD, LUTON
Bedfordshire LU2 0DJ..01582 481114
e: sales@red-radio.co.uk
w: www.red-radio.co.uk

Rg Jones Sound Engineering Ltd
16 ENDEAVOUR WAY, WIMBLEDON, LONDON
Greater London SW19 8UH 0208 971 3100
e: info@rgjones.co.uk
w: www.rgjones.co.uk

Richmond Film Services
BUILDING 11, SHEPPERTON STUDIOS, STUDIOS ROAD, SHEPPERTON
Middlesex TW17 0QD..020 8940 6077
e: bookings@richmondfilmservices.co.uk
w: www.richmondfilmservices.co.uk

Roland Systems Group UK
ATLANTIC CLOSE, SWANSEA ENTERPRISE PARK, SWANSEA
SA7 9FJ...01792 702701
e: simon.kenning@rolandsg.co.uk
w: www.rolandsystemsgroup.co.uk

Roy Truman Sound Services
UNIT 2 HARP BUSINESS CENTRE, APSLEY WAY, LONDON
Greater London NW2 7LW.....................................020 8208 2468
e: rtss@rtss.biz
w: www.rtss.biz

S2 Events
141- 143 NATHAN WAY, LONDON
Greater London SE28 0AB.....................................020 7928 5474
e: info@s2events.co.uk
w: www.s2events.co.uk

Sabre International Ltd
UNITS 5, 6 & 7 HEADLEY PARK 8, HEADLEY ROAD EAST, WOODLEY, READING
RG5 4SA 0118 938 0683
e: sales@sabre-international.com
w: www.sabre-international.com

Serious Stages Ltd
TOR HILL WORKS, DULCOTE, , WELLS
Somerset BA5 3NT 01749 899 188
e: info@stages.co.uk
w: www.stages.co.uk

Shades Events & Discotheques
4 DEAKIN LEAS, TONBRIDGE
Kent TN9 2JU...01732 363675
e: shadesevents@me.com
w: www.shadesevents.com

Show Hire
UNITS 19 & 20 BORDON TRADING ESTATE, OLD STATION WAY , BORDON
Hampshire GU35 9HH 01483 414337
e: info@showhire.co.uk
w: www.showhire.co.uk

Show Partners
481 QUARTIER INDUSTRIEL, LOTISSEMENT AL MASSAR, ROUTE DE SAFI, MARRAKECH, MOROCCO
40 100... +212 524 35 58 91
e: showpartners@gmail.com
w: www.show-partners.ma

Shure Distribution Uk
SHURE DISTRIBUTION UK, UNIT 2 THE IO CENTRE, WALTHAM ABBEY
Essex EN9 1AS 01992 703058
e: info@shuredistribution.co.uk
w: www.shuredistribution.co.uk

Silver Streak Events
12 STOKE MEADOWS, BRISTOL
BS329BG.. +44 (0) 1179116806
e: info@silverstreakevents.co.uk
w: www.silverstreakevents.co.uk

Skan Pa
THE MERIDIAN BUILDING, 1 BROOKWAY HAMBRIDGE LANE, NEWBURY
Berkshire RG14 5RY 01635 521010
e: enquiries@skanpa.co.uk
w: www.skanpa.co.uk

Smash Productions Ltd
50 ALBERT RD
Bristol BS2 0XW...0117 329 0109
w: www.smashproductions.com

Smile Events
392 GALLEY HILL,, HEMEL HEMPSTEAD,
Hertfordshire HP1 3LA 01923 750 525
e: info@smileevents.co.uk
w: www.smileevents.co.uk

Sonifex Ltd
61 STATION ROAD, IRTHLINGBOROUGH
Northamptonshire NN9 5QE 01933 650700
e: sales@sonifex.co.uk
w: www.sonifex.co.uk

S

Sound & Light Event Management
THE OLD ISOLATION HOSPITAL, VAUXHALL LANE,
TUNBRIDGE WELLS
Kent TN4 0XD 0800 083 8368
e: enquiries@soundandlightgroup.com
w: www.soundandlightgroup.com

Sound & Vision Av Ltd (edinburgh)
16 DRYDEN ROAD, BILSTON GLEN INDUSTRIAL ESTATE,
LOANHEAD, LOANHEAD
Edinburgh EH20 9LZ 0131 334 3324
e: edinburgh@visionevents.co.uk
w: www.visionevents.co.uk

Sound 2 Light Hire
.... 07092 316129 / 0845 128 5238
e: info@djequipmenthiredoncaster.co.uk
w: www.djequipmenthiredoncaster.co.u

Sound And Light Guys
36 CUMBERFORD CLOSE, BLOXHAM, BANBURY
Oxfordshire OX15 4HN 01295 720825
e: hire@soundandlightguys.co.uk
w: www.soundandlightguys.co.uk

Sound Artist Management Ltd.
UNIT B54, , 56 WOOD LANE, LONDON
Greater London W12 7SB..020 71129073
e: info@soundartistmanagement.com
w: www.soundartistmanagement.com

Sound Barrier Systems
UNIT 20, PALMERSTON BUSINESS PARK, NEWGATE LANE,
FAREHAM
Hampshire PO14 1DJ..07855 165 781
e: enquiries@soundbarriersystems.com
w: www.soundbarriersystems.com

Sound By Design Ltd
 21 ISLAND FARM AVENUE, WEST MOLESEY
Surrey KT8 2UZ 020 8339 3800
e: enquiries@deltasound.uk
w: www.soundbydesign.net

Sound Division
430 HIGH ROAD, LONDON
Greater London NW10 2DA 0208 3495 200
e: info@sounddivision.com
w: www.sounddivision.com

Sound Of Music Ltd
.... 08456 448 550 / 07946 739 384
e: info@pahire.com
w: www.pahire.com

Sound Support Ltd
UNIT A8 (5) PENNINGTON COURT, MOSS INDUSTRIAL ESTATE,
LEIGH
Leicestershire WN7 3PT..01942 607070
e: info@soundsupport.co.uk
w: www.soundsupport.co.uk

Soundbase Solutions
64 OLDHAM STREET, MANCHESTER
Greater Manchester M4 1LE 0161 238 8727
e: info@soundbasesolutions.com
w: www.soundbasesolutions.com

Soundfield Microphones
UNITS 1 & 2 FIRST AVENUE, GLOBE PARK, MARLOW
Buckinghamshire SL7 1YA .... +44 1628 564 610
e: enquiries@tslproducts.com
w: www.tslproducts.com

Soundstage One Event Services
61 STATION ROAD, THORNEY , PETERBOROUGH
Cambridgeshire PE6 0QE .... 084321 62026 / 07846 349063
e: info@soundstageone.co.uk
w: www.soundstageone.co.uk

Soundwave Audio
UNIT D1 LINCOLN PARK, BOROUGH ROAD, BUCKINGHAM ROAD
INDUSTRIAL ESTATE, BRACKLEY
Northamptonshire NN13 7BE 01295 298288
e: info@soundwaveaudio.co.uk
w: https://www.soundwaveaudio.co.uk

Southwest Sound & Light
THE OLD SMITHY, CHURCH ROAD, COCKWOOD, NR EXETER
Devon EX6 8NU...01626 890806
e: sales@swlighting.co.uk
w: www.swlighting.co.uk

Spectrum Hire
UNIT 1 HESTON INDUSTRIAL MALL, HESTON, MIDDLESEX
TW5 0LD 07944 001174
e: info@spectrumhire.co.uk
w: www.spectrumhire.co.uk

Spectrum Hire Ltd
UNIT 1 HESTON INDUSTRIAL MALL, CHURCH ROAD, HESTON
Middlesex TW5 0LD 2079936455
e: info@spectrumhire.co.uk
w: www.spectrumhire.co.uk

Spotlight Sound
UNIT 32B, LITTLE BOYTON FARM , BOYTON HALL LANE,
CHELMSFORD
Essex CM1 4LN 01245 206206
e: info@spotlightsound.co.uk
w: www.spotlightsound.co.uk

Spyder UK Ltd
UNIT 3, ATTRILLS YARD, THE DUVER, ST HELENS
Isle of Wight PO33 1YB 01983 779337
e: hire@spyderuk.com
w: www.spyderuk.com

Stage Audio Services
UNIT 2, BRIDGE STREET, WORDSLEY , STOURBRIDGE
West Midlands DY8 5YU..01384 263629
e: kevinmobers@aol.com
w: www.stageaudioservices.com

S

Stage Connections
UNIT 1B, ACTON STREET , LONG EATON, NOTTINGHAM
Nottinghamshire NG10 1FT....... 0115 938 6354 / 07976 00 5769
e: info@stageconnections.co.uk
w: www.stageconnections.co.uk

Stage Services Event Production
THE COACH HOUSE, MAYALLS FARM, WATERY LANE, UPPER
WELLAND , MALVERN
Worcestershire WR14 4JX........... 01684 560022 / 07719 730053
e: info@stage-services.net
w: www.stage-services.net

Stage Support Services Ltd
UNITS 2-3, WEST SHED,, QUINTON GREEN PARK,
Northamptonshire NN7 2EG 01604 870870
e: enquiries@stagesupportservices.com
w: www.stagesupportservices.com

StageCore
UNIT 6 EAST GATE BUSINESS PARK, ARGALL WAY, LONDON
Greater London E10 7PG.......................................020 3697 3888
e: info@stagecore.co.uk
w: www.stagecore.co.uk

Storm Events London Ltd
.... 0207 993 6077 / 07733 352631
e: messages@storm-events.co.uk
w: www.storm-events.co.uk

STS Touring Productions
GROUND FLOOR UNIT 1, APOLLO BUSINESS CENTRE, ARDWICK,
MANCHESTER
Greater Manchester M12 6AW 0161 273 5984
e: office@ststouring.co.uk
w: www.ststouring.co.uk

SXS Events
....0870 080 2342
e: hello@sxsevents.co.uk
w: www.sxsevents.co.uk

Synergy Audio
THE OLD BAKERY, FRAMLINGHAM
Suffolk IP13 9DT...07941 552418
e: info@synergyaudio.co.uk
w: www.synergyaudio.co.uk

System Sound & Light Ltd
1 LIDDALL WAY, HORTON ROAD, WEST DRAYTON
Middlesex UB7 8PG 01895 432995
e: design@systemsound.com
w: www.systemsound.com

Tannoy Ltd
ROSEHALL INDUSTRIAL ESTATE, COATBRIDGE, STRATHCLYDE
Lanarkshire ML5 4TF...01236 420199
e: enquries@tannoy.com
w: www.tannoy.com

Team Audio Ltd
168 CHURCH ROAD , HOVE
BN3 2DL...447811326475
e: mark@teamaudio.net

TEC PA & Lighting
PORTLAND BUILDING, UNIVERSITY PARK, NOTTINGHAM
Nottinghamshire NG7 2RD 0115 846 8720
e: info@nottinghamtec.co.uk
w: www.nottinghamtec.co.uk

TechST
....07767 366031
e: info@tech-st.co.uk
w: www.tajiri-events.co.uk

Thames Audio Ltd
UNIT 33 JOSEPH WILSON IND EST, WHITSTABLE
Kent CT5 3PS 01227 264204
e: info@thamesaudio.co.uk
w: www.thamesaudio.co.uk

The LED Studio
HANGER WAY, PETERSFIELD
Hampshire GU31 4QE 020 3617 1979
e: sales@theledstudio.co.uk
w: www.theledstudio.co.uk

The Noizeworks
UNIT 7, WENNINGTON HALL FARM, WENNINGTON ROAD,
RAINHAM
Essex RM13 9EF...441708523812
e: info@thenoizeworks.co.uk
w: thenoizeworks.co.uk

The PA Company Ltd
UNIT 7, THE ASHWAY CENTRE, ELM CRESCENT,
KINGSTON UPON THAMES
Surrey KT2 6HH...020 8546 6640
e: thepacompany@aol.com
w: www.thepaco.com

The Production Shop
55 WELLINGTON ROAD, EAST BRISBANE
4169.. +61 1300 099 492
e: sales@productionshop.com.au
w: www.productionshop.com.au

The Production Works
UNIT 5- EXMOUTH COURT, EXMOUTH ROAD, CHELTENHAM
Gloucestershire GL53 7NR 01242 807841
e: contact@the-production-works.co.uk
w: www.the-production-works.co.uk

The Small PA Company
NEWHAM
Greater London .... 020 8536 0649 / 077 8558 4279
e: ian@thesmallpacompany.com
w: www.soundengineer.co.uk

S

The Warehouse Sound (edinburgh)
THE WAREHOUSE, 23 WATER STREET, LEITH, EDINBURGH
Edinburgh EH6 6SU..0131 555 6900
e: sales@warehousesound.co.uk
w: www.warehousesound.co.uk

Thunder and Lightning
....01368 459457
e: enquiries@thunderandlightning.org.uk
w: www.thunderandlightning.org.uk

Total Live Sound Ltd
67 CHEWTON STREET, EASTWOOD
Nottinghamshire NG16 3GY 07977 048 097
e: info@totallivesound.com
w: www.totallivesound.com

Tower Productions
23 ALBERT ROAD , EDINBURGH
Edinburgh EH6 7DP .... +44 131 552 0100
e: enquiries@tower-productions.com
w: www.tower-productions.com

True Sound Hire
UNIT 2, MANOR PARK INDUSTRIAL EST, WYNDHAM STREET,
ALDERSHOT
Hampshire GU12 4NZ .... 01252 313154 / 01252 313154
e: info@truesoundhire.co.uk
w: www.truesoundhire.co.uk

Tube Uk Ltd
UNIT 9, CLAYTON COURT, CITY WORKS, MANCHESTER
Greater Manchester M11 2NB...............................0845 890 9990
e: info@tubeuk.com
w: www.tubeuk.com

Tusk Showhire
23 COLLUM LANE, SCUNTHORPE
Lincolnshire DN16 2SZ .... 01724 859541 / 07850 307162
e: info@tuskshowhire.co.uk
w: www.tuskshowhire.co.uk

Ultimate Acoustics Ltd
UNIT 2, TOP CAT INDUSTRIAL ESTATE, ESTATE ROAD NO. 8,
GRIMSBY
Lincolnshire DN31 2TG 0845 680 2079
e: info@ultimate-acoustics.co.uk
w: www.ultimate-acoustics.co.uk

VisionSound AV
751 SOUTH WEIR CANYON ROAD, SUITE 157-223, ANAHEIM, CA
92808..001 714 280 8201
e: sales@visionsoundav.com
w: www.visionsoundav.com

VNV Sounds
UNITS 10 AND 10A ASHLEY HOUSE, ASHLEY ROAD, LONDON
Greater London N17 9LZ.......................................0203 021 1370
e: info@vnvlive.co.uk
w: www.vnvsounds.co.uk

W1 Productions Ltd
UNIT 7 WOODLANDS BUSINESS PARK, BURY ST EDMUNDS
Suffolk IP30 9ND 0870 2405217
e: info@w1productions.co.uk
w: www.w1productions.co.uk

Warwick Corporate Events Ltd
UNIT 5 GLOUCESTER CRESENT, HEATHPARK INDUSTRIAL ESTATE,
HONITON, EXETER
Devon EX14 1DB...0845 3510392
e: enquiries@wce.co.uk
w: www.wce.co.uk

Wellpleased Events
11 BLAYDS YARD, LEEDS
West Yorkshire LS1 4AD.......................................0113 244 2720
e: info@wellpleased.co.uk
w: www.wellpleased.co.uk

Zeal Events
UNIT 6, BESSEMER PARK, BESSEMER ROAD, BASINGSTOKE
Hampshire RG21 3NB 01256 359264
e: info@zeallive.com
w: www.zealevents.com

Zenworks
114 CHEDDON ROAD, TAUNTON
Somerset TA2 7DW.. +44(0)7814754206
e: zenworksengineer@gmail.com
w: zenworks.wix.com/index

Zerodb Live
38 NIGEL HOUSE, PORTPOOL LANE, LONDON
Greater London EC1N 7UR 020 3332 0049
e: info@zerodblive.com
w: www.zerodblive.com

Special Effects

Aardvark FX
UNIT 21 AVON VALLEY FARM, PIXASH LANE, KEYNSHAM
Bristol BS31 1TS..................... 0 1179 863051 / 0 7891 509521
e: enquiries@aardvarkfx.com
w: www.aardvarkfx.com

Agog Special Effects Ltd
UNIT 10, GREEN FARM, FRITWELL
Oxfordshire OX27 7QU 020 3475 5745
e: hello@agogspecialeffects.co.uk
w: www.agog.tv

Annix Ltd
580 EASTSIDE COMPLEX, PINEWOOD STUDIOS, IVER HEATH
SL0 0NH 01753 656728
e: stuart@annix.com
w: www.annix.com

Applied Arts
22-27 THE OVAL, CAMBRIDGE HEATH, LONDON
Greater London E2 9DT..020 7739 3155
e: info@appliedarts.co.uk
w: www.appliedarts.co.uk

AVS Hire
UNIT 4, HIGHAMS FARM, SHEEPBARN LANE, WARLINGHAM
Surrey CR6 9PQ...01959 540 028
e: av_equipment_questions@yahoo.co.uk
w: www.avs-hire.co.uk

Blackjack Event Co
ALPHA 6, , MASTERLORD OFFICE VILLAGE WEST ROAD, IPSWICH
Suffolk IP3 9SX...08448 400 123
e: info@blackjackevents.co.uk
w: www.blackjackuk.co.uk

Colour Sound Experiment
ST LEONARDS ROAD , PARK ROYAL, LONDON
Greater London NW10 6ST 020 8965 9119
e: sales@coloursound.co.uk
w: www.coloursound.co.uk

Confetti Magic Ltd
ROCKET PARK, PEPPERSTOCK, LUTON
Bedfordshire LU1 4LL 01582 723502
e: ian@confettimagic.com
w: www.confettimagic.com

Continental Lasers (uk) Ltd
B105 PORTVIEW TRADE CTR, 310 NEWTOWNARDS ROAD,
BELFAST
BT4 1HE 028 9045 8658
e: info@continental-lasers.com
w: www.continental-lasers.com

Creative Lighting & Sound (CLS)
UNIT 6, SPIRES BUSINESS CENTRE, MUGIMOSS RD , ABERDEEN
Aberdeen AB21 9NY..01224 683 111
e: info@clsaberdeen.co.uk
w: www.clsaberdeen.co.uk

DAC Pro-Media Ltd
Surrey 01372 374 600
e: dcrisp@dacpromedia.co.uk
w: www.dacpromedia.co.uk

Dave Parkinson Murals
LANGSTONE, 6 AVENUE ROAD, ABERGAVENNY
Monmouthshire NP7 7DA.......................................07946 830446
e: dave@daveparkinsonmurals.co.uk
w: www.daveparkinsonmurals.co.uk

David Fitch Services Ltd
176 BEXLEY ROAD, ERITH
Kent DA8 3HF 01322 350351
e: contactus@davidfitchservices.com
w: www.davidfitchservices.com

Definitive Special Projects Ltd
HIGH TREE FARM, WOOD END
Hertfordshire SG2 7BB..01438 869005
e: info@laserlightshows.co.uk
w: www.laserlightshows.co.uk

East Anglia Leisure
UNIT 4, CIVIC INDUSTRIAL ESTATE, HOMEFIELD ROAD, HAVERHILL
Suffolk CB9 8QP 01440 714204
e: info@ealeisure.co.uk
w: www.ealeisure.co.uk

EMF Technology Ltd
....020 8003 3344
e: info@emftechnology.co.uk
w: www.emftechnology.co.uk

Emphasis Event Production Ltd
UNIT 14, BELGRAVE INDUSTRIAL ESTATE, SOUTHAMPTON
Hampshire SO17 3EA...023 8055 0557
e: enquiries@emphasiseventproduction.co.uk
w: www.prestech.co.uk

Especial Effects Company
UNIT 86 WOODHURST AVENUE, PETTS WOOD, BROMLEY
Kent BR5 1AT..07000 433332
e: espfx@specialeffects.uk.com
w: www.specialeffects.uk.com

Event FX Ltd
9 GOODWOOD CLOSE, BURGPHFIELD COMMON, READING
Berkshire RG7 3EZ..08000 787707
e: info@eventfx.co.uk
w: www.eventfx.co.uk

Flying by Foy
UNIT 4 BOREHAMWOOD ENTERPRISE CENTRE, THEOBALD
STREET, BOREHAMWOOD
Hertfordshire WD6 4RQ...02082 360 234
e: stephen.wareham@flyingbyfoy.co.uk
w: www.flyingbyfoy.co.uk

Flying By Foy Ltd
UNIT 4, BOREHAMWOOD ENTERPRISE CENTRE, THEOBALD
STREET, BOREHAMWOOD
Hertfordshire WD6 4RQ.......................................0208 236 0234
e: enquiries@flyingbyfoy.co.uk
w: www.flyingbyfoy.co.uk

Halo Lighting
98-124 BREWERY ROAD, LONDON
Greater London N7 9PG 0207 607 4444
e: info@halo.co.uk
w: www.halo.co.uk

Hamilton Ice Sculptors Ltd
54 WIMBLEDON STADIUM BUSINESS CENTRE, LONDON
Greater London SW17 0BA....................................020 8944 9787
e: info@icesculpture.co.uk
w: www.icesculpture.co.uk

S

Hands On Production Services Ltd
79 LOANBANK QUADRANT, GLASGOW
Glasgow G51 3HZ..0141 4402005
e: info@hands-on-uk.com
w: www.hands-on-uk.com

Heathrow Sound Hire
UNITS 9 & 10- POD BUSINESS CENTRE, HARRIS WAY,
SUNBURY ON THAMES
Surrey TW16 7EW........................ 0208 4322310 / 07834520290
e: enquiries@heathrowsoundhire.co.uk
w: www.heathrowsoundhire.co.uk

Hi-fli
18 GREEN COURT DRIVE, MANCHESTER
Greater Manchester M38 0BZ 0161 278 9352
e: mikefrost@hi-fli.co.uk
w: www.hi-fli.co.uk

High Lite Touring
MITROVICKA 359/45, OSTRAVA - NOVA BELA
72400...00420 596 731 034
e: info@highlite.cz
w: www.highlite.cz

Holomedia
156 IVYBANK   , MAIN ROAD , BAXTERLEY
Warwickshire CV9 2LG.............. 07979 771 360 / 01675 475 670
e: benjamin.field@holomedia.co.uk
w: www.holomedia.co.uk

Kirby's Afx Ltd.
8 GREENFORD AVENUE, HANWELL, LONDON
W7 3QP 020 8723 8552
e: mail@afxuk.com
w: www.afxuk.com/

Kudos Music
UNIT 10 TRADE CITY, COWLEY MILL ROAD, UXBRIDGE
 UB8 2DB...01895 207990
e: info@kudosmusic.co.uk
w: www.kudosmusic.co.uk

Laser Hire London
UNIT 4 - PACIFIC WHARF, HERTFORD ROAD, BARKING
 IG11 8BL .... 0844 664 4455 / 07999 559 995
e: info@laserhirelondon.com
w: www.laserhirelondon.co.uk

Laser Hire Ltd
FOLE SPRING FARM, FOLE, UTTOXETER
Staffordshire ST14 5EF 01889 507 067
e: info@laserhire.co.uk
w: www.laserhire.co.uk

LCI Productions Ltd
55 MERTHYR TERRACE, BARNES, LONDON
Greater London SW13 8DL....................................020 8741 5747
e: contact@lci-uk.com
w: www.lci-uk.com

Le Maitre Ltd
6 FORVAL CLOSE, WANDLE WAY, MITCHAM
Surrey CR4 4NE..0208 646 2222
e: info@lemaitreltd.com
w: www.lemaitreevents.com

Light The Way
UNIT 7 CAVENDISH COURT MILL, WEST STREET, BRADFORD
BD11 1DA...01422 250 819
e: hire@lighttheway.co.uk
w: www.lighttheway.co.uk

London Event Rentals
UNIT 7, WILLOW WALK, TOWER BRIDGE, LONDON
Greater London SE1 5SF 01252 313154
e: info@londoneventrentals.co.uk
w: www.londoneventrentals.co.uk

Lumacoustics Ltd
FOURTH FLOOR, 2-8 SCRUTTON STREET, LONDON
Greater London EC2A 4RT....................................020 7043 2632
e: hello@thisisluma.com
w: www.thisisluma.com

Lumiere Studios
3RD FLOOR, 10/11 LOWER JOHN ST, SOHO, LONDON
Greater London W1F 9EB 020 7287 1677
e: info@lumierestudios.co.uk
w: www.lumierestudios.co.uk

LX Communications Ltd
UNIT 36, WEST STATION YARD, MALDON
Essex CM9 6TS...01621 854075
e: info@lxcommunications.com
w: lightinghireessex.com/

Machine Shop
180 ACTON LANE, PARK ROYAL, LONDON
Greater London NW10 7NH 020 8961 5888
e: info@machineshop.co.uk
w: www.machineshop.co.uk

Matt Bunday Events
.... 023 8055 3736 / 07730 604 869
e: info@mattbundayevents.com
w: www.mattbundayevents.com

MCL Create
UNIT 500, CATESBY PARK, ECKERSALL ROAD, KINGS NORTON,
BIRMINGHAM
West Midlands B38 8SE..0121 433 8899
e: birmingham@mclcreate.com
w: mclcreate.com

Movetech UK
PART OF THE BRITISH TURNTABLE GROUP, EMBLEM STREET,
BOLTON
Lancashire BL3 5BW................... 01204 525626 / 01992 574602
e: info@movetechuk.com
w: www.movetechuk.com/rental

S

SPECIAL EFFECTS

PYROTECHNICS • EXPLOSIVES • FIRE • SMOKE
FIREDANCE • WIND • CO$_2$ • RAIN • WATER
FIREWORKS • AQUAGRAPHICS • SNOW & WINTER
HIGH VOLTAGE • CONFETTI & GLITTER

MTFX. The ingenious effects people.
01452 729903   info@mtfx.com   www.mtfx.com

MTFX

Velt House Lane
Elmore, Gloucestershire
GL2 3NY

t: 01452 729 903
e: info@MTFX.com

MTFX specialise in; Aquagraphics Water Screens, CO2, Confetti,
Fire, Fireworks, Flogo's, High Voltage, Hydraulics, Pyrotechnics, Rain,
Smoke, Snow, Streamers, Water, Wind and much more.

Welcome to MTFX, the ingenious special effects people.

www.MTFX.com

MTFX
VELT HOUSE, VELT HOUSE LANE, ELMORE
Gloucester GL2 3NY..01452 729 903
e: mark@mtfx.com
w: www.mtfx.com

MTFX Confetti Effects
VELT HOUSE, VELT HOUSE LANE, ELMORE
Gloucestershire GL2 3NY......................................01452 729903
e: info@mtfx.com
w: www.mtfx.com

MTFX High Voltage
VELTHOUSE, VELTHOUSE LANE, ELMORE
Gloucestershire GL2 3NY......................................01452 729903
e: info@mtfx.com
w: www.mtfx.com

MTFX Special Effects
VELT HOUSE, VELT HOUSE LANE , ELMORE
Gloucestershire GL2 3NY......................................01452 729 903
e: info@mtfx.com
w: www.mtfx.com

MTFX Winter Effects
VELT HOUSE, VELT HOUSE LANE, ELMORE
Gloucestershire GL2 3NY......................................01452 729903
e: info@mtfx.com
w: www.mtfx.com

Multiform Technology
SEEDBED BUSINESS CENTRE, VANGUARD WAY, SHOEBURYNESS
Essex SS3 9QY..01702 680021
e: sales@adelto.com
w: www.multiform-lighting.com

Philip L Edwards (Theatre Lighting)
5 HIGHWOOD CLOSE, GLOSSOP
 SK13 6PH..01457 862811
e: enquiries@pletheatrelighting.co.uk
w: www.pletheatrelighting.co.uk

Planet Gold Decor
UNIT 4 ROMARSH, FOWLSWICK BUSINESS PARK, , ALLINGTON
Wiltshire SN14 6QE...07747 015 170
e: info@planetgolddecor.co.uk
w: www.planetgolddecor.co.uk or www.

Projected Image Uk Ltd
UNIT 17 HOULTS ESTATE, WALKER ROAD,
NEWCASTLE UPON TYNE
Tyne and Wear NE6 2HL..0191 265 9832
e: gobo@projectedimage.com
w: www.projectedimage.com

Snow Business International Ltd
THE SNOW MILL, BRIDGE ROAD, EBLEY, STROUD
Gloucestershire GL5 4TR......................................01453 840 077
e: snow@snowbusiness.com
w: www.snowbusiness.com

Snowboy Systems Ltd
UNIT 10, GLEN INDUSTRIAL ESTATE, ESSENDINE, STAMFORD
Lincolnshire PE9 4LE..01780 752166
e: website@snowboy.co.uk
w: www.snowboy.co.uk

Stage Right
SHAW LODGE FARM, STONE ROAD, FRADSWELL, STAFFORD
Staffordshire ST18 0HA...01889 502222
e: info@stagerightcreative.co.uk
w: www.stagerightcreative.com

Storm Lighting Ltd
WARWICK HOUSE, MONUMENT WAY WEST, WOKING
Surrey GU21 5EN...01483 757211
e: hire@stormlighting.co.uk
w: www.stormlighting.co.uk

Street Advertising Services
69 MERE GREEN ROAD, BIRMINGHAM
West Midlands B75 5BY...0845 658 9940
e: mail@streetadvertisingservices.com
w: www.streetadvertisingservices.com

The Projection Studio
13 TARVES WAY, GREENWICH, LONDON
Greater London SE10 9JP.....................................020 8293 4270
e: info@theprojectionstudio.com
w: www.theprojectionstudio.com

The World Famous
BOUNDARY FARM, MAIDSTONE ROAD, HADLOW
Kent ME18 6BY...01732 852002
e: info@theworldfamous.co.uk
w: www.theworldfamous.co.uk

Theatresearch
DACRE HALL, DACRE
North Yorkshire HG3 4ET......................................01423 780497
e: office@theatresearch.co.uk
w: www.theatresearch.co.uk

S

Triple E Ltd
16 AIRPORT INDUSTRIAL ESTATE, MAIN ROAD, BIGGIN HILL
Kent TN16 3BW 01959 570 333
e: info@3-eee.com
w: www.3-eee.com

True Sound Hire
UNIT 2, MANOR PARK INDUSTRIAL EST, WYNDHAM STREET,
ALDERSHOT
Hampshire GU12 4NZ .... 01252 313154 / 01252 313154
e: info@truesoundhire.co.uk
w: www.truesoundhire.co.uk

UV Light Technology Limited
582-854 HAGLEY ROAD WEST, BIRMINGHAM
West Midlands B68 0BS...0121 423 2000
e: sales@uv-light.co.uk
w: www.uv-light.co.uk

Vortex Lighting
THE OLD CHAPEL, BILLY ROW GREEN, CROOK
Durham DL15 9TA .... 0845 486 7839 / 07971792398
e: sales@vortexlighting.co.uk
w: www.vortexlighting.co.uk

Water Sculptures Limited
UNIT 4 STEVANT WAY, WHITE LUND INDUSTRIAL ESTATE,
MORECAMBE, LANCASTER
Lancashire LA3 3PU...01524 37707
e: info@watersculptures.co.uk
w: www.watersculptures.co.uk

Specialist Advertising Services

Adby Creative Images
VOYAGE, GLENDALE HOUSE, READING ROAD, READING
Berkshire RG7 3BL 020 3239 1084
e: sayhello@adbycreative.co.uk
w: www.adbycreativeimages.co.uk

Alternative Advertising
ELM TREE FARM ESTATE , THE SHEEPWAY, PORTBURY
Bristol BS20 7TF..01275 371117
e: enquiries@alternative-advertising.co.uk
w: www.alternative-advertising.co.uk

Braidburn Property Management
BRAIDBURN PROPERTY MANAGEMENT, EDINBURGH
EH10 6ES 7518871496
e: margot@braidburnproperty.co.uk
w: www.braidburnproperty.co.uk

Geerings Print Ltd
COBBS WOOD HOUSE,, CHART ROAD, ASHFORD
Kent TN23 1EP..01233 633366
e: Info@geeringsprint.co.uk
w: www.geeringsprint.co.uk

Holomedia
156 IVYBANK , MAIN ROAD , BAXTERLEY
Warwickshire CV9 2LG............. 07979 771 360 // 01675 475 670
e: benjamin.field@holomedia.co.uk
w: www.holomedia.co.uk

LCI Productions Ltd
55 MERTHYR TERRACE, BARNES, LONDON
Greater London SW13 8DL....................................020 8741 5747
e: contact@lci-uk.com
w: www.lci-uk.com

Mediaco Graphic Solutions
CHURCHILL POINT, CHURCHILL WAY, TRAFFORD PARK,
MANCHESTER
Greater Manchester M17 1BS..............................0161 875 2020
e: customerservice@mediaco.co.uk
w: www.mediaco.co.uk

Ne Plastics Ltd.
1 RUXLEY CORNER IND. EST., EDGINGTON WAY, SIDCUP
Kent DA14 5BL 0208 308 9990
e: sales@neplastics.co.uk
w: www.neplastics.co.uk

Powell Outdoor Media
54 MILLMOUNT ROAD, SHEFFIELD
South Yorkshire S8 9EG 0870 005 3123
e: email@futurate.com
w: www.futurate.com

Regency Lettings & Property Management Ltd
RYSTEAD LODGE, BARN BUILDINGS, POCKFORD ROAD,
CHIDDINGFOLD
Surrey GU8 4XS 01428 684 540
e: lettings@rlpm.co.uk
w: www.rlpm.co.uk

Street Advertising Services
69 MERE GREEN ROAD, BIRMINGHAM
West Midlands B75 5BY..0845 658 9940
e: mail@streetadvertisingservices.com
w: www.streetadvertisingservices.com

The Advertising Bike Company
1 UNDERCROFT, YORK
Yorkshire YO19 5RP 07712 887551
e: sales@advertisingbikeco.net
w: www.advertisingbikeco.net

The Alternative.
2 VALENTINE PLACE , SOUTHWARK , LONDON
SE1 8QH..0207 803 0905
e: hello@thealternative.co.uk
w: www.thealternative.co.uk

The Projection Studio
13 TARVES WAY, GREENWICH, LONDON
Greater London SE10 9JP 020 8293 4270
e: info@theprojectionstudio.com
w: www.theprojectionstudio.com

The Searchlight Company
UNIT 9, CROMER HYDE FARM, SYMONDSHYDE LANE, HATFIELD
Hertfordshire AL10 9BB 01707 269681
e: enquiries@searchlight.co.uk
w: www.searchlight.co.uk

Tribe Marketing
UNIT 4, THE WOOL HOUSE, 74 BACK CHURCH LANE, LONDON
Greater London E1 1LX 020 7702 3600
e: info@tribemarketing.co.uk
w: www.tribemarketing.co.uk

Virgin Airship & Balloon Co
JESSON HOUSE, STAFFORD COURT, TELFORD
Shropshire TF3 3BD...01952 212750
e: sales@virginballoonflights.co.uk
w: www.virginballoonflights.co.uk

Sponsorship Agencies

Big Fish Music Partnerships
STUDIO 215, WESTBOURNE STUDIOS, 242 ACKLAM ROAD,
LONDON
Greater London W10 5JJ 020 7524 7555
e: info@bigfishmusicpartnerships.com
w: www.bigfishmusicpartnerships.com

Grand Plan Consultancy
....01608 654040
e: media@thegpc.co.uk
w: www.thegpc.co.uk

Maitland Sponsorship Consultancy
SIDEWAYS COTTAGE, CONFORD, LIPHOOK
GU30 7QW...01428 751195
e: info@sponorshiponline.com

Tenpast Events
27 TAVISTOCK SQUARE, LONDON
 WC1H 9HH................................ 020) 3143 3243 / 07490 390219
e: nh@tenpast.com
w: www.tenpast.com

Sports

Bac Sport
112 CLERKENWELL ROAD, LONDON
Greater London EC1M 5TW...................................020 7456 7100
e: info@bacsport.co.uk
w: www.bacsport.co.uk

Beyond Brilliant Events
54A CHURCH ROAD, BURGESS HILL
West Sussex RH15 9AE..01444 254350
w: www.beyondbrilliant.co.uk

Dubai Experience
ACORN BUSINESS CENTRE, 18 SKATERS WAY, WERRINGTON,
PETERBOROUGH
Cambridgeshire PE4 6NB.....................................0843 290 7092
e: sales@dubaiexperience.com
w: www.dubaiexperience.com

Esselle Sports Management
349 THE GREEN, ECCLESTON, CHORLEY
Lancashire PR7 5PH 01257 450991
e: esselle@essellesports.com
w: www.essellesports.com

Gamewagon Ltd
113 - 115 OYSTER LANE, BYFLEET
Surrey KT14 7JZ...0845 319 4263
e: julie.owen@gamewagon.co.uk
w: www.gamewagon.co.uk

Leisure Pursuits
BLACKLAND FARM, GRINSTEAD LANE, EAST GRINSTEAD
West Sussex RH19 4HP 01342 825522
e: mail@leisurepursuits.co.uk
w: www.leisurepursuits.co.uk

Mendip Outdoor Pursuits
THE WAREHOUSE, SILVER STREET, WESTON-SUPER-MARE
 BS49 5EY 01934 834877
e: info@mendip.me
w: www.mendipoutdoorpursuits.co.uk

Mwm Sports Management Group
144 HIGH STREET, HOLYWOOD BT18 9HS 028 9042 6633
e: info@mwmsports.co.uk
w: www.mwmsports.co.uk

Neon Arena Services
UNIT 305, THE ARGENT CENTRE, 60 FREDERICK STREET,
HOCKLEY, BIRMINGHAM
West Midlands B1 3HS..0121 236 5555
e: info@neonarenaservices.co.uk
w: www.neonsportsfloors.co.uk

Pennine Events
SUITE 1A, RIBBLE HOUSE, MEANYGATE, BAMER BRIDGE,
PRESTON
Lancashire PR5 6UP 01772 447 979
e: support@pennineevents.co.uk
w: www.pennineevents.co.uk

Pop Up Arena
50 QUEENS ROAD, LONDON
 SW19 8LR 020 8879 3030
e: info@popuparena.com
w: popuparena.com

Rushmans Ltd
PO BOX 2391, MARLBOROUGH
Wiltshire SN8 3EU...01264 852 010
e: info@rushmans.com
w: www.rushmans.com

S

Sportsworld Group Plc
DST HOUSE,, ST MARKS HILL, SURBITON
Surrey KT6 4BH 020 8971 2966
e: info@sportsworld.co.uk
w: www.sportsworld.co.uk

The Carter Company
THE RED HOUSE, COLLEGE ROAD NORTH, ASTON CLINTON
Buckinghamshire HP22 5EZ...................................01296 631671
e: hello@the-carter-company.com
w: www.the-carter-company.com

The Queen's Club
PALLISER ROAD, WEST KENSINGTON
Greater London W14 9EQ.............................020 7386 3400
e: marketing@queensclub.co.uk
w: www.queensclub.co.uk

TMB Events
2 KINGSTON BUSINESS PARK, KINGSTON BAGPUIZE, ABINGDON
Oxfordshire OX13 5FE...01865 822500
e: hello@tmb-events.com
w: www.tmb-events.com

VIP Adrenaline Ltd
9 EDGBARROW RISE, SANDHURST
Berkshire GU47 8QH...07734 391299
e: info@vipadrenaline.com
w: www.vipadrenaline.com

Stag Nights

Gamewagon Ltd
113 - 115 OYSTER LANE, BYFLEET
KT14 7JZ...0845 319 4263
e: admin@gamewagon.co.uk
w: www.gamewagon.info

Stage Construction

Actus Event Technology
UNIT 4, FULLERS YARD, SHEEPHOUSE ROAD, MAIDENHEAD
SL6 8HA 0844 736 5650
e: info@actusevent.com
w: www.actusevent.com

Alistage (t/as Aliscaff Ltd)
EARLS FARM, EARLS LANE, SOUTH MIMS, POTTERS BAR
Herefordshire EN6 3LT...01707 653245
e: sales@alistage.co.uk
w: www.alistage.co.uk

Blackfriars Scenery Ltd
33 BEAR LANE, LONDON
Greater London SE1 0UH 020 7928 6413
e: info@bsstaging.com
w: www.bsstaging.com

Bower Wood Production Services
UNIT 5 THE BILLINGS, 3 WALNUT TREE CLOSE, GUILDFORD
Surrey GU1 4UL 01483 300926
e: enquiries@bowerwood.com
w: www.bowerwood.com

Brilliant Stages
5 LANGTHWAITE ROAD, LANGTHWAITE , BUSINESS PARK, SOUTH KIRKBY, , WAKEFIELD
West Yorkshire WF9 3AP 01462 455 366
e: info@bstages.com
w: www.brilliantstages.com

C&E Structures scaffolding
NORTH MERSEY BUSINESS CENTRE/WOODWARD RD, KNOWSLEY INDUSTRIAL PARK, LIVERPOOL
Merseyside L33 7UY .... 0151 5484 492 / 07775 880 460
e: ian@candestructures.co.uk
w: www.candestructures.co.uk

Cardiff Theatrical Services
ELLEN STREET, CARDIFF
Glamorgan CF10 4TT...029 20634680
e: cts@wno.org.uk
w: www.cardifftheatricalservices.co.

Celtic Stage Crew
DRAGON HOUSE, LECKWITH QUAY, LECKWITH ROAD, CARDIFF
CF11 8AU 029 20225152
e: office@celticstagecrew.co.uk
w: www.celticstagecrew.co.uk

Centre Stage
23 IRON WORKS, 58 DACE ROAD, LONDON
Greater London E3 2NX.......................................01442 255170
e: hire@centrestage.org.uk
w: www.centrestage.org.uk

Concept Staging Ltd
WHITEHOLME MILL, SKIPTON ROAD, TRAWDEN
Lancashire BB8 8RA 01282 862777
e: enquiries@conceptstaging.co.uk
w: www.conceptstaging.co.uk

EC Creative Services Ltd
UNIT 1 LANSDOWNE ROAD, CHADDERTON, OLDHAM
Lancashire OL9 9EF...0161 628 7723
e: info@eccreativeservices.com
w: www.eccreativeservices.com

Fenwick Mobile Exhibitions Ltd
FENWICK BY-PASS, FENWICK
Ayrshire KA3 6AW...01560 600271
e: enquiries@fmx-ltd.com
w: www.fmx-ltd.com

Flat Earth Scenery & Staging Ltd
UNITS A & B, WHITE STREET, BRISTOL
Bristol BS5 0TS...0117 954 1102
e: info@flat-earth.co.uk
w: www.flat-earth.co.uk

S

Hall Stage
UNIT 4, COSGROVE WAY, LUTON
Bedfordshire LU1 1XL 01582 439440
e: info@hallstage.com
w: www.hallstage.com

HPSS Ltd
UNIT 5 DAIRYCOATES INDUSTRIAL ESTATE, WHILTSHIRE RD, HULL
East Yorkshire HU4 6PA..01482 221 810
e: webmail@hpss.co.uk
w: www.hpss.co.uk

Indalo Marquees
.... 0121 355 0005 / 07976 928 053
e: info@indalomarquees.co.uk
w: www.indalomarquees.co.uk

KC Lighting
123 PRIORWAY AVENUE, BORROWASH, DERBY
DE72 3HY .... 01332 674589 / 07860 669323
e: kev@kclighting.co.uk
w: www.kclighting.co.uk

LMS Events
UNIT 60C , BLACKPOLE TRADING ESTATE WEST, BLACKPOLE,
WORCESTER
Worcestershire WR3 8TJ.......................................01905 759 265
e: info@lmsevents.com
w: www.lmsevents.com

Media Structures
87-91, BEDDINGTON LANE, CROYDON
Surrey CRO 4TD 020 8683 3131
e: info@mediastructures.co.uk
w: www.mediastructures.co.uk

Metalworx Ltd
PONSWOOD INDUSTRIAL ESTATE, DRURY LANE,
ST LEONARDS ON SEA
East Sussex TN38 9BA..01424 446345
e: info@metalworx.com
w: www.metalworx.com

Nbm Timber Products
SITWELL STREET, HULL
East Yorkshire HU8 7BG 01482 323904
e: info@nbm-timberproducts.co.uk
w: www.nbmstagedecking.co.uk

Neon Arena Services
UNIT 305, THE ARGENT CENTRE, 60 FREDERICK STREET,
HOCKLEY, BIRMINGHAM
West Midlands B1 3HS..0121 236 5555
e: info@neonarenaservices.co.uk
w: www.neonsportsfloors.co.uk

Orbit Staging Ltd
UNIT 2 OUZLEDALE FOUNDRY, LONG ING LANE, BARNOLDSWICK
Lancashire BB18 6BN.. 01282 816500
e: info@orbitstaging.co.uk
w: www.orbitstaging.co.uk

Portable Stages
123, PRIORWAY AVENUE, BORROWASH, DERBY
Derbyshire DE72 3HY...07860 669323
e: kev@portablestages.co.uk
w: www.portablestages.co.uk

Prism Lighting
UNIT 5A, HAMPTON INDUSTRIAL ESTATE, MALPAS
Cheshire SY14 8LU 01948 820201
e: mail@prismlighting.co.uk
w: www.prismlighting.co.uk

Rudi Enos Design
SUITE 2, SEATON BUSINESS PARK, 65 DEEP LANE, SHEFFIELD
South Yorkshire S5 0DU 0114 257 7755
e: info@rudienosdesign.com
w: www.rudienosdesign.com

S2 Events
141- 143 NATHAN WAY, LONDON
Greater London SE28 0AB....................................020 7928 5474
e: info@s2events.co.uk
w: www.s2events.co.uk

Scenex Sets & Staging Ltd
FELDSPAR CLOSE, THE WARRENS INDUSTRIAL PARK, ENDERBY,
LEICESTER
Leicestershire LE19 4SD......................................0116 284 5999
e: hello@scenex.co.uk
w: www.scenex.co.uk

Serious Stages Ltd
TOR HILL WORKS, DULCOTE, , WELLS
Somerset BA5 3NT 01749 899 188
e: info@stages.co.uk
w: www.stages.co.uk

Showlite Ltd
SUITE 1, FOSSE HOUSE, EAST ANTON COURT, ANDOVER
Hampshire SP10 5RG 01264 365 550
e: info@showlite.co.uk
w: www.showlite.co.uk

Showscape Ltd
HOLLY FARM BUSINESS PARK, HONILEY
Warwickshire CV8 1NP 01926 484591
e: enquiries@showscape.co.uk
w: www.showscape.co.uk

Showstars
BRIDGE HOUSE, 3 MILLS STUDIOS, THREE MILL LANE, LONDON
Greater London E3 3DU 0208 215 3333
e: enquiries@showstars.co.uk
w: www.showstars.co.uk

Silver Stage Event Structures
THE OAKS, MILL DROVE, NORTHWOLD, THETFORD
Norfolk IP26 5LQ...01366 727 310
e: info@silver-stage.com
w: www.silver-stage.com

S

Silverback Events
THE SPACE PROJECT, 12 VAUGHN STREET, MANCHESTER
Greater Manchester M12 5FQ 08445 617 939
e: info@silverbackuk.com
w: www.silverbackuk.com

Spyder UK Ltd
UNIT 3, ATTRILLS YARD, THE DUVER, ST HELENS
Isle of Wight PO33 1YB 01983 779337
e: hire@spyderuk.com
w: www.spyderuk.com

Stage Miracles Ltd
WOODLANDS, SCHOOL ROAD, POTTERS BAR
Hertfordshire EN6 1JW 01707 662 500
e: mail@stagemiracles.co.uk
w: www.stagemiracles.com

Stage Systems
2 PRINCES COURT, ROYAL WAY, LOUGHBOROUGH
Leicestershire LE11 5GU..01509 611021
e: info@stagesystems.co.uk
w: www.stagesystems.co.uk

Stage Technologies
9 FALCON PARK, NEASDEN LANE, LONDON
Greater London NW10 1RZ 0208 208 6000
e: london@stagetech.com
w: www.stagetech.com

Stagecraft UK
ST QUENTIN GATE, TELFORD
Shropshire TF3 4JH 01952 281 600
e: sales@stagecraftuk.com
w: www.stagecraftuk.com

Stagerent.co.uk
SOUTH GARRON, SOWDEN LANE BARNSTAPLE
EX32 8BU 01271 329 225
e: ian@impactmm.co.uk
w: www.stagerent.co.uk

Staging Services Ltd
LEAMORE LANE, BLOXWICH, WALSALL
West Midlands WS2 7BY 01922 405111
e: info@stagingservicesltd.co.uk
w: www.stagingservicesltd.co.uk

Star Events Group Ltd
MILTON ROAD, THURLEIGH, BEDFORD
Bedfordshire MK44 2DF...01234 772233
e: info@StarEventsGroup.com
w: www.stareventsgroup.com

Steeldeck Rentals
UNIT 58 T MARCHANT ESTATE, 42 - 72 VERNEY RD, LONDON
Greater London SE16 3DH 020 7833 2031
e: rentals@steeldeck.co.uk
w: www.steeldeck.co.uk

Steely Trees
....01308 488574
e: info@steelytrees.co.uk
w: steelytrees.co.uk

Themobilestage.com
SOUND PERSPECTIVE LTD, 23 YOXALL DRIVE, DERBY
Derbyshire DE22 3SF...07970 076 753
e: info@themobilestage.com
w: www.themobilestage.com

Wango's Staging Concepts
OLD STATION HOUSE, INGHAM, BURY ST EDMUNDS
Suffolk IP31 1NS...077100 37997
e: info@wangos.com
w: www.wangos.com

Staging

24 Carrot Promotions
Y GAER, CWMCOU, NEWCASTLE EMLYN
Carmathenshire SA38 9PR.......... 01239 711854 / 07989 520637
e: info@24carrotpromotions.co.uk
w: www.24carrotpromotions.co.uk

3d Productions Ltd
UNIT 8, LOTHERTON WAY GARFORTH, LEEDS
West Yorkshire LS25 2JY 0113 236 3700
e: info@3dproductions.co.uk
w: www.3dproductions.co.uk

Abacus Stagetech
UNIT 9 BROOKLANDS TERRACE , SAYER STREET, HUNTINGDON,
CAMBS
PE29 3HE .... 01480455780 / 07961 140152
e: abacusstagetech@gmail.com
w: www.abacusstagetech.co.uk

Actus Event Technology
UNIT 4, FULLERS YARD, SHEEPHOUSE ROAD, MAIDENHEAD
SL6 8HA 0844 736 5650
e: info@actusevent.com
w: www.actusevent.com

Alistage (t/as Aliscaff Ltd)
EARLS FARM, EARLS LANE, SOUTH MIMS, POTTERS BAR
Herefordshire EN6 3LT 01707 653245
e: sales@alistage.co.uk
w: www.alistage.co.uk

All Access Staging & Productions Ltd
UNIT 12 WOKING BUSINESS PARK, ALBERT DRIVE, WOKING
Surrey GU21 5JY 01483 765 305
e: guyf@allaccessinc.com
w: www.allaccessinc.com

S

Audio Source Ltd
31 MONGLEATH AVENUE, FALMOUTH
Cornwall TR11 4PP 079/1 607172
.... 07867 525016 / 01326 3115
e: hire@audio-source.co.uk
w: www.audio-source.co.uk

Austen Lewis Ltd
UNIT DG, CHELWORTH PARK, CRICKLADE, SWINDON
Wiltshire SN6 6HE..01793 750599
e: info@austen-lewis.co.uk
w: www.austen-lewis.co.uk

BES Systems Ltd
155A SOUTH LIBERTY LANE, ASHTON VALE, BRISTOL
Bristol BS3 2TL......................... 0845 224 5967 / 07812 111 646
e: info@b-e-s.co.uk
w: www.bes-systems.co.uk

Big House Events Ltd
35 ST CLAIR STREET , EDINBURGH
EH6 8LB 0131 669 6366
e: tash@bighouse-events.co.uk
w: www.bighouse-events.co.uk

Big House Events Ltd
35 ST CLAIR STREET , EDINBURGH
EH6 8LB 0131 669 6366
e: tash@bighouse-events.co.uk
w: www.bighouse-events.co.uk

Big-TV (UK) Ltd
HUDSON HOUSE, THE HUDSON, WYKE, BRADFORD
Yorkshire BD12 8HZ..01274 604 309
e: info@big-tv.co.uk
w: www.big-tv.co.uk

Black and White Live
....0208 422 0042
e: info@blackandwhitelive.com
w: www.blackandwhitelive.com

Bower Wood Production Services
UNIT 5 THE BILLINGS, 3 WALNUT TREE CLOSE, GUILDFORD
Surrey GU1 4UL 01483 300926
e: enquiries@bowerwood.com
w: www.bowerwood.com

Brilliant Stages
5 LANGTHWAITE ROAD, LANGTHWAITE , BUSINESS PARK, SOUTH
KIRKBY, , WAKEFIELD
West Yorkshire WF9 3AP 01462 455 366
e: info@bstages.com
w: www.brilliantstages.com

Bristol (UK) Ltd
UNIT 1, SUTHERLAND COURT, TOLPITS LANE, WATFORD
Hertfordshire WD18 9SP 01923 779 333
e: tech.sales@bristolpaint.com
w: www.bristolpaint.com

C&E Structures scaffolding
NORTH MERSEY BUSINESS CENTRF/WOODWARD RD, KNOWSLEY
INDUSTRIAL PARK, LIVERPOOL
Merseyside L33 7UY .... 0151 5484 492 / 07775 880 460
e: ian@candestructures.co.uk
w: www.candestructures.co.uk

Cardiff M Light & Sound
UNIT 2, THE HIGHWAYMAN, CASTLEVIEW, BRIDGEND
CF31 1NJ 01656 767388
e: info@cardiffm.co.uk
w: www.cardiffm.co.uk

Celtic Stage Crew
DRAGON HOUSE, LECKWITH QUAY, LECKWITH ROAD, CARDIFF
CF11 8AU 029 20225152
e: office@celticstagecrew.co.uk
w: www.celticstagecrew.co.uk

Complete Avenue Ltd
OLD BARN, BLACKBIRD FARM,BLACKBIRD LANE, ALDENHAM
West Midlands WD25 8BS.....................................07854 007483
w: www.completeavenue.co.uk

Concept Staging Ltd
WHITEHOLME MILL, SKIPTON ROAD, TRAWDEN
Lancashire BB8 8RA 01282 862777
e: enquiries@conceptstaging.co.uk
w: www.conceptstaging.co.uk

Creffields (Timber & Boards) Ltd
UNIT 6, MARCUS CLOSE, TILEHURST, READING
Berkshire RG30 4EA 0118 945 3533
e: info@creffields.co.uk
w: www.creffields.co.uk

Daytona Stage Hire
PO BOX 43, HUDDERSFIELD
West Yorkshire HD8 9YU 01484 605555
e: office@daytonastagehire.com
w: www.daytonastagehire.com

DC3 Productions Ltd
37 BRAMBLE ROAD, HATFIELD
AL10 9RZ.................................. 020 8123 8765 / 07737 535886
e: dan@dc3productions.co.uk
w: www.dc3productions.co.uk

Devs AV Company
BARCELONA
.... +34 938010612
e: Barcelona@devsavcompany.com
w: www.avrentalspain.com

Devs Av Rental Group Europe
....34938010612
e: devs@devsavrentalgroup.com
w: www.devsavrentalgroup.com

S

DLC Events
STREET 22, AL QUOZ IND 3, DUBAI
PO Box 282841,.. +971 4 347 0484
e: office@dlcevents.com
w: www.dlcevents.com

Dynamic Production Solutions
UNIT 13E, BARTON BUSINESS PARK, NEW DOVER ROAD,
CANTERBURY
Kent CT1 3AA 01227 656 599
e: info@dynamicproductionsolutions.co.uk
w: www.dynamicproductionsolutions.co

East Anglia Leisure
UNIT 4, CIVIC INDUSTRIAL ESTATE, HOMEFIELD ROAD, HAVERHILL
Suffolk CB9 8QP 01440 714204
e: info@ealeisure.co.uk
w: www.ealeisure.co.uk

EC Creative Services Ltd
UNIT 1 LANSDOWNE ROAD, CHADDERTON, OLDHAM
Lancashire OL9 9EF..0161 628 7723
e: info@eccreativeservices.com
w: www.eccreativeservices.com

Emphasis Event Production Ltd
UNIT 14, BELGRAVE INDUSTRIAL ESTATE, SOUTHAMPTON
Hampshire SO17 3EA...023 8055 0557
e: enquiries@emphasiseventproduction.co.uk
w: www.prestech.co.uk

ES Global Solutions
UNIT G EAST COATE HOUSE, 1 Â " 3 COATE STREET, LONDON
Greater London E2 9AG.......................................020 7055 7200
e: info@esglobalsolutions.com
w: www.esglobalsolutions.com

Event Equipment Hire
UNIT 2, SYKES STREET, CLECKHEATON
Yorkshire BD19 5HA...01422 200960
e: sales@eventequipmenthire.co.uk
w: www.eventequipmenthire.co.uk

Firefly Audio Visual Solutions Ltd
UNIT 31 BARKSTON HOUSE, CROYDON STREET, LEEDS
West Yorkshire LS11 9RT 01133 320042
e: hire.leeds@fireflyav.co.uk
w: www.fireflyav.co.uk

First Network Ltd
ROWDELL ROAD, NORTHOLT
Middlesex UB5 5QR 020 8842 1222
e: info@first-network.com
w: www.first-network.com

Flat Earth Scenery & Staging Ltd
UNITS A & B, WHITE STREET, BRISTOL
Bristol BS5 0TS...0117 954 1102
e: info@flat-earth.co.uk
w: www.flat-earth.co.uk

G Stages Ltd
SPARROWS REST FARM, POPLAR TREE LANE, TROWBRIDGE
Wiltshire BA14 9NB 07976 239 181
e: info@gstages.co.uk
w: www.gstages.co.uk

Gain Audio
47 GORSEY LANE , CLOCK FACE , ST HELENS
WA9 4QS .... 08438861162 / 07896045416
e: justgainaudio@gmail.com
w: www.gainaudio.co.uk

Gallowglass Ltd
3RD FLOOR, 199 THE VALE, ACTON , LONDON
W3 7QS 0845 600 8966
e: events@gallowglass.co.uk
w: www.gallowglass.co.uk

GMC Professional
HOZA 51, WARSAW
00-681 .... 0048 507 164 924 / 0048 601 375 295
e: info@gmcpro.pl
w: www.gmcpro.pl

Gopak Ltd
RANGE ROAD, HYTHE
Kent CT21 6HG...01303 265751
e: gopakinfo@gopak.co.uk
w: www.gopak.co.uk

Gosh Staging
GOSH STAGING, LONDON
SE1 1PE..07970 833 654
e: ed@goshstaging.co.uk
w: www.goshstaging.co.uk

Gradav Hire and Sales Ltd
SHENLEY ROAD , BOREHAMWOOD
Hertfordshire WD6 1JG 020 8324 2100
e: office@gradav.co.uk
w: www.gradav.co.uk

Hall Stage
UNIT 4, COSGROVE WAY, LUTON
Bedfordshire LU1 1XL 01582 439440
e: info@hallstage.com
w: www.hallstage.com

Halo Lighting
98-124 BREWERY ROAD, LONDON
Greater London N7 9PG 0207 607 4444
e: info@halo.co.uk
w: www.halo.co.uk

Hands On Production Services Ltd
79 LOANBANK QUADRANT, GLASGOW
Glasgow G51 3HZ 0141 4402005
e: info@hands-on-uk.com
w: www.hands-on-uk.com

S

Hi-Lights
18E WHITEROSE WAY, FOLLINGSBY PARK, GATESHEAD
Tyne and Wear NE10 8YX......................................0191 495 0608
e: martin@hi-lights.tv
w: www.hi-lights.tv

Ideal Event Services
310 UNTHANK ROAD, NORWICH
Norfolk NR4 7QD 01603 280176
e: hello@idealeventservices.co.uk
w: www.idealeventservices.co.uk

Impact Production Services
29 MOUNT AVENUE , BLETCHLEY , MILTON KEYNES
Buckinghamshire MK1 1LS...................................01908 657950
e: enquiries@impactproductions.co.uk
w: www.impactproductions.co.uk

J & J Carter Ltd
UNIT 2, 34 WALWORTH ROAD, WALWORTH BUSINESS PARK,
ANDOVER
Hampshire SP10 5LH...01264 721630
e: sales@jjcarter.com
w: www.jjcarter.com

J&C Joel Limited (Head Office)
CORPORATION MILL, CORPORATION STREET, SOWERBY BRIDGE,
HALIFAX
Yorkshire HX6 2QQ...01422 833835
e: uksales@jcjoel.com
w: www.jcjoel.com

Jigsaw Events
104 ALMA LANE, UPPER HALE, FARNHAM
 GU9 0LP 0116 248 9421
e: info@jigsaw-events.co.uk
w: www.jigsaw-events.co.uk

Le Mark Self Adhesive Ltd
UNIT 1 HOUGHTON HILL INDUSTRIES, SAWTRY WAY, HOUGHTON
Cambridgeshire PE28 2DH....................................01480 494 540
e: info@lemark.co.uk
w: www.lemark.co.uk

Light The Way
UNIT 7 CAVENDISH COURT MILL, WEST STREET, BRADFORD
BD11 1DA...01422 250 819
e: hire@lighttheway.co.uk
w: www.lighttheway.co.uk

LMS Events
UNIT 60C , BLACKPOLE TRADING ESTATE WEST, BLACKPOLE,
WORCESTER
Worcestershire WR3 8TJ..01905 759 265
e: info@lmsevents.com
w: www.lmsevents.com

Location Audio
....07815 918398
e: locationaudiostage@gmail.com
w: www.locationaudiostagehire.co.uk

London Event Rentals
UNIT 7, WILLOW WALK, TOWER BRIDGE, LONDON
Greater London SE1 5SF 01252 313154
e: info@londoneventrentals.co.uk
w: www.londoneventrentals.co.uk

LS Live
UNIT 53, LANGTHWAITE BUSINESS PARK, SOUTH KIRKBY,
WAKEFIELD
West Yorkshire WF9 3NR.......................................01977 659 888
e: sales@ls-live.com
w: www.ls-live.com

Magnet Schultz Ltd
3-4 CAPITAL PARK, OLD WOKING, SURREY
Sussex GU22 9LD 01483 794700
e: sales@magnetschultz.co.uk
w: www.magnetschultz.co.uk

Matt Bunday Events
.... 023 8055 3736 / 07730 604 869
e: info@mattbundayevents.com
w: www.mattbundayevents.com

MCL (Glasgow)
UNIT C, MOORPARK CENTRAL, 40 DAVA STREET, GLASGOW
Glasgow G51 2BQ..0141 425 2016
e: glasgow@mclcreate.com
w: mclcreate.com

MCL (Manchester)
18 LORD BYRON SQUARE, STOWELL TECHNICAL PARK, SALFORD
QUAYS, MANCHESTER
Greater Manchester M50 2XH...............................0161 745 9933
e: manchester@mclcreate.com
w: mclcreate.com/

Mosaic FX Lighting
THE TYTHE BARN, DOG KENNEL FARM, THE CHARLTON ROAD,
HITCHIN. Hertfordshire SG5 2AB............................01462 434445
e: sales@mosaicfx.co.uk
w: www.mosaicfx.co.uk

Movetech UK
PART OF THE BRITISH TURNTABLE GROUP, EMBLEM STREET,
BOLTON
Lancashire BL3 5BW.................. 01204 525626 / 01992 574602
e: info@movetechuk.com
w: www.movetechuk.com/rental

Nbm Timber Products
SITWELL STREET, HULL
East Yorkshire HU8 7BG 01482 323904
e: info@nbm-timberproducts.co.uk
w: www.nbmstagedecking.co.uk

Omega Drapes
RIVERSIDE INDUSTRIAL ESTATE, THAMES ROAD, BARKING
Essex IG11 0ND 020 8591 4945
e: contact@omegadrapes.co.uk
w: www.omegadrapes.co.uk

S

On Event Production Co.
UNIT 16, WILLOW ROAD,, TRENT LANE INDUSTRIAL ESTATE,
CASTLE DONINGTON, DERBY
Derbyshire DE74 2NP 01159 222959
e: hello@on-productions.co.uk
w: www.lovingitlive.co.uk

Orbit Roofs And Staging
UNIT 2, LONG ING LANE, OUZLEDALE FOUNDRY, BURNLEY
BB18 6BN..01282 816500
e: info@orbitroofsandstaging.co.uk
w: www.orbitroofsandstaging.co.uk

Orbit Staging Ltd
UNIT 2 OUZLEDALE FOUNDRY, LONG ING LANE, BARNOLDSWICK
Lancashire BB18 6BN... 01282 816500
e: info@orbitstaging.co.uk
w: www.orbitstaging.co.uk

Overlay Events Ltd
54 OXFORD ROAD, UXBRIDGE
Middlesex UB9 4DJ..020 3693 4925
e: info@overlayevents.com
w: www.overlayevents.com

Panache Audio Systems
A5 SPECTRUM BUSINESS CENTRE, MEDWAY CITY ESTATE,
ROCHESTER
Kent ME2 4NP 01634 720700
e: sales@panacheaudio.co.uk
w: www.panacheaudio.co.uk

Portable Stages
123, PRIORWAY AVENUE, BORROWASH, DERBY
Derbyshire DE72 3HY...07860 669323
e: kev@portablestages.co.uk
w: www.portablestages.co.uk

Precise Events
UNIT K14 CLYDE WORKSHOPS, FULLARTON ROAD, GLASGOW
Glasgow G32 8YL 0141 255 0740
e: info@PreciseEvents.co.uk
w: www.preciseaudio.co.uk

Premier Solutions Ltd
11 ASCOT PARK ESTATE, LENTON STREET,, SANDIACRE,
NOTTINGHAM
Nottinghamshire NG10 DL 0115 9394122
e: info@premier-solutions.biz
w: www.premier-solutions.biz

Premier UK Events Ltd
UNIT 2, ROOKERY LANE, THURMASTON, LEICESTER
Leicestershire LE4 8AU..1162029953
e: ben@premier-ltd.com
w: premier-event-solutions.com

Pro Event Solutions
THEAKLEN DRIVE, PONSWOOD INDUSTRIAL ESTATE,
ST LEONARDS
East Sussex TN37 9AZ...8006127427
e: hello@proeventsolutions.co.uk
w: www.proeventsolutions.co.uk

Pro Productions Limited
CASTLEFIELDS FARM, HARVINGTON LANE, NORTON,, EVESHAM
Worcestershire WR114UJ.......................................01386 871901
e: hire@proproductions.co.uk
w: www.proproductions.co.uk

Prolyte Sales UK Ltd.
UNIT 1A, SHORTWOOD BUSINESS PARK, SHORTWOOD WAY,
BARNSLEY. S74 9LH 01977 659 800
e: info@prolyte.com
w: www.prolyte.com

RATstands Ltd
UNIT 3 WATERSIDE BUSINESS PARK, EASTWAYS, WITHAM
Essex CM8 3YQ 020 8741 4804
e: sales@ratstands.com
w: www.ratstands.com

Rock City Stage Crew
LANGSFORD HOUSE, 8 DARKLAKE VIEW, ESTOVER, PLYMOUTH
Devon PL6 7TL 01752 255 933
e: office@rockcitycrew.co.uk
w: www.rockcitycrew.co.uk

Rock-Tech Projects
UNIT 2, FRYORS COURT, MURTON
Yorkshire YO19 5UY 01904 481 700
e: info@rock-tech.co.uk
w: www.rock-tech.co.uk

Roustabout Ltd
FRONGOCH BOATYARD, SMUGGLER'S COVE, ABERDOVEY
LL35 0RG 01654 767 177
e: info@roustabout.ltd.uk
w: www.roustabout.ltd.uk

S2 Events
141- 143 NATHAN WAY, LONDON
Greater London SE28 0AB.....................................020 7928 5474
e: info@s2events.co.uk
w: www.s2events.co.uk

Salima Ltd
2A BACCHUS HOUSE, CALLEVA PARK, ALDERMASTON, READING
Berkshire RG7 8EN .... 0845 458 1699 / 07825 586 083
e: info@salima-ltd.co.uk
w: www.salima-ltd.co.uk

Scenex Sets & Staging Ltd
FELDSPAR CLOSE, THE WARRENS INDUSTRIAL PARK, ENDERBY,
LEICESTER
Leicestershire LE19 4SD.......................................0116 284 5999
e: hello@scenex.co.uk
w: www.scenex.co.uk

S

Serious Stages Ltd
TOR HILL WORKS, DULCOTE, , WELLS
Somerset BA5 3NT 01749 899 188
e: info@stages.co.uk
w: www.stages.co.uk

Set Creations Ltd
STUDIO HOUSE DELAMARE ROAD, CHESHUNT
Hertfordshire EN8 9SH..01992 789 759
e: connect@setcreations.com
w: www.setcreations.com

Sevens7
3RD FLOOR , 46A ROSEBERY AVENUE, LONDON
Greater London EC1R 4RP 020 3096 1348
e: info@sevens7.co.uk
w: www.sevens7.co.uk

Silver Stage Event Structures
THE OAKS, MILL DROVE, NORTHWOLD, THETFORD
Norfolk IP26 5LQ..01366 727 310
e: info@silver-stage.com
w: www.silver-stage.com

Soundbase Solutions
64 OLDHAM STREET, MANCHESTER
Greater Manchester M4 1LE 0161 238 8727
e: info@soundbasesolutions.com
w: www.soundbasesolutions.com

Specialist Lighting Co Limited
49 THE BROADWAY , CHEAM SUTTON
SM3 8BL...01202 700569
e: sales@slclightingonline.com
w: slclightingonline.com/

Spotlight Sound
UNIT 32B, LITTLE BOYTON FARM , BOYTON HALL LANE ,
CHELMSFORD
Essex CM1 4LN 01245 206206
e: info@spotlightsound.co.uk
w: www.spotlightsound.co.uk

SPS Productions
UNIT 1, LATHAM PARK, ST BLAZEY ROAD, PAR , CORNWALL
PL24 2JA...01726 817380
e: steve@sps-productions.co.uk
w: www.sps-productions.co.uk

Spyder UK Ltd
UNIT 3, ATTRILLS YARD, THE DUVER, ST HELENS
Isle of Wight PO33 1YB 01983 779337
e: hire@spyderuk.com
w: www.spyderuk.com

Stage Connections
UNIT 1B, ACTON STREET , LONG EATON, NOTTINGHAM
Nottinghamshire NG10 1FT....... 0115 938 6354 / 07976 00 5769
e: info@stageconnections.co.uk
w: www.stageconnections.co.uk

Stage Lighting Services Ltd
UNIT A, AVENUE PARK INDUSTRIAL ESTATE, CROESCADARN
CLOSE, PENTWYN, CARDIFF
CF23 8HE..02920 613 577
e: info@stagelightingservices.com
w: www.stagelightingservices.com

Stage Miracles Ltd
WOODLANDS, SCHOOL ROAD, POTTERS BAR
Hertfordshire EN6 1JW 01707 662 500
e: mail@stagemiracles.co.uk
w: www.stagemiracles.com

Stage Systems
2 PRINCES COURT, ROYAL WAY, LOUGHBOROUGH
Leicestershire LE11 5GU..01509 611021
e: info@stagesystems.co.uk
w: www.stagesystems.co.uk

Stage Technologies
9 FALCON PARK, NEASDEN LANE, LONDON
Greater London NW10 1RZ 0208 208 6000
e: london@stagetech.com
w: www.stagetech.com

Stagecraft UK
ST QUENTIN GATE, TELFORD
Shropshire TF3 4JH 01952 281 600
e: sales@stagecraftuk.com
w: www.stagecraftuk.com

Stageline Mobile Stage
700 MARSOLAIS, 827 L'ANGE-GARDIEN, L'ASSOMPTION, CANADA
J5W 2G9.. +1 450-589-1063
e: info@stageline.com
w: www.stageline.com

Stageplan London
UNIT 26-30, THE SWAN CENTRE, ROSEMARY ROAD, LONDON
 SW17 0AR 020 8944 0899
e: info@stageplanlondon.co.uk
w: www.stageplanlondon.co.uk

Stagerent.co.uk
SOUTH GARRON, SOWDEN LANE BARNSTAPLE
EX32 8BU 01271 329 225
e: ian@impactmm.co.uk
w: www.stagerent.co.uk

Staging Services Ltd
LEAMORE LANE, BLOXWICH, WALSALL
West Midlands WS2 7BY 01922 405111
e: info@stagingservicesltd.co.uk
w: www.stagingservicesltd.co.uk

Steeldeck Rentals
UNIT 58 T MARCHANT ESTATE, 42 - 72 VERNEY RD, LONDON
Greater London SE16 3DH 020 7833 2031
e: rentals@steeldeck.co.uk
w: www.steeldeck.co.uk

S

SXS Events
....0870 080 2342
e: hello@sxsevents.co.uk
w: www.sxsevents.co.uk

Tega AV
148 SCULCOATES LANE, HULL
East Yorkshire HU5 1EE..01482 444666
e: av@tega.co.uk
w: www.tega.co.uk

The Manchester Light & Stage Company Ltd
76-78 NORTH WESTERN STREET, ARDWICK, MANCHESTER
Greater Manchester M12 6DY..............................0161 273 2662
e: info@manchesterlightandstage.com
w: www.manchesterlightandstage.com

The Revolving Stage Company Ltd
CRONDAL ROAD, BAYTON ROAD INDUSTRIAL ESTATE, COVENTRY
Warwickshire CV7 9NH 024 7668 7055
e: enquiries@therevolvingstagecompany.co.uk
w: www.therevolvingstagecompany.co.u

Tusk Showhire
23 COLLUM LANE, SCUNTHORPE
Lincolnshire DN16 2SZ .... 01724 859541 / 07850 307162
e: info@tuskshowhire.co.uk
w: www.tuskshowhire.co.uk

UK Event Services
UNIT 56- ENFIELD INDUSTRIAL ESTATE, REDDITCH
Worcestershire B97 6DE .... 08456 43 48 49 / 08456 44 65 70
e: websitecontact@ukeventservices.co.uk
w: www.ukeventservices.co.uk

Velvet Twenty
....020 8675 4870
e: enquiries@velvettwenty.co.uk
w: www.velvettwenty.co.uk

Vision Events (Edinburgh)
16 DRYDEN ROAD, BILSTON GLEN INDUSTRIAL ESTATE,
LOANHEAD
Edinburgh EH20 9LZ 0131 334 3324
e: edinburgh@visionevents.co.uk
w: www.visionevents.co.uk

VisionSound AV
751 SOUTH WEIR CANYON ROAD, SUITE 157-223, ANAHEIM, CA
92808...001 714 280 8201
e: sales@visionsoundav.com
w: www.visionsoundav.com

VNV Sounds
UNITS 10 AND 10A ASHLEY HOUSE, ASHLEY ROAD, LONDON
Greater London N17 9LZ..0203 021 1370
e: info@vnvlive.co.uk
w: www.vnvsounds.co.uk

Wango's Staging Concepts
OLD STATION HOUSE, INGHAM, BURY ST EDMUNDS
Suffolk IP31 1NS...077100 37997
e: info@wangos.com
w: www.wangos.com

Zerodb Live
38 NIGEL HOUSE, PORTPOOL LANE, LONDON
Greater London EC1N 7UR 020 3332 0049
e: info@zerodblive.com
w: www.zerodblive.com

Standard / Luxury Vehicle Hire

Aston Martin Hire London (Season Cars)
45 HERTFORD STREET, , MAYFAIR, LONDON
Greater London W1J7SN...2071182345
e: enquiries@seasoncars.com
w: www.seasoncars.com

Auto Pavilion Coventry
COPPER BEECH CLOSE , COVENTRY
CV6 6LW.................................... 07815 510600 / 024 7627 9429
e: admin@autopavilion.co.uk
w: www.autopavilion.co.uk

Benchmark Leasing Ltd
....01753 867430
e: l.Wilson@benchmarkleasing.co.uk
w: www.leaseacar.co.uk

Bradshaw Event Vehicles
NEW LANE, STIBBINGTON, PETERBOROUGH
Cambridgeshire PE8 6LW......................................01780 782621
e: enquiries@eventvehicles.co.uk
w: www.eventvehicles.co.uk

Caddy Car Company
FARTHINGSTONE GOLF COURSE, FARTHINGSTONE, TOWCESTER
Northamptonshire NN12 8HA 01327 361423
e: info@caddycars.co.uk
w: www.caddycars.co.uk

Car leasing made simple
AUTOMOTIVE HOUSE, GRAYS PLACE , SLOUGH
Berkshire SL2 5AF 0800 458 0113
e: contactus@carleasingmadesimple.com
w: carleasingmadesimple.com

Civilised Car Hire Company Ltd
CAMBERWELL TRADING ESTATE, 117-119 DENMARK ROAD, LONDON
Greater London SE5 9LB.......................................020 77387 788
e: darren@londoncarhire.com
w: www.londoncarhire.com

Drive The Best Ltd
340 EASTCOTE LANE, HARROW, LONDON
Middlesex HA2 9AJ.................... 01235507007 / 078 8699 1906
e: info@drivethebest.uk
w: www.drivethebest.co.uk

S

Driven Executive Hire
MODA BUSINESS CENTRE, STIRLING WAY, BOREHAMWOOD
Hertfordshire WD6 2BW .... 020 8243 8873 / 07956 466 125
e: info@drivenexecutivehire.co.uk
w: www.drivenexecutivehire.co.uk

DYC Touring Ltd
DYC TOURING LTD, DOCK ROAD, BRENTFORD
Middlesex TW8 8AG...020 8560 5944
e: bookings@dyctouring.com
w: www.dyctouring.com

Event Buggy Hire
CASTLE GATE , PATRICK GREEN LEEDS
LS26 8HH 1133934100
e: brian@eventbuggyhire.co.uk
w: eventbuggyhire.co.uk/

Getup Front
....020 3475 7767
e: hello@getupfront.co
w: www.getupfront.co

Go Explore Motorhome Hire
CONWY RD, LLANDUDNO JUNCTION, CONWY
LL31 9LU..01492 583913
e: info@goexplore.biz
w: www.goexploremotorhomehire.co.uk

Golfbuggyhire Ltd
FLIXTON ROAD, CARRINGTON, URMSTON, MANCHESTER
Greater Manchester M41 6JE 0161 776 5927
e: info@golfbuggyhire.co.uk
w: www.golfbuggyhire.co.uk

GPS Logistics
LAKESIDE INDUSTRIAL ESTATE, COLNBROOK BY PASS,
COLNBROOK
Berkshire SL3 0EL 020 8150 3300
e: info@gpslogistics.co.uk
w: www.gpslogistics.co.uk

Grace Wedding Cars
UNIT 3 MAFEKING PLACE , ASHTON IN MAKERFIELD , WIGAN
WN4 9DE .... 01942 716106 / 07718 012555
e: graceweddingcarsmarketing@yahoo.co.uk
w: www.graceweddingcars.co.uk

Heli Adventures
THE OLD FIRE STATION, COTSWOLD AIRPORT, KEMBLE,
CIRENCESTER
Gloucestershire GL7 6BA 01285 719222
e: ops@heliadventures.co.uk
w: www.heliadventures.co.uk

Intelligent Car Leasing
SKYPARK 1, 8 ELLIOT PLACE, GLASGOW
Glasgow G3 8EP 0844 3872727
e: info@intelligentcarleasing.com
w: www.intelligentcarleasing.com

Kent & Medway Wedding Cars
NEWINGTON, KENT
....1622677846
e: graham@weddingcarskentmedway.co.uk
w: www.weddingcarskentmedway.co.uk

Lets Go Drive
4 KATHERINE CLOSE , CHARFIELD WOTTON UNDER EDGE SOUTH
Gloucestershire GL12 8TU 07971 198 008
e: steve@letsgodrive.com
w: www.letsgodrive.com

Magnet Hire Ltd
UNIT 2 , DAVISELLA HOUSE, NEWARK STREET, SNEINTON,
NOTTINGHAM
Nottinghamshire NG2 4PP...................................... 01159 243324
e: rob@magnetstudios.co.uk
w: www.magnetstudios.co.uk

Matt Snowball Music
UNIT 2, 3-9 BREWERY ROAD, LONDON
Greater London N7 9QJ 020 7700 6555
e: enquiries@mattsnowball.com
w: www.mattsnowball.com

MM Band Services Ltd
ACER GLADE, BLACK TUP LANE, ARNOLD, HULL
East Yorkshire HU11 5JA.......................................01964 563 464
e: enquiries@mmbandservices.co.uk
w: www.mmbandservices.co.uk

Northern Ferrari Hire
YONDERLEA, PORTENCROSS, WEST KILBRIDE
Ayrshire KA23 9PY 01244 43 44 55
e: info@northernferrarihire.com
w: www.northernferrarihire.com

Signature Car Hire
45 ROWDELL ROAD, NORTHOLT, LONDON
Greater London UB5 6AG 0845 370 2222
e: sales@signaturecarhire.co.uk
w: www.signaturecarhire.co.uk

South Lakes Motorhome Hire
....01229 440113
e: info@southlakesmotorhomehire.com
w: www.southlakesmotorhomehire.com

Studio Moves Ltd
54A CONINGHAM ROAD, BASEMENT FLAT, LONDON
Greater London W12 8BH........... 020 8746 9329 / 07970 518217
e: info@studiomoves.co.uk
w: www.studiomoves.co.uk

TFS Vehicle Leasing
25-39 SMALL HEATH HIGHWAY, BIRMINGHAM
B10 0HR................................... 01213285391 / 0800 910 1111
e: mo@tfsvl.co.uk
w: www.tfsvl.co.uk

S

Tiger Tours Ltd
81 - 83 WEMBLEY HILL ROAD, WEMBLEY
Middlesex HA9 8BU 0208 9021 006
e: info@tigertours.co.uk
w: www.tigertours.co.uk

Tilshead Caravans & Motorcaravan Hire
OAKLEY CORNER GARAGE, LOPCOMBE, SALISBURY
Wiltshire SP5 1BS 01980 863636
e: hire@tilshead-caravans.com
w: www.tilshead-caravans.com

Tractor Hire Ltd
LITTLE TY-COCH, ST. BRIDES WENTLOOG, NEWPORT
NP10 8SR 01633 680754
e: hire@hopkinsmachinery.co.uk
w: www.buggyhireuk.com

Vans For Bands Ltd
42 WOODSTOCK ROAD EAST, BEGBROKE, OXFORD
Oxfordshire OX5 1RG 01865 842 840
e: info@vansforbands.co.uk
w: www.vansforbands.co.uk

Steam Engines / Vehicles

Bluebell Railway
SHEFFIELD PARK STATION, UCKFIELD
East Sussex TN22 3QL 01825 720800
e: info@bluebell-railway.co.uk
w: www.bluebell-railway.co.uk

Great Central Railway Plc
GREAT CENTRAL ROAD, LOUGHBOROUGH
Leicestershire LE11 1RW 01509 230726
e: booking_office@gcrailway.co.uk
w: www.gcrailway.co.uk

Paignton & Dartmouth Steam Railway
QUEENS PARK STATION, TORBAY ROAD, PAIGNTON
Devon TQ4 6AF......................................01803 555872
e: pdsr@talk21.com

Steamreplicas Ltd
82 BIRMINGHAM ROAD , , GREAT BARR , BIRMINGHAM
West Midlands B43 6NT 0121 580 8893
e: enquiries@steamreplicas.co.uk
w: www.steamreplicas.co.uk

Vintage Trains & Shakespeare Express
670 WARWICK ROAD , , TYSELEY, BIRMINGHAM
West Midlands B11 2HL..........................0121 708 4960
e: office@vintagetrains.co.uk
w: www.vintagetrains.co.uk

Storage

Anglian Confidential Ltd
BENTINCK OFFICES, RHOON ROAD , TERRINGTON ST. CLEMENT, KING'S LYNN
PE34 4HZ .... 07747827991 / 01553 828203
e: jonathan@anglianconfidential.co.uk
w: www.anglianconfidential.co.uk

Bonded Services
UNITS 4/5, SPACEWAYE, FELTHAM
Greater London TW14 0TH.....................0 203405 5560
e: CustomerServices@bonded.co.uk
w: www.bonded.com

CEI Exhibitions
STONEBRIDGE HOUSE, 28-32 BRIDGE STREET, LEATHERHEAD
Surrey KT22 8BZ .... +44 (0) 1372 869849
e: darryl@ceiexhibitions.co.uk
w: www.ceiexhibitions.co.uk

Container Team Limited
UNIT 9 WESTLAND DISTRIBUTION PARK, WINTERSTOKE ROAD, WESTON-SUPER-MARE
Somerset BS24 9AB 01934 245027
e: contact@containerteam.co.uk
w: www.containerteam.co.uk

Dragon Cases
6 THE STUDIO, OLDBURY BUSINESS CENTRE, OLDBURY ROAD, CWMBRAN
NP44 3JU 01633 791590
e: info@dragoncases.co.uk
w: www.dragoncases.co.uk

ESE Direct
WENSUM WORKS, 150 NORTHUMBERLAND STREET, NORWICH
Norfolk NR2 4EE 01603 629956
e: sales@esedirect.co.uk
w: www.esedirect.co.uk

Event Locker Solutions
.... 0161 925 0095
e: info@eventlockersolutions.co.uk
w: www.eventlockersolutions.co.uk

Fly By Nite Conferences Ltd
THE FBN COMPLEX, SHAWBANK ROAD, LAKESIDE , REDDITCH
Worcestershire B98 8YN 01527 520 720
e: enquiries@flybynite.co.uk
w: www.flybynite.co.uk

Gorilla Marketing & Events Ltd
PAPER STOCK HOUSE, AMERSHAM ROAD, CHALFONT ST. GILES
Buckinghamshire HP8 4RU 01494 876 876
e: info@gorillauk.com
w: www.gorillauk.com

Integro Insurance Brokers Ltd
101 LEADENHALL ST, 3RD FLOOR, LONDON
City of London EC3A 3BP.....................................1615 193 000
e: stephanie.less@integrogroup.com
w: www.integrouk.com

Kennelstore
THE WESTON CENTRE CREWE
Cheshire CW1 6FL 1270212193
e: sales@kennelstore.co.uk
w: www.kennelstore.co.uk

KLD Man and Van
....7540553899
e: chris@kldmanandvan.co.uk
w: www.kldmanandvan.co.uk

LowCost Storage
33 HONEY STREET, RED BANK, MANCHESTER
Greater Manchester M8 8RG..... 0800 587 3711 / 0789 613 9451
e: enquiries@low-cost-storage.co.uk
w: www.low-cost-storage.co.uk

M.Brill Limited
55A MORTIMER ROAD , HACKNEY , LONDON
N1 5AR..................................... 020 7254 0333 / 07956 827 836
e: info@mbrillltd.co.uk
w: www.mbrillltd.co.uk

Matt Snowball Music
UNIT 2, 3-9 BREWERY ROAD, LONDON
Greater London N7 9QJ 020 7700 6555
e: enquiries@mattsnowball.com
w: www.mattsnowball.com

North London Piano Transport 2 Ltd
176 MILLICENT GROVE, LONDON
Greater London N13 6HS .... 07711872434 / 020 3441 9463
e: thenorthpiano@googlemail.com
w: www.pianomoveteam.co.uk

Peaks Storehouse Ltd
135 DITTON WALK, CAMBRIDGE
Cambridgeshire CB5 8PY 01223 210691
e: sales@peaks-storehouse.co.uk
w: www.peaks-storehouse.co.uk

Personal Storage Shepherd Bush
SHEPHERDS BUSH, LONDON
Greater London 020 3432 4207
e: a.adams@personalstorage.co.uk
w: www.magentastorage.co.uk

Priory Self Store
33 OZENGELL PLACE, EURO KENT BUSINESS PARK, RAMSGATE
Kent CT12 6PB 0184 3861 352
e: enquiries@prioryselfstore.co.uk
w: www.prioryselfstore.co.uk

Set-a-side Storage
14 DUNDONALD ROAD, LONDON
Greater London NW10 3HR 0333 8000 900
e: andy@setasidestorage.co.uk
w: www.setasidestorage.co.uk

Space & Places
PURLEY CHASE INDUSTRIAL ESTATE, ANSLEY COMMON, NUNEATON
Warwickshire CV10 0RG 02476 960 918
e: info@spaces-and-places.co.uk
w: www.spaces-and-places.co.uk

Spaces4business Ltd
FAIRACRE, SOUTH NEWINGTON ROAD, BLOXHAM, BANBURY
Oxfordshire OX15 4JB...........................01295 721640
e: davidpratley@spaces4business.co.uk
w: www.spaces4business.co.uk

Vision Logistical Solutions
36 BRUNEL WAY, SEGENSWORTH, FAREHAM
Hampshire PO15 5SA 0500 120013
e: info@vision-logistics.co.uk
w: www.vision-logistics.co.uk

Xpression Event Solutions Limited
3210 HEYFORD PARK , UPPER HEYFORD
Oxfordshire OX25 5HD 01869 233324
e: info@xpressionevents.co.uk
w: www.xpressionevents.co.uk

Street Entertainment

Electric Cabaret
107 HIGH ST, BRACKLEY
NN13 7BN 07714 089 763
e: info@electriccabaret.co.uk
w: www.electriccabaret.co.uk

Subtitling Services

Atlas Translations
8 SPICER STREET,, ST ALBANS
Hertfordshire AL3 4PQ 01727 812 725
e: team@atlas-translations.co.uk
w: www.atlas-translations.co.uk

Lunar Dragon
....7562939262
e: aybuke.kavas@gmail.com
w: www.lunardragonproductions.com

Newcom
UNIT 2, NEWCOM HOUSE, 125 POPLAR HIGH STREET, LONDON
Greater London E14 0AE.....................020 7193 8952
e: newcom@newcomgroup.com
w: www.newcomgroup.com

S

Omnititles
10 WENDOVER ROAD, BROMLEY
 BR2 9JX 020 8460 4101
e: omnititles@ukgateway.net
w: www.omnititles.co.uk

S

TUV

Team Building

Accolade Corporate Events
17 CHALFORD AVENUE, THE REDDINGS, CHELTENHAM
Gloucestershire GL51 6UF......................................01452 857 172
e: enquiries@accolade-corporate-events.com
w: www.accolade-corporate-events.com

Adventure Scotland Ltd
CROFT HOUSE, 12 CROFTSIDE, KINGUSSIE
Highlands PH22 1QJ..01479 811 411
e: info@adventure-scotland.com
w: www.adventure-scotland.com

All-terrain Services
GREETHAM VALLEY, WOOD LANE , GREETHAM, RUTLAND
Leicestershire LE15 7NP.......................................01792 862 669
e: info@4x4events.co.uk
w: www.4x4events.co.uk

Altitude Events Mobile Rock Climbing Walls
OLD BROOKHOUSE BARN, BROOKHOUSE LANE, FRAMFIELD
East Sussex TN22 5QJ..07832 227571
e: mail@altitudeevents.org
w: www.altitudeevents.org

Anglia Sporting Activities
HUNGARIAN HALL, , PETTISTREE, WOODBRIDGE
Suffolk IP13 0JF 01394 460 475
e: enquiries@angliasport.co.uk
w: www.angliasport.co.uk

Arena Pursuits Ltd
ROSEMARY HOUSE, ROSEMARY LANE, FLIMWELL, WADHURST
East Sussex TN5 7PT 01580 879 614
e: info@arenapursuits.com
w: www.arenapursuits.com

Ashcombe Adventure Centre Ltd
COLLEY LANE, , ASHCOMBE, NEAR DAWLISH
Devon EX7 0QD 01626 866 766
e: info@ashcombeadventure.co.uk
w: www.ashcombeadventure.co.uk

Avalanche Adventure
THE WRONGS, WELFORD RAOD, SIBBERTOFT,
MARKET HARBOROUGH
Leicestershire LE16 9UJ 01858 880 613
e: info@avalancheadventure.co.uk
w: www.avalancheadventure.co.uk

Awesome Events
ARGO HOUSE, ARGO BUSINESS CENTRE, KILBURN PARK ROAD
London N56 5LF 0845 644 6510
e: sales@awesome-events.co.uk
w: www.awesome-events.co.uk

Banzai Action Sports Ltd
STRATTON COURT BARN, POOL FARM, STRATTON AUDLEY,
BICESTER Oxfordshire OX27 9AJ...........................01869 278199
e: info@banzaievents.com
w: www.banzaievents.com

Circomedia
ST PAUL'S CHURCH, PORTLAND SQUARE, BRISTOL
Avon BS2 8SJ..0117 947 7288
e: info@circomedia.com
w: www.circomedia.com

Creative Action
69 HIGHGATE ROAD, WOODLEY, READING
RG5 3ND...0118 948 7058
e: andy@creative-action.co.uk
w: www.creative-action.co.uk

D&s Events
THE CIRCUIT OFFICE, DONINGTON PARK, DERBY
Derbyshire DE74 2RP 01332 810007
e: enquiries@dandsevents.co.uk
w: www.dandsevents.co.uk

Hatt Adventures
PO BOX 5157, BRIGHTON
BN50 9TW 01273 358359
e: adventures@thehatt.co.uk
w: www.thehatt.co.uk/adventures

Manby Motorplex
MANBY SHOWGROUND,, MANBY, LOUTH
Lincolnshire LN11 8UZ...01507 328855
e: info@manbymotorplex.com
w: www.manbymotorplex.com

Off Limits Corporate Events
EAST VIEW TERRACE, LANGLEY MILL
NG16 4DF..01773 766047
e: links@actiondays.co.uk
w: www.actiondays.co.uk

Priory Events
SANDY LANE, NUTFIELD
Surrey RH1 4EJ 01737 822 484
e: info@prioryevents.co.uk
w: www.prioryevents.co.uk

Progressive Resources
UNIT 6 DELL BUILDINGS, EFFORD PARK, MILFORD ROAD,
LYMINGTON
Hampshire SO41 0JD 01590 676599
e: info@teambuilding.co.uk
w: www.teambuilding.co.uk

Sno!zone Ltd
602 MARLBOROUGH GATE, MILTON KEYNES
Buckinghamshire MK9 3XS....................................01908 680824
e: eventsmk@snozoneuk.com
w: www.snozoneuk.com

**T
U
V**

Spy Games
COATES GROUNDS, SINGLEBROUGH, MILTON KEYNES
Buckinghamshire MK17 0RF.................................0845 1303 007
e: info@spy-games.com
w: www.spy-games.com

Sushi Team Building
....020 3287 2299
e: info@sushi-teambuilding.co.uk
w: www.sushi-teambuilding.co.uk

Team Building Solutions
UNIT 7, AMPRESS LANE, LYMINGTON ENTERPRISE CENTRE, LYMINGTON
Hampshire SO41 8LZ..0845 121 1194
e: info@teambuildingsolutions.co.uk
w: www.teambuildingsolutions.co.uk

Teamday.co.uk
THE POTTERS BARN, ROUGHWOOD LANE, HASSALL GREEN, SANDBACH, CHESHIRE
CW11 4XX 01270 884080
e: breakthemould@teamday.co.uk
w: www.teamday.co.uk

Wild Events Ltd
THE VALLEY, , LAMARSH, BURES
Suffolk CO8 5EZ...01787 269 819
e: info@wildevents.co.uk
w: www.wildevents.co.uk

Wingbeat Sporting Events
10 STRAWBERRY GREEN, WHITBY, ELLESMERE PORT
Cheshire CH66 2TX...0151 356 1208
e: wingbeat@lineone.net
w: www.wingbeatsportingevents.co.uk

Xtreme Vortex
85 CHESSINGTON AVENUE , BEXLEYHEATH
Kent DA7 5HF 07739 560990
e: mail@xtremevortex.co.uk
w: www.xtremevortex.co.uk

Technical Project Management

De-Risk ltd
PO BOX 504, FARNHAM
Surrey GU9 1AF .... 01252734222 / 07866 69981
e: contact@scscleaningservices.com
w: www.de-risk.com

Howat Avraam LLP
154-160 FLEET STREET, LONDON. EC4A 2DQ 020 78849700
e: info@hasolicitors.co.uk
w: www.howatavraamsolicitors.co.uk

iMAG Displays
30-31 HARWELL ROAD, NUFFIELD INDUSTRIAL ESTATE, POOLE
Dorset BH17 0GE..1202282202
e: karley@imagdisplays.co.uk
w: www.imagdisplays.co.uk/contact/

Lightwave Productions
....2034881455
e: info@lightwaveproductions.co.uk
w: www.lightwaveproductions.co.uk

Priava
LEVEL 4 282 OXFORD STREET , BONDI JUNCTION , AUSTRALIA
NSW 2022 .... +61 (0)2 8383 4333
e: sales.au@priava.com
w: www.priava.com

QED Productions
UNIT 11, SUMMIT ROAD, CRANBORNE INDUSTRIAL ESTATE, POTTERS BAR
Hertfordshire EN6 3QW.......................................01707 648 800
e: info@qed-productions.com
w: www.qed-productions.com

Scenograf
HENDY YNYSFOR, LLANFROTHEN
 LL48 6BJ................................ 07717 748 355 // 01766 238451
e: info@scenograf.co.uk
w: www.scenograf.co.uk

Whole Nine Yards Productions Limited
ST. NICHOLAS HOUSE, 31-34 HIGH STREET, BRISTOL
Bristol BS1 2AW... +44 117 315 5220
e: info@wny.uk.com
w: www.wny.uk.com

Temporary Internet Providers

Attend2IT
UNIT 8, PARK FARM INDUSTRIAL ESTATE, BUNTINGFORD
Hertfordshire SG9 9AZ..01763 877 477
w: www.attend2it.co.uk

Digital Avenue
STUDIO 80, 49 EFFRA ROAD, LONDON
Greater London SW2 1BZ.....................................0203 397 7999
e: enquiries@digitalavenue.co.uk
w: www.digitalavenue.co.uk

Fli-Fi
....07590 681878
e: will@fli-fi.co.uk
w: www.fli-fi.co.uk

Hubbub
....020 3432 1222
e: matt@hubbubwireless.com
w: www.hubbubwireless.com

Max WiFi (UK) Ltd
8 BELBINS BUSINESS PARK, CUPERNHAM LANE, ROMSEY
Hampshire SO51 7JF...0203 727 9520
e: events@maxwifi.co.uk
w: maxwifi.co.uk

T
U
V

Paralogic Networks
1D HADDENHAM BUSINESS PARK, PEGASUS WAY, HADDENHAM
Buckinghamshire HP17 8LJ....................................01844 293330
e: hello@paralogic.co.uk
w: paralogicnetworks.co.uk/

RockIT Networks
26 BROOM CLOSE, TEDDINGTON
Middlesex TW11 9RJ...07956 920581
e: marty@RockIT-Networks.com
w: www.rockit-networks.com

Simpli-Fi Ltd
UNIT 11, MOUNT ROAD, FELTHAM,
Middlesex TW13 6AR.................................. +44 (0) 8456 123 008
e: info@simpli-fi.co.uk
w: www.simpli-fi.co.uk

SimpliWifi
THE TELEPHONE EXCHANGE, 33 BRIDGE STREET, KINGTON
 HR5 3DW...01544 327 310
e: hello@simpliwifi.co.uk
w: https://www.simpliwifi.co.uk/

Wifinity Ltd
UNIT 13 TO 14, KINGSMILL BUSINESS PARK, CHAPEL MILL ROAD,
KINGSTON UPON THAMES
Surrey KT1 3GZ..020 8090 1290
e: support@wifinity.co.uk
w: www.wifinity.co.uk

Temporary Power

The Powerline
MARSHFIELD, CHIPPENHAM
Wiltshire SN14 8BB 1226 892 352
e: alistair@thepowerline.co.uk
w: www.thepowerline.co.uk

Temporary Structures

A&J Big Top Promotions
AMERICA FARM COTTAGE, OXNEY ROAD, PETERBOROUGH
Cambridgeshire PE1 5YR 1734 222 999
e: sales@ajbigtophire.com
w: www.ajbigtophire.com

Kayam Theatre & Concert Structures
ATTICBEST LTD T/A KAYAM THEATRE & CONCERT STRUCTURES,
THE LAURELS, FRONT STREET, WORSTEAD
Norfolk NR29 9RW 1693 536 025
e: richard@kayam.com
w: kayam.co.uk

Media Structures Ltd
87-91 BEDDINGTON LANE, CROYDON
surrey CR0 4TD 02086 833 131
e: andrew.wilson@mediastructures.co.uk
w: www.mediastructures.co.uk

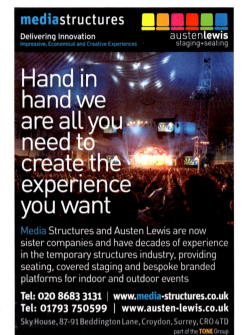
Theatrical

Backstage Supplies
1 EMPEROR WAY, EXETER BUSINESS PARK, EXETER
Devon EX1 3QS...01392 314042
e: mail@backstagesupplies.co.uk
w: www.backstagesupplies.co.uk

Bath Theatrical Costume Hire
UNIT 8 WALLBRIDGE MILLS, FROME , MENDIP
 BA11 5JZ..01373 472786
e: baththeatrical@talktalk.net
w: www.baththeatrical.com

Bryan Philip Davies Costumes
25 GLYNLEIGH DRIVE, POLEGATE, EAST SUSSEX
 BN26 6LU...01323 304391
e: bryan@bpdcostumes.co.uk
w: www.bpdcostumes.co.uk

Cameron Mackintosh Ltd
NUMBER ONE BEDFORD SQUARE, LONDON
Greater London WC1B 3RB 020 7637 8866
e: info@camack.co.uk
w: www.cameronmackintosh.com

**T
U
V**

Classworks Theatre
UNIT 12, BARNWELL BUSINESS PARK BARNWELL DRIVE,
CAMBRIDGE
Cambridgeshire CB5 8UY.....................................01223 210883
e: sue@classworks.org.uk
w: www.classworks.org.uk

Conference Engineering
....+44 (0)1625 426916
e: hello@conferenceengineering.co.uk
w: www.conferenceengineering.co.uk

Confetti Magic Ltd
ROCKET PARK, PEPPERSTOCK, LUTON
Bedfordshire LU1 4LL 01582 723502
e: ian@confettimagic.com
w: www.confettimagic.com

Costume Hire Direct
 UNIT 2, NEW BUILDINGS FARM, WINCHESTER ROAD, PETESFIELD
Hampshire GU32 3PB 01703 263094
e: hire@costumehiredirect.co.uk
w: www.costumehiredirect.co.uk

CSE / SSVC
CHALFONT GROVE, NARCOT LANE, GERRARDS CROSS
Buckinghamshire SL9 8TN....................................01494 874 461
e: info@bfbs.com
w: www.ssvc.com

David Fitch Services Ltd
 176 BEXLEY ROAD, ERITH
Kent DA8 3HF 01322 350351
e: contactus@davidfitchservices.com
w: www.davidfitchservices.com

eStage Production Ltd
71-75 SHELTON STREET, COVENT GARDEN, LONDON
 WC2H 9JQ 2071128903
e: chat@estage.net
w: https://production.estage.net

Field Services Ltd
UNIT 3, CUMBERLAND AVENUE, LONDON
Greater London NW10 7RX 020 8961 1225
e: enquiries@field-services.co.uk
w: www.field-services.co.uk

Film Rights Ltd
11 PANDORA ROAD, LONDON
Greater London NW6 1TS.....................................0208 001 3040
e: information@filmrights.ltd.uk
w: www.filmrights.ltd.uk

Fineline Limited
THE OLD QUARRY, CLEVEDON ROAD, FAILAND, BRISTOL
Bristol BS8 3TU...01275 395000
e: enquiries@fineline.uk.com
w: www.fineline.uk.com

Gradav Hire and Sales Ltd
SHENLEY ROAD , BOREHAMWOOD
Hertfordshire WD6 1JG 020 8324 2100
e: office@gradav.co.uk
w: www.gradav.co.uk

Harveys Of Hove
110 TRAFALGAR ROAD, PORTSLADE, BRIGHTON
 BN41 1GS..01273 430323
e: harveys.costume@ntlworld.com
w: www.harveysofhove.co.uk

Hirearchy Classic & Contempory Costume
45 PALMERSTON ROAD, BOSCOMBE, BOURNEMOUTH
Dorset BH1 4HW...001202 391661
e: hirearchy1@gmail.com
w: www.hirearchy.co.uk

Iogig Ltd
39 EQUINOX HOUSE, WAKERING ROAD, BARKING
 IG11 8RN..0207 1128 907
e: info@iogig.com
w: www.iogig.com

J&C Joel Limited (Head Office)
CORPORATION MILL, CORPORATION STREET, SOWERBY BRIDGE,
HALIFAX
Yorkshire HX6 2QQ..01422 833835
e: uksales@jcjoel.com
w: www.jcjoel.com

Jacqui Leigh Production Management Services
11 MAFEKING ROAD, ENFIELD
 EN1 3SS 07971 660089
e: jacqui@jacquileigh.co.uk
w: www.jacquileigh.com

John Slough Of London
OLD FORGE, PETERCHURCH, HEREFORD
Hertfordshire HR2 0SD...................................... 01432 277 237 /
07775 643 762

e: john@johnsloughoflondon.co.uk
w: www.johnsloughoflondon.co.uk

Just Add Water
6 FLITCROFT STREET, ST GILES IN THE FIELDS, LONDON
Greater London WC2H 8DJ...................................020 7557 4377
e: swim@sojustaddwater.com
w: www.sojustaddwater.com

Kave Theatre Services
UNITS 1 & 2, 55, VICTORIA ROAD, BURGESS HILL
 RH15 9LH 01444 245500
e: sales@kave.co.uk
w: www.kave.co.uk

Komedia Ltd
44-47 GARDNER STREET, BRIGHTON
East Sussex BN1 1UN 01273 647101
e: admin@komedia.co.uk
w: www.komedia.co.uk

T
U
V

Lee Batty Production Management
7A BLACKFEN PARADE, SIDCUP
Kent DA15 9LU 020 7839 8676
e: lee@leebatty.co.uk
w: www.leebatty.co.uk

Lee James Associates Ltd
P.O. BOX 61, MAIN STREET, YORK
North Yorkshire YO61 1WD...................................07739 227 687
e: leejamesltd@btconnect.com
w: www.leejamesltd.com

MTFX Confetti Effects
VELT HOUSE, VELT HOUSE LANE, ELMORE
Gloucestershire GL2 3NY 01452 729903
e: info@mtfx.com
w: www.mtfx.com

MTFX High Voltage
VELTHOUSE, VELTHOUSE LANE, ELMORE
Gloucestershire GL2 3NY 01452 729903
e: info@mtfx.com
w: www.mtfx.com

MTFX Special Effects
VELT HOUSE, VELT HOUSE LANE , ELMORE
Gloucestershire GL2 3NY 01452 729 903
e: info@mtfx.com
w: www.mtfx.com

MTFX Winter Effects
VELT HOUSE, VELT HOUSE LANE, ELMORE
Gloucestershire GL2 3NY 01452 729903
e: info@mtfx.com
w: www.mtfx.com

Multi-Lite (UK) Ltd
15 AIRLINKS, SPITFIRE WAY, HESTON
Middlesex TW5 9NR...020 8561 4501
e: sales@multi-lite.co.uk
w: www.multi-lite.co.uk

Pascal Theatre Company
35 FLAXMAN COURT, FLAXMAN TERRACE, BLOOMSBURY
 WC1H 9AR 020 7383 0920
e: pascaltheatrecompany@gmail.com
w: www.pascal-theatre.com

Priory Theatre
ROSEMARY HILL, KENILWORTH
Warwickshire CV8 1BN 01926 863334
e: marketing@priorytheatre.co.uk
w: www.priorytheatre.co.uk

Private Drama
ISLAND STUDIOS, 22 ST PETER'S SQUARE, LONDON
Greater London W6 9NW.......................................020 8749 0987
e: event@privatedrama.com
w: www.privatedrama.com

Roscolab Ltd
KANGLEY BRIDGE ROAD, SYDENHAM, LONDON
Greater London SE26 5AQ 0208 659 2300
e: contact@rosco.com
w: www.rosco.com

Royal Court Theatre
1 ROE STREET, LIVERPOOL
Merseyside L1 1HL 0870 7871240
e: admin@royalcourtliverpool.com
w: www.royalcourtliverpool.com

Samuel French Ltd
52 FITZOY STREET, LONDON
Greater London W1T 5JR 020 7387 9373
e: customerservices@samuelfrench-london.co.uk
w: www.samuelfrench-london.co.uk

Schoolplay Productions Ltd
15 INGLIS ROAD, COLCHESTER
Essex CO3 3HU...01206 540111
e: chrissie@schoolplayproductions.co.uk
w: www.schoolplayproductions.co.uk

Sculpture Studios
UNIT 3F HARVEY ROAD, NEVENDON INDUSTRIAL ESTATE,
BASILDON
Essex SS13 1DA 01268 726470
e: aden.hynes@hotmail.com
w: www.sculpturestudios.co.uk

Show Of Strength Theatre Company
74 CHESSEL STREET, BEDMINSTER
Bristol BS3 3DN...0117 902 0235
e: info@showofstrength.org.uk
w: www.showofstrength.org.uk

Showtex
EVERAERTSSTRAAT 69, ANTWERP
 2060..01706 819746
e: suzanne@showtex.com
w: www.showtex.com

Smiffy's
PECKETT PLAZA, CALDICOTT DRIVE, GAINSBOROUGH
Lincolnshire DN21 1FJ...0800 590 599
e: sales@smiffys.com
w: www.smiffys.com

Sonia Friedman Productions
DUKE OF YORK'S THEATRE, 104 ST MARTINS LANE, LONDON
Greater London WC2N 4BG 020 7845 8750
e: queries@soniafriedman.com
w: www.soniafriedman.com

Stage Management Association
89 BOROUGH HIGH STREET, FIRST FLOOR, LONDON
Greater London SE1 1NL.......................................0207 403 7999
e: admin@stagemanagementassociation.co.uk
w: www.stagemanagementassociation.co

**T
U
V**

Superhire
55 CHASE ROAD, PARK ROYAL, LONDON
Greater London NW10 6LU.....................................020 8453 3900
e: info@superhire.com
w: www.superhire.com

Theatre Tent Company
THE OLD POST OFFICE , BEATRICE ROAD
Leicestershire LE9 9FD...1163673791
e: redwagon@letsdotheshowrighthere.com
w: www.LetsDoTheShowRightHere.com

Uk Productions Ltd
BROOK HOUSE, , MINT STREET, GODALMING
Surrey GU7 1HE...01483 423600
e: mail@ukproductions.co.uk
w: www.ukproductions.co.uk

Varia Textiles Ltd
197 KINGS ROAD, KINGSTON-UPON-THAMES
Greater London KT2 5HJ.................................. +44 20 8549 8590
e: varia@variatextile.co.uk
w: www.varia-uk.com

Walk The Plank
WALK THE PLANK, 72 BROAD STREET, SALFORD
Lancashire M6 5BZ...0161 736 8964
e: info@walktheplank.co.uk
w: www.walktheplank.co.uk

Theatrical Supplies

Backstage Supplies
1 EMPEROR WAY, EXETER BUSINESS PARK, EXETER
Devon EX1 3QS..01392 314042
e: mail@backstagesupplies.co.uk
w: www.backstagesupplies.co.uk

Bath Theatrical Costume Hire
UNIT 8 WALLBRIDGE MILLS, FROME , MENDIP
BA11 5JZ..01373 472786
e: baththeatrical@talktalk.net
w: www.baththeatrical.com

Bryan Philip Davies Costumes
25 GLYNLEIGH DRIVE, POLEGATE, EAST SUSSEX
BN26 6LU...01323 304391
e: bryan@bpdcostumes.co.uk
w: www.bpdcostumes.co.uk

Confetti Magic Ltd
ROCKET PARK, PEPPERSTOCK, LUTON
Bedfordshire LU1 4LL 01582 723502
e: ian@confettimagic.com
w: www.confettimagic.com

Costume Hire Direct
UNIT 2, NEW BUILDINGS FARM, WINCHESTER ROAD, PETESFIELD
Hampshire GU32 3PB 01703 263094
e: hire@costumehiredirect.co.uk
w: www.costumehiredirect.co.uk

eStage Production Ltd
71Â "75 SHELTON STREET, COVENT GARDEN, LONDON
WC2H 9JQ 2071128903
e: chat@estage.net
w: https://production.estage.net

Fineline Limited
THE OLD QUARRY, CLEVEDON ROAD, FAILAND, BRISTOL
Bristol BS8 3TU...01275 395000
e: enquiries@fineline.uk.com
w: www.fineline.uk.com

Gradav Hire and Sales Ltd
SHENLEY ROAD , BOREHAMWOOD
Hertfordshire WD6 1JG 020 8324 2100
e: office@gradav.co.uk
w: www.gradav.co.uk

Harveys Of Hove
110 TRAFALGAR ROAD, PORTSLADE, BRIGHTON
BN41 1GS...01273 430323
e: harveys.costume@ntlworld.com
w: www.harveysofhove.co.uk

Hirearchy Classic & Contempory Costume
45 PALMERSTON ROAD, BOSCOMBE, BOURNEMOUTH
Dorset BH1 4HW..001202 391661
e: hirearchy1@gmail.com
w: www.hirearchy.co.uk

J&C Joel Limited (Head Office)
CORPORATION MILL, CORPORATION STREET, SOWERBY BRIDGE, HALIFAX
Yorkshire HX6 2QQ...01422 833835
e: uksales@jcjoel.com
w: www.jcjoel.com

John Slough Of London
OLD FORGE, PETERCHURCH, HEREFORD
Hertfordshire HR2 0SD...................................... 01432 277 237 /
07775 643 762
e: john@johnsloughoflondon.co.uk
w: www.johnsloughoflondon.co.uk

Kave Theatre Services
UNITS 1 & 2, 55, VICTORIA ROAD, BURGESS HILL
RH15 9LH...01444 245500
e: sales@kave.co.uk
w: www.kave.co.uk

MTFX Confetti Effects
VELT HOUSE, VELT HOUSE LANE, ELMORE
Gloucestershire GL2 3NY 01452 729903
e: info@mtfx.com
w: www.mtfx.com

MTFX High Voltage
VELTHOUSE, VELTHOUSE LANE, ELMORE
Gloucestershire GL2 3NY 01452 729903
e: info@mtfx.com
w: www.mtfx.com

T U V

MTFX Special Effects
VELT HOUSE, VELT HOUSE LANE , ELMORE
Gloucestershire GL2 3NY 01452 729 903
e: info@mtfx.com
w: www.mtfx.com

Multi-Lite (UK) Ltd
15 AIRLINKS, SPITFIRE WAY, HESTON
Middlesex TW5 9NR...020 8561 4501
e: sales@multi-lite.co.uk
w: www.multi-lite.co.uk

Roscolab Ltd
KANGLEY BRIDGE ROAD, SYDENHAM, LONDON
Greater London SE26 5AQ 0208 659 2300
e: contact@rosco.com
w: www.rosco.com

Samuel French Ltd
52 FITZOY STREET, LONDON
Greater London W1T 5JR 020 7387 9373
e: customerservices@samuelfrench-london.co.uk
w: www.samuelfrench-london.co.uk

Schoolplay Productions Ltd
15 INGLIS ROAD, COLCHESTER
Essex CO3 3HU..01206 540111
e: chrissie@schoolplayproductions.co.uk
w: www.schoolplayproductions.co.uk

Showtex
EVERAERTSSTRAAT 69, ANTWERP
 2060..01706 819746
e: suzanne@showtex.com
w: www.showtex.com

Smiffy's
PECKETT PLAZA, CALDICOTT DRIVE, GAINSBOROUGH
Lincolnshire DN21 1FJ...0800 590 599
e: sales@smiffys.com
w: www.smiffys.com

Superhire
55 CHASE ROAD, PARK ROYAL, LONDON
Greater London NW10 6LU....................................020 8453 3900
e: info@superhire.com
w: www.superhire.com

Varia Textiles Ltd
197 KINGS ROAD, KINGSTON-UPON-THAMES
Greater London KT2 5HJ................................ +44 20 8549 8590
e: varia@variatextile.co.uk
w: www.varia-uk.com

Themed Events / Party Planners

Abby Lacey Events
25 HILLTOP ROAD, TWYFORD, READING
 RG10 9BJ 07789 756656
e: info@abbylacey.co.uk
w: www.abbylacey.co.uk

ABZ Events
ABERDEEN...01224 515375
e: info@abz-events.co.uk
w: www.abz-events.co.uk

Accidental Productions
36 BARRATT AVENUE, LONDON
Greater London N22 7EZ......................................020 8881 8000
e: info@accidental.co.uk
w: www.accidental.co.uk

Action Hero Events
20-22 WENLOCK ROAD, LONDON
Greater London N1 7GU ....0845 003 5301 / 07957-667774
e: info@actionheroevents.co.uk
w: www.actionheroevents.co.uk

Added Dimension Events
6A SQUARE RIGGER ROW, PLANTATION WHARF, LONDON
Greater London SW11 3TZ....................................0207 978 7400
e: events@addeddimension.co.uk
w: www.addeddimension.co.uk

Amazing Parties Ltd
THE FORUM, 277 LONDON ROAD, BURGESS HILL
West Sussex RH15 9QU 0 2071 181 088
                                                                    / 01444 240 165
e: sales@amazingpartythemes.com
w: www.amazingpartythemes.com

American Theme Events Ltd
20 SHIRLEY AVENUE, OLD COULSDON
Surrey CR5 1QU..020 8668 5714
e: info@american-theme.com
w: www.american-theme.com

At Home
40 HIGH STREET, COBHAM
Surrey KT11 3EB 01932 862026
e: parties@athomecatering.co.uk
w: www.athomecatering.co.uk

Bamboo London
UNIT 12, THE TALINA CENTRE, BAGLEYS LANE, LONDON
Greater London SW6 2BW....................................0207 610 8606
e: contact@bamboolondon.com
w: www.bamboolondon.com

bars2you ltd
.... 01925 633 131 / 07709888809
e: chris@bars2you.co.uk
w: www.bars2you.com

BDD Events Ltd
PARK VIEW HOUSE, 79 BRIDGEWOOD ROAD, WORCESTER PARK
 KT4 8XR 020 8274 8274
e: enquiry@bddevents.co.uk
w: www.bddevents.co.uk

**T
U
V**

Bentleys Entertainments Ltd
7 SQUARE RIGGER ROW, PLANTATION WHARF, LONDON
Greater London SW11 3TZ 020 7223 7900
e: info@bentleys.net
w: www.bentleys.net

Best Parties Ever
UNITS 2 - 4 TRADE CITY, AVRO WAY, BROOKLANDS INDUSTRIAL
ESTATE, WEYBRIDGE
Surrey KT13 0YF..0844 499 4040
e: sales@bestpartiesever.com
w: www.bestpartiesever.com

Blue Ribbon Events Ltd
845 FINCHLEY ROAD, LONDON
 NW11 8NA..020 8455 2255
e: team@blueribbonevents.com
w: www.blueribbonevents.com

Bondini Events & Entertainment
LOW FARM, BROOK ROAD, BASSINGBOURN, ROYSTON
 SG8 5NT 01763 852691
e: doctor@bondini.co.uk
w: www.bondini.co.uk

Capability Events
MANOR FARM, LONGDON, TEWKESBURY
Gloucestershire GL20 6AT 01684 833133
e: events@capabilityevents.co.uk
w: www.capabilityevents.co.uk

Celebrationz
24 CHURCH HILL, LOUGHTON
 IG10 1LA................................ 0845 006 7333 // 020 8500 6542
e: enquiries@celebrationz.co.uk
w: www.celebrationz.co.uk

Chance Entertainment
321 FULHAM ROAD, LONDON
Greater London SW10 9QL....................................020 7376 5995
e: info@chanceorganisation.co.uk
w: www.chanceorganisation.co.uk

Chartwell Speakers & Literary Agency
14 GRAY'S INN ROAD , LONDON
 WC1X 8HN .... +44(0)7967175578
e: lisa@chartwellspeakers.com
w: www.chartwellspeakers.com/

Chase Dream Events
.... 07930 069 551 / 07985349861
e: info@chasedreamevents.co.uk
w: www.chasedreamevents.co.uk

Classic Crockery
CLASSIC CROCKERY HIRE, UNIT 10 - 11 MAPLE, FELTHAM,
WEST LONDON
Greater London TW13 7AW .... 020 3582 9818 / 07584 993 498
e: hire@classiccrockery.co.uk
w: www.classiccrockery.co.uk

Clockwork Entertainments & Leisure (London) Ltd
4 THE STABLES, BROADFIELD WAY, ALDENHAM
Hertfordshire WD25 8DG..01923 635536
e: sales@clockworkentertainment.com
w: www.clockworkentertainment.com

Collection 26
66 PORCHESTER ROAD, LONDON
Greater London W2 6ET 08450 553290
e: info@collection26.com
w: www.collection26.com

Complete Avenue Ltd
OLD BARN, BLACKBIRD FARM,BLACKBIRD LANE, ALDENHAM
West Midlands WD25 8BS.....................................07854 007483
w: www.completeavenue.co.uk

Crafts & Giggles
....07824 396645
w: www.craftsandgiggles.com

CS EVENTS
.... 01274 967950 / 07769 328428 / 0742602907
e: c-s-events@outlook.com
w: www.csevents.co.uk

Dancefloor DJs & Events
THISTLEY CLOSE, THORPE ASTLEY, LEICESTER
Leicestershire LE3 3RZ 0116 348 0146
e: dancefloordjs85@gmail.com
w: dancefloor-djs-events.com/

Dark Happenings
....07412 199971
e: dhenquiries@hotmail.com
w: www.darkhappenings.com

Dash of Sparkle
IDIT GINSBERG, DASH OF SPARKLE , 59 BEECH DRIVE,
BOREHAMWOOD , HERTS
WD6 4QX................................. 020 8905 2908 / 07877 927 246
e: office@dashofsparkle.com
w: www.dashofsparkle.com/

Delta Production Services
UNIT 4, SPRINGSIDE, LA RUE DE LA MONNAIE, TRINITY
JE3 5DG 01534 865885
e: info@delta-av.com
w: www.delta-av.com

Demon Wheelers
 132-154 HARVEST LANE, SHEFFIELD
South Yorkshire S3 8BX 01142 700 330
e: info@demonwheelers.co.uk
w: www.demonwheelers.co.uk

Department Of Enjoyment
21 BAR TERRACE, WHITWORTH, ROCHDALE
Lancashire OL12 8TB 0800 292 2049
e: events@enjoy.co.uk
w: www.enjoy.co.uk

T
U
V

Double Vision Events
....7580775517
e: doublevisionevents1@gmail.com
w: www.doublevision.events

Emma Boardman Consulting
KENSINGTON, LONDON
W8 6JW..07976 294604
e: ideas@emmaboardman.net
w: www.emmaboardman.net

Eurohire Sound & Light
UNIT 6, BESSEMER PARK, BESSEMER ROAD, BASINGSTOKE
Hampshire RG21 3NB 01256 461 234
e: jools@eurohiresoundandhire.co.uk
w: www.eurohiresoundandlight.co.uk

Evalpe Events Management
58 RUE DE LA TERRASSIÀRE, GENEVA - SWITZERLAND
1207.. +33 (0) 22 519 08 00
e: contact@evalpe.com
w: www.evalpe.com

Evenlogolists
SECOND FLOOR (ENTRANCE AT REAR) , 87 BELGRAVE ROAD
Leicestershire LE4 6AS .... 07932220016 / 07710 017 991
e: gerard@eventologists.co.uk
w: www.eventologists.co.uk/

Eventelle Limited
69 DUNVEGAN ROAD, BIRMINGHAM
B24 9HH..07961 067 546
e: info@eventelle.co.uk
w: www.eventelle.co.uk

Eventwise
AXE & BOTTLE COURT, 70 NEWCOMEN, LONDON
Greater London SE1 1YT.......................................020 7378 2975
e: hello@eventwise.co.uk
w: www.eventwise.co.uk

Evolve Events Ltd
6 FILMER ROAD, LONDON
Greater London SW6 7BW.....................................020 7610 2808
e: info@evolve-events.com
w: www.evolve-events.com

Fisher Productions
118 GARRATT LANE, LONDON
Greater London SW18 4DJ.....................................020 8871 1978
e: enquiries@fisherproductions.co.uk
w: www.fisherproductions.co.uk

Friday Island Ltd
POOLE KEYNES, CIRENCESTER
Gloucestershire GL7 6ED 01285 770082
e: its-great@friday-island.co.uk
w: www.friday-island.co.uk

funk:tion events
6 KINGS BUILDING, KING STREET, CHESTER
Cheshire CH1 2AJ...0161 341 0052
e: info@funktionevents.co.uk
w: www.funktionevents.co.uk

Gamewagon Ltd
113 - 115 OYSTER LANE, BYFLEET
Surrey KT14 7JZ..0845 319 4263
e: julie.owen@gamewagon.co.uk
w: www.gamewagon.co.uk

GDC Events Ltd
52 KINGSGATE ROAD, KINGSTON UPON THAMES
Surrey KT2 5AA 0208 9479915
e: info@gdc-events.co.uk
w: www.gdc-events.co.uk

Girl Friday Events
25 ROCHESTER TERRACE, LEEDS
LS6 3DF 0113 217 9966
e: info@girlfridayevents.co.uk
w: www.girlfridayevents.co.uk

Global Infusion Group
GLOBAL INFUSION COURT, NASHLEIGH HILL, CHESHAM
Buckinghamshire HP5 3HE 01494 790700
e: hello@globalinfusiongroup.com
w: www.globalinfusiongroup.com

Grid Girls Promotions
36 LANCING CLOSE, LANCING
West Sussex BN15 9NJ 1903537780
e: clothing@grid-girls.co.uk
w: www.gridgirlspromotions.com

Harrisons Events
THE MALTING BARN, MALTING LANE, DAGNALL, BERKHAMSTEAD
HP4 1QY 07846 380474
e: info@harrisonsevents.co.uk
w: www.harrisonsevents.co.uk

Havana Miss
40A ROYAL HILL, LONDON
Greater London SE10 8RT, ...020 8691 6001
e: enquiries@havanamiss.co.uk
w: www.havanamiss.co.uk

Holmsted Events
DRAY CORNER INDUSTRIAL CENTRE FOUR OAKS ROAD,
HEADCORN , KENT
TN27 9PB 07860 771914
e: bryanbryan@holmstedevents.co.uk
w: www.holmstedevents.co.uk/

iCatching Events
UNIT D, JOSEPH ADAMSON IND EST, CROFT STREET, HYDE
Cheshire SK14 1EE 0845 833 6372
e: info@icatchingevents.co.uk
w: www.icatchingevents.co.uk

Ice Box
UNIT A35/36, NEW COVENT GARDEN MARKET, LONDON
Greater London SW8 5EE......................................020 7498 0800
e: info@theicebox.com
w: www.theicebox.com

Ice Entertainment Uk
ICE ENTERTAINMENT UK, UNIT C-D DODD LANE IND ESTATE,
CHORLEY ROAD, BOLTON
Greater Manchester BL5 3NA................................0845 4751020
e: info@iceentertainmentuk.com
w: www.iceentertainmentuk.com

Inspiration Events
14 STANHOPE MEWS WEST , LONDON
Greater London SW7 5RB 020 7370 4646
e: info@inspirationevents.com
w: www.inspirationevents.com

Irvin Leisure Ltd
35 CURTIS LANE, MAIN STREET, HANWORTH, WEMBLEY
Middlesex HA0 4FW...020 8795 4282
e: info@irvinleisure.com
w: www.irvinleisure.com

Jay & I Services
WEMBLEY COMMERCIAL CENTRE, UNIT 4.6 4TH FLOOR,
BUILDING A, EAST LANE, LONDON
Greater London HA9 7PT .... 020 8908 4276 //
....020 8908 6943
e: info@jayandievents.com
w: www.jayandievents.com

Joffins (london) Ltd
SUITE 33, 10 BARLEY MOW PASSAGE, LONDON
Greater London W4 4PH...08000 723073
e: alan@joffins.co.uk
w: www.joffins.co.uk

Jongleurs Events
20B CHANCELLORS ST, HAMMERSMITH
W9 6RN 08700 111960
e: enquiries@jongleurs.com
w: www.jongleursevents.com

JSO Productions Ltd
THREEWAYS, RADNAGE COMMON RD, RADNAGE
Buckinghamshire HP14 4DF .... 0208 8407070 //
....01494 387 770
e: parties@jso.co.uk
w: www.jso.co.uk

JVP Events
64 WFIR ROAD, LONDON
Greater London SW19 8UG 020 8947 3410
e: hire@jvp.uk.com
w: www.jvp.uk.com

Kudos Music
UNIT 10 TRADE CITY, COWLEY MILL ROAD, UXBRIDGE
UB8 2DB..01895 207990
e: info@kudosmusic.co.uk
w: www.kudosmusic.co.uk

Lazer Lions / Laser Tag Birthday Parties
....07800 861767
e: Info@lazerlions.co.uk
w: lazerlions.co.uk

Lettice Party Design & Catering
18 STANNARY STREET, LONDON
Greater London SE11 4AA....................................020 7820 1161
e: stevie@letticeparty.com
w: www.letticeparty.com

London Corporate Event Solutions
REGENT SQUARE, BOW
E3 3HQ 020 8467 7185
e: jacqui@lcesolutions.co.uk
w: www.lcesolutions.co.uk

Lucy Attwood Events Ltd
26 BERENS ROAD
NW10 5DT 020 8964 2657
e: parties@lucyattwoodevents.com
w: www.lucyattwoodevents.com

Luk Events Limited
LUK EVENTS, EEKO'S BARN, HEVER
Kent TN8 7ET...0871 620 7063
e: enquiries@laplanduk.co.uk
w: www.laplanduk.co.uk

Lvlv Events Ltd
UNIT 17 & 21, 54-56 DOVER ROAD EAST, GRAVESEND
Kent DA11 0RG........................ 07534 921 310 / 01474 247 557
e: Info@eventsbylvlv.co.uk
w: www.eventsbylvlv.co.uk

MacEvents Event Management
HULTON HOUSE, 11 EWALD ROAD, LONDON
Greater London SW6 3NA .... 020 7736 6606 // 07973 667624
e: cm@macevents.co.uk
w: www.macevents.co.uk

Magical Quests
1A WALPOLE MEWS, OFF WALPOLE ROAD, COLLIERS WOOD
SW19 2DL 020 8417 0920
e: mail@magicalquests.com
w: www.magicalquests.com

Mango Pie
....01206 243 400
e: info@mango-pie.com
w: www.mango-pie.com

T
U
V

Masquerade Events
33 REGENTS DRIVE, REPTON PARK, WOODFORD GREEN
IG8 8RZ 07747 868 050
e: ade@masqueradeuk.com
w: www.masqueradeuk.com

Murder, Mystery And Mayhem
57 THE FAIRWAY, RUISLIP
Greater London HA4 0SP 020 8842 1284
e: info@mayhem.org.uk
w: www.mayhem.org.uk

Ninth Events Ltd
39 FEATHERSTONE STREET , ISLINGTON , LONDON
EC1Y 8RE 7879896725
e: info@ninthevents.com
w: www.ninthevents.com

Norah Sleep Events
NO 5, FIRST FLOOR, WESTFIELD HOUSE, MILLFIELD LANE, YORK
North Yorkshire YO26 6GA.......................01904 790123
e: enquiries@norahsleep.co.uk
w: www.norahsleep.co.uk

Nutty Party Productions
96 OXFORD GARDENS, LONDON
W10 6NG 7852403242
e: nuttypartyproductions@googlemail.com
w: www.nuttypartyproductions.co.uk

OPM Partnership
STUDIO A1, THE 1927 BUILDING, THE OLD GAS WORKS, 2
MICHAEL ROAD, LONDON
SW6 2AD 020 7731 1008
e: enquiries@opmpartnership.com
w: www.opmpartnership.com

Planet Gold Decor
UNIT 4 ROMARSH, FOWLSWICK BUSINESS PARK, , ALLINGTON
Wiltshire SN14 6QE................................07747 015 170
e: info@planetgolddecor.co.uk
w: www.planetgolddecor.co.uk or www.

Premier UK Events Ltd
UNIT 2, ROOKERY LANE, THURMASTON, LEICESTER
Leicestershire LE4 8AU.............................1162029953
e: ben@premier-ltd.com
w: premier-event-solutions.com/

Pretty Clever Events
BRIGHTWIRE HOUSE, 114 CHURCH ROAD, BRIGHTON
East Sussex BN3 2EB 0845 413 3030
e: info@prettyclever.co.uk
w: www.prettyclever.co.uk

Red Alligator Group Ltd
SUITE 313, DAISYFIELD BUSINESS CENTRE, APPLEBY STREET,
BLACKBURN
Lancashire BB1 3BL 0844 873 1966
e: info@redalligatorgroup.com
w: www.redalligatorgroup.com

Rhythm Masters Entertainments (RME)
29 FOURTH AVENUE, WATFORD
WD25 9QB............................... 01923 677358 / 07973 217226
e: info@rme-events.com
w: www.rme-events.com

Rockitfish Ltd
16 MEAD BUSINESS CENTRE , MEAD LANE , HERTFORD
Hertfordshire SG13 7BJ 01992 558820
e: hello@rockitfish.co.uk
w: www.rockitfish.co.uk

Seasoned Events
13 BISHOPSGATE
Greater London EC2N 3BA 020 7236 2149
e: hello@seasonedevents.co.uk
w: www.seasonedevents.co.uk

Smart Christmas Parties
30 MAIDEN LANE, COVENT GARDEN, LONDON
Greater London WC2E 7JS 0207 836 1033
e: enquiries@smartgroupltd.co.uk
w: www.smartchristmasparties.co.uk

Smile Events
392 GALLEY HILL,, HEMEL HEMPSTEAD,
Hertfordshire HP1 3LA 01923 750 525
e: info@smileevents.co.uk
w: www.smileevents.co.uk

SP Events
THE LILACS, STREET LANE, BEWERLEY, HARROGATE
North Yorkshire HG3 5HW .... 01423 711806 / 07976 402986
e: info@spevents.co.uk
w: www.spevents.co.uk

Steven Duggan Events London
6 SCRUBS LANE, LONDON
Greater London NW10 6RB 020 8960 3120
e: info@stevendugganevents.com
w: www.stevendugganevents.com

Straight Productions
TREYARNON HOUSE, WESTBEAMS ROAD, SWAY
Hampshire SO41 6AE...........................07802 753058
e: info@straightproductions.com
w: www.straightproductions.com

Studio 50 Floors
7 PORTAL CLOSE, CHIPPENHAM
Wiltshire SN15 1QJ.................... 01249 661078 / 07713 095975
e: info@studio-50.com
w: www.studio-50.com

Studio Megastar
UNIT 1.7 & 1.8, THE ARCHES INDUSTRIAL ESTATE, COVENTRY
West Midlands CV1 3JQ.......................02476 712 152
e: info@studiomegastar.co.uk
w: www.studiomegastar.co.uk

T U V

Swim Productions
24A HOLYWELL ROW, LONDON
Greater London EC2A 4JB.....................................020 7770 6160
e: jim@swimproductions.com
w: www.swimproductions.com

Target London Events
60 HARRISON'S WHARF, PURFLEET
 RM19 1QW..01708 868 109
e: info@target-london.com
w: www.target-london.com

Tastes Catering Ltd
....020 7232 2325
e: orders@tastescatering.com
w: www.tastescatering.co.uk

Team Spirit Event Management Ltd.
UNIT 16 BOARSHURST BUSINESS PARK, BOARSHURST LANE,
GREENFIELD,, OLDHAM
Lancashire OL3 7ER 01457 875878
e: hello@team-spirit.co.uk
w: www.team-spirit.co.uk

TechST
....07767 366031
e: info@tech-st.co.uk
w: www.tajiri-events.co.uk

TGM Solutions Ltd
SUITE 2, HARTCRAN HOUSE, CARPENDERS PARK, WATFORD
 WD19 5EZ................................. 0203 011 5555 / 07785 932351
e: info@tgm-solutions.com
w: www.tgm-solutions.com

The Embee Diamond Reception
69 NIGHTINGALE LANE, LONDON
Greater London E11 ....0207193 7090
e: info@embee-reception.com
w: www.embee-reception.com

The Lovely Party Company
WHITEFRIARS WHARF, TONBRIDGE, KENT
Kent TN9 1QP 01732 669812
e: hq@thelovelypartycompany.com
w: www.thelovelypartycompany.com

The Man In The Red Coat
JAMES HASLER, THE MAN IN THE RED COAT, C/O 7 STANSTEAD
GROVE, LONDON
 SE6 4UD..7773229909
e: james@themanintheredcoat.co.uk
w: www.toastmasterjameshasler.co.uk

Theme Traders Ltd
THE STADIUM, OAKLANDS ROAD, LONDON
Greater London NW2 6DL 0208 452 8518
e: enquiries@themetraders.com
w: www.themetraders.com

Transform Venue
UNIT 1 REAR OF 486 PORTSWOOD ROAD, SOUTHAMPTON
Hampshire SO17 3SP 02380 558923
e: info@transform-venue.co.uk
w: www.transform-venue.co.uk

TSC Events
WOODPOND FARM, BUCKINGHAM ROAD, WHADDON
 MK17 0EQ..01908 504766
e: pat@theshooting.co.uk
w: www.theshooting.co.uk

Ultimate Experience Ltd
AXE AND BOTTLE COURT, 70 NEWCOMEN STREET, LONDON
Greater London SE1 1YT 0207 940 6060
e: hello@weareultimate.co.uk
w: www.weareultimate.co.uk/

Urban Caprice
63-65 GOLDNEY ROAD, MAIDA VALE
 W9 2AR 020 7286 1700
e: events@urbancaprice.co.uk
w: www.urbancaprice.co.uk

Visual Impact
ST JOHN'S FOUNDRY, 12 ST JOHN'S ROAD, HAMPTON WICK,
KINGSTON UPON THAMES
Greater London KT1 4AN 020 8977 2577
e: info@visual-impact.co.uk
w: www.visual-impact.co.uk

Warrior Fire & Rescue Services
C/O 3 AMBULANCE HOUSES, SAXMUNDHAM
Suffolk IP17 1DZ...07544 920588
e: info@warriorfire.co.uk
w: www.warriorfire.co.uk

West End Events
27 OLD GLOUCESTER STREET, LONDON
Greater London WC1N 3AN 020 3740 1539
e: bookings@westendevents.co.uk
w: www.westendevents.co.uk

William Bartholomew Party Organising Ltd
20 BRIDGE STREET, HUNGERFORD
Berkshire RG17 0EG 0207 7318328
e: mail@wbpo.com
w: www.wbpo.com

Zest Mixology
4 DOLLY LANE BUSINESS CENTRE, DOLLY LANE, LEEDS
West Yorkshire LS9 7TU...01423 275 832
e: info@zestmixology.com
w: www.zestmixology.co.uk

T U V

Ticket & Box Office Services

Awkward Tickets
8 MARSDEN BUSINESS PARK, JAMES NICOLSON LINK, CLIFTON
Yorkshire YO30 4WX 01759 371786
e: john@awkwardentertainments.com
w: www.awkwardtickets.com

CrowdCanDo
....07860 848993
e: paul@crowdcan.do
w: beta.crowdcan.do

Eventbrite
24 GREVILLE STREET, LONDON
C1N 8SS 0800 652 4993
e: james@eventbrite.com
w: www.eventbrite.co.uk

FiloZilo
126 & 127 UDYOG BHAVAN, SONAWALA ROAD, GOREGAON EAST,
MUMBAI, INDIA
400063.. +91 224 220 0422
e: sales@filozilo.com
w: www.filozilo.com

Printmytickets
WINDSOR COURT, WINDSOR HOUSE,, TRENT VALLEY ROAD,
LICHFIELD
West Midlands WS13 6EU 01543 250446
e: orders@printmytickets.co.uk
w: www.printmytickets.co.uk

Sanver Sports Private Limited
126 - 127 UDYOG BHAVAN, SONAWALA ROAD, GOREGAON EAST,
MUMBAI, INDIA
400063.. +91 22 42200422
e: sales@sanversports.com
w: www.sanversports.com

Tickets.com Ltd
THE MEZZANINE, CBX2 WEST, 380 MIDSUMMER BOULEVARD,
MILTON KEYNES
Buckinghamshire MK9 2EA......................011-44-1908-232-404
e: sales@tickets.com
w: www.tickets.com

Toilets / Showers

A1 Loo Hire
SILVER BIRCHES, HIGHLAND AVENUE, WOKINGHAM
Berkshire RG41 4SP 01189 894 652
e: info@a1groupcomp.co.uk
w: www.a1loo-hire.co.uk

A1 Mobile Ltd
NEW FARM, HOVERINGHAM LANE, HOVERINGHAM, NOTTINGHAM
Nottinghamshire NG14 7JX...................................0844 850 8818
e: sales@a1mobile.co.uk
w: www.a1mobile.co.uk

Alide Hire Services
UNIT 46, BURNETT BUSINESS PARK,, BURNETT
Bristol BS31 2ED 01225 326 484
e: hire@alidehire.co.uk
w: www.alidehire.co.uk

Andyloos Limited
UNIT 22 HARTLEBURY TRADING ESTATE, HARTLEBURY
Worcestershire DY10 4JB 0845 671 1111
e: Hartlebury@andyloos.co.uk
w: www.andyloos.co.uk

Asles Toilet Rentals
82 BROADWAY, SHIFNAL, TELFORD
Shropshire TF11 8AZ 01952 461266
e: sales@asles.co.uk
w: www.asles.co.uk

At Your Convenience - Mobile Toilets
SHADES MANOR, 24 BONIFACE ROAD, UXBRIDGE
Middlesex UB10 8BU 07778 744292
e: del@aycuk.com
w: www.aycuk.com

Brandon Hire Plc
72-75 FEEDER ROAD, ST PHILIPS, BRISTOL
Bristol BS2 0TQ 0117 971 9119
e: info@brandonhire.co.uk
w: www.brandontoolhire.co.uk

Chew Valley Hire
WOODWICK FARM, BRISTOL ROAD, COMPTON MARTIN,
COMPTON MARTIN
Somerset BS40 6NQ 01761 221105
e: info@chewvalleyhire.co.uk
w: www.chewvalleyhire.co.uk

Classic Chambers
BRANSDALE COTTAGE, STILLINGTON ROAD, BRANDSBY
North Yorkshire YO61 4RS......................................01347 888262
e: info@classicchambers.co.uk
w: www.classicchambers.co.uk

Classic Conveniences Ltd
THE FORGE, DAY GREEN, HASSALL, SANDBACH
CW11 4XU 01270 872377
e: info@classicconveniences.co.uk
w: www.classicconveniences.co.uk

Classical Loo Company
AULD BARN HOUSE, FONAH, FORFAR
DD8 2SB...01307 818190
e: info@classicalloocompany.com
w: www.classicalloocompany.com

Classical Toilet Hire
UNIT 19, SHEPHERDS GROVE INDUSTRIAL ESTATE (WEST),
STANTON, BURY ST EDMUNDS
Suffolk IP31 2AR..01359 253 556
e: enquiries@classicaltoilethire.co.uk
w: www.classicaltoilethire.co.uk

T U V

Convenience Company Ltd
INKERSALL GRANGE FARM, NR BILSTHORPE, NEWARK
Nottinghamshire NG22 8TN 07527 547071
e: info@theconco.co.uk
w: www.theconco.co.uk

Coopers Marquees
BOLTON LANE, WILBERFOSS, YORK
North Yorkshire YO41 5NX.....................................01759 380190
e: info@coopersmarquees.co.uk
w: www.marqueesuk.co.uk

D & P Luxury Toilets
COLDHARBOUR COTTAGE, WINCHBOTTOM LANE, HIGH WYCOMBE
Buckinghamshire HP10 9QE 01494 526 065
e: info@luxury-toilets.co.uk / sales@luxury-toilets.co.uk

D-Tox Event & Waste Management
DAISY HOUSE, RED HOUSE INDUSTRIAL ESTATE, ANGLIAN ROAD, ALDRIDGE
West Midlands WS9 8EP 0800 999 2260
e: info@dtox.org
w: www.dtox.org/

Deluxe Loos
FLEET LANE, FINCHAMPSTEAD, WOKINGHAM
Berkshire RG40 4RN 0118 324 3200
e: hello@deluxeloos.com
w: www.deluxeloos.com

E-Toilet Services
UNIT 7 MILLBROOK BUSINESS PARK, HOE LANE, NAZEING
Essex EN9 2RJ...01992 899 453
e: info@etoiletsales.co.uk
w: www.etoiletsales.co.uk

Elegance Toilet Hire
.... 07733103644/0203 4781538
e: elegancetoilethire@gmail.com
w: www.elegancetoilethire.co.uk

Euro Loo Portable Toilets
EURO HOUSE, WEST HANNINGFIELD ROAD, CHELMSFORD
Essex CM2 7TA...................... 01245 475 700 // 0800 61 22 515
e: sales@euroloo.com
w: www.euroloo.com

Event Support Services
TRITLINGTON OLD HALL, MORPETH
 NE61 3ED 07974 949 756
e: enquiries@eventsupportservices.co.uk
w: www.eventsupportservices.co.uk

Event Tents Global
223 ARDGLASS ROAD, DOWNPATRICK
 BT30 7ED .... 02844 841 820 / 07872 501861
e: contact@eventtentsglobal.com
w: www.eventtentsglobal.com

Event Washrooms
DANIELS WATER FARM, DANIELS WATER, ASHFORD
Kent TN26 1JY...0800 2800 247
e: info@eventwashrooms.co.uk
w: www.eventwashrooms.co.uk

Festival Loo - Poonarnia
FERNHILL FARM, CHEDDAR ROAD, COMPTON MARTIN
Somerset BS40 6LD 07503 769188
e: squeak@festivalloo.co.uk
w: www.festivalloo.co.uk

Hallmark Event Hire
RYELAND FARM, WILDE STREET, BECK ROW
Suffolk IP28 8BT 01842 861070
e: office@hallmarkeventhire.co.uk
w: www.hallmarkeventhire.co.uk

Igloos
CHERRY PARK, ARDELEY, STEVENAGE
Hertfordshire SG2 7AH...01438 861418
e: 4u2p@igloos.co.uk
w: www.igloos.co.uk

James Dabbs Marquees
BRETFIELD COURT , BRETTON STREET INDUSTRIAL ESTATE , SAVILE TOWN , DEWSBURY
West Yorkshire WF12 9BB .... 0800 590460 // 01924 459550
e: sales@james-dabbs-marquees.co.uk
w: www.james-dabbs-marquees.co.uk

John Anderson Hire
UNIT 5 SMALLFORD WORKS , SMALLFORD LANE, ST ALBANS
Hertfordshire AL4 0SA...01727 822485
e: quotes@superloo.co.uk
w: www.superloo.co.uk

Justloos.com Ltd
PADDOCK BARN, MANOR FARM, ITCHEN STOKE
Hampshire SO24 0QT 01962 867 808
e: enquiries@justloos.com
w: www.justloos.com

Justloos.com.ltd
PADDOCK BARN, MANOR FARM, ITCHEN STOKE
Hampshire SO24 0QT 01962 867 808
e: enquiries@justloos.com
w: www.justloos.com

Liberty Event Suites
THE OLD AIRFIELD, BELTON ROAD, SANDTOFT
Lincolnshire DN8 5SX 08450 944487
e: sales@libertyguard.co.uk
w: www.libertyguard.co.uk

Loos For Do's Ltd
5 FARRINGDON BUSINESS PARK, ALTON
Hampshire GU34 3DZ 0845 123 2901
e: info@loos.co.uk
w: www.loos.co.uk

T U V

M L Environmental Services Ltd
HOLMES WAY, BOSTON ROAD INDUSTRIAL ESTATE,
HORNCASTLE, LINCS
LN9 6JW..1507524040
e: mlenvironmental@aol.com
w: www.mlenvironmentalservices.webs.

Midland International Hire Services Ltd
WALL HILL ROAD, ALLESLEY, COVENTRY
West Midlands CV5 9EL 024 7633 6411
e: hire@toilet-hire.com
w: www.toilet-hire.com

Midland Toilet Hire
BRIDGE HOUSE, 509 ALDRIDGE ROAD, GREAT BARR,
BIRMINGHAM
West Midlands B44 8NA 0800 999 2820
e: info@midlandtoilethire.com
w: www.midlandtoilethire.com

Mobile Thrones
TABRUMS FARM, TABRUMS LANE, BATTLESBRIDGE, WICKFORD
Essex SS11 7QX .... 01245 324901 //
07971 846227
e: info@mobilethrones.co.uk
w: www.luxurytoiletsforhire.co.uk/

Mobile Toilet Services
7 PESSALL FARM, PESSALL LANE, TAMWORTH
B79 9JL.................................... 01827 382 048 // 07590047758
e: mobiletoiletservices@aol.com
w: www.mobiletoiletservices.com

Oakwood Services
OAKWOOD HOUSE, LANE HEAD LANE, KIRKBURTON,
HUDDERSFIELD
HD8 0SQ..01484 604212
e: info@oakwoodservices.co.uk
w: www.poshtoilets.co.uk/

Pickerings Plant Ltd
ASHBY ROAD, MEASHAM, SWADLINGCOTE
Derbyshire DE12 7JW...01530 271618
e: accounts@pickeringsplant.co.uk
w: www.pickeringsplant.co.uk

Plush flush
....7921543935
e: alex@plushflush.co.uk
w: www.plushflush.co.uk

Porta Potty Direct
.... +1 877 240 4411
e: support@directrentalservice.com
w: www.portapottydirect.com

Portable Toilets Ltd
UNIT 12 ABERGARW TADING ESTATE , BRYNMENYN, BRIDGEND
CF32 9LW 08702 407 208
e: enquiries@ptl.uk.com
w: www.portabletoiletslimited.com

Posh-Loos
CHURCHLE, CHURCH FARM, CHURCH ROAD, HARBY, NEWARK
NG23 7ED............................... 0845 602 5062 / 01522 686 314
e: info@posh-loos.com
w: www.posh-loos.com/

Premier Toilets
21 ASPEN WAY, TELFORD, SHROPSHIRE
TF5 0LH..01952 541 133
e: premiertoilets@gmail.com
w: www.premier-toilets.co.uk/

Qdos Event Hire
FERNSIDE PLACE, 179 QUEENS ROAD, WEYBRIDGE
Surrey KT13 0AH 0845 862 0952
e: enquiries@qdoseventhire.co.uk
w: www.qdoseventhire.co.uk

Rawley Event Toilets
HARVEY ROAD, BURNT MILLS, BASILDON
SS13 1RP 01268 722300
e: info@rawley.co.uk
w: www.rawley.co.uk

Royle Flush Conveniences Ltd
WOOTTON PARK FARM, HALL END, WOOTTON
Bedfordshire MK43 9HT.............. 01234 766422 / 07811 449899
e: info@royleflush.co.uk
w: www.royleflush.co.uk

T U V

Search (Manchester)
DANIEL ADAMSON ROAD, SALFORD
Greater Manchester M50 1DT 0161 745 7319
e: events@wgsearch.co.uk
w: www.wgsearch.co.uk

Search (Sheffield)
191 WOODBOURN ROAD, SHEFFIELD
South Yorkshire S9 3LQ 0114 244 6521
e: events@wgsearch.co.uk
w: www.wgsearch.co.uk

Simply Loos
MANOR WAY, RAINHAM
Essex RM 13 8RH .... 0800 783 4710 // 020 8532 7878
e: info@simplyloos.co.uk
w: www.simplyloos.co.uk

Site Event
THE DEPOT, THE AVENUE, LASHAM
Hampshire GU34 5SU 0800 371994
e: hire@site-equip.co.uk
w: www.site-equip.co.uk/event

Smart Event Support
HECTON HOUSE, FRIDAY STREET,, FAST SUTTON,, MAIDSTONE
Kent ME17 3EA...01622 844 123
e: enquiries@smarteventsupport.co.uk
w: www.smarteventsupport.co.uk

Speedy Events
CHASE HOUSE, 16 THE PARKS, NEWTON-LE-WILLOWS
Merseyside WA12 0JQ .... 01942 720000 / 0845 609 9998
e: customerservices@speedyhire.com
w: www.speedyservices.com

Swift Loos
150 WALKDEN ROAD, WORSLEY, MANCHESTER
Greater Manchester M28 7DP.. 0161 790 3428 // 0161 703 8793
e: sales@swiftloos.com
w: www.swiftloos.com

Tardis Environmental Uk
COPPICE SIDE INDUSTRIAL ESTATE, BROWNHILLS, WALSALL
West Midlands WS8 7HB...................................... 0800 731 0589
e: info@tardishire.co.uk
w: www.tardishire.co.uk

The Elite Hire Company
10 OAKDALE ROAD, THE DALES, BRUNDALL, NORWICH
Norfolk NR13 5AF 07831 685522
e: info@elitehirecompany.co.uk
w: www.elitehirecompany.com

The Site Welfare Company
MK44 2BN...0800 999 2820
e: info@thesitewelfarecompany.co.uk
w: www.thesitewelfarecompany.co.uk

Tor Luxury Toilet Hire
PARK END FARM, WHITLEY LANE, WALTON
Somerset BA16 9RW 07702 497 484
e: torluxurytoilethire@gmail.com
w: www.torluxurytoilethire.co.uk

Wernick Event Hire Ltd
JOSEPH HOUSE, NORTHGATE WAY, ALDRIDGE, WALSALL
West Midlands WS9 8ST 0800 970 0231
e: enquiries@wernickevents.co.uk
w: www.wernickeventhire.co.uk

William G Search Limited
WHITEHALL ROAD, LEEDS
West Yorkshire LS12 6EP 0113 2639081
e: info@wgsearch.co.uk
w: www.wgsearch.co.uk

Wrekin Conveniences
21 ASPEN WAY, SHAWBIRCH, TELFORD
 TF5 0LH..01952 406399
e: info@wrekinloos.com
w: www.wrekinloos.com

Tours

AEG Live (UK) Ltd
ALMACK HOUSE, 28 KING STREET, LONDON
 SW1Y 6QW 0207 536 2626
e: help@aeglive.co.uk
w: www.aeglive.co.uk

Andrew Cheeseman Productions
LA GRANGE BLEUE, SALIGOS
 65120...0845 474 1992
e: info@acp-productions.co.uk
w: www.acp-productions.co.uk

Arlekino Production
KOSOVSKA 8, ZEMUN, BELGRADE, SERBIA
 11080... +381 63 22 95
11
e: office@arlekino.rs
w: www.arlekinoproduction.com

Artist Needs Ltd
41 ST PAUL'S STREET , LEEDS
West Yorkshire LS1 2JG 0113 244 0410
e: info@artistneeds.com
w: www.artistneeds.com

Bac Sport
112 CLERKENWELL ROAD, LONDON
Greater London EC1M 5TW...................................020 7456 7100
e: info@bacsport.co.uk
w: www.bacsport.co.uk

**T
U
V**

Black and White Live
....0208 422 0042
e: info@blackandwhitelive.com
w: www.blackandwhitelive.com

Book 'em Danno
2 GLASTONBURY CLOSE, SPENNYMOOR
DL16 6XP 01629 584 438
e: info@bookemdanno.com
w: www.bookemdanno.com

Diplomat Cruises
3 MORE LONDON RIVERSIDE, LONDON
Greater London SE1 2RE.....................................020 3283 4108
e: info@diplomatcruises.com
w: www.diplomatcruises.co.uk

Engineroom Production Services
4 BAILLIE STREET, NORTH MELBOURNE
.... +61 (0) 3 86858271
e: info@engineroom.tv
w: www.engineroom.tv

Esselle Sports Management
349 THE GREEN, ECCLESTON, CHORLEY
Lancashire PR7 5PH 01257 450991
e: esselle@essellesports.com
w: www.essellesports.com

GMC Professional
HOZA 51, WARSAW
00-681 .... 0048 507 164 924 / 0048 601 375 295
e: info@gmcpro.pl
w: www.gmcpro.pl

Incentivise Limited
.... 07741 254214 / 01925 211 400
e: paul.bradford@incentivise.co.uk
w: www.incentivise.co.uk/

Made Up Ltd
28 RAYMOUTH ROAD, LONDON
Greater London SE16 2DB 020 7231 7678
e: info@madeupltd.com
w: www.madeupltd.com

Millsea Production Services
2A ROTHERWOOD MANSIONS, 78 MADEIRA ROAD
SW16 2DE 07770 428 096
e: millsea@mac.com

Peter Kent Productions
78/12 PHATSANA SOI 2, EKAMAI SOI 4, SUKHUMVIT SOI 63,
PHRA KHANONG NUA, WATTANA
.... +66 802 307 477
e: peter@peterkent.com
w: www.peterkent.com

portmantravel
....44 800 731 1627
e: sales@portmantravel.com
w: www.portmantravel.com

Robbie Williams Productions
1 ANSELM ROAD
SW6 1LH 020 7381 1385
e: robbie@rwpltd.co.uk
w: www.rwpltd.co.uk

Sevens7
3RD FLOOR , 46A ROSEBERY AVENUE, LONDON
Greater London EC1R 4RP 020 3096 1348
e: info@sevens7.co.uk
w: www.sevens7.co.uk

Spires Of Oxford
P.O.BOX 24, WHEATLEY
Oxfordshire OX33 1RA 01865 875 539
e: info@spiresofoxford.co.uk
w: www.spiresofoxford.co.uk

The JWP Group
195 THORNHILL ROAD, SURBITON
Surrey KT6 7TG 020 8288 0246
e: web@jwp.co.uk
w: www.jwp.co.uk

Total Live Sound Ltd
67 CHEWTON STREET, EASTWOOD
Nottinghamshire NG16 3GY 07977 048 097
e: info@totallivesound.com
w: www.totallivesound.com

Tour Management Services (Nottinghamshire)
207 PARK ROAD EAST , NOTTINGHAM
Nottinghamshire NG14 6PS..................................07530 431 908
e: mike@tour-management-services.co.uk
w: www.tour-management-services.co.u

Tusk Showhire
23 COLLUM LANE, SCUNTHORPE
Lincolnshire DN16 2SZ .... 01724 859541 // 07850 307162
e: info@tuskshowhire.co.uk
w: www.tuskshowhire.co.uk

Universal Events Services Ltd
UNIT 27, SPACE BUSINESS CENTRE, TEWKESBURY ROAD,
CHELTENHAM
Gloucestershire GL51 9FL.....................................01242 530055
e: info@universalevents.co.uk
w: www.universalevents.co.uk

Trackway

AWA LTD
11 GREYCOAT PLACE, LONDON
Greater London SE1 1SB..1372 700 510
e: info@all-werheraccess.co.uk
w: awalimited.co.uk

Trade Union

Musicians Union - East & SE England Region
33 PALFREY PLACE, OVAL, LONDON
Greater London SW8 1PE......................................020 7840 5504
e: london@theMU.org
w: www.musiciansunion.org.uk/

Traffic Management

AA Signs
FANUM HOUSE, BASING VIEW, BASINGSTOKE
Hampshire RG21 4EA..0800 731 7003
e: aasigns@theaa.com
w: www.theaa.com/aasigns

City and Suburban Parking Ltd
8TH FLOOR YORK HOUSE, EMPIRE WAY, WEMBLEY, LONDON
Greater London HA9 0PA......................................020 8900 2405
e: sales@gotocsp.com
w: https://www.gotocsp.com

CJ's Events Warwickshire
THE COW YARD, CHURCH FARM, , CHURCH LANE, BUDBROOKE,
WARWICK
Warwickshire CV35 8QL..01926 800 750
e: info@cjseventswarwickshire.co.uk
w: www.cjseventswarwickshire.co.uk

Code 9 Security Ltd
80 HIGH STREET, WINCHESTER
Hampshire SO23 9AT...08442 448 448
e: enquiries@code9security.com
w: www.code9security.co.uk

Corvus Security Ltd
HEMSWELL, 4 CHESTNUT COURT , PARC MENAI, BANGOR
 LL57 4FH..0845 643 1514
e: info@corvussecurity.co.uk
w: www.corvussecurity.co.uk

CTIH Limited
UNIT 5 TWIGWORTH COURT BUSINESS CENTRE, TEWKESBURY
ROAD, GLOUCESTER
Gloucestershire GL2 9PG 0333 577 9501
e: sales@ctih.co.uk
w: www.ctih.co.uk

DC Site Services Ltd
FENLAND DISTRICT INDUSTRIAL ESTATE, STATION ROAD,
WHITTLESEY, PETERBOROUGH
Cambridgeshire PE7 2EY 01733 200713
e: admin@dcsiteservices.com
w: www.dcsiteservices.com

Destinations PTC Ltd
6 TEMPLE COURT, TEMPLE WAY, COLESHILL, BIRMINGHAM
West Midlands B46 1HH 01675 461800
e: operations@destinationsptc.com
w: www.destinationsptc.com

Eastern Events Ltd
DIGGENS FARM HOUSE, BUXTON ROAD, AYLSHAM
Norfolk NR11 6UB..01263 734711
e: info@easternevents.com
w: www.easternevents.com

Europalite
MILWARD HOUSE, EASTFIELD SIDE, SUTTON IN ASHFIELD
Nottinghamshire NG17 4JW...................................01623 528760
e: sales@europalite.eu
w: www.europalite.eu

Exclusec Security Solutions Ltd
THE GUARDIAN BUILDINGS, LONGBRIDGE ROAD, TRAFFORD
PARK, MANCHESTER
Greater Manchester M17 1SN...............................0333 344 3991
e: security@exclusec.co.uk
w: www.exclusec.co.uk

G4S Events
SOUTHSIDE, 105 VICTORIA STREET, LONDON
Greater London SW1E 6QT...................................0207 963 3100
w: www.g4s.uk.com

Green Light Traffic Management Ltd
UNIT 25, DEWSBURY MILLS, THORNHILL ROAD, DEWSBURY
West Yorkshire WF12 9QE 01924 463223
e: info@gltm.co.uk
w: www.gltm.co.uk

Perfect Guards Limited
TALON HOUSE PRESLEY WAY, MILTON KEYNES
 MK8 0ES...0844 4145616
e: info@perfect-guards.co.uk
w: www.perfect-guards.co.uk

Pirans Print Ltd
UNIT 1 SOUTHGATE TECHNOLOGY PARK, PENNYGILLAM WAY,
LAUNCESTON
Cornwall PL15 7ED 01566 779341
e: enquiries@piranprint.com
w: www.piranprint.com

Road Safety Services Ltd
BRACKENWOOD CENTRE, BRADSHAW LANE, GREENHALGH,
PRESTON Lancashire PR4 3HQ 01253 596388
e: shaun@road-safety.net
w: www.road-safety.net

RSS Events
BRACKENWOOD CENTRE, BRADSHAW LANE, GREENHALGH,
KIRKHAM
Lancashire PR4 3HQ 01253 596388
e: info@rssevents.co.uk
w: www.rssevents.co.uk

Securex Security Ltd
FIRST FLOOR, 962 OLD LODE LANE, SOLIHULL
West Midlands B92 8LN..0121 742 4333
e: info@securexsecurity.com
w: www.securexsecurity.com

T
U
V

SpaCES - Complete Event Services
SPA HOUSE, 23 IO CENTRE, , SALBROOK ROAD, SALFORDS ,
REDHILL
Surrey RH1 5GJ 0330 124 1541
e: enquiries@spacesuk.org
w: www.spacesuk.org

Sun Traffic Signals Ltd
SUN TOWERS, CARY COURT, SOMERTON BUSINESS PK,
SOMERTON BUSINESS PARK, SOMERTON
Somerset TA11 6SB 01458 274 100
e: info@suntraffic.com
w: www.suntraffic.com

Total Care Security Ltd
UNIT 3 , BRUNEL DRIVE, NEWARK
Nottinghamshire NG24 2DE 0800 917 47 67
e: info@totalcaresecurity.com
w: www.totalcaresecurity.com

Traffic Management Safety Solutions Ltd
AINLEYS INDUSTRIAL ESTATE, AINLEY BOTTOM, ELLAND, HALIFAX
West Yorkshire HX5 9JP 0844 686 1023
e: info@tmssltd.co.uk
w: www.tmssltd.co.uk

Traffic Management Services
AURILLAC WAY, , HALLCROFT INDUSTRIAL ESTATE, RETFORD
Nottinghamshire DN22 7PX....................................01777 705053
e: info@traffic.org.uk
w: www.traffic.org.uk

Trailer / Cabin Units

At Your Convenience - Mobile Toilets
SHADES MANOR, 24 BONIFACE ROAD, UXBRIDGE
Middlesex UB10 8BU 07778 744292
e: del@aycuk.com
w: www.aycuk.com

Blackburn Trailers Ltd
WHITESTONE FARM, MAIN ROAD, BIRDHAM
West Sussex PO20 7HU 01243 513550
e: trailers07@kompak.co.uk
w: www.kompak.co.uk

BlackDog games ltd
....01992 534448
e: peter@blackdoggames.co.uk
w: www.blackdoggames.co.uk

David Wilson's Trailers Ltd
JUBILEE PARK, HONEYPOT LANE, COLSTERWORTH, GRANTHAM
Lincolnshire NG33 5LZ...01476 860 833
e: info@dwt-exhibitions.co.uk
w: www.dwt-exhibitions.co.uk

Freeway Trailers Ltd
WIRELESS HILL SOUTH LUFFENHAM, 23 DILLINGTON, OAKHAM
Rutland LE15 8NF..01780 720435 //
07980 302149
e: info@exhibitiontrailer.co.uk
w: www.exhibitiontrailer.co.uk

Garic Ltd - Temporary Fencing Division
KINGFISHER PARK, AVIATION ROAD, PILSWORTH, BURY
Lancashire BL9 8GD 0844 417 9780
e: nfo@garic.co.uk
w: www.garic.co.uk

Hallmark Event Hire
RYELAND FARM, WILDE STREET, BECK ROW
Suffolk IP28 8BT..01842 861070
e: office@hallmarkeventhire.co.uk
w: www.hallmarkeventhire.co.uk

John Anderson Hire
UNIT 5 SMALLFORD WORKS , SMALLFORD LANE, ST ALBANS
Hertfordshire AL4 0SA..01727 822485
e: quotes@superloo.co.uk
w: www.superloo.co.uk

Lynton Trailers (UK) Ltd
ROSSINGTON INDUSTRIAL PARK, GRAPHITE WAY, HADFIELD,
GLOSSOP
Derbyshire SK13 1QH 01457 852700
e: sales@lyntontrailers.co.uk
w: www.lyntontrailers.co.uk

Mobex Ltd
UNIT 6 RIGESTATE INDUSTRIAL ESTATE, STATION ROAD,
BERKELEY
Gloucestershire GL13 9RL.....................................01453 511 210
e: exhibit@mobex.co.uk
w: www.mobex.co.uk

PW Hire
A5 CITY PARK TRADING ESTATE, DEWSBURY ROAD, FENTON
Staffordshire ST4 2HS 0844 854 8686
e: info@pwhire.co.uk
w: www.pw-hire.co.uk

Quentor Cases Ltd
UNIT 10, FITZMAURICE COURT, RACKHEATH INDUSTRIAL ESTATE,
NORWICH
Norfolk NR13 6PY 01603 721604
e: sales@quentor.com
w: www.quentor.com

Rollalong Hire Ltd
WOOLSBRIDGE INDUSTRIAL PARK , THREE LEGGED CROSS ,
WIMBOURNE
Dorset BH21 6SF 01202 824541
e: enquiries@rollalong.co.uk
w: www.rollalong.co.uk

T U V

Scott Medical (UK) Ltd
SCOTT HOUSE, BARRY'S LANE INDUSTRIAL ESTATE, SEAMER
ROAD, SCARBOROUGH
YO12 4HA 01723 363225
e: scott.andrew@btconnect.com

Search (Manchester)
DANIEL ADAMSON ROAD, SALFORD
Greater Manchester M50 1DT 0161 745 7319
e: events@wgsearch.co.uk
w: www.wgsearch.co.uk

Search (Sheffield)
191 WOODBOURN ROAD, SHEFFIELD
South Yorkshire S9 3LQ 0114 244 6521
e: events@wgsearch.co.uk
w: www.wgsearch.co.uk

Smart Event Support
HECTON HOUSE, FRIDAY STREET,, EAST SUTTON,, MAIDSTONE
Kent ME17 3EA...01622 844 123
e: enquiries@smarteventsupport.co.uk
w: www.smarteventsupport.co.uk

Tilshead Caravans & Motorcaravan Hire
OAKLEY CORNER GARAGE, LOPCOMBE, SALISBURY
Wiltshire SP5 1BS...01980 863636
e: hire@tilshead-caravans.com
w: www.tilshead-caravans.com

Torton Bodies Ltd
PILOT WORKS, HOLYHEAD ROAD, OAKENGATES, TELFORD
West Midlands TF2 6BB 01952 612648
e: sales@torton.com
w: www.torton.com

Vipex
NUNN BROOK ROAD , HUTHWAITE, SUTTON IN ASHFIELD
Nottinghamshire NG17 2HU 01623 441114
e: info@vipex.co.uk
w: www.vipex.co.uk

Wernick Event Hire Ltd
JOSEPH HOUSE, NORTHGATE WAY, ALDRIDGE, WALSALL
West Midlands WS9 8ST 0800 970 0231
e: enquiries@wernickevents.co.uk
w: www.wernickeventhire.co.uk

William G Search Limited
WHITEHALL ROAD, LEEDS
West Yorkshire LS12 6EP 0113 2639081
e: info@wgsearch.co.uk
w: www.wgsearch.co.uk

Winner Events
1 NORTH MOORS, SLYFIELD INDUSTRIAL ESTATE, GUILDFORD
Surrey GU1 1SE 0845 601 5427
e: sales@winnerevents.com
w: www.winnerevents.com

Translation / Interpretation Services

Atlas Translations
8 SPICER STREET,, ST ALBANS
Hertfordshire AL3 4PQ 01727 812 725
e: team@atlas-translations.co.uk
w: www.atlas-translations.co.uk

Conference Interpreters Uk
14 EATON MEWS NORTH, LONDON
Greater London SW1X 8AR.....................................0845 230 2450
e: info@conferenceinterpreters.co.uk
w: www.conferenceinterpreters.co.uk

French To English Literary Translations
280 IMPASSE DEHIOU, SOUSTONS
40140.. +33 558 417 783
e: contact@french-english-translator.com
w: www.french-english-translator.com

German Accurate Translations
81 CHAMBERS LANE, WILLESDEN GREEN, LONDON
Greater London NW10 2RN 020 8459 5023
e: michaelmertl@aol.com
w: www.mmertl.com

German Language Services
48 ST WERBURGHS PARK
BS2 9YS 07970 349 315
e: germaninterpreter@gmx.net

HL TRAD Limited
73 WATLING STREET, LONDON
EC4M 9BJ..2076297258
e: hltrad2015@gmail.com
w: www.hltrad.co.uk

Inbox Translation
86-90 PAUL STREET, LONDON
Greater London EC2A 4NE 020 7993 8080
e: info@inboxtranslation.com
w: www.inboxtranslation.com

Intonation Ltd
21-23 EAST STREET, FAREHAM
Hampshire PO16 0BZ................ 0800 0966 825 / 01329 828438
e: info@intonation.co.uk
w: www.intonation.co.uk

Isabelle Geesen-leigh French Translations
10 WENDOVER ROAD, BROMLEY
BR2 9JX 020 8460 4101
e: isabellegeesen@live.co.uk

Kwintessential
GROUND FLOOR, UNIT 1, CREWKERNE BUSINESS PARK,
NORTHERN WAY, CREWKERNE
Somerset TA18 7HJ 01460 279 900
e: info@kwintessential.co.uk
w: www.kwintessential.co.uk

T U V

M&R Communications Ltd
7 BELL INDUSTRIAL ESTATE, 50 CUNNINGTON STREET, LONDON
Greater London W4 5HB..020 8995 4714
e: office@m-rcom.com
w: www.m-rcom.com

Newcom
UNIT 2, NEWCOM HOUSE, 125 POPLAR HIGH STREET, LONDON
Greater London E14 0AE.......................................020 7193 8952
e: newcom@newcomgroup.com
w: www.newcomgroup.com

ProDubbing
UNIT 17, THE QUADRANT, 135 SALISBURY ROAD, QUEENS PARK, LONDON
Greater London NW6 6RJ.......................................020 81449980
e: info@produbbing.com
w: www.produbbing.com

Quadrillion TV
17 BALVERNIE GROVE, LONDON
Greater London SW18 5RR 01628 487522
e: enqs@quadrillion.tv
w: www.quadrillion.tv

Ros Schwartz Translations Ltd
34 HERIOT ROAD, HENDON
 NW4 2DG...020 8202 7877
e: schwartz@btinternet.com

Sally Walker Language Services
BANK HOUSE, 1 BURLINGTON ROAD, BRISTOL
Bristol BS6 6TJ..0117 973 4742
e: translations@sallywalker.co.uk
w: www.sallywalker.co.uk

Specialist Speakers
THE OLD FACTORY OFFICES, 8 HAWLEY ROAD, HINCKLEY
Leicestershire LE10 0PR...2030024125
e: jayne@speacialistspeakers.com
w: www.specialistspeakers.com/

The Living Word Language Services Ltd
51 ST JOHN STREET, ASHBOURNE
Derbyshire DE6 1GP 0845 8737 898
e: hello@livingword.co.uk
w: www.livingword.co.uk

TranslateMedia
4TH FLOOR, 292 VAUXHALL BRIDGE ROAD, LONDON
Greater London SW1V 1AE....................................020 8834 4840
e: antonio.catanese@translatemedia.com
w: www.translatemedia.com

Voice & Script International Ltd (vsi)
ARADCO HOUSE, 128 - 134 CLEVELAND STREET, LONDON
Greater London W1T 6AB.......................................020 7692 7700
e: info@vsi.tv
w: www.vsi.tv

Wiseguides Ltd
PO BOX 63, PRESTWICH, MANCHESTER
Greater Manchester M25 3DB...............................0161 773 0692
e: operations@wiseguides.co.uk
w: www.wiseguides.co.uk

Transport

Fly by Nite Conferences
SHAWBANK RD, LAKESIDE, REDDITCH
Worcestershire B98 8YN.......................................01527 520 720
e: carlreed@flybynite.co.uk
w: www.flybynite.co.uk

Trucking Services

Alpha Crew Ltd
28 GRAZEBROOK ROAD, STOKE NEWINGTON, LONDON
Greater London N16 0HS 020 8802 9227
e: info@alphacrew.co.uk
w: www.alphacrew.co.uk

Anglo Pacific International
5/9 WILLEN FIELD ROAD, PARK ROYAL , LONDON
Greater London NW10 7BQ 020 8965 1234
e: info@anglopacific.co.uk
w: www.anglopacific.co.uk

Bradshaw Electric Vehicles
NEW LN, PETERBOROUGH
Cambridgeshire PE8 6LW.....................................1782 782 621
e: sarahg@bradshawelectricvehicles.co.uk
w: www.bradshawelectricvehicles.co.u

C&C Exhibition Services Ltd
124 CEMETERY ROAD, HOUGHTON REGIS, DUNSTABLE
Bedfordshire LU5 5DE...07946 645591
e: info@candc-exhibition-services.co.uk
w: www.candc-exhibition-services.co.

Clipper Logistics Group
GELDERD ROAD, LEEDS
West Yorkshire LS12 6LT......................................0113 204 2050
w: www.clippergroup.co.uk

Conference Haul International Ltd
11 WINTERSELLS ROAD, WINTERSELLS BUSINESS PARK, BYFLEET
Surrey KT14 7LF...01932 353 057
e: terryg@conferencehaul.co.uk
w: www.conferencehaul.co.uk

Cross Transport Ltd
UNIT 3 LYNDONS FARM, POOLHEAD LANE, EARLSWOOD
Surrey B94 5ES 01564 700381
w: www.crosstransport.co.uk

T U V

CS Bull Ltd
PO BOX 872, CANTERBURY
Kent CT4 6WA...01227 831611
e: sales@csbull.ltd.uk
w: www.csbull.ltd.uk

E:d Truckin
20 MIDLAND ROAD, STAVELEY YARD, KETTERING
Northamptonshire NN14 4JR 01832 734490
e: info@ed-truckin.co.uk
w: www.ed-truckin.co.uk

Elev8 Access Platforms Ltd
UNIT 2B, CLAY STREET, SHEFFIELD
South Yorkshire S9 2PF...0845 274 3627
e: hiredesk@elev8hire.com
w: www.elev8hire.com

Fly By Nite Conferences Ltd
THE FBN COMPLEX, SHAWBANK ROAD, LAKESIDE , REDDITCH
Worcestershire B98 8YN 01527 520 720
e: enquiries@flybynite.co.uk
w: www.flybynite.co.uk

Hiremech
UNIT 1, TARIFF ROAD, TOTTENHAM, LONDON
Greater London N17 0EB 020 8880 3322
e: sales@hiremech.co.uk
w: www.hiremech.co.uk

HiTech Engineering
HEATHFIELD WAY, , UNIT 108-111 K2 HOUSE, NORTHAMPTON
Northamptonshire NN5 7QP .... 01604586175 /
.... 01604 757 414 / 078 94 62
e: office@hitecheng.co.uk
w: www.hitecheng.co.uk

KB Event Ltd
PLYMOUTH AVENUE, BROOKHILL INDUSTRIAL ESTATE, PINXTON
Nottinghamshire NG16 6NS 01773 811136
e: info@kbevent.com
w: www.kbevent.com

Lion Trackhire Ltd
CLAYLANDS AVENUE , WORKSOP
Nottinghamshire S81 7BQ....................................01909 212 214
e: enquiries@liontrackhire.com
w: www.liontrackhire.com

Logistics Un Ltd
55 MAIN STREET, LONG COMPTON
Warwickshire CV36 5JS.......................................0845 094 9944
e: contactus@logistics-un.ltd.uk
w: www.logistics-un.ltd.uk

Luckings Live Events Ltd
BOSTON HOUSE, 69-75 BOSTON MANOR ROAD, , BRENTFORD
Middlesex TW8 9JJ...0208 332 2000
e: Info@luckings.co.uk
w: www.luckings.co.uk

T
U
V

Matco Piano Transport
465 HORNSEY ROAD, LONDON
N19 4DR..020 7281 9555
e: piano@matcomoves.com
w: www.matcomoves.com

McGuinness Forwarding Ltd
4 ROEBUCK PARK, GOATSTOWN
Dublin 14...003531 296 2281
e: fiona@mcguinness.eu
w: www.mcguinness.eu

Motorvation (shows On The Road) Ltd
CHILHAM 3, STATION APPROACH, CHILHAM
Kent CT4 8EG 01227 738 266
e: info@motorv.com
w: www.motorv.com

Motorvation

Chilham 3 Station Approach,
Canterbury, Kent
CT4 8EG

t: 01227 738266
e: info@motorv.com

Specialists in UK and International Events Transport with 30 years' experience and a reputation for reliability. Our dedicated team of working drivers will assist with the build process to ensure your event is ready in time.

Call today for a quote.

www.motorv.com

Production Freight
UNIT 7, LAKESIDE INDUSTRIAL ESTATE, LAKESIDE ROAD, ,
COLNBROOK
Berkshire SL3 0ED...01784 472 600
e: derek@productionfreight.com
w: www.productionfreight.com

R Jameson Ltd
BENCOMBE COTTAGE, 13 MARLOW BOTTOM ROAD, MARLOW
Buckinghamshire SL7 3LZ .... 01628 483357 /
....07823 882394
e: lynne@rjameson-transport.co.uk
w: www.rjameson-transport.co.uk

Showforce
UNIT 001 STRATFORD WORKSHOPS, BURFORD ROAD,
STRATFORD, LONDON
Greater London E15 2SP.......................................0208 519 5252
e: info@showforce.com
w: www.showforce.com

Sound Moves (UK) Ltd
ABBEYGATE HOUSE, CHALLENGE ROAD, ASHFORD
Middlesex TW15 1AX .... 01784 424 471 /
....07785 735 045
e: martin.corr@soundmoves.co.uk
w: www.soundmoves.com

Southern Van Lines
RIVER WHARF BUSINESS PARK, MULBERRY WAY,
BELVEDERE, KENT
Greater London DA17 6AR 020 8310 8512
e: operations@southernvanlines.com
w: www.southernvanlines.com

Stagefreight Ltd
EVANSTON AVENUE, LEEDS
West Yorkshire LS4 2HR..0113 238 0805
e: info@stagefreight.com
w: www.stagefreight.com

Stagetruck Ltd
LARKWHISTLE FARM WORKS, LARKWHISTLE FARM ROAD,
MICHELDEVER
Hampshire SO21 3BG 020 8569 4444
e: enquiries@stagetruck.com
w: www.stagetruck.com

Stardes Ltd
ASHES BUILDINGS, OLD LANE, HALFWAY, SHEFFIELD
South Yorkshire S20 3GZ 0114 251 0051
w: www.stardes.co.uk

Team Relocations
DRURY WAY, BRENT PARK, WEMBLEY
Greater London NW10 0JN 020 8784 0100
e: uk@teamrelocations.com
w: www.teamrelocations.com

The Wicked Company
UNIT 2, BLACKETT ROAD, DARLINGTON
Durham DL1 2BJ .... 01325 789382 /
....07725 164507
e: info@thewickedcompany.co.uk
w: www.thewickedcompany.co.uk

Three Counties Contracts Ltd
....1525841404
e: Katie@threecountiescontracts.co.uk
w: www.threecountiescontracts.co.uk/

Transol Worldwide Logistics Ltd
UNIT 1 CRONDAL RD,, BAYTON IND EST, COVENTRY
Warwickshire CV7 9NH 02476 688 766
e: info@transoluk.com
w: www.transoluk.com

Truck School Ltd
4 ONSLOW ROAD, NEW BRIGHTON , WALLASEY, WIRRAL
Merseyside CH45 5AN ....

T
U
V

Vision Logistical Solutions
36 BRUNEL WAY, SEGENSWORTH, FAREHAM
Hampshire PO15 5SA 0500 120013
e: info@vision-logistics.co.uk
w: www.vision-logistics.co.uk

Xpression Event Solutions Limited
3210 HEYFORD PARK , UPPER HEYFORD
Oxfordshire OX25 5HD 01869 233324
e: info@xpressionevents.co.uk
w: www.xpressionevents.co.uk

Turnstiles

DLC Events
STREET 22, AL QUOZ IND 3, DUBAI
PO Box 282841,... +971 4 347 0484
e: office@dlcevents.com
w: www.dlcevents.com

Video Gaming

Gamewagon Ltd
113 - 115 OYSTER LANE, BYFLEET
KT14 7JZ...0845 319 4263
e: admin@gamewagon.co.uk
w: www.gamewagon.info

Vintage Vehicles / Car Displays

Coys Of Kensington
2-4 QUEENS GATE MEWS, LONDON
SW7 5QT 020 7584 7444
e: sales@coys.co.uk
w: www.coys.co.uk

Virtual Reality / Futuristic Games

Psw Events Ltd
THE OLD CHAPEL, 36 NORTH STREET, BURWELL, CAMBRIDGE
Cambridgeshire CB25 0BA....................................0845 3703 660
e: sales@pswevents.co.uk
w: www.corporate-entertainment-hire.

T
U
V

WXYZ

Waste Management / Recycling

A1 Mobile Ltd
NEW FARM, HOVERINGHAM LANE, HOVERINGHAM, NOTTINGHAM
Nottinghamshire NG14 7JX...................................0844 850 8818
e: sales@a1mobile.co.uk
w: www.a1mobile.co.uk

Aktrion Recycling And Waste Management
WINDSOR HOUSE QUEENSGATE, BRITANNIA ROAD,
WALTHAM CROSS Hertfordshire EN8 7NX 01992 712229
e: sales@aktrion.com
w: www.aktrion.com

Avanti Environmental Services
YARDLEY ROAD , INDUSTRIAL PARK, KNOWSLEY
Merseyside L33 7SS..0333 240 4027
e: info@avantienvironmentalservices.co.uk
w: www.avantienvironmentalservices.c

B.I.G. Recycling Consultancy
.... 01371 877 728 / 07787 291 554
w: www.bigrecyclingconsultancy.co.uk

Bywaters
LEA RIVERSIDE , TWELVETREES CRESCENT, BOW, LONDON
Greater London E3 3JG...020 7001 6000
e: info@bywaters.co.uk
w: www.bywaters.co.uk

D-Tox Event & Waste Management
DAISY HOUSE, RED HOUSE INDUSTRIAL ESTATE, ANGLIAN ROAD,
ALDRIDGE
West Midlands WS9 8EP 0800 999 2260
e: info@dtox.org
w: www.dtox.org/

DC Site Services Ltd
FENLAND DISTRICT INDUSTRIAL ESTATE, STATION ROAD,
WHITTLESEY, PETERBOROUGH
Cambridgeshire PE7 2EY 01733 200713
e: admin@dcsiteservices.com
w: www.dcsiteservices.com

Dunmow Waste Management
MID ESSEX RECYCLING CENTRE, REGIMENT BUSINESS PARK,
CHELMSFORD Essex CM3 3PZ.............................0800 030 6058
e: info@dunmowgroup.com
w: www.dunmowwaste.com

Emprise Services Plc
186 CITY ROAD, LONDON
Greater London EC1V 2NT....................................020 7549 0800
e: info@emprise.co.uk
w: www.emprise.co.uk

Festival Loo - Poonarnia
FERNHILL FARM, CHEDDAR ROAD, COMPTON MARTIN
Somerset BS40 6LD 07503 769188
e: squeak@festivalloo.co.uk
w: www.festivalloo.co.uk

Greens Environmental
HILLHOUSE INDUSTRIAL SITE, FLEETWOOD RD NORTH,
THORNTON-CLEVELEYS
Lancashire FY5 4QD 0800 458 8281
e: info@greensenvironmental.com
w: greensenvironmental.com/

Grundon Waste Management Ltd
THAMES HOUSE, OXFORD ROAD,BENSON,, WALLINGFORD
Oxfordshire OX10 6LX...01491 834 311
e: info@grundon.com
w: www.grundon.com

Haslehurst Waste Management & Recycling
606 KINGSTON ROAD, LONDON
Greater London SW20 8DN 020 8543 5088
e: mail@haslehurst.co.uk
w: www.haslehurst.co.uk

M.Brill Limited
55A MORTIMER ROAD , HACKNEY , LONDON
N1 5AR .... 020 7254 0333 / 07956 827 836
e: info@mbrillltd.co.uk
w: www.mbrillltd.co.uk

MJS Recycling
THE WARREN, ROWLEY LANE, WEXHAM
SL3 6PB .... 01753 429177 / 07535092443
e: info@mjs-recycling.co.uk
w: www.mjsrecycling.co.uk

More Bins
E2, DUCK FARM CRAFT WORKSHOPS, BOCKHAMPTON,
DORCHESTER DT2 8QL...01308 423349
e: sales@morebins.co.uk
w: www.morebins.co.uk

NG1 Skip Hire
UNIT 21,109 VERNON HOUSE, FRIAR LANE, NOTTINGHAM
Nottinghamshire NG1 6DQ...................................0800 612 7453
e: info@ng1-skip-hire.co.uk
w: www.ng1-skip-hire.co.uk

Nu Kleen Services
UNIT 2 ABBEY GRANGE WORKS, LONDON
Greater London IG11 8BL......................................020 8594 0800
e: sales@nukleen.com
w: www.nukleen.com

Pink Skips Manchester
PRINTWORKS LANE, LEVENSHULME TRADING ESTATE,
LEVENSHULME, MANCHESTER
Greater Manchester M19 3JP 0161 224 4222
e: enquiries@pinkskipsmanchester.co.uk
w: www.pinkskipsmanchester.co.uk

Speedy Events
CHASE HOUSE, 16 THE PARKS, NEWTON-LE-WILLOWS
Merseyside WA12 0JU .... 01942 720000 / 0845 609 9998
e: customerservices@speedyhire.com
w: www.speedyservices.com

Tardis Environmental Uk
COPPICE SIDE INDUSTRIAL ESTATE, BROWNHILLS, WALSALL
West Midlands WS8 7HB...................................... 0800 731 0589
e: info@tardishire.co.uk
w: www.tardishire.co.uk

Total Waste Management Ltd
HODEFIELDS AVENUE, BURNT MILL INDUSTRIAL ESTATE,
BASILDON
Essex SS13 1ED 01279 444406
e: skips@totalwastemanagement.co.uk
w: www.totalwastemanagement.co.uk

Waste Cost Reduction Services (WCRS)
UNIT 29 CHILDERDITCH INDUSTRIAL ESTATE , CHILDERDITCH
HALL DRIVE, LITTLE WARLEY , BRENTWOOD
Essex CM13 3HD 0844 846 2000
e: victoria.muirhead@wisg.co.uk
w: www.wcrsltd.co.uk/

WCRS Ltd
UNIT 29 CHILDERDITCH INDUSTRIAL ESTATE, CHILDERDITCH
HALL DRIVE, LITTLE WARLEY, BRENTWOOD
Essex CM13 3HD 0844 846 2000
e: findoutmore@wcrsltd.co.uk
w: www.wcrsltd.co.uk

Wood Waste Control (ENG) Ltd
....1628525290
e: info@woodwastecontrol.co.uk
w: www.woodwastecontrol.co.uk

Water / Ice Supply

All About Ice Europe Limited
PO BOX 1355 , HEMEL HEMPSTEAD
Hertfordshire HP1 9LF 0845 604 6547
e: sales@allaboutice.com
w: www.allaboutice.com

Glacial Art Ice Sculptors
UNIT 3A, NELSON'S BUSINESS PARK, LONG LANE, AINTREE,
LIVERPOOL
Merseyside L9 7BN..0151 521 5070
e: studio@glacialart.com
w: www.glacialart.com

Ice Box
UNIT A35/36, NEW COVENT GARDEN MARKET, LONDON
Greater London SW8 5EE......................................020 7498 0800
e: info@theicebox.com
w: www.theicebox.com

Liquiline Event Water Services
ASHTREE HOUSE, TARRANT HINTON, BLANDFORD
Dorset DT11 8JA 01258 830324
e: office@liquiline.co.uk
w: www.liquilineeventwaterservices.c

Show Site Services
UNIT 18 WEYBRIDGE BUSINESS CENTRE, 66 YORK
ROAD,, WEYBRIDGE Surrey KT139DY 01932 228 416
e: info@showsiteservices.co.uk
w: www.showsiteservices.co.uk

Water Direct Ltd
B26, EARLS COLNE BUSINESS PARK, EARLS COLNE,
COLCHESTER
Essex CO6 2NS..0845 345 1725
e: enquiries@water-direct.co.uk
w: www.water-direct.co.uk

Wicked Event Water Services Ltd
4 WILEMAN VILLAS, BECKINGHAM, DONCASTER
Nottinghamshire DN10 4PF...................................07909 771 996
e: info@wews.biz
w: www.wickedeventwaterservices.com

Wincanton Water Services
METHUEN PARK, CHIPPENHAM
Wiltshire SN14 0WT................................... +44 (0) 1249 710000
e: getintouch@wincanton.co.uk
w: www.wincanton.co.uk

Website / Designers

Charlie Apple
8 CEDAR WALK, KENLEY
Surrey CR8 5JL......................... 020 8668 6921 // 07973 987779
e: info@charlieapple.com
w: www.charlieapple.co.uk

Conference Websites
44 NEWTON ROAD, TUNBRIDGE WELLS
Kent TN1 1RU...01892 800 136
e: Conference-Websites@miramedia.co.uk
w: www.conference-websites.co.uk

MCCP Ltd
63 WINCHESTER STREET, BOTLEY, SOUTHAMPTON
Hampshire SO30 2EB 01489 782 535
e: GetInTouch@mccp.co.uk
w: www.mccp.ltd.uk

Mobius Media
SUITE 2, SAXON HOUSE,, ANNIE REED ROAD, BEVERLEY
 HU17 0LF 014 8224 0260
e: hello@mobiusmedia.co.uk
w: www.mobiusmedia.co.uk

Netpromote Web Design
....0161 9690605
e: info@netpromote.co.uk
w: www.netpromote.co.uk

New Media
ELCOT MEWS, ELCOT LANE, MARLBOROUGH
Wiltshire SN8 2AE...1672552352
e: hello@wearenewmedia.co.uk
w: www.wearenewmedia.co.uk/

W
X
Y
Z

One2Create
THE FLINT BARN ST CLAIRS FARM, WICKHAM ROAD, DROXFORD
Hampshire SO32 3PW...0844 8040 796
e: INFO@ONE2CREATE.CO.UK
w: www.one2create.co.uk

Photo Snap Marketing
128 CANNON WORKSHOPS, LONDON
Greater London E14 4AS.....................................020 7096 3966
e: info@photosnapmarketing.com
w: www.photosnapmarketing.com

Project Simply
THE SHARP PROJECT, THORP ROAD, MANCHESTER
Greater Manchester M40 5BJ 0161 408 1023
e: enquiry@projectsimply.com
w: www.projectsimply.com

Shorestream Media
EXETER PHOENIX, BRADNINCH PLACE, GANDY STREET, EXETER
Devon EX4 3LS.......................................07765 488101
e: james@shorestreammedia.co.uk
w: www.shorestreammedia.co.uk

SkyWeb Media
.... 0203 328 9917 / 0753 917 6000
e: will@skyweb.media
w: www.skyweb.media

Stable Creative
MEDINA YARD, COWES
Isle of Wight PO31 7PG 07885 774 666
e: ben@stablecreative.co.uk
w: www.stablecreative.co.uk

The UX Agency
12 MELCOMBE PLACE, MARYLEBONE, LONDON
Greater London NW1 6JJ.....................................020 7947 4940
e: enquiries@theuxagency.co.uk
w: www.theuxagency.co.uk

Union Street Media Arts
20 EAST UNION ST, MANCHESTER
M16 9AE...1618773124
e: roop@unionstreetmediaarts.com
w: www.unionstreetmediaarts.com/

VisualDialogue
16 PRUNUS CLOSE, WEST END, WOKING
Surrey GU24 9NU..01483 289009
e: info@visualdialogue.co.uk
w: www.visualdialogue.co.uk

Weddings

ABZ Events
ABERDEEN
....01224 515375
e: info@abz-events.co.uk
w: www.abz-events.co.uk

Acacia Marquees
3 ALBERT TERRACE, HEOL-Y-DWR, HAY-ON-WYE
Herefordshire HR3 5AS .... 01497 820 882 /
07795 958 421
e: mail@acacia-marquees.co.uk
w: www.acacia-marquees.co.uk

Akshyis Events Management Ltd
SOUTHEND ROAD, EASTHAM , LONDON
E6 2AA .... 02084771356 / 079 5141 8145 / 078 5227 5
e: akshyiseventsm@hotmail.com
w: www.akshyisevent.com/

Arabian Tent Company
RYE FARM, HOLLANDS LANE, HENFIELD
West Sussex BN5 9QY 0800 88 15 229
e: info@arabiantents.com
w: www.arabiantents.com

Aries Leisure
2 - 7 WEBBER ROAD, KNOWSLEY INDUSTRIAL ESTATE,
LIVERPOOL
Merseyside L33 7SW 0151 545 0599
e: info@ariesleisure.co.uk
w: www.ariesleisure.co.uk

bars2you ltd
.... 01925 633 131 / 07709888809
e: chris@bars2you.co.uk
w: www.bars2you.com

Bella Parties
LEESWOOD COTTAGE, FIR TREE HILL, CHANDLERS CROSS
WD3 4NA...7789833676
e: info@bellaparties.co.uk
w: www.bellaparties.co.uk

Bespoke by Bijou
....0345 130 9966
e: Yourday@bijouweddings.co.uk
w: www.bespokebybijou.co.uk

Bondini Events & Entertainment
LOW FARM, BROOK ROAD, BASSINGBOURN, ROYSTON
SG8 5NT...01763 852691
e: doctor@bondini.co.uk
w: www.bondini.co.uk

Bridgewood Manor
BRIDGEWOOD ROUNDABOUT, WALDERSLADE WOODS, CHATHAM
ME5 9AX...01634 201333
e: bridgewoodmanorevents@qhotels.co.uk
w: www.qhotels.co.uk

Brighton Sound System
BILLY WOOD LTD TA BRIGHTON SOUND SYSTEM, UNIT 2,
VICTORIA GROVE, HOVE
East Sussex BN3 2LJ...1273746506
e: info@brightonsoundsystem.co.uk
w: www.brightonsoundsystem.co.uk/

Carta Pojects Ltd
5 GEORGE ST, SNAITH
East Yorkshire DN14 9HY 07809 209950
e: martin@cartaprojects.co.uk
w: www.cartaprojects.co.uk

Chapman Holmes Events
UNIT 1 PEEL GREEN ESTATES, GREEN STREET, MANCHESTER
Greater Manchester M30 7HF 0161 7893262
e: events@chapmanholmes.co.uk
w: www.chapmanholmes.co.uk

Chuckle Pod Limited
....07770 692499
e: info@chucklepod.co.uk
w: www.chucklepod.co.uk

Clear and Loud
....0191 64 54 645
e: bookings@clearandloudpahire.co.uk
w: www.clearandloudpahire.co.uk

Collection 26
66 PORCHESTER ROAD, LONDON
Greater London W2 6ET 08450 553290
e: info@collection26.com
w: www.collection26.com

Crystal Marquee Hire
BRAMBLE FARM, SHERE ROAD, WEST HORSLEY, LEATHERHEAD
Surrey KT24 6ER 01483 283228
e: info@crystalmarqueehire.co.uk
w: www.crystalmarqueehire.co.uk

Dancefloor DJs & Events
THISTLEY CLOSE, THORPE ASTLEY, LEICESTER
Leicestershire LE3 3RZ 0116 348 0146
e: dancefloordjs85@gmail.com
w: dancefloor-djs-events.com/

Dash of Sparkle
IDIT GINSBERG, DASH OF SPARKLE , 59 BEECH DRIVE,
BOREHAMWOOD , HERTS
 WD6 4QX .... 020 8905 2908 / 07877 927 246
e: office@dashofsparkle.com
w: www.dashofsparkle.com/

Eastern Illusion
....07958 734311
e: info@easternillusion.com
w: www.easternillusion.com

Event Decor Group
UNIT 11 PARKROSE INDUSTRIAL ESTATE, MIDDLEMORE ROAD,
BIRMINGHAM
West Midlands B66 2DZ........... 0121 306 9412 // 07799 353 537
e: admin@eventdecorgroup.co.uk
w: www.eventdecorgroup.co.uk

Eventelle Limited
69 DUNVEGAN ROAD, BIRMINGHAM
 B24 9HH..07961 067 546
e: info@eventelle.co.uk
w: www.eventelle.co.uk

Firebird Events Ltd
UNIT 3, NIMBUS BUSINESS PARK, HERCULES WAY,
FARNBOROUGH
Hampshire GU14 6UU 01252 545654
e: enquiry@firebirdevents.co.uk
w: www.firebirdevents.co.uk

G & D Events
STUDIO 18, FINSBURY BUSINESS CENTRE, 40 BOWLING GREEN
LANE, LONDON
Greater London EC1R 0NE 020 3021 3333
e: ganddevents0@gmail.com
w: www.g-and-d-events.co.uk

Gamewagon Ltd
113 - 115 OYSTER LANE, BYFLEET
Surrey KT14 7JZ...0845 319 4263
e: julie.owen@gamewagon.co.uk
w: www.gamewagon.co.uk

Gamewagon Ltd
113 - 115 OYSTER LANE, BYFLEET
 KT14 7JZ...0845 319 4263
e: admin@gamewagon.co.uk
w: www.gamewagon.info

GIG...fyi
GLOBAL INFUSION COURT, NASHLEIGH HILL, CHESHAM
Buckinghamshire HP5 3HE 01494 790700
e: hellogigfyi@gigfyi.com
w: www.gigfyi.com

Gold Choice Wedding Cars
4 MCKAY PLACE, EAST KILBRIDE
 G74 4SP 01355 220 228
e: mail@goldchoiceweddingcars.co.uk
w: www.goldchoiceweddingcars.co.uk

Gorgeous Invites Ltd
189 BASFORD PARK ROAD, NEWCASTLE-UNDER-LYME
Staffordshire ST5 0PN 1782623670
e: info@gorgeousinvites.co.uk
w: www.gorgeousinvites.co.uk/

Grosvenor Classic Cars
LITTLETON HALL , LITTLETON LANE , LITTLETON, CHESTER
Cheshire CH3 7DJ................... 0800 999 5151 // 07776 248 592
e: classiccars@littletonhall.com
w: www.grosvenorclassiccars.co.uk

Hannah Emily Bridal
5A BEULAH RD, CARDIFF
 CF14 6LT 02921 152357
e: hannah@hannahemilybridal.com
w: www.hannahemilybridal.com

W X Y Z

Harrisons Events
THE MALTING BARN, MALTING LANE, DAGNALL, BERKHAMSTEAD
HP4 1QY 07846 380474
e: info@harrisonsevents.co.uk
w: www.harrisonsevents.co.uk

iCatching Events
UNIT D, JOSEPH ADAMSON IND EST, CROFT STREET, HYDE
Cheshire SK14 1EE 0845 833 6372
e: info@icatchingevents.co.uk
w: www.icatchingevents.co.uk

Ice Entertainment Uk
ICE ENTERTAINMENT UK, UNIT C-D DODD LANE IND ESTATE,
CHORLEY ROAD, BOLTON
Greater Manchester BL5 3NA................................0845 4751020
e: info@iceentertainmentuk.com
w: www.iceentertainmentuk.com

INAANIAH Limited
THE LANSDOWNE BUILDING , 2 LANSDOWNE ROAD , CROYDON
Surrey CR9 2ER 7533001780
e: earthvillageevents@gmail.com
w: www.earthvillageevents.co.uk

Jay & I Services
WEMBLEY COMMERCIAL CENTRE, UNIT 4.6 4TH FLOOR,
BUILDING A, EAST LANE, LONDON
Greater London HA9 7PT .... 020 8908 4276 //
020 8908 6943
e: info@jayandievents.com
w: www.jayandievents.com

JDB Events
GATEHOUSE TRADING ESTATE, LICHFIELD RD, BROWNHILLS,
WALSALL
 WS8 6JZ..0121 667 1444
e: info@jdb-events.co.uk
w: www.jdb-events.com

JSO Productions Ltd
THREEWAYS, RADNAGE COMMON RD, RADNAGE
Buckinghamshire HP14 4DF ..... 0208 8407070 // 01494 387 770
e: parties@jso.co.uk
w: www.jso.co.uk

Kent & Medway Wedding Cars
NEWINGTON, KENT

....1622677846
e: graham@weddingcarskentmedway.co.uk
w: www.weddingcarskentmedway.co.uk

Kudos Music
UNIT 10 TRADE CITY, COWLEY MILL ROAD, UXBRIDGE
 UB8 2DB...01895 207990
e: info@kudosmusic.co.uk
w: www.kudosmusic.co.uk

Lakeview Events Ltd
OLD BANK END ROAD, FINNINGLEY, DONCASTER
South Yorkshire DN9 3NT.......................................07731 510685
e: lakevieweventsltd@gmail.com
w: www.lakeviewevents.com

Life's Kitchen
....0800 915 0978
e: info@lifeskitchen.com
w: www.lifeskitchen.com

Lillingston
ONE FOLLY MEWS, 223A PORTOBELLO ROAD, LONDON
Greater London W11 1LU 020 7221 5820
e: info@lillingston.co.uk
w: www.lillingston.co.uk

Lvlv Events Ltd
UNIT 17 & 21, 54-56 DOVER ROAD EAST, GRAVESEND
Kent DA11 0RG......................... 07534 921 310 / 01474 247 557
e: Info@eventsbylvlv.co.uk
w: www.eventsbylvlv.co.uk

Mansion & Gardens, Port Lympne Wild Animal Park
PORT LYMPNE RESERVE, NR ASHFORD
Kent CT21 4LR...0844 842 4647
e: info@aspinallfoundation.org
w: www.aspinallfoundation.org

Meridian Marquees
READING OFFICE UNIT A, PARSONS FARM , CHURCH LANE,
FARLEY HIL
Berkshire RG7 1UY 0800 298 5955
e: meridianmarquees@googlemail.com
w: www.meridianmarquees.co/

Nexlevel Entertainment & Event Management
106A CLARENCE ROAD, HACKNEY
 E5 8HB...0208 985 3165
e: lekan.fakoya@nexlevel.co.uk
w: www.nexlevel.co.uk

Ninth Events Ltd
39 FEATHERSTONE STREET , ISLINGTON , LONDON
 EC1Y 8RE 7879896725
e: info@ninthevents.com
w: www.ninthevents.com

Norah Sleep Events
NO 5, FIRST FLOOR, WESTFIELD HOUSE, MILLFIELD LANE, YORK
North Yorkshire YO26 6GA.....................................01904 790123
e: enquiries@norahsleep.co.uk
w: www.norahsleep.co.uk

Olive Weddings
....07737 361168
e: ruth@oliveweddings.co.uk
w: www.oliveweddings.co.uk

W
X
Y
Z

Om-Creatives
....07599 888869
e: info@om-creatives.com
w: www.om-creatives.com

Paperchain Wedding Stationery
....0116 3183634
e: info@paperchainweddingstationery.co.uk
w: www.paperchainweddingstationery.c

PhotoLesk
4 GOLD STREET, TIVERTON
Devon EX16 6PZ..01884 798 070
e: lesk@photolesk.co.uk
w: www.photolesk.co.uk

Porter & Smith Event Planners
1 FOREST DRIVE, WOODFORD GREEN
Essex IG8 9NG...07796 966 805
e: info@porterandsmith.co.uk
w: www.porterandsmith.co.uk

Princess Days
5 FORT CRESCENT, MARGATE
 CT9 1HN...01843 227 838
e: princessdays@hotmail.com
w: princessdays.wix.com/princess-day

Sapphire London Ltd
.... 020 8127 5400 / 07895 007 951
e: info@sapphirelondon.com
w: www.sapphirelondon.com

Smile Events
392 GALLEY HILL,, HEMEL HEMPSTEAD,
Hertfordshire HP1 3LA 01923 750 525
e: info@smileevents.co.uk
w: www.smileevents.co.uk

South West Lakes Trust
LIDN PARK, QUARRY CRESCENT, PENNYGILLAM, LAUNCESTON
Cornwall PL15 7PF 01566 771930
e: info@swlakestrust.org.uk
w: www.swlakestrust.org.uk

Splash Events Ltd
PO BOX 3384, BARNET
Greater London EN5 9BT.......................................0208 447 5650
e: party@splashevents.co.uk
w: www.splashevents.co.uk

Story of Your Day
....07973 459058
e: emma@storyofyourday.co.uk
w: www.storyofyourday.co.uk

Sweet Pea Wedding Photography
....0145 2618 738
e: simonfennell697@btinternet.com
w: www.sweetpeaweddingphotography

The Chillout Furniture Company
RYE FARM, HOLLANDS LANE, HENFIELD,
East Sussex BN5 9QY 0800 881 5229
e: info@completechillout.com
w: www.completechillout.com

The Pearl Tent Company
UPPER TILTON BARN, FIRLE, LEWES
East Sussex BN8 6LL..0800 88 15 229
e: info@thepearltentcompany.com
w: www.thepearltentcompany.com

Transform Venue
UNIT 1 REAR OF 486 PORTSWOOD ROAD, SOUTHAMPTON
Hampshire SO17 3SP 02380 558923
e: info@transform-venue.co.uk
w: www.transform-venue.co.uk

Twisted Monkey Events Ltd
THE STABLES, HOLME PIERREPONT HALL, NOTTINGHAM
Nottinghamshire NG12 2LD 0115 933 4030
e: info@twistedmonkeyevents.co.uk
w: www.twistedmonkeyevents.co.uk

Upp
UNIVERSITY PARTNERSHIPS PROGRAMME , 40 GRACECHURCH
STREET,, LONDON,
Greater London EC3V 0BT.......................... +44 (0)207 398 7200
e: info@upp-ltd.com
w: www.upp-ltd.com

Wedding Bands Glasgow
73 ALBERT ROAD, GLASGOW
 G42 8DP .... 01414234863 / 07590693127
e: info@weddingbandsglasgow.com
w: weddingbandsglasgow.com/

Your Right Arm Events Ltd.
....0788 3033 552
e: mary@yourrightarm.co.uk
w: www.yourrightarmevents.co.uk

Wine / Wine Tasting / Champagne

Charles Salt Fine Wines
CORNER COTTAGE, 2 PARK ROW COTTAGES, DAWLISH
Devon EX7 9NP...0162 686 4381
e: salt@charliethewineman.co.uk
w: www.charliethewineman.co.uk

Grape Escapes Ltd
THE MANOR HOUSE, HIGH STREET, BUNTINGFORD
Hertfordshire SG9 9AB...08456 430 860
e: mark@grapeescapes.net
w: www.grapeescapes.net

Lovely Bubbly
PO BOX 330, NEWCASTLE UPON TYNE
Tyne & Wear NE3 1ZS 0845 2572754
e: info@lovelybubbly.co.uk
w: www.lovelybubbly.co.uk

W
X
Y
Z

Taste Of The Vine
JEROBOAM HOUSE, SANDY LANE, GRAYSWOOD, HASELMERE
Surrey GU27 2DG..01428 656319
e: events@tasteofthevine.co.uk
w: www.tasteofthevine.co.uk

The Tasting Quarter
WEST LODGE FARM, LOW ROAD, EASTON, NORWICH
 NR9 5EN...01603 340 084
e: info@thetastingquarter.com
w: www.thetastingquarter.com

Thirty Fifty Wine Tastings
24 CHESTNUT ROAD, TWICKENHAM
London TW2 5QZ 0208 288 0314
e: chris.scott@thirtyfifty.co.uk
w: www.thirtyfifty.co.uk

Vinisus Wines
LOVELETTS, GOSSOPS GREEN, CRAWLEY
West Sussex RH11 8EG 01293 734664
e: info@vinisus.com
w: www.vinisus.com

Vintellect
HERONSMERE, ASHTEAD WOODS RD, ASHTEAD
Surrey KT21 2ET..01372 272295
e: info@vintellect.co.uk
w: www.vintellect.co.uk

West London Wine School
2B SILVER CRESCENT, , CHISWICK, LONDON
Greater London W4 5SE 020 8144 2444
e: info@westlondonwineschool.com
w: www.westlondonwineschool.com

Winfield Wine Events
38 THE AVENUE
London W13 8LP..0208 997 4718
e: gilbert@winfieldwines.co.uk
w: www.winfieldwines.co.uk

Winter Effects

MTFX
Velt House Lane
Elmore, Gloucestershire
GL2 3NY

t: 01452 729 903
e: info@MTFX.com

**W
X
Y
Z**

MTFX provide a huge range of Winter Effects including Artificial Snow, Snow Machines, Tree Flocking and a Bespoke Winter Wonderland Service to create awe inspiring snow scenes! Welcome to MTFX, the ingenious special effects people.

www.MTFX.com